Contents

PART III Sport As an Institution 93

PART IV Sport and Culture 167

Social Issues in Sport

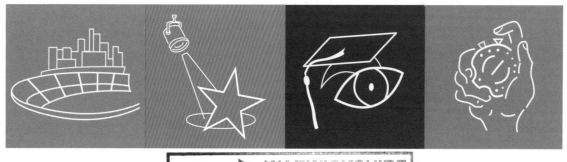

Ronald B. Woods, PhD

University of South Florida

Library of Congress Cataloging-in-Publication Data

Woods, Ron, 1943 Nov. 6-
    Social issues in sport / Ronald B. Woods.
        p.   cm.
    Includes bibliographical references and index.
    ISBN-13: 978-0-7360-5872-8 (soft cover)
    ISBN-10: 0-7360-5872-9 (soft cover)
  1. Sports--Social aspects.   2. Sociology.   I. Title
    GV706.5.W655 2006
    306.4 ' 83--dc22

                                                          2006019542

ISBN-10: 0-7360-5872-9
ISBN-13: 978-0-7360-5872-8

Copyright © 2007 by Ronald B. Woods

Permission notices for photos reprinted in this book from other sources can be found on page xiii.

The Web addresses cited in this text were current as of June 8, 2006, unless otherwise noted.

Acquisitions Editor: Myles Schrag; **Developmental Editor:** Amanda S. Ewing; **Assistant Editor:** Maureen Eckstein; **Copyeditor:** Jocelyn Engman; **Proofreader:** Anne Rogers; **Indexer:** Marie Rizzo; **Permission Manager:** Dalene Reeder; **Graphic Designer:** Robert Reuther; **Graphic Artist:** Kathleen Boudreau-Fuoss; **Photo Managers:** Sarah Ritz and Laura Fitch; **Cover Designer:** Keith Blomberg; **Photograph (cover):** © Streeter Lecka/Getty Images; **Photographs (interior):** © Human Kinetics, unless otherwise noted; **Art Manager:** Kelly Hendren; **Illustrator:** Kelly Hendren; **Printer:** Custom Color Graphics

Printed in the United States of America   10   9   8   7   6   5   4   3   2

Human Kinetics
Web site: www.HumanKinetics.com

United States: Human Kinetics
P.O. Box 5076, Champaign, IL 61825-5076
800-747-4457
e-mail: humank@hkusa.com

Canada: Human Kinetics
475 Devonshire Road Unit 100, Windsor, ON N8Y 2L5
800-465-7301 (in Canada only)
e-mail: orders@hkcanada.com

Europe: Human Kinetics
107 Bradford Road, Stanningley, Leeds LS28 6AT, United Kingdom
+44 (0) 113 255 5665
e-mail: hk@hkeurope.com

Australia: Human Kinetics
57A Price Avenue, Lower Mitcham, South Australia 5062
08 8372 0999
e-mail: liaw@hkaustralia.com

New Zealand: Human Kinetics
Division of Sports Distributors NZ Ltd.
P.O. Box 300 226 Albany, North Shore City, Auckland
0064 9 448 1207
e-mail: info@humankinetics.co.nz

Preface

This book critically and factually examines the sport (particularly in the United States) of today's society. I have compared the historical development of sport with our modern sports world. As you will see, sport participation and spectatorship in America have significantly changed and now lean toward a corporate model of sport.

In the past 50 years, major changes in society spilled over into the world of sports. Racial barriers gave way to dominance by African Americans in sports like basketball and football, while Latinos now account for a third of Major League Baseball players. Women and girls participate more in sports and agitate for equal opportunities as participants and spectators. The Special Olympics and Paralympics have become major sport events for people who have mental and physical disabilities. Finally, consumer sports are accommodating a surging population of older adults who look to sport to enhance their personal fitness, quality of life, and social interaction. Each of these changes promotes new sport outlooks and strategies and offers hope for the continued expansion of sport for every person.

Methods of studying sport have become more rigorous and insightful, as sport sociology has advanced as a science. University courses are plentiful for students wishing to study the sociology of modern sports, and hundreds of researchers and professors study the relevant issues. This book presents the controversies and status of sport in a sociological construct without dwelling on the theoretical constructs. This text is a look at sport from a longtime sport participant, observer, fan, teacher, coach, administrator, and critic who has tried to maintain a balanced approach to sport.

INTENDED AUDIENCE

This is a book for people who are looking at sport objectively for the first time. It seeks to help you understand sport, its place in society, and possible changes it may need in order to maintain a positive future. I hope you will become better acquainted with the historical and current role of sports. Regardless of your major course of study,

if you are a sport participant or fan you will find the information illuminating and in some cases surprising.

As you understand more about the sports world and its interaction with our society, you will be better equipped to decide what role sport will take in your life and your family. Whether you are a competitive athlete, enthusiastic participant, or spectator, after reading this book you will likely enjoy sport more, appreciate the challenges sport faces, and better evaluate the decisions of sport leaders. Sport can help unify or divide society, but clearly it has a better chance of helping if more people understand its value and limitations.

Although this book is founded in research and reflects various social theories, it is not written for academic colleagues and does not break new ground in theoretical constructs. Rather, it is intended to encourage students to delve more deeply into the issues and contradictions that characterize what sometimes is a love–hate affair between sport and many of us.

TEXT ORGANIZATION

Part I presents a framework for studying sport in society, defining terms and establishing the purpose and importance of sport study. It also looks at the overall field of sport science and how sport research contributes to knowledge in sport.

Part I also presents sociological methods for studying sport so that you will understand how knowledge is gathered and analyzed. It describes social theories and how these theories help in studying sport.

Part II examines the scope of modern sport and how it affects society. It clarifies the parallels and differences between sport participants and sport spectators, showing how popular sport differs between participants and spectators. It also examines and compares growth trends in various sports and distinguishes people who play participation or recreational sports from those who are devoted to high-performance sports.

Part II also presents the business side of sport at the professional and collegiate levels and discusses the issues of spending public funds for private gain. It considers how finances affect athletes, coaches, owners, and participants individually and collectively. You will gain appreciation for the huge economic investments made in sports and the influence of money on sport policies and programs.

Part II outlines the powerful symbiotic relationship between media and sport. It acknowledges the influence of sport media personalities and journalism and the continuing challenges of including minorities and females more often in sport media.

Part III looks at sport as an institution and how it functions within other institutions such as colleges and the Olympics. Youth sports outside of the school setting have become an adult organized activity for kids that permeates every community. Interscholastic sport teams continue to grow and prosper but face the challenges of integrating opportunities for girls in accordance with Title IX and constant funding pressures. Collegiate sports struggle to find their way under the economic pressure to support programs for a relatively few elite athletes who may or may not be comfortable in the academic setting.

The globalization of sports reflects our increasingly smaller world. International competition has increased as American sports have been exported around the world and soccer has finally begun to take hold in North America. The Olympic movement has propelled certain sports to international prominence and has taken on an originally unintended economic and political significance. Including professional athletes in the Olympic Games has changed the nature of the games and focused world attention on developing elite athletes who can compete for a gold medal.

Part IV of this text focuses on the interaction between culture and sport. Beginning with good sporting behavior and progressing to race, ethnicity, gender, and social class, this section lays out the significance of social issues in our sports world. The changing role of women and African Americans in society has revolutionized sports, while ethnic and social class continue to be powerful factors in who plays or watches sports particularly and generally.

Religion and politics interact with sport as they have for centuries. Both have affected the growth of sport and have used sport to their advantage. Athletes use religion in their sport and religious organizations use sport to promote their purpose. Government uses sport to promote identity and unity, social values, and nationalism.

A chapter unique to this book, "Special Populations and Sport," looks at groups who are physically disabled, mentally disabled, or aging and recognizes the effects of major societal changes regarding these populations in the past 25 years. As baby boomers age and life expectancy increases, we are seeing a significant change in our population demographics, with more of our population represented by older adults who view sports as recreation and a tool for a healthier lifestyle. Similarly, since the Americans with Disabilities Act of 1990, people who are physically or mentally disabled have seen their sport participation opportunities expand exponentially.

Deviant behavior in sport includes problems of violence, hazing, performance-enhancing drugs, and eating disorders. These behaviors are found among athletes of every age and affect individuals, teams, and institutions. Gambling on sport is also a growing concern despite organized professional and collegiate sports' firm stand against it, and unregulated Internet gambling on sport continues to be a problem.

Another chapter unique to this book, "Coaching Sport," acknowledges the influential role of coaches. As sports changed, so did the coaching profession, demanding higher standards in performance sports. Yet unsolved are the challenges of recruiting and training thousands of volunteer youth sport coaches needed each year, although some people are working to promote national and statewide standards for coaches.

The final chapter in this text looks to the future of sport in North America. Performance sport continues to compete with participation sport. Many youth have moved toward extreme sports that suit their needs better than the traditional, adult-organized sports. Older adults look to sports to enhance a longer life. American sport continues to face issues of finances, opportunities for women, and growing minority populations that are changing the face of society. The struggles among these interest groups will likely play out over the next 50 years.

LEARNING TOOLS

To facilitate student learning, each chapter starts with "Student Outcomes," which outline the chapter topics. Key terms are highlighted in bold-faced print and included in a glossary for easy reference. Each chapter ends with a summary of its main topics. Throughout the text, you will enjoy various sidebars:

"In the Arena With…" sidebars highlight key players in sociological change in sport.

 "Pop Culture" sidebars discuss current trends in the movies, books, magazines, and so on that highlight sociological issues in sport.

 "Expert's View" sidebars show how experts in sport sociology interpret sport issues, and then they raise discussion points for students.

 "Activity Time-Out" sidebars give students the opportunity to classify information, engage in friendly debates, or receive interesting information.

INSTRUCTOR RESOURCES

Several instructor resources are available to facilitate using this text in your class. The instructor guide includes chapter summaries, student objectives, chapter outlines, additional student activities, and supplemental resources. The text package includes more than 190 questions, including multiple choice and essay questions. The Microsoft© PowerPoint presentation package includes 295 slides that outline the text in a lecture friendly format.

CLOSING COMMENTS

I have spent more than 40 years studying sport and applying that knowledge as a professor, a coach, and an administrator. I've spent nearly 20 of these years on a college campus, teaching the psychosocial aspects of sport as well as coaching men's tennis at the Division I and II levels. Later I worked in various administrative roles for the United States Tennis Association, the governing body for tennis in the United States. I also spent 8 years on the coaching committee for the United States Olympic Committee that embraced the challenge of improving coaching in all sports in the United States. These experiences have given me a unique perspective on sport. It is my hope that you will enjoy that perspective and yet understand where it is limited.

Acknowledgments

I want to express my sincere thanks to hundreds of students who sparked my interest in evaluating the information on sociology of sport. They challenged me to make the information relevant to today's world of sport.

I'm indebted to Rainer Martens, who challenged me to accept this project and had confidence in me to produce a worthwhile product. Likewise, I appreciate the work of Myles Schrag, acquisitions editor, for his guidance in the conception and shaping of the manuscript. Amanda Ewing, in her role as developmental editor, offered insightful advice and helped keep me on target. I'd also like to thank Linda Ann Keeler for writing the PowerPoint presentation and instructor's guide.

Finally, my wife, Kathy, has been a tireless supporter throughout the project and encouraged me every step of the way. Without her interest and personal commitment to sport, it would have been a lonely undertaking.

Photo Credits

page 190 © Associated Press

page 194 © Sportschrome

page 195 © AP Photo/Eric Gay

page 197 © Sportschrome

page 199 © AP Photo/Koji Sasahara

page 200 © Sportschrome

page 205 © AP Photo/Francis Specker

page 211 © Getty

page 213 © Associated Press

page 214 © Associated Press

page 220, left, © AP Photo/Eric Risberg

page 220, right, © AP Photo/Laurent Rebours

page 222 © Sportschrome

page 223 © AP Photo/Kamran Jebreili

page 227 © AP Photo/Anja Niedringhaus

page 229 © Aurora Photos/Andoni Canela/ASA/IPN

page 232 © Sportschrome

page 235 © AP Photo/Charles Rex Arbogast

page 240 © Eyewire/Photodisc/Getty Images

page 243 © AP Photo/Thanassis Stavrakis

page 247 © Associated Press/HO/USOC, Joseph Kusumoto

page 249 © AP Photo/Alden Pellett

page 252 © Photodisc/Getty Images

page 255 © Associated Press

page 256 © AP Photo/Chuck Stoody

page 259 © AP Photo

page 261 © Associated Press

page 262 © Dale Garvey

page 263 © Getty

page 266 © Associated Press

page 267 © AP Photo

page 269 © Dale Garvey

page 271 © AP Photo/Lenny Ignelzi

page 276 © Eyewire\Photodisc\Getty Images

page 278 © Empics

page 282 © Photodisc Royalty Free

page 284 © AP Photo/Lawrence Jackson

page 287 © AP Photo/Daniel Luna

page 292 © AP/World Wide Photos

page 294 © AP Photo/Paul Connors

page 295 © AP Photo/Manu Fernandez

page 296 © AP Photo/Jack Smith

page 298 © AP Photo/Dieter Endlicher

page 300 © Sportschrome

page 301 © AP Photo/Amy Sancetta

page 306 © Aurora Photos/Melissa Farlow

page 308 © AP Photo/Kevork Djansezian

page 311 © AP Photo/Ann Heisenfelt

page 314 Courtesy of Bob Hurley

page 324 © AP Photo/John Russell

page 326 © Malcom W. Emmons/Sporting News/ Icon SMI

page 328 © AP Photo/Stephan Savoia

page 331, from *l* to *r:* © Human Kinetics, © Associated Press, © AP Photo/Alastair Grant, © Human Kinetics, © Human Kinetics, © Human Kinetics, © Human Kinetics, © AP Photo/Magnus Torle, © AP Photo/Clive Rose, © Human Kinetics, © Aurora Photos/Ed Kashi/IPN, © Human Kinetics, © Aurora Photos/ Andoni Canela/ASA/IPN, © AP Photo/ Thanassis Stavrakis, © Associated press, © AP Photo/Lenny Ignelzi, © AP Photo/ Daniel Luna, © AP Photo/Ann Heisenfelt

page 336 © AP Photo/Todd Bissonette

page 339 © Associated Press

page 341 © Getty Royalty Free Images

Studying Sport in Society

The opening chapters set the stage for studying sport from a socio-logical perspective by pointing out the integral relationship between sports and society in North America. The first chapter defines salient terms such as *play, games, sports,* and *work* in terms of purpose, organization, and complexity. As sport moves from *partici-pation sport* played by amateurs to *high-performance sport* played by professional athletes, it moves away from recreation or leisure play activities and takes on the characteristics of work.

In chapter 1 we also look at why people study sport, and we review the sport sciences that form the basis for the scientific knowledge upon which coaching and training are based.

Chapter 2 presents the typical methods of studying sport. It defines several social theories and gives examples as to how they might apply to sport research and interpretation. While sport psychology tends to focus on one individual, sport sociology looks at groups of people and how they interact and affect one another. The emerging field of sport sociology is described along with tools for learning more.

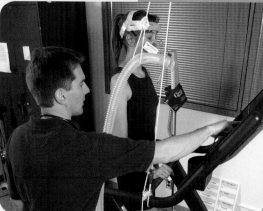

What Is Sport and Why Do We Study It?

On Thursday, April 15, 1954, I realized that baseball was important in the world. On that day Baltimore, Maryland, got its own Major League Baseball team and opened the spanking-new Memorial Stadium. The Orioles, spawned from the lowly St. Louis Browns franchise, marked the entry of my home city of Baltimore into the big leagues! Although just a kid, I knew that day was special since city hall closed for half the day, most businesses shut down, and best of all, school closed for the day so that everyone could enjoy the city-wide parade.

The city of Baltimore was about to embark on its golden age of sports concurrent with my childhood. We rooted for moderately talented sports teams at first, but soon Hall of Famer Brooks Robinson led the Orioles while the magical arm of Hall of Famer Johnny Unitas guided our football team, the Colts. Having two superstars like Unitas and Robinson performing in the same city was like having current stars Peyton Manning and Albert Pujols as your football and baseball heroes. I knew right then that I was falling in love with sports.

You probably have a similar story from your childhood of your introduction to sports. Once hooked, we never quite let go of our interest, loyalty, and devotion to sports and our heroes. In fact, the word *fan* derives from *fanatic*, and that's just what many of us have been or continue to be.

If you're like me, studying sports is fun and can also help you expand your understanding of the place of sports in North America and the world. Imagine if all sports were banned, as they have been from time to time in certain civilizations. Our lives would change dramatically in how we spend our discretionary time, money, and emotion.

Sports affect our lives every day. Strangers on the street stop to chat about their hometown sport successes, discussing the local high school, college, or professional team. Entire cities wake up the morning after an exhilarating win by their home team and feel proud to live where they live or wake up after a tough loss in a meaningful game and sink into mourning. Kids look up to sport heroes, memorize the lifetime statistics of each athlete, and dream of someday making it to their own fame and fortune. They copy the stance, mannerisms, and dress of their heroes as they grow up.

Sports also affect the cultures, traditions, and values of our society. Stories in the sports world help us clarify our stance on issues such as racial equality, gender opportunity, rights of citizens with disabilities and senior citizens, class mobility, youth development through physical activity, and creating a better standard of health and fitness for everyone. We examine these issues and more in the succeeding chapters. For now, let's focus on what sport is and how it differs from play and games.

SPORT THROUGH THE AGES

Before we can analyze the effect of sport on society (and vice versa) we need to know what sport is and why we should study it. *Sport* is derived from the Latin root *desporto,* which means "to carry away." Sport has been used throughout the ages to describe physical activities that are competitive and organized

Games and sport have been a vital part of every civilization, dating back to the ancient Greeks as shown on this vase from the 5th century BCE.

and that divert people from everyday activities producing economic gain or sustained life.

Sport and games have fulfilled various roles in societies throughout the centuries. The early Greek civilization used sport and games in celebrations, to honor the gods, or as part of funeral ceremonies. The great Greek poet Homer described sport in his *Iliad* and *Odyssey*. Typical contests of physical prowess included running races, chariot races, wrestling, boxing, and leaping. Hunting was also a sport of the ancient Greeks. In the ancient city-state of Sparta, sport and games helped young men refine their wartime skills. In contrast to Sparta, the city-state of Athens educated young men in grammar, music, and gymnastics to fully develop their physical and mental capacities. The difference between Sparta and Athens in the approach to sport was the beneficiary of the sporting skill: In Sparta the state benefited while in Athens sport aided the perfection of the individual man.

Other ancient civilizations showed evidence of the role of sport and games through paintings, carvings, and other historical documents. Running, swimming, and jumping have been part of every culture. Combat activities like boxing, wrestling, and other martial arts such as those originating in the Far East are part of every culture's history. Games with a ball were popular in diverse civilizations, including the Egyptians and the American and Canadian Indians, and various forms of football can be traced to ancient China.

In the Roman Empire, physical fitness and skill were taught to young boys to prepare them for the military. Their physical training included using the spear, sword, shield, and javelin along with horsemanship and swimming. Near the end of the Roman Empire, chariot races, gladiatorial contests, and other forms of combat were popular entertainment performed by slaves to amuse wealthy citizens. Eventually, the Romans rejected the Olympic Games founded by the Greeks as a pagan festival to honor the Greek gods and therefore in conflict with Christianity (Rice, Hutchinson, and Lee 1958; Spears and Swanson 1978).

Sport and games are still used today as celebrations and as examples of athletic prowess. But what is sport?

DEFINITION OF SPORT

The **sport pyramid** is a helpful way to think of sports (see figure 1.1). The pyramid contains four elements of human activity—play, games, sport, and work. These terms are often confused because of the interchange and overlap of ideas. Let's look at each element individually and then examine the interrelationships.

Play

Play forms the base of the pyramid since it is the physical activity of childhood and continues throughout life in various forms. Play is a free activity that involves exploration, self-expression, dreaming, and pretending. Play has no firm rules and can take place anywhere. The outcome of play is unimportant other than giving pleasure. Over the years, many people have postulated theories of play, including Dutch historian Johan Huizinga (1950), who described play as free of form, separate from ordinary life, and with no specific purpose. He considered games and sport to be specialized forms of play with more formal rules and purposes and an emphasis on the outcome.

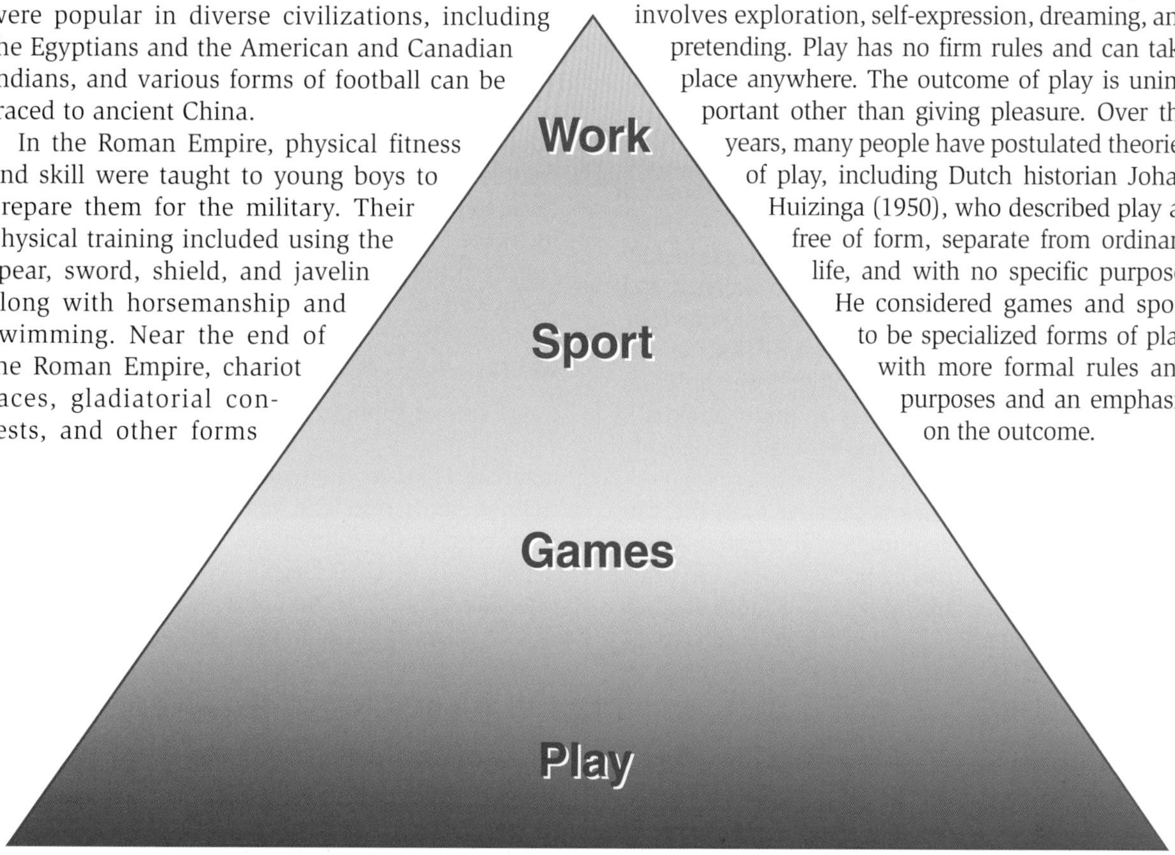

FIGURE 1.1 The sport pyramid.

Play is unstructured fun, with no rules.

Games

Games are an aspect of play that have greater structure and are competitive. Games have clear participation goals that are mental, physical, or a combination of both; are governed by informal or formal rules; involve competition; have outcomes determined by luck, strategy, skill, or a combination thereof; and result in prestige or status. Inactive games include board games like Monopoly, card games like hearts, and video games like Madden NFL, Texas hold'em poker, or Halo. Active games include stickball, relays, capture the flag, touch football, dodgeball, and street hockey.

The category of games is broader than the category of sport (described next), and actual sporting events such as a football or hockey game are often described as games. Taken by itself, a football game is a game, but when it is part of a league with rules, standings, and sponsors, as a college football game is, it becomes sport.

An example of the variation in games is the work of Dale Le Fevre, who developed and popularized the New Games that emphasize cooperation, participation, creativity, and personal expression rather than competition. New Games are being used in physical education classes, in youth camps, by religious groups, and by businesses to teach team building. Le Fevre's latest book, *Best New Games* (2002), is popular around the world. In many of his workshops, traditionally adversarial groups have successfully come together to play and have fun: Arabs and Israelis in the Middle East; Catholics and Protestants in Northern Ireland; mixed races in South Africa; and Serbs, Croats, and Muslims in Croatia and Serbia.

Sport

Sport can be thought of as a specialized or higher order of play or as games with certain special characteristics that set them apart. Various authors have defined sport over the years, and generally their ideas contain the following characteristics (Coakley 2004; Leonard 1980; Sage 1998; VanderZwaag and Sheehan 1978). The first and perhaps most critical is that sport must involve a physical component. Unlike play or games, which may or may not be physical, sport must include physical movement and skill. Sport typically involves physical coordination, strength, speed, endurance, and flexibility. Following this definition, a game of chess cannot be a sport, whereas games such as billiards and darts can be classified as sports although the physical skill required is fairly limited to eye–hand coordination.

The second common characteristic of sport is that it is competitive, with outcomes that are important to those involved and often to others such as families, fans, sponsoring organizations, and the media. Winning and losing are a critical part of competition and powerfully motivate participants to train faithfully and compete using their best effort.

The third common characteristic of sport is that it involves institutionalized games. Sports are governed by an outside group or institution that oversees conduct and results and enforces rules. In the United States, the National Football League (NFL) governs professional football, the National Collegiate Athletic Association (NCAA) governs collegiate sports, and local Game and Wildlife Commissions set the rules for hunting and fishing. So a pickup baseball game at a local park is just a game, but a Little League baseball game with rules, customs, standards for play, officials, coaches, and records of wins and losses is a sport.

The fourth common characteristic of sport is that it almost always requires specialized facilities and equipment. While this may be less true of sports such as cross country running or distance swimming across a natural body of water, most sports require a field with set boundaries, a pool, a gymnasium, a court, a golf course, or a similar facility. Equipment becomes particularly important at the professional level where athletes critically depend on the quality of their sled, skates, vaulting pole, tennis racket, golf clubs, or baseball bat.

Sport, then, is typically defined in North America as institutionalized competitive activity that involves physical skill and specialized facilities or equipment and is conducted according to an accepted set of rules to determine a winner.

The definition of sport in a given society reflects the culture, beliefs, and attitudes of that culture toward warfare, manhood, survival, and honoring the gods. In a society emphasizing cooperation more than competition, sports would differ from those in our North American society. In fact, the rise of alternative sports among our youth (see chapter 6 on youth sport) demonstrates the changing definition of sport within a given culture.

For most people, attaining high performance and a professional career in sport is not an option.

Sport is an institutionalized competitive activity.

Instead, we play sports for the love of the game, as a hobby; we play as **amateurs,** which stems from the Latin word for love. We gain intrinsic satisfaction, competing to improve our fitness, refine our physical skills, work in a team, or embrace the challenge and excitement of testing our skill against nature or other competitors. For amateur athletes, participation is the key rather than the outcome. Sport participation is recreation that differs greatly from work. We participate to rejuvenate our spirit, without needing other extrinsic rewards.

Sport can vary to accommodate people with physical or sensory impairments. Program directors who value the inclusion of people with disabilities use modified sports such as wheelchair basketball, tennis, soccer, and volleyball to blend those with disabilities and those without disabilities in sport competition. We'll look at sport for people with disabilities in chapter 14.

Work

Work is purposeful activity that may include physical or mental effort to perform a task, overcome an obstacle, or achieve a desired outcome. Often, people earn their living through work by trading it for compensation that provides for existence. Work appears at the top of the pyramid in figure 1.1 because sport can take on the characteristics of work at the professional level. Professional athletes are paid to perform work by training their physical skills to the highest level for competition with other elite athletes. Although all professional athletes begin their lives with childhood play and then participate in games and eventually sports, they may begin to regard sport as work after many years of facing competitive pressure, fighting through injuries, and living up to the expectations of their employer, their fans, and the media.

At the highest level of organized sport, athletes and coaches may earn millions of dollars for their performance along with endorsement fees for the use of their appearance or name to promote particular products. Once they accept financial remuneration for their athletic skills, they are deemed professional athletes, hired to perform in their sport.

Athletes of any age who aspire to become professional athletes may be described as **high-performance athletes.** They develop their composite athletic skill so they can perform at the highest level possible and perhaps earn a living doing so. Children as young as age 10 may decide to follow their dream of becoming a star athlete and submit to a regimen of training and competition that prepares them for a professional career. Even at young ages, if the goal is a professional career, playing sports can take on the characteristics of work, which can lead to burnout and boredom for a child who is more interested in playing a sport for the fun of it.

Activity Time-Out: Sport or Game?

Would you classify each of the following activities as a game or a sport? Test your understanding of the differences between sports and games and then compare your answers with those of other students. Mark S for sports and G for games:

____ Flying a kite	____ Street hockey	____ Boccie
____ Throwing a Frisbee	____ Weightlifting	____ Tap dancing
____ Croquet	____ Ballroom dancing	____ Cheerleading
____ Roulette	____ Jumping rope	____ Jogging
____ Juggling	____ Fishing	____ Bowling
____ Skateboarding	____ Riflery	____ Bicycling

If you had trouble classifying some of the activities, it may be that they fit neither sports nor games. They may involve physical activity, but their primary purpose is for entertainment. For example, professional wrestling involves two people who perform carefully choreographed moves that may appear to be competitive but in fact are pure entertainment. A Broadway show may entertain you with skillful dancing and singing, but that does not qualify the dancing as a sport. Evaluate the activity against all the classification criteria before judging whether it fits the definition of sport.

For the amateur, golf is a sport, but for professional athlete Tiger Woods, it is work.

sums of money to support their athletic teams even though the players can only receive scholarships in return for their services. Similarly, even some youth programs take on the characteristics of professional sport by requiring kids to train year round, specialize in one sport at a young age, and perhaps risk a career-threatening injury in the heat of competition.

Only a small percentage of athletes can ever hope to reach the professional level. The health and welfare of society are clearly affected by the amount of its exercise and activity, yet the attention in sports is typically on the gifted few. As our population ages, obesity increases, and physical fitness becomes a national concern, perhaps participation in sport by the masses will command more attention, funding, and publicity.

It is only in the United States where *amateur* and *professional* are defined so specifically. This delineation is largely due to the unique presence of thousands of collegiate sports teams that have maintained an amateur label. In the rest of the world, this distinction is unnecessary because universities generally do not field sports teams or offer athletic scholarships. In European countries, Russia, or Africa children as young as age 10 may sign professional contracts and deals (with parental consent) that provide coaching and training expense money from a sporting goods manufacturer or from government sport agencies. In the United States people would say that these athletes had "turned pro" while in their country no such distinction is even considered.

Given the discussion on sport and work, we might represent the top levels of the sport pyramid as shown in figure 1.2.

The reality of the pyramid as shown in figure 1.2 is that much of the attention on sport in North America is focused on the highest level of sport performance. Professional sport is a business and decisions at this level often reflect the goal of earning money. The line between professional and amateur becomes blurred at the highest levels of collegiate sport where universities commit large

Work

Professional sports ↑ High performance

Sport

Amateur sports ↑ Participation

Games

Play

FIGURE 1.2 Detailed sport pyramid.

In the Arena With . . . *Jim Thorpe*

Jim Thorpe was born in Oklahoma in 1887 to Hiram Thorpe, a farmer, and Mary James, a Potawatomi Indian. He attended school at the American Indian School in Carlisle, Pennsylvania, where he was selected as a first team All-American in football in 1909 and 1910. He won gold medals in the 1912 Olympic Games in Belgium in both the pentathlon and the decathlon, and he set world records that stood for decades. After his Olympic performance, Thorpe signed on to play baseball for the New York Giants, and in the off-season he also played professional football. In 1950 he was named the greatest overall male athlete of the first half of the 20th century by the Associated Press, and a few years later ABC's Wide World of Sports named him the Athlete of the Century.

But Thorpe also came afoul of the delineation between amateur and professional. Shortly after his triumphant Olympic victories, information came out that he had played two semiprofessional seasons of baseball, accepting modest pay. Even though his semiprofessional play was in another sport, he was stripped of his Olympic medals and his records were removed. By playing for pay Thorpe broke the rules of the Olympic Games at the time and he paid the price. Eventually, the rules of the Olympic Games were changed as attitudes toward professional athletes changed. It wasn't until 1982 that the medals were restored to Thorpe posthumously and his records were put back into the books. Support from the media, notably the *New York Times,* and constant pressure from his family and heirs secured his Olympic legacy (Thorpe 2005).

In recent years, two notable American athletes have turned pro at young ages. Freddy Adu debuted in his professional career in 2004 at age 14, playing for Major League Soccer franchise D.C. United. He is the youngest professional player in modern team sport history and carries the burden of America's hope for an international soccer star. Golfer Michelle Wie turned professional in 2005 just days before her 16th birthday. She immediately became the world's highest paid female golfer, with a reported $8 million U.S. in endorsement fees. Because of their decision to become professional, these young athletes are not eligible to participate in college athletics in their sport, but for these exceptional athletes this is not a severe consequence. The athletes who do suffer from the eligibility rules are borderline professionals who may wish to someday go to college. In the United States, this demarcation between amateur and professional can have far-reaching consequences for young athletes who are uninformed.

STUDY OF SPORT

Now that we know what sport is (physical competition according to a set of rules that determines a winner), we can look at why its study is worthwhile. There are three main reasons why people learn about sport and physical activity:

- Personal development
- Scholarly study
- Professional practice

Many people enjoy learning about the science of sport and physical activity because they are attracted to sports and are intrigued enough to want to expand their understanding. There are millions of sports fans in any country, many of whom are experts at sport trivia, but there are few who truly understand sports from a scientific viewpoint.

According to Hoffman (2005), at least 10,000 people worldwide engage in scholarly study of physical activity, and these people spend an estimated $100 million U.S. to acquire knowledge in the field. The growth of interest in sport study is evident in the remarkable explosion in the number of scholarly sport journals and societies that has occurred the past 50 years; the number of journals has multiplied about eight times while the number of societies has grown fourfold.

Much of the study of sport occurs in universities. You can find departments devoted to specific sport sciences or to the overall field of kinesiology or physical education. At the undergraduate level, most students acquire a general overview of the field. At the graduate level, students seeking a master's or doctoral degree often concentrate their studies in one or two of the field's subdisciplines (discussed later in this chapter on page 12).

Professional practice within sport and physical activity has grown and developed over the years to serve others through sports. Many students study the generic field of kinesiology in college and later fashion a career by specializing in a subdiscipline or its application in everyday living. Often competency or certification tests are required for legitimately practicing within a specialty. Career options can be grouped as the following:

- Teaching or coaching
- Sport management
- Sport research
- Program directing
- Sport promotion and publicity
- Recreation and leisure
- Therapeutic exercise
- Sport business
- Health and fitness

Sport Sciences

In the United States, the study of physical activity was typically labeled *physical education* and the major goal of colleges offering majors in physical education was to prepare teachers and coaches. In recent years, labels such as *exercise and sport science, health and human performance, movement science,* and *sport and leisure studies* have been adopted to more accurately describe the study and function of physical activity.

Happily, many universities have adopted the term *kinesiology,* leading the trend toward greater unanimity in labeling the field of study of physical activity. After extensive study and debate additional support for using *kinesiology* came from other prestigious academic associations such as the American Academy of Physical Education. Although you may not include the term *kinesiology* in your typical daily language, you should understand who studies physical activity and where to seek information about it. Sports are a part of physical activity, although many other forms of movement are included under the field of kinesiology.

During the last 35 years, the study of sport has remarkably changed as scientific study has expanded its base of knowledge. Sport study has been divided into subdisciplines, each with its own devotees, researchers, and practitioners. The emerging subdisciplines, based on scientific inquiry, slowly changed the perception of sport and physical activity and gave rise to a broader, more concrete overall discipline. It will help you to understand each of these subdisciplines,

Activity Time-Out: Careers in Sport and Physical Activity

Identify at least three people who work in sport or physical activity, each from a different category listed above. Interview each person face to face or by telephone to learn the following:

- Why did you chose a career in sport and physical activity?
- How did you narrow down your interests to select your specialty?
- What education or certification was required? Do you think the standards for your specialty should be more stringent and if so, how?
- What is the average yearly compensation in your field?
- Do you see the job opportunities for your specialty expanding or shrinking in the next 10 years and why?

how they relate to each other, and how to integrate their information. The subdisciplines of sport science are typically divided into three domains:

- Biophysical
- Psychosocial
- Sociocultural

Let's look at each of the sport sciences.

Biophysical Domain

The **biophysical domain** focuses on physical activity from the sciences of biomechanics, physiology, and medicine. Areas of study within this domain include the following:

- **Biomechanics** is the study of the structure and function of biological systems by applying principles of physics to human motion to understand how the body uses gravity, inertia, balance, force, or motion to produce speed, power, or distance.
- **Exercise physiology** is the study of human systems to enhance strength, speed, and endurance

Conducting $\dot{V}O_2$max tests is an area that falls within the biophysical domain.

in performance toward the Olympic ideal of higher, faster, and stronger.

- **Nutrition** is sometimes studied as part of physiology to understand how food and drink affect performance. An athlete's diet and hydration habits under varied climates, contest durations, and environmental conditions are investigated.
- **Sports medicine** examines the prevention, care, and rehabilitation of injuries caused by participation in physical activity and sport. Research in sports medicine may also affect recommendations for training.

Psychosocial Domain

The **psychosocial domain** focuses on physical activity from the science of psychology. Areas of study within this domain include the following:

- **Sport psychology** is the study of human behavior in sport, including enhancing performance and treating disorders that affect optimal performance.
- **Motor learning and behavior** is the study of relatively permanent changes in motor behavior that result from practice or experience. It focuses on how people learn to perform motor skills and patterns efficiently and retain that ability even under pressure.
- **Pedagogy** is the study of the art and science of teaching. It focuses on the teacher or coach who creates the learning environment and assists the learning of sport skills.

Sociocultural Domain

The **sociocultural domain** focuses on physical activity from the sciences of history, philosophy, and sociology. Areas of study within this domain include the following:

- **Sport history** is the study of the tradition and practices of physical activity and sport over time and within different countries, cultures, and civilizations.
- **Philosophy of sport** examines the definition, value, and meaning of sport. Understanding your philosophy of physical activity will help you create your coaching style or prescription for sport participation.
- **Sport sociology** is the study of sport and physical activity within the context of the social conditions and culture in which people live. Since this book focuses on the sociology of sport, it can help you identify the role of sports in your society and world. Whether you are an elite athlete, a recreational athlete, a prospective coach, a prospective athletic trainer, or a sports fan, you can deepen your understanding of the issues and possibilities in the

Activity Time-Out: Effects of Physical Activity

Since sports are a physical activity, they can affect the physical well-being of the population. Physical health has grown more important as our population ages and continues to live longer. Let's look at some alarming statistics from the U.S. Surgeon General (U.S. Department of Health and Human Services 2001):

- **Overweight** and **obesity** may soon cause as much preventable disease and death as cigarette smoking causes.
- Currently, approximately 300,000 U.S. deaths per year are associated with obesity and overweight (compared to 400,000 annual deaths associated with smoking).
- In 1999, an estimated 61% of U.S. adults were overweight, along with 13% of children and adolescents. Obesity among adults has doubled since 1980, while overweight among adolescents has tripled.
- Less than one-third of Americans meet the federal recommendations to engage in at least 30 minutes of moderate physical activity at least 5 days a week, while 40% of adults engage in no leisure activity at all.

Given the statistics, it makes sense to evaluate the promise of sport as a physical activity that could ameliorate such health concerns.

sports world. Studying sport sociology may help you determine what role you want sports to play in your life, your family, and your community. Once you clearly understand that role, you can create a positive force for change, growth, and continuing prosperity for sports.

Sociology is the study of a society, its institutions, and its relationships. It relies on a systematic study of the development, structure, interaction, and collective behavior of a group of human beings (Merriam-Webster's 2001). Mature societies are likely to be more complex. In a modern society like ours, sociological analysis of sport is broad and deep since its study ranges from families to sport participants to sport spectators to even those who gamble on sport. Sociology provides us with the tools to better understand sports as they exist in our lives. Analyzing institutions such as schools, colleges, clubs, churches, youth sport organizations, and professional sport organizations and studying social processes such as commercialization, institutionalization, mass communication, conflict, and change are essential to thoroughly understanding the dynamics of how sport operates.

Growth in Sport Sciences

Now that you better understand the overall field of sport science and its subdisciplines, you may suspect their influence on the field's recent growth in volume and complexity. More importantly, the explosion of knowledge in the sport sciences has improved the average citizen's experience of sport and physical activity. The knowledge acquired through the sport sciences allows us to do the following:

- Understand the historical precedents in sport and fitness, avoid mistakes of the past, and plan a healthier future
- Enhance competition performance through better training methods and produce record-setting performances that challenge us all
- Provide better motivation for citizens through understanding of the value of physical activity and help citizens plan for physical development
- Teach people new activity skills faster and more efficiently and thus convince them of their ability to successfully perform an activity
- Prevent physical injuries and speed up the recovery process following injury
- Understand the influence of sport on our culture and use sport and activity to promote equality, fairness, and success for all citizens
- Help people deal with stress and anxiety through sport
- Promote good health at all ages that allows people to function with high energy

Understanding the history of sport and physical activity falls into the sociocultural domain.

- Understand how training for sports expands and challenges our physical systems and strengthens them to deal with emergencies
- Provide healthy activity for youth that enhances their maturation into productive adults
- Offer a better quality of life in later years as the life expectancy extends

You can see the many ways the sport sciences can positively influence our lives. You can see why their growth affects the expansion of sport and physical activity. There is a slight risk that people will use information from the sport sciences out of context because looking at the complete picture is too time consuming or daunting. However, the knowledge gained in all of the sport sciences needs to be integrated to achieve the best understanding of sport and physical activity.

CHAPTER SUMMARY

The sport pyramid is a good way to look at sport. The pyramid starts with play, which is informal, free activity that begins in childhood and continues throughout life. The second level of the pyramid is games, which are more structured than play and have specific goals and outcomes through competition. Sport is a higher order of games and has specific characteristics. The characteristics of sport include (1) a physical component, (2) competition to determine a winner and loser, (3) an outside group or institution that governs the conduct and results of the sport and enforces its rules, and (4) specialized facilities and equipment.

Sports can be further defined as professional sports that focus on the high performance of athletes who are rewarded extrinsically with money, fame, and prestige and as amateur sports in which people compete for the love of the game and value their participation for the excitement, physical exertion, test of skill, or benefits to their personal health.

Sport is studied for personal development, scholarly study, and professional practice. Through studying sport we can recognize historical precedents in sport, health, and physical activity and can advocate changes in the society around us. The 10 individual sport sciences belong to three domains: (1) biophysical, (2) psychosocial, and (3) sociocultural. Integrating the knowledge from the different sport sciences allows us to better interpret their collective information.

How Do We Study Sport?

Student Outcomes

After reading this chapter, you will know the following:

- Types of research methods and data
- Sociology theories used to analyze sport
- How sociology theories apply to the study of sport
- How to use theories to interpret sport and decide on necessary changes in sport

You may have watched, read about, and played a lot of sports during your lifetime. You probably know what it means to be a participant or spectator in a sport setting. But you may not know that you have been asking the questions sport sociologists have asked for years. When your high school athletic program was in danger of losing district funding and you defended it on the grounds that sport teaches a strong work ethic, did you know you were speaking as a functionalist? Or did you know you were a critical theorist when you suggested intercollegiate athletes be compensated as workers for the millions of dollars they bring to their universities? That you might be considered a feminist when you argued that women tennis pros winning a Grand Slam final should be paid the same amount as the men who win? These and many other examples show how sociocultural issues pervade the sports world, both locally and globally.

From chapter 1, we know that sports are physical competitions that follow a set of rules to determine a winner. We also know that we should study sport so we can recognize trends and apply that information to the current world. But *how* do we study sports? First, we collect data through research. Then we analyze the collected data using different social theories, all of which view the world differently.

RESEARCH METHODS

In order to study sport or physical activity, the research scientist must have tools for collecting data that can be organized and analyzed. Many times a researcher will use more than one tool at a time. The sport sociologist generally uses two types of tools: **quantifiable studies** producing data that can be counted and analyzed statistically or **qualitative data** collected through interviews and observations of individuals or groups or through analyzing societal characteristics and trends. Examples of different research methods are the following:

- **Survey research** through questionnaires is popular for determining sport participation and comparing spectator habits. With this method large quantities of data can be collected, analyzed for trends, and then generalized to the entire population if random sampling is used. However, this approach relies on self-reports by athletes or spectators that may or may not be accurate. Furthermore, unless the data are discrete enough to segregate responses from different groups of people, they may be misleading. For example, large surveys often combine all age groups to determine trends when separation by age might produce very different responses. Similarly, not accounting for race, gender, ethnic group, or income level may affect data interpretation. Surveys can also limit the choice of responses and thus miss the true feelings of respondents.

- **Interviews** with individuals or small groups (called *focus groups)* offer more in-depth questioning and can elicit unexpected answers from open-ended questions. When designed correctly with sampling from various ethnic groups, geographical locations, income levels, genders, and other variables, an interview can provide a deeper analysis. However, interviews are time consuming, expensive, and often rely on small sample sizes because of time and cost.

- **Content research** involves collecting information or pictures from articles, magazines, and TV programs and assigning the data to categories around a particular theme. For example, in content research the ideal feminine body type for sport could be inferred from the frequency of photos of various body types appearing in the major sports pages. A drawback is that information is not provided directly by athletes, but rather by others reporting on them. Content research has been useful, however, in assessing the amount of coverage the media give to females in sport over a specified duration.

- **Ethnography,** which is based on observation, involves data collected by researchers who immerse themselves in an environment and keep recorded conversations or notes. Topics such as "Life on the Pro Tour" or "Life in the Minor Leagues" lend themselves to ethnography. Researchers use detailed notes of their observations, personal interviews, and other sources of data to gather a full picture of their subject. The obvious weakness in this approach is the time and cost required for a complete analysis. Yet some of the most interesting and helpful studies in sport have used this method to provide an inside view of a particular sport or class of athletes.

- **Historical research** involves looking at trends in sport over time. Often, the value of such research

Activity Time-Out: Using Research Methods

Imagine you are part of a research team looking at trends in youth sport participation in rural communities. Which research methods would you use to collect data? If you were looking at trends in youth sport participation in inner cities or suburbs, would your research methods change? Explain your answers.

is to compare trends in sport with trends in society. For example, the changes in female participation in sport during the second half of the 20th century closely paralleled the push for equality and women's rights in the United States. While historical research is helpful, it is usually limited to large societal trends.

■ **Societal analysis** uses social theories (described in the next section) to examine life from a social point of view. For example, a researcher can apply a critical feminist model to professional sports to compare the opportunities for women and men who are professional athletes, including financial compensation for similar work.

The risk of using only one theory is overlooking other salient facts such as race, income level, and historical precedent (Hoffman 2005).

No matter the research method, once the data are collected they need to be analyzed. Several social theories can be used to analyze data.

SOCIAL THEORIES

Social theories are used to compare the trends in sport with an overall social theory and thus conclude when sport reflects the larger culture or acts as a change agent. Theories of sport sociology help

Looking at this polo match as a functionalist theorist, you would see the benefits of fair play and teamwork. But would you see the lack of economic diversity that typifies polo?

organize our thoughts about a particular issue. They involve describing existing social situations, analyzing them from various perspectives, and formulating certain beliefs based on the findings. A theory can be explained to others, who can compare it to their analyses. As theories gain acceptance, they may become the basis for predicting the future or for calling for change within sport.

Analyzing sport with a social theory helps us consider the larger picture of how sport exists throughout society. It forces us to examine all aspects of the sport experience, including the seat of power within a sport, the values that are embraced, and the interaction of various groups involved. Sports become much more than a competitive season with a beginning and an end when examined within the context of larger social issues. Most social theories are rooted in the concept of enhancing and preserving the status quo or looking at the need for change. Table 2.1 lists the six theories discussed in this chapter; let's discuss each of them now.

Functionalist Theory

Functionalist theory looks at sport as a social institution that reinforces the current value system in a society. Sports are seen as maintaining the status quo by positively benefiting a community or nation striving to work and play together. The traditional American values of hard work, discipline, and competition are perpetuated through sports and reinforced as the path to success.

Functionalist theorists see sport as contributing to the smooth functioning of a society by helping people promote common values, which in turn leads to stability within communities and the nation. At the same time, as social changes occur, sport can take a leading role in promoting those changes and thereby reinforce the dominant social value system.

The weakness of functionalist theory is that what is good for the architects of sport, who are often the economically or culturally privileged few, may not benefit society at large. Further, sport may positively benefit the average citizen while it discriminates against other groups (such as women, Hispanics, or people who have physical disabilities) that are typically underrepresented in sport.

A proponent of functionalist theory may embrace the traditional American emphasis of winning at all costs in sport. Americans celebrate winners and reward them lavishly until the next great team or

In the Arena With . . . the National Federation of State High School Associations

The National Federation of State High School Associations (NFHS) conducts annual research through its member state associations, who track the participation of high school students in cocurricular activities including sports. NFHS data list the number of athletes who play competitive varsity sports, record which sports they play, and highlight the most popular sports. They also compare participation levels over time and typically extol the virtues of sport by pointing out the continuous growth in participation over the past 15 years, especially the rapid growth of female participation, which is lauded as significant social progress (see www.nfhs.org).

Overlooked in their statistics are the trends in participation by specific populations such as racial groups, trends in opportunities for people with physical disabilities, and trends in the increasingly worrisome participation cost that affects varsity sport opportunities.

NFHS research tends to reinforce the status quo of varsity sports participation by a relatively small percentage of high school students without acknowledging problems in society such as the rising obesity rates partially caused by the lack of physical activity of youth. While varsity sports may be flourishing, intramural or community-based sports cannot be growing if so many youth are sedentary. For example, since 1994, participation in high school lacrosse has increased by 188%, making it the fastest growing sport according to the NFHS as reported by the U.S. Lacrosse Association in its annual report for 2004 (United States Lacrosse Association 2004). However, statistics do not address the question of why lacrosse has grown so rapidly (see chapter 11 for more details).

ABLE 2.1 Social Theories for the Study of Sport

Theory	How it looks at the world	Preferred method of research	Major concerns as it looks at sport	Shortcomings
Functionalist theory	Maintain the status quo and equilibrium.	Quantitative survey research	Sport is a valuable social institution that helps build character and instill values. Competition is valuable and high performance is a critical outcome of sport participation.	Tends to overemphasize the positive consequences of sport while ignoring those who are disenfranchised or overlooked such as women, people who are economically poor, certain racial groups, and people who have physical disabilities.
Conflict theory	Economic interests shape the world. Those who have power exploit those who do not. Change is inevitable and struggle by repressed classes is expected.	Societal analysis	Sport benefits the individuals and organizations in power to the detriment of the participants and working class. Athletes should have more control over their sport destiny and quality of experience.	Relies too heavily on economic factors and ignores the importance of race, ethnicity, gender, and age. Underestimates the effect of groups that empower individuals in a capitalist society. Tends to overlook participation and recreational sport for healthy living.
Critical theory	Life is complex and diverse. Order is obtained through struggles over ideology and power. A better life for all citizens is the goal. Sports do not simply mirror society; they provide opportunity to change society.	Societal analysis	Sports must change to be fair to everyone, more democratic, and sensitive to diversity. Sports can help us improve our outlook toward gender, physical or mental disability, sexual orientation, and physical talent.	Critical theories are varied and sometimes confusing. They tend to encourage resistance against the status quo to protect special interests even when doing so is not advisable. They work better for specific cases than for forming an overall ideology.
Feminist theory	Social life is based on a patriarchal ideology and controlled by men in powerful positions. Feminine virtues are ignored or undervalued.	Quantifiable questionnaires, societal analysis, ethnography, and content research	Females lack equal opportunity in sport. There is a lack of women in coaching and leadership positions. Traditional masculine traits of competitiveness and aggressiveness conflict with traditional feminine traits like sensitivity and nurturing.	Similar weaknesses to those of other critical theories. Also weak in addressing other categories that are connected to gender such as age, race, social class, and disability.
Interactionist theory	View the world from bottom up rather than from top down. Focus on social relationships between people. People make conscious decisions on how to respond and act toward the outside world.	Qualitative ethnographic research	How people choose to participate in sports. What the experience is like for the athlete. Encourages open and democratic sport organizations. Youth sport should fit the needs and desires of kids.	Focuses on the individual to the exclusion of the overall structure of sport. Does not address issues of power in sport as critical theories do.
Figurational theory	Emphasizes the connections between people and their interdependence. Views change that occurs over time.	Historical research	Historical and long-term view of sport within society. Tends to focus on masculinity and male power. Helpful in understanding global influence on sport development.	Devotes little attention to current issues by focusing on the long-term picture. Reduces the urgency to press for changes. Tends to emphasize the male power in societies.

player knocks them out of the winner's circle. In professional sport, the emphasis on winning reflects the business approach to competition. However, when the preoccupation with winning seeps down to collegiate, scholastic, and youth sport programs, the results can be damaging. The overinvolvement of parents in youth sports is one reoccurring result that has been well documented through the headlines on the sports pages.

Sports that emphasize high achievement tend to dominate the American culture, attract media coverage, and attract live spectators and TV viewers. However, the majority of Americans who are involved in sport spend most of their time participating in recreational sport rather than seeking high performance. When the values of high performance are applied to the recreational setting, confusion and conflict are certain to occur among players, coaches, and officials (Leonard 1980; Loy and Booth 2004).

Conflict Theory

Conflict theory also reinforces the status quo as it exists in the United States. Conflict theory is based on the theories of Karl Marx and views sports as being built on the foundation of economic power. In a capitalistic society such as that in the United States, it is easy to point to the owners of sports teams, who benefit financially at the expense of athletes, coaches, and spectators. Likewise, many view bureaucratic organizations that operate sport like the football bowl alliance, the NCAA, governing bodies of sport, and the International Olympic Committee (IOC) as promoting sport to gain power, status, and money. Conflict arises when sport participants or spectators resist the apparent domination of controlling individuals or groups.

Unlike the functionalist theories that are based on societal imbalances, conflict theories focus on the disruptive forces that produce instability and disorganization. Sports are looked at in relation to changes in society. Nothing is as certain in life as the constant change produced by struggles between groups of different interests. In the middle of the 20th century, many sport sociologists moved toward the conflict theory approach and away from the more traditional functionalist point of view that tended to simply reinforce the existing status quo.

Much of conflict theory is directed at those sports that dominate spectator sports. Advocates of this theory would place more influence in the hands of sport participants and promote sport at the local community level so that it benefits all classes of people rather than the elite few. The working class would have more influence over sport than the rich have. Conflict theorists favor player unions that confront owners and support other organizations that guard against using public monies to build luxurious stadiums that benefit owners of professional teams.

The controversial bowl championship series in the United States stays intact because of money interests even though it is widely considered a poor system for determining the best football team of the year. This is a classic example of conflict theory.

Looking at sport from a critical theory forces us to explore newer sports.

Conflict theorists also campaign for athlete representation at all levels of decision making in sport organizations. Olympians would vote on policy questions concerning the staging of the Olympic Games. Student-athletes would help their colleges in coaching searches, and even athletes in youth sport would provide input into decisions made by league officials and coaches (Leonard 1980; Rigauer 2004).

Critical Theory

Sociologists describe theories that study culture and determine the source of authority that one group has over another as **critical theories.** These theories examine how a culture operates and its struggles in the search for a better life for all citizens. A critical theorist is especially attuned to combating structural conditions in a society that lead to exploitation, oppression, or social injustice. Rather than shifting power to sport participants as conflict theorists do, devotees of critical theories agitate to effect change where it is warranted.

Critical theorists conclude that sports do not simply mirror a society (as the functionalists or conflict theorists believe) but instead offer the opportunity to create society by affecting how people think and feel about social conditions. For example, it is possible that eventually people will understand

the far-reaching benefits of regular physical activity in improving quality of life well into older ages. In America's recent history, physical activity has often been relegated to the role of fun and recreation, a worthy use of leisure time. However, the evidence keeps mounting that sport and activity should in fact be a regular part of life in order to maximize disease resistance, maintain energy, control body weight, improve appearance, and reduce the costs for health care.

One critical theory of interest is **hegemony,** which is largely based on the ideas of Italian political theorist Antonio Gramsci. Hegemony focuses on dominance, which is the power that one individual or group has over others. Coaches may fit into hegemony descriptions. In professional sport where the goal is winning above all else, the authoritarian coach can usually survive so long as the team makes the play-offs. Bill Parcells, former coach of the New England Patriots and the New York Giants and current head coach of the Dallas Cowboys, is one example of a strong, authoritarian coach.

Analyzing sport with critical theories may lead us to new ways of looking at our sport and our role within sport. It should also help us understand the plight of others whose sport opportunities may differ from those we have. The goal of critical analysis is to make sports more democratic and sensitive to diversity and to provide access to anyone regardless of ethnic background, social class, or financial status. Sport can lead us to new understanding of gender, sexual orientation, and physical talent.

Critical theories take a more objective view of the conventional wisdom about sport in American society. Using critical thought, we challenge the status quo, analyze its effects on society, and propose beneficial changes. At the same time, we look objectively at the weaknesses of our current economic system including how we treat people who are poorer or socially disadvantaged (Hargreaves and McDonald 2004; Sage 1998).

Feminist Theory

Feminist theories evolved from dissatisfaction with cultural traditions that emphasize males and either ignore females or reduce them to a subservient role. A feminist analysis of sport forces us to confront our sexuality and define our expectations of males and females and to openly discuss homophobia.

Feminist theories force us to analyze the status of women in sport. In American society, people may rejoice in the gains yet acknowledge the remaining work needed to ensure equal opportunities for both genders. For example, the dearth of women in coaching deprives half of our youth sport population of role models. A lack of women in leadership positions in sport organizations affects decisions made in sport by disenfranchising a majority of our population.

An obvious weakness in analyzing sport with feminist theories is the tendency to overlook the influence of other factors such as race, religion, ethnicity, and economic class. Clearly these factors can be equally powerful, but when ignored, they doom us to inadequately evaluate sport (Birrell 2004; Coakley 2004; Sage 1998).

Interactionist Theory

Those who ascribe to **interactionist theories** view society from the bottom up rather than the top down. They focus on the social interactions among people that are based on the reality people choose to accept. Rather than simply respond to our world, we make conscious choices about how we will behave based on the effect our actions will have on ourselves, other people, and our society.

Research by interactionists involves extensive interviewing and ethnography to elicit how athletes think and feel about their sport participation. This approach helps us understand how people choose sports and how they define themselves as athletes within the culture of a particular sport. Interactionists create sport experiences that focus on the athlete rather than the business, institution, or leaders. Interactionists put kids' needs first in youth sports rather than allow sports to be defined by adults who think they know what kids need.

Interactionists focus on the human experience of African American athletes rather than on their athletic performance. Interactionists would confront the exploitation of college athletes who never earn a degree but serve the university's purpose as an athlete for hire and encourage women who seek to develop traditional masculine and athletic virtues

Expert's View: The Sexualization of Women

Margaret Duncan, a professor of human movement at the University of Wisconsin at Milwaukee, has led the way as a critical feminist by focusing on how the media portray women in sport. One of Duncan's causes has been the "sexualization" of women when they are portrayed in sports. As women's sports have gained in popularity, the media has featured more women, but often in a sexualized way. According to Duncan, the message sent to young girls is that their value as people lies in their physical attractiveness.

Duncan published landmark studies in the *Journal of Sport Sociology* comparing the differences in photographs of males and females in the 1984 and 1988 Olympic Games. She also studied the presentation of women in *Shape* magazine and critically analyzed televised women's sport. She has provided expert commentary in the media about the lack of women's sports on television since 1989. She criticized the presentation of women's sports by comparing the graphics, lead-ups to events, and advertising of events to those of men's sports (Duncan and Messner 2005).

Do these athletes exhibit traditional female virtues? An interactionist theorist explores this question.

such as aggressiveness that conflict with traditional feminine values.

Interactionist theorists rely on the methods of psychology by probing the feelings and understandings of the individual rather than looking at the structured world outside. They also study subcultures within sport such as those reported in a classic text by Ball and Loy (1975). This text devotes four chapters to the subcultures of college coaches, professional baseball players, hockey players, and wrestlers.

Since the 1990s, the interactionist approach has become more popular and productive among sport sociologists because of the rich in-depth analyses it favors. For example, survey research has long established that more males than females are involved in sport and physical activity, but it was left to the researcher to speculate on why this was true. By refocusing research through ethnographic observations, the reasons behind the trends became more understandable (Donnelly 2004).

Figurational Theory

Figurational theories are rooted in Europe, particularly England, but are rarely used in North America.

They emphasize interconnections between people that are called *figurations*. The crux of these theories is that we are all connected by networks of people who are interdependent on one another by nature, through education, and through socialization. Over time, the interconnections change as we mature, move in different circles, and absorb more information. While looking at sports from this perspective, figurational theorists study the historical processes through which people change.

The interrelationships in our life are dynamic and change frequently. Figurational theories require a long-term analysis to completely understand social influences. If we are fully engaged in changes in our culture, our perspectives, including those on sport, change as we age. For example, consider the warm camaraderie among senior athletes who compete furiously but also view the game differently from the way the youthful athlete views it.

Figurational theories have helped researchers study the amazing rise of soccer in Europe and around the world. The rise of violence by players and spectators has been instructive from this perspective, and in the early 2000s, figurational theory was used to view the reports of officials who had taken bribes to influence the outcomes of soccer matches.

Perhaps the most critical contribution of figurational theories has been a fuller understanding of the global processes at work in a shrinking world. As the connections between people and between nations strengthened worldwide, sports prospered in unimaginable ways through international training, competition, and coaching courses.

A weakness of figurational theory is that it tends to reduce the urgency for change. Since social problems are viewed over the long term, there is little chance to confront social problems within sport in a timely manner. By the time we understand what has happened and perhaps why it happened, new changes have taken place (Murphy, Sheard, and Waddington 2004).

Summary of Theories

After reviewing these six theories, you may wonder how they all fit into the sociology of sport. Each theoretical approach was developed over time and has helped sport sociology develop as a legitimate academic discipline with a discrete body of knowledge. Each of these theories has contributed to our understanding of the world of sport and exercise as it presently exists. Some generalizations may help you absorb the significance of each theory:

▪ Most people who extol the virtues of sport as it has existed traditionally use the *functionalist* approach. While this approach may have been useful in the past, it does not help identify existing social issues or provide any hope of solutions. People who work within existing sport organizations may adopt this approach in the interest of maintaining the status quo.

▪ *Conflict theories* have impressed upon us the influence of social class and the power structure within sport. These theories have pointed out conflict within sport and have often led to dramatic proposals for change.

▪ Since the 1970s, *critical theories* have been the most helpful in clarifying the challenges in making sport more accessible to people from all backgrounds and abilities. One specific critical theory, *feminist theory,* has enabled us to understand the issues that women faced before Title IX (see chapter 12 for an in-depth discussion about Title IX) and their ongoing struggle to claim a share of the sporting world and make it people oriented rather than male oriented.

▪ *Interactionist theories* allow us to look in depth at sport from the athlete's point of view and to add a qualitative bent to our analysis. Since the 1990s, North American researchers have adopted this approach more than any other.

▪ *Figurational theories* have been especially helpful in Europe in long-term analyses of sporting subcultures and in understanding global expansion of sport.

CURRENT STATUS OF SPORT SOCIOLOGY

Although the study of sociology as a discipline became popular around the turn of the century, sociology was not applied to sport for another 50 years. In 1964 the International Committee for Sport Sociology was created as an outgrowth of the International Council of Sport and Physical Education and the International Sociological Association of UNESCO. This organization (presently named the International Sociology of Sport Association) has published the *International Review of Sport Sociology* annually since 1966, meets every year, and attracts scholars from around the world.

The second major organization for sport sociology is the North American Society for the Sociology of Sport. It was founded in 1978, holds annual conferences, and since 1984 has published the *Sociology of Sport Journal.* The third group, the Sport Sociology Academy, is more casually organized as a unit of the National Association for Sport and Physical Education (NASPE), which falls under the large parent organization, the American Alliance for Health, Physical Education, Recreation and Dance (AAHPERD), which is located in Washington, DC. This large organization includes teachers, researchers, and professional

In the Arena With . . . *Richard Lapchick*

Richard Lapchick founded the Institute for the Study of Sport in Society at Northeastern University in 1984 and subsequently moved to the University of Central Florida where he established the Institute for Diversity and Ethics in Sport in 2002. He has published an annual *Racial and Gender Report Card* for professional and collegiate sport for many years. His work at the University of Central Florida became the gold standard for reporting on the progress in providing equity among gender and racial groups. His reports include not only athletes but also coaches, administrators, officials, and other staff. You will see references to his reports in later chapters of this text that discuss gender and racial issues in sport. In his research, Richard Lapchick meticulously accumulates data from athletic teams, institutions, and professional leagues and presents them in descriptive statistics using percentages. He also compares his results with statistics from previous years so that changes over time can be analyzed. No reporter would consider writing on race or gender in sport without consulting his yearly report card (Lapchick 2004).

practitioners of all fields relating to health, fitness, and sport. At the annual meeting, research papers are presented in the field of sport sociology.

As the popularity of sport increases, more researchers are drawn to the interrelationships between sport and society. Most large and many small universities now offer courses such as Sport and Society, Sport Sociology, Social Science of Sport, and Social Issues in Sport. Students from different fields of study are drawn to such a course as an elective because of their interest in sports.

The media rely on research in sport sociology for their articles and features on athletes or a particular sport. Along with reporting current events, the media provide the color commentary to help people understand the underlying causes, relationships, and struggles of their sport heroes. Without solid grounding through sociological research, much of their writing would be limited to their own experience, knowledge, and bias.

CHAPTER SUMMARY

In this chapter we laid out the plan for looking at sport through sociology, using its methods and theories. Methods for collecting data include interviews, surveys, content research, historical research, and ethnography. Once the data are collected, they can be analyzed with functionalist theories, conflict theories, figurational theories, interactionist theories, feminist theories, and critical theories. We've presented the essential elements of each of these theories, compared them, and suggested how each is applied to the world of sport.

The researcher can analyze the data and interpret the resulting evidence within the context of the theories. Doing so organizes large amounts of data that can be examined in detail and from an overall perspective. Using scientific methodology reduces the influence of our own bias and preconceived notions about sport.

Scope and Effect of Sport on Society

This part begins in chapter 3 by clarifying the distinction between sport participants and sport spectators. Since the two groups overlap, combining them to assess the popularity of particular sports leads to faulty assumptions. Those who participate in a particular sport are also likely to be spectators but those who are spectators often are not participants. Think of the millions of NFL and college football fans who watch football but do not play it.

A further refinement is made between people who participate in sport as recreation and those who strive for high performance. High-performance or elite athletes are usually younger athletes, while older adults primarily participate in recreational sports. However, increasing numbers of youth are also turning toward recreational models of sport.

Marketing opportunities through sport are presented and examined for trends. Sport is evaluated as a corporate venture in chapter 4, which also looks at how sport affects national economy. The benefits to owners of professional sports teams are documented and the questionable value of financing sport stadiums with public monies is discussed. The laws that allow sport leagues to operate as virtual monopolies are presented and the way colleges and universities may profit from sport is examined. We also take a realistic look at the earning power and job conditions of athletes who play corporate sports.

Finally, in chapter 5, this part looks at the close relationship between the media and sport. Televised sports continue to bring sport entertainment to our homes through ever-increasing hours of sport broadcasts. Sports pages are a critical part of daily print

media, although print media still cover more elite male sports than women's sports or local sports. Worldwide access to the Internet has changed the delivery of sports and there are hints of even more dramatic changes in the future as technology is refined.

We examine how sport and the media affect each other and how through the media sport influences societal ideology and values. Careers in sports journalism are described along with the substantial challenge of increasing access for women in the sport media and how the imbalance between males and females affects decisions in sport media.

Participants Versus Spectators

Student Outcomes

After reading this chapter, you will know the following:

- Who a sport participant is, and what affects the decision to participate
- Who a sport spectator is
- Trends for both participants and spectators
- How marketing efforts follow participant and spectator trends

Participating in sports is quite different from watching sports. Yet in sport studies, these two activities are often lumped together statistically and anecdotally. Combining them only adds to the confusion of the value of each, leads to suspect conclusions, and interferes with the assessment of the overall influence of sport. For example, many people would rate tackle football as the most popular sport in the United States. Based on *spectator* interest, this is a reasonable conclusion. But if we look at *participation*, football is popular only through high school and only with boys. Beyond age 18, tackle football is not a reasonable option due to the number of players required, lack of equipment, and risk of injury. Thus it is more accurate to say that football is the most popular spectator sport in the United States but rates far down the list in participation.

Some evidence supports the claim that watching sports and playing sports significantly interact. Young people are often attracted to sport participation because they see famous athletes on television or perhaps in live action (Harris 2004). Youth who participate in a sport are more likely to watch that sport in later years because they understand it (Kretchmar 1994). Without question, many people who play a sport also watch that same sport and in fact are likely to watch other sports as well. Their experience as an athlete helps them empathize with competitors in other sport activities. Common athletic skills and strategies that exist across sports are fun for the sport competitor to observe and admire.

The argument has been made for years that spectators who watch favorite performers in sport are more motivated to participate in sport than those who are not fans. Particularly young people seem to naturally imitate their sport heroes in a pickup game, on the playground, or in the gym. Many sports without the role models of elite athletes languish and have low participation.

SPORT PARTICIPANTS

An understanding of **sport participation** requires that we look closely at the characteristics of sport participants, their motivation, and the outside factors that influence their decisions.

High-Performance Versus Participation Athletes

As we introduced in the sport pyramid in figure 1.1 (see chapter 1), people who play sports can be classified as high-performance athletes or as participation athletes. The difference in motivation, training, and attitudes toward competition are marked for these two groups of athletes, no matter their age. Athletes who seek high performance (as characterized by the Olympic motto of "Faster, Higher, Stronger") train intensively, compete aggressively, and aspire to a professional career that brings **extrinsic rewards** such as money and fame. Athletes who value participation are motivated by **intrinsic rewards** such as fun and fitness. They use sports as recreation to enhance their quality of life, escape from work responsibilities, and socialize with family and friends.

About 65% of all Americans have integrated participant sports into their lifestyle (Leisure Trends 2004), thus making recreational sport the overwhelming dominant group in sports in our society. However, the human preoccupation with excellence, competition, and performance has vaulted high-performance sports to dizzying heights of popularity fueled by business interests and the media even though a relatively few athletes are elite. Of course, spectator sport feeds off the popularity of high-performance sport, as people enjoy watching exceptional performers match skill, wit, and courage.

We can also classify athletes by age, keeping in mind the two tracks they may follow toward high performance or recreation. At times these two paths overlap, providing some confusion for athletes, coaches, parents, and sponsoring organizations.

Youth Sport Athletes

Youth sport athletes typically fall between ages 4 and 13. Participation opportunities are usually community driven and seasonal, with an emphasis on team sports. Parents encourage their children to play so they can learn the skills of a particular sport, socialize with other children, and experience physical activity. Many parents are involved as team coaches, chauffeurs, and fans. Most youth sports encourage participation by everyone regardless of skill and

What motivates this player? How does her motivation differ from that of a high school varsity tennis player or a professional tennis player?

strive to offer low-key competition and to generate an interest in sports that will last a lifetime.

Some parents, however, may push their children into sports, hoping that their child will be the next youth superstar. Children as young as 10 may join specialized high-performance programs that emphasize competition, rankings, traveling teams, national events, and specialization in one sport year round. These programs are clearly dedicated to developing elite athletes. (Youth and sport are covered in chapter 6.)

High School Varsity Athletes

Athletes at this level may still participate for reasons similar to those of youth sport athletes—they like to socialize with their peers and want to continue to improve in their sport. The choice to participate is usually made by the athlete rather than the parents. Participation can also be motivated by a desire to receive a college athletic scholarship for one or a few sports or to progress directly into professional play. (For a further discussion about high school sports, see chapter 7.)

By definition, high school varsity sports sponsor competition against other schools. Most teams are limited in size, so the majority of high school students do not play varsity sports and must rely on intramural or community-based sports. Some high school sports such as football, basketball, and baseball may be high-performance programs that truly prepare athletes for college sports. In other sports, particularly Olympic and individual sports, high school teams are more recreational and elite athletes must look outside the school setting to private development programs and competition sponsored by the national governing body of that sport.

College Varsity Athletes

College athletes are an even more select group than are high school athletes. High school varsity athletes numbered 6.9 million in 2004 while the number of college varsity athletes was just 375,000 (NCAA 2004b; NFHS 2004b). Competition for positions on collegiate varsity teams is intense, especially at large institutions. Most high school athletes face the fact that they are not good enough to play at the intercollegiate level and join campus intramural programs or club teams that offer more recreational competition. (For further discussion of college sports, see chapter 7.)

The most intense high-performance programs are found at the large universities that are categorized as Division I by the NCAA. Most of their athletes receive a full or partial athletic scholarship and are expected to produce athletically to justify the expense to the university. Other colleges compete at the lower divisions of II or III where the competition is less intense, the commitment to athletics is more modest, and the financial investment by the institutions is lower.

Many college students who have grown up playing sports find themselves shut out of sport opportunities simply due to the competition. They may turn to the on-campus intramural teams and sports clubs, and many turn to community-based sports in their hometowns during the summer to satisfy their competitive and recreational urges.

Professional Athletes

Professional athletes compete in sport for the extrinsic financial rewards offered to them such as salaries, prize money, or product endorsements. Virtually every sport holds professional tournaments and leagues somewhere in the world, including the Olympic Games. While professional athletes may compete in their sport because they enjoy it, the longer they compete at the professional level, under pressure to perform, the closer sport moves toward work.

For most adults, recreational sporting opportunities are the only option for sport participation. The ability and option to turn professional simply doesn't exist.

Except for a few sport prodigies, most athletes do not qualify for professional sports until they are young adults. Professional careers have limited duration because of the exceptional physical skills they demand. As their physical skills decline in the late 20s and 30s, most professional athletes are forced to retire from competition.

Master Athletes

While older competitors typically cannot compete with younger competitors who are at the height of their physical prowess, master athletes may be focused on the highest level of performance within their prescribed age group. Competition is staged in categories beginning as young as 35 and older and ending up as old as (in some sports) 90 and older. The competition is intense, the athletes train year round, and often sport events are staged at local, national, and even international levels. As health, training regimens, and medical care advance, master athletes continue to break records and grow in number. The difference between master athletes and their professional counterparts is that generally their financial rewards are modest. While some

sports offer prize money, most only offer good competition, an opportunity to travel, and an expanded social network.

Adult Recreational or Participation Athletes

At every age, beginning with youth sports, some participants play simply for fun. They enjoy socializing with friends, being physically active, and playing the game. But they may not have the physical or psychological attributes needed to compete at high levels. We often spend our childhood years testing our physical limits, and by the time we reach adulthood, very few of us can compete at the elite levels of sport. Yet more than half of the U.S. population still enjoys playing sports. As we age, we tend to move away from collision sports such as football, soccer, wrestling, or boxing and toward sports that offer less risk of physical injury or stress on the body. Team sports become more difficult to organize in an adult world, and so many people turn to sports for individuals or a smaller number of contestants.

Participation athletes spend a relatively smaller amount of time practicing and training for competition. Since their time is limited by work and family commitments, most recreational athletes just play when they can. Winning or losing does not affect their life as much as it might have at a younger age or affect their reputation within their occupation.

FACTORS AFFECTING SPORT PARTICIPATION

Now that we have an idea of who participates in sport, let's look the factors that influence participation as well as the conflicts between the different levels of participants.

Pursuit of Excellence

The attitudes of some youthful competitors who may be encouraged by their parents and coaches are oriented toward producing the best physical performance possible. It could be argued that youth sports in general discover the best potential competitors through a progression of competitions promoting survival of the fittest. Athletes who do well at a young age play on all-star teams, are exposed to advanced training and coaching, and sometimes even compete at international or national competitions. Because of their early success, these athletes often have sport experiences that help them increase their edge over other kids their age.

One of the difficulties with designating *elite athletes* at a young age is that their dominance may simply result from maturing early. Once their peers catch up with them physically, they lose confidence and motivation quickly as kids they used to defeat routinely overtake them.

Of course, the American preoccupation with high achievement spills over into youth sports. Parents hope their child will be chosen for the elite, select, or traveling team. In many sports, the number of youngsters chosen for these teams may amount to as many as 30% of the participants in order to cast a wide net for future superstars. After several years in these high-performance programs, it becomes clear that only about 5% of the athletes will emerge at the top of their competitive level (NCAA 2003).

Schools, businesses, sponsors, and the media often focus on the quest for high performance in sports. This quest reinforces the pioneering spirit of humans to break barriers of human existence and performance. Schools and colleges spend huge sums of money to support athletic teams whose primary purpose is to defeat their rivals.

Money, fame, media attention, and hero worship are part of the reward to athletes who sacrifice to perform at the highest level. Commercial sponsors, professional teams, college teams, and Olympic organizations all support athletes dedicated to excellence in sport.

Recreation Through Sport

A different attitude toward sport is that participating for recreation is the ultimate goal regardless of the level of skill or achievement. This approach is more suited to the masses since by definition very few can truly reach elite levels. Sport participation is founded on the principle that people need diversion from their work, and recreation provides this diversion and recharges their natural energies. In many instances, what we call *participation sports* are commonly called *recreational sports.*

Participation in sports emphasizes their social side. People enjoy a friendly game of golf, tennis, or volleyball or going fishing as a way to spend time with family and friends. While high-performance athletes aim to defeat one another, participation athletes typically root for each other and help out whenever they can.

Commercial sponsors of sport who operate facilities, sell sport clothing and equipment, or run sport associations realize that participation athletes far outnumber those dedicated to high performance. To attract average people to sport participation, these commercial groups modify their sport to make it friendly to players of all ages, skills, and income levels. Here are a few examples:

- Golf is one of the few sports in which players of different skill levels can enjoy competing against

In the Arena With . . . *Freddy Adu*

In 2005, Freddy Adu became the youngest player ever to play in the all-star game of any professional sport. He plays soccer for D.C. United, with whom he signed at the tender age of 14 for $500,000 U.S. per year, the highest salary in the league. Add in $1 million U.S. per year for endorsing Nike and Freddy is doing quite well. He completed his requirements to graduate from high school in 2005, a few years early.

The Adu family won a lottery and emigrated from Ghana to the United States when Freddy was 8 years old. Forced to work two jobs to support the family after her husband abandoned them, Freddy's mother Emelia has been his sole support, cheerleader, and confidant. Thanks to Freddy's soccer income, she's now in a new house and retired from her jobs.

Where will this story end? Freddy is now a millionaire, an athletic prodigy, a media darling, a U.S. citizen, and perhaps America's first male soccer superstar. He has a chance to popularize the game in the United States that is unlike that of any other soccer athlete. And his international influence could be unsurpassed if he lives up to the hype (CBS News 2004).

Not all activity is driven by competition. The pursuit of relaxation and fun often motivates people to be active.

each other by altering the scoring system. Participants may play a scramble format or award points for each hole depending on which player reaches the green first or holes out first.

▪ Tennis has been adjusted to local recreational situations through altered lengths of play. The winner may be declared after a certain time limit to accommodate indoor play. Shortened sets have also become popular and include using tiebreakers at the end of a set instead of playing a traditional third set.

▪ Recreational volleyball and softball leagues sponsor coed teams that require a set number of females to field a team. Spiked shoes are banned from softball and sliding into bases is prohibited to reduce injuries.

▪ Soccer is played by smaller teams, such as teams of three, so that each player gets more action and the game can be played on a smaller field.

High Performance and Participation Tug-of-War

There seems to be a perpetual tug-of-war between the supporters of high-performance participation and those of recreational participation. National associations and governing bodies often pour their financial reserves into developing high-performance athletes, to the detriment of the average sport participant. Debates rage about the percentage of resources that ought to be expended for either purpose.

Consider the **Amateur Sports Act of the United States** of 1978, in which the U.S. Congress established the United States Olympic Committee (USOC) and outlined its responsibilities. The act listed the 12 purposes of the USOC numerically. Approximately half of the list addresses the issue of amateur sport participation. Number six states, "To promote and encourage physical fitness and public participation in amateur athletic activities." The law was amended in 1998 to become the Olympic and Amateur Sports Act primarily due to the strong advocacy of Senator Ted Stevens. The internal changes in the act particularly addressed the needs of elite Paralympic athletes. The proportion of time, effort, or budget dedicated to the various purposes is not prescribed by the U.S. Congress but left to the USOC board of directors (Stevens 2005).

Likewise, rules, boundaries, equipment, and clothing are often debated from two different points of view. New equipment may allow ordinary performers the thrill of better performance and keep them hooked on the sport. But that equipment may be illegal for high-performance athletes who must compete in stadiums of a certain size and within international rules.

Professional baseball players are not allowed to use aluminum bats, while amateur college players are. The pro golf tour has considered using a special tour ball that is less lively than current golf balls to put more of a premium on accuracy as opposed to power and distance. Golf legends like Jack Nicklaus and Arnold Palmer support such a move, as they believe the game has developed into a power game with less emphasis on accuracy and skill. Yet the average weekend player thrills to the whack of a golf ball that flies further than he ever thought possible.

Attitudes toward sport at the youth and high school level can tilt heavily toward high-performance or participation depending on the leaders of the school or league. It becomes self-defeating to lean too heavily toward the high-performance model since doing so limits the number of participants.

College baseball players are allowed to use aluminum bats; professional baseball players must use wooden bats. How would Major League Baseball change if professionals were allowed to use the bats of college athletes?

Sport participation is often suggested to improve quality of life, help fight obesity, and keep people stronger and healthier. As health concerns rise and the population ages, the balance of spending and publicity may tip more toward sport participation. Support for emphasizing sport participation is emerging from the health community, sport organization leaders, advocate organizations for the aging, and youth sport organizations. Comments and position statements such as that quoted from the Olympic and Amateur Sports Act are beginning to appear in the media and invade the public consciousness.

The conflict between performance sport and participation sport is not unique to America. The ninth World Sports for All Congress (2002) held in the Netherlands was devoted to this topic. Close to 450 participants from 95 countries attended and after much debate concluded that it is in the interest of both participation and performance sport to cooperate to enhance a lifetime of sport and physical activity so that every individual can be physically active and participate in sport at their own level, from recreational to elite. Rather than compete for time, facilities, and money, the two camps of sport should become complementary to better serve all citizens.

Social Influences on Sport Participation

People of all ages consciously decide to participate in sports or not. If they choose to participate, they must make another decision, conscious or unconscious, of whether to continue their participation or to drop out. If they decide to continue, they must decide on their dedication and performance intensity.

Expert's View: Elite Performance and Obesity

In "Elitism in Youth Sports Yields Physical Fatness," Ken Reed suggests that the current preoccupation with elite performance for kids contributes to the increasing obesity crisis. The Centers for Disease Control and Prevention reports that the number of overweight children has increased nearly 300% in the past 25 years. "There's a disparity in sports, the fact that there is so much at the top and not enough at the bottom," said Tom McMillen, a former congressman and basketball player. Richard Lapchick, founder of the Center for the Study of Sport in Society at Northeastern University, adds, "The biggest problem is that kids don't make the high school or junior high school team and drop out. They think their career is over and they stop doing anything physical" (Reed 2004).

The solution may lie in modeling European countries, where there is a local sports club for everyone. If you are a premier athlete, there is a club for you. If you are athletically challenged, there is a B, C, or D level of play that might suit you (Reed 2004).

Activity Time-Out: Performance Versus Participation Sport

As you examine the potential for conflict between performance and participation sport, do you think it is possible to support both? If you were responsible for a budget for youth sports in a community, what proportions of funding would you allocate to high-performance and participation sport? Justify your answer and give specific examples. In making your recommendation, consider that approximately 5% of the population qualifies for high-performance sport while the other 95% is relegated to participation sport.

These decisions about whether to participate for fun or for high performance are heavily influenced by outside factors and people combined with internal feelings, thoughts, and aspirations. The interaction of external and internal forces helps us come to our current decision, although we may certainly change our minds as we develop or the external conditions change.

In order to remain a participant, you must enjoy the sport you play.

When we are young, our families influence us more than outsiders do. If your parents played sports, took you to sporting contests, helped you learn basic sport skills, and encouraged you to participate, chances are you gave sport a try. In some cases, other family members such as grandparents, aunts, uncles, or older siblings may have encouraged you in sport.

Once you tried sports, the critical factors that influenced your continued participation may have been whether you felt comfortable in the environment created by the coach and other athletes. Your own success or failure in competition certainly helped shape your attitude about sport. Teachers, camp counselors, coaches, and older children can powerfully influence us as we try to figure out what is important in our lives.

Your environment also influences your choice of sport. For example, certain choices are a natural part of city life. Recreational facilities need to be accessible, affordable, and comfortable. Climate, tradition, and even your neighborhood will help determine the available choices. Your parents and siblings affect your earliest choices and continue to affect whether or not you sustain those interests. A pervasive influence, however, is your peers, especially as you mature and depend less on your family for decisions and support.

Once you are involved in sport, key factors that affect your decision to continue include your aptitude and the reinforcement you receive from coaches and friends. Athletes who experience success are more likely to crave that emotional support and rely on it.

Heroes and role models may help kids socially adjust to sports. By watching heroes and imitating their behavior, work ethic, and love for sport, kids learn what is expected of athletes. They often imitate their role models to see if that role fits them.

Children who struggle in sports often reject them. Who wants to play right field, bat last, be picked last, or ride the bench as a substitute? Coaches may make insensitive remarks, encourage rough play, or otherwise make the experience unpleasant. Even talented athletes often withdraw from the sport scene if they do not measure up to expectations or, in the case of high-performance programs, lack the drive and intensity that are expected.

As we mature, new factors affect our sport participation. Other facets of life interfere, friends drop out of sport, social cliques develop within and outside of sport, and economic costs of continued participation drain resources. Adults have the added burden of work responsibilities, less discretionary time, anxiety about their abilities, and difficulty in finding playing partners.

Geography, Age, Gender, and Social Class

In addition to family, friends, and coaches, other factors that affect our sport participation include the geography of the area where we live and what sports are available. Winter sports are most popular in the northern reaches of the country, and water sports thrive in areas near lakes, rivers, or oceans. Interestingly, not all intuitive patterns based on geography and weather hold true. For example, the highest participation rate in tennis does not occur in Florida, Texas, or California, the three U.S. states most often guessed. The highest rate actually occurs in New York City and its surrounding counties in Westchester, northern New Jersey, and southern Connecticut. The reason for the greater rate is economic affluence. There is a higher correlation between economic level and tennis participation than there is between weather and tennis participation.

Age also affects sport participation. As we age, the demands of many traditional sports become daunting. Loss of flexibility, strength, and endurance along with weight gain affects most adults as they age. Only those who devote hours to training are able to ward off the physical effects of aging. Sports that are popular with young people such as gymnastics, figure skating, wrestling, tackle football, lacrosse, and track and field simply are not easy to sustain after the teenage years. The stress on the body is too debilitating for most people.

Popular youth sports tend to be team sports. Team sports present a special problem for adults who are unable to arrange their schedules around work for practice or competition. Individual sports begin to attract more participants simply because they are easier to organize and schedule. Football, soccer, basketball, and baseball participation rates drop sharply after people leave their 20s and naturally move into lifetime sports such as golf, tennis, and swimming.

Gender affects sport participation due to tradition, interest, and sometimes body structure. Girls generally do not play tackle football, rugby, or other collision sports. Some athletes in boxing, wrestling, and weightlifting have broken down traditional barriers. Now these sports are even contested by women in the Olympic Games, although the contestants are admittedly few.

The Title IX legislation in 1972 opened up female participation in many sports that were traditionally male oriented. Soccer, basketball, cross country, and lacrosse are now seen as equally accessible for males and females. Spirit squads, which were formerly called cheerleading squads, now include both boys and girls although the majority of participants are still female.

Perhaps no factor influences sport participation more powerfully than social or economic class. Some traditions of participation are based on custom and accessibility while others are simply a matter of economics. There are always exceptions to the overall trends, but there are some sport favorites by economic class (Coakley and Donnelly 1999; Eitzen 2003; Gruneau 1999).

People with a high income, high education, and high-status occupation tend to participate in individual

Activity Time-Out: Encouraging Lacrosse

Investigate the growth of lacrosse in the United States in the past 10 years. How does the growth rate compare with those of other sports? How does the growth rate compare across genders, age groups, and geographical areas of the United States? List reasons that explain growth rate in each circumstance. If you were in charge of increasing the growth rate of lacrosse, what strategies would you employ, and why would you choose those strategies?

Where we live and travel to greatly influence the types of activities in which we participate.

sports such as golf, tennis, sailing, and skiing. They are able to arrange their schedule to play and can afford the cost of club memberships, travel, and equipment or clothing.

People in the middle-income group focus on sports that are publicly accessible at modest cost, are school or community sponsored, and do not require memberships in expensive clubs. Families of skilled workers often choose sports that tend toward competition, power, and machismo. The working class supports sports such as football, wrestling, auto racing, and boxing.

People who struggle to make a living tend to have little time for sports or recreation. Often their work involves physical labor, so they have little energy left for physical games. Their discretionary time and income are the lowest of those in society, and so they find it difficult to choose any recreational activity.

One of the ironies of elite competition, particularly in individual sports and many Olympic sports, is that athletes tend to come from wealthy backgrounds (Coakley 2004). The financial sacrifices required to fund a young athlete's development, particularly for sports like sailing, tennis, gymnastics, equestrian events, and skiing, which are not offered in public

schools, are simply beyond the reach of the average family. Team sports that are offered in public schools at little cost to participants are financially feasible for average families, and thus you see athletes of all social classes competing in track and field, soccer, basketball, baseball, wrestling, and similar sports.

TRENDS IN SPORT PARTICIPATION

The sports that people participate in change over the years. As a new sport gains popularity and more people participate in it, participation in other sports falls off. Let's look at some general trends in sport participation over the past 16 years. Table 3.1 shows data collected from the Sporting Goods Manufacturers Association (SGMA). These data include all persons age 6 or older that have participated in the sport at least once per year.

Trends in Adult Recreational Sports

When looking specifically at adult participants we can see clear differences between male and female preferences. The following are the top 10 recreational activities for men and women age 16 and older, as reported in August of 2004 by Leisure Trends:

Women	Men
1. Walking	1. Golf
2. Basketball	2. Lifting weights
3. Aerobics	3. Basketball
4. Lifting weights	4. Football
5. Exercise	5. Walking
6. Golf	6. Hiking
7. Biking	7. Jogging
8. Swimming	8. Fishing
9. Jogging	9. Biking
10. Tennis	10. Hunting

According to this same report,

▪ 65% of Americans say they participate in a sport or recreation of some kind, with the gender breakdown as males = 69% and females = 61%, and

▪ in 1990, the top activities for men were fishing, hunting, and golf. The top activities for women were swimming, walking, and golf.

A look back at the top-ranked adult participant sports of 25 years ago shows some differences from today. Statistics from 1978 listed the top 10 sports for men and women combined (Leonard 1980):

1. Swimming	38.5 million
2. Tennis	34.7 million
3. Fishing	30.3 million
4. Bowling	27.7 million
5. Baseball or softball	26.4 million
6. Golf	18.7 million
7. Basketball	15.0 million
8. Hunting	12.6 million
9. Running	10.0 million
10. Football	9.7 million

Sports such as bowling, tennis, and baseball or softball have decreased in popularity while activities that are more fitness oriented have gained. In light of our aging population, it seems that more people who exercise do so for the fitness benefits and are less interested in organized sports.

According to Mediamark Research (2003), over the past 12 years the number of people aged 45 to 65 who participated in conditioning activities 11 or more times in the last 30 days climbed to 34% from 19%.

Conditioning sports include running, swimming, weightlifting, walking, and bicycling. Walking is the most popular activity for physical conditioning.

Youth Participation in Sports

Youth sports rank somewhat differently in participation simply because many sports are more suitable for the young. As people age, they tend to move away from team sports, since those sports do not fit into the demands of their lifestyle. The following are the 12 most popular organized sports for youth aged 6 to 17 (participants in millions) (SGMA 2000):

1. Basketball	10.0
2. Soccer	9.5
3. Baseball	7.4
4. Slow-pitch softball	3.5
5. Tackle football	2.8
6. Swimming and diving	2.7
7. Track and field	2.5
8. Volleyball	2.3
9. Cheerleading	1.8
10. Touch football	1.4
11. Fast-pitch softball	1.3
12. Tennis	1.0

The percentage of participants by gender shows 59% boys compared with 48% girls. Together male and female participants accounted for 53.9% of all children in their age group.

As children age, they may change sports, particularly as they realize which sports best fit their natural talents and interests. Dropout rates become significant, especially among girls as they enter the adolescent years and their bodies and interests change. Further, youth are showing an explosion of interest in extreme or action sports that are not included in the research cited above. For more information on youth sport participation, refer to chapter 6.

As youth move on to interscholastic sports at the high school level, the popularity of most of their favorite childhood sports remains intact. Tackle football replaces touch football for boys and is by far the most popular high school sport for boys. Track and field enters the top three for both boys and girls. Golf also appears in the top 10 for both genders. For a complete list of the most popular sports among high school students, see chapter 7.

Now that we've thoroughly looked at sport participants and trends in sport participation, let's turn our attention to those who watch sport—the sport spectators.

TABLE 3.1 Trends in Sport Participation

Activity	1987	2003	Percent change over 16 years
Fitness activities			
Aerobics	21,225	16,451	−22.5
Fitness walking	27,164	37,945	+39.7
Running/jogging	37,136	36,152	−2.6
Fitness swimming	16,912	15,899	−6.0
Pilates training ('01)	2,437	9,469	+444.5
Stretching ('98)	35,120	42,096	+19.9
Yoga/tai chi ('98)	5,708	13,371	+134.3
Equipment exercise			
Free weights	22,553	51,567	+128.6
Resistance machines	15,261	29,996	+96.6
Rowing machine	14,481	6,484	−55.2
Stationary bicycle	30,765	30,952	+.6
Treadmill	4,396	45,572	+936.7
Stair-climber	2,121	14,321	+575.2
Elliptical trainer ('98)	3,863	13,415	+247.3
Team sports			
Baseball	15,098	10,885	−27.1
Basketball	35,737	35,439	−.8
Cheerleading ('93)	3,257	3,596	+17.6
Ice hockey	2,393	2,789	+16.5
Football ('01)	19,199	17,958	−4.1
Lacrosse ('98)	929	1,132	+22.2
Soccer	15,388	17,679	+14.9
Softball ('98)	21,123	16,020	−25.0
Volleyball	35,984	20,286	−43.6
Racket sports			
Badminton	14,793	5,937	−59.9
Racquetball	10,395	4,875	−53.1
Tennis	21,147	17,325	−18.1
Personal contact sports			
Boxing ('01)	932	945	+4.5
Martial arts ('98)	5,368	6,883	+28.2
Wrestling ('01)	2,360	1,820	−28.5

Activity	1987	2003	Percent change over 16 years
Indoor sports			
Billiards/pool	35,297	40,726	+15.4
Bowling	47,823	55,035	+15.1
Table tennis ('93)	17,689	13,511	−32.7
Wheel sports			
Roller hockey ('93)	2,323	2,718	+17.0
Roller skating, 2×2 wheels ('93)	24,223	11,746	−56.7
In-line skating ('93)	13,689	19,233	+309.6
Skateboarding	10,888	11,090	+1.9
Other recreational sports			
Bicycling ('98)	54,575	53,710	−1.6
Golf	26,261	27,314	+4.0
Swimming ('98)	94,571	96,429	+2.2
Walking ('98)	80,864	88,799	+9.8
Camping	50,386	51,007	+1.2
Hiking ('98)	40,117	40,409	+.7
Mountain biking	1,512	6,940	+359.0
Fishing	58,402	52,970	−9.3
Shooting sports			
Archery	8,558	7,111	−16.9
Hunting	25,241	15,232	−39.7
Shooting trap/skeet	5,073	4,496	−11.4
Target shooting	18,947	19,788	+4.4
Winter sports			
Ice skating ('98)	18,710	17,049	−8.9
Cross-country skiing	8,344	4,171	−50.0
Downhill skiing	17,676	13,633	−22.9
Snowboarding ('93)	2,567	7,818	+269.5
Water sports			
Canoeing ('98)	13,615	11,632	−14.6
Jet skiing ('98)	11,203	10,648	−5.0
Sailing	6,368	5,232	−17.8
Scuba diving	2,433	3,215	+32.1
Surfing	1,459	2,087	+43.0
Wakeboarding ('98)	2,253	3,356	+49.0
Waterskiing	19,902	8,425	−57.7

All numbers in thousands (e.g., 21,225 = 21,255,000). Numbers in indicate the first year other than 1987 that data were collected.

Reprinted, by permission, from SGMA, 2004, *Sports Participation Topline Report*. (North Palm Beach, FL: SGMA International), 2-4. Available: http://sgma.affiniscapte.com.

Earl Anthony was the most familiar face in bowling in the 1970s and the first player to break the $1 million U.S. barrier in winnings. Today, bowling no longer makes the top 10 most popular sports among adult participants.

SPORT SPECTATORS

Watching sports has become part of the American way of life. Since the 1920s, commercial sports have steadily attracted more and more **sport spectators** primarily because people have more leisure time and more money to spend. The number of people who watch sports rises each year, and the money generated from sport spectators, sponsorships, advertising, and products has increased dramatically.

Unlike participating in sports, watching or listening to sports doesn't take much effort or talent. It is a form of entertainment that appeals to millions of people for a variety of factors. A spectator may enjoy the particular sport itself, may formerly have played or currently play that sport, or may simply enjoy the competition and drama of superior athletes demonstrating their prowess.

While the number of spectators who watch live events continues to increase, the most significant growth results from the availability of sports on television and on the Internet. Televised sports began in the late 1940s when there were fewer than 190,000 TV sets in the country. NBC broadcast the World Series of baseball, heavyweight boxing matches, and the Army–Navy football game. In the early years of TV sports, spectator growth was enormous, and as television improved the technical presentation, the popularity of sports continued to explode. As more people watched, advertisers spent huge amounts of money to reach a sport audience that was primarily younger men. Great moments in sports were shared with millions of viewers and became the topic of discussion at work. Televised sports not only promoted sports viewing but also helped grow the TV industry to heights not even imagined in the early days.

In the last two decades, viewing of network sports has generally declined, as cable and all-sports channels offer more choices and interest has expanded to a wider variety of sports. Despite the sharp drop in baseball viewing and the relatively flat viewing statistics for football, overall sport entertainment on TV continues to thrive. College sports, high school sports, and even some youth sports are now televised nationally. Fans can tune into a variety of sporting events at almost any hour or check up-to-the-minute scores on the Internet. As the sport audience grows, so does the willingness of commercial sponsors to pay for an advertisement during events such as the Super Bowl—as much as $2.5 million per 30 second ad for the 2006 game (PR Web 2006).

Social class and economic status affect spectatorship as they do participation. Most white-collar workers are college graduates and therefore are natural supporters of college sport teams. Long after graduation, they assiduously follow their college team, donate money to athletic programs, and buy season tickets to major sport events. In contrast, people who do not attend college have little affinity for college sports and focus instead on professional sports.

The most affluent spectators, besides watching college sports, identify with sports like polo, yachting, sailing, sports car racing, and thoroughbred racing. The upper-middle class tends to enjoy tennis, golf, sailing, and skiing. The working class leans toward auto racing, wrestling, bowling, pool, boxing, demolition derby, and roller derby.

The high cost of attending many popular sporting events prohibits those of modest means from regular attendance. A family of four attending a professional basketball game in a metropolitan city may pay about $200.00 U.S. just for modest seats. For example, for an Indiana Pacers home game, tickets for the cheap seats in the upper deck are $30.00 U.S. each, tickets for the medium priced seats in the lower deck are $45.00 U.S. each, and tickets for good seats on the lower level are $100.00 U.S. each. If you add in the cost of parking at $10.00 U.S. and food at $10.00 U.S. per family member, the minimum cost is about $175.00 U.S. for a family of four (Indiana Pacers 2005). Over the basketball season, the average family may be able to afford tickets for one or two games.

Interestingly, professional baseball, usually thought of as a workingman's game, attracts spectators from all social classes. Perhaps its mass appeal has contributed to its long-held reputation as America's national pastime. Likewise, professional football attracts spectators of all incomes.

Perhaps the fact that baseball and football stadiums can accommodate fans of all economic levels adds to their appeal. Affluent spectators may ply their guests with food and drink in luxury suites that cost thousands of dollars for one game, or they might sit right by the action, at field level behind home plate or on the 50-yard line. Meanwhile, at the same game, the less affluent can save up for the more modest fare for seats in the bleachers, the end zone, or the upper rows of the stadium.

The general socioeconomic trends just described are based on live attendance at sporting events. If you factor in watching sports on television, which mitigates the expense of sport viewing for most people, spectators choose their sports by interest, history, and familiarity rather than by expense. People watch sports they identify with through previous participation or watch performers with whom they feel a connection. Television has brought spectator sports and the performances of the world's finest athletes to every home in the United States.

The increase in the number of televised sporting events greatly expands your opportunity to watch the sport of your choice.

Today commercial sponsors reach audiences of rich or poor, male or female, young or old.

The interest girls and women have recently shown in watching sports caused a major shift in the cross section of sport spectators. The tremendous change in female sport participation due to Title IX has produced a new generation of women who enjoy watching sports, can identify with the athletes, and include sports in their life. Gone are the days when the men retired to the den to watch sports while the women retired to the kitchen or living room.

The women's movement in the 1970s improved the place of women in the workforce and politics and changed the traditional feminine role. Traits such as vigor, strength, competitiveness, and poise under pressure were added to the more traditional feminine traits of nurturance and support. The feminist movement reveled in seeing women display athleticism, grit, and courage in competitive sports on television. Hundreds of thousands of women donned sneakers and workout clothes to exercise, sweat, and improve their body images and athletic skills, modeling the exceptional athletes they admired on television.

Racial background influences spectators. Certain races have traditionally participated in particular sports that produce heroes with whom other members of their race can identify. For example, Hispanics are proud of their superstars in boxing and Major League Baseball (MLB), while African Americans love to see their heroes dominate in professional basketball and football. Of course, sometimes nontraditional heroes emerge, such as Tiger Woods in golf or the Williams sisters in tennis, attracting nontraditional spectators wanting to follow their struggles and achievements.

TRENDS IN SPECTATOR SPORTS

Spectator sports can be divided into two major categories: those watched live or those followed through media such as the TV, Internet, and radio. Accurately counting the total number of viewers of a sport is somewhat difficult compared to tracking the attendance at a sport event, particularly a professional event. Amateur sports such as youth sports and most high school sports do not charge admission and therefore cannot provide attendance records.

One overall statistic is clear: Sport watching has grown steadily in recent years and the availability of sports on television has contributed to that growth. Certain sports have enjoyed a recent boost in popularity, including figure skating and women's college basketball. Of course, the televised Olympics, alternating Summer and Winter Games every two years, clearly boosts sport interest.

Let's look at general numbers for in-person attendance at the most popular spectator sports in the United States (table 3.2).

Just as we did for participant sports, we can compare today's numbers with those from several decades ago. Looking at the top spectator sports of 25 years ago (Leonard 1980) shows the following:

1.	Thoroughbred racing	50.7 million
2.	Auto racing	49.0 million
3.	Major League Baseball	38.0 million
4.	College basketball	35.7 million
5.	College football	32.9 million
6.	Harness racing	31.2 million
7.	Pro hockey	23.0 million
8.	Greyhound racing	19.0 million
9.	Minor League Baseball	13.0 million
10.	Pro football	11.0 million
11.	Pro basketball	8.2 million
12.	Pro boxing	3.0 million

Which changes jump out at you? Which sports have increased in popularity and which have declined? Horse racing suffered as different forms of gambling became available in many states. Perhaps its main attraction for the average citizen was its legalized gambling aspect, so that once other avenues for gambling opened up, attendance at racetracks fell dramatically.

According to a recent Harris poll, auto racing is the third most popular spectator sport topped only by football and baseball in the United States (Harris Interactive 2005). In fact, worldwide, auto racing may have overtaken soccer (football) as the top sport in attendance. Unfortunately, auto racing was not included in the U.S. Census statistics since it does not meet the U.S. Census Bureau's definition of a sport.

MARKETING TO PARTICIPANTS AND SPECTATORS

The business of sport generates significant income for educational institutions, the USOC, the assigned national governing bodies of each sport, television, and corporate sponsors. Cities pour millions of dollars into facilities for professional teams as well

TABLE 3.2   Trends in In-Person Attendance at Spectator Sports

Sport	1985	1990	1994	2001
Baseball				
Major League	47.7*	55.5	71.2	73.8
Basketball				
College men	26.6	28.8	28.3	28.9
College women	2.1	2.8	4.6	8.8
Professional men and women	11.5	18.5	19.3	21.4
Football				
College	34.9	35.3	36.5	40.4
Professional	14.0	17.6	14.8	20.5
Hockey				
Professional	11.6	12.3	15.7	20.3

*Numbers in millions. Numbers do not include TV viewing.
From U.S. Census Bureau, Statistical Abstract of U.S. 2003.

as facilities used by their residents. Manufacturers of sporting goods produce equipment, uniforms, and footwear. The clothing industry designs casual apparel that can be worn on the street and is acceptable for physical activity.

All of these groups have a strong interest in promoting their products and services to sport participants, spectators, or both. The dollars they spend on marketing have increased exponentially over the years as sport popularity has ballooned. Universities now offer degrees in the business of sport and emphasize sport marketing as a career path.

Sport marketing must adapt as various sports rise or fall in popularity, new classes of potential participants or spectators emerge, and demographic patterns shift. One example of the changing marketplace is the opportunity to globalize sport marketing. Soccer is the most popular sport worldwide, with tennis next in popularity. The global reach of these sports exposes the products of their sponsors worldwide. Likewise, American sports such as football, basketball, and baseball have worked hard to expand into overseas markets to increase revenue. Satellite television has allowed events to be seen around the world, has helped popularize sports and their athletes, and has attracted huge sponsorship dollars.

Organizations intending to market their sport or product to sport participants need to carefully

After winning Wimbledon in 2004, Maria Sharapova began advertising Canon cameras. Her international appeal helps market the product to a wide audience.

By sponsoring NASCAR driver Kasey Kahne, Dodge achieves good product placement aimed at their target audience.

research the historical perspective of potential participants, identify potential customers, and launch marketing campaigns specifically targeting those audiences. For example, not long ago many sport advertisements featured male athletes. Organizations wanting to attract the potential female consumers had to change the advertising by presenting female athletes as role models. Female athletes such as Chris Evert, Anna Kournikova, Brandi Chastain, Lisa Leslie, and Mia Hamm began appearing in commercials.

Professional athletes who are at the top of their sport earn more money from commercial endorsements than they do from playing. Sport icons such as Tiger Woods, Michael Jordan, and Andre Agassi, who represent clothing companies like Nike, earn millions a year in endorsement fees. In fact, some athletes became more famous from their commercial endorsements than they did from playing, including Joe DiMaggio for endorsing Mr. Coffee machines, Jim Palmer for endorsing men's underwear, and Rafael Palmeiro for endorsing Viagra.

Another example of the changes in sport marketing is the impetus by sports like tennis and golf to reach out to African Americans. The success of Tiger Woods and Serena and Venus Williams provided the perfect opportunity for these sports to demonstrate openness to people of all racial backgrounds and to actively recruit them for advertising. In a former generation, Zina Garrison, who ranked number four in women's tennis, couldn't command a clothing endorsement contract for most of her career. Instead she chose to wear fellow player Martina Navratilova's signature line until eventually Reebok offered her a contract near the end of her career. Twenty years ago, companies saw little value in Zina as a role model for advertising their clothes since few African Americans were interested in tennis.

Sponsors support the sports that attract participants or spectators that most closely parallel the consumers of their product. Thus Mercedes or Lincoln luxury cars sponsor professional tennis, Chevrolet trucks sponsor auto racing, and Miller or Budweiser beers sponsor professional football. Manufacturers of women's products naturally select women's sports to reach their market. At the same time, advertising in sports like football that attract a strong male audience tends to use attractive women in sexually suggestive ads that might pique the attention of male viewers.

Sports, trying to present an inclusive environment, are careful to design ads with pictures of all ethnic and racial groups, both genders, and all ages. Showing this variety is tricky in the advertising business, where visual pictures of one or two athletes are more powerful than a collage of smaller images.

Similarly, on television, ads for sport products use music and speech patterns that match those of the potential customer. An ad targeting youth uses styles, sounds, and performers the youthful audience recognizes and admires.

If marketing for fitness activities desires to reach out to people age 50, the models in the ads must look like the people in this audience or at least look how the audience would like to look. Watching a buff model who is 25 years younger does nothing to attract an older person.

CHAPTER SUMMARY

Sport participants range from youth league athletes to Olympic athletes. People at each level of play participate for different reasons. In spite of the fact that the overwhelming number of participants play simply to have fun, the majority of attention and funding is lavished on the small number of athletes who make it in high-performance sport.

Trends in adult sport participation show that fitness-oriented activities are now more popular than competition activities. Trends in youth sport participation show that a significant number of girls reaching adolescence drops out of sport. Trends in youth sport also show increased participation in extreme sports.

Sport spectators come from all ages, races, and economic backgrounds. College graduates are more likely to support their college teams, while those who did not attend college tend to support professional teams. Working-class spectators often enjoy the more violent sports, and people with higher incomes are drawn to sports that are traditionally supported at private clubs and are more expensive to watch or play.

Trends in sport spectators show that baseball continues to attract the largest number of in-person spectators among traditional team sports, although football is close behind, and if television viewers were added, football would be number one. Auto racing continues to be extremely popular both in the United States and worldwide. The popularity of horse racing dropped in recent years as people turned to other avenues for gambling.

Finally, trends in sport marketing are based on the changing demographics in society, the sport preferences, and the separation of marketing to potential participants from marketing to potential spectators.

Business of Sport

After reading this chapter, you will know the following:

▪ The powerful economic influence of sports

▪ How professional sports affect national and local economies

▪ How collegiate athletic programs profit

Sport is big business in the United States and around the world. By every measure, the money generated by sport events, spent by consumers, and allocated for sport sponsorship has increased dramatically in recent years. Of course, the amount of money spent on recreational sports is modest compared with the amount generated by professional sports. For that reason, most of this chapter focuses on the business of professional sports, sometimes referred to as **corporate sport.** We'll also look at career opportunities recently produced by the rapid economic growth of sport.

If you recall the detailed sport pyramid (figure 1.2) that shows the progression of play, games, sport, and work, you know that within the category of sport, there are different levels. For example, while college athletics are reputedly an amateur venture, the business aspects of collegiate athletics at large Division I universities are undeniable. In this chapter, we'll also look at the business of college sports.

SPORT AND THE ECONOMY

Entertaining people during their time off from work has always been a primary role of both participation and spectator sport. Although in the past sport entertainment was usually casual and relaxed, today's sport is often organized, mechanized, marketed, and administered as a business. Commercial interests influence virtually every decision in collegiate and professional sports. Events are rated by television audience share, ticket sales, Web site hits, concession sales, sponsor revenue, and media coverage. Wins and losses are important because they influence all of these standards of measurement.

How did this happen? When did commercialization begin to take over sport?

In the 19th century, almost 90% of working Americans were farmers or workers in skilled trades. As our society became industrialized, many workers quit self-employment to join larger companies. The worker became one piece of the larger machine, helping to produce whatever goods or services the company provided (Leonard 1980; Rice, Hutchinson, and Lee 1958; Spears and Swanson 1978). In other words, the worker fit into the overall hierarchy of the larger corporation.

As sport grew more businesslike, the corporate model crept into the organization of every sport franchise and governing body. Athletes were encouraged to provide their services for the good of the larger entity, to contribute to the bottom line, and to share in the profits at the end of the year with the head or owner of their sport organization. Coaches became the supervisors of athletes who were sometimes asked to go against their personal choices for the good of the team or organization. Players who demonstrated a good work ethic, exemplary moral character, and a willingness to sacrifice for the good of the team were admired and held up as role models. Those who deviated from that path were labeled malcontents and given limited playing time or cut from the team.

As the sports industry grew in economic power, it attracted commercial interests who could benefit from that power by influencing its organization. As the industry developed, the role of the athlete became to serve the organization. But the growth of commercial sports would not have occurred without other conditions supporting rapid expansion:

▪ People need time away from work to participate in or watch sports. The life of a farmer left little time for activities outside of work, but industrialization changed the worker's opportunity for leisure time.

▪ People also need money to spend on sport. A society has to generate an economic level at which the majority of its people can afford to be sport consumers.

▪ People must live in concentrated areas so that they can use sport facilities, travel to sport events, and identify with a local professional sports team. Small cities and rural areas can rarely support professional teams and rely instead on local college or high school sports.

▪ Media such as newspapers, radio, and television must provide access to sports and athletes in order to sustain the interest in professional sports.

▪ Facilities that can present professional sports must be constructed, financed, and refurbished to maintain the sport revenue stream.

When we moved from an agrarian society to an industrial society, we increased our leisure time. This leisure time could then be spent attending sporting events, thus increasing the role of sport in our economy.

OWNERSHIP OF PROFESSIONAL SPORTS

For the most part, professional sport franchises are owned by extremely wealthy Americans (overwhelmingly male) who benefit from ownership personally and financially. They may use their teams to increase their personal wealth or to serve as a tax advantage to offset other business gains.

Originally, owners of professional sports teams were people who loved the game. They spent much of their personal time and money promoting the game and strengthening their teams and the leagues as a profitable business. The next wave of owners were men like Tom Yawkey of the Boston Red Sox (owner from 1933-1976), Phil Wrigley of the Chicago Cubs (owner from 1932-1977), and Augie Busch Jr. of the St. Louis Cardinals (owner from 1952-1989). Their dedication to baseball was genuine, and they did not use their professional team to promote their other businesses. As this generation of owners died off, a new breed of ownership began to emerge.

Growing numbers of owners are corporate conglomerates that purchase sport franchises to help market and promote their other products. Some organizations, such as the Green Bay Packers football team, are owned by the general public, who hold shares in the team. Club owners have evolved into corporate managers who may or may not consider the welfare of the team or the host city in their decisions, which they make with the bottom line in mind. Player depreciation, capital gains tax laws, and potential income are guiding forces behind ownership decisions. In 1984 the Baltimore Colts, a storied, proud franchise, was surreptitiously moved to Indianapolis to benefit the owner, Robert Irsay, with financial inducements and a new stadium. In 1996, 12 years later, Baltimore retaliated by enticing Art Modell and the Cleveland Browns to forsake Cleveland and move to Baltimore to become the Baltimore Ravens.

Individual club owners sometimes own a professional sport franchise to find fun and excitement, boost the ego, or gain a sense of power. Others enjoy being around famous athletes. Some owners are actively involved in the day-to-day operations, standing on the field with the athletes and consulting with coaches on decisions. Others leave the sport to the professional coaches and managers and stick to the business side of the franchise.

Making Money From Professional Sports

Let's look at the ways an owner might make an investment in a sport franchise worthwhile. Not all

Early team owners like Tom Yawkey used their personal money to turn teams into profitable businesses. Today's owners have many options when it comes to earning money on their sports franchise.

team owners take advantage of all of these factors, but many do.

Investment

Professional team franchises **appreciate,** growing in value every year. Clubs that were once purchased for hundreds of thousands dollars are now bought for hundreds of millions. No owner has ever lost money on the initial capital investment, and putting money into a professional team has always paid off in the long run. And, if an owner is able to construct a new stadium with sources of income other than his own, he can automatically increase the value of the franchise by $30 to $40 million U.S.

To give you some idea of the value of an NFL franchise, consider that between 1993 and 1997, seven teams were sold in the price range of $158 to $212 million U.S. In the years since then, the average selling price for a franchise has shot up to $578 million U.S., topped by the $800 million U.S. Daniel Snyder paid for the Washington Redskins (Wall Street Journal 2004a).

Taxes

While some owners may show a loss in their franchise's bottom line at the end of the year, they usually go into the year expecting that outcome. In fact, they may balance those losses against significant profits made in their other businesses, thereby saving money by reducing their overall tax liability. For example, if an owner earns a profit of $1 million U.S. in another business such as a manufacturing company, he can subtract the losses from his sport franchise from his $1 million U.S. in other profits and only pay tax on the remainder. The resulting tax savings could be significant. While losing money each year to gain tax write-offs may seem like bad business, remember that the value of the franchise steadily increases each year, and once the owner sells, he will see significant profits. Don't be fooled by owners who claim they are losing money with their team. If they really see the team as a loss, they'll sell.

Depreciation

Depreciation has always been a mainstay of American business. Assets such as equipment, tools, and athletes (in sports) have a life expectancy. Their annually decreasing value is described as *depreciation.* American tax laws allow businesses to reduce the book values of their capital assets each year, and so businesses can show depreciation as a loss against their profits and again reduce their tax liability, even if the actual values of the **capital assets** have increased. Depreciation may be one of the least understood characteristics of owning a professional sport franchise. The players who are under contract to the team are valued at a certain level each year. Because their values decrease over time as they age and their careers wind down, federal laws allow clubs to annually depreciate the value of their stable of players.

Here's how an owner may depreciate players for tax benefits. Suppose a sport franchise breaks even in yearly income versus yearly expenses, but the owner can depreciate the value of his players by $1 million U.S. If his other businesses show a profit of $2 million U.S., he can apply the depreciation of $1 million U.S. against that profit and pay tax only on the remaining million.

Ticket Sales

Ticket sales account for about 23% of all revenue generated by NFL franchises, and each club retains the money it earns in sales (Bell 2004). Total ticket sales are affected by the seating capacity of the stadium, the prices set for each level of seating, and the attendance at each game. Many NFL teams with winning traditions routinely sell out their seating and have a waiting list of customers wanting to purchase season tickets. In MLB, demand may be similar, but

In the Arena With . . . *George Steinbrenner*

George Steinbrenner, owner of the New York Yankees, may be the most well-known club owner of the last half century. Born in 1930, Steinbrenner, a shipping magnate from Cleveland, Ohio, purchased the Yankee franchise in 1973 for $10 million U.S. The worth of the Yankees was estimated at $950 million U.S. in 2005 by Forbes.com, making it the most valuable sport franchise in the world.

According to George, "Winning is the most important thing in my life, after breathing. Breathing first, winning second." Some people admire his style, some dislike him and his Yankees, but all admit he has been the most successful owner in professional sports that we have seen. How does he do it?

One way is by spending money. Steinbrenner paid big bucks to lure Jim "Catfish" Hunter to the Yankees in 1974 and Reggie "Mr. October" Jackson in 1976. He believed that you have to spend money to make money. His teams routinely outspend every other competitor in payroll in spite of rules that penalize a team for spending too much on players. Owning a big-market team with all the advantages of a base in New York City, "The Boss" simply buys the best players available whatever the price tag, and when the team goes over the threshold for combined salary that was set for MLB teams, he just pays the luxury tax and keeps going.

Perhaps George Steinbrenner is best known for firing team managers. He changed managers 20 times during his first 23 years as team owner. That includes hiring and firing one manager, Billy Martin, five different times. After some missteps, Steinbrenner reconstituted the New York Yankees in the mid-1990s and created MLB's most dominant team. The Yankees went on to win the World Series in 1996, 1998, 1999, and 2000.

As the years passed, George mellowed a little, his managers lasted a little longer, and perhaps he became more conscious of his legacy. He has unselfishly given time and money to support the Olympics, youth sport programs, and other worthy causes, particularly those in the Tampa Bay area that he calls home. You might not like him or his Yankees, but you've got to respect what he's done with his team (Baseball Almanac 2005).

a game rarely sells out simply because a baseball team plays 162 games per year, while a football team plays only 16 games a season.

Stadium Revenues

Stadium revenues include income from luxury boxes, concessions, and parking. Most recently built stadiums include luxury boxes that are typically the most expensive seats available. They often include food service, have private restrooms, and feature televisions showing the game in progress. Most luxury boxes are bought by corporations and are deducted as a business expense since the corporations use them to entertain clients.

The food and souvenir concessions at most ballparks and arenas also generate significant profits for the local team. Most venues ban outside food and drink, forcing fans who wish to eat or drink to patronize the concession stands during the game. Parking also produces revenue since most fans drive to the venue and like to park near the facility. In the NFL, the league-wide stadium revenue is estimated at $1 billion U.S., or 21% of total league revenues (Bell 2004). The local franchise typically retains these stadium revenues, but in the case of publicly financed stadiums, the sponsoring agency such as the city may share in these revenues in return for financing the stadium in the first place.

Media Revenues

Media revenues include income from radio, TV, cable, and pay-per-view broadcasts. They account for the largest single source of income for the NFL and were estimated at 52% of total NFL revenue for 2004. Happily for most NFL franchises, that revenue is shared equally by all 32 teams. In contrast, income from television accounts for less than 20% of revenue for national hockey league (NHL) owners since their product cannot command the same level of compensation as professional football can (Bell 2004).

Whereas television income generates nearly 60% of each NFL team's revenue, in other sports that percentage may be as low as 15 (Sage 1998). Revenue sharing among teams in the league enhances their total bargaining power and helps balance the differences in various markets due to size, tradition, and competition from other recreational activities.

Licensing Fees on Team Merchandise

Professional sports teams sell team jerseys, caps, T-shirts, and every imaginable souvenir. The NFL has been the leader in capitalizing on such merchandise by establishing NFL Properties to market the league and license merchandise. The revenue from these sales was shared equally among all NFL teams. Some team owners balked at this arrangement, particularly if their team traditionally generated more sales than other, less popular teams generated.

The amounts of these revenue streams vary greatly from team to team, city to city, and sport to sport. Some leagues such as the NFL mandate **revenue sharing** among all teams, while others allow each franchise to keep what it generates or cap earnings and penalize franchises for exceeding the cap. The NFL and its franchises generate about $5 billion U.S. annually and share roughly two thirds of that amount equally. In contrast, MLB teams share about one third of their total revenue (Bell 2004). So in baseball, the large-market franchises in New York, Los Angeles, Atlanta, Houston, and Chicago fare better than their counterparts in smaller cities like Green Bay, Indianapolis, Miami, or Kansas City. This is one factor that tilts the competitive advantage toward a team like the Yankees that can spend more each year on player salaries and also afford the resulting penalty.

Naming Rights

Another major source of income for cities or teams is the selling of the **naming rights** to their stadium. In the past, stadiums were named after former owners, celebrities, or the local city. For example, Joe Robbie Stadium in Miami, which honored the former owner, and Connie Mack Stadium, former manager of the Philadelphia Athletics, have been replaced by Pro Player Stadium and Lincoln Financial Stadium, respectively. Now we are accustomed to names like Raymond James Stadium, American Airlines Arena, Pepsi Center, Tropicana Field, Safeco Field, and Ericsson Stadium. The largest stadium naming rights are shown in table 4.1.

A new or refurbished stadium increases the value of a professional sport franchise. As mentioned, an owner may see his franchise appreciate by $30 or $40 million U.S. without spending a dime if outside public or private funding finances a new stadium. The owner then pockets the increased value when he decides to sell.

Stadium Financing

Financing of stadiums or playing arenas has been under public debate for years and the discussion is sure to continue. Because of the need for constant refurbishing, upgrading, and redesign, constructing a new facility is often a better option than remodeling an old one. The cost of a new facility easily exceeds several hundred million dollars, and thus the source of that funding is a point of debate. Many creative minds have developed various financial packages to support these new facilities. Let's look at some of the packages.

The percentage of **public** and **private funds** used for construction varies in each situation. The 15 MLB parks constructed since 1991 on average received 75% of their financing from public funds. During a similar time frame, professional football stadiums averaged about 65% of public financing (Sage 1998). Public sources include sales taxes, proximity and beneficiary taxes, general obligation and revenue bonds, and tax increment financing. Private sources include owner contributions, league contributions, bank loans, loans from local businesses, and personal seat licenses.

The majority of stadiums are publicly owned by local governments or by special stadium or sport authorities. These groups oversee the operation of the facility, negotiate leases with the sports teams that use it, and may also supervise nearby ancillary construction such as shops, restaurants, and other amenities. A few stadiums such as Bank of America and Gillette were privately financed and are privately owned. The Bank of America Stadium, home of Carolina Panthers football, was completed in 1996 at a cost of $248 million U.S. (Ballparks 2006a). The Gillette Stadium in Foxboro, Massachusetts, has been home to the New England Patriots since 2002 and was funded entirely by owner Robert Kraft at a price of $325 million U.S. (Ballparks 2006c). The inducement for the owner to fund the facility is the ability to depreciate the asset. Over several years, the tax savings from such depreciation can be significant.

For years Florida has assessed a **bed tax** on hotel guests who are from out of state. For every room night, $1.00 U.S. goes into a special fund to help finance public sport stadiums around the state. The state government decides which sport in which city is due for support and allocates a portion of the bed tax revenue for that project. As you might suspect, football, basketball, baseball, tennis, and

TABLE 4.1 Deals on Stadium Naming Rights

Facility	Location	Deal value (in U.S. millions)	Deal length (years)
Reliant Park	Houston	$300	30
FedEx Field	Virginia (DC)	$205	27
American Airlines Center	Dallas	$195	30
Minute Maid Park	Houston	$170	28
Philips Arena	Atlanta	$168	20
INVESCO Field at Mile High	Denver	$120	20
PSINet Stadium	Baltimore	$105.5	20
Staples Center	Los Angeles	$100	20
Gaylord Entertainment Center	Nashville	$80	20
Xcel Energy Arena	St. Paul	$75	25
Compaq Center at San Jose	San Jose	$72	18
Savvis Center	St. Louis	$70	20
Pepsi Center	Denver	$68	20
Bank One Ballpark	Phoenix	$66	30
Comerica Park	Detroit	$66	30
Edison International Field	Anaheim	$50	20
Pacific Bell Park	San Francisco	$50	24
Tropicana Field	St. Petersburg	$46	30
Air Canada Centre	Toronto	$45 (Canadian dollars)	15
MCI Center	Washington, DC	$44	13
American Airlines Arena	Miami	$42	20
Miller Park	Milwaukee	$41.2	20
Conseco Fieldhouse	Indianapolis	$40	20
CoreStates Center	Philadelphia	$40	29
First Union Center	Philadelphia	$40	31
Ford Field	Detroit	$40	40
Safeco Field	Seattle	$40	20

Adapted, by permission, from Fried, G. 2005. *Managing sport facilities*. (Champaign, IL: Human Kinetics), page 205.

other sports lobby heavily for access to these funds. The beauty of this plan is that residents are mollified at the use of public money since it comes from the pockets of tourists or out-of-state businesspeople. Of course, some people might wonder what other uses the money could be put to, such as education, housing for the poor, hurricane relief, or coastline refurbishing.

Personal seat licenses (PSLs) are an interesting financing option in which fans pay for the right to purchase specific seats in a stadium. If the owner of a seat decides not to purchase the seat for a particular

Busch Stadium III, home of the St. Louis Cardinals, cost $344.8 million U.S. to build and was financed by both public and private financing. Public financing of $45 million U.S. was from a long-term loan from St. Louis County. Private financing of $299.8 million U.S. came from many sources: the Cardinals, interest earned on the construction fund, and bonds to be paid over a 22-year period by the team. Anheuser-Busch also agreed to a 20-year naming rights deal (through the 2025 season), which helped offset construction costs (Ballparks 2006b).

game, the seat can be sold to the general public. This plan has been popular and has raised significant capital in cities like San Francisco ($55 million U.S.), Chicago ($70 million U.S.), Green Bay ($92 million U.S.), and Charlotte ($122 million U.S.) (Steeves 2003).

Public tax funds provide funding for construction and maintenance of most professional sport stadiums. These publicly financed stadiums may be financed by tax-free public bonds, thereby depriving the government of a source of revenue that critics of such financing argue could be better applied toward improved living conditions for residents, especially the most needy. In many cases, the city may tax ticket sales, refreshment sales, and parking fees, although each of these items depends on the negotiated agreement with the sports franchise. Most cities also charge the team a rental fee that may range from several hundred thousand dollars a year to a nominal $1.00 U.S. The fee depends on the

negotiation between the professional sport franchise and the current city officials.

You might wonder how cities or states justify spending public funds to build stadiums and arenas that clearly benefit the team owners. Here are the major justifications that are typically told to the taxpayers:

■ The general public will benefit from the presence of professional sports teams because the area will be regarded as major league, real estate values will increase, and residents will take pride in their team identity and enjoy the recreational value of following the team.

■ The city will see revenue from tourists who attend the games, restaurants and hotels will see increased traffic, and the city government will realize tax revenue on all the money spent locally, which will go back into city coffers.

▪ The city and region will see priceless publicity that will attract potential residents, especially potential businesses looking to relocate offices and groups of employees or new businesses that provide jobs for local residents.

▪ National media attention will attract tourism and local businesses will flourish because of exposure and a chance to sell their products nationally or at least regionally.

▪ Special events like play-offs and championships may prove an added benefit. They provide added exposure, and the revenue generated from just one such event can easily be $50 million U.S. or more.

▪ The sport franchise creates jobs and income for local people who work directly or indirectly for the team. Ushers, ticket takers, refreshment stand workers, cleanup crews, and maintenance workers all derive income from the facility.

Detractors of public financing for these facilities argue just as vehemently that these benefits are modest when compared to the actual costs to the cities and their taxpayers. Over the years, various opposing groups have mounted campaigns to block public financing by drawing attention to alternative fund uses that might better improve the quality of life for a city's residents. Housing for the poor, educational services, public infrastructure improvements, medical research and care, and many other services are offered as reasonable alternatives.

Who wins the debate usually depends on the amount of money spent on the campaign for public support. The owners of sports teams expend significant amounts to hire the best "spin doctors" to present their case to the public. Local politicians, business leaders, and media often happily support the new proposal by reporting its positive benefits to the public. Opposition forces on the other hand are often a small group of local citizens with limited financial resources to publicize their point of view.

Sport owners may also subtly or not so subtly threaten to simply move their team to another city if the residents don't want the team badly enough to finance it. Although such threats are a form of blackmail, they have carried the day in many cities around the country. The actions of Art Modell in Cleveland, Robert Irsay in Baltimore, and Al Davis in Oakland have proven that such a threat is not just idle chatter (Turco and Ostrosky 1997).

Organizations as Owners

Many sporting events and even some professional sports teams, such as the Green Bay Packers, are owned by a group or organization. The dynamics of group ownership significantly differ from those of individual ownership since decisions have to be made by group members or at least by the elected governing board of directors. If the group is a public corporation its financial records are open to public scrutiny, an unpalatable prospect for professional sport leagues that would prefer to keep their finances private.

One of the most successful group ownerships of a professional sport event is the United States Open tennis championships at Flushing Meadow, New York. The annual tennis tournament is owned and operated by the United States Tennis Association (USTA), the appointed governing body (NGB) for tennis in the United States. As the NGB for tennis, the USTA was granted that right by the USOC, which based its decision on the Amateur Sports Act of the U.S. Congress. The USTA has a membership of approximately 700,000 people who pay a modest yearly due of around $35.00 U.S. But the real moneymaker for the USTA is the U.S. Open. About 85% of the annual revenue for the USTA comes from that two-week tournament. In recent years, the USTA's annual operating budget has been upward of $160 million U.S., so the Open must earn $135 to $140 million U.S. annually (USTA 2004).

By constitution and bylaws, the USTA is a not-for-profit organization that must spend the money it takes in each year to promote tennis. It does so by operating tennis leagues for adults and kids, developing community tennis programs, supporting elite junior players who promise to be successful professionals, and fulfilling its traditional role as a tournament organizer for every possible age group, ability level, and gender.

Several years ago, the facilities at the National Tennis Center in New York, the home of the U.S. Open, received a total face-lift at a cost exceeding $250 million U.S. The USTA bore the total cost of that expense, with no expenditure of public funding. Compared to other sport owners who have their facilities built for them, the USTA stands alone as self-supporting.

The only New York team that earns more money than the U.S. Open is the New York Yankees, and they accumulate their earnings over a season of 81 home games. During its two-week tournament, the U.S. Open earns more than the Jets, Giants, Knicks, Rangers, or Islanders. How does the USTA do it?

The U.S. Open derives its income about equally from three sources: ticket, food, beverage, and merchandise sales; corporate sponsors; and television rights worldwide. Other professional tennis events

The U.S. Open is an example of organizational sport ownership earning 85% of its total revenue in two weeks.

around the country operate similarly, although on a much smaller scale. Some of them are owned by organizations such as the International Management Group, the sport organization founded by Mark McCormick that represents players and also owns tennis events. Other tournaments are owned by individuals or local sporting groups who secure the sanction of the men's or women's professional tour to ensure that their date is not set on that of another event.

SPORT AS A MONOPOLY

Some people argue that professional sports in America are unique in that they are clearly a monopoly. No other business in the United States operates under the same favorable set of rules. Let's examine this argument, beginning with a review of history.

In the 1890s, President Grover Cleveland became concerned about the influence of the Standard Oil Company on the economy and influenced the U.S. Congress to pass the Sherman Antitrust Act, which made illegal "every contract, combination in the form of trust or otherwise, or conspiracy in restraint of trade or commerce among the several states or with foreign nations" (Michener 1987, p. 386). Although this bill did not directly target baseball, it significantly affected the sport. Professional baseball was conducting interstate commerce and restrained trade since players couldn't move from one team to another and the owners conspired to keep players' salaries at their desired level. Over the next 30 years, various interests challenged the Sherman Antitrust legislation, and in 1922, Supreme Court Justice Oliver Wendell Holmes declared that baseball was not in violation of the Sherman Antitrust laws. Numerous court suits have been filed since with minor changes to this momentous decision. Naturally, other professional sports fell into the same favorable position due to the similarity of their businesses.

How have professional sports used this favorable ruling to operate as a monopoly? Let's look at a few of the ways:

▪ Team owners formed leagues like the NFL to control how teams compete against each other for fans, players, media revenues, sales of licensed merchandise, and sponsorships.

▪ The leagues, including the MLB, National Basketball Association (NBA), NFL, and NHL, also work together to eliminate competition from new leagues that try to cash in on their sport.

▪ Using a draft system for hiring players, owners force players to negotiate only with the team that drafts them, thereby keeping the prices for athletes down.

▪ New or expansion teams cannot join the league without paying substantial fees to all the other owners, and one owner cannot relocate his team to another city without the approval of the other owners.

▪ Owners of individual teams cannot sell merchandise from their team. In professional football, NFL Properties markets all the business properties of the NFL as a unit. NFL Properties has been wildly successful in negotiating sponsorships, licensing agreements, and television contracts. However, Jerry Jones of the Dallas Cowboys, the most popular team in America, wanted to merchandise Cowboy paraphernalia himself. He didn't see why he should support other franchises with sales of Cowboys hats, jerseys, and so on. Jones forced the NFL to modify the monopolistic stance it had operated under for years, although the league still retains the majority of its power.

Television revenue is a huge source of income for most sports teams, but the potential revenue for each team depends on the size of its market. The NFL restricts individual teams from negotiating local TV contracts, but the MLB does not. Hence, the New York Yankees can sell their local TV rights for $75 million U.S. a year while a team like the former Montreal Expos was lucky to command $1 million U.S. Among other things, this inequity in potential income helped convince the Expos to relocate to Washington, DC, in 2005. You can see the disparity that different markets create between teams, which throws the teams' power and competitiveness off balance. The NFL remains a true monopoly by negotiating as one entity.

Management Versus Labor

Team owners restrict the options available to the workforce in their sports. First, they limit the choice of teams a player can sign with. Each league conducts an annual draft and players are assigned teams based on their selection by a team. A player who grew up in California and thrives in warm weather may be drafted by the Green Bay Packers and has no choice but to go to Green Bay if he wishes to play professionally in his sport. Also, by assigning players to teams, leagues reduce the players' negotiating leverage and therefore limit players' salaries.

Imagine if a young lawyer just out of school was drafted by a law firm and assigned to work there regardless of her preferences and the salary offered. That's how professional athletes go into their work. Those who support athletes' rights would say that athletes who spend their whole lives preparing to play professionally ought to have the rights of other citizens who can offer their services to the highest bidder. Team owners argue that a league draft fairly distributes sport talent and allows every team a shot at signing the best players. Since the draft begins with the team who had the worst record the previous year, the theory is that the team can strengthen itself by hiring the best new talent. This argument may be more fitting for basketball, where one 7-foot (2.1-meter) player can dominate the court, than for other sports.

When Kara Braxton was drafted by the Detroit Shock, did she have a choice to play for that team?

Second, team owners used to own the services of their athletes for life if they wished. Curt Flood in baseball was the first to challenge this reserve clause, and at great sacrifice to his personal career, he changed baseball forever. Now baseball players can become free agents after a certain amount of time and can bargain with other teams for their services. Football and basketball have at various times used an *option clause*, which requires a player to play one more year after his contract expires, typically at 90% of his previous year's salary, before he becomes a free agent, able to sell his services to another team. Each new collective bargaining agreement between owners and the player's union sets the terms of option clauses during the length of the agreement that may or may not include option clauses. Of course, when a player and his agent negotiate a contract, they also have the right to agree to an option clause in exchange for other favorable provisions such as a sizable signing bonus. Many teams try to trade a player once he announces he is playing out his option, as they figure it is better to get something in return than to lose a player's services without any compensation at all. A trade gives the player's current team some value in return compared to losing him with nothing to show for it once his obligation is satisfied and he is free to negotiate with any other team. Thus you see established players with significant careers traded for fringe players, future draft choices, or the famous "player to be named later."

Over the years, strong leadership from union officials and former athletes with backing from the player union have effected some favorable changes for athletes. Minimum pay levels have been established for rookies and veterans, options set for players who cannot agree with the team that drafts them on a contract, and the freedom established for players who have fulfilled their original contract to negotiate with other teams for their services.

The owners gave in grudgingly to each of these player demands, arguing that allowing players to sign with the highest bidder at any time would upset the balance of competitiveness. Large-market teams like the Yankees would pay the highest salaries, attract the best players, and have the best teams year in and year out. Small-market teams left with poorer players would see fan attendance tumble and be at economic risk. The final irony would be that the large-market teams with deep pockets would eventually have no other teams to play and the sport would put itself out of business.

The Yankees already contend for the championship every year, beating up on their competition. In 2005, the average salary for a New York Yankee was $5.8 million U.S. while the average salary of players from other teams in their division, like the Tampa Bay Devil Rays, was only $600,000 U.S. The total payroll for the Yankees was over $208 million U.S., while Tampa Bay's total was just $29 million U.S. (USA Today 2005).

Player Compensation

Before feeling too sorry for the professional athletes, let's look at their yearly compensation. According to the United States Department of Labor (2005), in 2004 the median annual earnings of athletes were $48,310 U.S. The lowest 10% earned less than $14,160 U.S. while the highest 10% earned more than $145,000 U.S. These statistics include all profes-

Not all athletes make exorbitant salaries. Minor-league players may make as little as $14,000 U.S. for a season of play that is typically shorter than a major-league season. Minor-league players often play in another league the rest of the year or take another job just to make a living.

sional athletes at all levels of play for pay. Statistics also show that there are only about 17,000 jobs in total for all levels of professional sport athletes in the United States. While you read about the multimillion-dollar contracts of top athletes in the news, hundreds more are struggling to make ends meet in the minor leagues, hoping for a chance at the big leagues.

Once athletes in major sports such as baseball, football, or basketball reach a certain level of performance, they are rewarded with a contract that may extend for several years or, in the case of superstars, up to 8 to 10 years. Since these athletes typically are in a high tax bracket, federal, state, and local taxes take a big chunk out of these earnings. Many athletes are required to pay state taxes in the state where their team is based and in states where their team competes, even if their residence is in a different state. The task of accounting and filing returns in a dozen states is daunting.

The average career in professional sports lasts less than 10 years. Most athletes need the income they earn in these years to last a lifetime and so must invest their money wisely to grow their nest egg. You might argue that athletes can find other jobs once their career ends. However, professional athletes often fall victim to relying on their athletic prowess and have no other marketable skills. Sport-related jobs like officiating, coaching, scouting, and working in the front office are limited and demand training and experience. The income potential for those jobs is very modest, much less than that the athlete has learned to live on. Some of the most successful athletes move into television reporting and broadcast work. These careers can be very lucrative, but the competition for these spots is intense, and sustaining these jobs requires excellent skills. During the 20s and early 30s, when most of us are carving a niche for ourselves in our chosen profession, honing our craft, and perhaps seeking additional education, professional athletes focus completely on their athletic careers.

Professional athletes face extreme competition to make it as an athlete, and that competitiveness rarely goes away. In some sports like professional tennis or golf, players earn prize money in tournaments. If they don't play well or suffer an injury, their income stops while their expenses continue. There are no guarantees in professional tennis or golf, so athletes have to prove themselves at every event, year after year.

The day-to-day work of a professional athlete is extremely demanding, even in the off-season. Athletes are constantly challenged at their physical and mental limits. They often travel extensively and spend long times away from spouses and children. If their team trades them, they are forced to uproot their families and start life in a new city.

Media coverage of athletes is very intense, and sports writers often criticize performances they judge as wanting. Very few occupations and performances are reviewed publicly, especially on a daily basis. Athletes must develop a tough skin to deal with the constant criticism and scrutiny.

Table 4.2 shows the top wage earners in football, baseball, and basketball, while the top wage earners in all sports are shown in table 4.3. Although these salaries are extremely generous when compared to that of the average wage earner in the United States ($39,795 U.S. in 2005; United States Department of Labor 2005), athletes are not ordinary people. Their athletic talents are extraordinary, and if they can combine that talent with good business sense, they may earn double and triple their salary in endorsements, appearances, and other activities.

In the Arena With . . . *Arnold Palmer*

With careers that may last only a few years and salaries that need to last a lifetime, many athletes find alternative ways of supplementing their income. Arnold Palmer is one such athlete; he parlayed his amazing success as a professional golfer into a second career as a successful businessman. He is president of Arnold Palmer Enterprises, a multilevel division structure that involves global commercial activity. He is also a leader in golf course design and has fashioned more than 200 courses around the world. A signature line of leisure clothing, teaching academies, golf equipment, country clubs, and automobile and aviation service firms all supplement the income he earned from his 92 golf championships (Palmer 2006).

TABLE 4.2 Top Wage Earners in Football, Baseball, and Basketball

Athlete	Team	Earnings (in U.S. millions)
Pro football (2004)		
Peyton Manning	Indianapolis Colts	$35
Chad Pennington	New York Jets	$19
Jevon Kearse	Philadelphia Eagles	$16
Grant Wistrom	San Diego Chargers	$16
LaDamian Tomlinson	Seattle Seahawks	$15.5
Pro baseball (2005)		
Alex Rodriguez	New York Yankees	$26
Barry Bonds	San Francisco Giants	$22
Manny Ramirez	Boston Red Sox	$22
Derek Jeter	New York Yankees	$19.6
Mike Mussina	New York Yankees	$19
Pro basketball (men; 2004-05)		
Shaquille O'Neal	Miami Heat	$27.6
Alan Houston	New York Knicks	$17.5
Chris Webber	Philadelphia 76ers	$17.5
Kevin Garnett	Minnesota Timberwolves	$16
Jason Kidd	New Jersey Nets	$14.7

Data from *USA Today* 2005.

TABLE 4.3 Top 2004 Wage Earners in All Sports

Athlete	Sport	Earnings (in U.S. millions)
Males		
Tiger Woods	Golf	$80.3
Michael Schumacher	Auto racing	$80
Peyton Manning	Football	$42
Michael Jordan	Basketball	$35
Shaquille O'Neil	Basketball	$32
Females		
Maria Sharapova	Tennis	$18
Serena Williams	Tennis	$9.5
Venus Williams	Tennis	$8.5
Annika Sorenstam	Golf	$7.4
Lindsay Davenport	Tennis	$6.0

Reprinted by permission of *Forbes Magazine* © 2006 Forbes, Inc.

Like athletes, construction workers have demanding jobs, face tough mental and physical challenges, and can spend long times away from their families. Should they be paid the same as athletes? Why or why not?

The average Joe Fan may get disgusted with the exorbitant pay of top athletes, particularly when the athletes don't play up to expectations. However, a fair way to look at their compensation is to regard them as entertainers in the sport industry. When compared to earnings of entertainers in music, stage, and film, their wages are not so amazing—Oprah Winfrey easily outearns most of the top athletes. Following is a list of the top 10 celebrities, including athletes, ranked by earnings and publicity (as measured by indexes such as the number of appearances on magazine covers; Kafka 2004):

1. George Lucas $290 million U.S.
2. Oprah Winfrey $225 million U.S.
3. Mel Gibson $185 million U.S.
4. Steven Spielberg $80 million U.S.
5. Tiger Woods $75 million U.S.
6. Madonna $50 million U.S.
7. Elton John $44 million U.S.
8. Johnny Depp $37 million U.S.
9. Shaquille O'Neil $33 million U.S.
10. Tom Cruise $31 million U.S.

Limits on Athlete Earnings

After years of wildly escalating salaries, professional sport owners decided to set a **total salary cap** on the amount each team could spend on player salaries in order to save money and ensure competitive balance in the league. The NFL enforces the toughest version of this cap, while baseball allows some wiggle room. When a baseball team exceeds the total cap, it has to pay a luxury tax on the amount of money they pay over the cap. As mentioned, the New York Yankees do exceed the cap most years and pay the fine.

Because of the salary cap, every team employs experts who figure out the implications of every player contract and how it will affect the team cap in the years ahead. Veteran players sometimes agree to renegotiate their contract and postpone earnings in order to free cap space so the team can sign a desirable free agent who might help the team win now. In other cases, a team may retire a veteran player with a contract in order to avoid having to count his entire salary in the cap totals.

Team administrators compile all the available data, scout for the best players, sign them to contract while staying under the cap, and try to keep everybody happy. Making everyone happy doesn't happen very often due to the competitiveness of the athletes, their agents, and the team officials.

COLLEGIATE SPORTS AS MONEYMAKERS

Let's step down from professional sports and look at intercollegiate sports. Born out of student activities, college sports have evolved into big business on many university campuses. Particularly in major or **revenue-producing sports** like football and basketball, the amount of money major universities earn and spend makes operation of the athletic department a business proposition. While the specific purpose of an athletic program may not be to make money, it sure is clear that the department cannot lose money. Amateur sport has become big business for several reasons:

- The student body enjoys having high-profile athletic teams on campus for entertainment and recreation.
- The university administration recognizes the power of the free publicity schools that compete at high levels receive in the sports pages of newspapers and periodicals.
- Sport publicity helps universities recruit applicants. Receiving more applications raises the competition for admission and improves the quality of students schools attract.
- Alumni enjoy identifying with their alma mater through sports, especially if they take pride in their athletic achievements. They are also more likely to return to campus to attend athletic events.
- Alumni are more likely to donate significant sums of money to their university. Some restrict their gifts to the athletic program, some donate to the general fund used at the administration's discretion, and others earmark their money for specific campus projects.
- Revenue from a high-profile sport like football can support a complete athletic program with a full complement of offerings for both men and women.

The University of Connecticut (UConn), a small regional university that was not even widely regarded as the best university in New England, moved into national prominence by dominating college basketball. The state of Connecticut invested a billion U.S. dollars over five years to refurbish the campus, build new facilities, and generally upgrade the school environment. Both the men's and women's basketball teams aided the emergence of UConn as a nationally competitive university. During the late 1990s, both teams steadily garnered titles, including a national championship. But in 2004, both teams won the national championship in basketball, making UConn the first university to achieve that feat. Afterward, the number of applications for admission continued to explode, the standards for admission were upgraded, and pride among alumni and students soared.

Sources of Revenue

College athletics collect revenue from a myriad of sources. Big universities sell tickets to football games

Wearing clothing with your school's name or mascot demonstrates team loyalty; it also represents thousands of dollars in licensing fee revenue for your school.

in stadiums that seat more than 100,000 fans. They add to their income through parking fees, concessions, souvenirs, and the luxury boxes that come with substantial fees for alumni or businesspeople who want to entertain clients.

Television rights can be a bonanza, provided the team is good enough. Notre Dame has been so well known in football for so long that it negotiates its own football package with TV and refuses to join a league and share its profit with other football teams. Most schools benefit from league membership and receive revenue from all televised league games. Play-offs or bowl games are another income source for the schools that earn those trips.

Most colleges charge every student an athletic fee that helps support the sport program. Athletic departments also charge many of their expenses to other university programs, budgets, or cost centers, making it difficult to track the actual cost for university athletics. For example, a new weight training facility may be built as part of a general fitness facility and not charged directly to athletic programs. Football stadiums and basketball arenas at large state universities are often financed with public funds or tax-free bonds available for public purchase.

Corporate sponsors also contribute significantly to big-time college sports with cash or with donations of clothing, equipment, and services. Local physicians often donate medical services in return for the publicity they receive as the team doctor.

Licensing fees on merchandise can also be a major source of income, particularly if athletic teams are successful. College bookstores that are allegedly filled with books for students are now often filled with sweats, caps, shirts, running gear, souvenirs, and any imaginable item with the university name or mascot on them. The books are often an afterthought, located in the back of the store.

High-profile athletic programs receive so much publicity that many people assume they are typical of universities. But a close look at the statistics reveals that a relatively small number of college athletic programs operate as high-profile programs. Only about 50% of all Division I men's football and basketball programs reported revenue in excess of expenditures in the 2000 to 2003 seasons. Less than 20% of most sports, including Division I women's sports, report that they actually made money (Parker 2004).

Annual budgets for college athletics vary from a couple hundred thousand to over $60 million U.S. Highly competitive athletic programs are designated as Division I, while less-competitive programs fall into Division II or III. Of the 1,200 collegiate institutions in the United States in 2003, only 325 met the qualifications for Division I. Those 325 are further subdivided: 117 schools have IA football programs, 123 schools have IAA programs that are smaller based on stadium size and average attendance, and 85 schools without football have IAAA programs that concentrate on basketball (NCAA 2005b).

There is a lot of money invested in college sports. Large programs offer athletic scholarships to attract the best athletes in the hopes of producing winning teams that will please the students, fans, alumni, and administration. However, not all college athletic programs fit the high-profile model, and we must clarify the levels of athletic program and commitment before lumping all college sports together.

There are hundreds of colleges where sports are simply a diversion from studies, and they attract athletes who play for the fun and experience. One

Expert's View: Pay College Athletes for Their Play

Peter Plagens, the Mellon distinguished visiting professor at Middlebury College in Middlebury, Vermont, an art critic for *Newsweek* magazine, and a self-proclaimed college sports fan, says the current practice of universities making money off of athletes amounts to little more than a plantation system. He proposes that it's time for big-time college sports to conduct their business in a socially honest way by paying athletes to play. Plagens suggests that colleges keep their million-dollar entertainment industry by making it an "age 23 and under professional league. Hire the players as college staff (as building and grounds workers are staff) at moderate salaries plus room and board. Grant players the perk of free academic classes for as long as they want till they attain a bachelor's degree, even after their playing days are over" (Lederman 2005).

such school, Swarthmore College, a tiny liberal arts school in Pennsylvania founded by Quakers and renowned for academics, even made it a point of pride when their football program lost game after game. Their losses symbolized to their students that football was not overemphasized on their campus. Of course, the players on that team did not have much fun or a positive experience. Losing year after year makes a player wonder if the effort is worth it.

We'll look more at collegiate sports in chapter 7. We mentioned them here since some major athletic programs truly are big business.

RECREATIONAL SPORT AS A BUSINESS

Recreational sport measures its economic effects through the sales of sport equipment like golf clubs, tennis rackets, balls, boats, and fishing rods. Sales also include athletic footwear and clothing that often serve the dual purposes of active wear for sport participation and leisure wear. The Sporting Goods Manufacturers Association estimates annual U.S. expenditure on sport clothing and equipment at upward of $50 billion (SGMA 2004).

Another way to measure the expenditures for sport recreation is to tally the amount of land in natural settings for boating and fishing, sport fields, public parks, and private sport facilities throughout the country. As the national economy advances, people have more discretionary income to spend on recreation, and facilities must be constructed or maintained to meet this demand. Every community spends a portion of its annual budget maintaining public recreational areas, often at significant expense to its citizens.

Even public facilities often charge a user fee to help cover the cost of operating their facilities. As municipal budgets are squeezed, recreational services are often among the first to be reduced and replaced with fees to support facility maintenance and operation. Golf courses, whether public or private, charge greens fees and cart fees and sell golf merchandise to help support their operation. Many public park systems have managed to remain solvent by treating their operations like businesses, including leasing out facilities to private contractors who guarantee an agreed-upon rate of return.

Tied in with local recreational activities are youth sports and the facilities needed for youth soccer, swimming, tennis, football, basketball, and so on. Virtually every town maintains community facilities to allow their kids to play sports for modest user fees. Arguments occasionally spring up about priorities of creating playing fields for kids or undisturbed, passive parkland for nature lovers, but essentially the public foots the bill for either choice. As kids join school sports in middle and high school, the sport facilities in some towns appear as miniature versions of professional complexes. Astroturf football fields with lights and commodious grandstands are common in football-crazy towns. Immaculate playing fields grace many suburban communities, and school-based athletic facilities may support community sport programs in the summer.

Let's look at how the individual consumer might contribute to the business of sport. I recall getting my first baseball glove, smacking it to build the pocket, oiling it to make the leather supple, and sleeping with it just to get used to the feel of it. Next came my very own baseball bat, a football, a basketball, a soccer ball, uniforms, sneakers, a bicycle, roller skates, a Wiffle ball and bat, swim gear like flippers and a mask, soccer and baseball shoes with spikes,

Activity Time-Out: How Much Do I Spend?

List the approximate costs of all sport equipment, memberships, fees, shoes, and clothing and of all tickets to sport events that you have purchased in the past year. Total the figure and compare your total with those of at least two other students. Judge whether you are about average, high, or low in your economic support of sports. Are you surprised by the result? Why or why not?

Multiply your total by 280 million people. This grand total estimates what U.S. residents spend annually on sports, assuming that you are a somewhat average consumer. What proportion of the gross national product is your projected sport expenditure?

How much money has this recreational golfer contributed to the business of sport?

CHAPTER SUMMARY

In this chapter we looked at the economics of sport in our society. We learned that owners of professional sport franchises tend to be wealthy people who have been successful in another business and purchase a team to minimize their tax liability, to associate with athletes, and to enjoy the excitement and high visibility of ownership. Some sports teams are owned by groups, conglomerates, or, in the case of the Green Bay Packers, the public.

To ensure the quality of the facility in which their team competes, franchise owners often upgrade or replace the facility to create a state-of-the-art stadium. Public funds are often a major source of stadium financing though the public may receive little direct benefit from the deal. The value of a franchise increases significantly with a new stadium, making the franchise a solid investment. Some organizations, like the United States Tennis Association, own and operate professional sport events.

We reviewed the tenuous relationship between sport management and labor and concluded that owners seem to wield most of the leverage. In recent years, athletes have acquired some control over their professional sport careers. We also looked at player compensation and compared it with that of others in the workforce in terms of longevity and earnings spread over a lifetime. We looked at the working conditions of professional athletes and the odds of making it to the big leagues. While a career in sports is very attractive to young people, the odds of cashing in on a big sport contract are long indeed.

Collegiate sports at the major institutions classified as Division 1A operate as another form of professional sport, except that they do not pay athletes for participation except through athletic scholarships. Only about 100 schools out of over 2,500 colleges operate their athletic program as a big business. However, these schools get the media attention and the notoriety.

Finally, we saw that the amount spent on recreational sports has escalated rapidly in recent years as more people participate in athletic activities. Annual purchase of sporting goods has exceeded $50 billion U.S. in the past few years. Millions more are spent in providing facilities and services to average citizens who participate in sport for leisure.

a tennis racket, and finally golf clubs. Children of families with at least modest incomes go through a similar progression of sport equipment, and over a lifetime a family may expend thousands of dollars on toys for sport and recreation.

Recreational sports generate revenues through the services they provide to people of all ages, incomes, and skill levels. Program administrators and coaches can earn a living through using their services to organize and implement recreational sport programs. Fees from renting sport facilities or equipment are collected at the community level to maintain current facilities and in some cases to build new ones.

Sport clubs and other commercial sport facilities charge fees for use by recreational participants. Golf courses, tennis clubs or centers, bowling alleys, fitness clubs, shooting ranges, swimming pools, equestrian facilities, skating rinks, and country clubs represent millions of dollars spent for recreational sport and a source of employment and income for the people who work there.

Media and Sport

Student Outcomes

After reading this chapter, you will know the following:

- The evolution of media in presenting sport
- How the media affect sport and sport affects the media
- How sport affects ideology
- Careers in sport media

It is natural to follow a discussion on the business of sport (chapter 4) with an analysis of the role that mass media play in sport. The media have a tremendous influence on sport in terms of creating revenue by supplying free publicity and advertisements. Equally substantial is the influence of sport programming on the media—it is the reason many media outlets exist and is a healthy source of revenue for all media outlets. Clearly, the economic effects of this interrelationship are significant in the overall business of sport.

Sport media fulfill a number of functions for consumers of sport:

- The media help create excitement about sport events leading up to the contest, describe the action during the event, and offer analyses and criticism at the conclusion of the event.

- The media convey to fans the significance of the game, players, history, and individual matchups. We rely on the media to give us the information that makes each of us a quasi-expert on the game, able to discuss it with friends and strangers who also are quasi-experts with their own opinions.

- Personal emotional attachments are developed through media features of athletes, coaches, and teams leading up to seasons or specific contests. We pick our favorite performers based on our own biases and experiences. Athletes with compelling personal stories, such as struggling to overcome injuries, often capture the imagination of fans and develop large fan clubs. Underdogs are always favorites, as are rookies, aging veterans, and athletes who have a knack for delivering peak performances under pressure.

- Preoccupation with sport is a healthy form of recreation and entertainment for many people and helps them escape from everyday life. Rooting for their favorite team or players often provides emotional excitement and drama.

The media that cover sport usually fit into two broad categories: the **print media** and the **electronic media.** Print media include newspapers, magazines, and books. More pervasive in modern society, electronic media are led by television, radio, and the Internet. Each of us has a bias toward certain media that we enjoy and feel comfortable with, but all of us are exposed to sport coverage in all types of media as technological advances encourage integration across media types. In the 1920s and 1930s, print media and radio delivered sport news. In the 1950s, television began to dominate sport delivery and maintained that position through the end of the century. At the end of the 20th century, the Internet began to open new ways to relay sport news, and perhaps in the future it will dominate other media as technology opens up new opportunities for sports fans.

As consumers of professional sport, we can be categorized as either direct or indirect spectators. **Direct spectators** attend live sporting events at a stadium, an arena, or some other venue. **Indirect spectators** listen to or watch sports by radio, television, or the Internet. Although direct spectators continue to increase in record numbers, the increase is relatively modest compared with that of indirect spectators.

Electronic coverage, particularly television, has opened up sport viewing to millions of fans around the world. Major sporting events are now broadcast live across time zones and into diverse cultures that often rearrange their sleep patterns or daily activities to catch a live telecast of events like the Super Bowl or Olympic Games. Consider, for example, the power of the 2004 Super Bowl, which attracted roughly 75,000 direct spectators but more than 144.4 million indirect spectators worldwide. Overall, the Super Bowl accounts for 7 of the top 10 telecasts of all time; of the top 40 telecasts since 1961, all but 6 were Super Bowls (Nielsen Media Research 2006).

Sport and large corporations are inextricably linked through the media since television stations are owned by corporations. The complex interrelationships that sprung up as a result of this link influence the decisions of which sports and events attract support and how they are presented.

In this chapter, we'll look at these interrelationships and how the media affect sport and sport affects the media.

We'll conclude the chapter by examining careers in sport media and some of the challenges women in particular face in this field.

EVOLUTION OF SPORT MEDIA

Growing up in the 1950s, I relied on news of professional sport from two major sources: newspapers and radio. A few times a year, I convinced my dad to

Before the mass availability of television, most families received their news and entertainment via the radio.

purchase tickets to a live game and thrilled at seeing my favorite players in person. Nothing compared to seeing a game in person, but most of the year, I was entertained by poring over the daily sports pages for game results, writers' opinions, and team or individual statistics. Games were broadcasted regularly on radio, and families or groups of fans gathered round to listen to the play-by-play broadcast. I spent many nights alone in my room, listening to radio broadcasts of an endless season of baseball games through the spring, summer, and fall.

Without the radio or newspaper, few of my generation would have become avid sports fans. These media provided our link to each game, stimulated our dreams and conversations, and helped form our attitudes toward sport and life. Professional sport boomed in popularity through exposure and an expansive fan base, and advertisers took advantage of that popularity to sell their wares through newspapers and radios.

Radio transmissions of sport events began in the 1920s, which just happened to be the golden age

of sport, and eventually sport helped make the late 1920s and early 1930s the golden age of radio. By the end of the 20th century, radio stations in the United States broadcast over half a million hours of sports events annually. Many stations converted to an all-sport format, and by 1998, there were 160 such stations. In addition to broadcasting live action, sport stations began to provide talk shows that sparked exchanges of opinions, particularly about local teams or well-known athletes (Sage 1998).

The first sports pages appeared sporadically in the second half of the 19th century in the big-city dailies. William Randolph Hearst, publisher of the *New York Journal*, is credited with establishing the first modern sport section. As Hearst acquired newspapers in other cities, he spread the sport section to Los Angeles, San Francisco, Boston, and Chicago. Sports pages in newspapers thrived during the 1920s. As professional baseball and football rose in popularity, horse racing and boxing thrived, and golf and tennis gained an audience, the public thirst for sport news demanded more and more information.

Today, virtually every major newspaper boasts a significant sport section staffed by a small army of researchers, beat writers, columnists, feature editors, photographers, and design editors.

By the end of the 1950s, television had become a fact of life in homes throughout the United States. In 1955, 67% of American homes had a television set. Just five years later that figure jumped to 87%, and by 2000 it had risen to 98% (Neuman 2005). With the single invention of TV, sport in America changed forever. The indirect consumer of sport via television gradually became king of the fans. Millions of sports fanatics sat glued to their TV sets, watching live-action sport. The end of the 1950s was marked by what many consider to be the "greatest game ever played," the 1958 NFL championship between the Baltimore Colts and the New York Giants. It was the first overtime championship in the NFL and the dramatic win by the Colts propelled professional football to an unprecedented run of popularity that has endured almost 50 years.

Television networks latched on to sport to fill up weekends with programming that they did not have to invent or stage. Workers and their families who were looking for entertainment and relaxation sat down in front of the TV. Advertisers lined up to sponsor sport events to reach the attractive audience of males who were often decision makers for their families and businesses. It seemed that television couldn't broadcast enough sport events to satisfy the demand until finally, in 1980, ESPN (the Entertainment and Sports Programming Network) was born as the first full-time sport station. All day, every day sport events are available on ESPN, which has expanded with ESPN2. Newer all-sports networks include Fox Sports and regional networks such as Madison Square Garden and Sun Sports. Over the next several decades, stations devoted to a single sport such as golf or tennis came on the air and promoted their sport to their niche audience.

Mass media disseminate information to large numbers of geographically dispersed people.

Satellites and other advances in technology make it easier to broadcast local sports to a worldwide audience.

Through television, people across the country and around the world can view sport contests in real time. They learn about the sport, the specific game, and the players through the live telecast, the announcers who provide play-by-play descriptions, and the color commentators who point out highlights and background information.

Just as television changed the way families in the 1950s interacted with sport, the Internet has given fans yet another way to experience sport. The Internet gives sports fans virtual access to sport in real time and on demand and allows them to create personal, specific methods of interaction. By 2004, two thirds of Americans had access to the Internet (compared to 98% who had access television) and used it on a regular basis. Internationally, the United States is the leading country in Internet usage, followed by China and Japan (Pearson Education, Inc. 2005).

Most of us use the Internet to supplement televised sport and newspaper accounts. We visit the Web sites of favorite teams, check for scores, listen to games in progress, order tickets, browse for stories, read sport blogs, or enter chat rooms to discuss the latest event results. Fantasy leagues attract some of us, and online betting on games attracts others. We can track the progress of sport events anywhere in the world. Stories by sports writers are published on the Internet so that we have access to perspectives from sports newsrooms around the country.

The rise of the Internet is likely one of the causes for the declining circulation of major newspapers. Newspaper circulation has been slowly falling since the 1980s, but recently that descent seems to be accelerating. According to the Audit Bureau of Circulations (2005), average weekday circulation for U.S. newspapers fell 2.6% during the six months ending in September of 2005. That topped a 1.9% decline of the previous six months. Among the top-20 selling newspapers, only the *New York Times* posted an increase of .46% in the Audit Bureau's report, while all other papers posted decreases. Even *USA Today* posted a loss of .59% and the *Wall Street Journal* posted a loss of 1.1%. One of the key reasons given in the report for the decline is the increasing consumer interest in getting news from the Internet.

As technology improves and access to the Internet increases, Web sites will fight to win consumers. Media corporations will enter the fray and try to entice consumers by offering exclusive data and entertainment on their site. Eventually, Internet access may allow us to design our own sport entertainment by giving us access to novel event presentations with unique camera angles, favorite announcers, instant replay on demand, and player or coach interviews. The interactive nature of such experiences will draw us closer to the action and make us more involved than the average spectator.

INTERPLAY OF SPORT AND MEDIA

Professional spectator sports depend on the media for survival. Ticket sales to live events simply cannot generate enough money to make professional events profitable without media support. The overwhelming bulk of revenue sport generates from the media

Pop Culture: Sports Photography

Advances in technology haven't just changed how spectators view games; technology has also changed how games are photographed. Sports photography relies on digital cameras and computers to transmit images instantly to the media. Digital images are astounding in their clarity, detail, and color. Pictures of great athletes that capture special moments are priceless, but there is no instant replay. You either get the shot or you don't.

Careers in sports photography in the United States range from 400-500 full-time positions. Other photographers work on a part-time freelance basis and seek out local events that can use their photographic expertise. Majoring in photojournalism and finding a mentor in sports photography are both good ways to advance in this field.

But, sports photography equipment isn't cheap. Most experts estimate that a professional sports photographer will need to spend at least $35,000 U.S. on equipment that includes several cameras, fast telephoto lenses, wide angle lenses, a good laptop computer, software, tripods, lighting, and carrying cases (Lodriguss 2005).

comes from television fees. For example, the New York Yankees generated over $60 million U.S. in 2004 from their local broadcasting agreements with Yankees Entertainment and Sports (YES) network (O'Keefe and Quinn 2005). That figure is on top of the league-wide revenue earned by MLB and shared by all clubs. Considering the team's annual payroll of $200 million U.S., you can see the importance of television fees to the Yankees. Other media forms, including print media, help support professional sport, but not by providing guaranteed income.

Amateur sport has a much more casual link with the media. For the most part, the media restrict their attention to occasionally featuring certain amateur events, particularly events that serve a public service, or to reporting on local amateur sport events to encourage local readership.

Let's look at the ways sport and media affect each other.

How Television Affects Sport

In his seminal book titled *Sports in America* (1987), James Michener estimated that television expended over $200 million U.S. on sport. That amount seemed unbelievable then, and the current annual rights fees swamp that figure (NCAA men's basketball in 2003, and contracts that expire in 2003 for the NHL, 2005 for the NFL and MLB, and 2008 for the NBA) (Ackman 2005):

NFL	$2,200 billion U.S.
NBA	$760 million U.S.
MLB	$560,417 million U.S.
NASCAR	$412 million U.S.
NCAA (men's basketball)	$216 million U.S.
NHL	$120 million U.S.

Add to these figures the fees for college football, women's professional and collegiate sports, tennis, golf, and the Olympics, and the total package adds up to a significant amount of money that television networks pay to broadcast sport.

Television viewing can expand dramatically through better marketing, presentation of the event, outreach to new audiences, expansion to include more female fans, and general worldwide expansion as American sports gain popularity in other parts of the world and internationally popular sports are broadcast in North America. Technology has helped expose American sports in other countries and has fueled the expansion of the uniquely American

Even the largest arena can only hold so many people. Without the money generated from television audiences, the Olympics wouldn't be nearly as profitable.

sports of baseball, basketball, and football. The major professional leagues have been able to expand to Europe and other countries as the popularity of the sports has grown.

The Olympic Games have grown into a huge moneymaker for the International Olympic Committee (IOC) through expanding television coverage around the world. In 1980, the broadcast rights for the summer Olympic Games in Moscow cost $87 million U.S., which grew to $793 million U.S. for the Athens Games in 2004. The winter Olympic Games in Lake Placid, New York, produced $15.5 million U.S. in rights fees in 1980 and grew to $613 million U.S. in Turin for the 2006 Games. These are broadcast rights fees just for the United States; the IOC also collects fees from every other major country televising the Olympic Games (International Olympic Committee 2006).

Perhaps the most important factor affecting income for professional sport is the potential marketplace televised sport provides. There is a limit to the number of spectators that can attend any given event, and there is a limit to the amount ticket prices can increase without cutting into demand. Let's review what television means to sport:

▪ Television networks pay significant broadcast rights fees to professional sport leagues, organizations, and franchises.

▪ Advertisers pay for rights to advertise their product to viewers during sport events.

▪ Sport owners or leagues can afford to pay athletes huge salaries due to the guaranteed income from television.

▪ Ticket sales and other game-day revenues pale in comparison with the income derived from television rights.

▪ Money is the most significant link between the media and professional sport. As rights fees increase, professional sports rely more heavily on television for their revenue stream. Television's influence over sport grows, and TV increasingly affects how sport events are presented to viewers.

How Media Affects Sport

Few people would dispute that the media can positively affect sport (aside from guaranteeing income through television rights). The media can

▪ affect the popularity of sport,

▪ provide free publicity for local teams, and

▪ present player personalities and build fan allegiance to teams and individual players.

The popularity of collegiate and professional sport exploded as more and more American homes gained access to television. People who had little or no interest in sport couldn't help but catch bits of games as they surfed the channels. They didn't even have to leave their chairs to see the games. Sports announcers hyped each contest to draw viewers in, and once they caught the viewers' attention, they enthusiastically and concisely described the game, making it exciting to watch.

Expert commentators work hard to educate viewers who know little about the sport without insulting diehard fans. For people who enjoy history, statistics, individual matchups, and record-setting performances, TV presentations offer all that and more. You don't need to lift a finger to find out more about a particular event than you ever wanted to know. You can just sit back, relax, and let the game come to you. With several options such as TiVo or DVR now available for viewing games on your own

Peyton Manning is perhaps most well known for his NFL career, but he is also well known for his volunteer work, as recognized by receiving the 2005 Walter Payton NFL Man of the Year award.

schedule, you can even decide when you want to spend time watching sport. The media expanded the popularity of sport by making sport spectatorship easily accessible, fun, and convenient for all.

Free publicity for the local professional team is a major contribution from all media outlets, both print and electronic. Imagine what it would cost team owners to purchase all the publicity they receive from the local newspapers, news broadcasts, magazines, and radio. The larger the market, the more media outlets there are. Local businesses also help publicize sport by advertising their support of the local teams in hopes of attracting customers who are fans.

Players depend on the media for publicity. Star players are given a public face in their community, receiving recognition for their sport performances and perhaps also kudos for visiting local schools or supporting local charities. Fans develop heroes, seek their autographs or pictures, follow their careers, join their fan clubs, and wear their jersey numbers. Kids imitate their style of play. The star player's lifestyle is often scrutinized, and dedicated family athletes are praised and held up as role models. Of course, for those who appear in the news for less attractive reasons, the media can also be harsh critics. Without the media's presentation of athletes, though, fans would have little opportunity to relate to them; uniforms tend to make one player look like all the rest.

In newspapers across the country, local headlines feature the fortunes of the local team on the front page. Local radio talk shows invite callers to comment on the home team. Interviews with coaches and top athletes on television help local fans understand a team's attitudes toward a game before, during, and after play. The local media, who unabashedly root for the home team, nourish hometown pride and spirit.

But the media can negatively affect sport, too, by changing the way sports are presented to the audience. Traditionalists generally oppose any change in sport, claiming that changes ruin the integrity of the game. Depending on your point of view, you may see these changes in sport as negative developments or simply signs of progress. Let's look at the way sport has changed over the last 25 years.

Rule Changes

Sport events that are unpredictable in length wreak havoc with station schedules. Television has pressured sports to revise their format to ensure that contests finish in a predictable amount of time. In response, collegiate football instituted overtime formats in which teams try to score from the opposition's 25-yard line and the other team is allotted an opportunity to match that score. The excitement generated by this approach has been a pleasant byproduct of the attempt to regulate game times.

The NFL has adopted instant replay to ensure that officials' calls are correct, and although each coach is limited to two challenges, the time spent reviewing the plays for the challenges has lengthened NFL games. College football has also begun to use instant replay, although on a limited basis. Halftimes have been modified to keep the viewer

Pop Culture: The *Heidi* Game

Perhaps the most well-known example of the conflict between sport and television schedules is the November 17, 1968, football game between the Oakland Raiders and the New York Jets. With 65 seconds left in the game, the Jets were up 32 to 29 heading into a commercial. When the commercial was over, viewers in the eastern and central time zones found the movie *Heidi* playing on their television. What they missed was a 43-yard touchdown pass by the Raiders, giving them a lead of 36 to 32. The next kickoff spurted free, and the Raiders picked it up and ran into the end zone for yet another touchdown.

The reason for the switch from the game to *Heidi*? NBC had sold the *Heidi* advertising to Timex and was obligated to start the movie at 7:00 p.m. eastern time, and the football game had overrun its 3-hour time limit. After that game, networks changed their practice to stay with a football game until its conclusion. The program to follow now starts in its entirety rather than being joined in progress—*after* the game is completed.

From www.nfl.com/news/mostmemorable10.html. Accessed January 6, 2006.

glued to the game by including game summaries, features, and analyses rather than the traditional marching bands that lose much of their entertainment value on television.

Tennis instituted the tiebreak in which the first player to win 7 points and be ahead by 2 points wins the set. This change ensured that a set would at least end after the equivalent of 13 games rather than last the 22 to 20 games a set could expand to under the old rules. The tiebreak at least contributes to the predictability of match lengths, which helps television producers plan their programming accordingly. Of course, the excitement generated by the critical tiebreak turned out to be a positive thing for the sport from the spectator's point of view.

Golf has moved almost exclusively to medal play, which means that the golfer with the lowest score wins, rather than match play with each hole counting for 1 point for the winner of that hole. The difference between the two systems is that the outcome is in doubt longer using medal play and may not be decided until the final hole.

The 3-point shot in basketball was adopted to put more emphasis on long-range shooting and reduce the dependence on large bodies pounding the ball inside to score. Additionally, the size of the lane or key under the basket was expanded to help push big players out from the basket, which opens up the game scoring to more athletic moves. A shot clock was also instituted to ensure that a team had to shoot the ball within the prescribed amount of time and to negate the time-honored tactic of one team freezing the ball when ahead near the end of a game. These changes help make a basketball game more exciting and action-packed to audiences who love watching great players and dramatic action.

MLB revised the strike zone and instituted the designated hitter for the American League in order to add more offense to the game. While purists contend they enjoy low-scoring pitcher duels, the average television fan is more interested in hitting and a barrage of home runs.

Perhaps the most annoying changes for television viewers are the numerous time-outs that allow for

Instant replay in the NFL lengthens games. How does this benefit or hurt the network? The fans?

commercial breaks. Rallies are interrupted, momentum is lost, and needed rest is given because the station is obliged to fulfill their promise to commercial sponsors. Watching football sometimes seems like watching a series of time-outs with some action squeezed in between. However, when you calculate the financial benefit of commercial time-outs, you can see why they have become standard practice. During the 2004 Super Bowl, a 30-second time-out cost commercial sponsors $2.3 million U.S. (Nielsen Media Research 2006). Of course, normal NFL games do not produce that kind of income, but they still generate critical revenue.

Attendance Declines Due to Televised Sport

In some markets, the presentation of games on television has affected attendance in the stadium. As a result, many professional football teams have adopted a blackout rule that means the game cannot be broadcast within a range of roughly 150 miles (241 kilometers) of the stadium unless all tickets are sold. The owners contend that without this rule, many fans would simply stay home to watch games on television rather than buy a ticket. Of course, when the game is blacked out, free access is denied to the

millions of fans who cannot afford to buy tickets or who prefer not to deal with the hassles of parking, uncertain weather, traffic, and so on. Die-hard fans get around blackouts by purchasing games on a pay-per-view basis that still creates revenue for the media and teams or by signing up for satellite programs that provide access to all NFL games on a given day.

Professional sports are so accessible on television that fans become spoiled watching superior athletes and often lose interest in the athletes on local minor league, college, or high school teams. A case in point is the demise of Minor League Baseball. In 1939, attendance at Minor League Baseball games exceeded that of MLB games with 15 million for the minors and 11 million for the majors. Lots of medium-sized cities across the country sponsored local teams and local fans supported them. Then came television, and it became easy to watch the top players in the country. Attendance dropped quickly for Minor League franchises and the number of Minor League Baseball teams fell from nearly 500 around 1950 to about 150 teams 25 years later. Eventually, the role of player development traditionally assigned to Minor League Baseball teams was filled by collegiate teams, who stepped up as the training ground for aspiring players (Leonard 1980).

Of course, Minor League Baseball was not the only victim of televised sport. Local college and high school sports also suffer when pitted against a professional team on television. The relatively few colleges with big-time football teams that are broadcasted on TV often draw fans away from the hundreds of other colleges that offer smaller football programs. High school games have avoided some of the conflict by scheduling football games on weeknights and Friday nights, times that do not conflict with professional sport and maximize the opportunity for fans to attend games in person.

Conflicts With Scheduling

The interests of television rather than the interests of players or spectators often determine the scheduling of games. Let's look at a couple of examples.

▪ World Series games are typically scheduled on October nights so as to attract the maximum television audience on both coasts. Selling out the ballpark for a World Series game is not a problem since only about 45,000 fans are needed; the largest fan base and income potential is the television audience. Night baseball is not popular with most players, but they are accustomed to such games throughout the regular season. Late starting times on the East coast mean that many potential fans, particularly children, are unable to watch because

Who should decide what time a match begins? The players? Television officials?

they have to go to bed. The late start allows people on the West coast to get home from work or school to watch the game, which balances the loss of fans on the East coast.

- Monday Night Football suffers from the same dilemma—the second half starts after bedtime for many East coast fans, but starting late does allow many fans on the West coast to watch the game.

- The NCAA basketball championships start after 9 p.m. on the East coast, thus shutting out young people and many adults as well.

- The U.S. Open schedules tennis matches through negotiations between four main parties: tournament officials, representatives of the men's and women's tours, and television. Guess who has the most leverage in deciding which match to feature at what time? Players' preferences are largely ignored, and tournament officials know that the money from the TV rights pays their bills. A match featuring a well-known American player such as Andre Agassi is likely to be set in a prime-time spot rather than a matchup of two lesser-known international players—that's just the logical schedule for television programming.

- Olympic telecasts are a critical source of income for the IOC and thus events are broadcast in order to attract maximum audiences in various countries. Featured events such as gymnastics, swimming, and track and field and recently women's team sports such as soccer, softball, and basketball get the prime spots in the United States.

Gambling

Gambling has always been part of the sport world. The posting of odds on each game in newspapers and on television increases the interest in winners and losers, point spreads, and possible upsets. There is no way to tell how much local betting occurs between neighbors and friends, at bars, or in office pools. At play-off time, it's rare for an office not to have at least one betting pool.

More serious betting is aided by the media reports on odds set in Las Vegas by bookmakers, picks by experts on television shows, injury and status reports of players in daily papers, and articles online predicting outcomes. Those who worry about the unhealthy influence of gambling in society wish the media did less to accommodate those who gamble (Brown 2000; Jenkins 2000). We'll consider sport gambling in chapter 17.

Free Publicity for Some Universities

Big-time college football on television and the endless publicity the media give the top schools with rankings, bowl speculation, and awards for best performances raises the public's awareness of a relatively few colleges based on their football success. Free publicity for those colleges typically means more student applications the next year, which allows them to be more selective in their admission. Although football success is unrelated to academic excellence and a host of other factors that are important when choosing a college, there is no question that the publicity helps universities with top-ranked football teams. During a televised game, the two competing schools get a spot on television to trumpet their virtues. They also get appearance money for being on TV, which is often split with the other teams in their conference. Games are scheduled according to TV commitments and are often changed to accommodate TV networks.

HOW SPORT AFFECTS THE MEDIA

The previous section documented how the media has been a primary support for the rapid expansion of big-time college and professional sport. However, this has not been a one-way street. Sport has provided the media with enormous, predictable audiences that are attractive to advertisers both in the United States and around the world. The revenue from sport coverage has been a major source of income for various media, but particularly for newspapers, television, and specialty magazines. Let's consider each in turn.

Newspapers have thrived on comprehensive sports sections for more than a century. For many readers, reading the sports pages is the first priority and may be the primary reason for purchasing the paper. Even though they watch the sport contests in person or on television, most fans love to read the accounts in the next day's paper, evaluate the opinions of the sports writers and compare them to their own, and search for inside information that they might not otherwise have access to.

Most major newspapers in North America devote more space to sport than any other topic, including business, politics, and world news. They have found that formula to be popular with readers and therefore attractive to advertisers. The primary audience for the sports pages has typically been males between the ages of 25 and 50 who have an above-average income (Coakley 2004). Advertisers for products that are targeted to that demographic have seized the opportunity to reach their potential customers through appearing in sports sections.

Newspapers also publicize local professional teams. Although newspapers might not derive advertising income directly from the publicity they offer, the number of readers they attract is heavily influenced by the public's interest in the local team. It is one way to guarantee a core group of faithful readers.

Printing stories on social concerns related to sport helps attract readers, stimulating their thinking and maintaining interest in lively debates. Sports pages that simply print event results and basic accounts of contests may not hold readers' interests, particularly as more people turn to the Internet or television to learn results. Social issues that are debated in the newspapers include

- racism among coaches, players, or organizations;
- economics of sport, including owner profits, union demands, club-versus-club payrolls, extravagant player compensation, and public financing of facilities;
- moral issues such as gambling on sport events, fan behavior at events, beer and cigarette sponsorship, and athletes as role models;
- gender bias, equal pay for women, appropriate attire for women, and attitudes of female athletes toward competition;
- changes in technology, such as improved surfaces, equipment, and apparel, and their effect on the integrity of the sport;
- training regimens and equipment and the effect of training on injury prevention; and
- use of ergogenic aids, drugs, drug testing, and penalties for those who fail drug tests.

While television thrives on live game-day action, newspapers are more suited to in-depth analysis of social topics that require significant research, clear presentation, and a slant that will challenge the reader to think.

Magazines that cover sport have responded to growing interest in specific sports. Most general news magazines rarely cover sport unless there is a major human-interest story involved. Publishers of magazines have found that appealing to fans of a specific sport guarantees a more stable audience of subscribers who are likely to support that magazine for a length of time. A quick check of www.magsonthenet.com reveals over 150 specific-sport magazines offered for subscription. General sport magazines such as *Sports Illustrated, The Sporting News,* or *ESPN: The Magazine* seek to attract the committed fan. These magazines rely on major sports for their bread and butter but include some stories on less popular sports for interest and to broaden the exposure of their readers.

Because magazines are published monthly or several times a year, they lend themselves to stories that take time to develop. Stories that examine trends in sport or the social issues listed previously are prime fodder for monthlies. On the other hand, because of their infrequent publication and lead time of several months, magazines are poor sources of information for up-to-the-minute news. By the time the reader receives the magazine in the mail, the news it contains may be out of date. Players have been traded, franchises remade, predictions proved false, and players released or injured. Keeping the readers happy under these conditions requires an astute editorial staff.

Of course, no media form has been affected by sport more than television. From its beginnings in the 1950s, television has included sport coverage as a critical part of programming. Although the camera angles were crude, replay did not exist, and many sports had not yet adjusted to television, the base was set for a happy and profitable relationship.

Television executives figured out that fans would watch TV on weekends when looking for some

Activity Time-Out: Advertising to the Target Audience

If you were in charge of soliciting advertising for the sports section of a metropolitan newspaper, what products would you seek for advertising? Remember, the typical reader is a male between the ages of 25 and 50 who has an above-average income. List at least 10 products you believe would interest this demographic.

Next, pick up a copy of your local newspaper and a copy of *USA Today.* Review the advertising in the sports sections of both papers. Did the ads match the categories you had suggested?

relaxation and diversion. Hours of ready-made weekend programming could be had by securing the rights to sport events paid for by corporate sponsors. Television executives learned that sport events minimized production costs, came with predictable ratings, and could be used to advertise the next event to the target audience. Soon televised sport included Monday Night Football, college football on Saturdays, and special events like the Olympics, tennis tournaments, golf tournaments, and NCAA basketball championships.

Special sport events are beamed around the world. Of the top 25 ranking network telecasts through 2005, 13 were sport events, including 12 Super Bowls and the 1994 Winter Olympics (table 5.1). When ranking the top 25 sports programs of all time through 2005, Super Bowls dominated with 22 spots. The Winter Olympics of 1994 claimed two spots, as did one NFC championship (table 5.2) (Television Bureau of Advertising 2005).

It may seem surprising, but the largest television audience in the world has been for World Cup soccer. When you consider that soccer is easily the

TABLE 5.1   Top 25 U.S. Network Telecasts

Program and ranking	Date	Network	Household rating*
1. *M*A*S*H* (final episode)	2/28/1983	CBS	60.2
2. *Dallas* ("Who Shot J.R.?")	11/21/1980	CBS	53.3
3. *Roots,* part 8	1/30/1977	ABC	51.1
4. Super Bowl XVI	1/24/1982	CBS	49.1
5. Super Bowl XVII	1/30/1983	NBC	48.6
6. XVII Winter Olympics	2/23/1994	CBS	48.5
7. Super Bowl XX	1/26/1986	NBC	48.3
8. *Gone With the Wind,* part 1	11/7/1976	NBC	47.7
9. *Gone With the Wind,* part 2	11/8/1976	NBC	47.4
10. Super Bowl XII	1/15/1978	CBS	47.2
11. Super Bowl XIII	1/21/1979	NBC	47.1
12. Bob Hope Christmas Show	1/15/1970	NBC	46.6
13. Super Bowl XVIII	1/22/1984	CBS	46.4
14. Super Bowl XIX	1/20/1985	ABC	46.4
15. Super Bowl XIV	1/20/1980	CBS	46.3
16. Super Bowl XXX	1/28/1996	NBC	46.0
17. *The Day After*	11/20/1983	ABC	46.0
18. *Roots,* part 6	1/28/1977	ABC	45.9
19. *The Fugitive* (final episode)	8/29/1967	ABC	45.9
20. Super Bowl XXI	1/25/1987	CBS	45.8
21. *Roots,* part 5	1/27/1977	ABC	45.7
22. Super Bowl XXVIII	1/29/1994	NBC	45.5
23. *Cheers* (final episode)	5/20/1993	NBC	45.5
24. *Ed Sullivan* (the Beatles)	2/9/1964	CBS	45.3
25. Super Bowl XXVII	1/31/1993	NBC	45.1

* Household rating is the percentage of all homes with televisions that tuned in to watch the program.
Television Bureau of Advertising based on data from Nielsen Media Research.

most popular sport worldwide, however, that statistic begins to make sense. Nations of every continent and fans of every economic level flock to live soccer games and follow them on television. Recent success by the U.S. women's soccer team and the emergence of certain superstar players such as Mia Hamm have buoyed the interest in soccer in the United States, and even the men's U.S. World Cup team is beginning

to attract a following. According to FIFA, the international governing body for soccer, the 2002 World Cup drew over 30 billion television viewers overall, and the finals between Brazil and Germany attracted 1.3 billion. Other worldwide sport events from 2004 are shown in table 5.3.

As we've seen, the more people watch sports, the more the media cover sports. This includes women's

TABLE 5.2   Top 25 U.S. Network Sport Telecasts

Program and ranking	Date	Network	Household rating*
1. Super Bowl XVI	1/24/1982	CBS	49.1
2. Super Bowl XVII	1/30/1983	NBC	48.6
3. XVII Winter Olympics	2/23/1994	CBS	48.5
4. Super Bowl XX	1/26/1986	NBC	48.3
5. Super Bowl XII	1/15/1978	CBS	47.2
6. Super Bowl XIII	1/21/1979	NBC	47.1
7. Super Bowl XVIII	1/22/1984	CBS	46.4
8. Super Bowl XIX	1/20/1985	ABC	46.4
9. Super Bowl XIV	1/20/1980	CBS	46.3
10. Super Bowl XXX	1/28/1996	NBC	46.0
11. Super Bowl XXI	1/25/1987	CBS	45.8
12. Super Bowl XXVIII	1/29/1994	NBC	45.5
13. Super Bowl XXVII	1/31/1993	NBC	45.1
14. Super Bowl XXXII	1/25/1998	NBC	44.5
15. Super Bowl XI	1/9/1977	NBC	44.4
16. Super Bowl XV	1/25/1981	NBC	44.4
17. Super Bowl VI	1/16/1972	CBS	44.2
18. XVII Winter Olympics	2/25/1994	CBS	44.1
19. Super Bowl XXIII	1/22/1989	NBC	43.5
20. Super Bowl XXXI	1/26/1997	FOX	43.3
21. Super Bowl XXXIV	1/30/2000	ABC	43.3
22. NFC championship game	1/10/1982	CBS	42.9
23. Super Bowl VII	1/14/1973	NBC	42.7
24. Super Bowl IX	1/12/1975	NBC	42.4
25. Super Bowl X	1/18/1976	CBS	42.3

* Household rating is the percentage of all homes with televisions that tuned in to watch the program.
Television Bureau of Advertising based on data from Nielsen Media Research.

women's soccer, began to claim more programming hours. Female announcers gradually were included in the broadcast teams and efforts were made to present sports in a style that was friendlier to female viewers. Gratuitous shots of female cheerleaders, sexist beer commercials, and commercials for pickup trucks were toned down, although not eliminated. Women's golf and tennis were featured at prime-time hours to attract larger audiences.

As more women's sports appeared on television, young girls in youth sport began to identify with their athletic heroes and copy their behavior. Women's soccer helped grow women's collegiate soccer and youth soccer. The emergence of Venus and Serena Williams in tennis opened up the sport to a new generation of Black females who might never have considered giving tennis a try. Inner-city high schools with predominantly African American populations suddenly had 50 girls trying out for the tennis team. Michelle Wie, who at 14 years of age was competing in selected professional golf events for men, suddenly became a constant story in sports pages. Her success not only among women in professional golf was amazing, but her challenge to qualify for male events made her a riveting story as well. It will be interesting to see if her success increases the popularity of golf among young girls.

sports as well, and the media has slowly begun to reach out to female viewers. For decades, sports were a man's world, and television presentations showed a strong bias toward the male viewer. Once the networks realized more than half the population was female and many were embracing sports, sports that were most popular with women, such as figure skating, gymnastics, tennis, and

TABLE 5.3 Top 10 Sporting Events of 2004

Event	Number of viewers (in millions)
Soccer—European finals, Portugal vs. Greece	153
Olympics—Opening ceremony	127
Olympics—Closing ceremony	96
Super Bowl	95
Olympics—Men's 100-meter final	87
Olympics—Men's 200-meter freestyle	66
Formula One—Monaco Grand Prix	56
Soccer—Champions League final	56
Basketball—NBA finals	25
Tennis—Wimbledon finals, women Tennis—Wimbledon finals, men	21 21

Data from Media Guardian, 12-23-04

IDEOLOGY OF SPORT THROUGH THE MEDIA

The media emphasize certain sport-related behaviors that affect the next generation of athletes and spectators. The presentation of sport in the media tends to emphasize behaviors that include certain values, attitudes, and beliefs that mirror the history of sport and maintain the status quo. Generally, sport media are owned and operated by large conglomerates such as the following (Sage 1998):

- Disney (e.g., ABC, ESPN)
- General Electric (e.g., NBC, MSNBC, CNBC)
- Time Warner (e.g., AOL, *Sports Illustrated,* CNN)
- News Corporation (e.g., Fox, Fox Sports, Madison Square Garden, Sunshine Network)
- Viacom (e.g., CBS, MTV, BET, Comedy Central)
- Bertelsmann (various European television networks)

These conglomerates are dedicated to maintaining their powerful position and are unwilling to venture into controversial positions. Some conglomerates own professional sport franchises, such as the following (Sage 1998):

- Disney (e.g., NHL Mighty Ducks, MLB Anaheim Angels)
- Time Warner (e.g., MLB Atlanta Braves, NBA Atlanta Hawks)
- Cablevision (e.g., NBA New York Knicks, NHL New York Rangers)
- Comcast (e.g., NBA Philadelphia 76ers, NHL Philadelphia Flyers)
- Paul Allen Group (e.g., NBA Portland Trail Blazers, NFL Seattle Seahawks)

In order to appeal to mass audiences, the sport media tend to reflect the opinions of the majority of Americans in order to curry their support. Social scientists would classify the media approach to sport as *functionalism* (as described in chapter 2). The media tend to reinforce commonly held values. Controversy, cutting-edge opinions, and creating discussion are typically not part of mainstream media productions.

A few significant ideologies that pervade North American sport are worth pointing out. For example, winning is worshipped in the sport media, and all the excitement they generate is toward that objective. Athletes who advance to the finals of a championship event only to lose are regarded as losers. Consider that in the U.S. Open tennis championships, 128 men and 128 women start out contending for first place. Of these players, 127 men and 127 women are destined to be losers, according to the media, and all attention is focused on the one winner.

Professional football teams or coaches who reach the Super Bowl, even several times, are branded as losers until they win the big game. The effect on youth sport, future athletes, and armchair quarterbacks is predictable; kids may give up and drop out of a sport when they realize they are not going to win the big game.

Athletes who are cooperative team players receive reinforcement from the media and are praised as leaders and role models. Individual athletes who deliver clutch performances are idolized and revered for their fortitude and success under pressure. On the other side, the press criticizes athletes who question coaching decisions, celebrate individual achievements over team performance, or do not cooperate with the press.

The history, traditions, and past heroes of the game are revered by the media. Coaches emphasize hard work and discipline and the media reinforce those values. Players who persevere and play even while injured are labeled courageous and team players. For example, Terrence Owens was praised for his rapid comeback from serious injury

Activity Time-Out: Winners or Chokers?

As coach of the Buffalo Bills football team, Marv Levy led the team to an amazing four Super Bowls, but he failed to win any of them. It became a running joke in the media and with fans that his teams were chokers and simply couldn't win big games. During that same time, most of the other teams in the league were wallowing in mediocrity, yet they earned no such label. Simply by reaching the Super Bowl, Levy's teams should have been revered rather than shunned as also-rans. What do you think?

to play effectively in the 2005 Super Bowl for the Philadelphia Eagles. However, a few months later he was crucified in the press and by fans for criticizing teammate Donovan McNabb and trying to renegotiate his contract. Athletes who appear cocky, self-absorbed, or selfish get less favorable attention. Owen's image as a spoiled player was so disruptive to the team that he was suspended for the second half of the 2005 season despite his courageous performance the previous year. There are no long-term guarantees as to how a player will be portrayed by the media.

Some cultural values of media executives, team owners, and league administrators clash with those of athletes. Issues of race, gender, and sexual preferences are often at the root of different attitudes toward sport and life, but the media realize their audience and benefactors have fairly mainstream values, so they tend to present and reinforce those same values. Let's look at some of the general themes about sport the media deliver.

Participation in Sport and Physical Activity

The importance of physical activity for everyone is well documented. With the alarming increases in obesity recently reported in the media for both youth and adults, you might guess that the media would take a strong stance regarding sport participation as an antidote for excess body weight.

Research to date has not supported the conclusion that watching sports on television affects sport participation one way or the other. Evidence is mixed: On one hand, many people who are already active report that their interest is heightened by watching great athletes perform, and many young people want to emulate their sport heroes on the playground or ball field. On the other hand, most adults who watch sports on television do not exercise regularly and have no plans to do so (Coakley 2004; Sage 1998). In fact, the amount of time spent in front of

the television is often cited as a primary reason for inactivity.

Traditional Values

Certain traditional values have become part of our culture. Americans generally believe in the ideal of individualism, that one person can make a difference. Even team achievements are traced back to the success or failure of key players. We also expect players to work cooperatively and extol the virtues of team chemistry and working cohesively as a unit. Players who put their own welfare first quickly fall out of favor with owners, coaches, and fans. At times, individual achievement and teamwork clash, creating conflict for players.

Harry Edwards, an influential critic of sport and a prominent sport sociologist in the 1970s, reviewed various publications in the media and organized the dominant social values attributed to sport. His work listed the following key values:

- Character building
- Religiosity
- Nationalism
- Discipline
- Mental fitness
- Competition
- Physical fitness

The place of each of these values in North American sport has been discussed since the 1970s, and generally these values have stood the test of time. Other behaviors that are more specific have been added over the years by other researchers, but Edwards' classic list covers the broad categories (Edwards 1973).

Winners and Losers

American society looks for winners, builds them up, showers them with praise for at least a day, and then looks to the next year. Fame is fickle. The message is clear—if you haven't won the big one, you don't count for much in sport. Some of our greatest athletes and coaches in history have failed to win the ultimate contest and so are considered failures. Other athletes who are less talented and productive over their careers have been considered successful because they won a big game. The win may have been due to luck, teammates, or inferior opponents, but they won. Super Bowl heroes never heard from before or after their one shining moment go down as winners in history.

For some fans, the preoccupation with winners grows tiresome. Veteran fans prefer to watch a well-played or exciting contest. One-sided games, predictable outcomes, defensive struggles, and sloppy play are all reasons for discontent. Television producers look for ways to minimize the chances for such disappointment by emphasizing possible upsets, possible rallies by the losing player or team, and possible contests that will end in tiebreakers.

Yet the beat goes on. Even athletes who deliver an illegal hit are lionized for their competitive spirit as long as they are not caught or the penalty is a minor inconvenience to their team. Other athletes who reenter a game after a painful injury, concussion, or exhaustion are lauded for their courage. Young people watching professional sport may start to believe that winning a contest is more critical than good health or common sense.

Gender

Hegemonic masculinity has predominantly been portrayed by the media in sport. Power, dominance, and violence are male characteristics that have been reinforced and admired. This is not surprising considering that male athletics predated the rise of female athletics, but as women's sport gained a foothold in the 1970s and has continued to grow since then, you might have expected a change in the traditional sport media worship of everything male.

Outside of the Olympic Games, women's sports have taken a backseat to media coverage of men's sports. While socially acceptable women's sports like gymnastics, figure skating, tennis, and golf have continued to get media attention, recent attention to women's soccer and basketball has begun to tip the balance slightly toward more equal media attention to female and male athletes. Yet the statistics of the imbalance that still exists between coverage of men and women in sport are revealing.

Since 2000, television coverage of women's sports has declined. The percentage of stories and airtime devoted to women's sports is nearly as low as it was in 1990, when women's sports received approximately 5% of the coverage. In 1999, the coverage reached 8.7%, but in 2004, the coverage percentage had declined to 6.3% (Duncan and Messner 2005).

During a 30-day analysis of ESPN's *SportsCenter* in 2002, ESPN ran 778 stories about males, 16 about females, and 13 that mentioned both—a ratio of more than 48 to 1 (Tuggle 2003).

National television coverage of college basketball in 2000 featured 270 men's games compared with only 29 women's games (Amateur Athletic Foundation of Los Angeles 2005).

Recent attention to collegiate women's basketball and televised games throughout the NCAA women's Division I tournament demonstrate at least a small

In the Arena With . . . *Dan Marino*

Dan Marino, quarterback extraordinaire for the Miami Dolphins, is by far the most productive passer in history. His career passing yardage is almost 10,000 more than his closest rival, and he has an edge of 78 more touchdown passes than the next closest player. He never won a Super Bowl, but he led his team to 147 wins and a winning percentage of 61%. Dan was a cinch for the football Hall of Fame despite the fact that his teams were not champions. Yet some Miami fans still faulted Marino for his inability to win the Super Bowl (Pompei 2000).

What factors other than gender influence what sporting events are televised? How much of an effect does the type of sport have on whether or not it's televised?

shift in emphasis. The scheduling and availability of games for women has essentially mirrored the attention given the men, although reading the media accounts in most daily newspapers, you might believe the women's games held little interest for readers. In spite of the apparent equality with men in television time, women's games still command significantly little attention in many newspapers.

Professional women's tennis has been well established for some years and the televising of the women's matches versus men's matches at Grand Slam events is nearly identical. Other sports can claim no such parity. Women's soccer, professional basketball, golf, and softball are only televised sporadically in comparison to their male counterparts. Similarly, women in the sports media are vastly underrepresented as discussed in the section on careers that follows.

Race and Ethnicity

Viewers' ideas about race and ethnicity can be influenced depending on what the viewers see and hear. Most sports journalists are careful to avoid language that could be interpreted as racist, and the few incidents that have occurred have been dealt with quickly. Yet some feel that racism in the media exists in less overt ways. For example, they feel that stories about Black athletes focus too often on their rise from poverty to wealth.

Historically, many Black athletes have felt belittled by the media's constant portrayal of them as physically talented while their White teammates are praised for their cool, strategic play. Those stereotypes have diminished, yet many Black quarterbacks in the NFL resent the emphasis on their running ability and want to be recognized for their leadership, courage in standing in the pocket, and coolness under fire like their White compatriots. Examples of NFL quarterbacks who have intimated such feelings include Randall Cunningham and Donovan McNabb, who both played for the Philadelphia Eagles; Kordell Stewart of the Pittsburgh Steelers; and Michael Vick of the Atlanta Falcons.

The dominance of Black athletes in the NFL and NBA has given rise to discussions of their influence on the younger generation. While it is fine to be represented in sport, some African Americans cringe at the thought of so many young Black people believing that sport is their cultural destiny. We'll look at this issue and others concerning race in chapter 11.

Ethnic insensitivities have always existed in sport, and while many have been eliminated, some persist. The use of Native American nicknames, chants, and cheers in violent ways in sport has become more offensive to the general population. Stereotypes of Asian Americans abound in descriptions of athletes such as Michelle Kwan, Michael Chang, Hideo Matsui, and others; comments about their self-discipline, intelligence, and methodical approach to sport do not necessarily apply to all Asian American athletes.

Finally, racial overtones are contained in the media's consistent coverage of African Americans as violent. The sport media have done much to portray the violent athlete in football and basketball. Stories about domestic beatings, drugs, and arrests at nightclubs after a fight often feature Black athletes. The public's impression is that Black men are to be feared or avoided. We'll talk more about race and deviance in chapter 17.

CAREERS IN SPORT MEDIA

Sports journalists may specialize in either print media or electronic media. Although the roles are

In the Arena With . . . *Bob Costas*

Bob Costas joined NBC in 1980 and spent 25 years covering the Olympics, World Series, Super Bowl, NBA championships, and collegiate basketball. He is extremely knowledgeable about sport, passionate about its problems, respectful of its history, and insightful in his analysis.

Costas has won 16 Emmy awards and has been selected by the National Sportswriters and Sportscasters Association as National Sportscaster of the Year eight times, more than any other sportscaster in history. His versatility is evidenced by his nomination for Emmys in five categories: play by play, hosting, writing, interviewing, and journalism. Perhaps Costas is more recognized for his reporting on the Olympic Games than any other activity. He anchored NBC's prime-time coverage of the Olympics in Barcelona (1992), Atlanta (1996), Sydney (2000), and Athens (2004). He also worked the 1988 Olympics in Seoul as a late-night host and the 2002 Winter Games in Salt Lake City.

Costas is equally at home reporting the action, conducting interviews, or offering commentary on sport issues. His books include *New York Times* bestseller *Fair Ball: A Fan's Case for Baseball,* and he served as narrator for *And the Crowd Goes Wild* and *The Fans Roared* (Speaker Series 2005).

similar in content, the method of communication is quite different. **Sports writers** tend to develop in-depth stories about athletic events or players. Their goal is to give readers as detailed a picture as they can within their space limits based on extensive research, personal observations, and interviews. Their focus is often the lifestyles, backgrounds, and personal situations of well-known athletes, presenting this information in a way that makes fans yearn to know the players better. The research can be a laborious process and articles may take months to complete. Journalists who weave some controversial material into their stories are the most popular, provided they avoid straying too far from acceptable standards.

Sports announcers on radio or television have a much different role that requires different skills. Their job is to excite listeners or viewers through their description of the game. Although they need to report play-by-play information, setting the viewers up for what they will be seeing or hearing is critical, as is a quick analysis after the play. Energy, wit, and a thorough understanding of the game are critical skills for sports announcers.

Many networks hire former athletes as announcers to establish the credibility of their comments. The public expects a former player in the sport to understand the game, the athletes' struggles, and the significance of the ebb and flow of the game. Some

athletes have done remarkably well even with little training as sportscasters. Another fertile ground for sports announcers is former coaches. Ostensibly, these coaches have an expert viewpoint to share and their communication skills are often better than those of well-known athletes simply through years of practice.

There is also a breed of professional sports announcers who have simply developed the skills of the craft, paid their dues with modest assignments, and risen to the top of sports announcing. These people, mostly males, often make their reputation in one sport and then branch out to others. Howard Cosell, Brent Musburger, Dick Enberg, Jim Nance, and Bob Costas have all made their mark in sports announcing. Although their personalities and styles vary, they all study sports and thoroughly prepare before the event so that they can convey the complete package to viewers.

A few sports announcers command a substantial salary because they are on the national stage broadcasting major events. But the average sports anchor on the local television station earns an average salary of about $50,600 U.S. per year. That is just a little less than the $69,800 U.S. average salary of news anchors and the $54,000 U.S. average salary of weathercasters. Radio announcers typically earn even less than their colleagues on television, although they often have an exceptional ability to describe the action so that the listener can picture the action just from the description (Journalism Jobs 2002).

There is a certain tension between sports journalists and the athletes they cover. Because they are looking for a story, many journalists will probe the personal life of an athlete and sometimes share the less flattering aspects. Other journalists tend to be critical of teams, owners, coaches, and players in order to stimulate readership. This situation often causes athletes to mistrust the press and resort to stock answers when queried. Consider how many clichés you've heard from athletes during interviews:

- It's just another game to us.
- We play them one game at a time.
- We're focused on the next game, not our record or the play-offs.
- My teammates made this all possible.
- We just didn't get it done.
- We came out a little flat and just never recovered.
- We need to get everyone on the same page.
- My serve let me down today.

- You've got to give them credit for their performance today.
- We've all got a job to do.
- We beat a great team today.
- No one player was responsible for the loss.

As women's sport has risen dramatically in participation and publicity, you might expect there to be a concomitant growth in the number of women reporting on sport. Between 1994 and 2000, the Association of Women in Sports Media (AWSM) more than doubled its membership from 400 to over 850 (Association for Women in Sports Media 2000). Likewise, within months of its founding, the Female Athletic Media Executives (FAME) organization claimed over 200 members (College Sports Information Directors of America 2001). In spite of these advances, the percentage of women in sport media remains alarmingly small. Among information professionals in college sports, the percentage of women occupying full-time positions actually dropped in the late 1990s from 14% to 9.5%. Similarly, Sally Jenkins, a well-known sports writer, estimated in 1991 that fewer than 50 of the 630 television sportscasters at over 630 network affiliate stations around the country were

Although the number of female sport reporters is on the rise, men still greatly outnumber women in the field of sport media.

women (Staurowsky 2000). In 2000, there were 335 male and 81 female sportscasters working in national network and cable television. ESPN numbers are not included because the network would not reveal the number of male announcers, although they did admit to 46 female announcers (Martzke 2000).

For many years, female reporters were banned from male locker rooms, and once they did gain access, they were mercilessly taunted and ridiculed for their efforts. Perhaps the most well-known case of sexual discrimination involved reporter Lisa Olsen, who was sexually harassed by three New England Patriot football players during the 1990s. Adding insult to injury, *Playboy* magazine not only carried a story on Olsen's experience but also offered her a pictorial layout in the magazine

The typical experience of female sportscasters in male locker rooms gained widespread publicity with the publication of *Never Let the Bastards See You Cry* by Toni Bruce (2000). Bruce's narrative is a fictional account of a female sportswriter's treatment by male athletes who taunted her, made lewd comments, and cautioned her against any "feminist crap."

Not only do women often find it difficult to secure positions in sports journalism, if they do manage to break down the barriers and get in, the challenge is not over. Once they are hired, they may face harassment or isolation in a sports environment populated mostly by males. They often are compensated at a lower rate than male colleagues and may find it difficult to secure promotions. Eventually, they may turn to other journalistic fields where the odds for advancement and success are more favorable (Dodds 2000). Johnette Howard, a *Newsday* sports columnist, observed, "I used to get mail saying 'You're a dumb broad and you don't know anything about sports.' Now they just say, 'You're a dumb broad.' I'd say that's progress" (McNamara 2000).

CHAPTER SUMMARY

In this chapter we examined how both the print and electronic media affect sports fans by increasing their knowledge, excitement, and interest in sport at all levels, but particularly professional sport. It is clear that the interrelationships between the media and big-time sport are inextricably intertwined and interdependent.

We examined the effect of the media on sport, from the free publicity they generate for teams and athletes to how they affect the popularity of specific sports or athletes. Similarly, the sport media have forced some dramatic changes in the presentation of sports, particularly on television since that is a major revenue source for professional sport.

Next, we looked at the relationship from the opposite point of view: how sports have affected the media. Both print media and the electronic media have turned to sport because it is guaranteed to produce interest and revenue. Millions of people worldwide thirst for the instant gratification of watching professional sport on television, and most of them enjoy reading about what they watched a day or week later in print. Of course, the print media have the disadvantage of timing, but they make up for that by having time to set the angle, tenor, and facts of their story before delivery.

Sport and the sport media have the potential to affect the ideology of a society in the way they present key values. We've looked at the effect of spectatorship on participation levels, attitudes toward gender, sexuality, and racial and ethnic groups. Since sport and the sport media have been almost exclusively the domains of White males, not surprisingly, the values presented in the media have typically been oriented toward White males and have not provided fair treatment for minority athletes or females. Although minorities and women have seen rapid gains as athletes in the past 50 years, their treatment by the media has lagged depressingly behind.

Finally, we looked at the careers of sports journalism and its status as a profession. It has become clear that changes in composition of sports staffs are occurring slowly. Women lag far behind their male cohorts in sports journalism opportunities.

Sport As an Institution

We begin in chapter 6 by looking at the trends in youth sport that show a steady increase in organized youth programs over the past 20 years. Of particular note is the recent rapid growth in participation by females. Yet as organized youth sport grows, informal sports and games that have been popular in other generations have declined dramatically due to transportation issues, safety issues, and competition from sedentary activities. The positive and negatives of youth sport programs that are organized by adults are examined and several problem areas are presented (such as the lack of well-trained volunteer coaches) along with potential solutions.

As shown in chapter 7, sport within the educational system has developed in North America unlike in any other place in the world. Although sports are designated as an extracurricular activity, they often serve their schools or colleges by unifying students, alumni, and fans. At universities they help attract more applicants, encourage alumni to donate funds, and generate lots of publicity for the college.

Interscholastic and collegiate sports have traditionally been extolled for their virtues, although many of these claims are not based on factual research. The percentage of students who actually make their high school or college teams is relatively small, while the cost to the institution per student is a significant expense.

Title IX has affected high school and college sport by requiring equal opportunities for females and males. The result has been a vast improvement in sport opportunities for girls. At the same time, budget allocations continue to be a source of debate and agony, especially as costs escalate as schools try to offer equal opportunities to both genders.

Chapter 8 examines sport from an international perspective and shows how sports are expanding worldwide. As communication and the media help shrink the world, sports spread quickly from one country to another. Favorite American sports such as football, basketball, and baseball have gained popularity throughout the world such that the United States no longer dominates world competition in basketball or baseball.

The opportunity to use sport competition to further relationships between countries has always been touted. Evidence suggests that athlete exchange programs between nations, world amateur competitions, and professional leagues that span the globe do help promote international understanding. However, claims that globalization through sport may alter political processes or governments seem to be more wishful thinking than reality.

No other sporting event has had a worldwide effect comparable to that of the Olympic Games, discussed in chapter 9. Steeped in the tradition of amateur athletes competing for the love of sport, the Olympics has evolved into big business. Including professional athletes has helped the Games popularize the events and attract huge amounts of television coverage and commercial sponsorship. The nationalism that has characterized the Games for the last 50 years is giving way to an economic model of competition.

All countries that compete seriously in the Olympic Games have organized national programs to help their best athletes. The United States Olympic Committee has recently struggled with its role. Unlike programs in several other countries, it receives no government funding and instead relies on private sponsors and donations. A by-product of strong Olympic development programs in many countries has been to make Olympic sports affordable and accessible for any talented athlete.

Youth Sport

Student Outcomes

After reading this chapter, you will know the following:

- The history of youth sport
- Current status of organization and participation in youth sport
- The distinction between athlete-organized sport and adult-organized sport
- Reasons why young people play sports
- Future modifications that may benefit youth sport

Youth sport significantly affects the development of young people simply because of the large amount of time they spend playing sports. Whether they choose to play informal games with their peers or join an organized program, almost all children experiment with different sports between the ages of 6 and 12. Those who are successful may continue with their sport through the teenage years; others may try other sport activities or drop out of sport completely.

Recent trends in youth sport participation have shown that the number of young people who play in organized programs continues to grow, and girls' participation especially is showing large increases compared to 20 years ago. The advent of both parents working outside the home has created a need for scheduled, supervised children's activities that keep kids after school. Sport has emerged as a natural child care activity and has the added advantage of delivering several benefits such as increasing physical activity and fitness, learning physical skills, and socializing with peers.

Lest we congratulate ourselves on the continuous growth of organized youth sport, a closer look reveals a steep decline in youth sport that is not organized. From 1995 to 2004, participation in bicycling, swimming, baseball, touch football, and fishing significantly declined. Kids no longer leave the house to spend the day playing pickup games in neighborhood parks or school playing fields as they once did. Some pundits attribute the decline to parents' hesitancy to allow their children freedom to roam unsupervised, while others point the finger at video games, the Internet, and television. Whatever the causes, organized sport for young people is growing while unorganized free play is declining (Cauchon 2005).

As adult-organized youth sport has grown, so too have criticisms of programs that emphasize winning, emphasize specialization in one sport, overschedule kids' time, overinvolve adults in structuring the program, and have a high cost. It's time to look closely at the current organization of youth sport and consider what changes should be made to enhance the role of youth sport in the development of young people.

Popular opinion concerning youth sport varies and depends somewhat on the influence of the media. While the media criticize excesses in youth sport, they also celebrate the successful performances of local teams and broadcast the Little League World Series into every home. Parents decry the negative influences of some coaches, but training and certification standards for youth coaches are nonexistent and it has been difficult to demand certification without enthusiastic support from parents. Organizers often recruit young people to play and stress how much fun they will have but then structure the experience to teach conformity to rules and coaching directions and reward winning teams and athletes for exceptional performances.

A *Youth Sports National Report Card* was released in 2005 by the Citizen Through Sports Alliance, a national coalition of sport organizations that includes, among others, the four major professional leagues in the United States (baseball, basketball,

Many children attend summer camps to develop their fitness and rugged individual spirit, but during the school year, they expect their mom or dad to drop them off.

football, and soccer), the NCAA, and the International Olympic Committee (IOC). The report card reflected some harsh criticism of youth sport. Grades were given from A to F in five categories:

Child-centered philosophy	D
Coaching	C–
Health and safety	C +
Officiating	B–
Parental behavior	D

The ratings were given by youth sport experts from across the country and focused on community-based sport for children aged 6 to 14. Some specific findings of the report were that youth sport has lost its focus on the child; suffers from the actions of overinvested parents; fails to recruit and train quality coaches; focuses too much on early sport specialization; and fails to listen to the voice of the child who wants to play sport for fun, friendships, fitness, and skill development.

HISTORY OF YOUTH SPORT

Youth sport programs became a huge factor in American society during the past 50 years. Before then, few programs existed and most children organized their own games. Children who grew up in cities spent hours playing different variations of baseball, such as stickball, curbball, wireball, and Wiffle ball. They filled in the time by jumping rope, playing hopscotch, and shooting baskets. Those who lived in rural areas were more likely to choose recreational sports that took advantage of the woods, lakes, mountains, and back roads of their environment. Hunting, fishing, boating, hiking, mountain climbing, bicycling, and running were popular outdoor pursuits.

Youth sport programs in the years following World War II were dominated by Little League Baseball, which was founded in 1939 in Williamsport, Pennsylvania. It was a community-based program in which each team was funded by local businesses. Along with teaching baseball skills and strategy, Little League was looked upon by parents and organizers as a way to teach young boys life skills, proper values, discipline, and adherence to rules. Along with the Boy Scouts, youth sport programs were invested with training the boys of America for adulthood (www.littleleague.org).

Youth sport in the 1950s and 1960s was primarily for boys and was heartily endorsed by most people, particularly those in the middle class, as a worthy use of time to learn athletic and social skills. Community leaders asserted that young men would learn the lessons of life on the ball field during competition.

Pop Culture: The Pinky Ball

For city kids in the 1950s, one of the most prized possessions was the pinky ball. For about 15 cents, you could buy a pinky ball at most toy stores, sporting goods stores, or even corner drugstores. The pinky ball first showed up in the late 1940s when tennis-ball manufacturers rejected the inner rubber core of some tennis balls and simply sold the rejected cores on their own.

Spalding pinky balls were nicknamed Spaldeens and Penn pinky balls were known as Pennsy pinkies. The ball was perfect for a single player. You could see if you could catch it, throw it as high as the rooftops, hit the telephone wires, bounce it off the front steps, or hit it with a broomstick. Games were invented and passed down in the neighborhood. No adults coached or umpired or ever got involved except when a window was threatened.

Bases were parked cars, trees, fire hydrants, or manhole covers and time was called when a car dared to approach from down the street. Kids could play all day with the pinky ball, going from one game to another. The pinky was perfect for wireball, curbball, stickball, wallball, four-square, handball, and hundreds of other games.

In those days, a "roofer" was a pinky ball caught on the roof, and if you wanted to guarantee that everyone in the game had to pay up for a lost ball, you called out "chips" before play began. If the cry "Cops!" rang out, it meant old lady Ginovski had called the police to break up the game. Play was postponed while everyone ran and the officer surveyed the situation, and 10 minutes later play resumed (Anastasio 2000).

Perhaps the most dramatic change in youth sport programs in the last 25 years has been the explosion of opportunities for girls that came with the passage of Title IX in 1972. Before Title IX, girls were cheerleaders, pom-pom girls, or majorettes or participated in a few ladylike sports such as gymnastics, figure skating, equestrian, swimming, and tennis. Once Title IX was passed, girls showed up in record numbers at softball fields, basketball courts, field hockey and lacrosse fields, and soccer fields.

Since the 1970s, family life in North America has endured many changes. A significant change has been the increase in the number of mothers working outside the home, from 40% of mothers in the 1970s to 66% in 2004 according to the U.S. Census (United States Census 2005a). As mentioned previously, this change meant that kids needed someplace safe to go after school. Sport filled that void with the added bonus that kids were getting exercise and life lessons in winning and losing, self-confidence, and good sporting behavior.

A second factor has been the increase in child abductions and sexual predators that frighten parents and make them fear for their children's safety (Cauchon 2005). With their children actively engaged under adult supervision in a sport program, parents can feel some comfort that their children are safe.

A third factor has been the belief, particularly in areas of high crime, that children are more likely to stay out of trouble if they are in an organized sport program. Before the age of 10, many children are exposed to drugs, sex, and crime on the streets. In a safe haven after school, children who live in dangerous neighborhoods can play sport free of worry, and in many programs they spend time completing homework assignments as well.

Finally, the emergence of specialized training for high sport performance at very young ages has encouraged parents to sacrifice their time and money to give their children a chance to become a great athlete. Kids are encouraged at early ages to commit completely to one sport, train hard every day, and focus on that one sport year round. Parents feel a sense of guilt if they do not support their child's one chance to be famous and make millions, so they sacrifice money, time, and sometimes even family happiness in the pursuit of athletic excellence.

SPONSORS OF YOUTH SPORT

The rise in youth sport occurred in large part because certain organizations lent their support. In broad categories, these are the groups that sponsored youth sport:

- Public community or parks programs
- Community organizations such as the YMCA or YWCA, Police Athletic League (PAL), Boys and Girls Club, and churches like Catholic Youth Organizations (CYOs)

In the Arena With . . . *Mia Hamm*

Mia Hamm learned to play soccer from her five siblings. She began to play youth soccer at age 7 and continued playing through high school. Mia's record of scoring 150 goals in international soccer competition is the greatest number in history for any soccer athlete, male or female. She played for 18 years on the U.S. national team, being the youngest player ever selected to the team at age 15. During her reign as queen of women's soccer, the U.S. team won gold medals at the 1996 and 2004 Olympic Games and earned the World Cup championship in 1999.

Mia Hamm carried the flag in the closing ceremonies of the 2004 Olympic Games, having been voted to the honor by her fellow team members. It was a fitting tribute to an athlete who helped change the face of sport for women and girls during the 1990s and catapulted the popularity of soccer for females around the world (Hamm 2005a, b).

- Nonprofit sport organizations such as Little League, Pop Warner football, United States Tennis Association, Amateur Athletic Union, and Youth Soccer
- Corporate sponsors of youth sport including national, regional, and local businesses
- Commercial sport or fitness clubs

One of the questions often raised is who should pay for youth sport. Once schools disengaged from sponsoring sport programs for young children, communities looked for other sources. One solution has been to use public funds to support community sport programs often through local parks or playgrounds. The rationale is that taxpayer money is well spent if it keeps children busy, out of trouble, and physically active. Most of these programs are available in the summer when school is not in session. Programs are often free or a nominal charge is assessed. Sport programs under this model tend to be introductory, recreational, and moderately organized.

When public funds are not available, other organizations such as YMCAs and YWCAs, Boys and Girls Clubs, and churches step in to fill the void. Funds are raised from public or private sources, memberships are established for modest fees, and donations are solicited. Youth sport programs clearly have a social component and are often targeted toward populations at risk. In some programs, tutoring and academic enrichment are combined with athletic activity.

Nonprofit sport organizations also began sponsoring youth programs to expose kids to their sport, build a solid base of fans, scout talent, and help develop elite players who might one day play professionally. These organizations largely finance youth leagues but also charge participants a modest fee to help cover the costs. Programs operated by these organizations tend to lean more toward skill instruction, greater emphasis on winning and losing, and development of elite performers.

Commercial sponsors of youth sports saw an opportunity to influence children and their families about their product. Local businesses know that sponsoring a team promotes goodwill in the community and at the same time allows them to advertise their business on the uniforms of players and on signs at ballparks. A few national sponsors latched onto programs such as the Punt, Pass, and Kick program.

Finally, commercial sport clubs have become a mainstay of the youth sport market. Local clubs offer swimming, tennis, soccer, basketball, and so on at

Sponsoring a youth athletic team spreads community goodwill for this local Kiwanis club and Mobil Super Pantry.

prices that are typically only affordable to the middle and upper classes. Programs are oriented toward high performance for serious young athletes who at the very least have a college scholarship as their goal if not a professional career. Summer camps specialize in one or two sports and draw thousands of youngsters from families who can afford to send their children to camp for weeks or even entire summers. The camps mix traditional camp activities with a heavy dose of sport instruction, drilling, and supervised play.

Depending on the organization that sponsors a youth sport program, the philosophy and expected outcomes vary. In general, the more intensive competitive programs are also more costly. The result is that kids of modest financial backgrounds often have limited opportunities to develop their natural talent without financial help or scholarships.

CURRENT STATUS OF YOUTH SPORT

With participation in youth sport at an all-time high, it would appear as if things are rosy in the sporting world of kids. A comprehensive survey in 2000 by American Sports Data found that 26.2 million youngsters age 6 to 17 played on at least one organized sports team. That figure represents 54% of the 48.5 million children within that age range in the United States. Another 10 million play team sports, but only in casual pickup situations, not as part of an organized team. Boys' participation totaled 14.7 million, and girls weren't far behind at 11.3 million (American Sports Data, Inc. 2000).

A follow-up to this study produced a mixture of good and bad news. It revealed that team sport participation peaks at age 11, basketball remains the most popular team sport, and participation in sport by girls has never been better—but frequent participation by both boys and girls in team sports is declining. A closer look, however, reveals a host of problems. Perhaps the most alarming statistic is that by some estimates, over 70% of participants drop out of youth sport programs along the way to high school. Speculation is rampant as to the cause, but no clear pattern has yet emerged. Some possible causes of youth dropouts in sport include the following (Cary 2004):

- Overemphasis on winning as the objective with resulting increases in pressure to win and achieve
- Stress on high performance that translates into longer hours of practice, longer seasons, and specialization in one sport at an early age

- Expenses of participation, traveling teams, sport camps, sport academies, coaching, and equipment that are out of reach of middle-class families
- Increased injury incidence due to inordinate demands on young bodies
- Increased participation in alternative sports by young people who are turned off by traditional adult-organized programs
- Lack of training for youth coaches and the resulting frustration of kids who take orders from well-intentioned but misguided coaches
- Earlier starts in youth sport (sometimes as young as 3 or 4 years of age); children simply grow bored of a sport after a number of years

Let's take a closer look at some trends in youth sport.

Decreased Physical Activity

USA Today ran a front-page story entitled, "Childhood Pastimes Are Increasingly Moving Indoors," that set off alarm bells among parents, teachers, and sport administrators (Cauchon 2005). It seems that the typical child spends more time indoors today than ever before, watching television, playing video games, or browsing the Internet. According to research by the Kaiser Family Foundation and the Centers for Disease Control and Prevention cited in

Activity Timeout: Researching Youth Sport

Many Web sites are devoted to youth sport. Take a look at the sites provided here or conduct your own Internet search and use these sites as you study more about youth sport.

- www.nays.org—Site for National Alliance for Youth Sports, a nonprofit organization that emphasizes making sport safe and positive for young people
- http://ed-web3.educ.msu.edu/ysi/—Site for the Institute for the Study of Youth Sports at Michigan State University, which sponsors research on youth sport and offers other educational materials
- www.momsteam.com—Site that offers information for mothers of children in youth sport programs
- www.asep.com—Site for the American Sport Education Program, a division of Human Kinetics; a premier coaching education site for coaches of youth sport
- www.sportsdonerightmaine.org—Site for the youth sport initiative of the state of Maine

the article, youths spend their recreational time each day in the following ways:

Watching television	4 hours, 10 minutes
Playing video games	1 hour, 5 minutes
Recreational computer use	37 minutes
Total time	5 hours, 52 minutes

Gone are the days of children leaving early in the day for outside play with the only requirement that they return in time for dinner. Suburban living has divided kids by miles, and parents fear for their children's safety. Air-conditioning in most homes negates the need to head for the local swimming spot to cool off in the heat of summer. Consider the evidence of reduced physical play:

- Participation in bicycling, swimming, baseball, fishing, and touch football has fallen dramatically in the past 10 years. Bike riding alone is down 31% in the past 10 years, and the sale of bikes fell from 12.4 million in 2000 to 9.8 in 2004, a 21% decline according to *Bicycle Industry and Retailer News,* an industry magazine.

- Little League participation has fallen to 2.1 million, down 14% from its peak in 1997, and participation in pickup games of baseball and other sports has declined nearly twice as fast according to SGMA studies (Cauchon 2005).

These are sobering statistics, especially when paired with the information that obesity has risen for children aged 6 to 11 from roughly 5% in 1963 to 16% in 2005. Children in rural areas show a 20% rate of obesity compared with urban kids, who are at the national average of 16%. The obesity rate for children in rural areas has been increasing about double the rate in urban areas. One possible explanation is that with increased mechanization of farms, children are burning fewer calories but still eating high-calorie meals (Sheehan 2005).

Explosion of Extreme Sport

Recent studies by the Sporting Goods Manufacturers Association (SGMA) and the National Sporting Goods Association (NSGA) show a dramatic shift in participation among teens and preteens from mainstream sports such as basketball and football to extreme or action sports (see table 6.1). Since 1990, participation in football, baseball, and basketball among 6- to 17-year-olds is down more than 30%, while participation in action sports like snowboarding, skateboarding, and in-line skating is up in excess of 600% (SGMA 2005a). Some additional facts quoted in these studies include the following:

Will the number of skate parks surpass the number of basketball courts? As participation in extreme sport continues to rise, it certainly is a possibility.

- In-line skating boasted more skaters than the combined number of baseball and tackle football players combined.

- Paintball participation has exploded more than 60% from 5.9 million in 1998 to 9.6 million in 2004.

- The average number of days of participation for skateboarding in 2004 was 48 days. That number is impressive compared to youth baseball where only 30% of players participated more than 52 times per year (SGMA 2005c).

By now you may be curious about the sudden shift toward action or extreme sport. Skateboarding legend Tony Hawk, now 37 years of age and a promoter of the X Games, says, "Kids like the freedom of what we do, no strict practice regimen, no coaches and it's an artistic pursuit as much as sport. It has constant action, no standing in the outfield waiting for something to happen" (Scheiber 2005, p. C8). A decade ago there were approximately 100 skate parks according to Ryan Clements, general manager of the Skate Park of Tampa. "Skateboarding used to

TABLE 6.1 Extreme Sport Participation Among Youths in 2004

Sport	Participants (in millions)
In-line skating	17.3
Skateboarding	11.5
Paintball	9.5
Artificial wall climbing	7.6
Snowboarding	7.1
Trail running	6.4
Mountain biking	5.3
Wakeboarding	2.8
BMX bicycling	2.6
Mountain/rock climbing	2.1
Roller hockey	1.7
Boardsailing/windsurfing	.418

Numbers are for participants age 6 and older who participated at least once.
Adapted, by permission, from SGMA, Extreme sports: Ranking high in popularity (North Palm Beach, FL: SGMA International). www.sgma.com.

be punk. Now it's normal" (Scheiber 2005, p. C8). The summer of 2005 marked the 11th anniversary of the X Games, which are no longer a novelty but part of mainstream youth culture. The X Games are even featured on ESPN. Another breakthrough was the agreement by NBC Sports and USA network to televise 32 hours of the 2005 Dew Action Sports Tour, the first season-long professional competition involving action sport.

The X Games feature wakeboarding, which evolved from waterskiing and surfing; motocross, which came from motorcycles and cross country running; surfing; BMX or bicycle motocross, which includes racing and jumps; and skateboarding. One thing all these sports have in common is racing, jumps, their own lingo, and an emphasis on creativity and athleticism. Action sports were once viewed as pursuits for outsiders, rebels, and geeks, but all that has changed; they're mainstream sports now. Participants say they pursue these sports for fun and because they like the fashion and lifestyle and just want to express themselves (Scheiber 2005).

Changes in Sport Preference

Over the past decade, several changes have occurred in the sports that youths prefer to play. As discussed earlier, baseball and football used to be the most popular sports. While they are still popular, other sports have made more dramatic gains in participants. Basketball is now the nation's most popular team sport with over 10 million young participants, and it is followed closely by soccer (SGMA 2005c).

Basketball

Statistics for youth basketball show that it has become the most popular team sport for kids, with over 10 million participants in 2005 (SGMA 2005c). Basketball offers many of the same advantages as soccer, although as children get older size does become a major determinant of success. Courts are accessible, particularly in urban settings where space is at a premium. Heroes like Michael Jordan have inspired a generation of players. As women's professional basketball makes a solid foothold, players such as Lisa Leslie, Diana Taurasi, and Sue Bird have become role models for younger female athletes.

Soccer

Soccer has grown at unprecedented rates in the past 20 years in the United States. Since 1995, soccer participation increased 11%; play on high school teams rose 65% and play in U.S. youth soccer programs surged 76% (SGMA 2005c). The major impetus has come from community-based programs that are affiliated with the U.S. Youth Soccer Association, as well as the dual influence of Title IX and the liberation of girls to play soccer. That happy circumstance led to the success in world competition of the U.S. women's national team led by Mia Hamm, Kristine Lilly, Brandi Chastain, and a core group of others who have starred at the professional level for over a decade. Young girls have role models to emulate, and these women have been outstanding citizens, athletes, and promoters of their sport.

Soccer has some built-in advantages over other sports. No one body type is required for success, size is not a prerequisite, and the necessary skills to play are somewhat modest. Although youth soccer is marked by a swarm of players all moving toward the ball, players get good exercise; learn basic balance, running, and kicking skills; and enjoy the camaraderie of teammates. The cost per player is modest since 22 kids on one field is a cost-effective use of space and personnel.

Soccer programs start as early as ages 4 and 5, snatching up kids before other sports have a chance to recruit them. Kids only need to be able to run and kick a ball to begin soccer play compared to more complicated skills required for many other sports. Recreational leagues that play within their own league structure are plentiful, and traveling teams, a next step up in competition, are offered in most communities. Up

Soccer is a sport accessible to youth of all ages, races, genders, and economic levels. What other youth sports fit those categories?

the workforce and have less time to devote to such activities. Fields are expensive to develop and maintain, particularly in urban settings. Scandal has also touched youth baseball, with several cases of players lying about their age to compete in divisions for which they were too old. However, if you combine all participants in baseball, fast-pitch softball, and slow-pitch softball, the total exceeds that of every other sport, including basketball.

Olympic Sports

Participation in Olympic sports like figure skating, skiing, tennis, and gymnastics has held steady but has shown little growth. The primary obstacle for all of these sports is the expense of practice and play. While some community programs are available for young people just starting out, elite programs are mandatory for athletes aspiring to higher performance. Various families have estimated that it costs them between $20,000 and $25,000 U.S. per year to support one child in an elite program. That figure includes expenses for coaching, equipment, and travel to competition for both the child and a parent chaperone.

For those select few who choose to attend a sport academy away from home, the tab can come to over $40,000 U.S. a year when you add the expenses of room, board, and schooling to the expenses already listed. These prices are out of reach of the average family (United States Tennis Association 2003), and only a select few can afford the high-performance programs without risking the family finances (see chapter 13). Some parents are so consumed by the possible pot of gold in professional sport that they are willing to risk everything in hopes that their child will reach payday. Imagine the pressure children feel when the family finances depend on them!

A corollary to the dilemma of the finances of high-performance sport programs is that minority families are typically underrepresented just because of the cost. That fact tends to produce artificial social environments for players who associate only with other players from families like their own.

ORGANIZED YOUTH SPORT

Sport at the youth level is organized by one of two groups: the youths themselves or adults. Both types of organization have shown growth in recent years and the question is whether one will dominate the other.

There are significant differences in the intent of the sport, the application of traditions and rules, the social influences, and the cost depending on which

to 30% of participants are identified as elite players and offered advanced training and coaching. Although we know that number is inflated, at a young age many players show potential to develop and parents eagerly support their children's talent.

Baseball

Participation in baseball has fallen off, particularly in urban settings and among African Americans. The number of players declined 26% during the 1990s, although the number who played frequently (at least 52 times per year) remained unchanged at 3.2 million (SGMA 2005c). A game that was once America's pastime has begun to play a much more modest role. A litany of reasons has been suggested with no clear answers. Some people blame the decline on the bitter feuds between professional players and owners that resulted in various strikes or lockouts. Other say the game is too slow and boring. Also, the steroid controversy and the exposure of several professional stars as users of illegal substances generated a lot of negative publicity (see chapter 17).

At the youth level, baseball more than any other sport has relied on parents as coaches and team administrators. In many families, both parents are in group is organizing the sport. Sports that are orga- nized by adults seem to be more reflective of adult and professional models of sport. They offer kids a glimpse into the adult world of sport and socialize young people into a system that prepares them for continued play in high school, college, and beyond. Sport programs that are organized by young people, on the other hand, are accepted as an end in them- selves, offering an opportunity to have fun, enjoy competition, and control the level of involvement, dedication, and control.

Athlete-Organized Sport

Athlete-organized sport includes sports and games that developed naturally over the years as children went outside to play. Free from school, parents, and other adult supervision, children choose an activity, agree on the rules, and settle disputes among them- selves. Games begin and end by mutual agreement or when the child who provided the equipment decides to go home.

Natural leaders who are often the best players or the oldest kids choose sides. The hurt feelings of those chosen last are ignored and kids learn where they stand in the evaluation of their peers. The most popular games provide lots of action for every player and flexible rules to mitigate imbalances due to size, age, or experience. For example, younger children who might often strike out in baseball-type games are often given a chance to bat until they actually hit the ball.

Disputes are creatively solved by one side giving in, negotiating between team leaders, or allowing a certain number of gimmees or do-overs during a game. In playground basketball, for example, the team with the ball can often call a foul on the oppos- ing team without the foul being open to question. Rules are agreed upon before play begins but may be changed by agreement during play. They also often change from game to game depending on the participants. Some sandlot football games are tackle, some are touch, some are two-hand touch, and some are flag. In some pickup basketball games the win- ners take the ball while other games give the ball to the loser of the last basket.

Uneven numbers between teams are often solved by one player serving both teams as pitcher, catcher, or some other position. Girls are accepted as part of games but typically are treated no better or worse than their male counterparts. More skilled athletes typically choose the most active positions crucial to the game such as pitcher, shortstop, quarter- back, receiver, goalkeeper, or point guard. Positions are shifted during the game to balance out the action.

The advantages of youth- controlled activity are that young people learn how to work within group dynam- ics, make decisions, and get along with their peers. As players come and go, lopsided scores develop, or bad feelings arise, players are forced to be creative and flexible if the game is to go on.

As discussed earlier, a more recent trend toward athlete-centered sport has been the rapid rise of alter- native sport, including in- line skating, snowboarding, and so on (see page 101 in this chapter). One appeal of these activities is limited

Free of adult supervision, athlete-organized sport is less formal in its rules and outcomes.

Activity Timeout: Extreme Kids

Locate at least three kids who have participated in an alternative sport and interview them to determine the reasons they chose that activity, why they like it, their expectations for their future in the sport, and how they think their sport compares with more traditional sports. Share your findings with others in class and discuss the implications for the future of youth sport.

adult supervision. Although there are some inherent dangers in these sports, young people are flocking to them as an alternative to traditional sport.

Adult-Organized Sport

At about age 6, many children begin playing soccer, munchkin tennis, tee ball or biddie ball, or flag football in adult-organized programs. Often parents are heavily involved in the practices and games, serving as coaches, partners, pitchers, or base coaches. The rules are modified to suit the ability of the players so that their introduction to the sport is successful. Rules are established to protect the safety of each child, ensure fairness of playing time, and control the length of games.

Since physical development proceeds at different rates, many children are not ready or able to perform precise skills when they enter an organized sport program. Frustration and lack of confidence can easily turn off children for life when pushy parents force them into a no-win situation too early. We often read about champion athletes who started in their sport at age 3 or 4, but clearly they are the exceptions. Plus, who knows what their beginnings in their sport were like. They may have been simply hitting a tennis ball against a wall or playing a game of catch with parents or peers.

Adult-organized sport is primarily concerned with teaching kids the following:

- Skills of the game
- Rules of the game
- Proper playing of positions
- Importance of following adult directions, strategy, and training methods

Adult coaches and parents are usually the key figures who determine the success of the experience. They set the tone and the level of competitiveness, arbitrate rule infractions, determine who plays where and when, and offer encouragement or disapproval. Since their role is so important, several national organizations (e.g., National Alliance for Youth Sports, American Sport Education Program, Institute for the Study of Youth Sports) have been established to offer training for coaches or parents involved in youth sport. The challenge is great since there is a new crop of adults every season to train and educate.

When coaches or parents are not trained, the risk to athletes is great. Lack of knowledge of safety in sport, of healthy competition, and of the emotional needs of children can do real harm. Inability to teach sport-specific skills can slow down the learning process and lead to frustration for the aspiring

The role of coaches in youth sport is vital. Poor behavior by coaches can take the fun out of sport.

players. Great strides in coach and parent education have been made, but the task is daunting—nothing is more crucial to ensure a positive experience for kids in adult-controlled youth sport.

Since kids are used to adult instruction and judgment at home and at school, the athletic field seems little different. To be successful, they need to please the adults, conform to the rules of the game, stay in position, and follow the strategy set by the coaches. Failure to do these things usually results in punishment, reprimands, or benching.

Spending time with friends is a key part of youth sport. Trips for pizza or ice cream are often more important than the game results for some kids. Celebrating success with friends produces enthusiasm and reinforcement that keep players coming back. On the other hand, a team that rarely wins a contest needs a wise, creative leader to salve wounded egos and maintain a healthy approach to competition.

If Pete Rozelle, the former commissioner of the NFL, were around to share his wisdom, I'm sure he would advise youth sport leaders to design the competitive balance between teams as he did in the NFL so that every team contends for honors until the end of the season. Parity among teams produces some wins and losses for every team and helps kids learn to deal with both scenarios. Too much winning often produces cockiness and unrealistic expectations.

Too much losing undermines confidence, encourages placing blame, and may sustain a self-fulfilling prophecy or defeatist attitude.

Key Role of Parents

Youth sport has the potential to become a terrific, positive influence on family life or a divisive, painful experience for all. Parents need to do some reading, attend orientation sessions, and talk to other parents in order to understand what the sport philosophy, policies, and expectations are of local sport programs before their children are old enough to participate in sport. That way, when their children come home and say they want to sign up for soccer because their friends are doing so, the parents are armed with information.

If parents get involved as coaches, league officials, or chaperones, chances are they will get a better picture of the experience and be prepared to counsel their child when problems arise. However, once a practice or game is over, parents need to let it go and resume normal family life. Kids don't need to feel constant pressure from family about their performance on the ball field. Attending home games as fans, providing transportation to away games, and joining in team celebrations deliver a message of strong parental interest and support. Plus, parents get to meet their child's friends, the team's coaches, and the parents of other kids.

When parental involvement in youth sport is well balanced and positive, athletes can gain more from the sport.

Watching kids play their chosen sport gives parents insight into the type of child they have raised. Rarely do they get to watch their children at school, but on the athletic field, they see their children in their peer environment. Many opportunities arise for reinforcing children's attitudes toward teammates, opponents, adult coaches and officials, and good sporting behavior.

If there is more than one child in the family, time and money must be balanced so that each one gets a fair share. By nature, some activities are more expensive than others, but kids need to understand the general expense and appreciate the family commitment.

Parents who take a relaxed view of the importance of competition can relieve the pressure on kids. Parents need to set expectations for good effort, improvement in skill or strategy, healthy physical activity, and cooperation with coaches and teammates. By reinforcing positive actions in these areas, they send a powerful message about what is important in sport and in life.

Finally, most parents whose children have been through the experience of youth sport would counsel parents approaching those years to have fun with them. Before they know it, those precious hours of growth and challenge will be gone for their kids, and they won't get the chance for a do-over.

WHY KIDS PLAY SPORT

Most kids are first attracted to sport because their friends are involved. The chance to spend time with peers; make new friends; and escape from the adult world, school, or boredom all factor into the attraction of sport. In addition, kids seem to enjoy the physical challenge of games and activity. In the typical suburban household, friends are separated by geography, and sport offers friends an opportunity to spend time together. There is little doubt that if children's parents have a favorable attitude toward sport, as most parents do, they are more likely to be encouraged to join a team or a program (SGMA 2001).

Virtually every survey that investigates why kids play sport reveals that they say they enjoy it (SGMA 2003, 2005b). In 1990, the largest study of youths' feelings about sport (over 10,000 students age 10 to 18) was sponsored by the Athletic Footwear Association and conducted by the Youth Sport Institute of Michigan State University. The results showed that the number one reason young people play sport is to have fun! The top 10 reasons also included to

improve skills, to stay in shape, to do something they're good at, to enjoy the excitement of competition, to be part of a team, and to enjoy the challenge of competition. For many, these reasons are also part of fun (Ewing and Seefeldt 1990).

Another study suggests that other benefits of participation include growth and maturation effects, increased fitness, improved self-worth, increased social competence, and enhanced moral development (Malina and Cumming 2003).

When sport ceases to be fun, youths are likely to drop out. But what does fun mean to the typical kid? Adults ascribe all types of motivations to young people and tend to try to convince them that having fun means playing like the pros with sharp uniforms, hard work, dedication, and a commitment to success. Conversations with young people, on the other hand, reveal that they are more likely to describe fun as the result of the challenge of the game, the skills they learn, the exercise they get, the time they have to be with friends, and the excitement of competition (Ewing and Seefeldt 1990).

There are also deeper reasons for sport participation other than fun. Gould (1993) suggested that young athletes' perception of their own competence or ability is crucial. If they see their own competence at a low level in comparison to their peers, they tend to become discouraged and drop out of sport. The most critical time for youths dropping out of sport is the onset of adolescence at age 11 or 12. By then, they have evaluated their own skill competence and decided whether the activity is fun and how they respond to competition and coaching. The major reasons they drop out of sport are changing interests, interest in another activity, the sport is no longer fun, or the coach is a poor teacher or plays favorites (Seefeldt, Ewing, and Walk 1992).

BURNOUT IN YOUTH SPORT

Burnout is simply a natural reaction to chronic stress in young athletes. Kids who have burned out seek to reduce the stress by withdrawing from the sport. If they know that their parents and coaches will be disappointed in them, the stress is simply heightened and they may feel forced to take drastic measures such as faking an injury or illness. In fact, the pressure they feel may actually produce an illness.

Stress isn't all bad; we often learn valuable life lessons after dealing with stressful situations. Consider the stress of being the last batter in a baseball game when your team is down in the score, there are

Involvement in youth sport shouldn't cause undue stress; rather, the involvement should be fun and provide positive, rewarding experiences.

runners on base, and there are two outs. Sure, the batter and pitcher feel stress, but the one who comes out on top gains confidence. The one who suffers in this situation may learn from his mistake, and at least he'll know that his friends, teammates, and coaches still value him as a player if they are smart.

Still, too much stress can creep into youth sport and may eventually lead to burning out and then dropping out. Athletes who worry too much about outcomes of games, have performance anxiety or low self-esteem, or believe that their parents attach too much importance to games may be at risk for burnout. Year-round sport programs, specializing in one sport at a young age, overdoing physical training, long practices, too many games without days off, and overemphasis on winning all contribute to feelings that sport is no longer fun.

Parents and coaches need to learn how to listen to kids and address potential burnout symptoms before they are irreversible. According to Waldron (2000), the signs include feelings, thoughts, behaviors, and physical symptoms. Specifically, observers may notice that players feel anxious or moody; often

mention thoughts about mental errors or lack of attention; cry easily or bite their nails; or experience physical symptoms like headaches, upset stomachs, or a racing pulse.

Youth sport organizers and coaches must be sensitive to signs of burnout by learning about the effects of stress on youngsters and be prepared to deal with the causes or refer the athletes to others with more training. The scars from a negative sport experience can turn happy, well-adjusted kids into withdrawn, unhappy kids. Parents also need to learn to recognize when kids are showing signs of burnout, which may include avoiding practice or games, never smiling, frequent physical ailments, lack of caring about performance, emotional outbursts, or other behavior that is atypical for that child. Once burnout is suspected, intervention by trained professionals may be necessary to plot a path back to normalcy that may or may not include the particular sport.

Sport psychologists who are trained in dealing with youth sport problems are likely the best source of help. They may be able to teach athletes, parents, and coaches specific strategies to combat the feelings of burnout if the damage is not too extensive. Certainly they will be able to help young athletes reassess their reasons for playing their sport and work toward a healthier approach that includes physical activity and perhaps other sports (Gould 1993; Smith 1986; Weinberg and Gould 1995).

Dropping Out Due to Burnout

A significant dropout rate has been documented in sport participation. Statistics show that over 40 million athletes participate in youth sport but only 6 million go on to compete in interscholastic sport. That nets out to 34 million kids who abandon their active participation as they enter their crucial teenage years. The average number of years of participation in one sport is about five, according to the 2000 SGMA research. The results from the Youth Sports Institute of Michigan State University cited earlier showed that 45% of Americans were involved in sport at age 10, but by age 18 only about 20% had any involvement in sport outside of school (Ewing and Seefeldt 1990).

Burnout can often to lead young athletes to drop out of sport. According to Ronald Smith, professor of psychology at the University of Washington, "The No.1 reason kids drop out of sports is: It's not fun. The next five reasons all have to do with parents' or coaches' behaviors" (Condor 2004, p. 2). Drawing from the sources cited previously in this chapter, here are a few common mistakes of parents that lead their children to burn out and potentially drop out of sport:

- Choosing a sport that they like rather than allowing their children to decide after trying several activities.
- Insisting that their children follow one sport season with another, when the children may just want a little free time for a change.
- Putting too much emphasis on the results of competition. For example, the first thing parents often ask is, "Did you win?" That question conveys the message to their child that winning is the most important thing.
- Forcing their children to compete even at the risk of physical injury from overuse of certain parts of the body.
- Becoming overinvolved in the game or team. When parents say *"We've* got a game tomorrow," they're too wrapped up in the child's sport.
- Arguing with officials, parents from opposing teams, or coaches.
- Not reinforcing the positive experiences children are looking for from sport, such as learning new skills, staying active, being with friends, achieving independence, and improving self-confidence.
- Pushing children to the next level of competition even when they resist.

Coaches of youth sport may be parents, volunteers, or paid professionals. One major concern with youth coaching is the lack of standardized training, and a second concern is the rapid turnover of coaches and the continual need for training of new coaches. Based on the recommendations of ASEP and other youth sport organizations such as the Youth Sports Institute of Michigan State, here are some of the common mistakes youth coaches need to avoid:

- Emphasizing winning rather than building skills and improving performance.
- Spending more time on and allocating more playing time to more skilled athletes at the expense of average or below-average players.
- Expecting kids to absorb rules and strategy that may be too advanced for their level of development in terms of understanding or skill.
- Using physical punishment as discipline.
- Arguing with officials or parents in inappropriate ways.

- Neglecting to create an atmosphere of fun for practices or games.
- Expecting families to sacrifice time, money, and priorities for the sports team.
- Encouraging kids to specialize in one sport at an early age to the exclusion of other sports or school-related activities.
- Using an authoritarian coaching style or imitating the coaching style of coaches of professional athletes.

In addition to coaches, other youth sport administrators include league organizers, publicity staff, governing board members, officials, and sponsors. All have an important role to play for a youth sport league to be successful, and they can even have a detrimental effect if their vision is not clear and the league policies are not set in writing for anyone to examine. According to the experts cited previously (Ewing and Seefeldt 1990; Weinberg and Gould 1995), typical issues concerning league-affiliated adults include the following:

- Failing to establish a philosophy for the league from which policies naturally follow.
- Failing to communicate the philosophy and policies to parents, coaches, and players through training days, newsletters, and Web sites.
- Putting too much emphasis on winning, playoffs, and all-star squads rather than a healthy program for all kids.

Poor coaching practices, such as using physical activity as punishment, can lead to dissatisfaction and burnout, which may eventually cause athletes to drop out of the sport.

- Requiring an unrealistic financial commitment from families, particularly those who have several children competing at the same time.

- Extending seasons by having preseason, postseason, and off-season programs that force kids to choose between one sport and other activities.

- Lacking proper safety procedures, training for coaches, and support from medical personnel to deal with emergencies and chronic health problems of players.

- Failing to provide safe, clean, and attractive facilities for practices and games.

- Adopting a casual attitude toward the hiring and training of league coaches and officials.

- Failing to balance the level of competition between teams to facilitate excitement.

Elite Teams and Burnout

An article that appeared June 7, 2004, in *U.S. News and World Report* was titled "Fixing Kids' Sports: Rescuing Children's Games From Crazed Coaches and Parents" (Cary 2004). The article relied heavily on an interview with Fred Engh, the founder of the National Alliance for Youth Sports, who has spent a lifetime trying to educate youth sport leaders on the need to make team sport "less pressurized, safer, and more child friendly." He created a training manual for coaches, and his organization has certified over 2.1 million volunteer coaches. But Engh realizes his accomplishments aren't enough. He extols the virtues of training everyone involved, including parents, administrators, and officials.

One of the major problems described in the article is the phenomena of so-called travel teams, where kids who are judged to be above average are placed on club, select, or elite teams to travel to nearby towns for tournaments or games. These teams often practice twice a week, play two games a week, and absorb participants' every weekend. Parents usually provide the transportation by carpooling.

The pitch to families is that if kids don't join one of these elite teams, their chances of making high school varsity teams is diminished considerably. If they fall behind their peers in skill development, they'll never catch up. Of course, Michael Jordan and many more like him have proved that you don't even have to make your high school team to go on to play professionally. Jordan got cut from his high school team in ninth grade!

Too much emphasis on playing just one sport can lead to miserable kids. In the misguided attempt by league officials and parents to make their kids more competitive, traditional seasons are extended into year-round programs. Baseball is extended into fall and winter seasons in warm climates, basketball is year round, tennis and golf are stocked with one-sport athletes, and swimmers hit the pool for workouts regardless of the month on the calendar. Some of the potential results of this overspecialization at a young age include the following (Wendel 2005):

- Kids lose interest and playing is no longer fun simply due to overexposure.

- When kids hit a performance barrier in their sport of choice, there are no other sports to turn to for activity.

- Friends tend to be limited to those they associate with on a daily basis in their sport.

- Complementary athletic skills that might be developed by cross-training in other sports are neglected.

- Kids are not exposed to a variety of coaching and training methods.

- Overuse injuries occur due to repeated stress demands of one sport.

Pressure builds on kids and families to commit time, money, and long seasons and off-seasons to one sport. Private instruction and summer sport camps add to the expense and pressure. If more than one sibling is involved, families are forced to juggle time, transportation, and finances.

Some parents justify their actions by saying, "I know the chances of my kid making the pros are small, I just want to give them a chance to earn a college scholarship." However, if you pay between $10,000 and $20,000 U.S. per year, as many families do, for one child in swimming, tennis, skating, or another sport, wouldn't it make a lot more sense to invest that money in a college savings plan? There's no guarantee that athletic scholarships will even be available in the sport in the next 10 years as colleges trim budgets and support scholarships only for revenue-producing sports.

REFORMS FOR YOUTH SPORT

Now that we have traced the history of youth sport and considered some of the current issues, perhaps you believe changes should be made. It's natural to try to improve an experience for children, whether it involves education or recreation. Kids need to be able to adjust to the world they will live in, not the one we lived in the past. Different skills are needed, new experiences should be embraced, and opportunities for positive social experiences through sport activity should be eagerly sought.

A society's core values tend to endure, and those for youth sport are no exception. Kids want to participate in sport programs that are designed to be a fun, positive experience and in which they can invest energy and enthusiasm. In 1979, two leaders in youth sport training, Rainer Martens and Vern Seefeldt, developed the Bill of Rights for Young Athletes (see figure 6.1) in response to growing concern about abuse of young athletes (Martens and Seefeldt 1979). This seminal work is still used and is available from many sport organizations.

Based on the bill of rights in figure 6.1, it is clear that there are some concerns that must be addressed in youth sport. Earlier in the chapter, we outlined some of the typical characteristics of adult-controlled youth sport, which obviously conflict with some of the rights listed here. It is likely that many local community programs do not exhibit all the characteristics of adult-centered sport or all those of athlete-centered sport but fall somewhere in between. If the athlete's bill of rights is accepted and implemented, the experience of youth sport will be enhanced for all children.

The keen interest in youth sports in the United States has spawned various organizations to provide educational services to coaches, parents, and officials. Perhaps the most inclusive organization is the National Council of Youth Sports (NCYS), a multisport corporation established to foster the continued education of youth sport administrators and to support the growth and development of young people through participation in organized youth sport. The NCYS represents more than 60 organizations and 45 million participants. By their estimates, the total number of coaches involved in youth sport is 2.4 million and the number of volunteers has ballooned to 7.6 million. When added together, over 55 million kids and adults are involved together in youth sport programs (National Council of Youth Sports 2006).

Athlete Bill of Rights

1. Right to participate in sports.

2. Right to participate at a level commensurate with each child's maturity and ability.

3. Right to have qualified adult leadership.

4. Right to play as a child and not as an adult.

5. Right of children to share in the leadership and decision making of their sport participation.

6. Right to participate in safe and healthy environments.

7. Right to proper preparation for participation in sports.

8. Right to an equal opportunity to strive for success.

9. Right to be treated with dignity.

10. Right to have fun in sports.

FIGURE 6.1 Bill of rights for young athletes.

Guidelines for children's sports (1979), reprinted with permission from the National Association for Sport and Physical Education (NASPE), 1900 Association Drive, Reston, VA, 20191-1599.

Pop Culture: Who Is Killing Kids' Sports?

Parade magazine, which reaches over 75 million readers around the United States, recently published an article titled "Who's Killing Kids' Sports?" A number of major problems with youth sport are highlighted, including high dropout rates, overemphasis on winning, and negative behavior of parents or coaches. Instead of just decrying the existence of problems, the state of Maine has launched a major initiative to rectify those problems and the article describes their initiative.

The statewide initiative, funded by a grant from the U.S. Senate and supported by the University of Maine, is called Sports Done Right. More than 30 other states have expressed an interest in Maine's groundbreaking project. The main targets are communities, schools, and all those involved in youth sport, including players, officials, coaches, and parents. Educational programs are the key to helping everyone understand what seems to work and what detracts from the experience of youth sport.

Some recommendations of the initiative are continuing education of coaches and parents, resisting specialization in one sport at young ages, promoting good sporting behavior, reducing pressure to win, and developing policies that keep more kids active in sport for a lifetime.

The project director, former Maine education commissioner J. Duke Albanese, says, "If I had to sum up the crisis in kids' sports, I'd do it in one word—adults" (Relin 2005). For more information on the project, see www.sportsdonerightmaine.org.

The SGMA (2000) identified the following reasons for the decline in team sport participation in 2000:

- The invention of in-line skating, which grew 494% during the 1990s to include nearly 28 million participants

- The increase in time devoted to television, video games, computers, and the Internet

- The tendency of parents to overschedule kids, cutting into time for spontaneous sport and play

- The reduction of school physical education programs and even recess

- The growing tendency of young athletes to specialize at an early age, resulting in fewer multisport athletes

Based on the research of the current issues in youth sport, here are some modifications that could be considered:

- Increase public funding of open fields and other facilities to support youth sport activities.

- Use community funding to supplement organizations that sponsor youth sport to provide after-school programs that are safe, affordable, and supervised by knowledgeable adults.

- Limit specialization in one sport at an early age and encourage kids to sample several sports when they are young in order to broaden their athletic development and choice of activities as they mature.

- Insist on continuous coaching certification programs for volunteer and paid coaches alike.

- Offer and support sport programs at various levels of skill, commitment, and intensity, allowing parents and children to choose the level that fits their child.

- Offer affordable high-performance programs to kids who demonstrate the athletic talent and desire a more intense program. Currently, these programs seemed to be limited to athletes from more affluent families.

- Provide funding to make sport programs available to children of all economic, racial, and ethnic backgrounds.

- Ensure equal opportunities for both girls and boys.

Recent news decries the lack of physical activity and the increasing rise in obesity among people of all ages. Although we seem to be getting many children started in the right direction of fitness for life, we shut down their progress just as they enter adolescence. Youth sport seems to be more of an elimination process, selecting the most talented kids for later sport participation in high school and bar-

This child is on the right track to learning a lifelong fitness activity. What must his parents, schools, and community organizations do to keep him on this healthy track?

ring those with less talent, motivation, and drive to a life without organized sport.

Should we be organizing and promoting community-based activities that attract youths who do not play interscholastic sport? Should these programs be oriented toward lifetime activities such as self-defense or martial arts, tennis, volleyball, aerobic fitness, golf, and swimming? Offering these sports as coed activities would certainly increase the appeal.

CHAPTER SUMMARY

In this chapter we looked at the relatively recent historical development of youth sport and examined the reasons for growth. We also considered the current status of youth sport in terms of participation and popularity. The organizations that sponsor youth sport were identified and differences in program emphasis were considered.

The differences and popularity of sport programs that are organized by adults compared with those organized by the athletes themselves were described and analyzed. Regardless of who organizes sport programs, it is clear that many programs have problems and shortcomings that need to be dealt with. The recent rapid rise in alternative sport was noted and reasons for that phenomenon were explored.

Differences among various sports were described and the relative popularity trends for each sport were examined. Although overall participation continues to increase, there are troubling questions about affordability, time requirements, dropout rates, and coaches' training of youth sport.

We spent time discussing what kids say they want out of sport programs and comparing their needs to the offerings of adult-designed programs. One major theme that emerged from kids is that they want sport to be fun. However, it seems that *fun* can mean quite different things to different people depending on their motivation for participation and their individual needs.

Finally, we considered whether changes to youth sport are needed and what the likely challenges are for the future. Issues were identified and possible solutions suggested. Overall, youth sport programs seem to receive the approval of most parents, coaches, and players. However, that does not mean that significant improvements cannot be made, starting with the needs and rights of children for healthy physical activity and recreation.

7
CHAPTER

Interscholastic and Intercollegiate Sport

Student Outcomes

After reading this chapter, you will know the following:

- The connection between sport and education at the high school and college levels
- The trends of interscholastic sport, including positive and negative effects
- The trends of intercollegiate sport, including positive and negative effects
- Challenges facing sport in educational settings and possible changes

In the last century, sport has become an important fixture in virtually all high schools and colleges. Conventional wisdom is that sport helps complete the education of young people by emphasizing the development of physical talents, a healthy work ethic, and a moral code and attitude that conform to the expectations of society.

College athletics had a modest start with a rowing contest between students from Harvard and Yale in 1852. At first, sports were run entirely by students for their entertainment and benefit. As years went by, that system became supplanted by one that seems to benefit the school, alumni, and student body at large with questionable benefits for some of the high-profile athletes.

Interscholastic sport soon followed the trend set by college sport programs. Leaders in high school education supported sport programs as a means of raising youth fitness levels, which were judged to be alarmingly low during the first World War. They also felt that students would learn the value of hard work, citizenship, and good sporting behavior.

School-based sport became so popular that athletes were the most admired students in school. One might think that in an educational setting, those who performed best in academic work would be the most admired. However, various replicated studies have shown that athletes were most popular with peers while bright students who were nonathletes ranked ahead of students who were both bright and studious (Eitzen and Sage 1978; Hechinger 1980). Apparently it is acceptable to be a brilliant student as long as you don't work at it; conversely, athletes are admired for talent and their work ethic.

Perhaps the difference is that athletic success benefits the team, and indirectly the whole school, while academic success seems more self-centered. Another factor is that major athletic events are often key social occasions where students congregate, flirt with one another, discuss life, and rally round their school's team. Particularly for boys who play highly visible sports like football and basketball, performance enhances status.

Student culture at the typical American high school values athletic achievement and usually conveys status on successful athletes as admired members of the in-group. Likewise, popular students are usually members of an exclusive clique that may be based on economic status, appearance, and dress or possession of material things such as a cool car. Academic standouts are often the butt of jokes and are left out of the social group.

In the last 25 years, the status of athletes has changed dramatically with the entry of girls into the athletic arena. Many of the most successful athletes are also top students and popular with their peers. These changes have affected the prescription for social success for girls in high school from one that emphasized femininity, cheerleading, domestic aptness, and appearance to one that supports girls as students, athletes, and all-around achievers.

Intercollegiate athletics presents a different picture from that of the typical high school. First, the number of students who qualify for athletic teams in college dwindles dramatically compared to those who can play on high school teams. Second, the type of school and the way the institution views the athletic program have a huge impact on the philosophy and conduct of college sport. Big-time athletic programs labeled as Division I by the NCAA emphasize winning, entertainment, and revenue-producing sports. These programs make little apology for appearing to operate more as a professional sport model than an educational one. Conversely, hundreds of smaller colleges' field athletic teams purport to offer students an opportunity to develop their physical skills just like other students develop their skills in drama, music, art, and other extracurricular activities.

Sport in the educational setting is a phenomenon that is stronger in the United States than any other country in the world. Most other countries offer sport programs that are community based and supported by sport clubs in towns and cities. Education is seen as a separate endeavor and athletics are not intertwined with education. The American trend has likely produced both positive and negative consequences for society, depending on your point of view.

INTERSCHOLASTIC SPORT

For the purpose of this discussion, high school sport covers grades 9 through 12, although in many schools gifted athletes in 7th or 8th grade are eligible to play on high school teams. At the national level, the National Federation of State High School Associations (NFHS) provides education; publishes rules for sport competition, information, research; and provides guidance to the state associations (www. nfhs.org). Sport at both public and private schools is typically governed by local leagues and the state association to which they pay dues. They adhere to the rules established by the state association and therefore are eligible for regional and state play-offs. Some states separate public and private schools at state competitions, especially when private schools have consistently won state titles.

In this section, we'll take a look at trends in high school sport participation, reasons high school athletes choose to participate as well as reasons they stop participating, how high school sport and community-sponsored sport interact, and some positive and negative aspects of high school athletics.

Participation Trends

According to the NFHS, the number of students participating in high school athletics has increased for 15 consecutive years (see figure 7.1), and in 2003 to 2004 participation reached an all-time high. The total number of students who participated in 2003 to 2004 was 6,903,552. That number represents 55.4% of the total enrollment in schools that play varsity sports (NFHS 2004b).

According to the NFHS (2004a), since 1980, the percentage of students who play sports has increased from 46.7% to the present level of 55.4%, an increase of 8.7%. Following the trend of the last 25 years, girls' participation has continued to increase at a greater rate than that of boys'. The increases over the years have primarily been the result of consistent gains in the number of girls participating while boys' participation levels have remained relatively stable.

Consider that in 1971 to 1972, only 294,015 girls played high school sports compared with 3,666,917 boys. Following the passage of Title IX and its manda-

tory rules for providing equal opportunity for both genders, girls flocked to the fields and courts. Today the balance is still higher for boys, but it reflects tremendous growth for girls. The NFHS numbers for 2003 to 2004 show 4,038,253 boys compared with 2,865,299 girls.

Girls' participation in recent years has swelled by the inclusion of spirit squads as an athletic sport. The athletic gymnastics moves that are required of today's cheerleaders convinced officials that they deserved to be treated as athletes, too. For girls, the most growth in participation was in spirit squads, soccer, lacrosse, and cross country.

According to the NFHS, the participation of boys in high school sport reached an all-time high of 4,367,442 from 1977 to 1978. Numbers then declined for the next 10 years until they began to reverse the downward trend. The last 20 years have shown a gradual but steady increase in boys' participation back up to 4 million, still short of the high marks of the mid-1970s (NFHS 2004a).

The most popular sports as measured by the number of teams rather than participants show some interesting results. The top four sports for boys in order of popularity are basketball, track and field, baseball, and football. For girls, the top four in order are basketball, track and field, volleyball, and softball. Soccer is seventh in popularity for both boys and girls but has steadily moved up in the ranks.

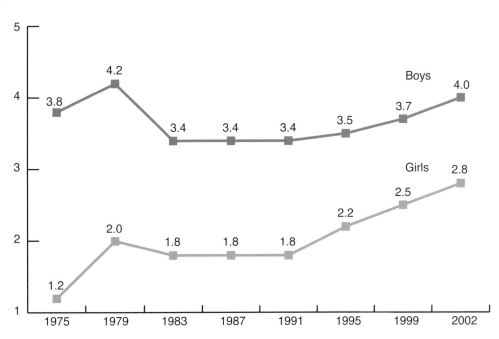

Figure 7.1 Boys and girls participating in high school varsity sport from 1975 through 2002. Numbers are shown in millions of participants.
Adapted from NFHS 2003-2004 High School Athletics Participation Survey.

These sports have shown the biggest growth in female participation. What other sports will see an increase in female participation?

Youth sport surveys that were discussed in the previous chapter show that approximately 26 million kids age 6 to 17 play on at least one organized team. That works out to a percentage of 54% of the population in those age groups (NFHS 2004b).

For boys, the largest increase was in soccer, followed by tennis, outdoor track and field, swimming and diving, and lacrosse. The most popular sport for boys in number of participants remained 11-player football, followed by basketball. Keep in mind that football teams typically attract and accommodate much larger numbers of participants than basketball. For girls, basketball continued to be the most popular sport, followed by outdoor track and field.

According to the NFHS, the most popular sports for high school students in number of participants in 2003 to 2004 were as follows (NFHS 2004b):

Boys

1.	Football	1,032,682
2.	Basketball	544,811
3.	Track and field (outdoor)	504,801
4.	Baseball	457,146
5.	Soccer	349,785
6.	Wrestling	238,700
7.	Cross country	196,428
8.	Golf	163,341
9.	Tennis	152,938
10.	Swimming and diving	96,562

Girls

1.	Basketball	457,986
2.	Track and field (outdoor)	418,322
3.	Volleyball	396,322
4.	Softball (fast pitch)	362,468
5.	Soccer	309,032
6.	Tennis	167,758
7.	Cross country	166,287
8.	Swimming and diving	144,565
9.	Competitive spirit squads	89,443
10.	Golf	63,173

It is interesting to note that if you eliminated over a million boys who play football, the overall numbers for boys and girls would be about equal. This issue has been a consistent point of debate both in high school and college in terms of interpreting the intentions of Title IX. We will revisit this point in chapter 12, which deals with gender and sport.

Activity Time-Out: Sport Dropouts

In spite of the participation percentages discussed in this chapter, various sources have decried the dropout rate from youth sport, estimating it to be anywhere from 50% to 70%. Since the percentage of participants seems relatively even from youth sport to high school sport, what is the explanation? Are youths dropping out of sport along the way, or are a similar number competing in high school as they did in youth sport programs? Justify your answer.

Another factor to consider when evaluating participation levels is that many sports by definition require fewer athletes to field a team. In many schools, numbers are limited to reduce expenses of playing space, uniforms, games, and coaches. Large squads are necessary for sports like track and field, soccer, swimming, and football. Smaller squads are required for cross country, golf, tennis, basketball, and volleyball. Most schools limit the number of participants in these sports. However, there may have been great interest for more athletes to play those sports had there been room.

Reasons for Sport Participation

In the landmark survey American Youth and Sports Participation (Ewing and Seefeldt 1990) cited in the previous chapter on youth sport, a sampling of approximately 4,000 students in grades 7 to 12 reported the reasons they played their best school sport:

Boys

1. To have fun
2. To improve skills
3. For the excitement of competition
4. To do something I'm good at
5. To stay in shape
6. For the challenge of competition
7. To be part of a team
8. To win
9. To go to a higher level of competition
10. To get exercise
11. To learn new skills
12. For the team spirit

Girls

1. To have fun
2. To stay in shape
3. To get exercise

4. To improve skills
5. To do something I'm good at
6. To be part of a team
7. For the excitement of competition
8. To learn new skills
9. For the team spirit
10. For the challenge of competition
11. To go to a higher level of competition
12. To win

In the same study, a sample of 5,800 athletes in grades 7 to 12 who had recently stopped playing a school sport or a nonschool sport admitted they would play again if the following conditions were met:

1. Practices were more fun.
2. I could play more.
3. Coaches understood players better.
4. There was no conflict with studies.
5. There was no conflict with social life.
6. Coaches were better teachers.

Although these generalizations are important for school officials, parents, and coaches to consider, not all students have the same motivations for playing sports in school. The study divided athletes into three groups based on their motivation.

▪ *Reluctant participants.* Approximately 25% felt they had to be in sports because of outside pressure. They joined because of current friends and in hopes of making new friends. They were less willing to play and practice hard. They were likely candidates to drop out along the way.

▪ *Image-conscious socializers.* This group represents about 40% of athletes and includes many good athletes. These athletes draw motivation from rewards or the approval of others. They like being perceived as good athletes, feeling important, winning trophies, being popular, staying in shape, and looking good. They may stick with school sports but are unlikely to be lifelong athletes.

▪ *Competence oriented.* Athletes in this group love playing sports and are likely to continue after their school days are over. They work hard, practice intensely, and play hard to improve their skills. Sport provides a means of self-achievement that they enjoy.

Partnerships
With Community-Based Programs

Most communities whose high school varsity teams have enjoyed success can point with pride to a community program that feeds their athletic teams. The wise coach who aspires to build a dynasty and ensure the popularity of a sport will get involved in youth sport programs to make sure that kids are introduced to the sport in their formative years. As young people enter high school, the coach then has the luxury of selecting athletes who have a strong background in the skills and strategies of the sport rather than having to teach them as beginning players.

In the summer, many community programs hire high school varsity athletes as coaches of youth sport programs. This helps strengthen the link between the high school and the community program. The varsity

athletes act as role models for younger children and can motivate them to try to achieve varsity status as they mature.

Many towns across the United States consistently produce generations of high performing athletes in certain sports. The tradition often starts with an enthusiastic high school coach who establishes and supports a community youth sport program. Year after year, kids graduate from the youth program and fill positions when players are lost to graduation. The head coach looks like a genius, but the key to success was simply giving time and effort to young participants in the sport.

Positive and Negative Effects
of Interscholastic Sport

A host of studies has supported the positive benefits of high school sport. Typically these studies have been conducted by school systems or other organizations such as the National Federation of State High School Associations (NFHS). Relying on data collected from athletes, principals, and parents, the studies make the case for the value of athletics as an educational endeavor.

The NFHS has summarized this research on their Web site in "The Case for High School Activities" (NFHS 2004a). The site quotes research that supports the value of athletics in promoting academic performance, moral development, good citizenship, gradu-

In the Arena With . . . *Bill Humes*

Bill Humes, a math teacher at Princeton High School, had an outstanding record as coach of the high school tennis team for both boys and girls in spite of the fact that he had little prior experience in the sport. The secret to his success was the work he did in the summer as a senior staff member of the Princeton Community Tennis Program (PCTP), founded by tennis visionary Eve Kraft. Drawing on the town's wealth of resources as the home of Princeton University, the PCTP gained access to tennis courts at the university along with a number of courts located in public parks. Private funds were raised to keep user fees low and virtually every child in Princeton was at least exposed to tennis during their childhood. Those who excelled went on to play on the high school teams.

Humes spent more than 40 years working in PCTP in the summers and went on to become a certified teaching professional by the Professional Tennis Registry and the United States Professional Tennis Association because he knew the value of creating skilled young players to stock the varsity teams. The program became a popular model, and the United States Tennis Association has replicated the Princeton model in community tennis organizations throughout the country.

ation rates, success in college, better attendance and graduation rates, fewer behavioral problems, higher achievement motivation, and resistance to drug and alcohol abuse. Leadership skills, decision making, social integration, and improved self-image are also mentioned as positive outcomes.

Some of the studies cited in the NFHS summary offered the following conclusions. Over two-thirds of parents support the value of cocurricular activities, including sport, according to the 29th annual Phi Delta Kappa–Gallup Poll of the Public's Attitudes Toward Public Schools. The Women's Sports Foundation consistently has supported the benefits of high school sport for young women including physical fitness, resistance to eating disorders, social acceptance, and academic success. Finally, more than three-quarters of high school principals are strong supporters of high school athletics, according to a study supported by a grant from the Lilly Endowment of Indianapolis and conducted by Indiana University in cooperation with the Association of Secondary School Principals. Both of these conclusions are cited in an NFHS summary (NFHS 2004a).

Influence of Athletics on Academic Performance

High school students who participate in athletics tend to have higher grade point averages, better attendance records, and lower dropout rates than the general student body. This conclusion has been drawn by various studies by the Women's Sports Foundation (1989); NFHS (1985, 2004a); and the states of Wyoming, North Carolina, Colorado, and New Mexico (Texas University Interscholastic League 1998).

Clearly there is strong support for interscholastic athletics from virtually every segment of the U.S. population. Sport as an educational experience continues to be a critical factor in the personal development of young people, and coaches must not lose sight of that goal if they hope to retain broad support of their programs.

However, a fair and comprehensive analysis of high school sport reveals both positive and negative effects of participation. One negative effect (which we'll discuss later in this chapter) is the possibility of creating disunity within the student body when athletes form cliques. Cocurricular sport is not for every student, although for some, they may be a critical factor in self-confidence, social acceptance, and physical development. High school athletics also have an influence on peer groups and the functioning of the student body, and hard choices often have to be made about how to finance athletic programs.

Character Development Through Athletic Participation

Supporters of high school sport have trumpeted its value in helping young people develop a strong work ethic, good moral behavior, healthy attitudes toward fitness, and improved academic performance. Let's see if those claims have been backed up by research.

Studies such as those by Dworkin, Larson, and Hansen (2003) and Gibbins, Ebbeck, and Weiss (1995) often compare the performance and attitudes of high school athletes to nonathletes and purport to demonstrate that athletes are superior to nonathletes in the traits just mentioned. However, what is not clear from the research is whether athletes already possessed these traits due to other influences in their life or if in fact athletics was a major contributing factor. Simply reporting that athletes appear to have higher levels of physical, social, or moral development compared to nonathletes does not prove that there is a cause-and-effect relationship between athletes' experience in sport and their academic performance, attitude toward fitness, moral behavior, and work ethic.

It is possible that athletes already display more progress toward a higher standard in these traits, and this progress helps them to perform successfully on athletic teams. Some studies such as those by Fejgin (1994) and Rees and Miracle (2004) have followed students over time and measured student performance. Generally, these studies showed that athletes are more likely to come from economically privileged backgrounds and have above-average cognitive skills, self-esteem, and academic performance. Of course it is also possible that students who are less privileged or weak in cognitive skills withdraw from sport or are excluded because of poor grades, thus affecting the results of such studies. These results are not that different from research on all students who participate in extracurricular activities in school. In general, students who choose to join musical groups, drama, debate clubs, school newspapers, and so on also show higher levels of development than the bulk of the student body.

Adults who have gone on to success in business or a profession often attribute their success to lessons they learned on the playing field. From their point of view, sport participation is vital for success in later life. A 1987 survey of individuals at the level of executive vice president or above in Fortune 500 companies indicated that 95% had participated in high school sport while 54% were involved in student government, 43% in the National Honor Society, 37% in music, and 18% in their school's

Activity Time-Out: Is Sport Participation Good or Bad?

What do you think? Does high school sport contribute to the development of the positive traits mentioned earlier? Find at least three studies that contribute to your conviction that sports do or do not have these positive effects. You might begin by researching the following Web sites:

NFHS.org

drugabuse.com

womenssportsfoundation.org

Summarize each of the studies in a paragraph, add another paragraph based on your personal experience in sport, and draw your conclusion based upon the evidence.

publications. It is possible that those people would have been successful regardless of their sport experience, but their personal belief and testimony can be a powerful argument (Texas University Interscholastic League 1998).

Most studies of high school students in sport have focused on the years of their participation. However, a comprehensive study by Carlson and Scott (2005) tracked over 25,000 high school athletes eight years after their senior year to see if sport participation had any lasting effects. The results showed that high school athletes are more likely than nonathletes to participate in physical fitness activities or recreational sport, graduate from college, be employed full time, and earn a higher salary and are less likely to be smokers. The most glaring negative factor associated with athletic participation was a tendency toward binge drinking. These results confirmed the conclusions of earlier studies (Barber, Eccles, and Stone 2001) that found higher rates of drinking and binge drinking among athletes compared to nonathletes.

Social Effects on the Student Body

In thousands of high schools, sport promotes school spirit; creates an "us against them" mentality; and offers natural social gatherings at pep rallies, sport events, and ceremonies. Attendance at sport events to root for friends and acquaintances strengthens the bonds between groups of students. Athletic teams often support each other by visiting each other's practices or games and cheering each other on.

Educators would point out that athletics are not the only school activity that have similar positive effects. In fact, the NFHS, which was cited previously, is not devoted solely to interscholastic sport, but includes all cocurricular activities. Its Web site devotes significant space to reasons to support all school-based cocurricular activities. For example, music and drama organizations often perform similar functions in after-school settings. Altogether, school activities outside of the academic curriculum cost an average of 1% to 3% of the overall school budget, according to the NFHS (2004a). However, across the United States, parents and communities have supported athletics more generously than any other school activity simply because of the number of students involved, the number of games, and the travel expenses incurred (Brady and Giler 2004b).

The social fabric of a school can also be negatively affected by the division between students who play sports and those who do not. Because athletes spend so much time together, are admired by other students, and receive plaudits from the community and media, they tend to socialize together, sometimes to the exclusion of other students. When the jock culture separates itself from the student body at large, envy and mistrust often sets in. Some misguided athletes interpret their social standing to mean that deviant behavior on their part is acceptable, and various offenses by prominent athletes often hit the front pages of local newspapers with tales of poor judgment and errant behavior.

Since many students envy athletes, particularly males, the emphasis on academic performance may suffer somewhat for all students. In spite of the fact that athletes seem to be on average better students than the norm, students who excel in the classroom are regarded as nerds in social circles. Fortunately, there are many examples of students who do well both in academics and athletics. This has been particularly true of female athletes.

Gender equity has transformed the scene in local high schools by including girls in the athletic culture. Young women now have many of the same

How much of a role does athletics have in school unity? How can athletics lead to disunity among students?

opportunities for self-development, competitive training, recognition, and college athletic scholarships that formerly were restricted to young men. Girls have to learn to balance academics, sport, and their social life in a way that didn't exist before the passage of Title IX in the 1970s. Conflicts between generations, tradition, and a society that used to encourage women solely toward a nurturing role in life have been inevitable. Girls are faced with acting as gutsy, tough competitors on the athletic field and then resuming a more traditional feminine role in their social environment where they are supposed to focus on clothes, personal appearance, and boys. For some girls, the challenge is intimidating and they often lack role models in teachers or parents because earlier generations simply did not have the same experiences.

Financial Issues

In recent years, as school districts face mounting budget crises, they often offer interscholastic sport and other extracurricular activities as areas to be cut, eliminated, or subsidized with user fees. An article by Brady and Giler in *USA Today* (2004a) recounted the dilemma in Fairfield, Ohio, where voters were asked to approve a higher tax levy with a budget increase that would support extracurricular activities, including sport. The tax levy was voted down and fees for all after-school activities were put in place. A parents group was organized to raise money to help support the activities, but they are having a tough time meeting the costs of the programs. Kids who choose a sport or other cocurricular activity have to pay a participation fee ranging from $100 U.S. to over $1,000 U.S. for some sports.

Fairfield's experience is not unique. The *USA Today* survey of states revealed that schools in 34 states charge for after-school activities, including sport (Brady and Giler 2004a). The numbers increased during the 1980s and 1990s as school budgets became tighter. Most often, the fees are levied in suburban towns where parents are used to paying for their children to play youth sport. Most schools that charge fees have waivers for those who can demonstrate an inability to pay.

It is easy to see that a family with several children who want to play multiple sports in public schools could easily be faced with a bill of several thousand dollars a year. The reality of this prospect is that eventually only middle- and upper-class students

When athletes are forced to pay for their athletic participation, unique fund-raising methods are often needed.

would be able to play sports. In many schools that charge fees to participate in sport, the number of athletes has dropped as much as 30% (Brady and Giler 2004b). This certainly conflicts with the prevailing educational policy for public schools of providing equal opportunity for children from all income levels in the United States.

Funding for cocurricular activities typically consumes only 1% to 3% of the total education budget. In the city of Chicago, that figure is even smaller. In 1999, the Chicago Board of Education had a total budget of $2.6 billion U.S., and activity programs cost $2.9 million U.S., or a miniscule one-tenth of 1% (.001) (NFHS 2004a). At the risk of seeming cynical, one could suspect that school officials and politicians often use sport as a bargaining chip in order to convince the public to vote for more money

for public schools. They cut athletics first, and when the predictable public outcry materializes, the politicians respond with the solution: Vote for the increase to save school sport. Sometimes this strategy works, but it often fails and sport programs are reduced, eliminated, or offered on a fee system.

Another effect of money on high school sport is that in affluent, suburban communities the athletic programs are typically more extensive, have better facilities, have more qualified coaches, and contend for state championships year after year. These communities spend more on facilities and teams, a key factor in the programs' success. Another key factor is that most kids grow up playing organized youth sport and taking lessons in various sports like tennis, golf, sailing, and so on.

COLLEGIATE SPORT

College sport has shown tremendous growth in the past 50 years. From the early days of student-supported athletic teams who played other local colleges, college athletics today is more diverse and offers opportunities for both men and women. Since the 1970s we've seen the following changes:

- Gender equity in response to Title IX, opening up doors for women including athletic scholarships
- Refinement of competitive divisions within the NCAA to Divisions I, II, and III along with similar divisions of play within the other organizations (NAIA and NJCAA)
- Support of championships for more sports for both men and women at all levels
- Separation of big-time college programs from the majority, which are more modest in expectation and expense and are closer to the original educational mission

For the purposes of this discussion, collegiate sport refers to those athletic programs at four-year institutions that are members of the National Collegiate Athletic Association (NCAA), by far the largest and most influential organization for college sport. Rules for conducting college sport are determined by NCAA member schools and enforced by their professional staff. There are 1,265 member institutions that represent approximately 355,000 student-athletes who participate in varsity intercollegiate sport. Approximately 44,000 athletes participate in 87 different NCAA championship events in 22 sports (NCAA 2004b).

Activity Time-Out: School-Supported Sport

Assume that both interscholastic sport and other cocurricular activities such as music, drama, and the school newspaper are positive educational activities. Make a case that they should be supported by schools without user fees in the same way that academic programs are offered in public schools. Be sure to justify the expense with some hard data rather than simply opinion and emotion.

The National Association of Intercollegiate Athletics (NAIA) includes about 300 smaller schools mainly in the South and offers national championships. Membership has declined as the NCAA has offered more opportunities for small schools. Over 100 Christian colleges also maintain membership in the National Christian College Athletic Association (NCCAA), although most have a dual membership in the NCAA. Two-year schools are governed by the National Junior College Athletic Association, which has 550 member institutions. All of these organizations have limited budgets, staff, and influence compared with the NCAA, which essentially controls the majority of college athletics.

In this section, we'll look at some participation trends in collegiate sport, the struggle for control of women's athletic programs, distinctions between different divisions, positive and negative effects of intercollegiate sport, and potential changes for the future.

Participation

Participation in NCAA college athletics has grown from a total of 231,445 students in 1981 to 1982 to 375,000 in 2003 to 2004 in sports for which the NCAA conducts championships. The most eye-popping figure is that women's participation has ballooned from 64,390 in 1981 to 1982 to 149,115, while men's participation is up from 167,055 to 206,573 (NCAA 2002). Equally impressive is the growth in the number of students who participated in NCAA championships: 21,904 students participated in 1992 to 1993 compared with 44,660 in 2004. That increase is primarily the result of an expansion of play-offs in all divisions of competition.

The number of women's championship sport teams has increased each year for 22 years while the number of men's teams has decreased 5 of the last 10 years up to 2004. There are more men's and women's teams in basketball than in any other sport (NCAA 2004b). The top sports are as follows:

Men

1. Basketball		5. Tennis
2. Cross country		6. Soccer
3. Baseball		7. Track and field
4. Golf		8. Football

Women

1. Basketball		5. Soccer
2. Volleyball		6. Tennis
3. Cross country		7. Track and field
4. Softball		

The average NCAA university sponsors approximately 17 teams, 8 for men and 9 for women. The trend of more teams for women began in 1997 and has continued to the present day. The sport with the most new teams added since 1988 is women's soccer with 551 new programs. Other sports for women that have been added, in order of most teams added, include golf, indoor track and field, cross country, softball, and outdoor track and field. For men, indoor track and field has the most new teams since 1988 with 289 new teams. In order of most teams added, other new teams are cross country, golf, outdoor track and field, and rowing (NCAA 2004b).

Since 1988, 2,161 men's teams were dropped compared with 1,462 women's teams. The women's sports that tend to be dropped in order of most dropped teams are cross country, golf, indoor and outdoor track and field, and tennis. For men, the sports that have been dropped in order of most dropped teams are indoor track and field, tennis, cross country, golf, rowing, outdoor track, swimming and diving, and wrestling (NCAA 2004b).

There have also been trends in the number of athletes participating who are from different ethnic backgrounds (see table 7.1). Notably, both male and female Black athletes have steadily increased their participation percentage in basketball and male Black athletes have done the same in football.

TABLE 7.1 Student-Athlete Ethnicity Percentages for 2003-2004

White		Black		Other	
Men	Women	Men	Women	Men	Women
All sports					
71.4	78.2	18.0	10.6	10.6	11.2
Football					
61.4		32.3		6.3	
Basketball					
49.6	64.2	42.0	27.0	8.4	8.8

Data from NCAA. www.ncaa.org.

Control of Women's Collegiate Athletics

In the 1960s, women in college athletics were governed by the Division of Girls and Women in Sport (DGWS) of the American Alliance for Health, Physical Education and Dance, who had taken the position of supporting low-key competition for women. Wary of the abuses and negative publicity (such as recruiting scandals, gambling on game outcomes, and paying of athletes with improper inducements) that had befallen men's programs, leaders in women's sport were determined to avoid the pitfalls. As the women's movement gained steam in the early 1970s, pressure began to build to offer intercollegiate competition for women similar to that enjoyed by men. A national organization, the Intercollegiate Athletics for Women (AIAW), was founded in 1972, including charter membership to 276 institutions. Within the next 10 years, AIAW boasted 971 member institutions and sponsored 42 national championships in 19 sports.

The AIAW was run by female administrators and coaches who were dedicated to an education-based model of competitive athletics. The goal was to create student-athletes with an emphasis on the sport experience rather than the scoreboard. Athletic scholarships were virtually nonexistent although a television contract with NBC to show women's sports was negotiated and implemented. The leaders of the AIAW were determined to forge their own path to benefit collegiate women and avoid the potential traps of men's collegiate athletics, including commercialism, sponsorships, competitive obsessions with winning, and devaluation of scholarship (Hawes 1999, 2001; Holway 2005; Katz 2005).

After just 10 short years, the AIAW went out of business in 1981 and merged with the NCAA, yielding to the pressure to embrace equal opportunities for women to compete for national championships and athletic scholarships as the men had long done. The leaders of the NCAA realized the potential benefits of including women's athletics within their umbrella, such as sponsorship recruitment. Suddenly, the future of women's sport changed dramatically and moved significantly toward the male model of college sports. Many female leaders lost their influential roles and were replaced by male administrators, although they did fight for representation on committees, on boards, and in athletic departments.

The merger of the AIAW with the NCAA heralded progress for women, but at a cost. While opportunities for women expanded, the philosophy of women's sport was sacrificed and replaced by one similar to that of men's sport. Women lost the power to set their own philosophy, rules, and agenda as they were absorbed into the powerful male-dominated NCAA. Yet as a social movement, the merger was a crucial step to help create a better collegiate athletic environment for all athletes regardless of gender.

With the adoption of Title IX and the eventual takeover of women's collegiate sport by the NCAA, athletic programs for both genders began on a path of equality. As new leadership, which now included some males, took over women's sport, they demanded equal rights, pay, and playing opportunities. Many men jumped at opportunities to coach

Activity Time-Out: Racial Groups in Sport Participation

Review the percentages in table 7.1 by racial groups and compare them to the percentages of racial groups in the United States according to the U.S. Census. Are some racial groups overrepresented in collegiate sport overall or just certain sports? If that is the case, what might be an explanation for the deviation from the overall averages?

women's sports and helped lead the charge toward equality.

Initially, women who had been in charge of women's athletics at their institution typically lost their power and were forced to serve under male athletic directors. It took several decades, but gradually, leaders in the athletic departments of many institutions included women in influential positions, and eventually pioneering women at various institutions took over full control of both men's and women's sports.

Divisions of Collegiate Athletic Programs

Fifty years ago, the NCAA divided all colleges into just two divisions, university and college, and championships were conducted at those two levels. In 1973, membership was divided into three categories, and in recent years, those divisions have been refined to include five. They include three at Division I: IA, which includes 117 schools with big-time football programs; IAA, which includes 123 schools with smaller football programs based on stadium size and average game attendance; and IAAA, which includes 88 schools without football teams. Colleges determine the level at which they will compete provided they meet the requirements of that level. For example, a school that chooses to compete in Division IA must schedule other Division IA opponents and support at least seven sports for men and seven for women. To participate in Division IA football, attendance of at least 17,000 at home games is required as is a stadium with permanent seats for 30,000.

Division II has 270 members and Division III has 410 members. Members of these divisions offer less ambitious athletic programs. Division III schools do not offer athletic scholarships, although they do permit grants based on financial need. Both divisions offer championships against other teams in the division, although in some smaller sports, the divisions are combined (NCAA 2005b). Separating out the big-time programs to the top Division I schools is still not the whole story. Of that number,

only about 100 schools make money on their football program. The remaining 128 schools actually lose money most years. The schools in Division IAAA choose to not even attempt football and instead stake their athletic reputation on men's basketball as their showcase sport. Generally, these are smaller schools that want exposure and name recognition without the attendant financial risk.

When you consider all Division I sports, only men's basketball and football can boast that about half of their programs actually report revenues that exceed expenses. Men's basketball had the highest percentage with 52% of programs earning revenue, while men's football showed 50% of programs earning revenue. No other sports are even close, with most sports averaging about 10% to 20% of programs that actually generate revenue (Sylvester 2004).

Sports pages abound with stories on college athletics, football factories, athlete abuse, coaching indiscretions, behavioral problems and deviance by athletes, and racial exploitation. Most criticism is directed at and emanates from big-time college programs; that's where the juicy stories that attract attention come from.

Clearly, the vast majority of colleges do not run big-time athletic programs or suffer from the same problems to the same degree. Particularly in Ivy League and Division III schools, athletic programs are more likely to maintain high academic standards, minimize expenses, compete locally rather than nationally, limit recruiting, and resemble the original educational mission of athletics. The original mission of college athletics was to support and enhance the educational and academic mission of universities. However, their influence at the NCAA level is modest since the larger Division I schools heavily influence much of the decision making.

Typically, the larger state universities that were land-grant institutions are the ones who dominate college football. Federal legislation required every state to set aside land for an educational institution. Thus, state-supported universities were founded

Activity Time-Out: College Versus Professional Sport

Investigate at least 25 states that have state universities and Division I football teams. Note the size of the town they are located in and how close the nearest professional football franchise is.

Activity Time-Out: Athletic Scholarships . . . Yea or Nay?

According to the NCAA, the estimated total for athletic grants-in-aid for 2000 was $975,000,000 U.S. (NCAA 2002). In no more than two pages, make a case for or against the awarding of athletic scholarships at collegiate institutions.

in the late 1800s, and in the next century many established athletic programs. The size of their budgets, facilities, available land, and geographic location were all positive factors. Typically located in geographically isolated spots, such as Gainesville, Florida, or Lincoln, Nebraska, college teams offered the only big-time sport in the area. Without competition from professional teams, university football teams became almost like a religion in the regions. In contrast, university-sponsored teams in cities typically have not flourished and just can't compete with the local professional franchise in terms of attracting fans, coverage by the media, or revenue.

Championships have grown in number and athlete participation over the past 20 years. The numbers show that in the past 10 years alone, the number of participants has doubled. Women's programs have begun to rival men's in some sports, particularly basketball and soccer (NCAA 2004b). NCAA Division II has experimented with a festival program of combining spring national championships at one location in an Olympic-type setting once every four years. By capitalizing on the economy of scale, media coverage, and the synergy of many sports in one locale, the experience for athletes is a memorable one.

The inaugural event was held in 2004 to rave reviews and plans call for these events to continue and expand to other sports in Division II (NCAA 2005a). Proposals are now being solicited for the 2008 event that will include more than 600 athletes in men's and women's golf, men's and women's tennis, women's softball, and women's lacrosse over a 10-day period. Research is under way to replicate this model for fall sports beginning in 2006.

Scholarships for Division I and II Schools

Many parents dream that their children will earn an athletic scholarship to pay for part or all of their college education. The reality is that a very small percentage of all children who start out in youth sport end up with college scholarships. However, athletic scholarships are not out of reach, especially if the child is in the right sport, is a good student, and is open to any school that offers financial aid. Many athletic scholarships go unclaimed each year, primarily for women, from colleges that are less known and less popular choices.

The number of athletic grants-in-aid rose from a total of 58,398 in 1992 to 70,619 in 2000. The largest change over that period of time was the proportion awarded to women. In 1992, only 33% of grants-in-aid were awarded to women while by 2000, 42% were awarded to women (NCAA 2002). Rules for scholarship limits are set by the NCAA for each sport in order to level the playing field. The number of scholarships is determined as a ratio of the number of starting players needed to field a team. Of course, the limits for football are by far the largest because schools claim that due to the violent nature of the game, schools need more athletes in a backup role. When schools award more than 90 scholarships for men in football, you can see how many spots for women in other sports are necessary to match that number. Sports like tennis, golf, archery, and so on may only allow eight scholarships. Thus the battle for equal distribution of scholarships for women and men is affected in a major way by football.

A particularly thorny issue in some sports such as track and field, tennis, swimming, soccer, and even basketball is the recruiting of international athletes and awarding them full athletic scholarships. The result in collegiate tennis has been an almost compete domination of the top 50 players in the collegiate rankings by players from other countries. American families who have spent thousands of dollars on their child's tennis development feel betrayed by a system that awards scholarships, often using public funds, to support foreign athletes rather than their children. Legal challenges have not held up in court and the issue persists.

You might ask why international athletes are chosen over their American counterparts. Most of the answer lies in the fact that in other countries, there is no such thing as an amateur player, and many tennis players accept money, play professional events, and have racket and clothing sponsors from a young age. Their experience, training, and financial support are limited only by their performance. American children, on the other hand, are not allowed to accept prize money or endorsements if they want to maintain their amateur status to be eligible for college athletics. The issue of international athletes in American colleges is complex and a solution doesn't seem to be in sight.

Revenues and Expenses for Collegiate Athletics by Division

The NCAA reports the total average revenues versus expenses for athletic programs in their various divisions. Based on the numbers in table 7.2, you might conclude that it pays to sponsor football at the IA level since at every other level with or without football, the expenses of the total program exceed the revenue. However, the total average budget for Division IA is four times that of lower-level programs.

Positive and Negative Effects of Intercollegiate Sport

As we've seen, it is impossible to lump all college athletic programs together since they vary widely. For the purpose of this section, we will divide our analysis into two primary groups: colleges that offer athletic programs that are modest in expense and intensity, representing around 800 colleges and universities, versus the group of roughly 300 highly competitive programs at schools where athletics follows a corporate structure and are classified as Division IA or IAA by the NCAA.

Pressure to Generate Income for the University

Major college sport programs are run as corporate businesses that pay no taxes. Typically, the university expects them to at least be revenue neutral, or break even. Of course, that means many schools have to secure an invitation to postseason play in order to earn the dollars guaranteed from bowl games or basketball play-offs to achieve a balanced budget.

Whether the budget is actually balanced is a source of discussion at many schools. It is often difficult to calculate the total expense for the athletic program when administrators assign various costs to other units of the college. For example, facilities are often charged to the state or other building funds, student activity fees support fitness and weight rooms, and stadiums are built or renovated using other development funds.

Whatever the cost, the expectations over the years at many notable universities have included outstand-

TABLE 7.2 Revenue and Expenses by Division for 2002-2003

Division	Average total revenue ($U.S.)	Average total expense ($U.S.)
IA	29,400,000	27,200,000
IAA	7,200,000	7,500,000
IAAA	6,200,000	6,500,000
II with football	2,600,000	2,700,000
II without football	1,700,000	1,900,000
III with football	N/A	1,570,000
III without football	N/A	900,000

Data from NCAA Report on Revenues and Expenses for Division I, II, and III. www.ncaa.org.

ing athletic teams, particularly in the major sports. You only have to check the last few years' football bowl games and NCAA basketball tournaments to compose a list of the top 50 schools that traditionally vie for national recognition.

Schools that support Division I athletic programs often justify their expenditures by pointing out that high-profile winning programs generate volumes of publicity for the university, contribute to school spirit among students, and increase donations from alumni and other prominent supporters.

Taking it one step further, some schools claim that based on the success of their athletic teams, more students apply for admission allowing them to select the very best of prospective applicants. In other words, successful sports teams also improve the academic level of the school.

Although several studies reviewed by Frank (2004) suggest these results are not likely, most of us know that generally people are drawn to winning programs. (See Athlete Recruitment on page 130 for more on this study.) We also can point to examples such as the University of Connecticut. In the mid-1990s, the University of Connecticut (UConn) was a modest regional institution that sought to be the finest university in New England. Not content with that modest goal, a few visionaries set higher standards to raise the profile of UConn to a nationally recognized university. The state legislature funded over $1 billion U.S. in new construction, transforming a utilitarian state university into an attractive modern campus. Next came success in men's and women's basketball, culminating in a national championship for both teams in 2004. UConn was on the map, and everyone in the country knew where it was. The

Activity Time-Out: Top 25

Without consulting any rankings or results, see if you can name at least 25 institutions that typically have successful football or basketball programs. Once you have your list, compare it with the lists of classmates and develop a composite list that includes the schools that were most often represented. Discuss the publicity benefits to these universities of their competitive results. Do the benefits justify the expenditures to support a top-level athletic program?

football team upgraded to Division IA and in 2004 received its first postseason bowl bid to the Motor City Bowl in Detroit, where it defeated the University of Toledo to conclude with a record of 8-4.

You might wonder if there is a correlation between all of this campus improvement, publicity, and sport success. The SAT scores for admission at UConn have increased steadily over the last five years. What used to be a safety school for state residents suddenly became the place to go. Can you think of other schools where a similar phenomenon has occurred? A few examples come to mind of schools that were virtually unknown before the exploits of one of their athletic teams thrust them into the public spotlight, if only briefly. Consider schools like Boise State, Gonzaga, University of South Florida, and University of Nevada at Las Vegas. An upset win on the football field or in the NCAA basketball tournament suddenly pushes schools onto the national stage.

Athlete Recruitment

William Bowen, former president of Princeton University, and Sarah Levin published a book, *Reclaiming the Game* (2003), in which they document the results of athletic recruitment and college outcomes of athletes compared to nonathletes at 33 highly selective academic institutions. Relying on data from Ivy League schools, Seven Sisters colleges, and other prestigious universities, Bowen and Levin expose the negative sides of college sport at schools that do not even offer athletic scholarships.

Some of the negative findings include the fact that athletes are four times as likely to gain admission to college as other students with comparable academic credentials. Their data also showed that athletes are substantially more likely to be in the bottom third of their college class than students who do not play sports. Recruited athletes also tend to underperform academically in college compared to the predictions based on their test scores and high school grades. Of

course, these are not the schools we think of when we think big-time college sport. It is rare when a team from Princeton, Harvard, or Yale contends at the national level.

In 2004, Robert Frank of Cornell presented a report to the prestigious Knight Commission on Intercollegiate Athletics. The report included an assessment of the effect of winning teams on applicants and on alumni donations. Citing a review of six studies conducted between 1987 and 2003, Frank reported that although there appeared to be several instances of small gains in admissions as measured by higher SAT scores, the increases were minor and not statistically significant. He also mentions the popular example of Boston College reporting a 12% gain in applicants after Doug Flutie chucked a miracle pass to win the 1984 Orange Bowl.

Frank also reviewed more than a dozen studies that measured the effect of athletic success on alumni donations. Although most studies showed little effect at statistically significant levels, one study did show that appearances at football bowl games and basketball tournaments do positively affect donations. Frank's conclusion, however, is that there is little empirical evidence to support the contention that it takes a winning team or program to secure alumni donations.

Historically, the Carnegie Commission for the Advancement of Teaching warned of the abuses in college athletics back in 1929. They cited corrupt recruiting practices, lack of professionalism of athletes, commercialism, and neglected education. Sadly, those same issues are being debated today in spite of numerous efforts to reform college sport.

One of the most comprehensive analyses of intercollegiate sport was conducted by the Knight Commission on Intercollegiate Athletics (2001) beginning in the early 1990s. The analysis was conducted because the foundation's board of trustees felt that

When recruitment violations are discovered, the fallout can be severe. For example, allegations of illegal recruiting practices at the University of Colorado led to the temporary suspension of then head football coach Gary Barnett in 2004 and to the resignation of athletic director Dick Tharp and university president Elizabeth Hoffman in March of 2005.

athletics were threatening the integrity of higher education. Some of the problems the commission cited as justification for its research were as follows:

- In the 1980s, 109 colleges were censured or put on probation by the NCAA. That included more than half of Division IA schools, or 57 out of 106.
- Nearly a third of present and former professional football players said they had accepted illicit payments while in college and more than half said they saw nothing wrong with it.
- Of the 106 institutions in Division IA, 48 had graduation rates under 30% for male basketball players and 19 had the same low rate for football players.

It seems there is a new scandal involving big-time sport programs nearly every month. Football and men's basketball are the magnets for most of the scrutiny and deservedly so. They're the big-money sports and temptations loom for athletes, coaches, and administrators.

The work of the Knight Commission has continued through the 1990s and the impact has been felt beyond 2000. Various reports on the study have been widely circulated in the media and pressed into the hands of college presidents and boards of trustees. Essentially, the Knight Commission advocated a one-plus-three model for reform that requires presidential control directed toward academic integrity, financial integrity, and independent certification that universities are meeting the standards set for athletic programs. Their view was that reform of college sport will never be achieved to everyone's satisfaction; it is an ongoing process that needs continuous work.

Although the Knight Commission has no formal authority, by 2003, the NCAA had adopted almost two-thirds of its recommendations. Most notable was the overhaul of the governance structure of the NCAA, which put college presidents in charge rather than athletic directors. That way if reform initiatives were to fail, it would be patently clear who should shoulder the blame.

The conclusion of the commission is that in spite of the changes to rules, the enforcement efforts of the NCAA, and the leadership of college presidents, the threat of college athletics operating without supervision or accountability to university leaders has increased rather than diminished. The commission calls on all members of the higher-education community to unite to address the problems and clean up college athletics.

One reformist group that has taken up the gauntlet is the Drake Group–National Alliance for College Athletic Reform (NAFCAR). Based out of Drake University in Iowa, NAFCAR is an alliance of college faculty members at various institutions who propose to

- eliminate the term *student-athlete,* thereby eliminating the special status often given to students who happen to play college sports;

- remove control of special academic counseling and support programs from athletic programs and make faculty senates responsible instead;

- publicly disclose academic information about all students, although not by name, as to courses enrolled in, grade point average, and course instructors;

- reduce the number of athletic contests; and

- eliminate athletic scholarships and expand need-based financial aid (Drake Group 2000).

Although there is not at this time a full-scale reform movement that is well organized or funded, the signs of a gathering storm are there. In general, the fight is against an increasingly commercialized and professional monopoly of college sport. As a training ground for a small proportion of eventual professional athletes, big-time college sport is simply a minor league.

Critics of the NCAA assert that while it talks about cleaning up college sport abuses, it simply goes about its business, perpetuating the status quo (Splitt 2004). It thus falls to various reform groups to pressure college presidents, boards of trustees, the public, and the media to call for reform (Lipsyte 2003).

Perhaps the most important step is simply to educate everyone on the facts of the matter. One group, founded by Richard Lapchick at Northeastern University, is the Institute for the Study of Sport and Society. Lapchick has now moved on to the University of Central Florida and has established a similar center there. His contribution has been to publish statistics on the graduation rates of college athletes, on race and correlates with graduation, on minority coach proportions, and on gender equity issues (Lapchick 2004).

Expert's View: Academic Standards in the Patriot League

John Feinstein (2001) is the author of *The Last Amateurs: Playing for Glory and Honor in Division I College Basketball.* Feinstein takes a look at the Patriot League, a team of seven schools including Colgate, Army, Navy, Bucknell, Lehigh, Lafayette, and Holy Cross. Although they are Division I schools and the league winner qualifies for the NCAA national basketball championship, this is not a conference populated with athletes in training for a professional career. Scholarships are few and are mostly based on need. The amazing thing is that none of these schools alters admission standards for basketball players, and one school, Bucknell University, has led the nation three times in graduation rates of men's basketball players (Bucknell University 2004).

Feinstein says, "Big-time college athletics are spinning out of control. I feel a great disconnect with big-time programs because 95% of the players are simply pros in training, and the term 'student-athlete' has become an oxymoron" (2001).

The only similar Division I athletic conference is the Ivy League. These two leagues have a different view of the role of athletics at their institutions compared to the big-time athletic schools. Although the games are intense, exciting, and fiercely competitive, the athletes are of a decidedly different caliber than those at schools that are stocked with players who hope to go pro.

Check out a copy of this book from your school library and see for yourself an alternative approach to the pervasive rush to semiprofessional college athletes and teams.

College As a Training Ground for Professional Athletes

Undoubtedly, one of the major factors that affects the academic performance and graduation rate of athletes in Division IA universities is that some athletes may have little or no interest or ability in school. Their motivation for going to college is to continue their training to become a professional athlete, and colleges offer the next step of training at no charge. Division IA college teams function like a minor league, or a development league, in football and men's basketball, the two big revenue-producing sports. These two sports are unlike baseball, which has had its own minor-league system for development of young players for many years although the number of minor league baseball teams has declined in recent years. Unfortunately, the odds of athletes making it from high school to top-level colleges to the professional ranks are extremely long. Consider table 7.3, which shows statistics published by the NCAA.

Out of approximately half a million boys and half a million girls who play high school basketball, only about 5,000 boys and 5,000 girls will play at a Division I institution. Those 5,000 boys will vie for 350 roster spots in professional basketball while the girls duke it out for only 168 spots. Of course, that includes beating out seasoned veterans who are already there.

The sad fact is, many young people, particularly from lower socioeconomic backgrounds, pin all their hopes on a successful career as a professional athlete. When that dream doesn't materialize, their absence of preparation for life through academics catches up with them. With limited skills and no college degree, their options are severely limited. We look more closely at this issue in chapters 11 and 13.

Social Issues and College Athletics

A number of social issues are constantly under scrutiny regarding college athletic programs, including the following (Splitt 2004):

- The differing standards for admission at many schools for athletes compared to other applicants. Although athletes must meet minimum requirements, at all types of institutions, including Ivy League schools, coaches often can recommend admission for a limited number of athletes who meet the minimum standard but not the average of other students who are offered admission.

- The recruiting practices to attract athletes to big-time programs, including lavish entertainment, parties, escorts, and other questionable practices. The University of Colorado made headlines in 2003 and 2004 when problems such as alleged football-recruiting violations, including use of sex, alcohol, and drugs to entice potential recruits; cases of sexual assault; binge drinking; and maintaining an athletic slush fund were exposed.

- The separation of athletes from the social fabric of campus life by having them live together in dormitories, eat together, attend required study sessions as a group, and workout in the weight room to the exclusion of a normal college life. The sense of entitlement that many athletes enjoy is only heightened in college, which may lead young men and women to act in socially unacceptable ways, sometimes even breaking laws.

- The encouragement by coaches or others for athletes to take minimum academic loads or less rigorous courses to ensure eligibility.

- The lack of female administrators and coaches in women's sports.

- The lack of coaches from minority groups except at historically Black colleges.

- Spotty attendance at classes due to frequent and sometimes sustained travel to compete in their sport.

TABLE 7.3   Professional Career Probability

	Men's basketball (%)	Women's basketball (%)	Football (%)	Baseball (%)	Men's soccer (%)	Men's ice hockey (%)
High school to NCAA	2.9	3.1	5.8	5.6	5.7	12.9
NCAA to professional	1.3	1.0	2.0	10.5	1.9	4.1
High school to professional	.03	.02	.09	.5	.08	.4

Estimated by percentage of students moving from one level to the next.

Diana Taurasi is one of the select few who made the transition from college athlete to professional athlete.

- The constant battle to meet the requirements of Title IX to ensure equal opportunity for sport participation for both men and women.

- The use of sport events by students as opportunities for binge drinking, wild parties, and rowdy behavior. When teams win or lose big games, it is not uncommon for students to get out of control on the field or in the community.

All of these issues have been addressed by the NCAA, various athletic conferences, and individual schools. Some progress has been made but vigilance must be consistent to prevent abuses (Brand 2004).

Equity Between Men's and Women's Sport

The rise in women's opportunities since the passage of Title IX in 1972 has still not resulted in equality between men and women. Fewer women play college sports than men and advocates for women contend that it simply isn't true that women choose not to play.

An unintended consequence of the enforcement of Title IX has led many colleges to drop men's sports that don't produce revenue in order to beef up their offerings for women. Cancellation of men's programs in wrestling, swimming, tennis, and others has raised the hackles of alumni, coaches, and governing bodies of those sports. For some Olympic sports, college provided the coaching and training for their athletes and the loss of programs hurts the United States' prospects in international competition. (See page 125 for some examples of dropped programs in both men's and women's collegiate sports.)

The crux of the matter is football. The expense and the huge number of athletic scholarships required make it difficult to offset with comparable women's sports. Some athletic leaders contend that if football were left out of the equation in enforcing Title IX, the sport opportunities would be quite comparable. Of course, keep in mind that only about 100 out of 1,200 colleges sponsor big-time football, and only half of those make money for the university.

The process of integrating equal opportunity for women into college athletics is a long, slow process. No easy solution appears imminent, but public pressure, legal battles, and changing expectations for girls starting in youth sport and high school sport may force gradual change as society changes. More on this issue will be discussed in chapter 12.

Issues for Discussion and Possible Changes in College Sport

Changes in college athletics have been called for since 1929 when the Carnegie Report on Big Ten athletics was published in the *Chicago Tribune* (Splitt 2004). In fact, many changes have been made over the years. Enforcement by the NCAA has been strengthened and college coaches are required to understand and abide by the prescribed rules when they are hired. Yet with the pressure to succeed, some coaches ignore the rules or bend them, especially when encouraged to do so by alumni or athletic boosters.

The infractions and failures of athletic programs and individual athletes make headlines in the sports pages with appropriate hand-wringing from college officials, coaches, and sports writers. Yet, the abuses go on and seem to move from conference to conference and school to school. Perhaps the solution does not lie in setting more rules and stepping up enforcement, but in reevaluating the value of college athletics, establishing the role of sport within an educational setting, and modifying policies to reflect that consensus.

The money that is at stake is enormous. As we have seen, big-time college sport, particularly football and basketball, is big business. Imagine the pressure on those who suggest changes that might affect the status quo.

Here are some of the most compelling issues that face college sport. Consider them and spend some time discussing with your classmates the possible changes to the current situation. If you were to prioritize change, what issues would be highest on your list? Would you start with the most difficult problems, or with smaller issues that hold promise for change in the shorter term?

Is cutting men's swimming to get the resources needed to add women's rowing a good way to implement Title IX?

▪ *Money.* Supporting college athletic teams is expensive, and it seems that many institutions are operating their athletic department as a corporate business rather than an educational endeavor. Decisions are often made with the bottom line in mind rather than the welfare of the athletes.

▪ *Gender equity.* Although females outnumber males on college campuses 53% to 47%, the number of female athletes is only 43% versus 57% males. In dollar allocation, the scales tip more heavily toward males in that recruiting money, operating budgets, and coaching salaries award two-thirds of the money to men's sport and only a third to women's sport (Suggs 2002). Thirty years after the adoption of Title IX, equality of opportunity for males and females has not yet been achieved.

▪ *Negative effect on academics.* Particularly in big-time programs, athletes are expected to put athletic performance first. School dropout and graduation rates in men's football and basketball programs are well below general student averages.

▪ *Racial bias.* Black athletes are often recruited for their ability to earn money and fame for the institution. However, they may be unprepared academically for college, and little effort is made to remedy that gap. Some accuse college athletic programs of simply using Black athletes and then discarding them before graduation.

▪ *Athlete rights.* Most athletic departments keep a close rein on their athletes by limiting their free time, expecting them to perform for the university almost as professionals without the accompanying financial rewards.

Should athletes be paid for their involvement in college sport? This is a question that will continue to be debated.

▪ *Conflict with educational goals.* Although athletic departments extol the virtues of sport for building character, independence, good decision making, and mental toughness, their practices and policies often stunt the development of these traits.

Athletes are expected to follow arbitrary rules and sacrifice their individual growth for the welfare of the team. While these practices may build character in a sense, perhaps the military is a more appropriate place to learn these life lessons than a college campus.

You may want to add issues according to your own research and experience. In any case, the question posed to all of us is, What can we do about these problems? Take some time to discuss possible solutions with your classmates, athletes, coaches, and administrators.

CHAPTER SUMMARY

This chapter looked at sport programs sponsored by high schools and universities. The major question considered at both levels was whether athletics is compatible with the educational goals of the institutions that sponsor them.

Evidence from research shows both positive and negative influences of athletics on the schools, the social structure, and the athletes themselves. Issues were presented with the hope that solutions can be found to preserve the best aspects of school-sponsored sport and mitigate some of the negative ones.

Over the past 20 years, participation in both high school and college athletics has increased, primarily due to a dramatic rise in participation by female athletes as a result of Title IX. Although opportunities for males and females are not yet equitable, they have moved significantly in that direction. As a result of new opportunities for girls, new problems have arisen, mostly centered on funding women's sport without paring back men's sport.

The issue of financial support for school-based sport was examined from a number of angles. In high school, while the proportion of total budget allocated for sport is modest, sport is often one of the first activities to be cut when schools face a budget crisis. The trend toward charging user fees for athletics threatens to put the sport experience out of reach for many students who come from modest economic backgrounds.

College sport was considered according to level of competition. The problems and publicity that make the sports pages typically involve abuses, cheating, and behavioral problems of athletes in Division I programs that are essentially businesses. Most collegiate athletic programs operate at a more modest level, suffer fewer problems of abuse, and more closely approximate the educational experience. However, those same schools wrestle with budget issues, gender equity, and racial imbalances.

At both the high school and college levels, the myth of the dumb jock has been discredited, although there are warning signs that some institutions encourage some athletes to emphasize athletic participation while allowing academic performance to lag behind. Socially, athletes are much admired by their peers, and their egos are sometimes inflated by adulation and praise from peers, coaches, and administrators. At some schools, the jock culture has become exclusionary and causes splits within the student body.

On balance, athletics in the educational setting are worth saving if educators and the public set clear goals, establish limits, and enforce standards for operation of sport programs within an agreed-upon framework and philosophy. Changes are likely to be gradual and will adjust to and reflect other societal trends including higher expectations from our educational system, eliminating racial and gender bias, and escalating costs to sponsor athletic teams out of university budgets.

International Sport

Student Outcomes

After reading this chapter, you will know the following:

- How and why sports have expanded globally
- How American sports, the Olympic Games, and nationalism affect worldwide sport
- How the media affect global sport expansion
- The roles of athletes and coaches as migrant workers in the sports world
- How sports affect the world at large

Although we have mostly focused on sport in North America and the United States, it would be a mistake not to consider the international role of sport. Competition between athletes from different countries has pushed every athlete to improve performance. The media revolution allows us to follow sports around the world and promotes sports in countries where they were once unknown. International travel by athletes, coaches, and others has helped us to learn about and appreciate different cultures and to forge ways of working together toward common goals.

As our world changes, it seems to shrink through technology connections and economic and political interdependency, and the sports world reflects our increasing globalization. Among the reasons for this trend in sport are the following:

- The media explosion that connects countries through the Internet, television, film, newspapers, magazines, and satellite transmission
- Marketing and retailing of sport equipment, clothing, shoes, and casual wear among countries
- The migration from country to country of athletes, coaches, officials, and sport administrators
- Exchange of values that reflect various cultures, attitudes toward competition, personal achievement, and socialization

GLOBALIZATION OF MODERN SPORT

The Greeks originated many of the athletic traditions practiced today. Most of the terms we use to describe sports come from Greek words such as *athlos,* which spawned *athletics.* Other words such as *gymnasium, stadium,* and *pentathlon* also are rooted in Greek.

Perhaps the most important contribution of ancient Greece was incorporating sport into their culture—a culture that has shaped much of our Western thought (Spears and Swanson 1978).

While modern sport is commonly credited to the Greeks, Great Britain had a huge hand in increasing the global popularity of sports. Great Britain had colonies in Africa, India, Singapore, Hong Kong, Australia, Canada, and the United States, and during the height of its influence in the 19th and early 20th centuries, "the sun never set" on the British Empire. Countries of the British Empire accounted for a quarter of the world's population. The British imported their language, customs, education systems, and law to their colonies. Each country belonging to the British Commonwealth was introduced to traditional English sports, and its citizens were encouraged to participate in sport as part of the preferred way of life. Competitions held within the British colonies attractively rewarded skilled athletes to further their ambition under the British flag (Maguire et al. 2002).

During the 17th and 18th centuries, the English developed the popular pastimes of the privileged, such as cricket, fox hunting, horse racing, and boxing, into sports and spread them to their colonies. During the 19th century, soccer (known worldwide as football), rugby, tennis, and track and field emerged as the next wave of popular sports. During the last 50 years, the sport system of the British Empire emerged as the dominant structure in worldwide sport competition. This system was founded on sports and games, highly skilled performers, and popularity with both participants and spectators (Elias and Dunning 1986).

Nationalism helped develop sport in countries whose popular sports were strongly rooted in their culture and stoked the competitive fires between nations seeking to demonstrate the athletic superiority of their citizens. Nations established sport competitions to promote their national spirit and pride. Geography influenced the national sports adopted by various counties as colder-climate countries naturally gravitated toward winter sports while more moderate-climate countries embraced warm-weather sports. Indoor sport arenas were constructed in more developed countries as a wider economic base encouraged sports based in indoor venues.

The Germans, Swedes, and Danish influenced gymnastics, while Norway helped develop winter sports such as skating and skiing. However, no country influenced modern sport as much as Great Britain did through its worldwide network of colonies and territories. Wherever the British went, they took their sports and games, which took root along with their government, law, and culture (Maguire 1999).

When the United States emerged as a world power, American sports began creeping onto the world stage. American football, baseball, basketball, volleyball, and lacrosse were uniquely American, while professional ice hockey flourished in Canada and then spread to the United States. Interchange among athletes, coaches, and officials of these sports and of traditional English sports promoted the globalization of both English and American sports. The influence of Western culture on world sport mirrored the political and economic dominance of the West. As the Communist world grew in importance, so did their influence on sports worldwide. During the Cold War years, Communist countries poured resources into high-performance athletes who captured worldwide attention as their governments claimed their success was rooted in their culture and political philosophies. Of course, the Western countries fought back to prove the superiority of their way of life.

Islamic and African countries have influenced worldwide sport the least. Generally, sports were incompatible with their culture, economic resources, religion, or attitudes toward gender roles. Efforts by international sport bodies to introduce sports in these countries have seen slow growth and isolated pockets of success. Track stars from Kenya are one example of a changing view of sports in Africa, and the growth of soccer in some countries has been significant.

In the last 20 years, the balance of power in worldwide sports has begun to shift. England has faded from contention on the international stage, and African, Asian, and South American countries have begun to dominate their former British mentors in sports like soccer, cricket, table tennis, and track and field. The Pacific Rim countries have emerged as a formidable force and fertile ground for development

Is the British colonization of India responsible for the popularity of cricket in that country? Or would cricket have arrived in India without the influence of Britain?

due to their population size, economic influence, and rising political power.

The selection of Beijing, China, as host of the 2008 Olympic Games was a remarkable departure from the norm. It was controversial because of China's history of Communism and because many people question China's record on human rights. Those concerns were balanced by recognition that China is a world power, home to nearly 20% of the world population and a huge engine in the world economy. Television broadcast rights were attractive and advertisers and sponsors eagerly entered what was a relatively new market for them. Four years after the 2008 Olympics, the Games will revert to a more traditional host, as London, England, won the bid to host the 2012 Summer Games.

Global Consumption of Sport

The worldwide emergence of companies such as Nike, Adidas, Puma, Reebok, and others has modified attitudes toward world consumers. Manufacturing of soccer shoes, balls, tennis rackets, sport uniforms, and so on has become a worldwide effort. Nike led

Although Morocco isn't known for its sport programs, Hicham El Guerrouj is arguably the greatest middle-distance runner in history. He won two gold medals in the 2004 Athens Olympics in the 1,500- and 5,000-meter events (O'Brien 2004).

the way, paying workers in developing countries 20 to 30 cents an hour to produce sport clothing (Kidd and Donnelly 2000). China, Indonesia, Thailand, and South Korea virtually cornered the market on manufacturing by supplying cheap labor and producing products at a fraction of the cost that they could be produced at in other countries. Multinational companies rushed to manufacture their products through these factories, added their markups, and sold their goods in developed countries at premium prices (Kidd and Donnelly 2000). As information leaked about the exploitation and low wages of these workers, especially children, Nike and other companies modified their practices to mitigate the resulting international outrage.

Sport clothing, starting with athletic shoes and eventually moving into casual wear, became a wardrobe staple in many societies. Starting with young people, athletic clothing began appearing at almost

any occasion. It's not uncommon to see retirees wear tracksuits in airports, malls, or anywhere else in public. The casual dress industry has captured the clothing market by focusing on comfort and encouraging a relaxed yet active lifestyle.

In some instances, economics may replace nationalism as the basis for choosing which teams and athletes to support, especially among people who profit from the success of sport clothing companies. Phil Knight, the founder and longtime president of Nike, admitted after recently stepping down in December of 2004, that he rooted for sport teams that wore Nike. Rather than cheering for the Americans in World Cup soccer in 1999, Knight picked his favorite teams by the uniforms they wore. Rather than look at the competition as U.S. versus Brazil, he saw it as Adidas versus Nike (Coakley 2004).

The United States Olympic Committee (USOC) accepts money from corporate sponsors to support the training and competition of American athletes. In return, U.S. athletes must wear the logo and warm-up apparel of the chosen USOC sponsor when competing in the Olympic Games. Imagine the outrage when a company like Nike, who paid millions to sponsor an athlete like Andre Agassi for years, finds out that during the Olympics Andre must shed Nike for the USOC brand.

Corporate sponsors also partially control the televised exposure of international sport. If the sponsors can promote their products by televising the sport, the sport gains terrific exposure in countries where the sponsor wants to advertise their product. If televising a sport doesn't benefit sponsors economically, spectators may have to find other media sources for following an international sport.

Popularity of Various Sports Worldwide

According to IPSOS World Monitor, a German sports research firm, the most popular sport worldwide in 2002 in both participation and spectatorship was soccer (or *football*, as it is called in other countries; see table 8.1). That is no surprise to anyone who has traveled the world and observed kids practicing their skills with the soccer ball, fields covered with players of all ages, and newspaper and television coverage of soccer games. World Cup soccer is the most watched international sporting event in the world. For the 2006 World Cup Finals held in Germany, 16 teams played in the qualifying that was eventually won by Italy over France. Telecasts of the games averaged over 93 million viewers worldwide, including a record 284 million for the championship game on July 9, 2006. Overall, 5.9 total viewers watched the World Cup on television in 54 global markets which

TABLE 8.1 Top Markets for Major Sports Among Watchers and Players

Sport	Watch			Play			Intend to watch or play	
Soccer	Brazil*	94%	(71%)	Brazil*	50%	(22%)	Mexico*	(27%)
	Mexico*	89%	(69%)	Mexico*	46%	(20%)	Brazil*	(17%)
	China*	82%	(72%)	South Korea	30%	(11%)	Italy	(7%)
Baseball	Japan	86%	(72%)	Japan	12%	(4%)	Japan	(4%)
	South Korea	71%	(47%)	South Korea	7%	(2%)	Mexico*/	(3%)
	United States	37%	(24%)	United States	5%	(3%)	United States	
							China*/	(1%)
							South Korea	
Football (American)	United States	68%	(44%)	United States	6%	(4%)	Mexico*	(5%)
	Mexico*	25%	(20%)	Mexico*	5%	(2%)	United States	(3%)
	United Kingdom	4%	(3%)				Germany	(1%)
Basketball	China*	45%	(39%)	Mexico*	27%	(11%)	Mexico*	(19%)
	South Korea	35%	(23%)	China*	25%	(13%)	China*	(9%)
	Mexico*/	28%	(22%/18%)	South Korea	15%	(5%)	Brazil*/	(5%)
	United States						United States	
Tennis	France	36%	(20%)	Japan	14%	(4%)	Japan	(11%)
	United Kingdom	20%	(14%)	France/Germany	8%	(4%/5%)	South Korea	(6%)
	Germany	18%	(14%)	Italy/South Korea/			China*/Germany	(5%)
				United States	7%	(2%/3%)		
Athletics	Germany	28%	(22%)	Mexico*	6%	(2%)	Mexico*	(4%)
	France	19%	(11%)	Italy	3%	(1%)	South Korea/	(2%)
	Japan	17%	(14%)	South Korea/	3%	(1%)	Italy/China*	
				France				
Golf	Japan	18%	(15%)	Japan	21%	(7%)	Japan	(13%)
	South Korea	16%	(11%)	United Kingdom/	11%	(6%/7%)	South Korea/	(7%)
	United Kingdom	14%	(10%)	United States			United States/	
				South Korea	5%	(2%)	United Kingdom	
							Germany	(4%)
Volleyball	Brazil*	44%	(33%)	Mexico*	10%	(4%)	Brazil*	(9%)
	China*	30%	(27%)	United States	5%	(3%)	Mexico*	(8%)
	South Korea	14%	(11%)	Brazil*	4%	(2%)	Japan	(3%)

Top three countries are based on total unaided mentions. Numbers in parentheses represent all consumers. * denotes urban-only samples.
IPSOS World Monitor.

is the equivalent of the television audience for 64 Super Bowls in American football. Those of us living in the United States may find the soccer frenzy puzzling because we are used to American sports. Only in the last 20 years has soccer taken the United States by storm, particularly in the youth market, and now ranks second only to basketball among youth (see chapter 5). In Latin America, soccer is part of the culture and boasts huge numbers of participants and spectators who embrace it with passion.

The second most popular sport worldwide is basketball (IPSOS World Monitor 2002), an American game that has infiltrated the international sporting population and produced cult figures such as Michael Jordan with the help of promotion by Nike. There are now professional basketball leagues in Europe, and an increasing number of star athletes

from countries other than the United States are now starting in the NBA. In the beginning of the 2005-2006 NBA season, there were 82 international players from 36 different countries on rosters led by stars such as Yao Ming of China, Tony Parker of France, and Manu Ginobili of Argentina (NBA 2005b). Critics of American players point to the players' playground origin, their preoccupation with individual play, and their lack of fundamental skills and team play. In international competition, American dominance has receded in recent years, and even when so-called American dream teams compete internationally, the outcomes of their games are in doubt.

The other American sport that has made international inroads is baseball. In Japan, 9 in 10 sport spectators watch baseball, and in South Korea that figure is 7 in 10. Central American countries send

Activity Time-Out: International Students As Athletes

International athletes have been a factor in college sports in the United States for many years, and the number of international student athletes keeps increasing, particularly in sports such as soccer, track and field, tennis, swimming, and more recently basketball. Often times, these athletes are offered athletic scholarships, which are often financed with university funds that ultimately come from either American taxpayers (for state universities) or private donors (for private colleges). Select a collegiate sport of your choice, research the effect of international athletes on that sport, and take a position for or against the practice of awarding athletic scholarships to international athletes. Share your findings with your classmates.

a steady stream of athletes to the major leagues in America, and 29% of players in MLB are international athletes.

Other sports that claim top popularity worldwide are tennis, golf, volleyball, track and field, and American football. Of course, the worldwide popularity of American football largely comes from its popularity in the United States, although the NFL has recently fielded teams in European markets with some success. Essentially, European teams operate as minor league teams, relying on players hoping to make it to the NFL. Canadian football has prospered for years although at a level of popularity below that of American football.

Tennis is played in more countries than any other sport except soccer, and it continues to grow in undeveloped nations due to sustained support from the International Tennis Federation. The Grand Slam tournaments, Wimbledon and the Australian, French, and U.S. Open, have supported tennis in developing nations for years. Ironically, athletes from some of those nations emerge to defeat players from the supporting countries.

Golf, baseball, and tennis appeal to higher economic groups worldwide. That makes them prime targets for corporate advertisers hoping to reach an audience with discretionary income. Golf attracts older participants and along with tennis and track and field relies on an older viewing audience as well. Soccer and basketball attract a younger population.

Worldwide, women still lag far behind men as sport participants. According to the IPSOS (2002) study, more men than women participate in the eight sports surveyed except in volleyball. Women spectators have increased, especially in tennis, volleyball, and track and field. American football claims a fair share of female spectators even though women do not compete in the sport.

AMERICAN INFLUENCE ON WORLD SPORT

While soccer has gained a huge foothold in America among youth in high school and college, American sports have had their own effect on the world. Professional leagues that thrive in the United States include American football, baseball, basketball, and ice hockey. The best players around the world come to the United States and to compete and test their skills against homegrown American players. International athletes have affected every American sport except football.

Ice hockey in the United States has been dominated for years by Canadians and a few great players from other countries. Some of Japan's finest baseball athletes have migrated to the U.S. to share in the wealth garnered by our MLB stars. Although Japanese baseball has lost some of its superstars, Japanese interest in American baseball skyrockets when one of their players competes in the playoffs or World Series. In Little League, international baseball teams are so successful that organizers divide the competition into two divisions to ensure Americans a place in the final rounds. Without the division, American teams would likely be eliminated early in the tournament, which would also eliminate potential interest and TV revenue.

Latin Americans have loved American baseball for years, and the proof of their talent is the high percentage of major-league players emerging from Latin America. In 2003, more than two-thirds of the combined major-league rosters were Latino or of Latino descent (Wendel 2003). While Latinos have always made their mark in baseball, the plethora of talent and all-star players in recent years has solidified their influence.

Sports such as tennis and golf that are not typical American powerhouse sports struggle to produce American players who can compete on the world stage. Yet the United States offers some of the most prestigious tournaments and biggest prize money. When non-Americans are in the finals of the U.S. Open, TV spectatorship can drop. For example, the 2004 finals of the U.S. Open saw the lowest television ratings in their history, with the men's finals at only 2.5 and the women's at just 2.2 (meaning that of all American households with televisions, 2.5% and 2.2% tuned in, respectively). The primary factor lowering the rating could quite possibly be the complete absence of American competitors, since the men's final featured Roger Federer from Switzerland defeating Lleyton Hewitt of Australia and the women's final showed Svetlana Kuznetsova defeating Elena Dementieva, both Russians. Just two years previously, when Venus and Serena Williams played for the women's championship, television ratings were the highest in history at 5.2. Of course, the Williams sisters' match was unique and added to viewing interest (Clarke 2005).

Yet hardcore tennis fans admire international athletes and are more apt to have traveled internationally due to higher economic status. Both tennis and golf rely on international professional tours, and competition takes place around the world. Since they are individual sports, fans are more likely to be attracted to specific athletes, regardless of nationality, than fans of team sports are.

OLYMPIC GAMES

Perhaps no event has promoted sport around the world more than the Olympic Games. The winter and summer games attract huge audiences from virtually every country and are a huge international event. Based on the original Olympic Games born in Athens, Greece, the modern Olympic Games were resurrected by Baron Pierre de Coubertin in 1896 (Henry and Yeomans 1984). Along with other organizers, Coubertin hoped that athletes competing on a world stage would open up communication between people of all nations, show that friendly competition could be exhilarating for athletes, promote understanding of different cultures and traditions, and serve as a model for nations working together. Those lofty goals remain a challenge, although it cannot be disputed that Olympic competition has promoted sport around the world.

The Olympic Games helped standardize rules for competition in all sports. Each sport has a designated international organization that determines the rules of play, stages world championships, records competitive records, sets drug-testing protocols, and helps conduct the Olympic events. National governing bodies in each sport take their cues from the international groups so that all countries play by the same rules of competition. For example, standards for the field of play, equipment limitations, and even scoring procedures are set by the international bodies to ensure consistency in every country. We will focus on the Olympic Games in chapter 9.

Pop Culture: The Dominican Republic As a Hotbed for Baseball

No country in the world has sent more players to MLB than the tiny Caribbean nation of the Dominican Republic, whose population is just over 7 million. Perhaps the most famous players have been Juan Marichal and the three Alou brothers, Felipe, Matty, and Jesus. Current stars include Vladimir Guerrero, David Ortiz, Manny Ramirez, Sammy Sosa, Miguel Tejada, and Adrian Beltre. These great athletes are just a few in a long list of players who escaped poverty and found fame and fortune in the United States through baseball.

All is not rosy, however, for the hundreds of kids who join local baseball academies, hoping to make the major leagues. In 2000, HBO's *Real Sports* aired a segment on the lengths athletes go to in order to make it to the big leagues. Many neglect their education in favor of baseball, and some lie about their age to attract scouts from major-league teams. While the success stories of those who make it are inspirational, they come at the expense of many families who are suckered into the dream of riches through baseball (Goldberg 2005; Munoz 2004).

EFFECT OF MEDIA ON THE GLOBALIZATION OF SPORT

We cannot ignore the media's role in expanding sport worldwide. Perhaps no other factor was more influential in spreading sporting events around the world and reducing former geographical and time constraints.

As discussed in chapter 5, sport and the media exist in a symbiotic relationship. Sporting events are a staple of both printed and electronic media. On the other side, sports receive millions of dollars in free publicity for their products, teams, and athletes. Sports are in the enviable position of being able to count on extensive media coverage without paying advertising fees.

Technological advances have opened up sports on television through satellite and dish broadcasting. DirecTV and the Dish network, the top two satellite networks in the United States, allow viewers to watch sport events from any American city and an increasing number of international sites. People who wish to watch soccer matches from other countries have immediate real-time access. Pay-per-view opens up a wide world of special sporting events.

The Internet allows us to visit favorite team Web sites, learn about games and players, and listen to interviews. Fans can listen to a game in progress that may not be accessible on television and can check the latest scores of games from anyplace in the world. As online newspapers continue to develop, we can read about games and events within a few hours of their completion to see what sports writers think of the results.

In addition to freely covering sports, the media pay huge amounts in broadcast rights to events such as the Olympics and NFL football, both of which have worldwide appeal. The Olympic Games rely on television rights as the major source of funding. NBC paid $456 million U.S. to broadcast the Atlanta Games, $715 million U.S. for the Sidney Games, $545 million U.S. for the Salt Lake Games, $793 million U.S. for the Athens Games, and $614 million U.S. for the Turin Games. That revenue goes to the International Olympic Committee and all the national Olympic Committees that help train and support athletes. NBC made an estimated $75 million U.S. net profit in ad revenue from the Athens Games. The television coverage in the United States was 198 million, meaning that roughly 71% of the American population watched some part of those Olympic Games (McCarthy 2004). However, the 2006 Winter Games from Turin, Italy saw a 37% decline from the viewing population of the Salt Lake Games and finished no better than fourth in the weekly ratings behind *American Idol* and *Dancing With the Stars* according to the Nielsen ratings.

The NFL may be the most successful sport at attracting television sponsorship. In 1998, the NFL secured a $17.6 billion U.S. contract with several TV networks wanting to televise its games. Every team in the NFL received in excess of $70 million U.S., or what amounts to nearly 65% of their total revenue (Miller and Associates 2005). The television networks in turn sell sponsorship time during the broadcast to recoup their expenditures. With Super Bowl advertising spots commanding more than $2 million U.S. for a 30-second advertisement, you can see how networks generate their revenue from corporate sponsors.

Events such as the NFL Super Bowl are routinely broadcast round the world to more than 200 countries. That publicity helps spread the popularity of the sport, promotes football players, and increases the sale of NFL merchandise. Due to the technological advances of delayed broadcast, satellites, and improved product delivery, fans across the globe can share in the drama and excitement of an American event. In the 10 countries IPSOS surveyed in 2002, American football ranked third in percentage of viewers, behind only soccer and baseball, even though American football is not even played in 8 of the 10 countries surveyed.

The relationship between TV and sport becomes more intertwined when you realize that if sports expect to command big bucks from television, they must be sensitive to the needs of the networks. Starting times are set to attract the largest audience, rules are modified to create drama, and coaches and athletes must make themselves available for interviews before, during, and after games.

Naturally the sports that command the most attention receive the widest TV distribution worldwide. Once networks choose their events, they do everything they can to advertise the event and increase their audience. Sharing international competition ensures viewership from the athletes' home countries, and the Olympic Games capitalize on the natural rivalries between fans from opposing nations.

American soccer can point to the broadcast of the World Cup for helping to popularize soccer in the U.S., particularly for women. The recent success of the American team has provided role models for girls and encouraged them to explore their own athletic prowess. Without the contributions of the media publicizing soccer by televising games, selling soccer to the American public was slow going and seemed destined for failure.

The emerging world markets are ripe for sport expansion. The percent of the population that watches sport on television in the following countries is high—greater than 50% in each (IPSOS 2002):

**Country and percent
of population watching sport**

Brazil	75%	Japan	84%
China	88%	Mexico	78%
France	57%	South Korea	66%
Germany	77%	United Kingdom	70%
Italy	65%	United States	65%

As countries such as China, Japan, and Mexico increase their participation in the global economy, the rise in sport involvement seems to indicate greater emphasis on personal lifestyle and leisure. In developed countries like the United Kingdom and the United States, growth potential appears smaller because the population is satisfied with their sport involvement and involvement has reached its peak. This is why marketing sports to emerging new markets is so critical to continued growth in sport popularity and revenue.

Looking at favorite sports in the countries that watch sports shows that the four most popular sports both in participation and spectating are soccer, baseball, American football, and basketball. Except for soccer, these sports were invented in America, and yet the United States ranks only 8 out of 10 in percentage of sport viewers (IPSOS 2002). American sports appear to rely significantly on worldwide broadcasting through television and radio for exposure and income.

Sports that are truly international at the professional level such as golf and tennis rely on television coverage because their events are staged in different parts of the world every week. The top competitors represent many nationalities, and world interest changes depending on the performance of favorite players. The four major world championships in professional tennis are referred to as the *Grand Slam tournaments.* They are played in Australia, France, England, and the United States. Worldwide coverage is critical to their success, and the television contracts are complicated multinational ones.

The spirit of nationalism can still be seen in fans today. How do fans from different countries show pride in their teams?

NATIONALISM VERSUS ECONOMICS

During the middle of the 20th century, international sporting competition was buoyed by strong feelings of nationalism. From Adolph Hitler's mission to create a superrace in Germany to the nationalistic tenor of the 1936 Olympic Games staged in Berlin, countries around the world used sports as a rallying cry of patriotism. Perhaps more than any other event, the Olympic Games thrived on the inherent nationalism built into their structure, publicity, and team medal count.

With the rise of Communism and the Cold War between the Soviet Union and its allies and the West, including Europe and the United States, athletic competition became more than who had the best athletes. Fueled by rhetoric by sport leaders and politicians, many people began to see sport contests as a validation of a more democratic or socialistic society. When high-profile athletes won medals at the Olympic Games, their country burst with pride at the proof of their society.

At the Olympic Games, the medals won by each country were totaled and a winning nation declared. That tradition faded significantly with the change in government in the Soviet Union but medal count by country still gets some play. Of course, winning gold medals in worldwide competition depends on many factors, including national sport tradition, economics, and support for athlete development.

As the Cold War faded and tension between the West and the former Eastern European Communist countries eased, the attitude in the sports world also changed. An **economic model** began to replace a nationalistic one in the Olympics and most other international sport events. The key factor in selecting a site for the Olympics is the financial package offered to support the Games, including the construction of millions of dollars worth of athletic venues and supporting transportation between sites. Choosing a site takes years: The site for the 2012 Summer Games was chosen by the International Olympic Committee in 2005 after thoroughly vetting all applicant cities, which consumed at least five years.

A city's potential attractiveness to corporate sponsors is also a key factor along with the proposed television package for broadcasting the Games. Consider for example the staging of the 1996 Olympic Games in Atlanta, home of Coca Cola. Corporate sponsors like Coke seize the opportunity to sell their product around the world by advertising through the Olympic Games. In recent years McDonald's has provided food in the Olympic Village for athletes, and Mars

In the Arena With . . . *IMG Academies*

Multinational training occurs at the International Management Group's (IMG) athletic training facility in Bradenton, Florida. This facility was originally a tennis academy founded by well-known coach Nick Bollettieri but was purchased by IMG about 15 years ago. IMG was founded by marketing visionary Mark McCormack with the help of Arnold Palmer, the legendary golfer. IMG added training facilities for multiple sports to attract elite athletes from around the globe. IMG Academies offers top-notch coaching, facilities, and competition to help serious athletes hone their skills in golf, tennis, soccer, baseball, or basketball. In a typical year, 11,000 athletes representing 75 countries attend. It is the largest and most famous sports academy in the world.

The annual cost of attending such a training academy is steep, usually in the range of $40,000 U.S. for room, board, coaching, and schooling. However, many of the international athletes are offered scholarships when spotted by IMG talent scouts around the world. Many top international players choose this route for athletic development as early as eight years old, and they are often accompanied by one or both parents, who seek local employment. The payday for IMG arrives when the child decides to become a professional and IMG is able to sign them as a client. If their career is successful, IMG more than recoups their expenses for training. Many world-class professional tennis players have opted for this route, and the academy hosts more international players than it does American players (www.imgacademies.com).

candy bars is a major sponsor with the goal of selling snacks and candy bars to a sporting public.

The economic model for international sports can also be illustrated by the fact that Roots, a Canadian clothing company, outfitted the 2004 U.S. Olympic team with warm-ups through a corporate sponsorship (www.roots.com). Most sponsors of sporting events are large multinational corporations dedicated to growing their business in as many markets as possible. Rather than be seen as provincial, these corporations seek to portray a global view. Because their sponsorship dollars have fueled the rapid economic expansion in sport, the sporting world depends on them to survive as a business.

ATHLETES AND COACHES AS MIGRANT WORKERS

People who make their living from sports include athletes, coaches, officials, agents, and organization officials and staff. Depending on the sport, they travel around the globe as a natural part of their employment. Most often, they are employed by specific sport organizations that rely on international exposure and operation. Of course, sports indigenous to one country or region of the world do not rely on international operation.

Athletes seek the highest level of competition and coaching in order to maximize their talent and earning power. They likely begin sport instruction near their home, but as they progress, they often travel to secure specialized coaching and train with other elite athletes. If their country offers a national program in their sport, they may attend a special school where training and academic education are combined. Some athletes living where their sport is not as keen or available may seek training in another country.

Athletes who train in the United States often become comfortable living there and eventually make it their home base. This is also true for their coaches, who travel with them. In sports like tennis and golf, in which world tours are the only way to make a living, both athletes and coaches are more like gypsies on the road. They move from city to city almost every week and live in hotels and out of suitcases. The cultural experience is unparalleled, and the excitement of visiting great cities on every continent is exhilarating.

Golfer Vijay Singh, originally from Fiji, now makes his home in Florida.

But the endless travel and lack of contact with family and friends can be lonely. Maintaining friendships outside of the sports world is very difficult and developing romantic liaisons can be a perplexing challenge. Also, if athletes spend too much time sightseeing to the detriment of their competitive performance, their earning power and career are threatened.

Coaches in individual sports must also be flexible and frequent travelers, and they often switch athletes as fortunes wane or players retire. Coaching on the road makes a family life difficult, and solitary nights spent in hotel rooms challenge most people, who crave relationships.

Coaches of international sport teams also find opportunities in various countries. Many undeveloped countries hire coaches from more developed nations to build their systems in sports like soccer, basketball, swimming, and track and field. Even among developed countries, coaches often move from one to another. In 1999 England hired a Frenchman, Patrice Hagelauer, to head the performance development program for tennis. Many of the leading tennis coaches in the United States originate from other countries. People are often intrigued by different coaching approaches and reach out to international coaches who offer alternative methods and perspectives.

Officials and administrators of world sport events also travel and often reside in foreign countries. They typically follow the world competition from venue to venue, although they may enjoy more time at home than athletes do. World championships, the Olympic Games, and similar events are not as frequent as the regular season or tour and are separated by weeks or months. Agents, on the other hand, usually travel constantly to attend events where their athletes compete. Since they typically handle more than one athlete, they can spend endless weeks on the road serving their clients and scouting for new talent to sign.

While many athletes from other countries play for American teams, many of the best U.S. rugby players, such as Todd Clever, play overseas where greater opportunities for professional contracts exist.

The result of all this global travel is that athletes, coaches, and officials become ambassadors for their home nation, learn about other cultures, and tend to develop a more comprehensive worldview. They probably do little to directly influence the countries where they travel, but as they develop followings, strong links may be spawned. Particular athletes may adopt or become fascinated with other cultures. Language barriers are reduced as people use more foreign phrases and expressions just to survive.

As professional athletes or coaches mature and start families, they often arrange for their loved ones to travel with them. Imagine the experience of such a family. The educational experience for kids from this background is priceless.

The countries of origin are not always happy when their athletes leave home to play professionally in another country. As mentioned, American baseball has increasingly attracted players from Latin American countries as well as some of the best-known Japanese players. The countries that lose the athletes lose some of their most charismatic and exciting competitors and see reduced interest in local baseball.

Over the past two to three decades in many European countries, sport leagues in soccer, ice hockey, and basketball have increasingly recruited players from other countries. The motivation is to find the best available players in the world to play for local clubs or teams. Some observers say that this recruiting hinders the development of young athletes in the home country, who see spots taken by athletes from other nations. Leagues take away jobs from home country athletes in the hope of producing a winning team (Maguire et al. 2002).

A parallel situation exists in many American colleges and universities. Once the top American athletes are signed to scholarships, the schools who didn't sign them recruit the best overseas athletes in hopes of competing with the leading American schools. Sports like swimming, track and field, soccer, and tennis have been particularly affected by this growing trend. Efforts to limit the number of international players have been struck down in the courts, and American families cry foul when their kids are denied athletic scholarships in favor of international players.

International competition in sports can provide a terrific opportunity for athletes, coaches, and others. On the other hand, complications in personal and family lives, burnout, and cultural shock also occur. Surviving this unusual life experience boils down to how grounded people are in their fundamental values and relationships.

USING SPORTS FOR BETTER WORLD UNDERSTANDING

In an ideal world, international competition is an opportunity for those involved to learn about each other and to connect on a personal level. Once people understand and appreciate the society and culture of others, the stage is set for people to live and work together. This valued outcome does happen in world competition, although it does not happen without dedication and effort from those involved.

Athletes of all ages may compete internationally if they earn a top ranking in their own country. World competitions for athletes 12 and under are staged in various sports, and athletes in their 50s and 60s also attend their own competitions. College athletes in many sports have also benefited from traveling abroad to compete. For many athletes, these experiences are eye-opening cultural excursions to countries they would not normally visit. Meeting athletes from around the world helps them appreciate the humanity of all cultures and may urge them to train harder to be the best in the world.

Some international competition balances sports and travel. High school students can sign up for tours of other countries during which they also compete at arranged sites along the way. Young people who take advantage of these tours may be sponsored by sport organizations, organizations promoting international understanding, or their families. Countries often establish exchange programs for young athletes. It is exhilarating for people who struggle to communicate to find a common bond in the language of sport.

The United States is a popular destination and most people who qualify to visit for a sport event seize the opportunity. In virtually every sport, young athletes from international countries visit and compete against U.S. kids while sightseeing and learning about American life.

Athletic coaches also have numerous opportunities to travel internationally. Most sports hold worldwide coaching conferences and each participating nation may designate several coaches as representatives. The concept of sharing coaching philosophies is not new, and countries that lead the world competition are in demand as speakers and teachers. Along the way, coaches from different societies interact and broaden their outlook toward the world.

The value of international sport competition may be narrowed if coaches and leaders focus entirely on their athlete's performance, losing the opportunity to learn about others. Coaches personally benefiting from international travel may view competition as more than what happens on the playing field.

People who schedule trips find that sightseeing is best left to the end of the trip when competition is completed and they can relax their single-minded focus on their sport.

Sports offer potential for understanding the larger world, but this opportunity may be lost unless we structure the experience with that goal in mind. One of the values we often trumpet to support sport participation is mocked if we do not establish international appreciation through competition.

CHAPTER SUMMARY

The English system of sports and games has largely affected the development of international sport. For centuries, Great Britain influenced countless countries to adopt their sports. In the last 50 years, other Western countries including the United States have added their influence. As the world population changes and countries like China embrace world sport, influence is likely to shift again.

Sports have become a global enterprise by standardizing rules, staging world competitions for athletes of all ages and abilities, and covering those contests through the media. Technological advancements have made sport events immediately available to fans worldwide.

Participation sport is historically popular in its nation of origin. The most popular sports worldwide are soccer and basketball, followed by baseball, tennis, golf, track and field, and volleyball.

The modern Olympic Games have helped significantly in developing sport worldwide. Most nations support the training and coaching of their athletes to ensure success in international competition. Extending the length and pageantry of the Games has attracted television viewers worldwide and generated millions of dollars for organizers and sponsors.

As multinational corporations realized the possibilities of advertising through international sports, they reached out to new audiences. Sport equipment and clothing companies discovered cheap labor in undeveloped countries and millions of consumers in developed countries.

The economics of international sport began to replace the nationalism that was the hallmark of competition during the Cold War. Olympic venues are now chosen by the potential revenue that can be generated. Athletes from competing countries are on the same team, in a sense, as they ply their trade with the backing of Nike, Adidas, Reebok, and others.

Opportunities for world travel, cultural study, and personal relationships with people of other countries have expanded for athletes and coaches. However, using sport to promote cultural understanding and harmony must be a valued goal if it is to progress.

Focusing exclusively on competition may improve performance but shortchange the travel experience for athletes.

Olympic Movement

Student Outcomes

After reading this chapter, you will know the following:

- A brief history of the Olympic Games
- The role of the modern Olympics in our global society
- How nationalism, economics, and politics influence the Olympics
- The role of the United States Olympic Committee
- How the Olympic movement has affected athlete development and coaching and training methods in the United States

No other sporting event in the last 100 years has had the widespread effects of the **Olympic Games.** Along with providing a venue for the finest athletes from a variety of sports, the Games provide opportunities for spectators to enjoy international competition in virtually every world nation. Through the years, nationalism developed in the Olympics as every nation took pride in its athletes and created heroes for youth to emulate.

In the more recent past, the fierce nationalism has been pushed aside by the economic effects of the Olympic Games for national Olympic organizations, corporate sponsors, and host cities. What was once an amateur competition has unabashedly morphed into a competition for the world's best professional athletes, many of whom financially capitalize on Olympic success.

By now most nations have established Olympic organizations, often under a governmental agency such as a Ministry of Sport. Relying on government funds and private donations, national Olympic organizations support the development of the country's Olympic candidates in hopes of boosting their performance as they return to the Games every four years. Sport in many countries has grown and flourished simply because of Olympic development programs that encourage young athletes.

HISTORY OF THE OLYMPICS

The ancient Olympics were founded as a festival to honor the king of the Greek gods, Zeus. The Games were held every four years for more than 1,000 years, from 776 BC to 393, AD. Only Greeks were allowed to compete, although athletes from Greek colonies in countries that are now Spain, Italy, Libya, Egypt, Ukraine, and Turkey gave the Olympics an international flavor (Henry and Yeomans 1984).

Although the origin of the Olympics is in dispute because of the plethora of unsubstantiated accounts of its beginnings, some general facts are known. At the height of their popularity, the games represented the culture that made Greece the undisputed mistress of the Mediterranean. Emerging from a religious festival that lasted one day, the games developed into a seven-day extravaganza that riveted the attention of the people of Greece and its colonies. Common men competed against soldiers and royalty for the glory of wining the coveted olive wreath symbolizing victory.

The original games featured just one event, a footrace down the length of the stadium of about 200 yards (183 meters). At the behest of the city-state of Sparta, more events were added, and the 18th Olympic Games featured a pentathlon that consisted of a long jump, spear throw, sprint, discus throw, and wrestling match. In succeeding years, boxing, chariot racing, footraces of varying lengths, and a pankration, a combination of boxing and wrestling, were added (Henry and Yeomans 1984; Leonard 1980; Rice, Hutchinson, and Lee 1958).

Even as the games expanded their physical contests and gained popularity, religious ceremonies were not forgotten. Religious ceremonies were always critical to the celebrations to honor the gods. Arts, including poetry recitations, singing, and dramatic productions, were also a vital part of the weeklong celebration. Every four years, the games turned a mosaic of religion, athletics, and arts into a national festival (Scheiber 2004).

As years went by, traditional Greek religion faded and the games lost their significance. The decline of the games has been blamed on the corruption of politicians and the wealthy. Athletes focused more on the prize money they could earn than on the honor of competing for the olive wreath. The rich history of morality and competing for the love of the contest was lost.

The last games were held in 393 AD, after which the Christian emperor of Rome, Theodosius I, banned pagan worship. The Olympic Games are one of the enduring contributions of Greek civilization. In addition to fostering a strong belief in the value of athletics, the games produced notable works of art, music, and culture and celebrated individual achievement. Those characteristics sparked the rebirth of the Olympics more than a thousand years later, in 1896. The Games began again in Athens, with just 14 countries competing in nine sports: track and field, cycling, fencing, gymnastics, wrestling, swimming, weightlifting, tennis, and shooting. These modern Olympic Games have continued through

The ancient Olympia Stadium built in Olympia, Greece, in 776 BC was an extension of an already existing religious sanctuary dedicated to Zeus.

political conflicts, world wars, and the passing of generations (Henry and Yeomans 1984).

The modern Olympic Games were revived by Baron Pierre de Coubertin, a French educator. His vision was to replicate worldwide the positive effects of the original Greek Olympics founded in Athens. According to the Olympic Charter, "Olympism is a philosophy of life, exalting and combining in a balanced whole the qualities of body, will, and mind. Blending sport with culture and education, Olympism seeks to create a way of life based on the joy found in effort, the educational value of good example and respect for universal fundamental ethical principles" (Olympic Charter 2004, p. 9).

Drawing from the holistic Athenian philosophy of a sound mind in a sound body, the Olympic movement wanted to help people understand and appreciate their differences through competition in sport. The hope was that by establishing a community of athletes, coaches, and organizers from every country in the world, international understanding and goodwill would be promoted (Henry and Yeomans 1984).

EFFECT OF THE OLYMPIC GAMES

The games profoundly affect their host city, the media who cover the contests, and the athletes who compete. This effect is felt in the years leading to the competition as well as during the staging of the competition, and in many cases it lasts for years afterward. Most Olympic competitors devote their early years to development and training in the hope of someday qualifying for the Olympics. Once they finally realize their dream, it becomes the defining factor in their life and sets the path for the years ahead. Many trade on their Olympic success as they move on to other professions.

Host City

Cities from around the world compete furiously to host the Olympic Games because of the potential prestige and financial benefits they offer. Sport venues are created or refurbished and endure once the Olympics end, used by athletes from the host country. Yet the costs of hosting can be daunting. The 2004 Athens Games cost an estimated $14.6 billion U.S., when the Greek government originally budgeted $5.9 billion U.S. based on previous Olympic Games. (For example, the Sydney Games cost $1.5 billion U.S. and the Atlanta Games $1.7 billion U.S.) But the challenges in readying the venue, construction snafus, and an unrealistic deadline along with increased security spurred by recent terrorist activities all jacked up the costs (Jenkins 2004).

In spite of the huge financial risks, the race for potential host cities has only heated up. Leading contenders for the 2012 Summer Olympics were Paris, London, New York City, and Moscow, with London finally securing the bid in a mild upset over favored Paris. Those cities underwent rigorous vetting and presented their plans to the International Olympic Committee in 500-page tomes boasting their assets and the benefits of awarding the bid to them. Past issues of bribery and lavish entertainment given to decision makers have resulted in a carefully monitored bid review and a transparency of process that had been recently lacking.

Beijing, China, is preparing to host the 2008 Summer Games by sprucing up the city, removing decaying slums, and constructing new high-rise buildings. Traffic and transportation are always a concern with so many people concentrated in one city during the games that new roads need to be built, transit systems refurbished, and travel capacity expanded (St. Petersburg Times 2005a).

New stadiums and athletic facilities are required for every Olympic Games. The host city begins by assessing the current facilities that are suitable and then constructs needed arenas, pools, and so on. The funding becomes complicated as various groups pitch in money in return for use or ownership of the facility long after the games end.

The 1996 Olympic Games in Atlanta, Georgia, significantly affected the long-term economics of the city and state. These Olympic legacies can be grouped into three categories: (1) the creation of world-class facilities; (2) the national and international recognition of the city through extensive media exposure; and (3) community benefits such as local volunteerism, job creation and training, youth programs, and funding for community development projects.

World-class athletic facilities from the Atlanta Games include the $189 million Olympic Stadium, the Georgia International Horse Park, the $17 million Wolf Creek Shooting Range, the tennis facility at Stone Mountain, and the $10 million Lake Lanier Rowing Center. New dormitories costing $47 million were built at the Georgia Institute of Technology (Georgia Tech) and Georgia State University to create an Olympic village to house athletes and coaches. An additional $24 million was spent to build a new aquatic center on Georgia Tech's campus, and $1.5 million was used to renovate the coliseum on campus to host the boxing events (Humphreys and Plummer 1996).

Expert's View: Floating Olympic Stadiums

The opportunity to be an Olympic host city is usually reserved for the wealthiest countries. The sheer volume of money needed to build facilities can be out of reach for many nations. A research team from Technion at Israel Institute of Technology has proposed the idea of a floating Olympic stadium built of a series of floating modules that are joined together for the Games and then dismantled and shipped to other locations. The modules would contain a central stadium equipped for up to 150,000 spectators; an auxiliary sport facility for various branches of sport; an Olympic village and accommodations for visitors; a center for administration, media, communication, and research; and a sports university campus (Play the Game 2005).

At the Play the Game 2005 conference, Michael Burt, a professor of architecture at the Israel Institute of Technology, said that the technology for a transportable stadium exists and that using such a stadium is the only way to erase the last discriminating feature of the Olympic Games, namely that not all countries can afford to host the events. The floating stadium would also help prevent what Burt called *Sydney's Olympic blues*—Olympic villages and facilities standing as ghost towns (Lausten 2005).

Media Effects

NBC paid over $3.5 billion for the U.S. rights to broadcast the Olympic Games from 2002 to 2008 (Miller and Associates 2005). The rationale from the network was that the Olympics, unlike any other event, can attract whole families to TV watching. The Olympics create a unique audience for sponsors to sell to. Unlike the Super Bowl, which lasts a few hours, the Olympic Games extend over 17 days, providing multiple time slots for advertising.

The Athens Games were televised by NBC and cable stations for 16 straight days in August of 2004. Most days, coverage began at noon and extended through the afternoon, with the best action airing from prime time up until midnight. The Olympics dominated TV viewership so thoroughly that NBC won every half-hour time segment in prime time for 17 straight days. An average audience of 24.6 million watched the Olympic Games, an increase of 14% over the previous audience who tuned in to the Olympics in Sydney. NBC's audience for the Athens Games represented about 198 million unique viewers, or about 71% of the U.S. population (McCarthy 2004). Can you imagine the relief of rival networks ABC, CBS, and FOX when the 17 days of Olympic Games finally ended?

Competing networks get into the action by inviting Olympic athletes onto talk shows, showing clips of their performances, and promoting their sponsors. Magazines and newspaper dailies devote pages to stories about Olympic athletes and coaches and the surrounding subplots of drug testing, romance, athletes' earnings, and judging controversies.

It seems that every two years, when either the Winter or Summer Games take the stage, the world steps back from other events to focus on the competition. That was the original idea of the Olympic Games, and it has endured for all these centuries.

Elite Performance Athletes

The motto of the Olympic Games is "*Citius, Altius, Fortius,*" which translates to "faster, higher, stronger." These are worthy goals for every aspiring Olympian who measures success by the winning

of gold, silver, or bronze medals. Of the athletes who compete, few come away with a medal, but most treasure the experience of competing with the world's best in their respective sports. Hundreds of thousands of aspiring youth around the world train and test their abilities in hopes of someday becoming an Olympian.

World championships are held in many sports under the aegis of that sport's international governing body, yet it is at the Olympic Games where almost all sports come together to stage the most unique, comprehensive, and lavish celebration of athletic competition yet conceived. The world attends to the Games, with audiences glued to their televisions for more than two weeks. The media have latched onto the Olympics as a significant world event that can attract huge audiences and hence hundreds of millions of dollars in corporate sponsorship. The Olympics have become the largest and most successful economic engine in the sports world.

The excitement of the Olympic Games focuses the world on the best performances of elite athletes in every Olympic sport. Winning a medal at the Olympics has achieved an almost mystical status among athletes. Rising to the occasion to win a medal or set a world record is the dream of every athlete. By

Training for the Olympics creates elite performance athletes. Do these athletes promote or hinder the ideals behind the Olympic Games?

Activity Time-Out: Who Gets the Money?

If you were in charge of the American Olympic team, with a goal of producing as many medals as possible but with a limited budget, would you restrict your financial support to athletes with a realistic shot at a medal? If so, how would you determine an athlete's odds at success? Or would you support any athlete qualifying for the Games according to the world standards? Justify your answer.

comparison, success at a world championship, while certainly notable, does not generate nearly the media attention or sponsorship opportunities as does an Olympic medal. The focus of world sport fans on the Olympic Games adds pressure along with instant fame for athletes who offer up a performance of a lifetime.

Famous athletes in their sport jockey for opportunities to rub elbows with athletes from other sports whom they admire. Olympic athletes are clearly not inured to the celebrity factor. They are sport fans who enjoy watching performers in other sports rise to greatness.

The emphasis on winning at the Games has become a double-edged sword. Successful medal winners are heroes and those who enter and come up short are labeled failures. In some countries like the United States, debate rages over whether athletes who qualify for the Games but are unlikely to challenge for a medal should be supported financially by their home country. In the United States, the goal of the United States Olympic Committee (USOC) is to accumulate the most medals possible in a particular game. Athletes who qualify but are unlikely to win a medal become something of a second-class citizen, and many people believe USOC resources are wasted on them. On the opposing side are those who believe that just competing in the Olympic Games is a right they have earned. Isn't competing to compete the point of it all?

The fascination with winning medals has produced an incentive plan for athletes in which they win cash awards for each medal won. Proponents of this plan believe that cash will encourage athletes to work harder. For professional athletes, the relatively modest reward of $25,000 to $50,000 U.S. is insignificant compared to their annual earnings and likely does not add motivation. Most donate the proceeds to a charitable organization.

The public acceptance of winning as the primary goal of Olympic athletes has fueled the concentration on elite athletic competition. Kids are steered

into elite development programs and encouraged to focus on preparing for a run at an Olympic medal. While some sport leaders believe it is healthy for kids to aspire to greatness, participation for fun may suffer and may lead to the high dropout rate in youth sports mentioned in chapter 5. Once kids realize high performance is not within their reach, they often give up competition and turn to other activities. Another by-product of the emphasis on winning is the increasing use of performance-enhancing drugs, which has resulted in stepped-up testing of winning athletes, both in and out of competition. Heading into the 2004 Olympic Games in Athens, speculations about which athletes were using illegal substances garnered as much media attention as predictions of athletic accomplishments. We'll spend more time on performance enhancement through drugs in chapter 17.

The demand to produce elite athletes who might someday compete for Olympic medals has spawned ambitious talent scouting in many countries. Children younger than age 10 have been tested for their athletic potential and offered government-funded training opportunities in the sport that seems to suit their body type, athletic skill, and temperament. These state schools produced many champion athletes in East Germany and Russia during the Cold War, when countries dedicated state monies to train athletes so they could prove the superiority of their culture.

Shift from Amateurs to Professionals

During the last 50 years, the Olympics shifted away from the idealistic notion that world-class athletes could compete solely for the love of the game and thus be dubbed *amateur athletes*. Juan Antonio Samaranch of Spain, president of the International Olympic Committee from 1980 to 2001, made it clear that his mission for the Olympic Games was to attract the best athletes in the world. Their standing as amateur or professional performers was irrelevant to him.

During the 20th century, sports were still supposed to be played for enjoyment, with no thought of financial reward. Only the economically well off could afford the time and expense of playing, so sport was limited to the privileged class.

As interest in watching sports grew, spectators became willing to pay admission fees and money became available to athletes. Commercial sponsors and television rights added to the available financial resources. Yet the athletes who performed often received a relatively small portion of this revenue.

American fans loved the idea of amateur athletes struggling to train and then succeeding on the world stage. But the amateur status was a front. College athletes received scholarships; athletes appeared in advertisements or were hired as spokespeople or consultants. Americans pointed to other countries, particularly Eastern European Communist countries, as ignoring the rules of amateurism, as the International Olympic Committee allowed each nation to determine what constituted amateur status.

The only athletes clearly excluded from the Olympic Games were professional athletes in basketball, tennis, ice hockey, and baseball who earned their living playing their sport. Rather than sending professionals, the United States sent college kids to compete in the Olympic Games. For some years, doing that worked since the United States dominated world competition anyway. But as other nations began challenging U.S. dominance, to keep winning the United States had to change its definition of amateur or the Olympics had to change its rules or open up competition to anyone—pro or amateur.

Over the last 25 years, all pretense of sending amateur athletes to the Olympics has been set aside. Now Olympic athletes include all professionals and in fact Olympic stars are expected to promote the Games and their sport for compensation. Stars from professional teams, leagues, and tours are welcomed into the Games.

The continuing stumbling block in the United States is the stance of the NCAA toward professionalism. The NCAA continues to define college athletes as amateurs, though college athletes receive athletic scholarships and other benefits. They require young athletes hoping to qualify for athletic scholarships to remain an amateur before attending college. This rule exists only in the United States, and it severely limits athletes in expensive Olympic sports from securing financial backers when young. The NCAA

Mary Lou Retton, who competed in the 1984 Olympics in Los Angeles, was considered an amateur athlete.

has an impossible task on its hands of regulating corporate sponsorship or support from organizations for young athletes. Supposed amateur athletes in youth sports cannot afford to compete unless their family has significant resources or they secure sponsorship of some kind. Fortunately, high school sports like basketball and American football provide development opportunities for younger athletes. But athletes in skating, equestrian, tennis, golf, gymnastics, and other Olympic sports have no such viable opportunity through the school system.

NATIONALISM AND THE OLYMPIC MOVEMENT

In the International Olympic Committee (IOC) there are currently 202 National Olympic Committees (NOCs) over five continents. These national committees promote the principles of Olympism within their country, support their athletes, and send athletes to participate in the Games. Modern Olympic Games have seen an increasingly nationalistic flavor, no doubt partly due to the fact that only NOCs are allowed to select and send athletes to the Olympic Games. Thus athletes feel, rightly so, that they are representing their country.

Team sports heighten the nationalism. At the Olympics the German team competes against the British team and so on. When athletes or teams win medals, they are presented the medal while their country's flag waves and their national anthem plays. The media show these ceremonies and note the tears of successful athletes who are testimony of their country's success.

The opening ceremonies of the Games include a huge procession with every athlete and coach marching into the Olympic stadium as teams representing their homeland. Usually their dress highlights their country's traditional garb or colors. Regardless of their competitive standing, medal chances, and financial status, athletes from one country march together.

Martin (1996) suggests that nationalism was catapulted into prominence by Adolf Hitler, who used the Olympic Games in Berlin as a propaganda show for Nazi Germany. Hitler's constant reference to the human *superrace* of White athletes was damaged by the heroic achievements of American sprinter Jesse Owens, a Black athlete who won four medals and dominated the competition in track and field.

After World War II and the Korean War, the world settled into 35 years of what was dubbed the *Cold War*. Essentially, the Cold War was a clash of cultures and ideas of governance between the Russian Federation and the United States. Although war was never declared between these two superpowers, it was always a threat and the tension was great. It was during the Cold War that nationalism peaked in the Olympic Games.

The two countries dominating the Olympic Games from 1948 to today have been the Russian Federation and the United States (see table 9.1). No other nation has finished as the top medal winner in all

Expert's View: Nationalism in the Olympics

According to Bruce Kidd (1996), a scholar at the University of Toronto at Canada and a former Olympian, politics and promoting nationalism have long been a characteristic of the Olympic Games. Sponsors and television have cultivated nationalistic feelings to promote public interest. But a different point of view would have the games emphasize cultural understanding, cooperation on world challenges, and nations working together. The switch to this view could start with the International Olympic Committee taking a stand to use the Olympics to promote friendship and peace. Athletes could be invited to the Olympics as global citizens and athletes, not as representatives of their countries. Country uniforms could be eliminated, the opening ceremony featuring athletes by country could be changed, and national anthems and flags could be outlawed. Sponsorship money and television airtime could be devoted to discussing responsible world citizenship. Athletes could be encouraged to use the competition as an opportunity to learn about their opponents and other cultures. Celebrating outstanding athletic performances by great athletes of the world could replace the jingoistic flavor of past Olympic Games and reestablish their original purpose.

TABLE 9.1 Top 10 Countries in Gold Medals Since 1948

Country	Total gold medals
Russian Federation	645
United States of America	632
Germany	338
Italy	162
France	117
People's Republic of China	116
Hungary	113
Australia	107
Sweden	98
Japan	96

Includes both Summer and Winter Games through Torino in 2006.
Data from International Olympic Committee website; www.Olympics.org

TABLE 9.2 Final Medal Count From the 2004 Summer Olympics

Country	Gold	Silver	Bronze	Total
United States	35	39	29	103
Russia	27	27	38	92
China	32	17	38	63
Australia	17	16	16	49
Germany	14	16	18	48

Data from International Olympic Committee Web site; www.Olympics.org.

that time. Since the breakup of the Soviet Union, the United States has won the medal race in three consecutive Summer Games. However, Asian countries are beginning to assert themselves. With the 2008 Games being hosted in Beijing, China, the Chinese are poised to challenge for the top spot. Wining 32 gold medals in Athens, China trailed the United States in the race for gold by just three medals (see table 9.2). Japan, Korea, Thailand, and Indonesia became significant factors in the medal race for the first time.

Nationalism peaked with politicians using success in the Olympic Games as an endorsement of a country's society and system of government. When Russia topped the standings, they crowed about the superiority of the Communist system. When U.S. fortunes rose, the United States trumpeted the

ideals of democracy. Most of the hype was not about developing athletes but was merely boasting that conflicted with good sporting behavior.

As you might suspect, the Olympic Games have seen their share of politics. The following are some instances of when countries used the Olympic Games for political purposes:

- World War II interrupted the Olympics in 1940 to 1944.
- Israel was excluded after a threat of an Arab boycott in 1948.
- In 1952, Taiwan boycotted the Olympics when Communist China was admitted to the IOC. East Germany was excluded because it was not a recognized state.
- In 1960, the IOC told North and South Korea to compete as one team. North Korea refused. Nationalist China was forced to compete under the name of Taiwan.
- In 1964 South Africa was banned for apartheid.
- In 1968 in Mexico City, South Africa was banned again. American sprinters Tommie Smith and John Carlos raised a Black Power salute during the American anthem and were banned for life from future Olympics.
- In 1972 in Munich, Palestinians murdered 11 Israeli athletes.
- In 1980, some 60 nations boycotted the Games in protest of the Soviet Union's invasion of Afghanistan.

Although people the world over decry the politics in the Olympic Games, sports cannot be separated from the world at large. In order for countries to come together peacefully, there must be at least some political cooperation between nations. The athletes are the ones who suffer when their countries withdraw and eliminate a lifelong dream they have trained for years to reach.

Transcending the nationalism were performances by exceptional athletes who achieved historic results and became part of Olympic folklore. They included Jesse Owens's four gold medals in Berlin in 1934; Emil Zatopek's triple victory in the 5,000 meter, 10,000 meter, and marathon in Helsinki in 1952; Bob Beamon's leap of 29 feet and 2 1/2 inches (8.90 meters) in Mexico in 1968; swimmer Mark Spitz's seven gold medals in Munich in 1972; and gymnast Nadia Comaneci's seven perfect 10s in Montreal in 1976.

Observers of the Olympic Games have written for years about the negative influence of nationalism on

In the Arena With . . . *Jesse Owens*

The Olympic feats of Jesse Owens are almost unparalleled. No individual ever dominated the sprint races as he did. In the 1936 Olympic Games in Berlin, Nazi Germany had just taken control of the government. One of their tenets was to prove the superiority of the White race over others, particularly Black races. Owens, a Black man from the United States, did more than any other athlete to disprove the German hypothesis. He broke the world record in the 100 meters although it was disallowed because of wind, set a new world record in the 200 meters, broad jumped more than 26 feet (7.92 meters) for the first time in Olympic history, and anchored the 400-meter relay team, which also set a world record. Owens's four gold medals took the wind out of the sails of the Nazis' racist propaganda (Henry and Yeomans 1984).

the spirit and purpose of the Games. If the competition is about athletes, their country of origin should not matter. Critics have suggested eliminating team sports to reduce the natural nationalistic fever. They suggest removing the flags, anthems, and opening ceremony march by nations and having an international body select athletes.

Over the past several Olympic Games, the debate over nationalism has been replaced by the debate over money. The economics of staging these massive events necessitate corporate sponsors and television for cash. The Games have become large and lavish, and viewers have come to expect that. Decisions are made to accommodate television broadcasting, recognizing the importance of attracting millions of viewers that in turn can translate into lucrative sponsorships.

UNITED STATES OLYMPIC COMMITTEE

In 1978, the U.S. Congress passed the Amateur Sports Act as federal law. The act appointed the United States Olympic Committee (USOC) as the coordinating body for all Olympic-related athletic activity in the United States. The vision of the USOC as stated on their Web site is "to assist in finding opportunities for every American to participate in sport, regardless of gender, race, age, geography, or physical ability" (United States Olympic Committee 2005).

The Amateur Sports Act also designated the national governing body (NGB) for each sport in the United States. Each NGB supports its athletes, sets the rules for competition, stages competitions, and selects athletes to compete in world championships and the Olympic Games.

The USOC is headquartered in Colorado Springs, Colorado, on land donated by the U.S. government that was formerly a military base. Over the years, state-of-the-art training facilities were constructed along with new offices for staff and housing for athletes. The weather and altitude, however, forced the USOC to also develop other training venues: Lake Placid, New York, for winter sports and Chula Vista, California, for summer sports.

USOC Funding

Unlike many other governments, the U.S. government does not help fund the Olympic movement or its athletes. Honoring its tradition of private enterprise, the United States has designated the USOC as its keeper of the Olympic flame.

The USOC relies wholly on private donations from Americans and sponsorships from corporations. The annual budget for the USOC has hovered near $100 million U.S. for some time, a modest amount compared to its mission. Part of those funds supports the national governing bodies that develop athletes in specific sports. The formula for how much funding each NGB receives is complicated and always a bone of contention. NGBs that do well financially on their own like the U.S. Tennis Association, which has an annual budget that surpasses the total USOC budget for all sports, still claims its share of Olympic funds.

The USOC has realized the value of the five rings Olympic logo as a trademark that can be loaned to corporations in return for financial support. Likewise, merchandise sales labeled with the Olympic logo are a consistent source of USOC income.

USOC Membership

USOC members are organizations from the following categories:

- NGBs such as USA Baseball, USA Gymnastics, and USA Swimming

- Paralympic Sports Organizations (PSO), a new category with membership still to be determined, for organizations that represent athletes who are hearing impaired, mentally disabled, or wheelchair users

- Affiliated sports organizations such as the U.S. Squash Racquets Association, U.S. Orienteering Federation, U. S. Trampoline and Tumbling Association, and Triathlon Federation USA

- Community-based multisport organizations such as the Amateur Athletic Union; American Alliance of Health, Physical Education, Recreation and Dance; Boys and Girls Club of America; YMCA and YWCA; and Native American Sports Council

Governance

Until 2004, the USOC was governed by a board of directors of over 100 members representing the various organizations belonging to the USOC. Another significant group within the board was the Athletes Advisory Council, who protect the interests of all Olympic athletes. An elected executive committee of approximately a dozen board members monitored the professional staff activity, oversaw the budget, and acted on behalf of the board between meetings. All of these representatives were volunteers, leaders in their sport that were either appointed or elected to serve on the USOC board.

Over the last 20 years a series of volunteer and staff conflicts, conflicts of interest among board members, and staff turnovers drew criticism from many different people, who pointed out that the USOC had morphed into an unwieldy bureaucracy that served no one, including the athletes. Pressure from the U.S. Congress in 2003 led to serious USOC self-evaluation, which in turn let the USOC to streamline its committees, policies, and board of directors. Essentially the reforms reduced the board to a size similar to that of the former executive committee and established four standing committees, annual reporting requirements, regular self-review, and whistleblower mechanisms beginning in 2004 (Borzilleri 2003; SportingNews.com 2003a).

The conflict between professional staff and volunteer board members or committee chairs has been an issue at the USOC just as it has been in many NGBs. Arising from different goals and styles of operation, the USOC volunteer–staff confrontations are like those in many not-for-profit organizations. Lines of reporting are blurred, personalities clash, and frequent changes in volunteer leadership and direction frustrate staff professionals who believe their careers are being affected by people who are consumed with the privileges and perks of their position. The recent changes in USOC governance place the staff supervision with the chief operating officer, separating it from volunteer leaders.

The role of the professional staff, which has exceeded 500 employees, is to provide athletes access to elite training programs, assist in training programs for potential Olympic athletes, and support athletes at Olympic events. Often the staff works closely with each NGB. Latest training methods, advances in sports medicine, and equipment research are all provided at Olympic training centers for use by NGB athletes and the results of the research with elite athletes is published and available. Along with funding, NGBs need advice on hosting competitions, training coaches, identifying athlete talent, and preparing athletes for world competition. The USOC acts as a clearinghouse for information on all these topics, identifies experts for consultation, and

Activity Time-Out: Medals Versus Participation

Reconcile the stated USOC vision with the goal of winning medals at the Olympic Games. Are these two goals in conflict? How might emphasizing one affect success in the other?

Once a competitive force in all Olympic sports, could American athletes soon see their dominance end?

produces educational materials that can be applied to multiple sports.

Pursuit of Medals

It may seem like the United States is in good shape to maintain dominance in Olympic competition. However, in-depth analysis reveals the challenges that lie ahead. Since the breakup of the Soviet Union, dozens of medals have gone to smaller nations once counted with Russia. In spite of that loss, Russia continues to snap at the heels of the United States.

The United States continues to be strong in swimming and track and field, where it won more than half of its 103 medals in 2004. But the United States is weakening in many other areas. USA Boxing has fallen on hard times and had its worst Olympics in more than 50 years in 2004. USA Diving went without a medal in the 2004 Olympics, and field hockey and men's soccer did not even qualify for the Games. Baseball also did not qualify—*baseball,* invented in the United States.

The nation to watch now is China, along with Japan, Korea, and other Asian countries. China is the most populous nation on the planet and by hosting the Games in 2008 has a strong stake in setting new records. China has almost tripled its medal production since returning to the Games in 1988. Asian governments are pouring resources into athlete training like they never have before and are likely to see the results in the near future.

Interestingly, if winning medals is the goal, then the smart strategy is to assess medal potential sport by sport and spend the money where it can do the most good. Some sports, such as tennis, only offer a few medals. Men's and women's singles and doubles are the only events offered, for a total of 12 potential medals. Other sports like swimming, track and field, and gymnastics offer multiple medals for individual and team events. To win more medals, the USOC should emphasize sports that offer greater medal potential and already have a strong base of athletic development within the country.

ATHLETE DEVELOPMENT

Since success is the goal of the USOC, it would seem that resources should be spent on developing American athletes. There are many factors the USOC must consider to maximize this development.

Activity Time-Out: Best Sport Options

As you examine the potential for conflict between performance and participation sport, If you were in charge of developing the best American Olympic team for winning medals, what sports would you fund? Find out the medal potential, the U.S. historical success and development tradition, and the current state of each sport, and then identify the five sports you would target for Beijing in 2008.

Talent Identification

National governing bodies must take responsibility for recruiting large numbers of kids into their sport, offering strong competitive events for every age, and assisting with training. By casting a wide net to find potential athletes, the NGBs increase their odds that talented athletes will emerge.

No one system of identifying future star athletes has been accepted in the sporting world. Certain athlete attributes have been identified as being critical in particular sports, but the many exceptions confound the experts. Maturation produces performance gains that simply cannot be predicted. Michael Jordan was cut from his high school basketball team and yet went on to become the finest basketball player in the world.

The key to talent identification as it stands today is to gather young athletes who exhibit the best potential in their sport, encourage them, and provide competition, including international competition, expert coaching, and financial support. Once the children develop, experts assess the natural talent and sport progress and predict future success.

Training

Training young American athletes is a crazy patchwork quilt of tradition, expediency, and entrepreneurship. The public schools offer sophisticated athletic programs in sports that are affordable and geographically accessible to any potential athlete. Other sports do not have interscholastic teams or are conducted more as recreational activities.

Community-based programs in many sports get kids started and provide excellent early training. By the time some athletes reach the critical age of 12 or so, they may have outgrown the local competition and coaching expertise and may need to travel or move to continue their athletic development. Here is where family income becomes a limitation.

The USOC has experimented with the idea of establishing minicenters to offer training in several Olympic sports in major metropolitan areas. The jury is still out on the viability of this approach, and funding the centers continues to be an issue. The geographical size of the United States makes competition between athletes from different regions expensive.

As athletes advance to within a few years of potential Olympic competition, they need to gather with the best athletes in their sport to train, compete, and focus on their goal. Many NGBs do not have the facilities, money, or even the commitment to provide this opportunity. Some sports rely on private training academies to provide this service, although money can still be a limiting factor. Other sports have located such programs at the Olympic Training Centers in California, Lake Placid, and Colorado Springs. Through economy of scale, these multisport facilities may offer more affordable operations, and athletes may interact with kids in other sports who might be easier to befriend than the ones they compete with every day.

Coaching

Although we will examine coaching in chapter 18, we will mention it briefly here, as it is essential to athlete development. Coaching is typically the key to the optimal development of any athlete. Most successful athletes are affected along the way by several coaches of different strengths. Coaches of introductory programs must understand youth, make sport fun, teach the fundamentals, and be willing to let go. Coaches of young athletes growing more dedicated to their sport must guide their development of competitive and physical skill, help them adjust to a changing physical body, offer a comprehensive training program, and recommend a coach for the next phase. Coaches of elite athletes aiming for world competition must understand that competitive world, capitalize on the athlete's strengths while minimizing weaknesses, tap into resources like specialists in sport science or advanced coaching as needed, and be sensitive to the total makeup of the athlete as it relates to athletic performance.

While serving on the USOC Coaching Committee for two quadrennials, I helped study the challenges the U.S. coaching profession faces. During the eight years I served from 1992-2000, we set the following goals:

- Improve the status and recognition of the coaching profession
- Ensure the competency of coaches at every level by encouraging each sport to develop desired coaching competencies and help their coaches acquire them
- Help the coaches desiring to research and apply sport sciences to formulate training and development programs

The USOC provided direction, materials, workshops, and consultants to NGBs wanting to improve their coaching performance. Results varied widely, depending on the sport, its traditions, available funds, and the quality of coaching opportunities.

CHAPTER SUMMARY

The modern Olympic Games have been a wildly successful international sporting event over the past 100 years. No other worldwide sporting event captures public interest, with the possible exception of the World Cup in soccer, which involves only one sport and sees fading interest in each country eliminated. At the Olympic Games, every country watches multiple athletes perform in multiple events lasting for more than a fortnight.

The Olympics have sparked athlete development programs in virtually all 202 nations that compete. Training elite athletes has become big business and is often supported by government funding. Athletes no longer need be amateurs who compete for the love of the sport. In fact, success at the Olympic Games ensures most athletes financial bonanzas, particularly if corporate sponsors choose them as spokespeople.

During the Cold War, a nationalistic spirit dominated the Games as countries vied for athletic supremacy to symbolically validate the superiority of their way of life. Gradually, the nationalistic fervor faded and was replaced by an economic tenor. The cost of staging the Games, opening the Games to professionals, and the race to exceed previous Games in breadth and quality drove organizers to enlist the financial support of major worldwide corporations.

Politics intertwine with Olympic Games, and over the years countries have used the Olympic Games for political purposes. Although many people are dismayed at the use of the Olympics for political statements, others view it as natural to seek world attention for issues such as apartheid and human rights that are simply incompatible with the lofty ideals of Olympism.

In the United States, the United States Olympic Committee (USOC) has the daunting task of developing Olympic athletes. While governments of many other nations devote funding to developing their Olympic athletes, the USOC raises money from private donations and corporate support.

The organization of the USOC has been under discussion in recent years. In 2004, several bills were put forth in the U.S. Congress to streamline the USOC governance, reduce bureaucratic overlap, and simplify the daily operations of this nonprofit organization that has an annual budget of $100 million U.S.

Athletes and coaches have benefited by efforts of the Olympic movement to provide better sport systems, talent scouting, support for potential Olympic athletes, and information and training for coaches. Through the national governing bodies, information is filtered and adapted to each sport.

Sport and Culture

Part IV begins with a look at how moral attitudes affect sporting behavior or are developed through sport. Most people believe that moral behavior can be taught through sport, but there is evidence that the opposite can occur unless a sport program has a clear philosophy, strong leadership, and enforcement of rules.

The next several chapters deal with the social classifications of people by race, gender, class, age, and disability. Each of these categories can have a powerful effect on sport participation. The exclusion of African Americans from the sport world mirrored the policies of segregation in the United States until the last 50 years; likewise, until Title IX was passed in the 1970s, sport opportunities for women and girls were severely limited. The inclusion of females and minorities has significantly changed the sport landscape in the United States. Participation has steadily increased, media coverage has expanded, and more money has been spent. While equal opportunities are not quite a reality, they are light-years ahead of where they were just a generation ago.

Social class tends to draw people to particular sports that fit their interests, available time, and economic ability to pay. Athletes who are more affluent are able to join private clubs, pay for coaching, and participate in expensive sports such as equestrian, skiing, and golf. Working- and middle-class families are forced to rely primarily on public or community programs and school athletic programs that are more affordable. Sports that include violence, such as auto racing, boxing, wrestling, and hybrids of sports such as roller derby appeal to the working class and the poor.

As baby boomers have reached retirement age, the proportion of the U.S. population over age 50 has exceeded 80 million, or nearly one-third of the total population. For most older adults, physical activity for health and lifestyle reasons replaces interest in competitive sport, although as spectators they still retain a commitment to competition. Another special population in sport is people with physical or mental disabilities whose opportunities in sport have expanded dramatically since passage of the Americans with Disabilities Act in 1990. Both the Special Olympics and the

Paralympics have become major worldwide events involving thousands of athletes who were previously left out of sport.

No culture has ever functioned without some form of politics and religion, and both influence attitudes of people toward physical activity and sport. Early religion in North America tended to favor development of the spirit rather than the body, but in this century, organized religion has embraced sport as a worthwhile use of time and a powerful socializing agent. Politics has long recognized the influence of sport on the masses and used it to entertain the masses, socialize them toward a particular way of life, and inculcate feelings of nationalism.

The chapter on deviance and sport tackles some of the more unpleasant aspects of the sport world. Emotion generated in sport can contribute to deviant behavior, but those athletes who are the most egregious offenders can claim no such excuses. Performance enhancement through the use of illegal substances is a recurrent problem that has finally attracted the attention of sport organizations and the government. Gambling through sport continues to be a thorny issue. Hazing in sport and eating disorders are other aberrant behaviors that we confront in this chapter.

Unlike most books of this type, the influential role of athletic coaches is acknowledged and considered. Coaches heavily influence many young people because they are often held in high esteem at a time when kids are looking for heroes other than parents. From youth sport to high school and college sport, coaches are often the most admired and respected adults by athletes. Their influence may go way beyond athletic training and extend into personal values, socialization into a group, and development of self-discipline and self-confidence.

Most coaches enter the profession because they want to lead young people, although many are not well equipped to do so. Coaching education is a major challenge, especially in youth programs where volunteer coaches are plentiful and the turnover rate is enormous.

In the concluding chapter, we explore the critical issues facing sport in view of larger social trends. An aging population and longer life spans are a reality. Many people look to sport participation and spectatorship to enhance their later years. At the same time, the population in general is facing a health crisis spurred by increases in overweight and obese people. Clearly, physical activity has to play a role in mitigating the effects of inactivity.

Attitudes toward sport participation based on race, gender, social class, disabilities, ethnicity, and sexual preference have changed. Power struggles are likely to continue between those who favor high-performance sport and those who prefer sport participation for recreation by large numbers of people.

Advances in science and technology will push the frontiers of sport performance ever higher and continue to cause records to fall. Sport will change as our society changes, and depending on which social theory you consult, those changes will come from within the sporting community or from outside based on larger social changes reflected in government and laws. What cannot be argued is that sport will change to reflect society.

CHAPTER

Sporting Behavior

Student Outcomes

After reading this chapter, you will know the following:

- What *good sporting behavior* means
- The relationship between learned moral values and sport
- Conflicting evidence for the positive or negative effects of sport on moral behavior
- How parents, coaches, and others affect children's sporting behavior

Grantland Rice, one of the preeminent sports writers of the early 20th century, once said, "For when the One Great Scorer comes to mark against your name, He writes not that you won or lost—but how you played the game" (Wikipedia 2005c). His quote has lived on as a motto for coaches and athletes who aspire to the highest levels of good sporting behavior.

Sporting behavior is quickly replacing the traditional term of **sportsmanship** to remove gender bias in describing human behavior in sport. For example, the Colorado High School Activities Association publishes a *Sporting Behavior Manual* (2005). Throughout this chapter you will see *sporting behavior* and *sportsmanship* used interchangeably, depending on the source. Sportsmanship has been defined as "the ethical behavior exhibited by a sportsman or athlete . . . generally considered to involve participation for the pleasure gained from a fair and hard-fought contest, refusal to take unfair advantage of a situation or of an opponent, courtesy toward one's opponent, and graciousness in both winning and losing" (Webster's Sports Dictionary 1976).

Sporting behavior has been a subject of debate and dissension for centuries. The ancient Greeks spoke about sportsmanship in Olympic competition. The Greek city-states of Athens, Corinth, and Argos valued courtesy and good sporting behavior. In contrast, athletes from the city-state of Sparta were encouraged to win at all costs, a philosophy for which they were despised by their opponents (Dunn 2005). The founder of the modern Olympics, Pierre de Coubertin, offered this famous quote:

"The important thing in the Olympic Games is not to win but to take part, the important thing in life is not the triumph but the struggle. The essential thing is not to have conquered but to have fought well. To spread these precepts is to build up a stronger and more valiant and, above all, more scrupulous and more generous humanity." (Henry and Yeomans 1984)

Acceptable standards of behavior have been extolled, ignored, and given lip service by many coaches and sport participants. This chapter takes a fresh look at what good sporting behavior actually is, whether it can be taught and practiced in sports, and the attitude of our society toward its importance. We'll look at how good sporting behavior is practiced at different levels of play, how moral development influences good sporting behavior, and how the examples of coaches, parents, other athletes influence good sporting behavior.

SPORTING BEHAVIOR AT DIFFERENT LEVELS OF SPORT

Performance sports in which competition and winning are paramount have dramatically influenced sporting behavior in recent years. As performance expectations increase, pressure to succeed rises exponentially. The value of winning may become such a seductive goal that all thoughts of moral behavior are temporarily put aside.

Professional athletes in all sports are role models for youthful competitors whether they want to be or not. Kids note their taunting, trash talk, disrespect, cheating, and bending or ignoring of the rules. The more successful professional athletes are, the more media attention they receive, in spite of boorish behavior or illegal acts. Professional basketball player Charles Barkley is notable for his well-publicized quote that "he isn't a role model." Barkley's point was that the responsibility for moral upbringing lies with parents, not with professional athletes (Brennan 2001).

Others may agree with Barkley, but the weight of the evidence shows that young people look to people they admire for clues about life. Athletes who are successful and on display impress youth who do not have caring parents and coaches to help them differentiate positive and unacceptable traits of famous athletes. Research shows that when children are systematically taught about fair play and moral development, character can be enhanced through sports (Gibbins, Ebbeck, and Weiss 1995).

The disconcerting influence of professional athletes at the top of their game is that kids may mistakenly believe that the athletes' questionable behavior contributes to their success. Young athletes may emulate that behavior to test its effectiveness, often with sad results that affect their athletic career. Media can contribute to the misunderstandings of youth by emphasizing winning above all else. Winners almost always get more photographs, more film footage, and more copy. The next most popular media themes are money, ownership, coaching, and the skills that helped win the game. Media coverage of fairness, honesty, or consideration for other athletes is almost nonexistent, giving the impression that these traits are unimportant (Fullerton 2003).

Participation sports tend to have a more balanced approach to winning. Playing hard and fair wins admirers regardless of the outcome of the game. As athletes age, they naturally tend to shift their emphasis from high performance toward participation. As we discussed in chapter 3, people who choose participation or recreational sport are more focused on enjoying the game, socializing with friends and opponents, and exercising. For millions of people who choose participation sports, even in youth, healthy sporting behavior is more naturally part of the social expectations of the sport since the focus shifts away from winning.

Athletes who are young have a lot to absorb just to learn the game. This learning includes proper behavior toward others in the sport. They may be too young to fully understand good sporting behavior, but they certainly can learn to follow coaches and officials in acceptable behavior. Then, as they mature intellectually, they become capable of understanding moral reasoning and emotionally able to control their feelings.

Since young people, particularly young people in performance sports, are malleable in attitude and behavior, most programs for promoting good sporting behavior focus on them. These kids also deal with the greatest pressure to perform at elite levels of sport and reconciling the conflicting behaviors of various role models. They need patience, clear guidelines, and consistent consequences for unacceptable actions.

Some people may laud the behavior of Rasheed Wallace, while others may question the example he shows to youth.

Clinical psychologist Darrell Burnett (2005) developed the following sample guidelines for kids:

- I abide by the rules of the game.
- I try to avoid arguments.
- I share in the responsibilities of the team.
- I give everyone a chance to play according to the rules.
- I always play fair.
- I follow the directions of the coach.
- I respect the other team's effort.
- I encourage my teammates.

As athletes age, they grow in their capacity to place sport competition within a larger framework of life. The physical limitations that come with aging help older adults focus on the befits of participation (Payne and Issacs 2005). As they revise their goals to a realistic level of expectation, the pressure to win drops. Their reasoning ability along with social experience allows them to form a code of behavior that reflects their personal value system. In most cases, people behave in a way that is acceptable to their social group if they want to continue in that group.

YOUTH ATTITUDES

According to Michael Josephson, president of the Josephson Institute of Ethics, a recent survey of 4,200 high school athletes revealed the following:

"Coaches and parents simply aren't doing enough to assure that the experience (in sports) is a positive one. Too many youngsters are confused about the meaning of fair play and sportsmanship and they have no concept of honorable competition. As a result they engage in illegal conduct and employ doubtful gamesmanship techniques to gain a competitive advantage. It appears that today's playing fields are the breeding grounds for the next generation of corporate pirates and political scoundrels." (Josephson 2004)

Here are some of the key findings of the survey (the survey form and complete data are available from www.charactercounts.org):

- Girls are more sportsmanlike than boys. Overall, boys are far more likely to exhibit cynical attitudes and engage in illegal or unsporting conduct.
- Coaches don't always set a good example. Most players felt that their coaches exhibited good sporting behavior, but when players were questioned about specific coaching actions, one-quarter to one-third of their answers revealed violations by coaches.
- Many high school athletes break rules and engage in unsporting conduct. Many think it is proper to (1) deliberately inflict pain in football to intimidate an opponent (58% males, 24% females), (2) trash-talk a defender after every score (47% males, 19% females), (3) soak a football field to slow down an opponent (27% males, 12% females), or (4) throw at a batter who homered last time up (30% males, 16% females).
- Winning is more important than sportsmanship. More than 37% of males agreed that it's more important to win than to be considered a good sport. When asked, 31% of males and 25% of females said they believe their coach is more concerned with winning than in building character and life skills.
- Cheating and theft seem acceptable to high school athletes. In the past year, (1) 68% of both males and females admit to having cheated on a test in school, (2) 26% of males and 19% of females said that they stole an item from a

store, and (3) 43% of males and 31% of females said they cheated or bent the rules to win.

- Hazing and bullying seem acceptable to high school athletes: 69% of males and 50% of females admit that they bullied, teased, or taunted someone in the past year, while 55% of males and 29% of females said they used racial slurs or insults.

The respondents in this study are high school athletes in a variety of sports in certain geographical locations. It is difficult to generalize these results to all athletes due to a wide variation in sport, location, coach, level of competition, and social class. Yet the results do indicate that the values systems of these high school athletes do not represent a developed sense of moral behavior.

Another study released in 2005 (Shields) by researchers at the University of Missouri at St. Louis, the University of Minnesota, and Notre Dame sampled 803 athletes ages 9 to 15 along with 189 parents and 61 coaches. Here are a few of their findings:

- Nearly 1 in 10 respondents admitted to cheating
- 13% had tried to hurt an opponent
- 31% had argued with an official
- 27% had acted like "bad sports"
- 7% of coaches had encouraged cheating

Now that we've looked at sporting behavior at different levels of sport, we can examine how good sporting behavior develops, beginning at moral development and following with how moral development and moral values affect sport.

DEVELOPMENT OF MORAL VALUES

The foundation of our behavior in sport is based on our level of moral reasoning. Many researchers have studied the development of moral values in society and have postulated various theories based on their findings. Many theories are similar while some take a slightly different view, but all link moral capacity to intellectual development. Jean Piaget, a famous Swiss psychologist, is renowned for his pioneering work in explaining the stages of mental development and later moral development. One of his devotees was Lawrence Kohlberg, who as a professor at Harvard University publicized his own theory of moral development beginning in the 1970s. Like Piaget, Kohlberg believed that children move through a

In the Arena With . . . *John Landy*

It was the 1956 National Championships in Melbourne, Australia, just before the upcoming Olympic Games. John Landy was the favorite in the mile run since he held the current world record of 3 minutes and 58 seconds. The crowd of 22,000 eagerly anticipated another world record.

As the race developed, the pace was fast and a world record seemed within reach. Ron Clarke, the former Australian junior champion, was in the third lap with John Landy just behind him. Another runner, Alec Henderson, tried to squeeze between the two leaders and tangled with Clarke, sending both runners sprawling. As Clarke fell, Landy leaped over him and inadvertently spiked him in the shoulder. The rest of the field ran around or jumped over Clarke and kept running. But John Landy stopped, ran back to the fallen Clarke, and said, "Sorry. Are you all right?" Clarke affirmed that he was OK and urged Landy to keep running.

Clarke got to his feet and he and Landy set off together, 60 yards (54.9 meters) behind the rest of the field. With the frenzied crowd chanting his name, John Landy sprinted down the homestretch and won the race with an amazing display of powerful sprinting. He didn't set a world record, but his win was unforgettable. The cheers and applause refused to die down during his victory lap.

Landy's pause to help a fallen competitor cost him 8 or 10 seconds and a world record, but it etched the importance of good sporting behavior in the mind of a nation. John Landy went on to set new world records and become a hero of the 1956 Olympic Games (Cochrane and Hoepper 2005).

series of stages before arriving at their capacity for moral maturity. Kohlberg's theory will serve as an example of moral development for our discussion on good sporting behavior (Crain 1985; Smart and Smart 1982).

Kohlberg demonstrated through studies that people progress in their moral reasoning through a series of stages. Kohlberg asserted that moral reasoning could only proceed with intellectual development and exposure to socialization. He classified the stages into three levels, placing two stages in each level:

Preconventional

1. Punishment and obedience
2. Pleasure or pain

Conventional

3. Good boy or girl
4. Law and order

Postconventional

5. Social contract
6. Principled conscience

Let's take a closer look at each of these stages and how they influence good sporting behavior.

Preconventional Stage

The **preconventional stage** is the base for moral reasoning. The first stage of punishment and obedience is the level of moral thinking typically found in elementary school. Young students and athletes behave according to socially acceptable norms because they are told to do so by parents, teachers, or coaches. Being right simply means obeying an authority. Disobeying the dictates of the authority results in punishment. This concept is within the intellectual grasp of children, and they can understand it. Whether they follow directions depends on the timing, manner of delivery, and punishment for disobedience.

The second stage involves thinking that the reason for behavior is to get pleasure for oneself. This hedonistic approach to moral choices is very self-centered as opposed to respecting the values of a group or society. Children at this stage realize that there is not always one right answer as decided by an adult authority and test their own conclusions. They expect punishment if their actions are wrong, but unlike in stage one, view punishment as simply a risk one takes for acting a certain way. Punishment does not necessarily occur because you were wrong.

At the preconventional stage of development, a youth sport athlete is more apt to trust the instructor and see the instructor as an authority figure.

Youth athletes in stage two may take certain actions because they have learned that doing so may be in their self-interest. Their idea is, "I'll scratch your back if you scratch mine." They reason as an individual rather than as a member of a community.

Kohberg believed that younger children typically use the preconventional level of morality because they can process it intellectually. As children mature and begin to understand how the world works, they adopt a more relative approach that does not accept rules as absolute but as changeable if the group agrees to change them. Children tend to change in moral capacity around age 10 or 11, at the time when many kids are heavily involved in youth sports. It is a wise coach who anticipates this development and assists it rather than limits players to simply following coaching dictates.

A good coach may enlist the help of her athletes in deciding appropriate punishment for players who break rules or behave inappropriately. When athletes participate in the process they must examine the seriousness of the offense, the number of occurrences, previous warnings, and possible sanctions or punishments. As they review the facts and consider alternatives, they establish a sense of moral decision making that will help them mature in their thinking abilities.

Unfortunately, some children get stuck in the preconventional level of moral development. They are the ones who often deviate from society and may end up in a correctional institution. Some adults still exhibit these lower levels of moral reasoning when justifying their actions, further confusing the young people who hear their opinions.

Conventional Stage

The **conventional stage** of moral reasoning is the level attained by most adults. The first stage in this level and the third stage of moral development is the one typically found in society. Behavior is guided by what is generally acceptable to friends, family, and community. Youth usually reach this stage in high school, and high school students often believe in good behavior that emphasizes love, caring, empathy, trust, and concern for others. They try on various behaviors to see how those around them respond and then typically either modify actions that do not conform to group standards or willingly pay the price for deviating from group standards.

The fourth stage is dubbed *law and order* because it is important to maintain laws, respect authority, and perform accepted duties so that society can function. Without the smooth functioning of a society, there would be anarchy. People need to follow the rules of society or work to change those with which they disagree.

The majority of any population fall into the two conventional categories because *conventional* categories are just that. Most of us stay at stage three or four for most of our life.

Postconventional Stage

The **postconventional stage** is a level most of us do not reach. The fifth stage is referred to as a *social contract* because those in this stage have an interest in the welfare of others. This is an autonomous, principled stage of thinking in which people adopt certain moral principles and hold to that behavior regardless of social punishment or reward. The concept of inalienable human rights enters here. So too does the idea of treating all people with dignity and respect regardless of their ethnic or racial background, economic class, or actions.

Kolhberg also postulated a sixth stage which relied heavily on humanistic principles of valuing human

At the conventional stage of moral reasoning, rules are followed to keep people safe. If you break the rules, you are punished.

life and feeling right with oneself. The principles of justice, fairness, and human dignity require compassion and ask us to treat all humans as individuals who deserve impartial love and concern. There are certain universal laws all religions accept that guide us toward appropriate actions. However, after a time, Kohlberg found so few humans he could point to who had reached this sixth level that he basically ignored it. Apart from great moral leaders such as Mahatma Gandhi, Martin Luther King Jr., or Nelson Mandela, few people reached the final level of moral development.

Barriers to Good Sporting Behavior

Because of the heavy emphasis on winning in sport competition, some athletes struggle with the choice between winning through any means and exhibiting good sporting behavior. With young children, it takes time to develop the intellectual understanding to move beyond simply playing by the rules to competing within the spirit of the game as well. With older youth and adults in the conventional stage, the barriers to good behavior may be customs within sports or the influence of coaches or spectators. Trash talk, verbally abusing opponents, and taunting have become a part of the social culture in some sports. Players who use these methods to distract their opponents may be rewarded with a victory that reinforces their actions.

Coaches or parents who understand good sporting behavior sometimes forgive athletes who offend because they want their team to win. The media glorification of winners helps reinforce the importance of winning and gives the impression that our culture admires winners, not necessarily good sports.

MORAL VALUES APPLIED TO SPORT

Now that we've covered the stages of moral development, let's look at how they affect sport. Sports can play a vital role in helping young people become socialized in their environment. **Socialization** is the process of interacting with other people and learning social customs, morals, and values. As we interact with others, we form opinions about what we believe and how we should act. Others do the same through their interactions with us. It is a dynamic process and our understanding of our social world changes as we accumulate experiences.

Many of the theories we discussed in chapter 2, including functionalism, conflict, and interactionist theories, describe how socialization occurs in society. Let's look at how each of these theories influenced current understanding of how athletes become socialized in sports.

Functional theorists view socialization as the process in which we develop the social characteristics that allow us to fit into our world. Using this approach, we would study the athletes being socialized, their likely guides, such as parents and coaches, and the outcomes of their process. Functionalist studies such as that by Shields et al., (2005) or Josephson (2004) elicit information from athletes about why they play sports and what changes occur as a result of their participation. Most of these studies have presented inconclusive or even contradictory evidence. It is difficult to generalize findings from a restricted sample size due to the wide variation of possible athletic experiences.

Conflict theory offers another approach to socialization. Advocates of this theory assume that people

Activity Time-Out: Moral Reasoning and Sport

What does Kohlberg's theory have to do with sports? Consider how you would answer the following questions on moral decision making in sport. For each question, list your answer as well as the level of moral reasoning you used.

1. Assume you are a football player who runs for a touchdown on the last play of the game and scores for the margin of victory. As your coaches and teammates mob you in celebration, you are torn because you know you stepped out of bounds during the run but the referee did not see it. Should you continue celebrating or stop to talk to your coach and the referee?

2. While your softball team is playing a game, the opposing team taunts your pitcher, heckles every batter, and talks trash at every opportunity. They win the game 10 to 2. A few weeks later you have a rematch. Your coach and team decide to get the jump on the other team by returning the behavior and recruiting your fans to help harass the opponents. Would you join in the trash talk and heckling?

3. During a tennis match without any line umpires, your opponent keeps calling balls out that you clearly saw as in. After this happens half a dozen times, you decide to take action. What do you do?

with economic influence use it to maintain their status in privileged positions within society. Most research as described by Coakley and Dunning (2004) using this approach has focused on how highly organized sport programs with authoritarian leaders and coaches have helped develop athletes who conform to their system in order to be accepted within the group. Athletes who come from lower socioeconomic classes may be exploited by this system. In spite of poor academic skills, athletes may be pushed through college as long as they have eligibility remaining but may never actually graduate.

The work by Fine (1987) is an example of research that has evolved to more interactionist models for studying athlete participation. Interactionist models emphasize the mutual interaction occurring between athletes and their environment as the athletes form their traits of socialization. Typically, this research has been more clinical, based on qualitative, in-depth interviews with athletes. The goal is to accumulate information in a natural field setting in order to understand what happens to an athlete during socialization through sports. This method significantly departs from the large samples of people who are questioned objectively and asked to report on their experiences.

Whatever the theory, the fundamental question of this chapter is whether sport participation builds character or negatively influences character. Or perhaps it exerts little influence at all. For years, we

have accepted the premise that sports build character with little evidence to support that claim. Let's look at the data that have been collected so far.

Sport As a Character Builder

Do sports build character? This question is much more difficult than it appears. Experts cannot agree on what character is and even if they did precisely define it, it would still be difficult to measure. Some studies (Beller and Stoll 1994) have compared those who play sports with those who do not and have concluded that the positive traits exhibited by athletes prove that sports are beneficial. However, it could be that those who play sports already possess those positive traits. Likewise, those who do not play sports could certainly attain positive character traits through other experiences. A clear cause-and-effect relationship has been very difficult to confirm.

Another confounding variable is that not all sport experiences are inherently similar. They depend on whether the emphasis is on participation or competitive excellence. Sport experiences also depend on the athletes' age, ability to make moral decisions, and opportunities to make such decisions. Coaches may greatly influence moral decision making, depending on their philosophy of coaching and openness to athlete-centered activity versus coach-centered activity.

Consider the different feelings about moral behavior that could arise from teammates who play very different positions. Contrast the attitude of a

Pitchers are sometimes encouraged to throw at a batter who hit a home run last time up. What stage of moral reasoning does this behavior fall in? How would a functional theorist explain this behavior? A conflict theorist?

defensive end who relies on aggressiveness to rush the passer and perhaps is urged to physically hurt the opposing quarterback with that of a reserve placekicker who rarely engages in physical contact but instead deals with constant mental pressure to focus on kicks in critical situations.

Likewise, athletes who compete in big-time sports at universities adopt a moral code of behavior that fits with their ultimate objective of competing at the highest levels of their sport. Although relatively mature intellectually, these athletes tend to embrace a simple, practical approach of playing within the rules to avoid punishment and progress to the next level of competition.

Athletes who compete for a Division III college with no scholarships have to determine the role of sports in their life and balance their time and effort with other life goals related to their studies and career. For these athletes, sports may be more social, a physical outlet and a chance to test their skills. Moral behavior is more about comfortably fitting in with their teammates and coaches.

Table 10.1 shows the results of a survey that questioned high school athletes about their attitudes toward sporting behavior. Although the majority of high school athletes viewed these negative behaviors as unacceptable, the fact that one-quarter to one-half of the respondents thought the behaviors were OK is significant. Apparently the athletes were simply reflecting the moral values they were taught, behaviors perhaps reinforced through sports. If we asked professional athletes the same types of questions, do you think the results would be similar? If not, how would they differ?

Character Development in Sport

As discussed, performance sports emphasize winning, pursuit of excellence, and attaining the highest possible level of performance. Opponents are often seen as enemies to be dominated, demoralized, and defeated. Hard work, dedication, sacrifices, and physical risks are all acceptable and expected.

In contrast, participation sports emphasize game play, the enjoyment of physical movement, and con-

TABLE 10.1   High School Attitudes Toward Sporting Behavior

Question	Percentage of athletes who deem behavior acceptable
1. A coach orders a player to attack a preexisting injury of the top scorer on the other team.	20%
2. In baseball, a key player for team X is hit by a pitch. In retaliation, X's coach orders his pitcher to throw at an opposing hitter.	20%
3. In football, a lineman deliberately seeks to inflict pain on an opposing player to intimidate him.	42%
4. In football, a coach's team is out of time-outs in a crucial game. He instructs a player to fake an injury to get the time-out.	31%
5. A basketball coach teaches players how to illegally hold and push in ways that are difficult to detect.	35%
6. In softball, a pitcher deliberately throws at a batter who homered the last time up.	24%
7. In ice hockey, a coach sends in a player to intimidate opponents and protect his own players.	67%
8. After scoring, a player does an elaborate showboat dance in front of the opponent's bench.	40%
9. On the winning point of a volleyball game, a player touches the ball before it goes out, but the referee misses the touch. The player says nothing.	48%
10. A coach argues with an official, intending to intimidate or influence future calls.	41%

Adapted, by permission, from M. Josephson, 2004, *Character Counts: Sportsmanship survey* (Los Angeles, CA: Josephson Institute of Ethics). www.charactercounts.org.

nections between mind and body, between athlete and nature, or between one athlete and another. Decisions are typically made democratically and all players regardless of ability get to participate in the action.

Performance sports clearly produce a lot more pressure on athletes and coaches. When people are stretched to their limits, their moral decisions may be affected until winning and great performance are more important than anything else. Many youth sports are conducted more like performance sports than participation sports, although in the long term the athletes may not be suited to performance sports.

Pickup games in neighborhoods have existed for generations. Kids learned to function as a group to agree on what game to play, what rules to follow, who would play what position, and how to handle disputes. The outcome of the game was less important than getting to play. If the group couldn't agree, the game simply didn't happen. Players learned to call their own fouls or risk social isolation. Players who hogged the ball were chosen last for future games. Moral codes of behavior were established and enforced by the group. Kids worked out disputes without coaches, umpires, or league organizers.

Defining Character in Sports

The concept of *character* changes with the times and the society in which it exists. For America, good character tends to be based on the ideals espoused by the founders and the Puritan work ethic. People were admired for working hard to survive a life that demanded hard work. Collectively, people expected others to conform to societal customs, obey parents and leaders, exhibit self-discipline as well as loyalty toward family and friends, and respect external rewards. Those same virtues constitute good sporting behavior.

Young people should be able to transfer the life lessons they learn in sports to the workplace as they enter the adult world. Thus a major achievement of youth sport is to teach young people to act in socially acceptable ways and so those lessons hopefully carry over to their adult years. Most articles, Web sites, and manuals (Ariss 2000) on good sporting behavior list the following attributes as essential:

- Knowing and following the rules of the game
- Respecting teammates, opponents, officials, and coaches
- Never using or threatening physical violence
- Abstaining from taunting, bragging, or excessive celebration

Pop Culture: *Friday Night Lights*

The popular book and movie *Friday Night Lights* (Bissinger 2003) chronicles a season of high school football in a small Texas town obsessed with football. The film shows the good, the bad, and the ugly of high school sports that emphasize winning above all else. The players and townspeople struggle or celebrate depending on the results of every Friday night football game. The football coach tries to put a bit of reality into the expectations for his young charges in a stirring halftime speech:

"Being perfect is about being able to look your friends in the eye and know that you didn't let them down, because you told them the truth. And that truth is that you did everything you could. There wasn't one more thing that you could've done. Can you live in that moment, as best you can, with clear eyes and love in your heart? With joy in your heart? If you can do that, gentlemen, then you're perfect."

- Avoiding profanity or other hurtful language
- Demonstrating honesty and resisting the temptation to cheat
- Accepting responsibility for personal actions
- Treating others as you expect to be treated

Some evidence (Beller and Stoll 1994) reveals that participating in high school sports may actually hinder the development of moral character. Researchers set out to compare the moral reasoning ability of athletes with that of nonathletes. They included data from more than 1,300 students in grades 9 through 12 and found that

- athletes scored lower than nonathletes on moral development and
- moral reasoning scores of athletes declined from 9th to 12th grade whereas scores for nonathletes increased.

At the end of the day, the evidence on whether sports build character conflicts. The concept of character is too vague and the effect of sports participation is so variable depending on the athlete's age, situation, and social dynamics in his sport. Social psychologists Miracle and Rees (1994, p. 96) conclude, "Research does not support either position in the debate over sport building character."

Sport Ethic

A dominant sport ethic is not a new concept in sports but it is one that constantly changes to reflect a system of values for coaches and athletes. It represents the behavior norms that are acceptable and praised within the sporting culture. Athletes who eagerly endorse the prevailing sport ethic are warmly embraced by sport owners, the media, coaches, and teammates. Those who rebel against the norms find it difficult to exist in that same world. In team sports,

The trouble with being a good sport is that you have to lose to prove you are one.

The rules of appropriate behavior differ greatly for these flag football players and for NFL players.

one generally accepted rule is that a player should not publicly criticize teammates. Terrell Owens, an outstanding wide receiver for the Philadelphia Eagles, publicly criticized quarterback Donovan McNabb. Along with other issues, this behavior contributed to his suspension without pay for the remainder of the 2005 season.

High-performance sports tend to have more clearly defined expectations for athletes. Dedication and sacrifice are expected and required of athletes to ensure success. There is little room for athletes to question prevailing norms if they want to be respected by teammates and competitors.

Coakley (2004) analyzed the culture of high-performance sport and saw dominant themes emerge:

- Striving for excellence is the hallmark of performance athletes. Athletes are expected to compete to win, train to exhaustion, sacrifice to meet their athletic goals, and put other areas of life aside in a single-minded pursuit of excellence in sport.

- Love of the game is expected and athletes must demonstrate it. Without a genuine love of the game, many athletes could not endure their sacrifices, hours of training, or exclusion of other areas of life. Commitment to the team, teammates, and coaches is preached by coaches and athletes who accept that mantra and are held up as role models.

- Playing with pain and adversity is a badge of courage for an athlete. As soldiers are admired for their bravery in battle and courage in facing death, so athletes are expected to deal with physical and psychological pain as the price they pay for respect.

Athletes must decide to embrace the current sport ethic or to struggle against the system. Young athletes in particular are susceptible to the exhortations of coaches and respected teammates as they search for behavior that will earn them acceptance, praise, and respect in a world they admire. Without a strong sense of personal identity, young athletes eagerly adopt the athletic code simply because of their age and inexperience.

Those who benefit the most from the current American sport ethic are those who gain in money or reputation when their affiliated athletes succeed. Owners of teams, the media, and coaches have a stake in the performance of their team and reward those who readily accept the prevailing values system.

Players who play with pain are labeled courageous even if they risk permanent injury. Those who overtrain may be admired for their dedication until their overtraining interferes with their performance. Eating disorders, particularly among female athletes, are prevalent in certain sports where body weight is a factor even though these disorders may lead to death.

Physical courage is expected, particularly for males, as proof of their manhood. Risk taking without regard for the consequence is admired. Players who shy away from physical danger are labeled unworthy of the fraternity of male athletes.

Unquestioned acceptance of the prevailing sport ethic sometimes is a form of deviant overconformity. Athletes may adopt behaviors that are outside the norms of society because their insulated world of sport has its own brand of ethics. The sport ethic may be reinforced by fans and the media who encourage athletes to pursue athletic excellence at any cost.

When the athletic ethic succeeds in building special bonds between teammates to the exclusion of bonds with others, the athlete's interpersonal relationships outside of sport may suffer. Marriages, families, and friends are all excluded from the special circle. Athletes may become so cocky that they believe themselves to be special and immune to rules of behavior to which others are expected to conform. The sport pages are rife with examples of athletes who expect special privileges and preferential treatment and who display a sense of entitlement. Adults and fans idolizing these athletes encourage this antisocial behavior and then wonder what went wrong when the athletes disappoint them.

Linking Good Sporting Behavior to Mental Toughness

One of the important connections made in recent years is that between emotional control and good sporting behavior. In the heat of battle, many athletes lose control of their emotions and subsequently behave poorly. They are also likely to perform poorly since highly aroused negative emotions usually harm competition.

Sport psychologists and coaches have found that teaching athletes how to control their emotions can help them compete in an ideal state of emotional arousal. In that state the athletes clearly focus on the task at hand, block out distractions, relax tense muscles, and regulate breathing. Other skills for achieving this state include rituals, positive self-talk, and visual imagery.

Since all athletes want to maximize their success, they are very receptive to learning skills to improve their mental toughness. A strong by-product of improved mental toughness may be better sporting behavior. Athletes are much more likely to ignore opponents' poor behavior and the vagaries of bad luck during play if they are under emotional control and focused on their performance.

Learning the rules of competition is still the foundation for good sporting behavior. But to develop further, athletes must understand the spirit of the rules: a commitment to fair play and socially acceptable behavior from all athletes, coaches, and fans.

The sport ethic of high-performance sport dictates that this athlete should play even though injured. Is the sport ethic correct?

MORAL VALUES TAUGHT THROUGH SPORT

In spite of the lack of convincing evidence, most people still assume there is value in linking good sporting behavior with competition in sports. Certainly it allows contests to exist under a common framework of rules and customs. Without those, chaos would reign.

It is also true that young people learn moral behavior as they mature. Sports can be one of the arenas that inform them of acceptable and unacceptable attitudes and behavior. As they gain intellectual maturity, their ability to process this information grows and a personal moral code emerges.

In the critical teenage years, most kids rely on their peers for guidance in acceptable behavior. Originally they rely on their parents, teachers, and other adults for that information, but as they begin the struggle into adulthood, being accepted by their peers becomes paramount. They exhibit the conventional level of "good boy or girl" or "law and order" moral reasoning.

Recognizing the powerful influence of sports on youth, many organizations have begun aggressive

Activity Time-Out: Locker Room Slogans

Make a list of at least 10 locker-room slogans that you have seen or read that reinforce the sport ethic. Consider the impact of those slogans and decide which ones should be banned and which ones have value. Then, come up with five new slogans that you believe would be healthier and reflect a more enlightened view of sports.

campaigns to promote good sporting behavior. For the last 15 years the Institute for International Sport has sponsored National Sportsmanship Day on the first Tuesday in March. The celebration involves youth sport organizations; elementary, middle, and high schools; and colleges in the United States and in more than 100 countries. It promotes awareness of good sporting behavior by stimulating dialogue between all those involved in sports (www.internationalsport.com/nsd/nsd.cfm).

By registering to participate, schools or organizations receive posters, role-playing scenarios, games, sport quotes, discussion questions, and other ideas for involving students, parents, teachers, and administrators. Some schools proudly display their banners and include good sporting behavior as a goal of their athletic teams. Outstanding high-profile athletes are carefully screened to serve as role models and make appearances on behalf of the organization.

In Colorado, the sporting behavior program for high school athletes takes the position that sport participants are placed in a unique context of competition that can develop the values of self-respect and respect for others. They list the values as follows (CHSAA 2005):

Respect for self	Respect for others
Self-esteem	Teamwork
Discipline	Loyalty
Courage	Compassion
Responsibility	Tolerance
Integrity and honesty	Courtesy
Ethics	Fairness
Pride	Integrity
Poise	Humility

Other organizations have similar programs to alert sport participants of the value of good sporting behavior. Almost every youth sport organization, including those of the Olympic movement, incorporate good sporting behavior in their offerings for players and coaches.

STRATEGIES FOR GOOD SPORTING BEHAVIOR

Clearly sports can be an opportunity for youth to learn the precepts of good sporting behavior. Due to the dynamics of play and the natural situations of competition, athletes may be tested hundreds of times in a season of play and thus develop their sense of a moral code in sports. Many of their attitudes will come from early life experiences, but the ones they learn on the athletic field are just as likely to transfer off the field and become part of their moral behavior.

If we hope to positively influence good sporting behavior, we have to adopt it as a key goal of youth sports. All of the significant sporting organizations for youth have done so, but in some cases their good intentions are simply not followed up. Colorado appears to have a model program that is comprehensive in concept, clear in purpose, and practical to apply. Schools in Colorado are asked to adopt and promote the program, recognize athletes who are good models, and educate players, coaches, and parents.

Parents are the first teachers of good sporting behavior. What lessons are these parents teaching?

Expert's View: Playing by the Rules

Michael Josephson (2004), founder of the Josephson Institute of Ethics, once received a letter from a high school football coach saying his team had reached the state finals; however, an English teacher had caught three of his players cheating on an exam they needed to pass to stay eligible for play. The teacher told the coach he had passed the players anyway "for the good of the school."

The coach realized that if these three athletes failed the test, they were ineligible, and all games those three students had played in would have to be forfeited, disqualifying the team from the state championships. The coach asked, "What good would it do to report the situation?" Everyone would lose—these three students, the football team, the fans, the school, and the coach.

Wouldn't it be better to just keep quiet about it?

Josephson's response was, "Of course not!" Although it would take moral courage to play by the rules and accept the consequences, that is exactly what has to be done. A coach is bound by his position to uphold the rules and send a message about honor and integrity to the school officials, coaches, players, and fans. It's a high price, but the path of honor will be an enduring gift to the community.

Parents are usually the first to teach their children fair play. From their parents, young athletes learn to share, take turns, accept agreed-upon rules of the game, and accept winning or losing. As they join youth teams and leagues, they learn to follow directions from coaches and officials or suffer the consequences that usually mean exclusion from play. Parents continue to model good behavior during games by admiring play by both teams, controlling their emotions, and respecting decisions of coaches and officials. After the game, parents need to help the athletes focus on the good aspects of their performance and not become consumed with the outcome.

Coaching behavior powerfully influences a team of young players. Along with teaching the rules, coaches must model good sporting behavior at all times. That means they must treat everyone with respect, make fair decisions, and positively reinforce good behavior. If coaches verbally abuse the referee from the sideline, they send a clear message to their players that such behavior is OK.

Coaches also need to help players modify their behavior when it does not meet acceptable standards. Good kids sometimes are bad sports. Kids become frustrated, lose patience, get overly emotional, react to poor behavior from opponents, or allow other issues in their life to affect their decisions. A wise coach can spot the possible cause for poor decisions through insightful questioning and suggest alternative methods of dealing with the situation.

At some levels of play, the fans can also influence the atmosphere through unacceptable behavior. Small groups of fans such as parents can be cautioned that their behavior is becoming a negative influence. Larger crowds simply require crowd control to ensure safety, and disruptive fans should be forcibly removed from the scene. The effects of too much alcohol consumption before and during athletic events are well documented. Limits must be publicized and enforced to prevent alcohol from turning a fan into a disruptive, rude, or dangerous instigator.

The power of sport role models cannot be overlooked. Young athletes often model their heroes in college and professional sport. If they see NFL players taunting each other and celebrating excessively after a good play, you can bet that they'll imitate those actions during their Pop Warner League football game. Leaders of professional sport need to be pressured to eliminate poor sporting behavior from their games. Rule enforcement, fines, and suspensions are all actions that can gain attention and help athletes change their behavior. Generally, most sport organizations do act on bad behavior, but often not until public outcries inspire them to do so.

We can also do much by rewarding those athletes who do exhibit good sporting behavior. Most organizations and leagues seasonally recognize certain athletes for their exemplary behavior. Even in fiercely competitive professional sports there are numerous players who deserve admiration for their good sportsmanship. No young girl who has watched the last 10 years of U.S. Women's Soccer could come away with anything less than a healthy respect for exemplary sporting behavior.

CHAPTER SUMMARY

Good sporting behavior has been defined as ethical behavior exhibited by athletes. Some studies have shown that that today's athletes are confused about the meaning of fair play and sportsmanship and have no concept of honorable competition. On the other hand, there is also evidence that sports provide a fertile ground for developing good sporting behavior, provided that it is an agreed-upon outcome accepted by coaches and players. The active occasions for moral decision making in sport make sport an ideal venue for learning moral behavior.

Highly competitive sports are more likely than participation sports to produce poor behavior. Males are more likely than females to exhibit poor behavior. Violent and contact sports have a strong history of poor sporting behavior. Various research projects with youth sport athletes and high school athletes have revealed an alarming understanding of acceptable levels of moral choice and decision making.

The stages of moral development as outlined by Kohlberg give us insight into how sporting behavior develops. The relationship between moral behavior and intellectual development in sport was examined. Young people in particular can be socialized into groups through their experience in sports and adoption of acceptable moral behavior.

Because athletic situations vary widely, there is no definitive way to declare that sport teaches either positive or negative sporting behavior. However, an increasing number of youth sport programs, state athletic associations, and school districts are adopting clear statements of intent to promote good sporting behavior and following that with concrete programs that include publicity, education, enforcement, rewards, and recognition for exemplary behavior in sports.

Race, Ethnicity, and Sport

Student Outcomes

After reading this chapter, you will know the following:

- How race and ethnicity are defined
- Sport participation by various ethnic populations
- How sport is both a positive and negative force in society for promoting racial and ethnic equality
- Strategies to combat challenges to racial diversity in all levels of sport

The face of professional sport in the United States has changed dramatically in the last 50 years through the inclusion of African American, Latino, and Asian athletes and their subsequent record-setting performances and domination of certain sports and positions. Where White males once dominated sport, the balance in major team sports such as basketball and football has now shifted to dominance by Black athletes. African Americans and Latinos have both increased their representation in Major League Baseball and many have achieved superstar status.

Despite the integration of athletes of all races into sport, there are still challenges:

- Opening opportunities in all sports to people of all races and ethnic backgrounds, especially for youths
- Integrating athletes from all races and ethnic groups into the social fabric of the sport world and capitalizing on the diversity of participants
- Recruiting and training sport leaders, such as coaches, managers, and owners, of all races and ethnic backgrounds

In this chapter, we'll take a look at sport participation by various racial and ethnic groups, sport participation as both a positive and negative factor in social change, and strategies for increasing participation by minority groups at all levels of sport. Before we take a look at these issues surrounding race, ethnicity, and sport, let's first take a look at what we mean by race and ethnicity and then look at some census numbers.

CLASSIFICATIONS OF RACE AND ETHNICITY

The terms **race** and **ethnicity** are often interchanged in describing various groups of people. However, it is more accurate to use *race* when referring to attributes that are passed along genetically from generation to generation and to use *ethnicity* to describe the cultural heritage of a group of people. All groups except Whites are also referred to as **minorities** since they constitute a smaller percentage of the population in the United States than the majority group (White Americans). Although these definitions may differ slightly depending on the discussion, they are a good starting point for this chapter.

Race is not as easy to define as you might think. Due to the mixing of many generations of different races, more Americans are of a mixed racial background than an unmixed one. Historically, many people used the so-called one-drop rule when describing racial origins, meaning, for example, that those who had even one drop of blood from an African American ancestor were considered African American. Of course, in popular culture, skin color, facial features, or type of hair might define members of a minority group. Adding to the confusion is the classification by the U.S. Census of Hispanics or Latinos, who are tallied as a single group with a footnote that they may be of any race (U.S. Census 2005c).

The term **racism** refers to the belief that race determines human traits and characteristics and that racial differences result in the superiority of a particular race. Groups that have been victims of discrimination due to racism have typically been minorities. The dominance of White males of European origin in the early days of the United States resulted in the belief that Whites were superior to those of other racial backgrounds.

The U.S. Census of the population in 1930 showed that 88.7% identified themselves as "White," while just 9.7% identified themselves as "Negro." There was no Hispanic or Latino category, but there was a category labeled "Mexican," who numbered only 1.2% of the population. Take a look at table 11.1, which shows the current percentages of racial groups as of 2004—they are markedly different from 75 years ago.

The forecast by the U.S. Census Bureau is that both Latino and Asian populations will triple by 2050. At the same time, the White population will drop to just 50% by 2050, the lowest in the nation's history. The decline appears to be due to declining birth rates among Whites and to immigration of minority groups. Additionally, the African American population is projected to increase at a rate of 71% by 2050. These eventual changes will mean that groups who were formerly minorities in the United States will actually be in the majority.

Another striking pattern is emerging in where minority groups choose to live in the United States. According to William Frey, demographer at the Brookings Institution in Washington, D.C., "Blacks are returning to the South while Hispanics are dispersing throughout the country where there are jobs" (Overberg and El Nasser 2005). In the 1990s, most Hispanics immigrants entered the country through five gateways: California, Texas, Illinois, New York, and Florida. Today, Hispanics make up at least 5% of the population in 28 states, up from 16 states in 1990. For Blacks the pattern is different, with over 17 million—almost half of all Blacks—living in the 11 states that were in the Confederacy, an increase of 1 million since 1990. Another significant trend is the addition this year of Texas to Hawaii, New Mexico, and California as states where minorities exceed 50% of the total population.

The concentration of various minority groups in particular areas of the country will likely have an effect upon the popularity of various sports in those regions. Both in participation and in spectatorship, racial groups tend to favor certain sports and ignore others. An example of this effect is the heavy recruiting by major colleges in the southeastern United States for football players. Football recruiters know that since a higher percentage of Blacks live in the southeast that it makes sense to recruit there.

The size and location of minority groups are significant when considering the numbers of minority athletes in particular sport. When compared with their percentage of the general population, minorities are heavily represented in certain sports at elite levels and are virtually nonexistent in others. A question to consider is whether these imbalances are the result of race or simply a function of opportunity and culture. In the following sections, we'll look closely at who is participating in what sports and what factors influence that participation.

SPORT PARTICIPATION AMONG RACIAL AND ETHNIC MINORITIES

In this section we will consider each of the major racial groups and examine their sport participation. As a result of the civil rights movement and elimination of many racial barriers, African American athletes have assumed a dominant place in certain

TABLE 11.1   United States Population by Racial Group—2004

Racial group	Population (in millions)	Percent of population
White	236,058	80.3
Hispanic or Latino*	41,322	14.0
Black or African American	37,502	12.7
Asian	12,326	4.1
Two or more races	4,439	1.5
American Indian, Alaska Native	2,825	.9
Native Hawaiian, Pacific Islander	506	.1
Total	293,655	

* Persons of Hispanic origin may be of any race.
www.census.gov/statab/www/racehisp.html

sports at the college and professional levels. Yet overall, Blacks are underrepresented in the vast majority of collegiate sports. Much of the data in this section deal with the challenges and triumphs of Black athletes in the last 50 years simply because their struggle has been studied and debated widely. To a lesser extent, Hispanics, Asians, and Native Americans have affected sport; however, each of these groups has always had key contributors to sport and is continuing to battle its own set of barriers.

As you read this chapter, it will be helpful to refer periodically to tables 11.2 and 11.3, which show detailed information on participation in collegiate and professional sport by racial groups. You will notice some stark differences between the percentages of participation by different racial groups at the various levels of collegiate and professional competition. It is also instructive to compare the percentage of racial groups in sports to their percentage of the U.S. population. Significant cases of overrepresentation and underrepresentation in various sports are obvious.

African American Athletes

A quick look at the history of sport reveals how African Americans have not only moved into prominent roles in the major American sports but have reached a point of domination. In his definitive history of the Black athlete, Arthur Ashe divided history into three volumes (1988). The first volume dealt with Black athletes from the 1600s up to the time of World War I. As sport entered its golden age in the United States in the 1920s and 1930s, a few Black athletes made their mark, including Jesse Owens in track and field and Joe Louis in boxing. But it was not until after

TABLE 11.2 Participation in Collegiate Sport by Racial Group

Racial group	Male (%)	Female (%)
Division I athletes		
White	62.3	70.6
Hispanic	3.6	3.3
Black	24.6	14.9
Asian	1.6	2.3
Native American	.4	.3
Other	3.2	3.7
Nonresident alien	4.4	5.0
Division II athletes		
White	67.3	77.5
Hispanic	4.3	4.6
Black	22.6	12.1
Asian	1.0	1.4
Native American	.5	.5
Other	2.7	1.3
Nonresident alien	3.1	2.7
Division III athletes		
White	83.3	87.3
Black	8.8	4.9
Asian	1.6	2.2
Native American	.3	.2
Other	2.3	2.5
Nonresident alien	.8	.5
Overall percentage of Division I, II, and III athletes		
White	71.4	78.2
Black	18.1	10.6
Asian	1.4	2.0
Native American	.4	.3
Other	2.5	2.8
Nonresident alien	2.7	2.9

Data from NCAA. *Student athlete ethnicity report: NCAA for 2003-04.* www.ncaa.org.

TABLE 11.3 Professional Players by Racial Group, 2004

Racial group	NFL (%)	NBA (%)	WNBA (%)	MLB (%)	MLS (%)
White	29	22	33	63	64
Black	69	76	66	9	17
Latino	.5	1	1	26	14
Asian	1.2	1	0	2	1

Data from Lapchick 2004.

World War II that integration became a reality in most American sports and Black athletes began to achieve a level of prominence. Most historians would agree that one of the major events in this period was the breaking of the color barrier in Major League Baseball by Jackie Robinson.

The Black athlete has been studied, written about, admired, scorned, and persecuted in American sport. Because of notable success by Black athletes, a great deal of attention has been given to the reasons behind this success. Conventional wisdom ranges from "White men can't jump" (compared to Black men) to "Blacks have brawn, not brains."

If you were to ask John Q. Public about Black athletes, chances are he would say they dominate American sport. However, out of 35 million African Americans in the United States, nowhere near the expected percentages are involved in sport. In most sports, they are woefully underrepresented or completely missing—consider, for example, sports such as sailing, ice hockey, tennis, golf, swimming, diving, soccer, cycling, figure skating, softball, volleyball, water polo, and almost all winter sports. It's in the major American sports of basketball, football, and baseball that African American males tend to participate in large numbers. Because those sports gobble up a huge proportion of attention, money, media, and television, we assume that Black athletes dominate sport.

African Americans in Professional Sport

In the early 1940s until the conclusion of World War II, there were no Black athletes in Major League Baseball, professional football, or the National Basketball Association (NBA). Outstanding Black athletes were relegated to playing in the Negro Leagues or other competitions organized for African Americans. In the latter part of the decade, each sport made the move to sign a Black athlete, marking a change in American sport that was to have far-reaching implications for the next 50 years. For

Black athletes, the five years following the end of World War II were the most memorable in their sports history (Ashe 1988).

By the end of the 1950s, African Americans had moved to a percentage of participation in the major sports equal to their percentage of the national population, which was approximately 11% to 12%. The civil rights movement, which eliminated segregation in public places, schools, and the workplace, no doubt had a major effect on the phenomenal rise of the Black athlete. If we fast-forward to 2002, just over 40 years later, the percentage of African Americans in professional sport is quite different (Lapchick and Mathews 2002):

Baseball	13%
Football	65%
Basketball	78%
Women's basketball	64%

Even sports that traditionally have not included Black athletes have begun to show some signs of inclusiveness. The sport of tennis boasted its first Black champion in Althea Gibson, who won Wimbledon in the 1950s. Arthur Ashe followed on the men's side, but Black athletes had few other champions in the next couple of decades. The arrival of the Williams sisters, Venus and Serena, however, touched off an explosion of interest in tennis in the African American community in the late 1990s. Suddenly a sport that was traditionally for the White and privileged had a pair of role models who were from modest means. They burst on the tennis scene without traveling the hard and expensive road of junior tennis and instead chose to vault right into professional play.

The effects of the Williams' sisters success is that tennis now ranks fourth in popularity among African Americans, following only football, basketball, and

From the 1920s through the 1940s, the Negro League was one of the only opportunities for African Americans to participate in sport.

In the Arena With . . . *Jackie Robinson*

He thrilled fans with his play, shattered the color barrier in baseball, and helped change the face of sport. In 1947, segregation ruled in the United States. There were separate schools, swimming pools, drinking fountains, hotels, restaurants, and baseball leagues for Blacks and Whites. Jackie Robinson helped change all that by becoming the first Black man to play Major League Baseball.

Branch Rickey, the owner of the Brooklyn Dodgers, chose Robinson for his amazing physical skills, his courage, and perhaps most important, his ability to turn the other cheek when faced with hateful behavior. According to a tribute by Hank Aaron, holder of the all-time home-run record, Jackie had to "endure teammates who petitioned to keep him off the club, pitchers who threw at him, opponents who dug their spikes into his shin, fans who mocked with mops on their heads and death threats" (Aaron 1999, p. 2).

"Robinson could hit, bunt, steal and run," says Roger Kahn in *Boys of Summer* (Schwartz 2005b, p. 2). "He passionately wanted to win, could intimidate opponents and burned with passion." Robinson's debut for the Dodgers in 1947 came a year before President Truman desegregated the military and seven years before the Supreme Court outlawed segregation in public schools.

He earned the Rookie of the Year award and two years later won the Most Valuable Player award based on a year in which he batted .342 and stole 37 bases. His lifetime batting average was .311 and he was voted into the Baseball Hall of Fame in his first year of eligibility.

Robinson was dogged by diabetes and was nearly blind by middle age. He died of a heart attack at age 53 in 1972. His final request: "We ask for nothing special. We ask only to be permitted to live as you live, and as our nation's Constitution provides" (Schwartz 2005b, p. 4).

---

baseball, and African Americans are the most avid tennis fans of any racial group. Approximately 11% of African Americans say they are avid tennis fans, nearly twice as many as Whites (5.7%). That compares with 39% of African Americans who pick football, 37% who pick basketball, and 18.2% who pick baseball for their avid sport support (Lapchick 2001b).

Similarly, Tiger Woods boosted the popularity of golf by 14% in the late 1990s when he began to dominate the game, and he has continued to be one of the dominant golfers. However, only 7% of African Americans describe themselves as avid golf fans (Lapchick 2001b).

African Americans in Collegiate Sport

In collegiate sport, African Americans dominate NCAA Division I basketball for both men and women. Likewise, Black men dominate football, and the next most popular sport for African Americans is track and field. A quick look at table 11.2 reveals some stark differences between Division I, II, and III athletes. The percentage of African Americans in Division II is similar to Division I, but in Division III the percentage drops drastically and well below their percentage of the population as a whole. Keep in mind that Division III schools are typically smaller, private schools and cannot offer athletic scholarships.

According to NCAA statistics (2003-2004, as shown in table 11.2), 23% of all athletic scholarships went to African Americans, which exceeds their size of the population at large (13%). In virtually all other collegiate sports outside of basketball, football, and track and field, African American athletes are underrepresented.

Change in collegiate sport has not come quickly, but gradually Black athletes have made their presence known. The Southeastern Conference was the last major athletic conference to integrate in 1966. In the late 1960s, there were still no Black athletes at several schools in the conference, including Alabama, Auburn, Florida, Mississippi, Mississippi State, Louisiana State, and Georgia. By 1972, though, more than 100 Black athletes were playing football in the conference, and by 1975 the University of Alabama started five Black athletes in basketball. This fact is somewhat remarkable when you consider the attitude of former Alabama governor George Wallace, who used physical restraint to block African Americans from attending the university in 1963. Ten years later, in 1972, several teams in the Southeastern Conference even had Black starting quarterbacks, an anomaly in those days.

Race and Athletic Dominance

Do Black athletes dominate certain sports because of race? Numerous studies such as those cited by Entine (2000, 2004) have been conducted to examine this issue from every perspective. The proportion of fast-twitch and slow-twitch muscle fibers has been used to explain the jumping ability of Black athletes. Explosiveness on the track is also attributed to the muscular makeup and high proportion of fast-twitch fibers of Black athletes. However, Ethiopian and Kenyan Black athletes have dominated distance running for the last generation. Kenyans and other East Africans are born with a high number of slow-twitch fibers. They tend to be ectomorphs, short and slender, with a large natural lung capacity.

In contrast to East Africans, athletes of West African ancestry, including most North American, British, and Caribbean Blacks, are generally poor distance runners. Rather, they tend to excel in sprinting and other sports where explosiveness, speed, and power rule. Thus, if we simply define race according to skin color, in this case Black athletes, there is significant variation between different groups of Blacks (Entine 2000).

According to S.L. Price writing in *Sports Illustrated* in 1997, "Generally accepted research has shown that African-American children tend to have denser bones, narrower hips, bigger thighs, lower percentages of body fat and tests also show that they run faster and jump higher." However, these are generalized observations that have not included extensive study of all types of Black athletes at the world-class level. And there are certainly exceptions such as Charles Barkley and Karl Malone in basketball and Warren Saap in football who certainly don't have the characteristics that Price listed in his article but have been eminently successful in professional sport.

Some people believe Black athletes have longer arms or reach compared with their White counterparts. Others believe that Black athletes are mentally tougher and more relaxed under pressure. However, no matter how thorough the testing is, it is difficult to isolate factors and ascribe them exclusively to race. In fact, if you were to take a random sampling of youth athletes of all racial groups, it is unlikely that you would find significant differences.

A complicating factor is that within any prescribed definition of race, huge differences in variability exist because race is not a precise factor. The question of who is a Black athlete is not a simple one when you realize all the possible ancestral origins of Blacks and variations in skin color. The most well-known golfer today is Tiger Woods, whom many classify as a Black athlete. However, Woods proclaims to be "cablinasian," which describes his Caucasian, Black,

Expert's View: Race and Sport

In 2000, journalist Jon Entine published *Taboo: Why Black Athletes Dominate Sports and Why We're Afraid to Talk About It.* Entine's book was based on an NBC documentary written and produced by Tom Brokaw, titled *Black Athletes: Fact and Fiction,* which was named Best International Sports Film of 1989. In his book, Entine confronts the difficult questions about race and sport performance with a mix of scientific research and anecdotal information. He debunks the myth of the dumb jock, which was used by some people when Black athletes began to dominate certain sports. Entine quotes noted sports writer Frank Deford, who once said, "When Jack Nicklaus sinks a 30 foot putt, nobody thinks his IQ goes down." Entine's book is not shy about taking on sensitive issues about race and sport and supplies helpful information and thoughtful reasoning.

American Indian, and Asian heritage. Although many observers herald Woods' ascension to the top of golf as a landmark of the Black athlete once again proving superiority, it seems that Woods would not attribute his success to his genetic makeup.

Another possible explanation for the dominance of Black athletes in certain sports is the environment in which they grow up. Because Blacks are a minority group, their choices in life may be fewer because they have fewer economic resources and less hope of landing a well-paying job as an adult. Young Blacks see successful athletes and imagine following that path. A survey of 4,500 African American male youths by Assibey-Mensah (1997) reported that when asked about their role models

- 85% of 10-year-olds and 98% of 18-year-olds picked athletes or sport figures,
- of those who picked athletes, 63% of 10-year-olds and 90% of 18-year-olds picked basketball players, and
- no child picked an educator.

A lack of role models for young Black males may be due to the absence of a father or the presence of a father who is unemployed. According to the U.S. Census (2005b), African American single mothers account for one-third of single-mother households in the United States. Black youths who live in inner cities may be particularly hard-pressed to find alter-

native role models as successful local businesses are scarce and many potential role models have fled to the suburbs in search of a better life. Add to these complications the fact that African Americans are the racial group with the highest percentage of families below the poverty line, and you can see why young Blacks would yearn for high-profile, high-paying careers in sport whether they are a realistic goal or not.

Sports like football, basketball, and baseball are relatively affordable and are usually offered by schools that provide coaching, uniforms, and equipment to athletes. Minority athletes are naturally drawn to these sports at school because they are accessible and affordable. On the opposite spectrum, sports that are expensive such as skiing, water polo, equestrian eventing, or those offered primarily through private clubs such as golf and tennis are often out of reach of minority athletes.

African American culture, particularly in urban settings, has drawn Black youths toward the basketball court and the draw has been reinforced by friends and heroes. Television offers plenty of opportunities to watch professional role models compete in basketball, football, and baseball. Basketball courts are plentiful, are relatively inexpensive to build, and can accommodate lots of players at a low cost. Playground basketball and recreational leagues that are free or low cost have been the training ground for thousands of city kids.

Stacking in Sport

The concept of stacking was coined by activist Harry Edwards, who is widely recognized as a leading authority on issues of race and sport. Edwards has been a longtime professor of sociology at the University of California at Berkeley and a consultant for Major League Baseball, the Golden State Warriors, and the San Francisco 49ers on issues of racial diversity in sport. **Stacking** refers to an unusual distribution of White and Blacks in certain sport positions that cannot be explained by a random distribution. For example, in football, the position of quarterback has typically been dominated by Whites while running backs and wide receivers have been predominantly Black. In baseball, pitchers and catchers have been predominately White while outfielders have tended to be Black. In basketball, centers and guards are more likely to be White and forwards are more likely to be Black. Many of these percentages have changed

There are nearly twice as many Black doctors as Black athletes, yet most children cite athletes as role models. Is this just the way kids are, or are there larger social issues at work?

in recent years as the overall percentage of Black athletes has risen dramatically, but there is still the historical aberration that gave rise to the suspicion that Black athletes were excluded from certain positions on a team.

Various explanations have been offered for the apparent existence of stacking. One such explanation is the centrality theory, which places White athletes in the center of the lineup or the middle of the team. In baseball this means Whites are pitchers, catchers, shortstops, and second basemen while in football it means Whites are quarterbacks, centers, middle linebackers, and offensive guards. The idea was advanced that the so-called White positions require more thinking and decision making central to the outcome of the game while Blacks are drawn to positions that require more raw physical talent.

Another theory is that as Blacks and Whites tend to be attracted to certain positions and that children follow the lead of their role models and seek out similar positions in youth sport. A similar theory is that coaches move players into certain positions based on race where they think the athletes would be most successful. Those positions are ones that require a relatively higher level of physical talent and speed and a lesser amount of cognitive ability.

As Black athletes have moved into professional sport in large numbers, the concept of stacking has received less attention and sparked fewer debates. Black quarterbacks have now led teams to Super Bowls and Blacks have become All-Stars in the positions of pitcher and catcher. Still, the concept endures, and a look at the statistics from as recently as the late 1990s reveals some surprising results (table 11.4; Lapchick and Mathews 1999).

If Black athletes are restricted from playing certain positions, then a case can be made for racism within professional sport. Such racism may result in the loss of earnings due to the fact that players in certain positions such as quarterback and pitcher tend to command greater compensation because they are so valuable to their team. Another factor is that the positions dominated by Black players tend to require greater strength, speed, and explosiveness. Since those attributes are often the first to decline with age, Black players may have shorter careers and thus less earning power. In fact, the positions held most often by Blacks—running back, cornerback, and wide receiver—tend to have the shortest careers. Overall, it was concluded by researcher Clayton Best that "experience and career length in professional football [are] the effects of positional segregation" (Best 1987). Consider that players who

occupy positions typically held by Blacks have a career expectancy of about three years in the NFL compared with four years for positions typically held by White players. That difference may seem inconsequential, but it means that Black athletes may have careers that are 25% shorter on average, thus affecting their earning power.

Of course, limiting Black athletes to certain positions also affects their long-term prospects for coaching or managing teams. Athletes who play in the central positions that require decision making and game understanding obviously have a leg up on others. The dearth of Black coaches, especially in football, has been a long-standing issue for many Blacks.

Exploitation of Black Athletes

An unfortunate outcome of opening sport participation to Black athletes has been the shameful way

TABLE 11.4 Stacking in the NFL and MLB

Position	Percent of Black athletes
NFL*	
Running back	87
Wide receiver	92
Offensive guard	29
Center	17
Quarterback	8
Cornerback	99
Safety	91
Defensive end	79
Linebacker	75
MLB	
Outfielder	48
First baseman	16
Second baseman	15
Shortstop	13
Third baseman	7
Pitcher	5
Catcher	4

* Note: Blacks represent approximately 65% of players in the NFL.

Data from Lapchick and Mathews 1999.

some schools, coaches, and universities exploit them for their athletic talent. Leaders in the Black community speak out against exploitive practices, use the media to publicize infractions, and warn athletes to watch their backs. But the potential to exploit talented Black athletes often starts at an early age.

As early as middle school, when the adolescent growth spurt is in full flower, teachers, coaches, and administrators notice the gifted athletes who demonstrate exceptional talent, size, or strength. They may be given the benefit of the doubt in the classroom in spite of lackluster academic performance because of their athletic potential or their importance to the school team. At the end of the year, they may be promoted to the next grade in spite of substandard academic performance. A few minority athletes who made it through college without ever learning to read, such as James Brooks, star running back at

Are we shortchanging high school athletes, like LeBron James, who turn pro immediately after high school graduation? Is a college education worth more than a multimillion-dollar contract? Who should decide?

Auburn University, are the most dramatic cases in the media (Muse 2000).

When colleges recruit top athletes and offer them scholarships, they believe their investment entitles them to protect it. It is normal practice at Division I institutions that compete at the national level to encourage athletes to choose relatively easy majors and courses, take a lighter academic load during the season, attend mandatory study halls, use a tutor when necessary, and delay their academic progress to gain another year of eligibility to play. All of these practices are susceptible to abuse and coaches who are caught lose their job and reputation. However, many are not caught and the result is the low graduation rate of minority athletes. Even those who graduate may have learned little and have no employable skills. If they don't make it as a professional athlete, their future is bleak.

On the other hand, the professional leagues have conspired to keep college-aged athletes from playing in the pros. While most athletes are not ready physically or mentally to compete at a young age, some, like LeBron James in basketball, are not only ready to play but also to be a star. Of course, colleges don't want to lose athletes, in whom they have invested time and money, to a professional team before the athletes' collegiate eligibility is up. So professional leagues and colleges work together to keep players in school (e.g., forcing players to wait until their class graduates to turn professional), even if the athletes have no interest in it and want to turn professional. The barriers have fallen in basketball and exceptions have been made in football, however. Baseball has always signed young players and often encouraged them to join minor-league teams rather than go on to college.

The decision to turn professional rather than play one more year of college usually has to do with the potential for a lucrative contract. If an athlete is offered millions of dollars, he takes a terrible risk if he rejects it to return to college and then sustains a serious injury. That injury may be the end of his career and long-term financial security for his family. In the end, if the deal is good enough, most athletes leave for the pros. Even if another year in college would have been good for their athletic development or academic career instead of sitting on the bench for a professional team, the temptation and security of a contract is often too great.

While athletes of all racial backgrounds are susceptible to exploitation in professional sport, because Black athletes make up a large percentage of players in the major American sports, they are disproportionately at risk.

Double Jeopardy
for African American Female Athletes

Despite being in the majority in schools and colleges, female athletes only comprise 35% of all high school athletes and less than 34% of all college athletes. Although enormous progress has been made in the last 25 years due primarily to the passage of Title IX legislation, women still have not achieved parity in participation or resources at any level of sport.

The case of Black women is doubly discouraging. They are discriminated against twice, because of gender and because of race. African American females represent less than 5% of high school athletes, less than 10% of college athletes, less than 2% of all coaches, and less than 1% of all college athletic administrators according to Donna Lopiano, PhD, executive director of the Women's Sports Foundation (Lopiano 2001).

Lopiano says that "the African-American female is a victim of sport discrimination and positional stacking within sports. She is generally restricted to basketball, track and field and the least expensive sports. (Unlike for boys, football is not an option.) Within the sports she does play, she is underrepresented in the skill/outcome positions of setter in volleyball or point guard in basketball" (Lopiano 2001).

Elite Black female athletes are offered fewer speaking engagements, endorsements, and sponsorships. They have not been at the forefront of the civil rights movement or the feminist movement because sport has been seen as trivial or reflective of a male model that should not be emulated. The two notable exceptions have been Venus and Serena Williams, who have captured huge sponsorships from Reebok and Nike, respectively. If Serena meets performance-related bonuses over eight years, she could earn upward of $55 million U.S. from her Nike deal. That is all added on to several million a year in prize money! That is an amazing achievement for a Black female athlete.

Lopiano proposes a series of actions to rectify the situation of Black female athletes. Using lessons learned from civil rights battles and gender equity battles already fought, she proposes building and maintaining accurate data of participation percentages of Black females at all levels of play to be used in an annual report card. With the gathered data, she suggests using media pressure to announce and pursue a national agenda targeting specific groups such as high school athletes or coaches and demand action from sport organizations and associations to fulfill their public responsibilities to seek equal opportunity in sport for everyone regardless of race or gender (Sabo et al. 2004).

Latinos and Hispanics

Hispanic is used to describe all people whose ethnic heritage can be traced to Spanish-speaking countries. *Latino* typically refers people of Latin America, including Central and South America and the Caribbean. This is a diverse group in ancestry and language and their skin color may be black or white. As noted previously, Hispanics and Latinos have recently nudged ahead of African Americans as a percentage of the U.S. population and the forecast is for the percentage to increase steadily over the next few decades.

When asked to think of athletes who are Latinos, most Americans think of baseball first. In recent

The All-Time Latino Team is a milestone for a culture that has greatly influenced the game of baseball.

years, Latinos have claimed a higher percentage of major-league players than African Americans and seem to be on an upward trend. On opening day of the 2005 baseball season, the number of foreign players in American professional baseball reached an all-time high of 29.2%. This included 91 players from the Dominican Republic, 46 from Venezuela, and 34 from Puerto Rico—all Latinos. The newest team, the Washington Nationals, has the most foreign Latinos on their roster with 16 foreign players (*St. Petersburg Times* 2005b).

In Major League Baseball from 2004 to 2005, the percentage of White players decreased 3% while the percentage of Latino players increased 3%, mirroring trends in recent years. At the same time, the percentage of African Americans dropped to only 8.5%, the lowest number in the past 26 years.

As more players find success in Major League Baseball, young Latinos look up to them as role models and pour their energies into honing their baseball skills. Young men from modest economic backgrounds can see few opportunities to achieve success and economic security for their family more attractive than becoming a star baseball player.

Major League Baseball has established baseball academies in many Central American countries and made top coaches and competition available for promising prospects. While the vast majority of Latinos who have made it to the major leagues in baseball are from Central American countries, their successes have attracted a huge following of American Latinos who identify with their origins.

The Dominican Republic has a long tradition of sending players to the major leagues, as illustrated by their lock on half of the spots on the All-Time Latino Team. The team was announced during the 2005 World Series after selection by fans. Voting was sponsored by Major League Baseball for 60 players from seven different countries and territories. The final selections included 12 players, one at each infield position, three outfielders, three starting pitchers, and one relief pitcher. The team was as follows (Sanchez 2005):

Ivan Rodriguez, Puerto Rico, catcher

Albert Pujols, Dominican Republic, first base

Rod Carew, Panama, second base

Edgar Martinez, Puerto Rico, third base

Alex Rodriguez, Dominican Republic, shortshop

Roberto Clemente, Puerto Rico, outfielder

Manny Ramirez, Dominican Republic, outfielder

Vladimir Guerrero, Dominican Republic, outfielder

Pedro Martinez, Dominican Republic, starting pitcher

Juan Marichal, Dominican Republic, starting pitcher

Fernando Valenzuela, Mexico, starting pitcher

Mariano Rivera, Panama, relief pitcher

The Chicago White Sox, World Series champions in 2005, claim a Latino as their manager, Ozzie Guillen. A three-time All-Star player, Guillen spent most of his 16-year career as a shortstop for the White Sox. He is the first native of Venezuela to manage in the big leagues. Other Latino managers in 2005 included Felipe Alou of San Francisco and Tony Pena of Kansas City (Lapchick 2005b).

Soccer is the most popular sport in the world and clearly king of sports among Latinos. But Major League Soccer (MLS) in the United States has been a tough sell. Unlike American football, basketball, and baseball, American soccer is not the best in the world. According to some estimates, it may be the 10th best league in the world, well behind European, South American, and Latin American leagues. A quarter of its spectators are Latino, and in 2001, almost 25% of players were Latino as well. That number fell in 2004 to just 14% (Lapchick 2005a). Part of the reason is the cap of five foreign players on any one team.

Soccer is clearly the choice of Latinos. A miniseries entitled *Raices (Roots)* aired in July of 2005 on the History Channel. The six-part series was hosted by Pablo Mastroeni, a member of the 2004 MLS All-Star team and a native of Argentina. The series highlights the greats of the game from Brazil, Mexico, Argentina, Uruguay, and Columbia including players such as Pele, Garrincha, Romario, Ronaldo, and Alfredo di Stefano. As the Latino population grows in the United States, the owners and organizers of professional soccer plan to market American soccer to them.

In March 2006, the first National Hispanic Games for recreational athletes was staged in Tucson, Arizona. More than 2,000 athletes competed in an Olympic-style tournament featuring the sports of basketball, soccer, baseball, and boxing (Tornoe 2005). Even the sport of NASCAR is moving full throttle into the Latino market. Led by youngster Carlos Contreras and racing legend Adrian Fernandez of Mexico, the sport is reaching out to the growing Latino market through marketing initiatives. Presently, Latinos account for close to 9% of NASCAR's fan base, and between 1999 and 2002, their number increased at a rate of 23%. NASCAR has founded the Drive for Diversity (D4D) program to train and encourage female and minority drivers. Cuban-born Armando Fitz owns Fitz-Bradshaw Racing along with his wife, Mimi, and Hall of Fame football player Terry Bradshaw. Although it is the only present Hispanic-owned NASCAR team, the future promises more to come.

Interestingly, according to NCAA statistics, Hispanics are underrepresented in virtually all sports at the college level with the lone exception of men's volleyball. That may be due to the heavy concentration of Hispanics in California, where volleyball is a popular sport (NCAA 2004b).

Asian Americans

Asian Americans are the fastest-growing population in the United States, but their participation in sport has been slow to develop. Compared with other racial groups, famous athletes of Asian descent are relatively few and participation in sport generally has been lower than that of other groups. It is difficult to generalize about the sport participation of Asian Americans due to their varied countries and backgrounds. Many came to the United States already highly educated and in the middle or upper-middle classes. They did not reach out to sport as a means to greater economic, social, or educational goals. Becoming a doctor, lawyer, scientist, or other professional is instilled in their youth by their parents and culture rather than becoming a sports hero, according to Central Florida professor Yun-Oh Whang, a native Korean (Lapchick 2003). Recent census data support the notion that Asian Americans have a higher household income and higher graduation rate in high school and college than any other group, including Whites. However, Asian Americans can boast a number of star athletes in a variety of sports:

Sammy Lee, diving

Ichiro Suzuki, baseball

Michael Chang, tennis

Tiger Woods, golf

Amy Chow, gymnastics

Se Ri Pak, golf

Kristi Yamaguchi, figure skating

Apolo Anton Ohno, speed skating

Jim Paek, hockey

Michelle Kwan, figure skating

Yao Ming, basketball

Hideo Nomo, baseball

Vijay Singh, golf

Michelle Wie, golf

Dat Nguyen has made a career playing professional football.

According to the NCAA (2002), just half of 1% of all Asian or Pacific Islander students were also athletes in college, compared to nearly 6% for African American students and 2.6% for White students. But in large population centers where there are usually more Asian Americans, the anecdotal evidence suggests that Asian American children are becoming more interested in sport both as spectators and participants.

Compared to the overall percentage of Asian Americans of the population at large (4.1%), they are overrepresented in collegiate sport at Divisions I, II, and III in women's archery, women's badminton, men's and women's fencing, men's and women's gymnastics, women's soccer, women's squash, men's and women's water polo, and men's and women's tennis. Most of these sports do not require a large physique and they put a premium on skill; perhaps they are more suited to the traditional body types of Asians.

Asians also tend to be attracted to martial arts because such sports are part of their cultural heritage. Martial arts have been some of the fastest-growing activities among the general population in recent years. Participation in yoga and tai chi increased 134% between 1987 and 2003, while martial arts, such as judo, taekwondo, and karate, grew by 28% (SGMA 2004).

Native Americans

Native Americans and Alaska natives made up .9% of the U.S. population in 2003 with just over 2.7 million people. With this relatively small percentage of the population, you would not expect them as a group to have had much of an impact on sport, but they have produced some notable athletes over the years.

The Olympic Games have produced several sport heroes for Native Americans. Probably the most famous is Jim Thorpe, who was featured in chapter 1 (see page 10). In the Tokyo Olympic Games in 1964, Billy Mills won the gold medal in the 10,000-meter race. A fellow Olympian in the Games at Tokyo was Ben Nighthorse Campbell, who captained the U.S. judo team and had been the U.S. champion in judo three times. Campbell later went to the serve in the U.S. House of Representatives and the U.S. Senate. Altogether since 1904, there have been 14 Native American Olympians (NASC 2005).

In 2005, Native American professional athletes actively engaged in their sport numbered about 20 (NASC 2005). Their sports range from the traditional American sports like baseball (6) to the less traditional sports like the Iditarod (5). Other sports include speed skating, golf, bowling, ice dancing, rodeo, and auto racing. None of these athletes has achieved wide acclaim, but all make their living in professional sport.

The Native American Sports Council (NASC) is part of the Olympic movement, an affiliated organization of the USOC, and conducts community-based sport programs for Native Americans to encourage community participation. It also provides financial assistance for Native American Olympic hopefuls.

The North American Indigenous Games are a celebration of sport and culture for aboriginal peoples of Canada and the United States. In 2002, 6,136 athletes and 1,233 coaches participated in the games held in Winnipeg, Canada (NASC 2005). The following sports were included:

Archery	Basketball	Lacrosse	Swimming
Athletics	Boxing	Riflery	Taekwondo
Badminton	Canoeing	Soccer	Volleyball
Baseball	Golf	Softball	Wrestling

The next games are scheduled for 2006 in Denver and Colorado Springs.

In the United States, the National Native American Games have been held in the state of Arizona and drew over 1,000 participants in the inaugural year of 2003. The competition is open to all tribes and athletes must be one-quarter Native American to compete. Sports include basketball, cross country, adult softball, track and field, and volleyball.

Sport participation has not been easy for many Native Americans in today's world. Poverty rates are nearly 50% on many reservations and in many urban areas where Native Americans live. Time, money, and access to sport are limited, and the cultures also limit assimilation into the American sport scene. Discrimination against Native Americans is widespread and the athletic field is often just another battle for respect and acceptance. Native Americans have been stereotyped, displaced from their land, restricted to reservations, and saddled with poor economic status (King and Fruehling 2001).

Coaches have expressed frustration with Native Americans who have been enculturated to cooperate rather than compete with each other. Many Native Americans simply are not comfortable with the "winning is everything" mentality and may withdraw rather than try to change their beliefs. White coaches who have worked with Native Americans have been frustrated with the attitude of their players toward the importance of winning athletic contests (Bloom 2000).

Legacy of Lacrosse

There is no more significant Native American contribution to sport than the game of lacrosse. Considered to be America's first sport, it was created by North American Indians and embraced by non-Native Americans and Canadians alike. Lacrosse is a combination of basketball, soccer, and hockey that rewards skill, speed, and agility rather than brawn.

Since 1994, lacrosse has been growing at a rate of over 10% nationally, and in both college and high school, it is the fastest-growing sport for men and women in the past decade. Here is how participation broke down in 2004:

Youth (under 15)	186,048
High school	133,857
College	23,162
Club	8,635
Professional	150

At the college level, lacrosse has grown by 54.8% for men and women in the past 10 years. In high schools, the growth rate has been an astounding 188.6% for boys and girls. Traditional hotbeds for lacrosse such as Long Island, Baltimore, and Philadelphia are now being challenged by teams from other areas of the country (United States Lacrosse Association 2004).

Native American Mascots

In recent years, the use of Native American mascots by professional teams and by schools has come under scrutiny. The complaint is that the use of stereotypical team names, mascots, and logos perpetuates an ideology that dehumanizes and demeans the cultures of Native Americans. Students of American history will recall that Native American tribes were settled in North America long before the Europeans "discovered" America. As more Europeans came to the "new world," Native American tribes had their lands taken and their lives changed irreparably by these new settlers. Many Native Americans paid with their lives to defend their land, civilization, and culture. Years later, Euro-Americans labeled their athletic teams at schools, universities, and in professional sports with Native American logos, names, cheers, and mascots. Defenders of such names and

mascots claim that these actions were and are meant to honor the legacy of Native Americans and perpetuate memories of brave and heroic warriors. However, the objections to Native American mascots and symbols in American sports have been based on the blatant stereotyping of the Indian persona, ignoring the racist attitudes and displacement of populations of Native Americans, and encouraging white Euro-Americans to arbitrarily define the Native American culture, experience, and, in some cases, even claim to be part of that heritage (King 2004).

The first group to take aggressive action has been the NCAA (Brown 2005); starting in 2008 it will limit the use of Native American mascots and imagery at NCAA championships. The limits are only for NCAA championships and have no application to regular-season or conference competition. The policy specifically forbids the displaying of hostile and abusive racial, ethnic, or national origin mascots, nicknames, or imagery. Moreover, some 19 schools with team names such as the Braves, Redskins, Indians, Tribe, Savages, and so on have been put on notice to make changes before 2006 or risk ineligibility for future

The Washington Redskins have received criticism for their team name and mascot. Are Native American names and symbols ever honoring rather than offensive? This is a question that continues to be debated.

NCAA championships. The changes these schools make will be the result of self-study to ensure their use of mascots do not violate the hostile or abusive standard as judged by the NCAA. For example, schools that use the generic term Warriors without referring to Native American culture have been deemed to meet the compliance standard.

The NCAA relied on its core principles regarding diversity and inclusion when they made the recommendation to eliminate nicknames that may be considered abusive or hostile. Following the action of the NCAA may take some time and courage for other athletic bodies, but the trend is growing. Publicity and pressure from a variety of sources has focused on this issue and scholars, journalists, and leaders against discrimination in any form have joined forces. In 2001 the U.S. Commission on Civil Rights, an independent bipartisan federal agency, issued a statement encouraging non-Indian schools and universities to stop using Native American mascots, nicknames, and imagery. Progress is being made slowly but surely.

SPORT AND PROMOTING EQUALITY

Although you have just read about the roles of minorities in sport, the more important question may be whether sport participation is a negative or a positive force for those groups in achieving racial equality. Let's look at both sides of the issue.

Negative: Sport As an Unrealistic Dream in the Black Community

In spite of the relatively high percentage of Black athletes in the professional sports of basketball,

In the Arena With . . . *Arthur Ashe, Jr.*

Arthur Ashe was a great tennis player in the 1960s and 1970s, but he was also a social activist, author, coach, and philanthropist. In the predominantly White world of tennis, he was a lone Black man who endured racial prejudice that none of his contemporary tennis compatriots had to deal with. A quiet, introspective man with strong convictions and impeccable character, Arthur blazed a trail where no Black man had gone before.

He is the only Black man to win a Grand Slam singles championship, and he won not just one but three: the U.S. Open (1968), the Australian Open (1970), and Wimbledon (1970). He also played and coached the U.S. Davis Cup team over 15 years and compiled an outstanding record. His world ranking in the top 10 players for 12 years earned him a place in the International Tennis Hall of Fame in 1985.

A longtime protester against apartheid in South Africa, Ashe was eventually granted a visa to compete there and was the first Black man to win a title there. His association with Nelson Mandela influenced him, and over the years Ashe lent his name, time, and money to various progressive causes.

After retiring as a player, Ashe turned to writing a three-volume definitive history of Black sport titled *A Hard Road to Glory,* which was published in 1988. His second book, *Days of Grace: A Memoir* was published in 1993. In his spare time, Ashe helped found numerous inner-city tennis programs that bear his name, raised money for the United Negro College Fund, served on various corporate boards, and received several honorary doctorates. He also chaired the United States Tennis Association's player development committee.

In 1979, Arthur suffered a heart attack and underwent quadruple-bypass surgery five months later. In 1988, he learned he had contracted HIV through a blood transfusion during heart surgery. He died in 1993 at age 49. His body lay in state in his hometown of Richmond, Virginia, where more than 5,000 came to pay their respects. In an HBO special on Ashe, Bryant Gumbel said, "He was an ambassador of what was right, of dignity and of class."

football, and baseball, the odds of making it to the professional level are exceedingly small. (See chapter 7 and table 7.3 for the specific odds of transitioning from youth sport to the pros.) Regardless of the odds of success, young Black athletes still dream of being professional athletes.

In the words of William Ellerbee, basketball coach at powerhouse Simon Gratz High School in Philadelphia, "Suburban kids tend to play for the fun of it. Inner city kids look at basketball as a matter of life and death" (Price 1997). Professional sport seems like a way out of a life marked by economic struggle, educational challenges, and poor prospects for a successful career. Sport is something young people can understand, relate to, and almost taste. The problem is that there are just not enough spots to fulfill all the dreams.

In 1990, Blacks made up about 9% of all professional athletes, while there were nearly three times more Black physicians. A decade later, the number of Black professional athletes had jumped to approximately 20%; however, the number of doctors had also risen to twice the number of Black athletes. Of course, that's just one profession, and there are many more possible choices. Many Black youngsters are just not as tuned in to the possibilities of other careers.

Leaders in the Black community, such as Arthur Ashe, have spoken out about the need to keep Black children interested in school and committed to attending college. However, a survey by Indiana University researchers of more than 1,000 Black teens found that the majority of athletes chose their university not for the academics but to increase their chances of being drafted by the pros. They admitted that they would do only the minimum required to stay eligible in school and if drafted would leave before graduating (Hutchinson 2004).

The graduation rates of Black athletes at most Division I institutions reflects the apparent determination of many Black athletes to use college as a training ground for a professional career. The most recent graduation rates posted by the NCAA on its Web site are for 1994 to 1995. They show that male students graduate at a rate of 54% and student-athletes at a rate of 51%, but African American student-athletes graduate at a rate of only 42%. The results are significantly better for females. Women graduate at a rate of 59% while female student-athletes graduate at a rate of 69%. African American female student-athletes graduate at a rate of 59%. It appears that being a student-athlete tends to be a positive factor for females and a negative factor for males.

Football players at Division I schools who played in a bowl game in 2004 generally had poor academic records. In spite of extensive tutoring, mandatory study halls, reduced credit hours, and easy courses and majors, the graduation rate for football players is under 50% for more than half of the top 60 schools. If we consider only Black football players in this group, only about 12 of the more than 50 schools that played in a bowl game graduated more than 50% of their Black football players, including such school as Boston College, Syracuse, Notre Dame, Virginia, and Southern Mississippi. The bottom of the list includes Pittsburgh at 20%, Northern Illinois at 24%, and Minnesota and Louisville at 27% for Black football players (St. Petersburg Times 2004).

Universities needn't shoulder all the blame. Arthur Ashe toured predominately Black high schools in the late 1980s and early 1990s as he was gathering information for his three-volume history of the Black athlete, *A Hard Road to Glory*. Ashe reported that he was "thunderstruck" by the emphasis placed on sports at the schools he visited.

Activity Time-Out: Changing Youth Obsessions

What steps do you think could be taken to change the apparently harmful obsession with a professional sport career held by so many Black youngsters? Assuming families and schools can work together to influence young Blacks, what strategies would you suggest? List at least 10 strategies, including who would be responsible for implementing them and at what age kids should be exposed to them.

He went to on to report that "Black families are eight times more likely to push youngsters into athletics than are White families. The disparity is glaring, if you think of the Black parents' involvement at a sporting event compared to participation in a PTA meeting. We need to turn that around" (Houston Chronicle 2004).

Similarly, former NBA player Charles Barkley has said, "Sports are a detriment to Blacks . . . not a positive. You have a society now where every Black kid in the country thinks the only way he can be successful is through athletics. People look at athletes and entertainers as the sum total of Black America. That is a terrible, terrible thing, because that ain't even one-tenth of what we are" (Shields 2002).

Barkley has used his platform as a former basketball star to get the attention of the Black community. His message is echoed by Gary Sailes, a sport sociologist at Indiana University who provides life-skills training to high school and college athletes. Says Sailes, "About 95% of NBA players need to find a job after their careers end and about 81% of those players are bankrupt when they retire from the sport." In spite of the millions of dollars commanded by superstars, not all professional players make that kind of money and the temptation to spend lavishly is often hard to resist (Sleek 2004).

Positive: Sport As a Force for Racial Equality

Sport at every level of competition can have a positive effect on the quest for racial equality in society. The helpful outcomes of sport participation should be considered in balance to the negative effects, which are often sensationalized in the media.

Harry Edwards, who has been a racial activist for over 30 years, has a unique perspective on the value of sport for Black youths. He offers the opinion that in the next 30 years, we will see a decline of Black athletic participation. Edwards expects the Black youth community to split into two groups, middle-class and poor, and each group will shy away from sports. Middle-class kids will go on to become professionals, doctors, lawyers, and businesspeople. But he believes that Black youngsters from poorer communities are dropping out of society and landing in gangs, on the street, or in jail. Edwards still believes that sport offers hope for a way out of poverty, crime, and disillusionment. In his mind, sport may be the last chance to reach out to disaffected Black youth (Leonard 2000).

Success in sport can have a dramatic effect on the self-image and self-confidence of young people from minority populations. Their exploits on the playing field earn them respect and admiration from peers and the community and reassure them of their worthiness as individuals.

Achievement in sport can also earn players respect and admiration from peers who are outside the minority group. Minority athletes are more easily integrated into the mainstream of their contemporaries who are members of the majority group through team membership, leadership, and the critical roles they play.

Many communities have instituted after-school sport programs to care for youths who have no parental supervision at home when school is dismissed. Kids look forward to physical activity and playing with friends after a day of inactivity in school.

Adding an academic component to after-school

After-school and community programs help children learn new skills as well as increase self-confidence and scholastic achievement.

Pop Culture: Remember the Titans

"People say that it can't work, black and white; well, here we make it work every day. We have our disagreements, of course, but before we reach for hate, always, always, we remember the Titans" *(Remember the Titans* 2000).

Remember the Titans was a popular movie that attracted huge crowds at theaters across the country. The plot was based in Alexandria, Virginia, on the coaching careers of Bill Yoast, who lost his position as head coach of a public high school populated by Whites when the town's two schools were merged in the early 1970s. African American Herman Boone, the coach for the predominately Black school, was appointed head coach of the merged school and Yoast had to either assist him or leave. The movie shows the struggle to integrate athletes from different races and backgrounds into a harmonious unit. Naturally, after confronting numerous challenges and setbacks, the team came together to win the state championship, a remarkable feat. The possibilities for cooperation and compromise between two markedly different racial groups that this real-life example showed were inspirational and instructional.

sport programs in minority communities has encouraged kids to complete homework, learn about computers, and explore other academic interests in addition to the time allocated to playing sports. The message conveyed to these young children is that school and sport do mix and both can help them learn skills for future application.

A number of sports have begun outreach programs to attract minority youngsters. Among them, tennis and golf have probably initiated the most ambitious programs. Traditionally, both sports have been played by affluent families and marketing efforts have been directed toward those audiences as well as toward corporations that also seek to reach a consumer group with household incomes well above the average. However, in an effort to reach larger audiences and open the sports to a more diverse population, programs for young people have been established and subsidized to introduce them to tennis or golf.

Arthur Ashe and businessman Sheridan Snyder founded the National Junior Tennis League (NJTL) in the 1970s with a unique philosophy for tennis development. The concept was called *instant competition* and got urban youths actually playing tennis from their first day at the courts. As they tried to play and realized it took certain skills to be successful, the kids asked for help in techniques such as serves and ground strokes. This was a radical departure from traditional tennis instruction found in country clubs at the time. Twenty-five years later, game-based teaching became all the rage among tennis coaches, a philosophy of teaching not far from the pioneer-

ing concept of the NJTL. Perhaps the most notable characteristic of NJTL programs was the requirement that they had to be free or inexpensive so that all kids had access to tennis. Public parks, foundations, and fund-raising projects provided funding.

Interscholastic sport, supported by tax dollars from the public, offers sport opportunities for youngsters of all racial backgrounds at no charge or for modest fees. Black and Hispanic youths can play on a team, receive coaching, and have all expenses paid for, including equipment and uniforms. For those drawn to football and basketball, for example, school programs have been helpful for minority families who have modest discretionary income or none at all. Other sports that require training or competition outside of school continue to require huge financial investments from families and thus are out of reach for many Black and Hispanic households.

Integration of young people from all racial and ethnic backgrounds occurs naturally in sports where teammates are forced to work together for success. Even when athletes of different races compete against each other, they learn to respect and admire competent athletic performance of opposing players. The lesson young athletes learn may be that success is based on achievement in any field, regardless of heritage or skin color.

As a coach of tennis at a primarily White college in Pennsylvania, I consistently scheduled at least one match each spring with a historically Black college during our annual trip through Virginia or the Carolinas. When our team of White players set foot on a campus of African Americans, they were

Activity Time-Out: Is Sport Positive or Negative for Change?

Based on the information presented in this chapter, do you believe sport plays a positive role or a negative role in promoting diversity and equal opportunity? List the pros and cons of each view and then decide which list is more powerful.

curious and a bit uneasy, and when they entered the college dining room to eat, all eyes were on them. They gained a bit more empathy for the minority students back home who dared to enter a mostly White university. After our tennis match, their appreciation for the skill and competitive spirit of athletes from a different background was enhanced. The visit was often a highlight of an educational experience that offered more than simply a tennis competition.

Exceptionally talented minority athletes have opportunities for travel, educational scholarships, and experiences outside their community. These experiences open them to new possibilities and to attitudes that are characterized by hope and possibility rather than bitterness and discontent.

Kids who play sports are more likely to stay out of trouble with law enforcement and are less likely to become dependent on drugs or alcohol. While athletes as a group are not immune from temptations or antisocial behavior, the time and dedication that excellence in sport requires often takes precedence over other activities that typically result in unacceptable behavior. In addition, they run the risk of losing the chance to play the sport they enjoy if they violate rules for conduct and behavior.

Black athletes who do beat the odds and forge successful careers in professional sport have the opportunity to better themselves financially, sometimes in amazing ways. Other opportunities as spokespersons or employees in businesses or sport organizations often materialize once their athletic career has ended. Upward mobility through sport has been demonstrated repeatedly by a generation of Black athletes.

Once they reach the peak of athletic performance, many Black athletes have used their prominence to speak out for causes they believe in. For example, improved race relations were a theme of the proposed Olympic boycott in Mexico City in 1968. When the boycott fell through, African American sprinters Tommie Smith and John Carlos instead used the award ceremony to call attention to the plight of Afri-

can Americans in the United States. Although they were criticized heavily for using sport to promote their personal point of view, their actions were no different from those of many other influential people who do the same.

Michael Jordan, perhaps the greatest basketball player of all time, demonstrated the global reach of sport success through his role as a spokesperson for Nike. Kids the world over adopted the mantra of "Be like Mike" and consumed Nike products from shoes to clothing in hopes of emulating Jordan's performances. He also showed how fame in one field can be transferred to the business world through ownership of a basketball franchise and through other business ventures.

Minority athletes become role models for the next generation of athletes. Their fame is not limited to children from a single racial background; children choose their heroes based on their performance, flair, and personality rather than race. Although some athletes reject their role as models for youths and simply want to be accepted as an athlete, the dynamics of the media, fans, and kids simply won't allow it. Their actions, lifestyle, and values are scrutinized and embraced or rejected simply because they are in the public spotlight. They can choose to be a positive force for improving society or a negative example of behavior that should be abhorred.

As the struggle for racial integration continues, sport offers a fertile ground for exposing the futility of erecting artificial barriers to integration, for embracing athletes from all backgrounds based on talent and conduct, and for promoting understanding and appreciation of people from all different backgrounds.

MINORITIES AS SPORT LEADERS

Virtually anyone who has studied the situation of minority athletes has come away believing that leadership in sport has to change for progress to occur. The lack of minority leadership in key positions in sport is sobering and shows few signs of improving in the near future. However, change can still happen. In the following sections, we'll look at some ways to increase the presence of minority groups in all levels of sport. Most of the examples are based on African Americans since their role as athletes in certain sports has been so dominant. Increasingly, though, people are also becoming more sensitive to the need for leaders from other minority groups as well.

Minorities in Leadership Positions in Collegiate Sports

With the statistics showing the dominance of African American athletes in the collegiate and professional sports of football, men's and women's basketball, and track and field, you might expect to see similar gains in the coaching ranks. However, the proportion of African American coaches is well below the proportion of African Americans in the population at large and is much lower than the proportion of African American athletes playing the major revenue sports. According to Lapchick and Mathews (1999), excluding historically Black institutions, the percentage of African American head coaches at NCAA member institutions in 1999 was as follows:

Karl Dorrell, head football coach at UCLA, is one of two Black head football coaches in Division 1-A football. Why are he and Sylvestor Croom, head football coach at Mississippi State, the only two Black head football coaches at the Division 1-A level?

- 4.4% for men's teams
- 4.4% for women's teams
- 8.6% for men's revenue sports
- 6.4% for women's revenue sports

By 2004, in men's sport Whites held 89.5% of head coaching positions in Division I, 90.5% of the positions in Division II, and 93% of the positions in Division III. African Americans held 7.7% of the positions in Division I, 3.4% in Division II, and 4.1% in Division III. Latinos held 1.6% in Division I, 3.4% in Division II, and 1.5% in Division III. Asians and Native Americans had almost no representation (NCAA 2004b).

In women's sport, the most startling data were that women still only claimed 41.9% of all head coaching positions in colleges after more than 30

years since the passage of Title IX. That said, the following results refer to both men and women who are head coaches of women's collegiate sports. In Division I, Whites held 91.3% of head coaching positions in women's sport; 90.8% in Division II, and 93% in Division III. African Americans held 5% of the positions in Division I, 3.7% in Division II, and 4% in Division III, while Latinos held 1.7% in Division I, 3.1% in Division II, and 1.2% in Division III. Asians held 1.2% of the positions in Division I, 1% in Division II, and 1% in Division III, and Native Americans had almost no representation (Lapchick 2004).

Compared with the approximately 13% of African Americans and 13% of Latinos in the U.S. population, these percentages are woeful. But if you match them with the percentage of Black athletes in basketball, 55% for men and 35% for women in Division I, the results are even worse.

The recent firing of several high-profile Black football coaches, including Tyrone Willingham at Notre Dame after only three years, sparked the criticism once again of the lack of Black coaches in major college football. At the end of the 2004 season, there were only two Black head football coaches in Division I football.

TABLE 11.5   Blacks and Latinos in Noncoach Positions

Position	African American (%)	Latino (%)
Athletic director	3.4	1.2
Associate director or assistant director	6.0	.7
Senior administrator (women)	8.9	0
Professional administration	5.9	2.3

Numbers exclude historically Black institutions for NCAA Division I schools for 2004. Other minority groups were barely mentioned.
Data from Lapchick 2004.

TABLE 11.6   Black Coaches as of 2004

Position	NBA (%)	NFL (%)	MLB (%)	WNBA (%)
Head coach or manager	37	9	10	31
Assistant coach or manager	29	30	12	45

Data from Lapchick 2004.

Since 1996, only one African American male each year has been hired to fill head football coaching positions—out of 142 openings (Harrison 2004). Report cards on the searches to fill these positions included whether universities had communications with the Black Coaches Association or the chair of the Minority Opportunity Interest Committee, the number of minorities on the search committee, the number of minorities who received interviews, the length of time it took to hire a candidate, and whether the search committee documented adherence to their institution's affirmative action policy.

The results showed that 40% of the schools (11 in 2003-2004) received a grade of C, D, or F. Only Cornell earned an A in every category and received an award of excellence.

One popular explanation for the dearth of Black coaches is the small percentage of athletic directors and other administrators in universities who are Black. It has been theorized that White administrators know fewer Black coaches, are less comfortable with them, and thus resist placing key programs in their hands. According to Lapchick and Mathews (1999), Black athletic directors in 1996 to 1997 were present in just 3.2% of Division I institutions. The numbers were somewhat better in some adminis-

trative positions other than the head person (see table 11.5).

Minorities in Leadership Positions in Professional Sport

In professional sport, the percentage of Black athletes is even higher than in college (see table 11.6). Those responsible for recruiting and hiring Black coaches are the owners of professional sport franchises. In 1999, according to research by Lapchick and Mathews, there were no minority owners of any professional sport franchises. There were, however, a number of limited partners in various leagues, the most notable among them Magic Johnson with the Los Angeles Lakers. Since then, Michael Jordan has joined the Washington Wizards, and Robert L. Johnson, who made millions from BET television, has acquired majority ownership of the Carolina basketball franchise, an expansion team that began competing in 2004. He also owns the Charlotte Stings of the WNBA, making him the first African American majority owner of a professional sport team.

By 2004, the picture had begun to change. Baseball had its first Hispanic owner, Arturo Moreno of the Anaheim Angels, and three other minorities had shares of teams. The NBA showed six minority limited partners in addition to Robert L. Johnson as a majority owner. The NFL had five minority limited partners and the WNBA had one majority owner.

In response to public pressure through the media and other sources, owners have actively recruited Black administrators for their teams, most notably as directors of community relations. While the percentage of other Black administrators lags behind the percentage of Blacks in the population, African Americans hold 45% of the positions of director of community relations in the NBA, 23% in the NFL, and 30% in MLB.

As for soccer, the 2004 report showed some dramatic changes in the racial and gender report cards (Lapchick 2005a). Although MLS was cited for dramatically improved hiring relative to gender, the percentages of White male players increased while the number of Latino and African Americans decreased. The results showed that 17% of players were African American and 14% were Latino. People of color held 24% of the professional positions in the league. However, there were no people of color as coaches or general managers.

Strategies to Promote Racial Diversity in Sport

From the discussion in the previous section, it is clear that one key strategy to promote racial diver-

Activity Time-Out: Out: Promoting Racial Diversity

The possible strategies for promoting racial diversity listed in the text are intended to get you thinking. See if you can come up with at least a dozen new strategies for sport at any level to eliminate racism and increase the number of minorities who participate. If you prefer, you may narrow your recommendations to one sport that you are familiar with.

sity in sport is to improve the hiring and retention of minority coaches in both college and professional sport. Institutions must follow guidelines for affirmative action that include strategies for recruitment of minority candidates, inclusion of minorities in the hiring process, and a "good faith" effort to evaluate minority candidates objectively and fairly. Other possible strategies include the following:

- Agree on the need to improve the percentages of minorities in all sports and all sport leadership positions. Targets should be set based on percentages in the population at large and within the sport community.

- Leaders in sport must help collect data such as that provided currently by Dr. Richard Lapchick of the University of Central Florida, which details the participation and presence of minorities at all levels of sport. Without a baseline number to work from, efforts to improve diversity will be impossible to measure. The process should be unbiased, objective, and transparent and the results should be widely disseminated.

- Leaders in minority communities and heads of sport organizations should confront any instance of discrimination or racism when they become aware of it and take steps to rectify the situation.

- Major sport organizations, both amateur and professional, should adopt statements of inclusion of minorities for their players, coaches, and administration staff.

- Major media outlets including television, radio, magazines, and newspapers should actively recruit minorities for their staff and aggressively endorse the need for change in sport.

- All sport organizations should develop standing policies of inclusion in pictures, graphics, and media representations.

- Politicians should adopt laws to ensure that public money is used for projects and orga-

nizations that are committed to providing opportunity for all and improving minority representation.

- Prominent minority athletes must assume the responsibility to point out inconsistencies and inequities and use their popularity to improve the future for other minority athletes.

- Local communities and youth sport organizations should adopt strong policies on nondiscrimination and should actively recruit minorities to participate in sport as players, coaches, leaders, and organizers.

- Minority-owned businesses should expect action by the organizations they support financially through sponsorship and marketing.

CHAPTER SUMMARY

In this chapter, we have reviewed the meaning of racial and ethnic background in sport. The differences in physical prowess between races were examined and the issue of whether differences were due to genetics or environment was considered. At the present time, there is no clear evidence either way, although research is ongoing. It is likely that both factors will prove to be crucial in most sports.

Participation by minority groups at various levels of sport was compared to the number of minorities in the general U.S. population. Generally, the data show that Black athletes dominate major American sports such as basketball and football at both the college and professional levels. Baseball also has a high proportion of Black athletes, although they are slowly losing ground to Hispanics. However, in all other sports, Whites overwhelmingly dominate in terms of participation at every level of play.

The history of minority athletes was briefly reviewed and the exceptional influence of outstanding Black athletes was noted. Most gains in participation by minorities have occurred since the second World War when college and professional sport opened to Black athletes. Latino athletes are exceedingly well represented in professional baseball, surpassing even Black athletes by percentage. In other sports, Latinos are generally poorly represented, as are Asians and Native Americans.

Both the positive and negative contributions of sport to racial and ethnic equality were presented. Sport has shown the potential to be a positive force for racial integration, although progress has not always been smooth. On the other hand, we considered some of the negative aspects, including minority preoccupation with sport at the expense of schooling and alternative career choices.

The struggles of Black athletes were pointed out even as they dominate some college and professional sports. Their participation tends to be limited to just a few sports and access to the majority of sports is still limited. The tendency of powerful sport institutions to exploit the physical abilities of Black athletes at the expense of their potential for a fulfilling life after sport was discussed.

Strategies for lessening the present inequities in sport were presented along with an opportunity for readers to add creative strategies of their own. For the progress of the last 50 years to continue at the same rate, a collective commitment to racial diversity in sport must be accepted at every level of play.

Women and Sport

After reading this chapter, you will know the following:

- The historical roles of women in and out of sport
- How Title IX affected women's sport participation
- How increased sport participation by females affected society
- Current challenges in women's sports

One of the most consistent forms of discrimination is the social role forced upon women throughout history. From the time of the ancient Greeks to the present day, societies have relegated females to subservient roles revolving around child rearing, family, and sex. Changes in American society in the last 35 years have dramatically altered the roles for women, but the quest for equalizing women's opportunity in society is still short of its goal.

A majority of women in the United States are now in the workforce. According to the 2005 U.S. Census, 58% of women work, compared to 71% of men (U.S. Census 2005a). In 1960, the percentage of working women was just 36%. Along with fighting for greater equality in employment opportunities, women have campaigned for and significantly progressed in admission to institutions of higher education, rights in marriage, roles in the armed forces, and opportunities for sport participation. The sporting world changed greatly with the passing of Title IX, which granted females equal participation in sports. With this foray into the sporting world, however, females faced new forms of discrimination.

In this chapter, we'll look at the factors that have affected women's participation in sports, the sweeping changes that have occurred in sport over the past 35 years, and the challenges women in sport still confront.

HISTORICAL ROLE OF WOMEN

To understand the magnitude of the first female breakthroughs in sport, you need to appreciate the context in which these pioneering women accomplished them. Since the times of the ancient Greeks and Romans, the family was based on a patriarchal model wherein the male was the absolute ruler. He alone could own property and enter into business contracts, and if his wife violated social customs or his wishes, he could punish her. In many societies, if a husband determined that his wife was guilty of infidelity, he could have her put to death.

The institutions of society reinforced the subjugated role of women throughout history. Even the church made it clear that the male was the head of the family and often portrayed the female as an agent of the devil whose role was to tempt the male. Women could not act as clergy and were expected to adhere to the teachings of men.

The prescribed role for women stayed the same for centuries. The male was always the leader, the provider for the family, and the center of power. The female was the child bearer and nurturer and keeper of the home. Females were not allowed physical exercise other than that required by their domestic roles. They were expected to look attractive to men, dress prettily, and be well mannered. Women were expected to depend on the men.

WOMEN AND SPORT BEFORE TITLE IX

Sports have reflected the limited role of women by excluding them from participation for centuries and resisting change to include them. Girls were ignored, ridiculed, and disciplined for their efforts to compete in sports (Rice, Hutchinson, and Lee 1958; Spears and Swanson 1978). It wasn't until the mid-1800s that women even ventured into physical activity programs founded at universities such as Mount Holyoke and Vassar. Medical doctors dedicated to improving the health and fitness of students typically led the early programs of physical education. Exercise for girls was carefully controlled and emphasized graceful, ladylike movements. Competitive sports were ruled out as simply inappropriate for women.

A few women dared to participate in individual sports such as tennis and golf. Figure skating, gymnastics, and swimming, considered a more feminine sports requiring grace, beauty, and coordination, were gradually accepted for women. Power and strength sports were deemed inappropriate and even the Olympic Games banned women from most track and field events. Running, jumping, and throwing heavy objects were not consistent with the social view of the female. In the modern Olympic Games that began in 1896, women were not allowed to compete. In 1920, the Olympics invited only 64 women, compared with more than 2,500 men. In the Berlin Games in 1936, the number of female participants swelled to 328 while male participants boosted their number to 3,738 (Fanbay.net 2005).

A few female athletes gained fame during the 1920s and '30s. Glenna Collett Vare was a remarkable amateur golfer who won the U.S. Open Amateur Championships six times between 1922 and 1935. Helen Wills Moody dominated women's tennis in the '20s and '30s by winning eight Wimbledon titles, eight U.S. national titles, and every set she played in competition between 1927 and 1932. The most famous and perhaps best athlete was Mildred "Babe" Didrikson Zaharias. In 1950, Babe was voted the greatest female athlete of the first half of the century by the Associated Press. Her accomplishments included two gold medals and one silver medal in track and field events at the 1932 Olympics. As a golfer, she dominated both the amateur and professional field. She was also a tennis player who could compete with the best players in the United States. Other women also made their mark in professional sports. The popular movie *A League of Their Own* chronicles the trials of the All-American Girls Professional Baseball League during World War II. You also might want to view the documentary, *Dare to Compete: The Struggle of Women in Sports,* which traces the history of women in sports.

These outstanding female athletes blazed the trail into the sports world. But their successes would not open up sport opportunities for the majority of women until society changed its general view of the woman's role. The following are some of the reasons society gave for excluding women from sport.

Females Aren't Interested

Lack of interest was in hindsight an irrational justification for excluding girls from sport. Since girls had little access to sport, few sport role models, and no encouragement to play sport by social institutions such as families, schools, and churches, of course they appeared uninterested. They were expected to become cheerleaders, pom-pom girls, and majorettes and to play in the band and fill the stands to cheer on the boys.

Physical Activity Harms the Female Body

In the last century, led by physicians and physical educators at universities across America, people gradually awakened to the positive benefits of physical activity for girls. Although limited to certain ladylike physical activities, girls were encouraged to become aware of their bodies for reasons of health and appearance. Research began to show that girls could train their bodies to become stronger and faster and endure longer without damaging their physique. It wasn't until the late 1970s that experts began to affirm the positive values of sport participation for females. In 1978, Klafs and Lyon said, "Let it be stated here, unequivocally, that there is no reason,

The All-American Girls League played in the Midwest from 1943 to 1954.

either psychological, physiological, or sociological, to preclude normal, healthy females from participating in strenuous physical activities, nor does such participation accentuate or develop male characteristics. Strenuous activity for the well-trained and well-conditioned female athlete results in good health and accentuates the very qualities that make her a woman" (Klafs and Lyon 1978, p. 10).

Although female leaders in sport forged a brave path toward physical activity for girls, they also held girls back. Up through the 1950s, leaders of women's sports limited the types of acceptable sport and encouraged girls not to become too competitive. Playdays or sports days on college campuses were the norm in the '50s. Women from several different colleges gathered at one campus and were assigned to teams for that day. The events were largely informal and encouraged mass participation. Several sports were typically played and competition was low-key and usually in round-robin format. The closing event was a tea or social hour when girls could talk with each other (Spears and Swanson 1978). When the NCAA threatened to take over women's sports, the leading female coaches and administrators fought against it. They preferred the more ladylike approach to sports in which girls were athletes tempered by good manners, winning was deemphasized, and femininity was maintained.

Remnants of this ladylike approach are team monikers such as *Lady Lions, Lady Vols,* and *Lady Tigers.* Imagine if the men's teams were called *Gentlemen Bears, Gentlemen Gators,* or *Gentlemen Warriors.*

Women Cannot Compete With Men in Sport, So They Don't Deserve Equal Opportunity to Play Sport

Objections about the relative skill and physical prowess of girls versus boys were a natural outcome of a few girls daring to compete against boys. My high school boys' tennis team competed against a young girl named Tory Fretz, who played first singles on the boys' team for Harrisburg High School and went on to a professional career. She defeated every boy in the conference, usually by lopsided scores. Her performance was an eye-opener for adolescent boys and humiliating for her victims, who endured teasing and taunting.

But unlike Tory Fretz, most girls were at a disadvantage when competing against boys once puberty set in. Before puberty, girls can compete equally with boys in any sport. But once the relative size, strength, and body proportions change, the comparative athletic ability also changes. To achieve equal opportunity in sports, women needed a whole new structure for girls' sports, starting from little history, equipment, or tradition.

Girls With Natural Talent in Sports Are Probable Lesbians

Girls who gravitated toward sports were often suspected of lesbian tendencies long before the term *lesbian* was even used in polite society. Women who liked sports and seemed to have more testosterone were viewed askance by males and females alike. The average person had little notion of the balance of testosterone and progesterone that exists in both male and female bodies. Women who were stronger and faster or could hit harder excelled in women's sports, leading some to suspect that they were really men disguised in women's bodies.

In the Olympic Games, testing for gender was an issue for years as a result of the masculine appearance of many great female athletes. **Gender verification** was required for nearly 30 years until after the 1996 Atlanta Games, when all gender verification was discontinued at the urging of virtually all professional medical associations including the American

Activity Time-Out: School Nicknames

Investigate your school and others in your league to see if *Lady* still precedes the team nickname. If it does, ask a few coaches, administrators, players, and students on campus why the *Lady* still exists and how they feel about it.

If your school does not fall into that pattern, use the Internet or library to research schools that do. Can you find a pattern in the type of school, size of school, church affiliation, public or private status, or geography? For example, is *Lady* more prevalent in the American south than in the northeast or on the west coast?

Medical Association. The extensive procedures being used for verification were too complex, uncertain, and expensive. Furthermore, very few athletes actually failed the tests that were administered. With the advent of doping control policies that included voiding urine under direct supervision, it became virtually impossible for male athletes to escape detection if they tried to pose as women (Genel 2000).

Social attitudes toward women and lesbians continued from the first half of the 20th century to be heavily weighted against equal participation of women in sport. Consider this quote from Woody Hayes, a famous football coach at Ohio State:

> *"I hear they're even letting w-o-m-e-n in their sports program now (referring to Oberlin College). That's your Women's Liberation, boy—bunch of goddamn lesbians. . . . You can bet your ass that if you have women around—and I've talked to psychiatrists about this—you aren't gonna be worth a damn. No sir! Man has to dominate . . . the best way to treat a woman . . . is to knock her up and hide her shoes." (Vare 1974, p. 38)*

TITLE IX

Social change throughout the 1950s and '60s helped change women's sports. The women's movement of the 1960s and organizations such as the National Organization for Women and the Women's Action Group helped further the movement for equality of men and women. In the sports world, however, it was the passage of **Title IX** that ultimately gave women an even playing field with men. (For a comprehensive work on the substance, effects, and challenges of Title IX, consult *Title IX* by Carpenter and Acosta [2005]). Title IX, passed in 1972 by the U.S. Congress, stated the following:

The sentiments expressed by Woody Hayes were typical rhetoric pre-Title IX. How have social attitudes toward women's sports changed over the past 30 years?

> *"No person in the United States shall, on the basis of sex, be excluded from participation in, be denied the benefits of, or be subjected to discrimination under any education program or activity receiving federal financial assistance."*

When Title IX was passed, there was little immediate outcry since America was in the throes of ensuring equal protection for all students, regardless

Activity Time-Out: Memories of Title IX

Interview at least one male and one female over the age of 50 about their recollection of the 1972 passage of Title IX. See if they recall the discussion and emotional debates that ensued. Ask women about their attitude toward sports for girls and their sport experiences before 1972. Ask both males and females their current feelings about equal opportunity in sport. How have their opinions changed over the years?

In the Arena With . . . *Billie Jean King*

Billie Jean was a champion tennis player and an outspoken advocate of gender equality in sports. Over the years, King's actions made her the center of attention in debates over the equality between the sexes, amateurism versus professionalism in sports, and gay and lesbian rights. Her crusading led *Life* magazine to recognize her in 1990 as one of the "100 Most Important Americans of the 20th Century." She was the only female athlete on the list and was one of only four athletes along with Babe Ruth, Jackie Robinson, and Muhammad Ali.

As a tennis player, Billie Jean won Wimbledon six times, won the U.S. Open four times, and was ranked number one in the world five times. In 1971, she was the first woman in any sport to earn more than $1 million U.S. in a single year. In 1972, *Sports Illustrated* named her the first Sportswoman of the Year.

Perhaps Billie Jean is most remembered for her 1973 "Battle of the Sexes" match against Bobby Riggs, a 55-year-old male tennis champion. Watched on television by nearly 50 million fans, King defeated Riggs decisively 6-4, 6-3, and 6-3 in the Houston Astrodome amid a media circus. Her victory convinced even skeptics that a female athlete can survive pressure at the highest levels and that men are just as vulnerable to nerves as women are.

Upon retirement, Billie Jean did not slink to the sidelines. She helped found the Women's Tennis Association during her career and later the Women's Sports Foundation and *WomenSports* magazine. With her husband, Larry, she also fulfilled a dream of a coed team tennis league by founding World Team Tennis at the professional level, a league that is still growing in popularity.

In the 1990s, she turned to coaching as the United States Fed Cup captain and Olympic coach. After years of criticizing the U.S. Tennis Association for its narrow-minded, antiquated policies, King joined the association as an adviser and in-house critic to work for change (Schwartz 2005a; World Team Tennis 2005).

of race or gender, in public education. Most parents agreed that their daughters should have the same right to a fine education that their sons had. It wasn't for some time that people understood that sports were included in the decree and that big changes would have to be made.

The imbalance in sport participation between boys and girls was dramatic up until the 1970s. At that time nearly 3.7 million boys were playing varsity high school sports compared with just 295,000 girls. Out of every dollar spent on sports, boys received 99 cents while girls received just 1 cent. In college, there were approximately 180,000 men playing varsity sports versus just 32,000 women.

Title IX raised many questions about what it really meant and what specific changes had to be made. Did it mean girls had to have as many teams as boys had? Did girls get half the money spent on sports, thereby reducing funding for boys? While many people thought girls should have an equal chance

to play sports, few wanted to see programs for boys cut. What a dilemma!

After much debate and foot dragging, in 1975 the Office for Civil Rights published guidelines clarifying what it meant to comply with Title IX. To be eligible for federal funding, schools and colleges had to meet any of three tests:

1. Proportionality test—If a school is 50% female, then no less than 45% of its athletes should be female. The 5% deviation was deemed the allowable margin.

2. History of progress test—A school demonstrates progress toward expanding women's programs, particularly over the last three years.

3. Accommodation of interest test—A school shows that it has fully accommodated the interests and needs of the underrepresented (female) sex. Inequality exists due to lack

of interest or to inability to field additional teams for athletic competition.

As these clarifications were issued, female athletes and their advocates began filing legal suits. In one of the lawsuits, the U.S. Supreme Court surprisingly ruled that Title IX did not apply to sports since sports were not supported by federal funds. Three years later the U.S. Congress overturned this decision by passing the Civil Rights Restoration Act that clarified that it did indeed intend Title IX to apply to sports. President Reagan vetoed the law, but Congress overrode his veto.

Massive changes in high school and college sports began shortly after the passage of Title IX. While most schools and colleges were slow to respond, the process had nevertheless begun. Supporters of male athletics initiated numerous lawsuits to delay the inevitable, but gradually women began to assert their rights and demand sport opportunities at every level.

WOMEN AND SPORT AFTER TITLE IX

In the 30 years following Title IX legislation, the numbers of girls and women playing sports changed dramatically:

- In 2002, girls made up 44% of all organized youth sport teams (SGMA 2003).

- More than half of all frequent (100 or more times annually) fitness participants are female. Females make up at least 45% to more than 50% of all tennis players, bowlers, and hikers. Women represent 91% of step exercisers, 73% of aerobic exercisers, 71% of kickboxers, 62% of exercise walkers, 62% of ice skaters, 58% of traditional roller skaters, 58% of badminton players, 54% of swimmers, 53% of volleyball players, 52% of in-line skaters, and 52% of people exercising with equipment (SGMA 2003).

- Women showed remarkable gains in participation in high school and college sports and in the Olympic Games. Look at tables 12.1 to 12.4 to see their progress. In the past 30 years, women's participation in U.S. teams has drawn nearly equal to that of men.

- Olympic performances by women improved dramatically as training intensified and the pool of competing athletes enlarged. Joan Benoit Samuelson's time for the marathon in Los Angeles in 1984 was faster than all men's

TABLE 12.1   High School Sport Participation by Gender

Year	Boys	Girls
1971	1 out of 2	1 out of 27
2001	1 out of 2	1 out of 2.5

Data from NFSHSA and Department of Education 2001.

TABLE 12.2   College Sport Participation by Gender

Year	Men	Women
1981	156,131	68,062
2004	216,991	160,650

Data from NCAA 2004b.

TABLE 12.3   Women in the Summer Olympic Games

Year	Percentage of participants who were female
1900	1.6
1960	11.5
1984	23
1996	34
2000	38
2004	44

Data from www.fanbay.net/olympics/women.htm.

TABLE 12.4   American Women in the Olympic Games

Year	Percentage of females making up the U.S. team
1972	21
2004	48

Data from www.fanbay.net/olympics/women.htm.

times before 1956. In Olympic swimming, the women's record in the 100-meter freestyle, set in 1992, was faster than all men's times before 1964. In cross-country skiing, the Olympic record for women in the 15-kilometer race, set in 1994, was faster than all men's records before 1992.

The following are several outcomes resulting from the increased presence of females in sport and physical activity.

Women As Sports Fans

As women's participation in sports exploded, females also became avid sports fans. Many females began watching sports to track the performances of their heroes and appreciate the contest not just as spectators but as fellow participants. The following statistics are from the Women's Sports Foundation (2004a).

- In 2003, 7 out of 10 fans at a WUSA game were female, and 89% of fans under the age of 18 were girls. The largest crowd to watch a women's soccer game was at RFK Stadium in Washington, DC, with 24,240 fans.
- Roughly 40% of the annual 6.6 million people attending Winston Cup races are women.
- Women make up 47% of MLS fans, 46% of MLB fans, 43% of NFL fans, 40% of NHL fans, and 37% of NBA fans.
- Over the Atlanta, Barcelona, and Seoul Olympic Games (1988-1996), viewership among women increased more than it did among men across all age groups, especially in the 18 to 34 age group (39%).

Perhaps because of their increasing interest in sports both as participants and spectators, women have become powerful consumers of athletic apparel. According to the Sporting Goods Manufacturers Association, women buy 81% of all athletic apparel, including 91% of sport clothing for children and 50% of sport apparel for men (Women's Sports Foundation 2004a). From 1992 to 1999, sales in women's athletic footwear increased by 37%, while sales in men's footwear increased just 5%. *Self* magazine reported that 88% of its readers indicated that it is very important or important in their purchase decision that a company provide a product or service that supports girls and women in sports and fitness activities (Women's Sports Foundation 2004a).

Popularity of Women's Sports

Women's sports at every level of competition have begun to attract large numbers of spectators. Here are some landmark attendance figures:

- In 1973, at the height of the women's movement, Billie Jean King defeated Bobby Riggs to win the "Battle of the Sexes" before 30,472 fans, still the largest crowd to attend a tennis match (Women's Sports Foundation 2004a).

- The 2001 U.S. Open singles final featuring Venus Williams versus Serena Williams drew a 6.8 television rating on CBS. The prime-time final outscored NBC's Notre Dame versus Nebraska football game that recorded a 4.8 rating (Women's Sports Foundation 2004a).

Women's collegiate sports have exploded, and schools with successful women's teams enjoy stellar attendance. Some college women's teams such as the women's basketball team at the University of Connecticut even have lucrative cable television contracts for the broadcast rights to their games. Here are some of the most remarkable collegiate viewership statistics as compiled by the Women's Sports Foundation (2004a):

- The University of Tennessee's Lady Vols led the nation in women's basketball total attendance at 232,646 and averaged 15,510 fans per game for 2000 to 2001.
- The NCAA Division I women's college basketball championship game of Connecticut versus Tennessee received a rating of 4.3, making it the most-watched women's basketball game in ESPN's history.
- The University of Utah's women's gymnastics team has consistently averaged more than 10,000 fans per meet since 1992 and is the only revenue-producing women's sport on campus.
- The 2003 WNBA championship game between the Detroit Shock and the Los Angeles Sparks drew a record crowd of 22,076.

You probably won't be surprised by the spectator figures for women's soccer given its huge popularity since the 1980s. More than 650,000 tickets were sold to the 1999 women's World Cup. The final match drew a women's sports record of 90,185 to the Rose Bowl in California. The same World Cup final between the United States and China earned an 11.4 Nielsen rating, with 11,307,000 households, or a 31% market share, watching. This was the most-watched soccer game (male or female) in U.S. television history, with more than 40 million viewers tuning in (Women's Sports Foundation 2004a).

Men As Fans of Women's Sports

Men deserve some credit for contributing to spectatorship in women's sports. According to the Harris Poll in 2001, the following percentages of fans watching women's sports are male (Harris Interactive 2001):

Male fans are a huge factor in the increasing popularity of women's sports.

WNBA	47%
LPGA	58%
Women's soccer	66%
Women's tennis	42%
Women's college basketball	56%

For the 1999 women's World Cup mentioned in the previous section, 49% of those viewing the final game were adult men, compared with 36% who were adult women and 15% who were children under 18 (Women's Sports Foundation 2004a). Men enjoy watching women compete for a variety of reasons. Some like the novelty of women competing; some like to root for the underdog (such as professional golfer Annika Sorenstam when she competes against men on the pro golf tour); and others enjoy watching fit, attractive women in action. Some men, particularly as they age, relate better to the level of athleticism of women in a sport like basketball, where men's play is dominated by athletes who appear as giants to most of us. Women's tennis tends to produce longer rallies than those found in men's tennis, just like the sport many of us play does.

The style of play can also attract male viewers. Women's basketball tends to feature more passing and teamwork than its male version does. This style appeals to basketball purists who appreciate a game built on teamwork over the modern male version that emphasizes individual play and slam dunks.

There is no substitute for results. The U.S. women's soccer team garnered a large audience, both male and female, simply because of its excellence of play lasting over 10 years. Their capture of Olympic gold medals and the World Cup championship thrilled us and inspired patriotic pride. We admire star players such as Mia Hamm, Brandi Chastain, Kristine Lilly, and Michele Akers. Men's soccer may be more popular worldwide, but in the Unites States no soccer team had ever captured the attention of the nation as these women did. The media declared the 1996 Olympic Games in Atlanta to be the "Year of the Women" (NewsSmith 1996). Female athletes reached the pinnacle of participation: 3,800 female athletes from around the world competed. Women represented 34% of all the athletes in the Games, and for the first time women contributed more than a third of the participants. Just eight years later, that percentage rose 44%, and female participants are rapidly approaching a number equal to that of men.

Expert's View: Women's Sports Benefit Men, Too

Richard Lapchick, who founded the Center for the Study of Sport in Society, in his article, "A Grandfather's Take on Women's Sports," makes the point that women's sports benefit men. Besides being entertaining to watch, sports help wives, daughters, and granddaughters become smarter, healthier, and more self-confident. Men who appreciate women's sports are less likely to be abusive, violent, and misogynistic. They are more likely to share the pressures of life and family with their wives and not expected to be the caretaker of the family. They respect women who achieve in sports and value them for their abilities in yet another arena. Dads who enjoy girls' sports spend more time with their daughters than they ever did before, shooting hoops, playing catch, dribbling a soccer ball, or rallying a tennis ball. Girls and their fathers can connect through sports in a way that used to be available only to boys (Lapchick 2001a).

Fine performances by American female Olympians also captured the attention of the media and spectators. The American team won gold medals in the Olympic debut of softball and soccer in the 1996 Olympic Games. Female gymnasts and the American women in both singles and doubles tennis also claimed the gold in the 1996 Games. Swimmer Amy Van Dyken became the first American woman to win four gold medals in a single Games, and the women's basketball team also captured the gold medal.

SOCIAL ISSUES IN WOMEN'S SPORT

As sport opportunities and fitness activities for women have increased, so, too, have unique social issues. Prior to women's participation in sport and physical activity, issues such as women's health and fitness and clothing designed specifically for a woman's body weren't topics that warranted study and attention. In this section, we'll explore several social issues that have emerged as women have entered the playing field.

Women's Health

Donna Lopiano (1994) of the Women's Sports Foundation has summarized the benefits that women's sport advocates claim sports and physical activity can have for females. Psychosocial, physical, behavioral, and emotional benefits have been identified and substantiated. Research has shown that introducing girls to sports and physical activity early is essential for them in making exercise a lifelong habit. In fact, Linda Bunker of the University of Virginia asserted that if a girl does not participate in sports

by the time she is 10, there is only a 10% chance she will participate when she is 25 (Women's Sports Foundation 2004a).

The amount of physical activity that a young girl gets relates to her race and culture and the influence of those who surround her. White girls (with 59% participation) are more likely than Black (47%) or Hispanic (49%) girls to participate in sports (Center for Disease Control and Prevention 2000).Girls who come from middle- and upper-middle-class homes are also more likely to participate in vigorous physical activity. Girls who grow up in a culture that ascribes relatively narrow female roles oriented toward childbearing and families value the sport experience differently. Likewise, families who are struggling economically are more likely to encourage girls to spend time helping in the home and caring for younger siblings. Girls who grow up in poor, urban settings may face daunting barriers to sport participation. See chapter 13 for more information on the specific challenges.

Research has shown that teenage female athletes are less likely than nonathletes to use marijuana, cocaine, or other illicit drugs, to be suicidal, or to smoke and are more likely than nonathletes to have positive body images (Women's Sports Foundation 2004a). These results mirror those of male athletes and speak to the value of encouraging young people to take better care of their bodies and develop a strong self-concept that helps them resist peer pressure.

Teenage female athletes are less likely to get pregnant, more likely to abstain from sexual intercourse, and more likely to experience sexual intercourse at a later age (Women's Sports Foundation 1998). One might wonder if the lack of sport participation among economically disadvantaged girls correlates with their significantly higher rate of teenage pregnancy.

Women who are active in sports as girls feel greater confidence and pride in their physical and social selves than do women who are sedentary as kids (Health and Human Services 1997). Sports and exercise reduce the incidence of osteoporosis, breast cancer, and stroke. According to data in a special issue of the *American Journal of Health Promotion* (Anspaugh et al. 1996), exercise lowers blood pressure, blood sugar, and cholesterol. Furthermore, exercising women report that they feel happier, have more energy, and feel healthier. Exercisers also missed fewer days of work. The only potentially negative influence of sport participation is the possible exacerbation of eating disorders or exercise addictions that develop in some girls.

As our culture has begun to encourage women to join the workplace and even contend for leadership roles in society, the lessons of the playing field appear to be just as helpful to girls as they are to boys. Experiences in leading, dealing with pressure, taking pride in accomplishment, and working on a team equip women with some of the critical skills needed for successful careers. Linda Bunker (1988) found that 80% of women identified as key leaders in Fortune 500 companies participated in sports during their childhood. Another similar study reported that more than four out of five executive businesswomen played sports growing up, and the majority claimed that lessons learned on the playing field contributed to their business success (Game Face 2002).

The evidence overwhelmingly shows that exercise and sport participation are good for women and girls. It may make you wonder why it took so long for society to realize this fact and encourage healthy activity for the female sex. To learn additional information and the latest facts and figures on women in sports, visit the Web site of the Women's Sports Foundation: Women's Sports & Fitness Facts & Statistics at www.womenssportsfoundation.org.

Lesbian Athletes

While the stereotype that all strong, female athletes must be lesbians is false, it is true that athletes who are lesbians still face misunderstanding and discrimination in the sporting world. Some famous female athletes, such as Billie Jean King and later Amelie Mauresmo of France, have been frank with the media about their sexual orientation. Billie Jean was a founder of the Women's Sports Foundation, an icon for women's liberation, and a role model for many in spite of her bisexuality. While she is

popular with women, her fan base among men is much smaller. In 2005, some fans were stunned when Sheryl Swoopes, three-time most valuable player for the WNBA, revealed her homosexuality. Although she was previously married and has a son, Swoopes told the world that she currently has a female life partner.

Pat Griffin was a pioneer in exposing and clarifying the issues surrounding lesbian athletes. Pat has been a top athlete, coach, and spokesperson against prejudice and homophobia in sports. In her book *Strong Women, Deep Closets,* she analyzed the lesbian experience in the sports world. In it she

Studies show that girls who are active in sports have better self-esteem, are less likely to use drugs, and have better graduation rates than male student athletes. What barriers keep girls from playing?

admitted to once dating a male wrestling coach to cover up her lesbianism and save her coaching job. Strong leaders like Pat Griffin have given voice to the conflicted lesbian athletes who fear showing their homosexuality will damage their career (Griffin 1998).

Not all discrimination against lesbian athletes comes from outside women's sports. This fact was highlighted at Penn State University in the early 1990s when women's basketball coach Rene Portland created a furor by stating in the press that she did not recruit or allow lesbians on her team. The controversy escalated in 2005 when a former player, Jennifer Harris, filed a federal discrimination lawsuit. Attempts to mediate the situation were unsuccessful and an internal investigation by the university fined Portland $10,000 U.S., ordered her to take professional development courses devoted to diversity and inclusiveness, and warned she would be dismissed for any future violations (Associated Press 2006b, 2006d). In spite of growing acceptance in society at large, lesbian athletes are still at risk for harassment, exclusion, or perhaps expulsion if their coaches or teammates disapprove of their lifestyle.

Sportswear

As girls and women moved into sports, they sparked changes in sport clothing as they demanded clothing that fit their unique needs. Apparel companies raced to design sport clothing for women, and the marketing campaigns followed to attract buyers of athletic gear designed specifically for women. The economy of sports business was affected along with cultural attitudes toward females in sports. Let's look at two significant developments in sport clothing.

Sports Bra

The sports bra was invented in 1977 to give women playing sports the same kind of physical support that men had enjoyed for years. Hinda Miller and Lisa Lindahl created a prototype for the sports bra by imitating the male athletic supporter that "pulled the body parts closer to the body" (Sharp 1994). Eventually their idea was labeled the *jogbra,* and

In the thrill of the winning moment, is the removal of Brandi's shirt any different from the removal of Andy's shirt?

females quickly adopted it for comfort, safety, and a way to limit embarrassment and perform uninhibitedly during vigorous activity.

It wasn't long before clothing companies began marketing versions of the sports bra that not only facilitated physical activity but also looked attractive. Women began wearing sports bras under their jerseys, but soon they shed their jerseys in the gyms, on the courts, and on the fields. Female athletes found the comfort and freedom exhilarating.

When Brandi Chastain ripped off her jersey to celebrate the 1999 U.S. Women's victory in the World Cup soccer championship, a seminal moment in sports was born. Her action was captured on film and her image was viewed round the world. Brandi's sports bra somehow symbolized to different people all that was right or wrong with women in sport.

Brandi Chastain's disrobing was accepted by many as an expression of pure joy at victory. After all, the gesture had been made previously by male soccer players and tennis players, notably Andre Agassi and Andy Roddick of the United States. Yet her action also ignited a storm of criticism.

Some saw Brandi Chastain's act as a striptease, as if she were offering her body to male viewers. Others thought her action was calculated to draw attention. Still others simply saw it as a celebration of a strong, muscular woman proud of her body. Whatever the opinion, her act stimulated debate and exposed the conflict in both male and female opinions about women's bodies and their acceptability in public view.

Athletic Shoes

As girls and women flocked to sports participation in the past 30 years, improper athletic footwear was a recurrent issue. Forced to wear sneakers designed for the male foot, female athletes suffered in silence until the 1990s when athletic shoe companies began designing and marketing shoes specifically designed for the female foot. Women basketball players, who typically are well above average in size, had previously been forced to wear men's sneakers for basketball. The women complained of the heaviness, bulk, and the width of the male shoe (Brown 2001). Basketball player Sheryl Swoopes became the first women to endorse her "Air Swoopes" during the Atlanta Olympics in 1996. By 2001, at the inaugural WNBA All-Star game with the best female basketball players in the world gathered, it became a celebration of how far women in sport had come. Five of the All-Stars wore basketball shoes designed specifically for them.

On average, the female foot is narrower and thinner than a male foot. Although foot shape varies from one female to another, generally a woman's foot has a wider forefoot and narrower heel than a male's foot. Orthopedists have attributed poor fitting shoes to the high incidence of sports injuries in women and girls, particularly in the knee, ankle, and lower leg (Sports Doctor 2006).

The modern athletic shoe development, led by Nike, Reebok, and Adidas, has introduced the public to terms such as *pronation, stability,* and *motion control.* New concepts in design have helped absorb shock, stabilize the foot, and reduce injuries in high performance athletes as well as casual recreational athletes (Pribut and Richie 2002). Shoes are made to accommodate the differences between the feet of male and female athletes.

The athletic shoe industry totaled $13.74 billion U.S. in 2000, with women's shoes accounting for 46% of sales, men's shoes for 40% of sales, and children's shoes for 11% of sales. The dominance of women's footwear is a fairly recent phenomenon when you realize that women's athletic shoe sales increased by 37% against only a 5% increase for men between 1992 and 1999 (Women's Sports Foundation 2004a).

But the shoe industry for women still has a ways to go. The feet of females are getting bigger . . . but not the shoes. That's the headline from an article originally published in the *Wall Street Journal* (2004b). Sports were cited as a reason for increased sizes of feet: "The biggest single contributor to the big-foot phenomenon may be the rise in participation in girls' sports since Title IX 32 years ago." As girls walk, run, and play sports, their feet become larger, stronger, and more muscular.

The average foot size has jumped from an American size 7 or an 8 to an 8 or a 9. (European sizes would be 37, 38, and 39.) According to Marshal Cohen, senior analyst for the NPD Group, more than 33% of women now wear a size 9 or larger, compared with just 11% in 1987. A survey by Carol Fry at the University of California at Los Angeles showed that 10% of high school girls now wear shoes larger than size 10. The population is generally increasing in size. Also, the baby boomer generation is aging, and with age the feet tend to enlarge as ligaments stretch and feet flatten out (Wall Street Journal 2004b).

Shoe manufacturers have not yet adjusted to the need for larger shoes and are still making the bulk of their shoes in an "average" size that's now outdated. Many women squeeze their feet into shoes that are simply too small. The resulting poor fit causes foot

Good athletes tend to be in good physical shape. Should this make them sex objects?

problems, and eventually pain spreads throughout the body.

The problem for manufacturers is that producing larger shoe sizes means creating new molds and using more goods in each shoe, both of which will drive prices up. Manufacturers are hesitant to begin producing larger shoes, waiting for the market to prove substantial enough to warrant producing larger size shoes. Since many manufacturers are located overseas where people tend to be smaller, the demand for larger sizes is unusual for them.

Objectification of Female Athletes

As strong, independent women delve into the sports world, they attract many types of attention. The female athlete's body is strong and agile, with defined musculature, and muscles are a magnet for thousands of viewers. As clothing trends changed, women moved from dowdy dresses, boxy pinnies,

and kilted skirts to formfitting swimsuits, gymnastics leotards, and skimpy outfits on the tennis court. And, although the sports bra was a technical improvement for women and serves a utilitarian purpose that allows them to move freely, it has symbolized the duplicity of society's view of women as strong athletes and sex objects for men (Schultz 2004).

Female athletes may be looked at as sex objects, whether they want to be seen that way or not. Successful female athletes are often judged more by their appearance than their athletic success. Jan Stephenson was more famous for her physical attractiveness than for her golf game, even though she was a fine golfer. In 2004, Maria Sharapova burst on the scene by winning Wimbledon, but the focus was more on her looks than her tennis ability.

But are female athletes partially to blame for this objectification?

The 2004 Olympic Games produced a plethora of ads featuring female Olympic athletes in various stages of undress. Swimmer Amanda Beard, who captured hearts at the 1996 Games by posing with her teddy bear at the starting blocks, posed in a white bikini on the cover of *FHM* in September 2004 and wore even less on the inside pages. Beach volleyball player Misty May, track star Marion Jones, and Amanda Beard were also featured in the men's magazine *Maxim*. High jumper Amy Acuff and swimmer Haley Cope Clark were featured in *Playboy* while wearing almost nothing (Topkin 2004).

Stuff magazine showed water polo player Jackie Frank, swimmer Kaitlin Sandeno, Misty May, and others in high heels and underwear. Perhaps the most photographed athlete of the Games was softball player Jennie Finch, who was voted the Hottest Female Athlete in an ESPN.com poll. A few years ago, swimmer Jenny Thompson posed in *Sports Illustrated* while covering her breasts with her fists. Holly McPeak, of beach volleyball fame, appeared nude in an artistic pose for a 2000 issue of *Life* (Brownfield 2004; Levy 2005). The ultrapopular swimsuit edition of *Sports Illustrated* demonstrates what most people already suspect: that women's bodies help sell magazines. Until recently these types of bodies didn't belong to female athletes (Topkin 2004).

Many female athletes are conflicted about posing to show off their bodies. Some favor it, believing that it helps promote their sport through publicity, while others think it dispels the notion that you can't be sexy just because you're an athlete (Topkin 2004). When female athletes do intentionally display their bodies, some people may question whether such images are appropriate for public viewing, especially by younger children. Suggestive images of both male and female athletes can be controlled and standards of decorum can be established, but only if the market demands it. The cutting-edge advertising agency will do whatever attracts attention and gains publicity, as they were hired to do.

GLOBAL STATUS OF WOMEN IN SPORT

While the numbers of women in sport continue to rise in the United States, that trend is not typical around the world. The social system in many countries, particularly Arab countries, discourages women from sport participation. Their adherence to the traditional role of women as subservient to men and focused on the home does not allow girls to explore their physical side through sports and activity.

As shown in table 12.3 on page 215, the percentage of women in the Summer Olympics has increased steadily from 34% in 1996 to 38% in 2000 to 44% in 2004. At the 2000 Olympic Games, 36 countries, or almost 30% of the 123 participating nations, sent no female athletes. By 2004, the number of countries entering an all-male team was 9. Female participation rates have not universally grown in all countries, especially in those countries where women's rights in general lag behind those of men. In countries where poverty, famine, political instability, and religion dominate, females are virtually excluded from participation in sports. Countries such as Ethiopia, Saudi Arabia, Algeria, Kenya, and Nigeria are beset with wider social problems than women in sport. Followers of Islam are blocked from participation because of a decree that women should be covered in public, and wearing this covering makes it difficult if not impossible to play sports. Women who seek to participate in sport are seen as threats to the social, moral, and religious codes of their societies and to repudiate their culture in favor of the Western influence.

The recent success of 18-year-old Sania Mirza of India in women's professional tennis holds promise for other Muslim women. She skyrocketed from a virtual unknown to a world ranking of 34 in just a year on the professional tour. While wearing traditional tennis clothing that exposes her arms and legs, she retains her spiritual values by praying up to five times a day. She is an example of a modern Indian woman who stands for progressive thinking while respecting her religious background. Her success is the antithesis of the straitlaced image of a backward, illiterate, conservative Muslim woman hidden behind a veil (Bahri 2005).

Similarly, 13-year-old swimmer Rubab Raza was the first female swimmer from Pakistan to represent her country in the Olympic Games by competing in Athens in 2004. Recent advances in full-body swimsuit design promise to enhance swimming efficiency by imitating the skin of a shark. They may also allow Muslim women to jump in the pool, something they have not been able to do because of the requirement to keep their bodies covered.

In the 2000 Sydney Olympics, more than 110,000 people saw Nouria Merah-Benida win the 1,500 meters, following up on the 1992 Olympic championship performance of her Algerian countrywoman Hassiba Boulmerka. These two runners have sparked debate about whether women may break out of the mold of Arab tradition and enjoy athletic success. Perhaps with time, change accommodating the culture and the hopes of Arab female athletes will occur.

Worldwide, the story in developed nations mirrors that in the United States. White women from middle-class backgrounds are most likely to be supported by their families and communities to participate in sport, strive for excellence, and embrace physical activity. Enhanced self-image, better health, and

Sania Mirza has found balance between her religion and her sport.

greater resistance to disease through sport should be available for all women, but some must still fight against the repressive customs of their society to enjoy these benefits.

BARRIERS FOR WOMEN IN SPORT

Learning about the rapid gains of women in sport during the last 30 years may lead you to think there is not much more for these women to accomplish. But a closer look reveals changes that must still come to truly create an equality of opportunity in sports for females. We review these changes in this section. Perhaps progress will come from outside the sports world as women gain power and influence in business and affect more of what is portrayed in the media. As society changes, so do women's sports. Yet sports can also be a catalyst for change led by confident, determined females who have a public stage on which to share their beliefs and dreams.

Title IX Challenges

The most perplexing question facing Title IX enforcement on college campuses focuses on American football and the 85 athletic scholarships for football awarded at most Division I schools. These schools must provide 85 women's scholarships just to match the football total. Once the 85 men's and 85 women's scholarships have been awarded, a university then decides how many other scholarships they can afford for other sports.

Most athletic directors have completely dropped the less popular, non-revenue-producing men's sports like wrestling, tennis, golf, gymnastics, and swimming. Programs rich in tradition, some of which earned national championships, have suddenly disappeared from college athletic programs. The governing bodies for these sports such as wrestling and tennis have mounted campaigns to reinstate those sports. Although they are careful not to criticize Title IX, the underlying mumbling blames women. Dropped sports are called *unintended consequences,* recognizing that the authors of Title IX never intended to harm men's sports by opening up women's sports (Lapchick 2004; National Women's Law Center 2002).

"Where is the money going to come from?" That's the plea of every athletic director and college president faced with Title IX compliance. We've taken their athletic budget, which was largely devoted to men's sports, and asked them to split it down the middle for men and women. On top of that, they are unwilling to reduce support for football, the main revenue sport at 131 Division I institutions and the source of publicity, pride, recruiting, and alumni donations. It would simply be unthinkable to reduce the number of football scholarships, even though some may ask why, if it only takes 22 men to play football, 11 on offense and 11 on defense, 85 scholarships are needed.

The football picture at the high school level may be very similar, although athletic scholarships are not a factor. Instead, the focus is on budgets for uniforms, equipment, fields, coaching salaries, and publicity. In every category, football is still a huge expense.

Physical Activity Participation

Physical activity participation among women of all ages continues to lag behind that of men. Whatever the reasons, here are some pertinent statistics:

- More than 60% of adult women do not complete the 30 minutes of recommended daily physical activity. More than 25% of women are not active at all according to the Center for Disease Control and Prevention (2000).
- The National Osteoporosis Foundation (1997) estimates that 23 million U.S. women are

Activity Time-Out: Football and Title IX

Some people have proposed colleges leave football out of Title IX compliance. Proponents of this view contend that football is a different animal and that there is no such comparable activity for girls. At large Division I institutions where the football team actually makes money, those revenues can help support other sports.

Is leaving football out of Title IX an equitable solution? If not, what other ideas would you offer an athletic director who faces increasing costs without an increasing budget?

What must we do to motivate more women to complete the recommended daily amount of physical activity?

affected by osteoporosis or have low bone mass.

- Boys are more likely than girls are to regularly watch televised sports (33% boys versus 7% girls). Girls are more than twice as likely to watch talk shows (25% versus 10%) (Children Now 1999).

- Ninety percent of U.S. boys regularly or often watch televised sports with a fundamentally male cast of players, coaches, and commentators. Commercials during these televised events tend to target the male viewer, reinforcing male stereotypes and gender roles (Children Now 1999).

Women As Leaders in Sport

Women still occupy a small percentage of leadership roles compared with their proportion of the sports or at-large population. Perhaps the most disappointing percentage is that of female coaches of collegiate women's sports. The 2004 percentage of 44% is close to the lowest percentage in history, and 25 years ago, women coached 90% of women's teams (Acosta and Carpenter 2004). Here are some other percentages of women in significant leadership roles in high school, college, and Olympic sports (Acosta and Carpenter 2004):

Coaches of collegiate women's sports	44%
Women athletic directors at colleges	18%
College sports information directors	12%
Head athletic trainers at colleges	30%
Senior staff at NCAA	26%
Heads of state high school athletic associations	6%
Members of International Olympic Committee	7%
Members of United States Olympic Committee	18%

Additional information including the percentages for professional sports can be viewed in the Gender and Racial Report Card for 2004 published by Richard Lapchick at the University of Central Florida.

Equal Pay for Equal Play

The opportunities for women in sport have expanded significantly in tennis, golf, basketball, and soccer, where professional careers are a realistic goal. Other sports such as gymnastics, track and field, figure skating, and swimming offer prize money and endorsement possibilities since the Olympics have recently allowed professional athletes. Yet compared with men, women still struggle to make a career in professional sport because in many cases, the financial compensation barely covers their expenses.

Traditionally at the four Grand Slam events in tennis, Wimbledon and the Australian, French, and U.S. Opens, the purse of prize money for men exceeded that of women. In recent years, only the Australian and U.S. Open have offered equal prize money for men and women, although the French Open finally succumbed to pressure in 2005 and did the same, leaving Wimbledon the lone holdout. The argument against paying women the same amount as men is usually as follows:

- Women don't play the same level of tennis as men. Head to head, a good collegiate men's player would defeat most women on the pro tour. (Probably true.)

- Women are not as strong, don't hit the ball as hard, and play mostly a baseline game featuring rallies rather than an exciting, power game. (True, although short points dominated by powerful serves can be boring to watch. Fans do like the rallies in women's tennis.)

■ Women only play three sets in championship matches whereas men play the best of five and therefore have to work harder. (Men do play five sets, but who wants to watch a match that takes five hours between exhausted competitors? Two out of three has more excitement because every point affects the outcome of the match.)

■ Fans come to see the men and ticket revenue should be the basis of the prize money. (For years the men argued this point, until the women's game and superstar personalities started to grab the headlines. Suddenly, the men backed off this statement.)

Here are other notable facts on pay for female versus male athletes (all amounts below are in U.S. dollars; Women's Sports Foundation 2004a):

■ In basketball, the minimum salary for a WNBA veteran is $42,000 and salaries have been capped at $622,000 per team. In the NBA, a first-round pick in his second year earns a minimum of $512,000.

■ In soccer, a third-place finish for the women in the 2003 World Cup netted $25,000 for each team member. Players on the men's team each received $200,000 for reaching the quarterfinals.

■ In golf, during the five years from 1996 to 2000, the LPGA annual prize money rose 45% from $26.5 million to $38.5 million. In the same time period, the men's PGA prize money rose 141.7% from $69.1 million to $167 million, an increase of 30%.

■ Golfer Annika Sorenstam signed a deal with Cutter and Buck that could earn her up to $600,000 per year. That figure is approximately 60% of what a male golfer can demand for a typical apparel contract.

■ Although huge endorsement deals are scarce for women, tennis star Venus Williams signed a five-year, $40 million deal with Reebok. Her sister, Serena, topped her a year later with a contract with Nike that could make her the richest woman in sport if she meets the performance-related bonuses, with a possible net income of $55 to $60 million. Of course, this income doesn't include any of the on-court prize

money both sisters are likely to win in the coming years. Maria Sharapova, who won Wimbledon in 2004, was the top female wage earner in tennis, pulling in an estimated $18 million.

■ According to Forbes.com, in 2004 the top 50 paid athletes were all male. Males in team sports dominated the list, although golfer Tiger Woods topped all athletes.

While the endorsement deals for female tennis players may stun the average fan, the amounts commanded by women compared to men still differ significantly. Although the Williams sisters and Maria Sharapova earn handsome incomes, male tennis player Andre Agassi earned over $28 million in 2004 and made the Forbes Top 50 list. He has collected more than $200 million in endorsement fees in nearly 18 seasons as a pro player.

Media Coverage of Women's Sports

More media coverage of women's sports would likely boost their popularity and enhance the opportunities for girls and women to see role models in action. There have been notable successes in televising women's sports. During the first quarter of 2002, the 10 highest rated broadcasts on network television included the winter Olympic women's figure skating long program, which ranked third behind only the Super Bowl and Super Bowl kickoff show. The Women's Final Four Championship game, featuring UConn versus Oklahoma, was the third-ranked sports broadcast on cable television. In contrast, the men's championship game of Duke versus Maryland, aired on network television, ranked only sixth (WomenSport International 2006).

A quick look at table 12.5 confirms that when compared to men's sports, women's sports are poorly represented in media coverage. According to Gibbons (2003), the decisions on coverage are made in newsrooms across the country, where women

TABLE 12.5 Women's Sport in the Media

Sports coverage	Males	Females
ESPN, 30 days (June 2002)	778 stories	16 stories
Sports Emmy Awards (2002 and 2003)	31 nominees	0 nominees
ESPN Top 100 Athletes (20th century)	92	8
Sportscasters (2000)	335	81

Data from Tuggle 2002; National Academy of TV Arts & Sciences 2003; ESPN 2000; USA Today 2000.

in charge are in the distinct minority. Perhaps the news media will soon awaken to the opportunities to attract female sports fans. A national study from Scarborough Sports Marketing revealed that there are over 50 million female sports fans in the United States, and that percentage is growing. In 1998, the number of women over age 18 who identified themselves as very or somewhat avid sports fans was 28%. Just four years later, the number had more than doubled, reaching 58% (Gibbons 2003).

GOLDEN AGE OF SPORTS REBORN

Perhaps in this new century we'll recreate the excitement of another "golden age of sports" that this time around includes women and girls. To reach that goal, some significant changes are still needed in the world of sports. However, changes to promote equity in sports will never occur without concomitant changes in our society. The following are some of the changes that will promote equality.

The percentage of women in the workplace is nearing that of men. But salaries for females still lag behind those of their male counterparts. The glass ceiling also prevents many women from reaching upper management. Workplaces, government agencies, and the courts, although all dominated by men, can help eliminate these discriminatory practices.

Challenging the rigid sex roles that have historically guided our society, expanding our definitions of sexuality, and accepting those who are lesbian and gay will help us all find equal places in society.

Collecting data to show inequities in all forms, particularly for women's sports activities, will keep us aware of where we need to work to reach equality. Dr. Richard Lapchick, author of the Race and Gender Report Card, and Donna Lopiano, executive director of the Women's Sports Foundation, have taken it upon themselves to inform the public of salient issues and statistics about racism, sexism, and other related topics.

Leaders in women's sports along with sympathetic corporate sponsors need to challenge each other to press ahead. Advocates for women's sports must aggressively recruit, train, and mentor young girls and women into key positions of influence such as coaching, officiating, administration, athletic training, marketing, and media. By taking their place in these positions, women can become a more powerful influence on the sports world.

Women must aggressively pursue leadership positions in sports organizations at every level. In the

Amelie Mauresmo earned $1,145,638 U.S. for winning Wimbledon in 2006. Men's champion Roger Federer earned $1,191,000 U.S. Should they be paid the same amount for winning the same tournament?

last 10 years, Kathy Woods became the first female president of the United States Professional Tennis Association, a trade association of over 13,000 tennis-teaching professionals. A few years later, Judy Levering ascended to the presidency of the United States Tennis Association, again the first woman to do so. Anita DeFrantz of the United States became the first female elected to the International Olympic Committee. These trailblazers deserve appreciation and a new succession of women to follow their lead.

Leaders in women's sports must take the initiative and look for ways to make their sports revenue producing so that men become their allies rather than remaining their competitors. A few colleges have figured out how to earn money from women's basketball and gymnastics, but other sports and schools lag behind. Professional women's sports need to build on the attractiveness of their product of athletes and strong, independent women.

Finally, we must continue to educate people about the value of sports for women. Never underestimate the power of the mind in convincing people of the need to combat sexism in sports. In the early 1980s, as a college professor at a midsize state university, I was invited to join a semester course called "How to Combat Sexism in the Classroom." Five women who knew their stuff and could argue their case taught the class on Saturdays. Although few men attended, all of us, women and men, learned strategies to combat sexism, applied them in our classes, and received feedback from students and colleagues. Our lives have never been the same. Many of the lessons I learned over 25 years ago are still a vital part of my thinking and working character.

CHAPTER SUMMARY

We looked at women in sport, beginning with the ancient Greeks and Romans when women were virtually excluded from all sports including the Olympic Games. That exclusion lasted until the 1850s, when U.S. women gradually began to play selected games.

During the first half of the 20th century, physical educators encouraged women's sports and physical activity in colleges as a route to good health. However, competitive athletics were deemed too violent, competitive, and aggressive for young women. It wasn't until the late 1960s, when the women's movement took hold, that women realized that competitive athletics were another restriction to conquer.

In 1972, the U.S. Congress passed Title IX, which states that no person can be excluded from participation in sports on the basis of sex in any educational program receiving federal assistance. Title IX set the stage for years of lobbying by those in control of men's programs who did not want to give up any of their funding or perks to women. Numerous lawsuits were filed; and the law challenged, and in the end it was reaffirmed.

The next 30 years were exciting for girls and women as opportunities opened up in sports. The proportion of female athletes rose rapidly, proving that girls wanted to play sports, though some men had suggested otherwise. Women and girls became consumers of sports, bought equipment and clothing, watched sports on television, signed up for youth sport programs, and made their presence felt in high school and collegiate sports. Research has overwhelmingly attested to the benefits of physical activity for women. Numerous studies have shown improved academic performance, self-image, confidence, and physical health, all benefits similar to those enjoyed by boys for years.

Ideological roles for women had to be modified to fit their aggressive attitudes toward equal opportunity, equal pay, and equal representation as coaches, administrators, and leaders. The marketplace confirmed the popularity of women athletes as role models and awarded them with multimillion-dollar endorsement deals, particularly for tennis players. The ideal woman became strong, lean, and attractive. A nurturing, caring, and passive model of women in general began to pass from the scene.

Despite all the positive changes for women in sports in the second half of the last century, women are still underrepresented as sport leaders, in sport business, and in the media. Continued progress cannot be made without persistent effort and determination by women and the men they can recruit to assist them.

Social Class and Sport

Student Outcomes

After reading this chapter, you will know the following:

- The importance of social, economic, and cultural capital
- The different social classes and the typical characteristics of each
- Access or barriers social class places on sport
- Who controls amateur and professional sport
- The opportunity for social mobility through sport

"We hold these truths to be self-evident, that all men are created equal." In 1776, Thomas Jefferson penned these words as the opening of the United States Declaration of Independence. He was saying that all people are born with equal rights. A natural assumption that follows is that everyone has the freedom to get an education, find work, vote for our leaders, or even become a leader. Our society has traveled far to live up to those ideals, and yet the evidence suggests that equal opportunities do not exist for a large proportion of our population. Social class or perhaps race, gender, or disability may limit these opportunities.

Americans are divided according to economic class, with each class possessing different material goods, income levels, inheritances, educations, work descriptions, or influences over others. Regardless of how we define or divide these classes, each experiences real differences in opportunity. In this chapter we will define **social class** as a category of people who share similar positions in society based on their economic level, education, occupation, and social interaction. Although we pride ourselves as a classless society, our form of capitalism naturally allows for different possible levels of economic success.

Capitalism is an economic system that is based on the accumulation and investment of capital by individuals who then use it to produce goods or services (Sage 1998). We tend to downplay the idea of social classes because it conflicts with our American ideal of an equalitarian society. But we need to recognize that there are different economic classes that expand to also include our social system. The inequities in our society are obvious: power, prestige, and wealth. When we assign classes according to the levels of power, prestige, and wealth, we refer to **social stratification.** Other forms of stratification include race, gender, age, and disability, which are covered in other chapters.

Turning to the sports world, we can readily see how social class influences a family of four who decide to attend a professional football game. In 2005, the average ticket price to see the New England Patriots, previous Super Bowl winners, was $128 U.S. (New England Patriots 2006). For the family of four, the total cost of tickets is $512 U.S. Adding in parking at $25 and refreshments at $15 per person ($60 U.S. total) means the family spends $597 in all.

If this family belonged economically to the upper class, they would likely contact some friends who have a skybox, inquire about availability, and end up with seats with complimentary refreshments and possibly a parking pass. A middle-class family would likely save for a once-a-year excursion, perhaps buy cheaper seats, and treat the game as a special occasion. A working-class family would likely wait for special promotions or discounted group tours, or they would opt to attend a preseason game or scrimmage.

Both social capital and economic capital help people access different levels of society. Let's define the different kinds of capital. **Economic capital** refers to the financial resources a person has or controls. People inherit, earn, invest, and spend money depending on their background and occupational status. **Social capital** depends on family, friends, and associates and includes resources based on group memberships, relationships, and both social and business networks. **Cultural capital** comprises the skills and abilities people gain from education and life experiences. Cultural capital may include attitudes, expectations, and self-confidence (Bowles and Jenson, 2001; Wikipedia 2005b). Cultural capital affects how we see the world of sports, and sport participation offers an opportunity to develop cultural capital. For example, a young girl from the middle class may view sports as a way to be accepted into a social group. Her parents may encourage her interest in sports to promote her fitness, help her gain self-confidence, and perhaps help her earn a college scholarship. Her athletics coach will help her learn to set goals, employ self-discipline, and perform under the pressure of competition. Sports will help her form a self-concept as a skilled, fit competitor. All of these influences assist her during the confusing years of early adolescence by enhancing her cultural capital.

In America, we like to think that sport transcends social class. We believe that hard work and dedication ensures success and failure simply results from a lack of perseverance. In the land of the free, we are all free to play and watch sports. However, our economic, social, and cultural capital defines what sports we watch and participate in and affects our chances at success.

SOCIAL CLASSES

Most people gain their economic capital through their annual earnings. In the United States, the average family income for 2003 was $43,300 U.S. (see figure 13.1). Asian families had the highest average income and Black families the lowest average income.

Of the multitude of ways to divide people into economic classes, the *upper, upper-middle, middle,* and *lower* classes will be used for this chapter. The **upper class** makes up the top 1% of American households, and members of this class control approximately 35% of the nation's wealth. In fact, the top 10% of American households control approximately 71% of individual and family wealth. Members of this class have plenty of disposable income and many choices as consumers. Their children often attend the best private schools, their families are often members of exclusive clubs, and their children are often expected to mature to meet the expectations of their parents. People in this economic class essentially control much of the financial world and seek to maintain their position in society.

The **upper-middle class** is composed of professionals such as physicians, attorneys, and managers. Typically members of this class have significant amounts of discretionary income and join private clubs for social experiences. While most do not have the economic resources to exist without their earned income, as white-collar professionals they do supervise and influence others in the workplace. People in the upper-middle class often value education and strive for advanced degrees. They establish a network of contacts that serves them throughout life. They also often become leaders in government and can affect laws to maintain their position.

The **middle class** is the largest economic group in the United States. They must carefully choose their expenses for daily living and leisure spending. They often work as skilled laborers, as teachers, and in service industry positions. Their earned income provides their economic base, and many middle-class families rely on two wage earners.

The **lower class** is composed of unskilled laborers who essentially do work that is assigned and supervised by others. Their income barely meets the minimum wage standards set by the government and they have few chances to improve their economic level. In 2003, the official poverty rate for all U.S. citizens was 14.5%, or more than 35 million people (U.S. Census 2005b). To be considered below the poverty line, annual family income must be below $18,810 U.S. (see figure 13.2).

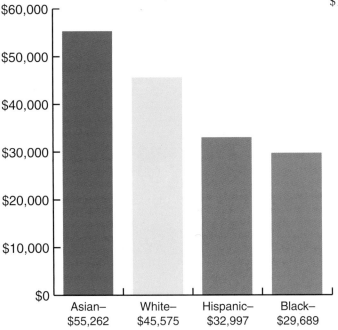

FIGURE 13.1 Average 2003 income for U.S. families.
Source: U.S. Census figures 2003. www.census.gov

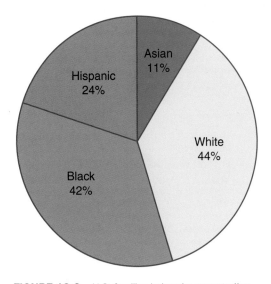

FIGURE 13.2 U.S. families below the poverty line.
Source: U.S. Census figures 2003. www.census.gov

SOCIAL CLASS AND SPORT ACTIVITY

There are wide differences in general access to sports and in which sports families of the various economic classes are likely to choose. Let's look at how social class affects sport participation and spectatorship.

Social Class and Choice of Sport

Sport participation has always been more popular and accessible within the upper class due to the availability of leisure time and money. Historically, people of wealth used sports as entertainment and as a way to demonstrate their wealth. They often use sports to build social capital through networks and contacts in business. Many of today's sports such as tennis, golf, equestrian, and sailing were traditionally pastimes of the wealthy, and many business deals were consummated after a round of golf or a set of tennis. Our current society is similar in that people of the highest income levels typically have the highest rates of sport participation. They also are more likely to attend a sporting event, and they even watch

more sports on television (Booth and Loy 1999). The upper and upper-middle classes have favored sports such as equestrian, golf, tennis, sailing, polo, skiing, and others that are typically performed at private clubs. Similarly, Olympic sports such as gymnastics, figure skating, swimming, riflery, and archery typically are the choice of the upper-middle class. As most of these sports are individual, they are often expensive to participate in. The facilities are often costly, the individual or family bears the training expenses, and traveling to compete consumes huge amounts of money.

The working class (lower-middle class) is more likely to choose community sports that are readily accessible and cheap. Community youth sport programs start kids in sport, and many kids go on to play on interscholastic teams that are subsidized by schools and taxpayers. Coaching and facilities are typically free and athletes with talent can enhance their performance at a modest expense to their families. Team sports dominate this class since they are cheaper to stage, accommodate more players on a field or court, and provide a social environment as well. Sports such as basketball, football, soccer, baseball, softball, and volleyball are popular. Parents

The toughness and uncertainty of boxing mirrors the lives of many at lower economic levels. Is this why many find boxing so appealing?

Pop Culture: *Cinderella Man*

The 2004 film *Cinderella Man* chronicles the life of James Braddock, an embattled ex-prizefighter and out-of-work family man during the Great Depression. Unable to pay his bills, he joined thousands of impoverished people in turning to public welfare just to exist. In an unlikely return to boxing, he miraculously won and kept on winning all the way to claim the heavyweight championship over the previously unstoppable Max Baer. In the end he paid back what he'd been given on welfare. His story of grit, determination, and unfailing spirit inspired a desperate generation.

often serve as volunteer coaches or officials to stay involved with their children and keep the expenses within reason.

The poor and working classes devote so much time to earning a living and taking care of basic needs that they have little time or money left to spend on sports. As our society's standard of living improved, blue-collar families have been able to participate in or watch certain sports that appeal to them and are readily accessible to the public, inexpensive to play, and available in public recreational facilities (Sage 1998).

Those who have higher levels of income and education and work in professional or managerial roles are the most ardent and frequent consumers of health and fitness activities and sports. They value physical fitness and enjoy leisure activity. In contrast, those who physically labor are less likely to feel the need or inclination to exercise or play sports. They are more likely to spend leisure time resting for the next day of work (Gruneau 1999).

The lower economic classes typically choose sports such as boxing, wrestling, weightlifting, auto racing, bowling, pool, and motorcycle racing. Most of these sports share the characteristics of violence and uncertainty based on physical strength and daring. They are often available at low costs and in urban areas and are accessible to all. They lean toward the masculine identity of toughness that is a trait for kids from modest backgrounds may find necessary for survival (Coakley 2004). Many people at lower incomes live in rural areas, and those people favor sports that are readily accessible such as hunting and fishing.

French sociologist Loïc Wacquant (2004) joined a gym on the south side of Chicago in a predominately Black neighborhood. There he learned the importance of boxing for boys from the lower socioeconomic class who are looking for a legitimate way to establish self-respect and a sense of masculinity.

The alternative to boxing for many kids in that neighborhood was "to end up in jail or dead in the streets." Boxing has traditionally appealed to the lower economic classes and to recent immigrants to the United States. Boys in the cities turned to boxing to try to escape lives marked by a lack of employment prospects. They preferred the controlled violence of the boxing ring to the random violence of the streets.

Basketball is unique in that it appeals to all classes and is popular in both the suburbs and the city. But at heart, it is a city game with its own history, hierarchy, and heroes. A driveway, an asphalt playground, or a parking lot with a hoop can provide the court. Anyone can play, and winners typically stay on the court to challenge all comers. The dream of escaping the ghetto through basketball has been the subject of articles, books, and motion pictures such as *Hoosiers, White Men Can't Jump,* and *Hoop Dreams.* A few players do make it to professional basketball, but the odds are miniscule for the millions of kids who dream of making it.

Social Class and High-Performance Sport

Young athletes who aspire toward high-performance sports have to invest large amounts of time and money into training and competition. If their family doesn't have the resources to support their dream, their chances of success are severely curtailed. The choice of sport is critical since the opportunities to develop within some sports depend highly on economic investment while other sports can be pursued at a more modest expense.

Young people from the upper-middle and upper classes typically do not develop strong motivation to succeed in highly competitive sport. Their exposure to a family that makes a living in business or profession influences their interests from their earliest days. Sports are seen as more of a diversion, played for fun. Family and friends encourage them in sports such as golf, tennis, sailing, and skiing so that they can acquit themselves admirably in social occasions. Many friendships are developed and business deals consummated on the golf course or tennis court. Family vacations often include these sports. A certain level of skill and understanding of such sports is expected, just like good table manners and other social graces are expected.

Young men from the middle class often see sports as a way to establish their masculinity and to gain social capital by acceptance in their peer group. Combined with the cultural capital instilled by their parents of self-discipline, hard work, and focus on achievement, middle-class youth often become high achievers in sports. Coaches of youth sports tend to reward the work ethic and reinforce the behavior of high-achieving athletes.

Families tend to support their kids' quest for excellence and often will sacrifice financially to support training costs. It is not unheard of for families to move to another part of the country to train with a better coach or better competition. In sports like tennis and golf, families with exceptionally talented kids often move to warm climates where the competition is strongest and academies are typically located. At the extreme, families even split apart, with one parent moving with the talented athlete and the other staying behind because of a job or other siblings.

Male athletes from lower classes also link sports to masculinity because sports provide a chance to exhibit fearlessness and aggressiveness. Since they often can't compete with young men from higher classes in school or in material possessions, their sport success becomes their badge of courage that defines them (Messner 2002).

Olympic Sports

Olympic sports were historically dominated by the upper classes, and many sports in the Olympic Games (both Summer and Winter) reflect that tendency. The leaders of the Olympic movement were typically males from well-to-do backgrounds. They promoted the sports indigenous to their social class and for years limited participation to amateurs. By excluding professionals, they restricted participation to athletes from their social class, since athletes with limited resources couldn't afford to train as amateurs. In fact, early definitions of *amateur* were based on social class, and athletes from lower economic classes were categorized as nonamateurs.

The problem with limiting the Olympics to amateurs was simply that doing so excluded some of the best athletes. Furthermore, there were extensive reports of athletes who violated the rules and secretly accepted money for training expenses. Some countries established free training schools that prepared their young athletes for the Olympics, virtually making these athletes professionals. The discussion on Olympic restrictions came to a head in the 1980s, and beginning in 1988 professional athletes were admitted to the Games (Amateur Athletic Foundation Olympic Primer 2005).

Most of the recent Olympic athletes have come from working or middle-class families who sacrificed to support their child's Olympic quest. David Hemery (1986), a former Olympian, studied 63 of the top performers, who included athletes from 22 sports and 12 countries. His sample, which was relatively small and focused on the best of the best, fell into the following class distribution:

Poor	2%
Working class	26%
Middle class	44%
Upper-middle class	3%
Upper class	0%

Athletes who aspire to compete in certain sports at the Olympic Games run into special problems. Many Olympic sports are not emphasized or even offered at high schools or colleges. High-performance athletes must pursue their athletic dreams through private academies and competition that are expensive and time consuming.

Olympic sports that require specialized training include gymnastics, swimming, judo, weightlifting, boxing, and almost all winter sports, although a limited number of schools and colleges offer varsity programs in winter sports. Families must often move to allow their kids to train with a top coach living in another part of the country. Athletes of modest means may seek employment to help them afford competition, travel, and coaching. Some corporate sponsors of the Olympic movement help provide jobs for prospective Olympians.

Another option for prospective Olympians is to train at one of the Olympic training centers at Colorado Springs or San Diego. Of course, athletes have to qualify for these programs, but if they do, the costs of training are generally borne by the U.S. Olympic Committee or the national governing body of that sport. In many countries, the expense of training future Olympians is borne by the government and administered by the minister of sports. Government financial support for training has been debated in the United States for many years.

Cost of High-Performance Sport

Many people are unaware of the financial investment it takes to compete at the highest levels, whether the Olympics or professional sport. Here is where parents of talented kids can put their social and cultural capital to good use to help circumvent the financial challenges of elite training. Perhaps the most expensive sports involve the equestrian events. Owning and caring for a horse can cost upward of $70,000 U.S. a year. Of course, the price can go up quickly when shipping the horse to competitions around the country (Veronica 1991).

Costs can run as high as $75,000 U.S. per year for a top figure skater and $30,000 U.S. per year for a top gymnast (Ryan 1995). Athletes aspiring to compete in professional tennis and golf may also pay around $30,000 U.S. a year. Let's look at the yearly expenses of a tennis player. If a tennis player attends 12 national tennis tournaments a year at a cost of $1,500 U.S. to travel to and compete in each, the player needs to budget $18,000 U.S. to start. If a parent or coach travels with the player, this expense doubles or triples, especially if the athlete pays the coach for his time. Weekly lessons, some group and some private, cost an average of $250 U.S., and athletes living in a cold climate pay more to practice on indoor courts. Then add in the expense of tennis rackets, shoes, clothing, and other incidental equipment at a cost easily greater than $2,500 U.S. a year (unless the player gets an endorsement deal with a clothing or racket company).

Many young athletes also use the services of a fitness gym or a physical trainer and perhaps a sport nutritionist or sport psychologist. Their fees can easily add several thousand dollars in expense. The total probably will exceed $25,000 U.S. a year for frugal athletes and may reach $50,000 U.S. if money is not a concern. Families with no financial worries may send their prodigies to a live-in academy in a warm climate where they play tennis half the day and attend a private school the other half. Expenses at such an academy typically start at $35,000 U.S. and can be

Competition at the national and international levels in many activities requires private coaching, putting high-performance competition out of reach for athletes in lower economic classes. Some schools, such as Madison Elementary School on Chicago's South Side, are bringing these high-performance types of activities into the classroom to give all students an opportunity to compete.

double that figure. Of course, athletes still have to pay to compete so they can acquire a ranking.

You can see how children of most families face limited opportunities in certain sports. The median income for families in 2004 was approximately $50,000 U.S. Families whose combined annual income exceeded $100,000 U.S. ranked in the top 5% to 10% of all American families. The average family with a total income of $50,000 U.S. can't begin to afford sports like professional tennis, and even top wage earners making six-figure salaries can't afford to expend a quarter or half of their family income on sport training for one child.

You can also see now why team sports and varsity high school teams are the most popular sports for most kids. The costs are reasonable and almost every family can finance sport participation if they are creative and frugal. Of course, every other family has also figured out that team sports are more affordable, so the competition is keen. Children whose families are well-off financially might find it better to develop skills in a more exclusive sport and compete for a national championship against fewer opponents.

Social Class and High School Sports

Children from lower-class families usually do not have much family support in playing sports since their families are struggling to make ends meet. Girls are expected to help out with household chores and care for younger siblings. Sport dropout rates are well over 50% for teenage girls from lower income levels (Dobie 2000). Research shows that "the most affluent high schools—those in the top quarter of the state of New Jersey—have won athletic championships at more than twice the rate of those in the bottom quarter" (groups based on the household median income of the school neighborhood and the percentage of students on federal free or reduced lunch; Brady and Sylwester 2004):

A. Top quarter   =   40%
B. Upper middle   =   22%
C. Lower middle   =   22%
D. Bottom   =   16%

Schools in wealthier neighborhoods tend to have better sport facilities, better coaches because the pay is better, money for equipment, weight rooms, and booster clubs to pay for extras. Athletes receive team jackets, shirts, uniforms, banquets, rings, and other goodies that are out of reach of other schools.

The training in youth sports in affluent communities tends to be better organized. Families typically start their kids early and encourage them to attend specialized coaching camps to refine their skills. The kids might go to a summer camp for tennis, soccer, golf, swimming, or the more traditional team sports like basketball, soccer, or volleyball. At such camps they are exposed to top coaching, and rubbing elbows with other talented kids from outside their neighborhood heightens cutting-edge concepts and their expectations.

The article from *USA Today* (Brady and Sylwester 2004) also specifically studied the high school in Glen Rock, New Jersey. Glen Rock won 13 state titles over the five years in the 10 core sports analyzed in the article. The state titles included four in football, four in girls' track, three in girls' soccer, one in baseball, and one in boys' track. The median income in the Glen Rock neighborhood was $120,000 U.S., more than double the statewide median. Similar sport statistics abound for suburban school districts in southern Connecticut like Greenwich, New Canaan, and Westport, neighborhoods that are within easy commuting distance to New York City and have high per capita incomes. This pattern in high school sport statistics is replicated around the country in affluent, typically suburban communities.

A glaring omission from the study cited is that the only sports included were basketball, soccer, outdoor track, football, girls' volleyball, girls' softball, and baseball. What do you think the study would have shown if tennis and golf had been included? Have you ever heard of an inner-city high school winning a state championship in tennis or golf?

The lack of golfers or tennis players in urban environments is not solely due to a lack of affluent families. The accessibility to golf courses or tennis courts is so limited in urban settings simply because of lack of space and the cost to build sport facilities. Renting indoor tennis courts in New York City can cost $100 U.S. an hour simply because they are so expensive to build and maintain. Golf courses, except for the few public courses in city parks, are likewise few and far between.

There are some exceptions to the general trends in high school sport statistics. Small rural communities sometimes excel in sports because their kids have few choices for entertainment and so most play sports. Some inner-city high schools have strong traditions of excellence in sports like basketball where playgrounds abound and kids follow history.

Some boys may learn that their role models in professional sport making millions of dollars came from a similar socioeconomic background. Sports give them hope and a roadmap to fulfill their dreams of upward mobility. They typically choose team sports since training can often be found close by at modest expense. As they mature, they can continue to improve their skills through high school varsity programs and eventually they can win an athletic scholarship to college. Sport programs at all levels set aside funds to provide scholarships for youth from poorer families and are eager to assist deserving and talented kids.

Solutions to Financial Barriers in Sport

Access to sports has somewhat opened up in the United States through community sport programs that are available to all kids in a community. Many programs are staged at public school facilities or parks that are supported with taxpayer funds. Although programs usually charge a modest user fee, families who qualify for scholarships based on income often can still send their kids to the programs. Usually recreation departments, again funded by taxpayer funds, provide facilities, provide some equipment, and pay for coaching. Most communities typically offer team sports that can accommodate large numbers of players at modest expense. Some communities also offer swimming or tennis as after-school or summer programs.

Some sports are promoted by nonprofit community organizations established to fund and organize programs in that sport. Often these nonprofit groups are assisted by their national governing bodies and supported financially by local donors, government grants, fund-raisers such as auctions and dinner dances, and business donors who want to help support their local community. Typically these nonprofit organizations provide programs at very modest fees and welcome every child regardless of ability to pay.

Other strong sources of youth sport programs are organizations such as the YMCA and YWCA, Boys and Girls Clubs, Catholic youth organizations, Jewish community centers, police athletic leagues, church leagues, Girl and Boy Scouts, and Big Brothers Big Sisters. All are dedicated to providing healthy recreational experiences for kids, and many concentrate in disadvantaged neighborhoods. Although their goal is not to produce high-performance athletes, if a talented child is spotted in the program, there are often ways to additionally support extended training or scholarships for specialized programs.

CONTROL OF AMATEUR AND PROFESSIONAL SPORT

People with power in the sports world can effect significant change or prevent change. The power in sports is different at every level of competition. In local community, high school, and recreational sport programs, a board of directors usually hires staff to administer the programs. Parents, politicians, and others in the community may join the boards or exert their influence from outside the organization. Typically, those who make program decisions even at the local level are adults who have their own biases and ideas about how a sport should be presented and run.

Organizations like the YMCA help break down the financial barriers to sport participation, even in sports like gymnastics.

At the national level of sport, the people who control the money make decisions on how to run the sport programs. Their economic capital is based on the organizations they head rather than on their personal wealth. However, most of the people who have a say at the national level of sports belong to the upper or upper-middle class by virtue of their income, background, and robust social and cultural capital. The *Sporting News* magazine has published a list of the most powerful people in sport every year since 1991. They have defined *power* as "the capability to effect significant change—or to prevent significant change—in the games we play" (SportingNews.com 2003b). This definition does not include athletic performance, winning, coaching, or popularity, but simply the power to make changes.

The people who have topped this list are for the most part familiar names to sports fans. They include Michael Eisner, formerly of Disney, Rupert Murdoch of News Corporation, and Ed Snider of Comcast, who *Sporting News* dubbed as "emperors" of sport. Others included are George Bodenheimer of ESPN and David Hill of Fox Sports Television Group. These men all represent vast media empires that deliver sports television and media coverage.

The next group appearing on the list contains the commissioners of the major sports leagues such as Paul Tagliabue of the NFL, David Stern of the NBA, Bud Selig of MLB, and Gary Bettman of the NHL. Also on the list are the heads of Nike, Anheuser-Busch, Pepsi, Coors Brewing Company, and Reebok, companies that are major sponsors of sport events. Finally, the list includes those such as Mark McCormack, the former founder of IMG who recently passed away.

All of the men cited above are White males, and the only female who has ranked in the top 25 people on the list is Dawn Hudson, president of Pepsi-Cola North America. The only athletes who have appeared on the list in recent years are Michael Jordan and Tiger Woods, both of whom had an unusual impact on the popularity of their respective sports. Interestingly, there are no coaches on the list (SportingNews.com 2003c).

At the United States Olympic Committee the traditional heads of the board of directors and the officers were often White males. In recent years women and Blacks were gradually included in the controlling group of the USOC, and Leroy Walker, a distinguished former coach of track and field, was the first African American to serve as president, while Sandra Baldwin from swimming became the first female president.

The people who control sports in America often base their decisions on the welfare of the organizations or businesses they head. They decide what sports will receive high visibility, what image of each sport to portray, and what accompanying messages to send to the sport consumers. Of course, they need to please the customer, and for the most part that means taking a conservative, mainstream position on all issues. They can be conscious of public sentiment and media criticism, but they also have the means to influence or deflect much of that.

Perhaps the best example of the powerful control of sport is Rupert Murdoch, chairman and CEO of News Corporation, a media corporation that owns Fox, FX, Fox News, Television Games Network, part of the Golf Channel, Fox international sports channels, and cable and satellite networks around the world. The company also owns major news-

Activity Time-Out: Power at Your University

Investigate your university to assess how sport decisions are made. Who gets involved in the big decisions: the college president, the board of trustees, politicians (if yours is a state university), significant donors, coaching icons, student leaders, athletes, the media, or fans? Interview at least three people in different positions who influence the decisions and ask them to list the five most powerful people in sports at your school. (Remember to use the definition of power as the ability to effect or prevent significant change.) To help the people you interview, you might ask who would have the most influence at this university on topics such as: adding or suspending a particular sport, building a new sport facility, increasing student fees to support sports, accepting a major new sport sponsor, allocating scholarships by sport, or accepting a bowl bid for the football team. Feel free to use your own examples.

papers across the country. They own major-league teams including the New York Knicks, the New York Rangers, the New York Liberty, and the Los Angeles Dodgers and several minor-league teams as well. At the same time, they own Madison Square Garden, Dodger Stadium, and Dodgertown. Fox has television contracts with every major sport and has shown remarkable growth in its coverage of NASCAR (Wikipedia 2006c).

It is easy to see the sprawl of Murdoch's influence in sport by looking at the breadth and depth of his companies' holdings in sport organizations. His decisions can have far-reaching effects on what, when, or where happens in sports on any given day. For example, in the case of a national or regional disaster such as the attack on the World Trade Center or a major earthquake, the News Corporation has considerable power over the response of the sports world, such as deciding what events to postpone or seasons to suspend.

Murdoch's purchase of the Los Angeles Dodgers was driven by his desire to create programming for his television holdings. A similar situation exists for the Atlanta Braves who are owned by Time Warner, the Anaheim Angels owned by Disney, and the Chicago Cubs owned by the Tribune Co. In fact, 22 of the 30 MLB teams have broadcasting deals with Fox Sports Net. The potential for conflict of interest between a media empire and baseball was illustrated during the potential baseball strike of 2002 when Rupert Murdoch could have collected $500 million U.S. in liquidated damages from his fellow baseball owners. That agreement was part of the NewsCorp deal for television rights to broadcast baseball games (Frankel 1998; Sandomir 1997).

Consider if Rupert Murdoch was a devoted fan of women's sports. How could he translate his cultural capital into promoting the cause? Could he forward women's sports by hiring women in prominent leadership positions within his businesses, owning women's sport franchises, or dramatically increasing the exposure of women's sport on television and in the newspapers?

CLASS MOBILITY IN SPORT

A part of the American dream has always been the ability to enhance your social or economic status in life through hard work and discipline. The popular corollary was that Americans who do not improve their status do not have the motivation or discipline to do so. Sports provide an opportunity to improve social and economic status through success on the playing field. Once again, the conventional wisdom is that hard work is even more important than talent in reaching the ultimate prize in a given sport.

The typical example illustrating social mobility through sport is that of football or basketball players or boxers who come from a low-income family and make their way to the professional ranks and command a huge contract. By earning millions of dollars, the athlete automatically joins the upper class, a society he may find difficult to fit into.

There are many dimensions to rising in class status through sport. The most obvious is through education that goes along with continuing a career in sports, even if a career in professional sports is not a reality. Most lower-class kids who passionately latch onto sports realize that maintaining their academic eligibility will allow them to pursue their sport. If they keep up their grades, they may also earn an athletic scholarship that opens up the possibility for higher education that their parents never had. The

In the Arena With . . . *Basketball Without Borders Africa*

In 2003, African Americans in the NBA joined together to launch an NBA outreach program, Basketball Without Borders Africa. Led in 2005 by Dikembe Mutombo of the Houston Rockets, Marcus Camby of the Denver Nuggets, and Mamadou N'diaye of Los Angeles Clippers, among others, the program included a trip to South Africa where 106 players under age 19 from 28 different African countries were hosted. The focus was on developing basketball skills along with promoting healthy living, AIDS awareness and prevention, leadership, and character. Similar tours have been staged in the United States, Brazil, Argentina, Canada, and China. Athletes share living quarters with others of different race or nationality, a unique circumstance for some of them (National Basketball Association 2005a).

knowledge and friends gained through their college education will set them up for employment opportunities beyond their social and economic class even if they never make it as a professional athlete.

Athletes who play sports in college seem to have more opportunities than nonathletes do. The reason for their success may be the sport experience, which teaches discipline, teamwork, and leadership. Of course, they may have innate capabilities that allow them to succeed in sports, and athletics simply enhance those abilities. Sport participation may also help them build their own social and cultural capital. Their education, personal expectations, and social network surely help them

Even with the right environment and training, what are the chances that this athlete will make it big?

in the business world. Numerous research studies have documented both male and female business leaders who participated in athletics and attribute their success at least in part to the lessons learned through sport (Acosta and Carpenter 2004; Carlson and Scott 2005).

In every sport, certain athletes stand out because they appear hungry to succeed. When these athletes come from lower socioeconomic families, people usually conclude that they are striving to escape a life of poverty. Many elite athletes on the world stage have emerged from poor countries to become international celebrities and economically wealthy compared to their countrymen.

How likely are young athletes to make it to the professional level? Evidence from the NCAA (2003) suggests that a small percentage of athletes actually make it from high school to college to professional sport. The odds of a high school athlete making a collegiate team are only about 5%. That means 95% of athletes have no chance of a career in sport beyond their high school years. Only 3% of college athletes make it to the pros. So of high school athletes, roughly .2% make it to a professional career. These are small odds indeed. In spite of many inspiring biographies of athletes who moved from poverty to the professionals, the percentages are stacked against such mobility.

When tracking athletic success, the sports involved may affect the results. We have already seen that many sports such as golf, tennis, swimming, and gymnastics tend to attract athletes from upper-middle class families. Their records are often lumped in with large-scale research studies on class mobility, but their chances of achieving upward mobility are limited since they're starting from a relatively high level. Similarly, female athletes have fewer sports through which to gain upward mobility due to the dearth of professional sports for women. Women in the WNBA earn a modest salary compared to the men in the NBA, and many great women athletes in track and field collect only modest prize money due to the limitations of the sport.

Understanding the limited chances for women to make it in professional sport only reinforces the amazing success of Serena and Venus Williams. Coming from Compton, California, an economically depressed area rife with crime and poverty, they have risen to the top of the sporting world in a sport usually reserved for the upper classes. Combining natural athleticism and talent with the savvy management of their parents, they managed to break into and dominate professional tennis. They accomplished all that without spending years and money in junior competition. Their simple formula was to play a few tournaments and practice under their father's tutelage until they were eligible to turn professional. The result has been Grand Slam championships for both girls and record-setting endorsements, which in the case of Serena, were worth over $50 million U.S.!

The losers in the quest for upward mobility through sport are the thousands of children who have an unrealistic view of their potential and misjudge the odds of realizing their dreams. Leaders in the African American community decry the tendency of young Black males to put all their hopes into a possible professional contract. Those goals are unrealistic for all but a special few, and when lower-class families emphasize sport over academics, most are setting their kids up for failure.

Arthur Ashe, Jr. (who we featured in chapter 11) shared his views on the importance of education in a *New York Times* "Open Letter to Black Parents" (Ashe 1977). Although the statistics have changed today, the sentiments have not. "Unfortunately, our most widely recognized role models are athletes and entertainers—'runnin'' and 'jumpin',' 'singin'' and 'dancin'.' While we are 60 percent of the NBA, we are less than 4 percent of the doctors and lawyers. While we are about 35 percent of major league baseball, we are less than 2 percent of the engineers. While we are about 40 percent of the NFL, we are less than 11 percent of construction workers such as carpenters and bricklayers. Our greatest athletes have been athletes such as Jack Johnson, Joe Louis, and Muhammad Ali. These were the ways out of the ghetto. We have been on the same road—sports and entertainment—too long. We need to pull over, fill up at the library, and speed away to Congress, the Supreme Court, the unions, and the business world" (Ashe 1977).

Yet the lessons learned through sport participation are valuable for young athletes even if a pro career is not in their cards. Hard work, determination, sacrifice, and teamwork can certainly be valuable assets in their future careers. Perhaps the optimistic view of social mobility through sport makes sense when viewed in this light.

CHAPTER SUMMARY

Although Americans prefer not to emphasize social classes, the economic differences between families in our society are clear. People in the upper socioeconomic classes of course prefer to maintain the status quo since they are comfortable with their position. In addition to economic capital, social and cultural capital affect which sports people choose to watch and play, and through sports people in lower classes may improve their social standing.

There are strong relationships between social class and the types of sports people tend to choose for participation or watching. People from the upper classes tend to choose individual sports and sports that are often played at private clubs that are not open to the public. They also choose sports that are more expensive to pursue, whether it be for recreation or high-performance training.

Most people in the middle or working class gravitate toward the team sports that are more affordable. Children can take advantage of free or low-cost programs at the community level to begin playing a traditional team sport and can continue their career in the public schools at no cost in most communities. Team sports emphasize the traditional American values of hard work, discipline, determination, and teamwork. Athletes who do well are admired for their All-American values while those who fail are criticized for laziness or lack of effort.

The people who control sport are often the people in charge of the large media conglomerates, the heads of the professional sport leagues, the heads of the Olympic Games, and the owners of professional franchises, stadiums, and facilities. Almost without exception these leaders in sport are White males who tend to perpetuate the status quo that has clearly favored them. They have the power to make or prevent change in sport.

The odds are against social mobility through success in sport. In spite of a few poster boys who have risen from poverty to great riches, the majority of athletes never play professionally. Using sports for academic motivation or funding for higher education may be the best ticket to improving social and economic class.

CHAPTER

Special Populations and Sport

Student Outcomes

After reading this chapter, you will know the following:

▪ Special populations in sport and the challenges they face in sport participation

▪ How the Americans with Disabilities Act affected special populations

▪ The role of the American Association of People with Disabilities

▪ Sport opportunities for people who are physically or mentally challenged and older adults

▪ Issues facing older athletes and athletes with physical or mental disabilities

This chapter includes three distinct groups of unique populations in sport: people who are physically challenged, people who are mentally challenged, and older adults. Each group faces unique circumstances and has had a different history of acceptance and accommodation within our society. Their participation in sports and recreational activities is relatively recent, and law at every level of government now supports their participation.

More than 54 million people in the United States have one or more physical or mental disabilities, and this number will increase as the average age of our population increases. According to the recent *Survey of Americans with Disabilities* (Harris Poll 2004), a fifth of American people have disabilities. Yet people with disabilities have had few chances to pursue their American dream of equality of opportunity.

Things began to change dramatically (such as requiring government buildings to be accessible to those with handicaps) when the federal government began to enact legislation that addressed various issues of discrimination, including Title V of the Rehabilitation Act of 1973, including discrimination against those with disabilities. And then in 1990 President George H.W. Bush signed the Americans with Disabilities Act (ADA), which became a landmark law and began to effectively limit long-standing discriminatory practices.

Older adults, or adults older than 50 years, are often included as people with disabilities as they begin to combat both physical and mental problems of aging. However, even for relatively fully functioning adults older than 50, the opportunities for sport participation are limited. Life expectancy has been steadily increasing, and the maturing of the baby boomers has resulted in an explosion of older adults. There are presently more than 80 million U.S. residents older than age 50, and the number is rising quickly. In the five years between 2004 and 2009, the number of Americans older than age 55 will increase by 70%, while the number of people younger than 55 will grow by just 1% (Coffman 2004).

As the population ages and seeks a better quality of life, the focus lands on physical health and fulfilling social relationships. Sports and physical activity can contribute to a healthier lifestyle, help fight diseases, and prolong life. Sport programs and physical exercise facilities are critically adjusting marketing and programming to serve this burgeoning population.

AMERICANS WITH DISABILITIES ACT

President H.W. Bush, marking a long and tedious battle to ensure the rights of all people with disabilities, signed the **Americans with Disabilities Act (ADA)** into law in 1990. Before this act, living with a disability was characterized by discrimination and segregation. The situation was not unlike that suffered for centuries by minorities or women. The ADA has been amended several times since its passage and will continue to be refined as court decisions clarify and interpret the law. Unfortunately, some recent Supreme Court decisions have eroded the ADA protections for people with disabilities by placing severe restrictions on the class of people who are protected, narrowed the remedies available to complainants, and expanded the defenses available to employers. However, in the 2004 decision of *Tennessee v. Lane,* the court ruled that the state of Tennessee must allow plaintiffs to sue for financial damages over inaccessible courthouses (United Cerebral Palsy 2004).

Let's review the history of laws preceding the ADA that removed barriers for various groups and laid the groundwork for a society that affirms the equality of people with disabilities. In the late 1960s, major civil rights legislation changed the face of America. Led by Dr. Martin Luther King Jr., who envisioned a society that was just and inclusive for all, as expressed in his now famous "I Have a Dream" speech, the civil rights movement created major changes in schools, businesses, public buildings, federal funding, transportation, and virtually every area of life.

Young people today have a hard time believing that until the 1960s, African Americans were excluded from playing intercollegiate sports and there were none in the professional sports leagues. Baseball player Jackie Robinson was the first to break

The ADA required public buildings to provide access for people with disabilities.

the color barrier, and within 30 years Black athletes dominated professional basketball and football.

In the 1970s, women's rights took the stage. Although women had the right to vote, their rights in the workplace were abysmal and their earning power was a fraction of that of males. Women began to claim an equal place in society and agitated for fairer opportunities. Title IX legislation established the equal rights of females for sport participation. Colleges, high schools, media, and the public slowly adjusted to a world where women could be fit, competitive, and champions just like men.

In the late 1960s, the last of the major antidiscrimination statutes of the civil rights movement was passed with the enactment of the Fair Housing Act. That act did not include people with disabilities in its protected classes. Likewise, Title VII of the Civil Rights Act prohibited discrimination on the basis of race, religion, national origin, and sex in the sale and rental of housing but again offered no protection for those with disabilities.

Finally in 1988, the Fair Housing Act was amended to add the new protected classes of people with disabilities and families with children. Two years later, President H.W. Bush declared at the signing of the Americans with Disabilities Act, "This Act is powerful in its simplicity. It will ensure that people with dis-abilities are given the basic guarantees . . . of freedom of choice, control of their lives, the opportunity to blend fully into the mosaic of the American mainstream" (Americans Disability Technical Assistance Centers 2004, p. 9).

The ADA addressed discrimination against those with disabilities in employment, state and local government, public accommodations, telecommunications, and transportation. The purpose of the law was to provide a clear and comprehensive national mandate to eliminate discrimination against individuals with disabilities and to establish standards that are clear, strong, and enforceable. Over the past 15 years, many advances have been made as courts have upheld the law and interpreted its application and organizations have adopted similar statements of inclusion for people with disabilities.

While reading this brief historical review, you may have noticed how recently the developments occurred for creating fairness for people with disabilities. Businesses, schools, churches, public programs, organizations, and of course governments have all adjusted their practices to conform to the law.

The current opportunities in sport participation emanate from the shift in attitude of our society. Why shouldn't people with disabilities have the same opportunities to enjoy sports and fitness activities

Activity Time-Out: Protecting Civil Rights

Develop a list of the three major legislative acts that were passed to protect the civil rights of minorities, women, and the physically or mentally disabled. Include the dates the laws were passed, the political climate preceding their passage, the short-term results, and their status today. Note the effects of each law on both sport participation and the general quality of life.

that others in society enjoy? The challenge is to welcome their participation and accommodate their needs within the sporting world.

Although in the last decade there have been quantum leaps in improving the quality of life for people with disabilities, they still face significant inequalities in key areas of living (Harris Poll 2004):

▪ Only 35% of people with disabilities are employed, compared with 78% of those without disabilities.

▪ Three times as many live in poverty, with annual household incomes below $15,000 U.S.

▪ They are twice as likely to drop out of high school (21% versus 10%).

▪ They are twice as likely to have transportation problems, and many go without needed health care.

▪ They are less likely to socialize, eat out, and attend religious services.

▪ Only 34% say they are very satisfied with life, compared to 61% of people without disabilities.

Sports and recreation opportunities are perhaps less important than issues of fair housing, access to buildings, access to schooling, fair employment opportunities, and access to health care. But sport participation, whether at the competitive or participation level, does enrich life for all of us.

AMERICAN ASSOCIATION OF PEOPLE WITH DISABILITIES

The **American Association of People with Disabilities (AAPD)** was founded in 1995 as a nonprofit organization to represent all Americans with disabilities. Family members and friends are welcome

to join the AAPD for an annual membership fee of $15.00 U.S. AAPD was conceived, advised by, and managed by people with disabilities for people with disabilities. It is not a government program. Although the mission of AAPD is much broader than fairness in sports, they do provide leadership and lobby to ensure that recreational opportunities exist for their constituency.

According to the AAPD, more than one in five Americans, or over 50 million people, have a disability. Nearly half of these people are of employable age, yet only one-third are employed. Government and private plans that support people with disabilities cost American taxpayers over $230 billion U.S. each year, and another $200 billion U.S. in earnings and taxes are lost because of their unemployment. The economic impact alone is striking (American Association of People With Disabilities 2005).

Many governing bodies for specific sports have expanded their programs for people with disabilities since the passage of the ADA. You may notice pictures of physically disabled athletes in their literature, videos, and materials for coaching courses. Whenever possible, athletes with disabilities are mainstreamed into regular sport programs, although athletes with severe disabilities require specialized coaching and rules for competition.

SPORT PARTICIPATION FOR ATHLETES WITH PHYSICAL DISABILITIES

According to the Americans with Disabilities Act, the term **disability** applies to any individual who has a physical or mental impairment that substantially limits one or more of their major life activities. In sports, physical disabilities can range from loss of limbs or loss of hearing or sight to physical impairment due to disease or accident. In sports, the degree of disability is taken into account to ensure fair competition.

Paralympics

The Paralympic Games are the second largest sporting event in the world, second to the Olympics. The inaugural Paralympics were staged in 1960 in Rome, Italy, and included about 400 athletes from 23 countries. Today, the Summer and Winter Games together include over 5,000 athletes representing 120 countries in the Summer events and 36 countries in the Winter events. The Paralympics feature competition in 21 sports, 18 of which are also contested in the Olympics (United States Paralympics 2005). The following sports are included in Paralympic competition:

Winter Games

Alpine Skiing	Nordic Skiing
Curling	Sled Hockey

Summer Games

Archery	Rugby
Men's Basketball	Sailing
Women's Basketball	Shooting
Boccie	Soccer
Cycling	Swimming
Equestrian	Table Tennis
Fencing	Tennis
Men's Goalball	Tack and Field
Judo	Men's Volleyball
Powerlifting	Women's Volleyball

Many of these sports, including fencing, volleyball, basketball, rugby, and tennis, are played in wheelchairs.

The mission of the U.S. Paralympics is: "To be the world leader in the Paralympic movement by developing comprehensive and sustainable elite programs for our athletes. To utilize our Olympic and Paralympic platform to promote excellence in the lives of persons with disabilities." Founded in 2001, U.S. Paralympics is a division of the USOC with a focus on enhancing programs, funding, and opportunities for persons with physical disabilities to participate in sport (United States Paralympics 2005).

This is a clear statement of commitment toward producing excellence in competitive sport by athletes with physical disabilities. Because the Paralympic movement is under the aegis of the USOC, it generally follows the Olympic model for the development of athletes and applies a similar philosophy and purpose.

In order to participate in the Paralympic Games, athletes have to meet eligibility standards established by the International Paralympic Committee. Eligible athletes include those with amputations, those who are blind or visually impaired, those with cerebral palsy, those with spinal cord injuries, those with multiple sclerosis, and those with dwarfism, along with other categories of disability.

The Paralympic division of the USOC manages 18 Paralympic sports. They also support the programs offered by USA Curling, U.S. Equestrian Federation, U.S. Sailing, and U.S. Tennis.

Elite athletes who have qualified through competitive performance are selected for financial support, coaching assistance, and training for the next Paralympic Games. They are required to comply with the

In the Arena With . . . *Erin Popovich*

Erin Popovich is a seven-time gold medalist. Her disability is achondroplasia, a genetic disorder that results in a usually normal torso and shortened limbs. She stands 4 feet (1.2 meters), 4 and 3/4 inches (12.1 centimeters) tall and weighs 105 pounds (47.6 kilograms), which is a bit larger than normal for females with her disability. A two-time Olympian from Silverbow, Montana, Erin won seven gold medals at the 2004 Paralympic Games in Athens, Greece. She won five individual titles: 220 IM, 100-meter freestyle, 100-meter breaststroke, 50-meter butterfly, and 50-meter freestyle. She also tacked on two more gold medals as part of the relay teams in the 4 × 100 freestyle and the 4 × 100 medley. As a bonus, she set numerous Paralympic and world records in several events. She was voted runner-up for the 2004 United States Olympic Committee SportsWoman of the Year.

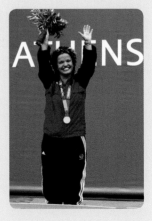

policies of the U.S. Anti-Doping Agency, including unannounced out-of-competition testing.

The USOC developed a comprehensive development plan in 2000 to ensure that American athletes with disabilities have every chance of performing to their highest potential. Funds in excess of $23 million U.S. were committed for 2000 to 2004 for soliciting sponsors for support, educating the media, and providing coaching training and support. Although this development plan is in its infancy, the promise for future success of our physically disabled athletes has never been brighter. American Paralympic athletes finished the Athens Games ranked fifth in the world and are likely to improve that finish in future competitions.

State and Community Development Programs

Elite athletes don't just pop up. They develop over many years and require nurturing through expert coaching, organizational support, competitive events, and financial assistance. Grassroots programs that provide opportunities for athletes with disabilities are scattered throughout the country and depend heavily on local leaders and dedicated coaches in each community.

The Paralympic Academy is supported by the USOC and is an annual event held in each state. The academies last one to two days and are designed to introduce sports to potential Paralympic athletes age 12 to 18. They also provide training for coaches, program administrators, families, and community leaders who are involved in local Paralympic sport programs. By attracting media attention, state academies help garner public attention and support for the mission.

At the community level is where the real work of ensuring equal opportunities for physically disabled athletes occurs. When practicable, programs should include all young athletes, with adaptations as required for athletes with disabilities. This practice provides economy of operation and viable competition for athletes who may not find local events to participate in or other athletes to train with. A national program is relatively easy to put in place because of the limited number of athletes involved, whereas these local programs need to flourish in every community in the country (United States Paralympics 2005).

SPORT PARTICIPATION FOR ATHLETES WITH MENTAL DISABILITIES

According to the Special Olympics, the people with mental disabilities include those an agency or professional has identified as having one of the following conditions: intellectual disabilities, cognitive delays, or significant learning or vocational problems due to cognitive disabilities that require specially designed instruction.

Pop Culture: *Murderball*

Fierce rivalry, violence, suspense, and huge personalities mark the documentary film *Murderball.* The winner of several prizes at the 2005 Sundance Film Festival, this film is about highly competitive rugby players who are "quads;" that is, people who have at least partial impairment of all four limbs. These guys add an unusual dimension to the violence and competitiveness of the naturally tough sport of rugby.

With the help of therapy and special wheelchairs, the athletes play a rough brand of rugby. The chairs, costing in excess of $2,000 U.S. each, are customized for sports, are built lower to the ground, and are wider than some doorways. With their special chair and lots of physical therapy, "quads" can drive, cook, have sex, and, as this movie shows, compete at the highest levels of athletics.

What *Murderball* helps us understand is the humanness we all share in spite of differences like physical disabilities. You might think that people with disabilities would be depressed by their physical limitations, but the athletes in this film show convincingly that they're just your average Olympic athletes who get up earlier, train harder, eat healthier, travel more, love, and win if they want to (Persall 2005).

The Special Olympics is an international organization involving 150 countries and more than 1.7 million people with intellectual disabilities that provides year-round sport training and competition. Founded in 1968 by Eunice Kennedy Shriver, the Special Olympics provides people with mental disabilities opportunities to develop their full potential, develop their physical fitness, demonstrate courage, and experience joy and friendship through sport. The athlete oath for the Special Olympics is: "Let me win. But if I cannot win, let me be brave in the attempt" (Special Olympics 2005).

Since its inception, the Special Olympics has helped its athletes improve fitness, develop motor skills, increase self-confidence, and enhance self-image. The same values that make sports attractive to all athletes have also helped Special Olympians develop physically, socially, and spiritually through participation.

People with profound disabilities can also participate in the Special Olympics through the Motor Activities Training Program (MATP). The MATP was developed by specialists and emphasizes training and participation rather than competition.

The worldwide participation in the Special Olympics can be seen in the Special Olympic World Games that are held every four years for both summer and winter events. The 2005 Special Olympic Winter Games were held in Nagano, Japan, and were the first Games held in Asia. More than 1,800 athletes from 80 countries competed in seven sports. The 2007 Special Olympic World Games will be held in Shanghai, China (Special Olympics 2006).The Summer Games include aquatics, athletics, badminton, basketball, boccie, bowling, cycling, equestrian, soccer, golf, gymnastics, handball, judo, powerlifting, roller skating, sailing, softball, table tennis, tennis, and volleyball. The Winter Games include Alpine skiing, cross-country skiing, snowshoeing, figure skating, floor hockey, snowboarding, and speed skating.

The Special Olympics is divided into seven world regions: Africa, Asia Pacific, East Asia, Europe and Eurasia, Latin America, Middle East and North Africa, and North America. In the North American region, most U.S. states have a Special Olympic office that offers and coordinates Special Olympic activities in all 26 sports. Funding is provided by the international organization along with local financial support.

The first Special Olympics was held in Chicago and attracted 1,000 athletes from the United States and Canada. The inaugural Winter Games were held in 1977 in Colorado and involved 500 athletes. By 1987, the Summer Games had grown to include over 4,700 athletes from 70 countries. A year later, the International Olympic Committee officially recognized the Special Olympics. The Games continued to expand, and more than 7,000 athletes from 150 countries competed in the Special Olympic World Summer Games in 2003 in Dublin, Ireland, the first Summer Games ever held outside the United States. From its humble beginnings as a summer camp in the backyard of founder Eunice Shriver, the organization has grown in numbers and prestige around the world (Special Olympics 2006).

Coaches, family members, and other volunteers are essential to the sport programs. Most donate their time to the athletes and are rewarded with smiles, hugs, and self-satisfaction. Hundreds of these dedicated volunteers are the lifeblood of the organization, and they allow it to offer programs and competition at no charge for participants.

The joy of competing is worth more than a gold medal.

State organizations in cooperation with various governing bodies in sport also train coaches and officials for the Special Olympics. Since many athletes require personal support and supervision, the demands of coaching and officiating are extremely people intensive and require adequate training.

Participation in the Special Olympics is valued regardless of the participant's skill. The Special Olympics offers both the performance and participation tracks; that is, events for highly skilled athletes and the same events are held for more modestly accomplished athletes (Special Olympics 2006).

SPORT PARTICIPATION FOR OLDER ATHLETES

As mentioned, older adults, or adults older than 50 years, are often included as people with disabilities due to disabilities associated with age. They also have organizations that advocate for their equal treatment. The largest and most powerful is the Association for Retired Persons (AARP), which has a membership of over 30 million people. AARP has a strong voice on issues such as taxes, insurance, health care, and social security that older adults often deal with as they leave the workforce. To date, AARP has not tackled encouraging more physical activity for older persons except for experimenting in the early 2000s with promoting triathlons and

promoting tennis in partnership with the United States Tennis Association. Due the wide diversity of the physical needs of its members, AARP has settled on a strategy of encouraging more Americans to get at least the minimum amount of physical activity as recommended by the U.S. surgeon general by walking several times per week (personal communication with Bill Novelli, CEO of AARP).

The International Council on Active Aging (ICAA) is a relatively new group that promotes quality of life, physical activity, and sport participation by older adults. They publish a newsletter and a bimonthly magazine, *Journal on Active Aging*. ICAA also hosts conferences to share research information and educate people on creative approaches to innovative programming, staff training, and product selection to assist in the aging process. Their more than 5,000 members include many commercial organizations and health clubs that are seeking to accommodate older adults in their programs and facilities and are looking for guidance (International Council on Active Aging 2006).

Performance Sport for Older Adults

In most sport organizations, senior divisions for competition have existed for years, although most of them included adults beginning at age 35 or 40. Today, with the changes in life expectancy, 35 to 40 hardly make an athlete a senior athlete. Senior divisions are now called **masters** divisions and usually begin at age 50. By that age, most athletes are unable to physically compete with younger people who are in their prime of physical ability, and they seek competition within their own age group for social reasons as well as competitive ones.

There are a few remarkable athletes such as Martina Navratilova, who turned 50 years of age on October 18, 2006, and was still competing on the women's professional tennis tour at that time. The Senior Olympics, Senior PGA Tour, and masters games in other sports give athletes for whom the competitive fires still burn the chance to test their skills.

The performance level of masters athletes is very high. How do these athletes change your perception of older adults?

In the Arena With . . . *Phillipa Raschker*

Masters athletes won't take a backseat to anyone when it comes to competition. Consider the case of Phillipa "Phil" Raschker, who was named one of five finalists for the prestigious Sullivan Award for top amateur athletes in 2003. She vied for the award with basketball star Lebron James, Olympic speed skater Apolo Anton Ohno, swimmer Michael Phelps, and University of Connecticut basketball star Diana Taurasi. This is the first time a masters athlete has been a finalist for the award.

At age 57, Phil is a remarkable competitor in track and field. She is a 13-time athlete of the year in track and field, holds 44 masters world records, and has set more than 200 United States and world track and field records. In 2003 alone, she set seven world and nine American records for the pentathlon, heptathlon, 60 meters, 200 meters, 400 meters, 800 meters, high jump, pole vault, and long jump.

At the award ceremony in New York, Phil shared some thoughts with the audience:

"I am 57 years new! We need never lose our competitive spirit and stay healthy and fit for a lifetime by competing in sports. This award is for all aging athletes out there. And who would dare rob them of the pure joy of competing? Everett Hosack is still setting track records at the age of 103. Margaret Hinton in her 80s is still pole vaulting. As Babe Ruth once said, 'It's hard to beat someone that never gives up.' She or he that attempts the impossible has little competition." (Weiner 2004)

In 2005, 10,400 athletes competed in 18 different sports at the National Summer Senior Games (Senior Olympics) held during 16 days in Pittsburgh, Pennsylvania. The minimum age to compete was 50 and athletes were divided into five-year age groups. The National Senior Games began in 1987 and now more than 35% of the competitors are female. Summer Games are scheduled for Louisville in 2007, San Francisco in 2009, and Houston in 2011 (National Senior Games Association 2005).

The Senior Olympics negotiated with the USOC to grandfather in the use of the Olympic name although the senior organization as a whole is now referred to as the National Senior Games Association. The association also sponsored Winter Games until 2001 and planned to resume with Winter Games in 2006 in even-numbered years. Other special events such as a National Senior Games Championship Festival for golf and tennis and the AARP Minnesota Senior Olympic Hockey Championships were held in the fall of 2006.

The Summer Olympics includes archery, bowling, badminton, basketball, cycling, horseshoes, racewalking, racquetball, road racing, shuffleboard, swimming, table tennis, tennis, softball, track and field, triathlon, and volleyball.

Competitors qualify for the national events through the state games held annually in their age division. Most of these athletes have been competing all their life and have slowed down the aging process by improving their diet, working on their fitness, and keeping up with the latest advances in sport science and sports medicine.

Participation Sport for Older Adults

All trends point toward an explosion in physical activity for people over age 50 as in the next few decades our population tilts toward older adults. Many people now consider 50 to be middle age and expect to live another 25 or more years. They want those years to be fun, vital, and active. Their health is a major concern and slowing the aging process is a top priority.

Recreational sports offer the best opportunity for older people to have fun, enjoy activity, test their skills, socialize with others their age, and keep fit. Every community offers free or low-cost programs for its citizens and now more of these programs are beginning to target adults age 50 and over.

Older adults are turning to sports that they can play for a lifetime, like swimming, walking, tennis, golf, dance, biking, skiing, bowling, yoga, and weight training. Some team sports such as softball, basketball, and volleyball are also thriving, using rule adjustments and age groups to equalize the competition. Sports that require maximum strength, quick bursts of energy, or body contact and carry the risk of injury tend to decline in popularity as people age.

Most people 50 and older crave the excitement of playing sports, want to stay fit, and enjoy the mental challenge of trying to outsmart an opponent. They gain confidence and still get a high from competing or moving vigorously. They value youthfulness, and sports help them attain that goal.

They may cut down the frequency, duration, or intensity of play that was customary in their younger days but enjoy playing even more. Rules, rankings, and awards are less important to many who achieved previously in their life, and just getting to play is its own reward.

In St. Petersburg, Florida, the legendary Kids and Kubs softball league has been around for more than 75 years. The club's 56 members gather in North Shore Park to play a doubleheader every Tuesday, Thursday, and Saturday beginning at 10:30 a.m. They divide into two teams and go at it. The age limit is 75 and older!

Paul Good, who just turned 95, says, "It adds years to your life and life to your years!" Some years ago, the club reached a landmark when George Bakewell at age 101 took the field along with his son Elton, who was 75. Ethel Lehmann broke the gender barrier in 2005 by joining the group at age 75 (St. Petersburg Times 2005c). The Kids and Kubs pay about $75 U.S. per year to play and look forward to exhibition games against local politicians, kids, or other older players, and they travel to other states to test themselves. A road trip to Pennsylvania and Ohio a decade ago resulted in nine wins in ten games. Since then, Kids and Kubs has sent teams to senior world championships around the country, winning the over-80 division in 1998 and finishing third in the 1999 Senior World Softball Championships the next year. Their next step is to establish feeder leagues in nearby communities like Tampa, Sarasota, and Bradenton to start training some youngsters who can eventually move up to their league.

ISSUES FOR SPECIAL POPULATIONS IN SPORT

Although many opportunities for special populations have opened up in sport, these opportunities for older athletes and for athletes who are mentally or

Lifetime activities, such as hiking, walking, and biking, are increasingly popular with older adults and help them lead healthier lives.

physically disabled must expand to meet the needs of this rapidly growing population. As the demographics shift to an older population, the proportion of people in these categories will increase, as will demand for the following:

- Widespread acceptance of the need for sport for special populations
- Funding support from public and private sources
- Organizational support by all sport bodies including the national governing bodies
- Programs offered at the community level through parks and recreation departments
- Training for coaches, officials, and sport administrators who understand and want to work with the target population
- Equipment and rule modifications that allow special populations to play sports
- Sport opportunities that include all athlete populations when appropriate
- Media support for publicity and information

All people should have access to participation in recreational sports regardless of their age or disability. While most people acknowledge that fact, conflict arises when programs do not exist or budgets do not permit expanded activities. In some sport activities, including special populations with the general population works well, but combining all populations is not always possible. Similarly, aging can prevent players from competing with younger players in any meaningful way. Public programs in schools and recreation departments should be required to provide access for older adults and athletes with disabilities.

Sport organizations at every level should seek ways to accommodate special populations. High school and collegiate sports have barely scratched the surface of possible inclusion. For example, numerous tennis players using wheelchairs have competed on their high school varsity teams and gone on to compete in college. In 2003, a wheelchair user from Oakville High School in St. Louis, Missouri, received his varsity letter after compiling a 15 to 3 win–loss record his senior year. The only concession to wheelchair players is that they may play the ball after two bounces rather than the customary one. This simple change has allowed nondisabled and physically disabled players to compete with each other, a perfect example of a policy of inclusion (Woods 2004).

Community sport programs typically cannot accommodate special populations due to a lack of participants in the age group or ability level, and need to explore creative methods of including these populations in existing programs. More and more programs for older adults are springing up due to the demand and the availability of so many older players.

Educational conferences and programs of study need to be sponsored by organizations for the physically disabled and elderly, sport organizations such as governing bodies, and colleges and universities. Coaches, officials, and sport administrators sorely need training to work with special populations. Those who have sport experience are good candidates to fill these roles, but more people are needed who have a special interest in serving these populations. Family and friends should be recruited, trained, and put to work.

Equipment advances have made sport participation possible for many physically disabled or older athletes. Sport wheelchairs that are lightweight and mobile permit athletes in chairs to play a variety of sports including basketball, tennis, fencing, volleyball, and rugby. Lighter bats, golf clubs, and rackets allow athletes to manipulate them easily. Artificial prostheses allow athletes without limbs to run, jump, and play sports in ways never imagined in the past. Aids for visual or hearing impairment allow athletes to track balls, run on their own, and play multiple sports.

Finally, the media must help educate the public on the needs of special populations. Television features on older athletes and those with disabilities are powerful tools for garnering public support for sport access for all athletes. Movies can significantly affect the general population's understanding and empathy for special populations. In 2004, the movie *Million Dollar Baby* highlighted the effects of quadriplegia. Other films that feature people with disabilities such as *Ray, My Left Foot, The Miracle Worker, Johnny Belinda, Children of a Lesser God, Rain Man, Elephant Man*, and *A Beautiful Mind* have typically shown people who triumph over their disability. Through these films, people became and continue to become enlightened and inspired by the challenges and successes of a population many know little about.

CHAPTER SUMMARY

We identified special populations as athletes who are physically disabled, mentally disabled, or older adults. Each of these groups faces different challenges that affect sport participation.

National laws to protect these three special populations were passed relatively recently. The Americans with Disabilities Act in 1990 spurred understanding of the need for accommodating people with special needs.

Physically disabled athletes may compete nationally and internationally under the supervision of the Paralympic Games. Much like the Olympic Games, the Paralympics are contested every four years and offer both winter and summer events. Medals are awarded in 21 sports and more than 5,000 athletes compete in each Paralympic Games.

Mentally disabled athletes may compete through the Special Olympics, which is typically held in the United States and hosts state, national, and worldwide competition. More than 1.7 million athletes are involved in the Special Olympic movement, and that number is expected to continue to grow worldwide.

Older athletes, often referred to as *masters* athletes, also compete worldwide. Age groups up to and including athletes 90 years old ensure equitable competition in various sports that are staged by the National Senior Games Association in the United States. The achievements of these older athletes are becoming increasingly inspirational to an aging population looking for challenges in their later years.

Participation sports for older athletes or athletes with disabilities are not as well organized as performance sports but nevertheless are offered throughout the United States. Typically, schools, recreation departments, or other local sport organizations sponsor these participations sports. The emphasis is on healthy physical activity to enhance quality of life. Efforts to include people with special needs in mainstream sport programs are growing and gaining acceptance.

Key issues need to be addressed to ensure continued progress in sports for special populations. Among these are consistent funding; education of coaches, officials, and sport administrators; publicity from the media; and support from sport organizations at every level.

Religion and Sport

Student Outcomes

After reading this chapter, you will know the following:

- How religion has affected sport throughout history
- Interrelationships between sport and religion
- How athletes use religion in sport
- How institutions and organizations use both religion and sport
- How coaches and sport organizers use religion
- Conflicts between religion and sport

Religion is the belief in a god or supernatural force that influences human life. Humans in every society on record have created belief systems about the supernatural. Such beliefs are essential to the core structure of a society and help humans understand their purpose for living and how they should spend their days, treat others, and deal with death and the afterlife.

Religion plays a central role in helping people find purpose and meaning in life, in allaying fears of the unknown, and in providing guidelines for interacting with others. It is the basis for a moral code that keeps society functioning and respectful of all persons. Religious customs can bind people together through common acts and unite them in spirit.

Religion and sport share a common trait in that both have been labeled as an "opiate of the masses" (Hoffman 1992). In the 1800s Karl Marx wrote in *The Communist Manifesto* that religion was an opiate that was used by governments to distract people from their miserable life and instead focus them on an afterlife. Similarly, people have accused political leaders of encouraging sport participation and spectatorship to distract citizens from economic or political concerns (see chapter 16).

At first blush, sport and religion may seem unrelated. But throughout history people have often linked the two and blended them into their belief systems. At times, organized religion has been at odds with sport and has considered games as not worthy of mankind. The belief was that people live on earth to develop their spiritual side and pursuing leisure through sport simply detracts from that mission.

One of the main reasons the Americas were explored and settled was the possibility of religious freedom. Although there have been many athletes in many sports who follow religions other than

Sumo wrestling originated as a performance to entertain the Shinto gods.

Christianity, no religion has dominated American sport as the Christian faith has. Thus, much of the information in this chapter will focus on Christianity although there are sections dealing specifically with the Jewish and Muslim faiths.

Polls by both Harris and Gallup show that in 2001, approximately 72% of Americans identified themselves as Christians. About 10% of the people surveyed labeled themselves as agnostic or atheist. Protestant believers were the religious majority, comprising 51% of the population, while the Roman Catholics were next at 25%. Those of Jewish faith accounted for 2%, while Orthodox churches made up less than 1% of the population (Adherents 2005). These statistics illuminate the strong influence Protestantism has had on the United States by virtue of their numbers.

In today's sports world, we may see athletes praying together before or after contests, making the sign of the cross before attempting a foul shot in basketball, crediting God for a victory, or quoting Scripture to justify their pursuit of excellence in sport. In the last century, organized religious leaders gradually embraced sport as another avenue to reach the masses and influence their behavior toward a worthy, godlike existence. That change in philosophy gave rise to the interrelationship between religion and sport that exists today. This chapter looks at the interplay between religion and sport, the use of sport within religion, and the use of religion within sport.

RELIGION AND SPORT IN HISTORY

The ancient Greeks mingled religion with athletics. Demonstrations of athletic prowess were a major part of their religious festivals. The Greeks portrayed their gods as perfect physical specimens who took pleasure in the pursuit of physical excellence. They held the Olympic Games and their athletic contests to honor Zeus, the king of the gods.

The Olympic Games were suspended by the Roman emperor Theodosius I, who as a Christian wanted to stamp out paganism. The Olympic Games in those days were a series of pagan rituals that featured many footraces along with some "sports" that were violent and life threatening. Chariot races in which horses and drivers risked life and limb were favorites. Also popular was the pankration, a no-holds-barred combat sport that melded elements of boxing, wrestling, and street fighting (Gertz 2004). Often animal sacrifices were also a part of the pagan religious festivals.

The early Christians did not think that sport was evil, as evidenced by the apostle Paul, who wrote approvingly of physical activity. But the history of paganism surrounding sport events caused the early church to separate itself from the sports played by the pagan masses. Some church leaders felt that the body was inherently evil and should be subordinate to the spirit. Therefore time spent in exercising the body took away from time that should be devoted to the spirit.

With the Protestant reformation in the early 16th century, the negative attitude of the church toward the body might have had a chance to wane. However, the Puritanical interpretation of religion that was eventually transported to America embraced a new asceticism that pushed the physical side even further in the background. The Puritans believed that the only purpose for the body was to perform the physical labor necessary for survival. They thought that no time should be spent in leisure pursuits, and they viewed pursuits that involved gambling, harmed animals such as in cockfighting, or pleased the participants as evil (Eitzen and Sage 2002).

By the mid-1850s, people in the United States began to change their attitude toward sport. As the population shifted from rural to urban and production shifted from manual labor to the industrial age, physical well-being became a concern. Led by physicians and, surprisingly, by ministers, the concept of a sound, healthy body through physical activity once

Activity Time-Out: Religion, Sport, and Other Civilizations

The ancient Greeks weren't the only early civilization to combine sport and religion. Take a look at some other civilizations (such as the Mesopotamians, Egyptians, or Mayans) to see how their culture, religion, and sport interacted. How have their customs influenced sport today? Compare your findings with those of others in the class.

again gained favor. Leading universities hired medical doctors to promote the health of their students, and those doctors in turn founded departments of physical education. Influential Christian men labeled as *muscular Christians* extolled physical fitness as a virtue that fit well with godly behavior as a means of glorifying God by taking care of the body. The founding of the Young Men's Christian Association (YMCA) near the end of the century capitalized on the emerging acceptance of the positive link between body and spirit.

Although churches still battled to keep the Sabbath (Sunday) as a holy day of rest, church leaders began to accept and even promote sport as long as it did not interfere with developing the spiritual side of people. The lone holdout to this trend was the Congregational Church from New England, which in 1957 became the United Church of Christ, which viewed sport and games as inconsistent with developing the soul.

In the 20th century, the bond between sport and religion expanded in the United States in ways never envisioned by the founding fathers. They became two institutions that often cooperated to promote a better life for their constituency. Churches sponsored sports and many sports promoted churches. Some people have even declared that sports are a religion, although that view is hard to substantiate.

CHRISTIAN INFLUENCE ON SPORT

Churches realized that they could attract people to their doors by offering social occasions that involved sports. They constructed gymnasiums, sponsored basketball or softball teams, provided playing fields, and encouraged people to join them for sports and stay for Sunday services. The Catholic Church founded the Catholic Youth Organization (CYO) to organize sport leagues for young people. Protestant groups supported the Young Men's Christian Association (YMCA) and the Young Women's Christian Association (YWCA). Housed in gymnasiums around the country, Ys became a powerful force in providing organized sports for youth while espousing a broader purpose of developing their minds and spirits. The famous triangle that shows mind, body, and spirit was the hallmark of the Y movement. The YMCA even established what is now Springfield College in Springfield, Massachusetts, to train its instructors. For many years, Springfield College was the preeminent institution for studying physical education and sport.

A major contribution to American sport emanated from Springfield and the YMCA when in 1891 Canadian James Naismith invented basketball, a game that became the most-played sport in America and is now taking off worldwide. Just a few years later, William Morgan invented volleyball at the YMCA in Holyoke, Massachusetts, just a few miles away from Springfield. Thus, two popular team sports indigenous to the United States are products of the YMCA.

The sports world welcomed the backing of religion since it promised to spread access to sports for the average citizen. Athletes also seized upon religion as a way of addressing their fears in the face of competition. While some athletes are simply superstitious, others use their religious beliefs to keep them safe, bring them luck, and calm their nerves. Many athletes admit to praying before important contests and to achieving focus through prayer.

Athletes also use religion to ascribe a deeper sense of purpose to their sport participation. Believing that it is God's will to develop your talent to glorify Him is a powerful motivator. Some athletes believe God has a plan for their life and to become a top athlete is fulfilling that plan. Others justify their consuming passion for sport by using their sport success to gain the attention of fans and witness their faith in God.

Christian athletes often quote Scripture to justify their complete dedication to sport and hard work as a way of glorifying God. A favorite verse some athletes use from I Corinthians 9:24 is: "Surely you know that in a race all the runners take part in it, but only one of them wins the prize. Run, then, in such a way as to win the prize." Another favorite is found in I Timothy 4:7-8: "I have fought a good fight, I have finished my course, I have kept the faith" (Deford 1976, p. 92-99).

Coaches and owners of sports teams often promote the link between sport and religion because it reinforces a code of conduct that they prefer for their athletes. The sports pages are full of tales of professional athletes involving violence, drugs, cheating, promiscuity, and alcohol abuse. In many cases, the athletes in these stories lack a strong moral code or a personal belief in religion that might have prevented dubious choices. Rehabilitation is often linked to an acceptance of a new moral code based on religious beliefs and reinforced by teammates and friends who are fellow believers (Coakley 2004).

Protestantism has always preached an absolute belief in the value of hard work, self-discipline, and striving for success. Indeed, in the United States, those characteristics are widely considered to be all-American and the very foundation of the nation.

Athletic coaches in America endorse those values beyond all others. Even talented athletes cannot reach their potential without at least a nodding acquaintance with hard work and self-discipline. The lessons learned on the playing field and extolled in the sanctuaries of churches are often identical: work hard, play hard, and do your best to win every day!

According to Overman (1997), traditional Catholic doctrine emphasized that the body was a "temple of the Holy Spirit" that should be kept pure rather than developed through physical activity. Protestants, on the other hand, trumpeted competition as an opportunity for people to prove their value through achievement and become the best they could be. In more recent times, both Catholicism and Protestantism have fully embraced sport as a special way of glorifying God by developing physical and competitive skill.

The belief systems of Protestantism, sport, and to some extent Catholicism are so closely intertwined that it is not surprising they have found a mutual synergy. They each reinforce the value system of the other and together help young people organize their lives and social system according to the code of church and sport. Both religion and sport often resist social change and seek to maintain the status quo that benefits both institutions.

SPORT AND RELIGIONS OTHER THAN CHRISTIANITY

Worldwide, religious faiths are distributed among Christianity (33%), Islam (21%), Hinduism (14%), and many others (Adherents 2005). Each religion directly affects the attitudes of its believers toward physical activity, sport, and competition and in many cases sets different standards for males and females. The result is that sport within each culture may be promoted or severely restricted according to the religious teachings.

Let's look at Judaism and Islam, which have significantly influenced North America as well as other parts of the world.

Judaism

Judaism has had a prominent role in the United States since its religious beliefs generally follow a Judeo–Christian heritage. The Old Testament recounts the history of the Hebrew people, and Jesus Christ of the New Testament was a Jew. The early Christians were essentially Jews, and the religion that developed and expanded around the world had its roots in Judaism.

Jews have played a somewhat obscure role in sport, probably because they make up a relatively small proportion of the U.S. population. Yet they have affected American sport through enviable success in boxing. Many Jewish athletes have also been celebrated for their achievements in the Maccabiah Games, a unique event similar to the Olympics but only open to participants from a Jewish background.

Perhaps the most well-known Jewish athletes in American sport have been Hank Greenberg, a slugger for the Detroit Tigers in the 1940s, and Sandy Koufax, the Hall of Fame pitcher for the Brooklyn/Los Angeles

How did athletes such as Sandy Koufax (left) pave the way for the success of current Jewish athletes?

Dodgers. Currently, Shawn Green of the Los Angeles Dodgers is the most prominent Jewish baseball player. He is currently number two in salary, behind only Alex Rodriguez of the New York Yankees. All of these athletes were challenged by fans and the media for their decisions not to play baseball on Yom Kippur, the holiest day of the year for Jews and a day when they atone for their sins. In spite of the pressure to play in the World Series or play-offs for their teams, these principled men chose to put their beliefs before their livelihood.

Other notable Jewish athletes include Sid Luckman, quarterback for the Chicago Bears, and Red Auerbach, a coaching legend who led the Boston Celtics when they dominated the National Basketball Association (NBA). Perhaps the most amazing achievement by any Olympic athlete was the performance by Mark Spitz, who won seven gold medals in swimming in the 1972 Olympic Games. Other Olympic champions who were Jewish include Keri Strug, a gymnast who won a gold medal in the 1996 Atlanta Games, and Sarah Hughes, a gold medalist in figure skating at the 2002 Winter Games. Professional tennis players who left their mark were Brad Gilbert and Aaron Krickstein as well as Eddie Dibbs and Harold Solomon, who were dubbed the "bagel twins" (Slater 2003).

The first half of the 20th century was blessed with the golden age of sport, particularly in the 1920s and 1930s. During that time, Jewish men dominated American boxing in virtually every weight class except heavyweight. Jews won more than 29 world boxing titles during that time. The most famous of these boxers were Benny Leonard and Barney Ross, who stood out in the 1930s. It may seem surprising that Jewish men pursued boxing, but they were no different from other poor immigrants in the United States who found hope through boxing. Other ethnic groups who dominated boxing at one time include the Irish and Polish, and recent champion boxers have been Puerto Rican and African American.

Jewish basketball players also flourished in inner-city basketball long before African Americans began to dominate it. During the 1940s, Jewish boys who were the sons of immigrants played street basketball in cities like New York and Chicago and laid the groundwork for the NBA. The first basket scored in the Basketball Association of America, the forerunner of the NBA, was credited to Ossie Schectman of the New York Knickerbockers in 1946.

Along with Schectman, Sonny Hertzberg, David Stern, and Red Auerbach were sources for *The First Basket*, a documentary film that explores the origin of inner-city basketball, the role of basketball in the lives of young immigrants seeking to become Americans, and the gradual decline of Jews in professional basketball through the early 1950s.

Young Jewish men in the 1940s honed their skills from synagogues and Young Men's Hebrew Associations (YMHAs) and throughout the Borscht Belt. Colleges in the cities were stocked with Jewish players, and at one time St. John's University in New York had a team starting five Jews. Other notable Jews who made their mark in basketball were coach Larry Brown, Washinton Wizards owner Abe Poling, and announcers Howard Cosell and Marv Albert (Porter 2004).

After the 1950s, as more Jewish families stabilized their economic base by establishing businesses and working as craftsmen, they encouraged their children, both male and female, to pursue their education to prepare for careers that were longer lasting and more socially acceptable.

Islam

Islam is second only to Christianity in world popularity and has been growing rapidly in the United States as more immigrants arrive from countries where Islam is the primary religion and as more African Americans are drawn to Islam. Muslims believe that every action they take must be to glorify Allah (God). Male Muslims have participated in sports for centuries and have had a history of success particularly in soccer and basketball. Females in Muslim cultures have largely been excluded from sport participation, primarily due to restrictions on their dress.

The Islam religion makes no prohibition against sport participation. Historically, sports and games were part of the expected teachings of parents to children. Muslims have always encouraged youth to run, jump, and engage in basic physical activities. Swimming and using weapons have long been a part of Muslim tradition. However, in conservative Muslim countries such as Saudi Arabia, sports for women have been largely ignored or banned.

In the Muslim culture, a female may not expose any skin in mixed company. The resulting clothing they wear limits or at least makes very uncomfortable sport participation. Recently, the trials of 22-year-old Muslim Andrea Armstrong in playing on the varsity basketball team for the University of South Florida were covered in the *St. Petersburg Times*, a daily newspaper. She sought permission from the NCAA to waive the uniform requirements so that she could play with a *hijab,* or headscarf, long pants, and long-sleeved shirts (along with her uniform) to conform to the tradition of her Muslim sect. Before the NCAA ruled on the matter, she quit the team due to

In the Arena With . . . *Muhammad Ali*

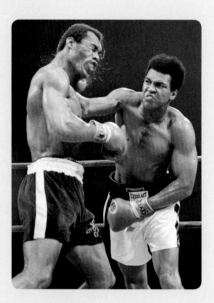

The notoriety of the Black Muslim sect rose immeasurably when Muhammad Ali converted to its religion in the 1960s. Born in 1942 as Cassius Marcellus Clay Jr., Muhammad Ali became the world's greatest boxer and was renowned the world over for his boxing skill, political activism, and religious beliefs. In 1999, he was named Sportsman of the Century by *Sports Illustrated,* and in 1987, *Ring Magazine* called him the greatest heavyweight champion of all time.

Cassius Clay won an Olympic gold medal in Rome in 1960 and went on to compile a professional boxing career record of 56 wins, 37 by knockout, and only five losses. But it was his political activism that captured worldwide attention. He renounced his Olympic gold medal in protest of racism in the United States. He was sparked, among other incidents, by an encounter in his hometown of Louisville, Kentucky, where he was refused service at a local soda fountain. Clay ranted that he had gone to Italy to represent the United States at the Olympics, had won a gold medal, and still could not get service at a local American soda fountain.

Soon after, Cassius Clay was inspired by human rights activist Malcolm X to convert to the Muslim faith and changed his name to Muhammad Ali, which means *beloved of Allah.* At first, Ali was not popular with White fans, and he referred to himself as the Black man's hero. He made outrageous comments to the media, such as using original rhymes to predict in what round he would knock out an opponent. He proclaimed himself "the greatest" and boasted that "I'm young, I'm pretty, I'm fast, and no one can beat me." Before he fought Sonny Liston in 1964 he declared that he would "float like a butterfly, sting like a bee." And he did, becoming the heavyweight champion of the world.

Because of his religious beliefs, Muhammad refused to be drafted into the army during the Vietnam War. Labeled a coward and un-American, Ali was stripped of his championship belt and his license to box and sentenced to five years in prison. He was released on appeal and his conviction was overturned three years later by the U.S. Supreme Court. Eventually Ali's religious views changed, and he began studying the *Qur'an* and eventually converted to Sunni Islam, rejecting the teachings of the Nation of Islam.

In later life, afflicted with Parkinson's disease brought on at least in part by his life of boxing, Ali traveled the world on behalf of human rights. Perhaps one of his most memorable moments was lighting the Olympic Flame at the Atlanta Olympics in 1996. As he mounted the steps with a television audience of 3.5 million collectively holding its breath, Ali's hands trembled with emotion and the effects of Parkinson's (Gale Group 1999; Wikipedia 2005d).

the negative publicity and scorn she was exposed to when her request became public. The university and coach of the team publicly supported her choice and right to apply for the clothing waiver, but some in the community and U.S. public clouded the issue with their racist comments and derisive actions including hate e-mails and negative comments on talk radio. Her case is not unusual for Muslim women who want to play sports in countries around the world and keeping sports open to everyone in the United States may require accommodating women such as her (Auman 2004; Matus 2004a).

Some summer sport camps for Muslim girls such as the one at Westridge School for girls in Los Angeles have sprung up in the United States. In these camps Muslim girls are free to wear what they like

The *hijab,* the traditional head covering of female Muslims, is starting to find a place in the sports world.

and learn to play all types of sports. They decide whether or not to wear a *hijab.* The reason these camps work so well for Muslims is that they exclude men and boys. As long as no men are around, girls can dress normally for sport (Issa 2001).

Muslim women have also made their mark on the Olympic Games. Algerian Hassiba Boulmerka was the gold medalist in the 1,500 meters at the Barcelona Games. But Muslim women have been few and far between due to the restrictive dress code of their religion. It is estimated that more than 500 million Muslim women around the world are essentially banned from sport participation. People attempting to change the culture and practices in conservative Islamic countries have been careful, realizing that by winning a few battles for women's

rights, they may lose the larger war. Still, change may come slowly as courageous women and men within Muslim cultures agree to allow more choices for women in all areas of society.

USE OF RELIGION BY ATHLETES

Now that we've examined the major religions that influence sport in North America, we can take a closer look at how athletes balance religion and sport. Athletes in competitive sports use religion in many ways:

- To justify their commitment to high-performance competitive sport
- To reduce pressure and uncertainty
- To enhance bonds with teammates
- To guide moral decisions

Judeo–Christian teachings in recent centuries have emphasized the obligation of individuals to fully develop their talent to "glorify God." Discipline, sacrifice, intense training, and commitment to high performance are religious principles that apply well to sport competition. Personal achievement is something to be valued and encouraged, and the intense dedication to winning is honorable and pleasing to God. It is not dissimilar to the belief that in a capitalistic society, individual achievement is a mark of success and hard work and looked upon favorably by God.

Athletes use their religious beliefs to reduce the pressure they feel in competition. Some adopt the point of view that the outcome is in God's hands and so they are free to relax and focus on their own execution. Others pray before or during a contest to ask for divine guidance during play. Some also might ask specifically for a favorable outcome (Eitzen and Sage 2002). Athletes use religious rituals such as touching a crucifix or making the sign of the cross before attempting a penalty kick in soccer. Football players sometimes point to the sky to acknowledge their gratitude to God when they score a touchdown or kneel in humble appreciation of the event.

Prayer is a powerful practice in which believers communicate with their god. The three major religions, Christianity, Judaism, and Islam, endorse prayer as a central practice of their faith. In recent years, sport psychologists have explored the implications of working with athletes who believe in prayer. Athletes who do believe in prayer should be encouraged to use prayer to help deal with the

Athletes often use signs of faith to help them perform better at their sport.

pressure, uncertainty, and depression that can arise from competitive sports. There is evidence that sport psychologists would be wise to recommend the use of prayer to those who are comfortable with it. Traditionally, prayer has been used to confess sins, express adoration, petition for needs, intercede for others, and offer thanksgiving. In sport, athletes tend to use prayer for three purposes (Watson and Czech 2005):

- To cope with uncertainty and anxiety
- To put life and sport into a proper perspective
- To provide meaning to sport participation

Many athletes use religious beliefs to strengthen their bonds with their teammates. When people share their personal beliefs and discuss weighty matters like the meaning of life, they take certain risks with each other and often develop strong trust and loyalty. Members of a team who share common religious beliefs may attend study groups and religious services together, pray together, and together support youth organizations or charities

that have religious affiliations. Each of these activities enhances their relationship with each other, and they hold one another accountable for actions both off and on the field.

All athletes face moral decisions in life and encounter many of these in sports. When young, people are taught to follow the rules and often do so unquestionably. But as they grow, they examine the meaning behind moral decisions, assess what is generally acceptable in society, and often use religious teachings as their guide. Questions about cheating, breaking the law, abusing drugs, intentionally harming an opponent, or behaving after winning or losing can all be guided by religious teachings. Many athletes use the popular phrase "What would Jesus do?" for guidance in everyday decisions made on and off the athletic field.

A popular religious justification for striving so hard to win is that fame through sport performance enlarges an athlete's sphere of influence. Athletes then have the opportunity to share their religious beliefs and influence people to follow their religious path. Thus, winning glorifies God and spreads His message. Athletes who are more famous automatically command a large audience who is more than impressed when listening to how the athletes live their life. Athletes who become role models can powerfully influence the behavior of young athletes as they struggle with growing up and making decisions in sport and life.

Athletes who come from a fundamental or evangelical religious orientation use the term *witness for Christ* to describe one of their primary responsibilities as a born-again Christian. They do not hesitate to share the specifics of their personal commitment to Christ, what that commitment means in their life, and how important that commitment should be in others' lives. They can be powerful recruiters for Christian organizations, schools, and churches where youth can join with others committed to following their faith.

Many athletes do much more than use words to promote their beliefs. Professional athletes who want to give back to their sport, community, or society often donate money to worthwhile causes or establish a charity in their name. Some choose charities that helped them or a loved one in a time of trouble. Others choose charities that help impoverished neighborhoods where they grew up. Of course, charitable organizations that promote certain religious beliefs are attractive to athletes who subscribe to the principles of that organization.

Some athletes are also generous with their time, especially in the off-season. They talk to fans, sign autographs, and make personal appearances to promote causes they believe in, often for no remuneration. Summer camps staged by Christian organizations such as the Fellowship of Christian Athletes (FCA) are natural opportunities to contribute to the overall development of young athletes and share their faith. Specialized sport camps can also teach skills and strategy, but often the most enduring lessons come from famous athletes sharing their beliefs with aspiring youngsters.

Celebrity athletes may use their religious beliefs to guide their choices of commercial products to endorse. Many religiously conservative athletes are uncomfortable endorsing products such as beer or balk at appearing in a commercial that includes sexual innuendo or is offensive to ethnic groups, races, or gender.

USE OF RELIGION BY COACHES, ORGANIZATIONS, AND OWNERS

Some athletic coaches use religion as social construct to unify their team. As pointed out in the previous section, when athletes share a belief system it pulls the team together and the athletes will do anything to avoid letting down their teammates. Like soldiers in warfare who count on each other for support, athletes have to know they can count on each other as they enter the athletic arena for battle.

Over the years, some coaches have invited informal team chaplains to lead their team in prayer before and after games. Typically, the chaplains pray for God's blessing on the contest by preventing serious injuries and allowing athletes to perform at the high level that justifies their athletic talents. These prayers emotionally affect team members who are religious and consider prayer an important part of their life. These athletes do not find prayer unusual since they pray regularly in private, in church, and in group Bible studies. More than likely they also prayed more than once as a former student, asking God to help them perform well on their exams.

Athletes are much more likely to use prayer in sport if they also use prayer in their daily lives. Coaches at private church-sponsored schools are also much more likely to use prayer before games than are coaches at public schools. Students enrolling at a secondary school or college that is church related also expect prayer to be part of the school culture, whereas students in public school do not.

Coaches also know that young athletes are susceptible to temptations in their lives. Some coaches establish a priority for their athletes that places God first, family second, academics third, and commitment to teammates fourth. This guideline helps the coach influence the decisions of young athletes to keep them out of trouble. Romantic attachments and partying fall further down the priority list, and their lower priority reduces the possibilities for poor choices.

Most coaches consider themselves as role models and molders of talent in the persons they coach. They believe that if their athletes adopt a system of values centered on spirituality, work ethic, respect for family, and academic learning, they will have performed a terrific service for the young athletes. For many coaches, teaching sport skills and strategies is their least important role.

Organizers of professional sports leagues have also encouraged prayer breakfasts and Bible studies between opponents in the off-season or before or after games. The sight of a couple of dozen NFL players kneeling in prayer on the field after a football game during which they tried to annihilate each other is at once thrilling and confusing. The players point out that in the larger game of life they are all brothers striving to do God's will and that they show respect for God, the game, and their opponents by praying together.

Does a strong faith make a better athlete? Some coaches think it does.

Organizers of the Olympic Games have also provided opportunities for athletes to gather together to share their beliefs and prepare for the competition. Young men and women from a variety of backgrounds and sports find that they share a common belief in spirituality and realize that they face similar temptations, trials, and uncertainties. While not endorsed by the Olympic organizers themselves, many religious organizations capitalize on the Games by hosting events such as prayer breakfasts featuring well-known speakers and former athletes, Bible studies, and prayer groups to interested athletes, spectators, and local citizens.

An example of religious outreach at the Olympic Games is Quest Australia More than Gold, a cooperative effort of denominational and parachurch ministries. Leading up to the 2000 Games in Sydney, their mission was to capitalize on the athletic spectacle to "reach and teach people about Jesus Christ" during the Olympic and Paralympic Games. They conducted youth sport clinics, staged 10 major evangelistic events during the Games, sponsored one citywide festival of believers, trained a mission team, and presented the gospel through creative arts at 500 performances around Sydney (Quest 2006).

Religious publications such as *Christianity Today* notified their readers of Christian athletes competing in the Games and offered these athletes' life stories or Christian testimonies. They encouraged readers support these athletes, such as basketball player Ruth Riley or triathlete Hunter Kemper, in the Sydney Games (Christianity Today 2000).

Many athletic contests begin with a ceremony to mark the significance of the occasion. In the United States, the two most common inclusions to the opening ceremony are the national anthem and an invocation. In recent years, praying at public events sponsored by schools has been questioned in its fairness to people who do not practice Christianity. Some who offer the prayers speak to the wide range of beliefs of the audience while others offend some listeners with entreaties to "Jesus Christ, Our Savior" or similar language.

In June of 2000 the U.S. Supreme Court ruled that public schools cannot constitutionally organize school prayers at regular sporting events. At the same time, they did reaffirm the right of players or fans to pray by themselves at such events and for students to pray together on their own accord. Separation of church and state only prohibits school officials from organizing prayer at regular school functions. For many Americans, this is a departure from a long-standing tradition of public prayer offered at official public functions of all kinds, including those of sports events (*Santa Fe Independent School District vs. Doe,* U.S. Supreme Court, 2000).Organizers of Minor League and some Major League Baseball teams, particularly of those located in the Bible Belt, use Faith Nights to attract spectators to their games. Local churches encourage their members to attend the games, which may feature Christian singers, players who share their testimonies, and faith trivia quizzes for prizes. Sport promoters are holding dozens of Faith Nights to attract record attendance. Faith Nights have been a marketing success for Minor League Baseball teams struggling to entice fans. Game attendance is also promoted by religious organizations such as Athletes in Action and the Fellowship of Christian Athletes and is heartily endorsed by parents and community leaders. To avoid offending spectators who do not care to participate in Faith Nights, the religious events are scheduled before the game perhaps in the parking lot. Cities involved include Hagerstown, MD; Johnson City, TN; Columbus, GA; Birmingham, AL; Nashville, TN; Mobile, AL; Tulsa, OK; and Portland, OR. Who would have thought that giving away bobble-head dolls of Moses, Noah, and Samson could cause such a stir by attracting fans to baseball games (Cherner 2005)?

USING SPORT TO PROMOTE RELIGION

Numerous Christian organizations have flourished in the United States over the past 50 years by combining religious teaching and sports. Perhaps the oldest and largest of these organizations that intertwine religion and sport is the FCA, established in 1954. It is still the largest interdenominational, school-based Christian sport organization in America. From its modest beginnings when founded by Don McClanen, Paul Benedum, Branch Rickey, and other Pittsburgh businessmen, it has grown to a nationwide organization of more than 6,598 huddles and more than 600 employees, most of whom are assigned to local communities. FCA summer camp attendance exceeds 15,000 annually.

The FCA was originally aimed at the major sports, and among the charter members were football great Otto Graham and baseball pitcher Carl Erskine. The FCA publishes a monthly magazine, *The Christian Athlete,* and it offers study guides, videos, and materials for Bible study and huddle meetings. They even have commercial sponsors,

In the Arena With . . . *Bob Richards*

Known as the *vaulting vicar* during his competitive days, Bob Richards was born in Champaign, Illinois, in 1926 and was an extraordinary athlete who made three Olympic Games in two events. He competed in the pole vault in 1948 and 1952 and added the decathlon in 1956. Richards is the only two-time winner in the pole vault, winning the gold medal in both 1952 and 1956. He was the second man to vault 15 feet (4.8 meters), and he made that vault without the aid of the now common fiberglass pole. He captured 20 national Amateur Athletic Union (AAU) titles while in college, 17 of which were in the pole vault. He was the Olympic ideal and the first athlete to have his face pictured on the front of a Wheaties box. His positive, energetic voice and wide smile made him the all-American Jack Armstrong.

After retiring from professional athletics, Richards became an ordained minister, and as Rev. Bob Richards, he gave speeches to youth, corporate leaders, and sport fans. His talks were motivational and carried a strong message of hope through effort and self-discipline (Wikipedia 2005a).

who currently include Chick-fil-A, Schutt Sports, and Krystal.

The mission of FCA (2006) is: "To present to athletes and coaches and all whom they influence the challenge and adventure of receiving Jesus Christ as Savior and Lord, serving Him in their relationships and in the fellowship of the church."

The basic organizational unit of FCA is the local huddle, which can be established at a high school, at a college, or in a community. Team members meet regularly in the huddle to study the Bible, follow devotional guides, or discuss their issues of Christian faith or sports. Most often, the huddle advisers are coaches who assist student leaders. Local huddles distribute opportunities through FCA such as the widely held summer camps. At the camps, famous athletes dedicate their time to teach sport skills, talk about their faith, and encourage young athletes to follow the precepts of FCA: integrity, serving, teamwork, and excellence.

Tom Landry, famous coach of the Dallas Cowboys, and one of his quarterbacks, Roger Staubach, were both key figures in the FCA and other organizations promoting sport and religion. They carried impeccable sport credentials as "winners" and used that platform to testify of the importance

of their faith in the "game of life." The personal dedication of these men and hundreds of others throughout the years has influenced hundreds of thousands of young people. No young person can help but be impressed by a famous athlete who they look upon as a hero.

Another Christian sport organization is Athletes in Action (AIA), a branch of Campus Crusade for Christ. AIA is a group of former college athletes who travel the country playing exhibition games against amateur teams including collegiate teams, especially early in the season. AIA has secured approval from the NCAA to compete against NCAA members, and typically they take advantage of the halftime and postgame to talk about their faith.

Sport missionaries like those from Athletes in Action generally try to convince young people to "follow the right path." They typically present a fundamental view of religion and rarely speak out on social issues such as discrimination against women or minorities, drug abuse, cheating, and violence in sport. They've been labeled as *jocks for Jesus* or as the *God squad* and tend to present God as desiring to become the master coach of the lives of all people who will let Him. Positive stories about good things that happen to Christian athletes, finding faith, and a higher reward tend to be their themes no matter the audience (Deford 1976).

There is also the Pro Athletes Outreach (POA) that sends professional athletes to meetings, camps, and events held by other organizations. At the events, pro athletes talk about sports and their faith and what faith means to everyday life.

Once limited to White, middle-class boys, these organizations have gradually included girls and some racial minorities. They tend to thrive in working-class communities among athletes playing traditional team sports. Perhaps not surprisingly, most of these religious sport organizations are strongest in the Bible Belt of the United States.

A final organization of note is the National Christian College Athletic Association (NCCAA), a national group that was founded in 1968 and now includes more than 100 colleges. It represents more than 13,000 collegiate athletes and 700 collegiate coaches and sponsors championships in 20 sports. The NCCAA divides itself into two divisions, with Division I encompassing liberal arts colleges and Division II comprising Bible colleges. Their athletic programs are dedicated to students and serve a larger purpose than simply winning athletic contests. Christian teachings are part of the total learning experience on their campuses and throughout their sport programs.

USING SPORT TO PROMOTE CHRISTIAN COLLEGES AND SECONDARY SCHOOLS

Since many colleges were founded by religious organizations, it is not surprising that some use sport to promote their school. Perhaps the most well-known university in America is Notre Dame, a Roman Catholic university famous for the exploits of its football team. Notre Dame has such a large fan base throughout the United States that it negotiates multimillion-dollar agreements for the rights to televise its football games on its own rather than through a league as most colleges do. Kids grow up knowing Notre Dame is the place to go for football, and the university has been fortunate to parlay their reputation into both sport and academic excellence, with a high graduation rate for its athletes. The Notre Dame allure was burnished during the years of Knute Rockne, a football coaching legend during the 1920s. Rockne stood

The success of Notre Dame football during the 1920s and 1930s helped dispel anti-Catholicism in the United States. What other sports or successful teams have helped to lessen religious discrimination?

Pop Culture: Sunday Morning Football or Church?

From the Institute for Global Ethics (Kidder 2002) comes this dilemma. In 2002, England was playing their opening game in the World Cup. The venue was South Korea and with time differences, the game would be televised at 10:30 Sunday morning in England. For fans who didn't attend church, there was no problem. But for those who did, the clergy felt compelled to advise. Some preached sermons with titles like "Make Jesus the Center Forward of Your Life." Others agreed to have a television nearby and to signal when England scored a goal.

The question was, should churches change their schedules to accommodate their members who wanted to attend church but also wanted to watch the game?

The Archbishop of Canterbury, head of the Church of England, declared that churches who wished were free to do so. "Worship comes first, of course," said the Archbishop, "but the World Cup comes round only every four years, so we can be flexible."

This may seem frivolous, but it is a clear case of principle and popularity. While many traditionalists would argue that Sunday morning worship should remain sacrosanct, others would bend to the popular will. After all, in the final analysis the churchgoers will have to make up their own minds about priorities.

Maybe TiVo is the answer?

up staunchly to the anti-Catholicism that prevailed in the United States at the time and to criticism from the Ku Klux Klan. In fact, the "more Rockne was exposed to prejudice around him, the more he was attracted to the religiosity around him at Notre Dame" (Robinson 1999).

Many other private schools have used sports to gain publicity, swell their pool of applicants, and attract an academically better-qualified student body. Smaller schools typically put their money into basketball since basketball is less expensive than football. Many small Catholic schools like St. Joseph's, LaSalle, and Immaculata (Philadelphia), St. John's (New York), Marquette (Milwaukee), Gonzaga (Spokane), Loyola (Chicago), and many others are well known in the basketball world. More recently, Oral Roberts University at Tulsa, Oklahoma, and Liberty University at Virginia have used sport promotion to get their schools early notice. Founded by Oral Roberts and Jerry Falwell, respectively, these schools find no conflict between their Christian values and winning games. In fact, winning draws more attention and allows them to spread the word of God.

Brigham Young University (BYU), founded by the Church of Jesus Christ of Latter-Day Saints (Mormons), also intertwines religion and sport, as expressed by the statement of purpose of their athletic department to "develop students academically, athletically, and spiritually." Over the past 20 years, BYU has consistently ranked in the top 25

nationally for the Director's Cup, which takes into account the overall performance of all varsity sports (Brigham Young University Athletics 2006). (Note: The Director's Cup is sponsored by the United States Sports Academy as a result of a joint effort by the National Association of Collegiate Athletic Directors and *USA Today*.)

Many private secondary schools founded as Christian schools have dedicated themselves to excellence in sport to help attract students. Since their funding relies on donations and private tuition payments, they need to show value for the money not only in academics but in all programs. They realize that top performance in sports attracts fans, builds school cohesion, and encourages boosters and donors. It is no accident that many top professional athletes have graduated from these schools over the years. Top high school athletes are recruited and often offered scholarships based on need or academic performance to gain their contribution on the field or in the gym.

Among the most well-known Catholic secondary schools are Christ the King in Queens, New York, and St. Anthony's in Newark, New Jersey. These schools have been perennial basketball powers. Another famed basketball team under the guidance of Coach Morgan Wooten is that of DeMatha in Hyattsville, Maryland, just outside Washington, DC. *Sports Illustrated* ranked DeMatha as number two out 38,000 high schools nationwide for excellence in total sport programs over the past 10 years (Huff 2005; Menez and Woo 2005).

The aggressiveness in some sports seems to conflict with the tenets of peace taught by most religions. Can it be justified?

CONFLICT BETWEEN SPORT AND RELIGION

Common conflicts seem to arise between religious beliefs and sports. For example, how is it an act of love for fellow man to put a bone-crushing tackle on an opponent, throw at the batter's head, slide hard into second base to break up a double play, or humiliate an undermanned opponent by running up the score? These actions are not unusual in most sport settings. Athletes with well-defined religious values often draw the line at certain behaviors they deem inappropriate. However, they might overlook the actions of coaches or teammates they have no control over. Their attitude is that they are only responsible for their behavior and for living according to their principles.

Stevenson (1997) researched the methods Christian athletes in high-performance sports use to reconcile the apparent contradictions between their religious beliefs and the demands of their sport. As mentioned, some declare their sport participation to be for "the glory of God" and reason that suc-

cess in sport gives them influence for spreading their Christian beliefs. According to Coakley (2004), some religious athletes also may reconcile conflict by refocusing on the ascetic aspects of sport, such as discipline and self-denial. These athletes believe that ascetic devotion morally justifies their sport experience.

Other athletes simply put their spiritual beliefs aside while playing sports. They follow the customs of their sport on the field and reengage in their spiritual beliefs off the field. While this approach is common, it can certainly provoke criticism if an athlete's on-field behavior does not square with off-field pronouncements of spiritual beliefs. While some actions in sports may be legal, they are not ethical. Usually, these actions are difficult to evaluate as they involve intent, which is hard to determine. For example, did the defensive end maliciously slam into the opposing quarterback with the preexisting injury? Or was slamming into the quarterback a coincidence during a routine pass rush? In sports like professional boxing, the intent is more straightforward, as the object is to win the fight by punching the opponent into submission.

Although Stevenson's (1997) study involved only 31 athletes who were also members of Athletes in Action, a third of these athletes admitted to reaching a crisis during their athletic careers in trying to reconcile the demands of their sport with their religious beliefs. Many found the question of the real value of sport difficult to answer. Even when winning trophies and recognition, they felt they were missing something more important in life. Of the 31 athletes, three eventually withdrew from elite sport, citing their inability to resolve the conflicts between the sport culture and their Christian beliefs.

These moral dilemmas are not unique to the sports world. People have fought more wars over religious differences than over any other cause. Consider the religious strife that's occurred for generations in Ireland or in the Middle East. Religions have always allowed for war against infidels. The religious justification for violence and inhuman treatment toward enemies has been a source of curiosity and confusion for people throughout the ages.

CHAPTER SUMMARY

Religion and sport have historically interacted in both negative and positive ways. Early religious festivals beginning with the ancient Greeks featured athletic contests. Over time, many religions began considering sport and games as mundane diversions that detracted people from spiritual development.

In the last 100 years, religion and sport have forged a mutually beneficial link, with each promoting the other. Churches have used athletes and sport to attract people, particularly youth, to their facilities and to recruit believers into their church family. Sports have used religion to justify sport competition as a worthy pursuit and to control the conduct of athletes. Coaches have promoted prayer to enhance performance and foster team togetherness. They have also reinforced religious values to encourage their athletes to work hard, show good teamwork, and commit to team goals.

Although Christianity, particularly Protestantism, has been the dominant religion in the United States,

other religions such as Judaism and Islam have had an impact on the sporting world, too. In some cases, religious beliefs have interfered with an athlete's sport participation when customs or expectations of the two institutions clashed.

Various organizations have developed over the years, spurred by the link between sport and religion. The Young Men's Christian Association and Young Women's Christian Association have built sport facilities across America and have organized thousands of sport programs for all ages. The Fellowship of Christian Athletes has grown steadily over the last 25 years and now boasts more than 6,000 organized huddles and employs a national staff of more than 600.

Christian secondary schools and colleges have also used sport to gain positive publicity and attract students and donors. They make no apologies for embracing the competitive ethic of striving for excellence. Liberty University and Oral Roberts University are two examples of universities following the path first trod by Notre Dame of football fame and Roman Catholic universities with a tradition of excellence in basketball. Secondary schools such as DeMatha, Christ the King, and St. Anthony's have capitalized on outstanding athletic teams to publicize their schools.

Athletes may use religion by asking for God's help in their performance, focusing on the competition through pregame prayer, and justifying their dedication to excellence. Many prominent athletes have also used their success in sports as a platform to share their religious beliefs and influence young athletes to stay on the "right path."

Religion has helped Americans justify their preoccupation with sport and has joined in that preoccupation, urging the pursuit of excellence through sport and convincing athletes that their religious beliefs should accompany them to the playing field. By promoting sport and using famous athletes to deliver their message, religious leaders are able to gain the attention of young men and women. Conversely, by applying the tenets of a worthy spiritual life to sport, participants can feel a powerful endorsement for what otherwise may seem a self-indulgent pastime.

16
CHAPTER

Politics
and Sport

Student Outcomes

After reading this chapter, you will know the following:

- How government and sport interact internationally, nationally, and locally
- How government may interact with sport to protect the rights of all citizens
- How governments use sport to promote identity and unity among citizens
- How governments use sport to promote social values
- How sport creates nationalistic feelings that reinforce the governmental policies
- How political groups within sport organizations can direct the development and delivery of sport to consumes
- Why sport personalities, athletes, and coaches may lean toward a conservative political philosophy

Politics is the art and science of government, of influencing governmental policy, or of holding control over a government. While there are some negative connotations of the term *politics,* politics is clearly a dominant component of any culture of people. This chapter examines the interrelationship between politics and sport from four primary perspectives.

The first perspective looks at how government uses sport to improve the quality of life for its citizens and regulates sport to protect the rights of its citizens. Currently in the United States, the government also regulates the conduct of sports, particularly when public monies and land are involved. The legislative and judicial branches also make decisions regarding antitrust issues in sport, levy taxes on the public to finance some aspects of sport, and referee the conflict among sport performers, owners, unions, and organizations.

A related area of interest is how communities build their identities through local professional sport teams, community teams, and even local university or high school teams. Political leaders may use sport to unify their citizens around a common interest such as attracting a professional franchise to their city. Rooting for the home team often links city residents who might otherwise feel isolated from government or fellow citizens. Governments also use sport to facilitate social integration. They may use sport to reduce juvenile delinquency, improve academic performance through after-school programs combining academics and sports, or to encourage healthy competition between disparate ethnic or racial groups.

The second perspective examines how sport can reinforce the prevailing political structure and status quo. Political leaders often use sport to promote self-interests or support for the government they lead. Generally, sport organizations, leaders, coaches, and athletes support the establishment that serves them well.

The third perspective focuses on how nations sponsor international teams in world sporting events to promote patriotic pride. National teams that successfully compete against other nations in the Olympic Games inspire a sense of identity and pride in their fellow citizens. As mentioned before, a by-product of international competition is using success in sport to justify a particular nation's government and way of life. International sport events are also used to advance political aims when certain nations boycott events or are restricted from participating by other countries that are offended by their social practices. Sport is also a way of maintaining good relationships or building understanding among nations.

The fourth perspective explores the politics of sport institutions. Within each sport, different interests struggle over who will set the policies and procedures and who will benefit from decisions—the team owners, athletes, or spectators. As with all organizations, the people who organize and govern particular sports or leagues develop political structures within their group. People in the political structure campaign to influence policy decisions, financial commitments, and competition rules. Leaders in sport organizations often must become consummate politicians in order to convince their constituency to follow their vision for the success of the sport and its organization.

GOVERNMENT IN PHYSICAL ACTIVITY AND HEALTH

Governments sometimes take on responsibility of the health and welfare of their citizens. In the United States a division of the federal Department of Health and Human Services, the Centers for Disease Control and Prevention (CDC) at Atlanta, Georgia, disseminates nationwide the latest information linking physical activity to better health. In its role of preventing and controlling disease, the CDC makes strong recommendations for every citizen to participate in physical activity: "Every citizen can benefit by engaging in moderate intensity physical activity for 30 minutes a day at least 5 days per week" (Center for Disease Control and Prevention 2006).

The official position of the U.S. government is that regular physical activity contributes to health, promotes well-being, and reduces the costs of medical care. It is in everyone's interest to use healthy activity as a means of ensuring a higher quality of life, increasing longevity, and reducing the expense and ravages of disease.

Research demonstrating the value of exercise for slowing the aging process has been a popular topic for the CDC, particularly since the U.S. population is tending toward increased longevity. Increasing longevity significant affects the U.S. government since it portends increased costs for health care and a greater need for long-term care facilities and it threatens the solvency of the social security system and Medicare.

In the 1950s, physical testing of military recruits made it clear that American youth were woefully lacking in physical fitness. Then, in a test of minimum muscular fitness developed by Hans Kraus and Sonya Weber, 56.6% of American schoolchildren failed one or more of the six tests. That percentage was compared to a failure rate of only 8.2% among schoolchildren in Austria, Italy, and Switzerland. The results became big news and President Dwight D. Eisenhower eventually founded the President's

Council on Youth Fitness, headed by Vice President Richard Nixon. The result was a series of publicity releases touting the virtues of physical fitness (Rice, Hutchinson, and Lee 1958).

In 1961, President John F. Kennedy established the President's Council on Physical Fitness and Sports to promote physical fitness and sport participation among Americans. The first recommendation from the President's Council was that all schools should provide daily a minimum of 15 minutes of vigorous exercise. At that time, 75% of the America's schools had no daily class for physical education. Perhaps the most enduring contribution of the President's Council has been to develop standards of fitness for schoolchildren. These standards have been in place in schools for more than 50 years (Hackensmith 1966; Weber 1956).

The President's Council on Physical Fitness and Sports has numbered among its leaders Bud Wilkinson, a famous football coach, and Arnold Schwarzenegger, a bodybuilder and movie star who later became governor of California. Although the organization has helped raise public consciousness toward physical fitness, its stature and funding have limited its impact to less than what its proponents

In the 1950s, more than half of American schoolchildren failed muscular fitness tests. Are today's schoolchildren faring any better?

Many school districts have their students complete the President's Challenge Physical Fitness Test, which tracks a student's fitness level in five exercises: the curl-up or partial curl-up, the shuttle run, the endurance run or walk, the pull-up or right-angle push-up, and the V-sit or sit-and-reach test.

desired. Perhaps the most effective policy of the council has been to award citations to schoolchildren who meet its standards in testing administered through the public schools.

GOVERNMENT IN SPORT

Many governments around the world, particularly those that have established a Ministry of Sport, aggressively promote sport participation, financially support high-performance athletes who represent their country in international competition, and help fund public athletic facilities. No such agency exists in the United States, and while some people would welcome the governmental support, most sport advocates believe American society is better off by keeping government red tape, endless discussion, and partisan bickering out of the sports world. Some citizens might even question the Constitutional right of the U.S. government to interfere in sport.

As mentioned in chapter 9, the U.S. Congress designated the United States Olympic Committee (USOC) to develop and conduct amateur sport and to train and support Olympic and Paralympic athletes. Although the government does not directly fund the USOC, it did donate a closed military base to provide the site for the USOC Headquarters and Training

Center. The USOC raises its own funds to conduct its business. Although the U.S. Congress does not normally interfere with the USOC, in 2003 it stepped in when the USOC met with scandal, breach of ethics, and internal strife. The resulting changes began to take effect in 2005 and the hopes are that the USOC will steadily progress in bringing itself under order (see chapter 9).

Safeguarding the Public

The U.S. government helps provide safety for its citizens. Sports that are dangerous or involve cruelty to animals are outlawed or discouraged. Bullfighting, cockfighting, and other so-called sports that abuse animals are punishable by fines or imprisonment. Sports that are inherently dangerous to participants, such as boxing, bungee jumping, skydiving, and auto racing, are carefully monitored and controlled by government regulations.

The U.S. government also regulates sports that may be reasonably safe within a controlled environment. Activities such as boating, fishing, hunting, using firearms, water sports, and bicycling have certain rules, require training for instructors and participants, and require certain protective equipment. The government also regulates outdoor activities that may affect the natural environment or endanger species. For example, the U.S. government regulates where, when, and how fishing can be done.

The U.S. government also strives to protect the public in sports when unruly fan behavior is a risk or when terrorist attack threatens the staging of large events. For many Americans in my generation, the first wake-up call to terrorism in sport came in 1972 when a Palestinian terrorist group took Israeli athletes hostage during the Summer Olympics in Munich, Germany. After a daylong standoff and a failed rescue attempt, 11 Israeli athletes, 1 German police officer, and 5 of the 8 kidnappers were killed by police (Wikipedia 2006b). The motion picture *Munich* recounts the story of a secret Israeli squad assigned to track down and kill the Palestinians who planned the massacre (Munich 2005).

Expert's View: Integrity in Professional Sports Act

Jim Bunning, a senator from Kentucky, is the primary sponsor of a proposed bill, the Integrity in Professional Sports Act, that would require professional sports leagues to adopt and enforce stringent policies on the use of performance-enhancing substances by players (GovTrack 2006). Major League Baseball would be directly affected by this bill, as it would require MLB and the players' union to adopt a policy that will deter players from using anabolic steroids and other similar performance enhancers.

Senator Bunning has a special interest in restoring integrity to the game of baseball; he is a former Major League Baseball pitcher and member of baseball's Hall of Fame. His career with the Detroit Tigers was exceptional, and following his retirement from baseball he entered the field of politics. Bunning is concerned about the effect professional athletes' behavior has on children who look up to and admire athletes. In his view, it has been disheartening to see other sports and the Olympic Games needing to adopt tough drug-testing policies in order to force athletes to play by the rules, with such penalties for offending athletes as long suspensions or even lifetime bans from competition (Library of Congress 2005; McCain 2004).

Interestingly, shortly after the approval of the Integrity in Professional Sports Act by both the U.S. House and U.S. Senate separately, in November of 2005 Major League Baseball did adopt much tougher policies on drug use along with severe penalties for offending players (Associated Press 2006a). It certainly appears that the threats of enforcement from politicians spurred MLB into action before the U.S. Congress stepped in. Jim Bunning is proud to have performed a service to the game that he loves.

Nearly 25 years later, at the Atlanta Olympics, a bomb went off in the Olympic Park and killed two people while injuring over 100 others. Panic set in, events were suspended, and spectators feared for their safety. But the Games went on, and five years later the main suspect, Eric Robert Rudolph, was found hiding in the mountains of North Carolina (Wikipedia 2006a).

The Olympics has always been a potential target for those with a political axe to grind and as a result, more than $600 million U.S. were spent on security for the Athens Games in 2004. More than 15,000 law enforcement personnel were employed to guard against attacks along with more than 8,666 supplemental military officials (Gebicke 1996). Terrorism really hit home in America when terrorists attacked New York City and Washington, DC, on September 11, 2001. In every sporting event since that time, security plans have been a major priority. College football stadiums filled with 100,000 fans on an autumn Saturday could be a prime target for terrorists. The Super Bowl has not only a live audience but also a worldwide television audience that could potentially witness an attack. Aircraft are routinely suspended from flying within miles of the stadiums on game days. Bomb searches, undercover police, alarm systems, and video surveillance have become commonplace. Everyone who enters the event facility may be searched, limits on what people may carry into the facility have become strict, and people who appear suspicious are quickly moved to the side for further inspection. The costs for these precautions have driven insurance premiums to more than $1 million U.S. a year for a typical NFL stadium. Security precautions and insurance protection have added significantly to the expenses of sport promoters, who have passed along those increases to fans.

Protecting the Rights of Citizens

The government can play a key role in protecting the rights of its citizens in sport. As mentioned in chapter 12, in 1972 the U.S. Congress passed Title IX, which declared that women and girls should have equal access to sport. Organizations that refused to meet the standards were denied federal funds of any type. In 1990 U.S. President George H.W. Bush signed the Americans with Disabilities Act (ADA), which protected the rights of athletes with physical or mental disabilities (see chapter 14). Public facilities, including sport facilities, now meet certain standards to accommodate people with physical disabilities, and the USOC provides sport competition and training for athletes with physical disabilities. Now, the Paralympics immediately follow the Olympic

The U.S. government regulates some sports to help protect both people and the environment.

Games in the same venue with full support of the International Olympic Committee and most national governing bodies.

Civil rights acts decreed that discrimination against persons of various racial, ethnic, and class preferences is illegal by governments who support or regulate access to sport programs. Although private clubs continue to have some leeway in determining their membership, any public facility or program must provide equal access for all persons. National governing bodies for specific sports are expected to develop policies that ensure equal access to all athletes. People who take issue with the conduct of any organization or facility can seek redress in a court of law and protection from discrimination based on race, creed, national origin, religious preference, or sexual orientation (see chapters 11-15).

Other U.S. laws protect the rights of children through child labor laws and protect the rights of athletes to play as professionals and to represent a specific country. Some laws regulate performance-enhancing drugs in sport. In 2005 the U.S. Congress held hearings on drug use in MLB and threatened to toughen the rules unless MLB significantly changed its policies on drug testing and penalties for infractions. Both the league and the players union quickly realized that tougher drug enforcement was necessary and approved much more stringent policies.

Protecting the Financial Interests of the Public

Sports are a huge economic engine in the United States and the money wrapped up in sport affects every citizen either directly or indirectly. In the past the U.S. government sometimes stepped in to direct and control the expansion of sports as they grew in power and significance. For example, in cities where proposals were advanced to use public monies to build stadiums or arenas that would benefit the owners of professional franchises, governments have stymied the proposals or put them to a public vote.

Historically, laws have been passed exempting professional sports leagues from antitrust laws (see chapter 4). MLB, the NFL, and the NBA have a virtual monopoly on their sports and wield tremendous influence over their athletes, ticket prices, television rights, and the sharing of revenue between teams and cities. The point to be taken here is that when government decides what is in the public interest, those who have economic power and influence are more likely to affect government decisions than those who have little power or influence. Also, owners of professional sport franchises are often able to further their business interests by claiming that their success will benefit the community and other local businesses such as hotels and restaurants.

Local governments often give huge tax incentives to owners of professional franchises in order to convince them to locate or keep their franchise in a certain city. When an owner loses money due to mismanagement, excessive player contracts, or changes in the economy, he may ask the city for a better tax deal or threaten to leave town for a more attractive financial package. For example, the Oakland Raiders football team relocated to Los Angeles in 1982 only to move back to Oakland in 1995 when it could not agree on a deal for a new stadium in Los Angeles. Oakland offered the team some $63 million U.S. in up-front incentives, loans, and other benefits to return (CNN Sports Illustrated 2001).

GOVERNMENT IN PROMOTING IDENTITY AND UNITY AMONG CITIZENS

Local, city, and state governments have long used sports to promote pride, identity, and unity among their citizens. By attracting a professional franchise, city leaders expect to capitalize on their financial investment by providing entertainment to residents and creating a bond among people of all backgrounds forged by a common interest in the home team.

On a given Monday morning during football season, the performance of the local professional team is a hot news item. Strangers use the fortunes of their local team to break the ice in conversations with others. If the team performs beyond expectation, fans feel a little bit prouder to be a part of their city and just a bit better about life. In contrast, an entire populace can be cast into gloom due to a seemingly unimportant detail such as a flubbed field goal in the waning seconds of play.

Even very large metropolises such as New York, Chicago, and Los Angeles rally round their home team. In strikingly diverse race and ethnic groups, the city residents and suburban dwellers join to support their teams. Although most residents never actually see a professional game, they form strong opinions concerning the team's performance and learn the details through the print media, radio, and television. Team jerseys and hats appear throughout the city and at every turn the team logo is displayed on billboards and auto stickers.

A particular type of fan support grows around pro teams that are cast in the image of their city and its historic ethnic groups. The Broad Street Bullies (as the Philadelphia Flyers were once known) emanated from their rough-and-tumble approach to the game of ice hockey that resulted in a world championship. The pride the city of brotherly love has been the Flyers, Iggles (Eagles), and the Phillies. In this city dominated by ethnic enclaves of immigrants, fans are unique in their approach to sport, fanaticism, and impatience with their heroes. This is a city that cheered the triumph of Rocky on the steps of the Philadelphia Art Museum and booed Santa Claus at an Eagles game.

Likewise, Baltimore and Boston teams have been in a love affair with their fans for decades. Generations of families have shared a special sport

In the Arena With . . . *World Police and Fire Games*

The World Police and Fire Games are second only to the Olympic Games as an international competitive sporting event. Established in 1985 and held every two years, the Games attract 10,000 police officers, firefighters, and custom and correction officers from 60 countries around the world to compete in over 70 sports and events of physical strength and skill. Events include traditional sports along with job-specific contests such as S.W.A.T. team competition, martial arts, motorcycle racing, shooting, and orienteering. Other novel events include tug-of-war, wrist wrestling, and paintball. The Games promote physical activity, and being physically fit better prepares law enforcement personnel to protect and defend the public order. Training and participating in competitive sports keeps them fit, skillful, and mentally sharp. The competition is free and open to public (World Police and Fire Games 2006).

fanaticism and even when younger generations moved away, they never lost their passion for their true home team. Meanwhile, teams relatively new to cities, such as teams in the Sunbelt, do not have the same hardcore fans. Some games don't even sell out on a Sunday simply due to a more modest passion for professional sport and a competition with too many other leisure activities, especially outdoor activities.

Special sporting events also can unify a city. Hosting the Super Bowl, the NCAA basketball play-offs, baseball's All-Star game, the Olympic Games, the Pan American Games, various collegiate championships, and even youth national championships can draw communities together, uniting businesses, media, and fans. The economic benefits the host cities accrue often more than compensate for the expenses of staging the event. Local volunteers often spend long hours helping operate the event in exchange for perks such as access to tickets.

A notable example of a city using sport to build an identity is Indianapolis, which labels itself the "amateur sports capital of the world." Through the entrepreneurial activities of a local sports commission, the city aggressively bids to host every imaginable amateur sport championship and has staged over 250 national or international sporting events. The city is also home to collegiate sports (NCAA) and high school sports (NFHS) and the American College of Sports Medicine. A dozen national sport organizations have their national headquarters located in Indianapolis. The city's business community has been steadfastly supportive and the financial bonanza to the city's economy has enabled the government to improve the downtown and add sport and recreation facilities that are the envy of similar cities. From 1977 through 1991, the amateur sports movement pumped $1.05 billion into the local economy (Indianapolis Chamber of Commerce 2006).

Even smaller cities use sport to build unity. They may focus on a particular sporting event, on a local college, or even on the local high school. State universities located away from large metropolitan areas usually garner tremendous fan support because they have no competition from professional sport events or teams. In a state like Texas where fans take their high school football seriously, the local football team is a source of town pride (see sidebar on *Friday Night Lights* in chapter 10).

The ADA requires facilities and stadiums to provide adequate seating for those who use wheelchairs.

In the Arena With . . . *Philly's Sports Fans*

They used to call it the "Nest of Death." Section 700 of the old Veterans stadium in Philadelphia, Pennsylvania, had a reputation for toughness and questionable behavior. Home to the Philadelphia Eagles football team and the Philadelphia Phillies baseball team, the "VET" has since been replaced by Lincoln Financial Field, which opened in 2003.

Bill Deery, a season ticket-holder of old section 700, operates a Web site, nestofdeath. com, devoted to the Eagles, including such things as mementos, listings of records, clothing for sale, and Eagles news. Deery says, "We like to put the fear of God in most teams and the fans that come into the stadium." Eagles fans have been notorious over the years for

- jeering Dallas Cowboys' receiver Michael Irvin for 20 minutes as he lay suffering from a neck injury,
- throwing "D" batteries at a St. Louis Cardinal's player who rejected the Phillies even though they drafted him and signed with the Cards instead, and
- showering Santa Claus with snowballs as he circled the field.

Section 700 was so rough, replete with drunkenness and fighting, that the city of Philadelphia opened up a court complete with a judge inside the stadium to deal with the rowdiness on-site. The stadium is gone, but Philly fans soldier on. Like many older rust belt cities, the fans are as tough as the teams they root for (Loverro 2002).

NATIONALISM AND SPORT

Sport events are replete with patriotic symbols that unify people by encouraging them to celebrate their shared heritage and common bonds. Games open with the national anthem, the presentation of colors by a military team, a military jet flyover, or a marching band playing rousing music and stage halftime ceremonies that feature music and dance celebrating the nation's culture and history.

One football game in America stands out for intertwining nationalism and sport. Up to 100,000 people attended the classic Army–Navy game usually held in Philadelphia, and the game enjoyed a national television audience. Decades ago, this game not only matched the two military academies but also boasted great football players. Both teams were among the elite in college football and featured superstars such as Doc Blanchard, Pete Dawkins, and Roger Staubach. Though recent years have seen a decline in the performance level of both teams, the Army–Navy game is still a memorable occasion. The pomp and circumstance of the game along with the hearty rooting sections of cadets and midshipmen create an atmosphere unlike any other in college sport. As the U.S. Air Force Academy has improved its sport programs, it occasionally dominates football among the three academies, but the Army–Navy game still has the cachet. America, soldiers, the brightest and best of the nation's youth, and an undeniable patriotic theme permeate the day and bestow significance on the game regardless of the quality of play.

Nationalism is an expression of devotion to one's country. In times of war or disasters such as the attack on the U.S. World Trade Center, expressions of nationalism take on a poignancy that unites all citizens. Shared tragedy helps create a strong bond among people of all backgrounds. When national symbols such as the American flag are displayed at sporting events and carried on live television, millions of people collectively take pride in their country in spite of their apparent differences.

As we discussed in chapter 9, perhaps no sporting event has traded on nationalistic feelings like the Olympic Games. Adolph Hitler staged the 1936 Olympics to demonstrate the superiority of the Nazi government and way of life. East Germany claimed 90 Olympic medals in the 1972 Games, more medals than any country in the world claimed in proportion to its size; consider that East Germany is the size of California. Their 90 medals are impressive compared to the 94 medals the United States won and 125 medals the Soviet Union won.

Since 1972, the system of selection and training that produced those medals has been discredited because of the abuse of young athletes and illegal drugs fostered by the East German government. The success of East Germany's Olympic athletes was a source of national pride that once exposed turned into a national embarrassment.

The Olympic Games have also been manipulated to publicize disputes between countries. The United States boycotted the 1980 Olympic Games staged in the Soviet Union to protest that country's invasion of Afghanistan. The favor was returned when the Soviet Union withdrew its athletes from the 1984 Games in Los Angeles, leaving Americans to claim a somewhat hollow victory.

The expulsion of South Africa from the Olympics in 1964 and 1968 affected world opinion and South Africa's long-standing apartheid. No doubt the resulting publicity pressured a major reform in a government that had repressed Black citizens for centuries. Similarly, the People's Republic of China was ostracized for its dismal record on human rights. In a remarkable change, Beijing was chosen as the host city for the Olympic Games in 2008. China believes that its selection shows other nations' stamp of approval on their progress to right the wrongs in their country.

SPORT IN PROMOTING SOCIAL VALUES

In the United States, sport is a conservative institution that promotes traditional values and can integrate people into the social construct. Generally, sport strives to maintain the status quo by teaching people mainstream values or perhaps by functioning as a distraction for people who are unsatisfied with their society or lives. Yet sport can also serve as a platform from which to point to the need for change.

In the United States, striving for excellence is critical social value and success is measured by achievement. Competition spurs Americans to perform to the maximum of their ability and to reach heights of excellence they may never have thought possible. The American recipe for success is to work hard, show discipline, and stay dedicated to personal goals. There is no shame in defeating or being defeated, for in striving to win against the competitor, both athletes are inspired to perform at their best.

In China, the values learned through sport can be very different. According to writers who studied Chinese attitudes toward sport in the 1970s, the prevailing attitude was not that winning is the ultimate goal. Rather, Chinese competition emphasized cooperation, working toward a group goal, friendship, and physical fitness. There was little emphasis on individual success, and athletes displayed devotion to success by the group (Johnson 1973a, 1973b, 1973c). Some of those attitudes changed in the decades since, and China has risen to a world power in competitive sport, a power culminating in Beijing's selection to host the 2008 Summer Olympics.

Adults use competitive sport to teach kids the lessons they believe necessary for later success in life. Kids learn that by trying their best to win in sport, they will develop the life skills to compete in the world. Those skills could also be developed through academic achievement, excellence in arts, or exploration in technology and invention. Yet sports are often the first thing that comes to the minds of people wanting to teach children the right habits for future success.

Sports are used throughout the world to socially integrate people from diverse backgrounds. For example, Northern Ireland has extensively invested in sport facilities to promote constructive interaction between Protestants and Catholics. In France, sports are often seen as a way of

Local high school teams can also create community pride.

regenerating French youth and improving social discipline. In many countries, including England and the United States, sports are used to combat urban unrest and to reduce crime and juvenile delinquency (Coakley and Dunning 2004).

Sport As an Opiate of the Masses

Various critics throughout history have charged governments with using sport to distract their citizens from the inequities in their society. These critics charge that the government used sport as an "opiate" to calm the masses, dull their senses, and distract their attention from their everyday social or economic problems. The hype given to sport literally puts the citizenry to sleep on matters of deeper significance. This charge has typically been leveled at authoritarian governments, especially those in countries with a large number of poor people (Eitzen 2004).

Developing countries have learned to use sport well. Powerful governments in the world's poorest nations have effectively rallied their citizens to support national teams representing their homeland. In most countries, the chosen sport is soccer, or what is referred to as *football* around the globe. Brazil is a good example of a nation that has embraced soccer as a national pastime and elevated its most famous son, Pelé, as a legendary hero. The exploits of the Brazilian soccer team have united rich and poor in a country beset with a myriad of social and economic tensions. Brazilian pride is stoked by every success fashioned by the national soccer team. Around the world, Brazil is respected for its tradition of excellence in world soccer competition.

Even in the United States, the charge of using sport as a distraction has been made by public figures such as Bill Bradley, a former All-American basketball player for Princeton University and later for the New York Knicks. After his basketball career, Bradley entered politics and became a U.S. senator. He was also a presidential contender in 2000. In the early days of his political career, he referred to sport as "a temporary fix, an escape from the problems of the world such as war, racism, and poverty that distracts the minds and saps the energies of people away from the problems of the lower classes" (Hoch 1972b, p. 12).

Typically, political activists seek changes in their present government by criticizing those in power of diverting attention from critical social problems. A contemporary example is that of Noam Chomsky, a brilliant political activist and professor of linguistics at the Massachusetts Institute of Technology. Chomsky has been acknowledged as one of the most influ-

ential voices in contemporary political discussions and is a left-wing critic of American foreign policy. He believes sport is an opiate of the masses:

"Sports keeps people from worrying about things that matter to their lives. Sports is a major factor in controlling people. Workers have minds; they have to be involved in something and it's important to make sure they're involved in things that have absolutely no significance. So professional sport is perfect. It instills total passivity." (Tsiokos 2005)

Social critics ask: How do you explain the American preoccupation with sport when they still face racial tensions, discrimination toward women and ethnic groups, a rising national debt, concern for long-term welfare of senior citizens on limited incomes, affordable health care, rising rates of obesity, continued assaults on the environment, and a deepening divide between the so-called red and blue states? Rather than facing a distrustful nation, the U.S. government may find it better to keep its citizens focused on the Super Bowl, the March Madness of college basketball, the start of spring training for baseball, and the next Olympic Games (Huston 2005).

Critics ask why cities spend millions to attract or retain professional sport franchises when those millions could be used to help the poor, build cheap housing, raise teachers' salaries and improve school facilities, fight crime, and provide quality health care.

It may be that people simply choose to focus their energy on more positive events. They may feel powerless or not know how to address the issues that social critics list as important.

Sport and the Status Quo

Generally in the United States, people associated with sport are politically conservative. These people include coaches, athletes, sportscasters, and sport owners or executives. Although there are notable exceptions of athletes and coaches who are politically liberal, they stand out because they are unusual In this context, *conservative* refers to those who adhere to traditional methods or views and generally seek to perpetuate the status quo. On the other hand, *liberal* refers to those who are not bound by authoritarianism, orthodoxy, or tradition, and they are open to and often seek change from the status quo (Merriam-Webster's 2001).

Owners of professional sports teams generally benefit from maintaining a political structure that supports them and that they have influence over.

Likewise, leaders in most sport organizations have no desire to change the social standards they used to work their way into their top positions.

Coaches at every level of competition tend to have a conservative outlook. They strongly believe in the traditional values of hard work, discipline, perseverance, and respect for authority. Regarding their society, coaches often favor the status quo and resist change. In fact, coaches in the United States often play an authoritarian role (Eitzen 1992). Athletic coaches are judged publicly on their job performance after every game. They are held responsible for their team's winning or losing, and if the percentage of losses is too great, they lose their jobs without discussion. As a result, coaches tend to control their own destiny by controlling the behavior of their athletes. They have strong opinions on how athletes should dress, act, wear their hair, represent their school, and interact with the media. Coaches may also have a direct interest in an athlete's academic performance, which affects athletic eligibility; an athlete's friends, who may get the athlete into trouble; and even an athlete's boyfriend or girlfriend, who might distract from athletic performance. We'll look at coaches in more detail in chapter 18.

Athletes often follow their coaches in their political leanings. They may not question their coaches, as these athletes are typically admired by their peers, fawned over by adults, and looked upon as heroes by younger kids. They enjoy a high social status, especially during their teenage years, and if they continue on to a professional career, their success explodes exponentially.

Typical athletes choose to participate in sports and submit to the direction of various coaches. They learn to push themselves physically and mentally in order to succeed and perhaps to punish their body. If they are successful, the reinforcement of winning encourages them to continue to punish their bodies so they can continue their success.

Athletes who are in the public eye are taught from an early age that they are representing their parents, peers, community, and school. Coaches warn athletes about aberrant behavior that might reflect negatively on those who rely on them. Athletes learn to act in ways that are socially acceptable and adhere to the standards of the existing community.

Particularly in team sports, team cohesion is part of the formula for success. Team members who think alike, share common goals, and are willing to sacrifice for the good of the group are popular with

As a female in a nonteam sport, is this athlete less conservative than a female basketball player?

coaches and other athletes. Those who march to a different drummer are only accepted if their athletic contributions are exceptional. So sport encourages conformity to normal behavior (Sage 1973).

In recent years in the U.S., the Republican party has generally tended toward a more conservative platform while the Democratic party leans toward a more liberal platform. However, it would be a mistake to classify all Republicans as conservative and all Democrats as liberal; there are many shades of gray on both sides that depend on the specific issues being debated or discussed.

As the 2004 U.S. presidential election loomed, the *Yale Daily News*, a student newspaper published at Yale University, featured an article titled "Many Elis Break From Norm, Lean Right" (August 2004). Yale has a long history of being a politically left campus. However, the "Elis," or members of the Delta Kappa Epsilon fraternity, broke tradition to lean right. Many players on the football team, baseball team, and soccer team belonged to the Delta Kappa Epsilon fraternity. One after the other said that they believed many varsity athletes on campus were politically conservative in contrast to the rest of the student body. In their view, athletes at Yale tended to vote Republican.

In a poll taken early in the year by the Yale Sport Publicity staff, 62 football players planned to vote for Republican candidate Bush, 27 planned to voted for Democratic candidate Kerry, and 11 were undecided. The conservative stance of many members of the football team might be due to more than sport participation. In fact, 20 players were from Texas, 35% were from southern states, and about 13% were from the Midwest, all regions that are traditionally Republican. Only four players called a northern city home. Perhaps their choice for president was not so surprising considering their origins.

According to the Center for Responsive Politics, a nonpartisan, nonprofit research organization that tracks money in politics, $2,300,724 U.S. was contributed to the federal campaign in 2004 by athletes, team owners, officials, and sport arenas. About 71%, or $1,628,630 U.S., was donated to Republicans. George W. Bush received $310,048 U.S. from these funds (Harris 2004).

Yet not all athletes fall neatly into the same niche. As professor William Kelly pointed out when interviewed for the *Yale Daily News* article, athletes in more individualized sports such as squash, tennis, track and field, gymnastics, and skiing are not necessarily as conservative as players in team sports. Kelly also stated that female athletes are often less conservative than male athletes perhaps because they are less satisfied with the status quo and desire change.

Using Sport to Change Society

Is it possible to change people's attitudes, feelings, and beliefs through the sport experience? Some people may respond quickly with personal examples while others may be more cautious. Over the years, sports have clearly been used to dramatize certain social inequities or injustices, racism, gender bias, and homophobia.

Champion athletes have a platform from which to share their views if they choose. Boxer Muhammad Ali spoke his mind on the draft, the war, and racial prejudice. Tennis player Arthur Ashe Jr. spoke on the same issues, though in a much different way than Ali used. Olympic athletes Tommie Smith and John Carlos used their Olympic success to raise the Black Power salute during the American national anthem in 1968 in Mexico City. Tennis player Martina Navratilova was open about her lesbian lifestyle throughout her professional career and still is wildly

Activity Time-Out: Encouraging Good Life Lessons

At a hockey game in Massachusetts in 2000, two dads watching their 10- to 12-year-old sons play ice hockey argued about the violent checking that was occurring on the ice. Their argument led to a physical confrontation that left Michael Costin, father of four, dead from the beating. The other dad, Thomas Junta, stood trial and was convicted of involuntary manslaughter (Relin 2005). Cases such as this shed light on how coaches and parents take athletics too far and set poor examples for youth athletes. What can governing bodies do to ensure that the behavior of adults sets a positive example for the youth? Come up with 5 to 10 ideas and share them with your classmates.

popular. Billie Jean King preceded Martina and in some respects gave Martina the courage to affirm her lifestyle publicly. Billie Jean was also a relentless pioneer for women's rights through the Women's Sports Foundation. Curt Flood basically sacrificed his outstanding baseball career to stand up for a player's right to free agency and some degree of self-determination as a professional athlete. He abhorred the idea that athletes could be bought and sold by team owners and had no say at all in the decision.

These examples demonstrate how some athletes used sport to agitate for change in their society. Whether they succeeded is not the point. They raised consciousness and inspired others to stop and question their views. In an institution that generally preserves the status quo, their outspoken actions are all the more remarkable.

Use of Sport by Politicians

American athletes who win a Super Bowl, World Series, or other significant event can bet on receiving a congratulatory phone call from the president of the United States. In the last 50 years, virtually every U.S. president has used his image as a sports fan to link himself to Everyman. Presidents have thrown out the first ball of the baseball season, attended the U.S. Open tennis championships, and graced the opening ceremonies of the Olympic Games with their presence. President Richard Nixon even suggested certain plays he thought the Washington Redskins should use in their quest for a Super Bowl title. Nixon was perhaps the first U.S. president to use sport contacts and his keen personal interest in sports to portray himself as a regular guy (Ball and Loy 1975).

For athletes who achieve notable success, one of the most coveted rewards is a visit to the White House following their victory. Young athletes are impressed with the experience and tend to rank it high among their personal highlights. The president and his invited political allies use the occasion to solidify their support and demonstrate a personal admiration for winners of significant competitive events.

At the local level, state governors, members of the state congress, mayors, and other political figures are never far from view at major sporting events in their state or city. Mayors almost routinely wager

Photo ops with athletes help politicians convey the idea of themselves as the Everyman.

on the outcome of the contests involving their city's team, and when they lose the wager, they award a symbolic prize indigenous to their region. The media pick up the news of the wager and the politicians manufacture a media opportunity both before and after the event. At the 2005 NCAA women's national basketball championships, Governor Jennifer Graham of Michigan and Governor Rick Perry of Texas wagered on the outcome of the finals between Michigan State University and Baylor University. When Baylor claimed the title, Governor Perry sent a Baylor team jersey, Blue Bell ice cream, and Dr. Pepper soda. Governor Graham was obliged to wear the jersey while sitting at her desk and consuming the ice cream and soda. The same two governors had bet on the outcome of the Rose Bowl earlier that year, when the University of Texas played the University of Michigan (Marot 2005).

Lest you get the impression that modern politicians invented the use of sport to enhance their image, they did not. For centuries, kings, queens, and heads of state seized upon athletic contests as opportunities for public relations. Current politicians are simply following a well-worn script.

Certain athletes have used their sport fame to propel themselves to political prominence once their playing days end. Notable examples include Jim Ryan, representative from Kansas and former Olympic distance runner; Jim Bunning, Hall of Fame pitcher for the Detroit Tigers and current Senator from Kentucky; Jack Kemp, quarterback for the Buffalo Bills and former representative from New York; Bill Bradley, basketball player for the New York Knicks and former senator from New Jersey; Jesse Ventura, a professional wrestler who became governor of Minnesota; and Arnold Schwarzenegger, a bodybuilder who became governor of California. On the local level, celebrities such as coaches at universities and high schools parlay their notoriety to enter public roles as mayors, commissioners, and community leaders.

POLITICS WITHIN SPORT

Every sport is controlled internationally by a governing body that sets the rules of play, defines age groups for competition, sanctions competitions, stages world championships, administers drug tests, and promotes the sport worldwide. The organization comprises representative governing bodies from every participating nation, and organizational officials are elected from within the membership. The process of electing members to the international

board of directors is clearly political and not unlike what transpires in other governmental elections. Powerful nations protect their turf and self-interests by forming liaisons with other nations, dispensing favors, and using their vast resources to advance their influence. Nations with less influence form coalitions to pressure for a place at the decision-making table.

The picture at the international level is replicated at the national level in every country. National boards wield awesome power, and aspiring leaders campaign for years to earn a place of prestige on the board. Depending on who is on the board, the mission of the organizations may tilt toward developing high-performance athletes, increasing participation by the masses, showing sensitivity to minorities, demonstrating compassion for athletes with physical disabilities, attracting more spectators, or generating more revenue through marketing the sport. In an ideal world, a national governing body would have the will and means to do all of the above and more.

Aside from national governing bodies, there are also organizations dedicated to youth sports. Some are multisport, such as the Amateur Athletic Union, while most focus on one sport. When more than one organization emerges in a single sport, such as in youth soccer, the result is a confusing war of words and political clashes over purpose, rules, and championships.

In the United States, the National Federation of State High School Associations loosely governs interscholastic sport. But as the name *federation* suggests, the organization has minimal control. It sanctions no national championships and allows each state to set its own rules of competition. The result is policies that differ widely from state to state and can be most confusing for athletes and their families, especially for those who move from one state to another.

Over the years, college athletics in the United States have endured several political battles between organizations fighting for control. The winner has been the National Collegiate Athletic Association (NCAA), which claims the bulk of colleges and universities as members. The NCAA has created different levels (I, II, and III) of competition and allows schools to choose their level provided that they meet certain standards. The philosophical differences between the three levels create controversy and political horse trading. Big schools want to be free to spend their money and conduct what amounts to a quasiprofessional sport program. Smaller schools where athletics are more student-centered demand more accountability from institutions, stronger academic standards for athletes, and emphasis on participation rather than high performance.

In U.S. professional sports, various competing leagues spring up to challenge existing professional leagues. Some competing leagues enjoy success, such as the American Football League, which eventually merged with the established NFL. The two football leagues found that together they could be more efficient, powerful, and attractive to commercial sponsors and television stations than two competing leagues could be.

Professional tennis has suffered from being divided into two organizations, one for women and one for men. Although women and men often play at the same tournaments, their separate organizations compete for facilities (e.g., practice courts, weight room, training room, press room), courts for matches, prize money to award champions, commercial sponsors, and fan loyalty. So far, politics and distrust mostly on the part of the women's tour have blocked a beneficial merger. The result is a fractured delivery of the professional game that confuses fans around the world and limits the appeal of both men's and women's tennis to potential commercial sponsors.

CHAPTER SUMMARY

In this chapter we discussed how sport and politics interact internationally, nationally, and locally. The U.S. government is responsible for protecting the rights of its citizens, and it enforces certain safeguards in sport, ensures that the rights of all citizens are respected in sport, and protects the financial interests of the public. Governments use sport to develop local, state, or national identities and promote unity among citizens. Governments and political leaders also use sport to promote dominant social values and encourage social integration of all citizens. Critics of government accuse politicians of using sport to distract citizens from other pressing issues or to reinforce the status quo. Politicians often use sport to enhance their personal image.

When athletes succeed in international competition, their excellence is often attributed to the superior way of life of their home nation. The Olympic Games have been used repeatedly to validate systems of government, generate support for political leaders, and prove the superiority of various ethnic or racial groups.

Sport events are typically staged with nationalistic displays that include the national anthem, marching bands, patriotic themes, and flag presentations. Citizens who take pride in their country are more likely to reelect current governmental leaders and feel content with their society.

In the United States, when young children are exposed to sport, they begin the socialization process of learning to respect authority, work hard, persevere, rebound from failure, and cooperate with others. Sport is just one way these traditional American values are passed to the next generation.

At times, sport can be a powerful agent in promoting change in society. The sports world constantly reminds the public, fans, and participants that changes are occurring. The emergence of the African American athlete on the public stage and later the rise of women's sports confirm recent landmark changes in U.S. culture.

Within sport organizations, politics influences the direction of the group and determines who leads the group. Those who advocate for radical change within a sport fight to select sympathetic leaders while those who do not want radical change rally around their chosen candidates. Most athletic groups have gradually begun to reserve a place at their decision-making table for females, minorities, and athletes with disabilities. Through diversity, sport can grow by reaching out to new populations of participants and fans.

Finally, we looked at the tendency for coaches and athletes to be politically conservative. Their training to respect traditional values and authority figures along with a belief in hard work, discipline, and good attitude tends influence their political philosophy. Those who succeed in sport or life often want to conserve the environment in which they excel.

Deviance and Sport

Student Outcomes

After reading this chapter, you will know the following:

- Breaking the rules in sport
- How emotion helps create deviant behavior
- Violence in sport on and off the field
- Performance enhancements and doping
- Eating disorders and hazing in sport
- Sports gambling

People in a society are expected to conform to the rules and norms of the group. People who do not conform are labeled as *deviant*. **Deviant** is an adjective that means deviating especially from an accepted norm. It does not mean that being deviant is either positive or negative. However, in U.S. popular vernacular, *deviant* is often equated with *devious,* which has a decidedly negative connotation. It is in this negative context that we will explore deviance in sport in this chapter. We will examine the relationship between sport and destructive actions such as generally breaking the rules, committing crimes, behaving violently against others, using drugs and other performance-enhancing substances, and finally gambling on competition outcomes.

Because there is so much publicity about the misconduct of college and professional athletes in the United States, it may seem that on the whole athletes clearly lack moral values and are out of step with mainstream America. This chapter will discuss whether that impression is justified and will compare the incidence of deviant behavior among athletes compared to that among others in society. We will also study the related question of whether athletics promote, encourage, or reward deviant behavior. Similarly, we will see if people who are attracted to athletics might be predisposed to deviant behavior.

Typically when we study deviant behavior, we study behavior that does not conform to normal behavior because of the person's unawareness or outright rejection of those norms. **Underconformity** describes behavior that does not conform to the generally accepted rules of sport. Such behavior includes breaking team rules, school rules, and competition rules. Many athletes use profanity, haze teammates, drink alcohol, argue with others, or bet others on the outcome of a sport event. It only when that behavior reaches a point outside of accepted limits that it becomes deviant.

Another form of deviance that exists in sport is an **overconformity** to the expectations of high-performance sport. Examples of overconformity are drastically altering food intake to gain or lose weight or using supplements to improve strength or bulk up muscles. Many athletes may engage in similar practices, but do not carry them to the extreme that qualifies as overconformity.

Excessive conforming may also take the form of following the rules and customs of sport too well. Particularly in high-performance training, athletes may put such a high priority on sport that they ignore or undervalue other critical areas of life. They may sacrifice friendships, ignore families, or neglect academic studies due to a single-minded dedication to sport training. In the long run, such behaviors are counterproductive.

Cheerleading in the United States is often an example of overconformity. Cheerleading has evolved from cheers for raising school spirit to exhibits of great gymnastics skill and athleticism. According to Shields and Smith (2005), during the 13 years between 1990 and 2002, 208,800 young people ages 5 to 18 were treated at hospitals for cheerleading-related injuries. Of these injuries, 40% involved the leg, ankle, and foot and were caused by violent and sometimes dangerous jumps and stunts. Although the participation in cheerleading grew just 18% during the 13 years reviewed, the number of injuries doubled. Overconforming to the demands of cheerleading has put both boys and girls at high risk for injury.

Another example of conformity is that of athletes who use physical violence within the rules of the game. While these actions may be legal in the boxing ring, on the football field, or in an ice hockey rink, similar actions used by everyday citizens would lead to jail. But in sport, a vicious blow delivered to an opponent draws cheers from the crowd, admiration from teammates, and exclamations of "Attaboy!" from the coaching staff.

RULE BREAKING

You have to learn the rules of the game in order to play a sport: You can't dribble with two hands in basketball, walk with the ball without dribbling, or hit the arm of an opponent who's shooting without causing a foul. You can't intentionally touch the soccer ball with your hands, run into an opponent without trying to play the ball, or commit a foul in the penalty box without giving up a penalty kick. You can't touch the tennis ball with your body or clothing, reach over the net, serve from inside the line, or throw your racket in frustration.

Sometimes rules are broken because players are unaware of them, do not understand them, or violate them accidentally. At other times, athletes may intentionally break the rules in hopes of not getting caught, to interrupt the opponent's flow, or to vent their frustration and anger.

Is rule breaking today occurring more, less, or about the same as it has historically occurred in sport? Athletes cheat in scoring, modify equipment illegally, commit fouls when officials aren't looking, participate in brawls, or call a phony injury time-out to get a strategic advantage. Students of sport history will remind us that such instances are not new and have always been a part of playing games. For decades baseball players have been accused of cheating by doctoring the baseball or throwing spitters that cause pitches to break unpredictably. Ice hockey has always been notorious for its inevitable fights and most fans are disappointed when fights don't break out. Although illegal, these examples of cheating were tolerated as part of the game unless a player was blatantly caught in the act.

In realty, there is probably less rule breaking during modern games due to improved officiating, clearer rules, television replays, immediate media comment, and a certain maturity that has evolved in most sports over the years of competition (Dunning 1999). When athletes or coaches do break the rules today, they often do so unintentionally or because they've concluded doing so may advance them toward their ultimate goal. For example, an offensive lineman may risk a penalty for holding to keep the opposing team from flattening and possibly injuring his quarterback.

More people seem to be following the rules also because of the rapid growth of organized youth sports. A coach's primary role in youth sports is to teach her young athletes the rules of the game and expect her athletes to abide by them. Organized programs such as the Citizenship Through Sports Alliance that promote good sporting behavior have also sprung up around the country. National programs backed by universities, youth sport organizations, or national governing bodies publicize and reward players who demonstrate good behavior. Books, Web sites, and videos on good behavior are widely

Even weight training can be a deviant behavior if carried to extremes.

available. Coaching clinics often feature sessions on teaching good sporting behavior. These tools help coaches, parents, and sport leaders explain the differences between acceptable and unacceptable behavior and suggest alternative actions for controlling frustration or aggressiveness. Athletes who learn these lessons when young develop positive habits that last a lifetime.

Most sport programs have always offered awards for good sporting behavior, often as a second thought for athletes who are not chosen as most outstanding, most valuable player, or team captain. Recently, these standard performance-oriented awards have been supplanted with awards for team behavior, and high schools have adopted an emphasis on good sporting behavior into their athletic philosophy. Banners hung in the gym proclaim the school's stance on good sporting behavior, slogans proclaim on good sporting behavior, and literature refers to good sporting behavior.

By the time most athletes reach high school, they have been exposed to several years of youth sports in which they learned the fundamental rules of the sport and the boundaries of acceptable behavior. As they move up in competitive level, the action becomes faster, the players become more skillful, and some rules become looser. Coaches make sure the athletes know they must abide by the rules or face disciplinary action including lost playing time.

Is faking an injury in soccer breaking the rules or just part of the game?

Myriad off-field regulations ensure fair competition and protect the rights of people involved in sports. Sport administrators and coaches must learn these rules, understand how to apply them, and make sure athletes follow them carefully.

Major deterrents and punishments for breaking the rules have evolved over the years, particularly in college sports. The most recent *NCAA Division I Manual* comprises more than 500 pages of rules, explanations of rules, and examples of decisions on breaking the rules. The manual devotes more than 50 pages to academic eligibility alone (National Collegiate Athletic Association 2004a).

The purpose of the NCAA rules is to protect the rights of athletes and coaches who are honest and to eliminate cheating. In the last 25 years, it has become the responsibility of all collegiate athletes, coaches, boosters, and athletic administrators to understand and obey the NCAA rules. Schools now hire specialists in rule enforcement to guide their athletic personnel and monitor actions to prevent unintentional or intentional rule breaking. A college that discovers rule violations is advised to turn

itself in for sanctions before the NCAA finds out and comes to investigate.

The penalties for violations have been stepped up in recent years. Coaches have been fired, athletes have been punished by suspension from games or even a season, and athletic programs have been severely hindered for years to come. When the media learn about the violation, the resulting publicity affects the reputation of the university and its people and affects admissions, fund-raising, and recruiting of future athletes. Schools also suffer huge financial penalties when banned from postseason play or bowl appearances worth millions of dollars.

In spite of the number of stories the media report on deviant acts of athletes, the percentage of athletes involved in such behavior is small when compared to the total athlete population. Rees and Miracle (2004) concluded that participating in high school sport does little to aid or harm the development of social values in adolescents. After reviewing research evidence, they also concluded that certain behaviors labeled as *delinquent* possibly represent positive deviancy within athletics. Behaviors considered devi-

Activity Time-Out: Tracking Deviant Behavior

Over the next two months, pick at least one major newspaper, online source, or television source and track the stories of athletes exhibiting deviant behavior. Record the athlete's name, the infraction, whether the athlete is a repeat offender, and the punishment given. Once you have assembled your list, look for trends and summarize your impressions. Following are some examples of what to look for:

- Players charged with infractions involving alcohol
- Players charged with violent or abusive crimes against another person
- Positive drug test results
- Illegal recruiting by high schools or colleges
- Illegal actions committed during play
- Coaches cited for unethical or illegal behavior
- Officials who helped fix games

ant in other social contexts seem normal in sport. Hazing, petty theft, and drunkenness seem part of the ritualized acceptance into the sport culture.

Violence seems to be increasing in American society, and the general public believes that athletes are leading the way. The media reporting of crimes committed by high-profile athletes sensationalizes the incidents and leads readers to believe that athletes, particularly African American males, are out of control. In his article "Race, Athletes and Crime" appearing in the *Sports Business Journal,* Richard Lapchick (1999) asserted that over a five-year time frame, nearly 100 athletes and coaches are arrested for assault against women. However, he goes on to point out that in a given year

- 3 million American women are battered,
- 1 million American women are raped, and
- 1,400 American women are murdered.

These statistics may include athletes, but the problem is not in athletics. The huge problem of violence against women cuts across race, economic class, age, education, and profession. American streets are more violent than in the past. Although the National Education Association has reported that generally the U.S. public believes schools are becoming more dangerous, the evidence contradicts that belief (National Education Association 2005). In fact, school violence in public and private schools remained stable from 2002 to 2003 and continued at about half the rate reported from 1992. However, there were an estimated 740,000 violent crimes against students in schools, with 150,000 of those

being the most serious violent victimizations (rape, sexual assault, robbery, and aggravated assault) (Department of Justice 2005).

EMOTION AND DEVIANT BEHAVIOR

The human emotions that are experienced through or within sport add flavor to our world. For the most part, we are taught to keep our emotions in check during our daily life, and particularly males subvert strong emotions as a requirement of masculinity. But in sports, we are free to express emotions as long as we do so within reason.

The excitement generated by an athletic contest of which the outcome lies in doubt down to the last second of play is unusual in daily life. While the excitement is energizing, it is also sometimes stressful. Nervousness, perspiration, clammy palms, headaches, and clouded thoughts can all result from the stress of the game. The more important the event seems, the more exciting and stressful it may be. Once the outcome is decided, the ecstasy of victory or the agony of defeat takes over. It may be hours or even days before the strong feelings subside and equilibrium returns.

When emotion overcomes us to the point where we stop thinking clearly, deviant behavior can result. An athlete who is consumed by the moment in a game may commit an egregious foul, let loose a stream of profanities, or become violent. Later, after cooling off, the actions committed in the heat of battle may seem immature, antisocial, and despicable.

Big-time sports exploit the emotional makeup of athletes. The stage is set before the game by the coach, who often psyches up his athletes using music, pep talks, slogans, films of moments of glory, or VIPs who exhort the players to perform. As the athletes jog onto the arena, the band fills their ears with stirring music, cannons or fireworks go off, and the crowd roars for the home team.

Some sports or some athletes may not prosper if their state of arousal is too heightened. Athletes who play highly skilled sports may need to lower their arousal to achieve best performance. But most American team sports thrive on excitement and energy.

Spectators are also affected by the emotional excitement. The traditional pregame cocktail party, tailgating, and consumption of alcohol have become synonymous with sport. Students seem to view big-time college football games as an excuse for binge drinking, and by halftime, some fans are barely able to function. Some families are so put off by the crude behavior exhibited at college football games or many professional sports that they do not feel comfortable bringing their children. Colleges and professional teams have experimented with limiting the number of drinks sold per customer, stopping sales after halftime, and restricting alcohol consumption to pregame tailgating. An increasing number of venues are banning alcohol, although some fans manage to hide their liquor. The University of Florida and University of Georgia no longer want to be known for throwing the "World's Largest Outdoor Cocktail Party" at their annual football game held in Jacksonville, Florida. Fans and the media affixed the label to the game in the 1950s. In recent years, the deaths of two students involving alcohol and an emphasis on responsible use of alcohol at both universities prompted Southeast Conference commissioner, Mike Slive, to request that CBS and ESPN consider dropping the use of the slogan during telecasts (Fox Sports 2006).

Fans, plied with liquor, boo the opposing players, taunt the officials, insult visiting fans, perform the wave, cheer their team's good plays, and try to get in front of a television camera. If the game is an important victory, a rush to pull down the goalposts often follows.

When the home team wins a championship, unruly fans often let their emotions carry over to the postgame celebration. In spite of increased security, mobs of fans sometimes get out of control, brawl, destroy property, and embarrass their city or school. Such behavior is no longer all in good fun.

In case you think such behavior is indigenous to the United States, let's take a quick peek at the behavior of fans at soccer games around the world.

Did alcohol contribute to this scene? Judging by the beer bottles littering the field, the answer is yes.

Soccer seems to inspire passion like no other sport, and because it is played worldwide and frequently matches country against country, the emotional investment people make in the games is huge. In countries where poorer or uneducated people make up the fan base, the behavior may be even worse than anything typically seen in the United States.

Hooliganism of British soccer fans has been a tradition for several hundred years. Usually, the label *hooligan* is applied to working-class men who disrupt soccer games with their antisocial behavior. They may direct their aggression against referees, opposing players, team owners, or other spectators. They may drink excessively, exchange insults, destroy property, and interrupt the game. Fans running on the field, throwing beer cans, pitching stones, and generally frightening other spectators became so pervasive that the British government became involved to control the growing violence. In spite of sensationalized stories in the British press, violence by fans at sporting events, particularly soccer, has reached alarming levels. In fact, because soccer is played worldwide and enjoys a passionate following, the incidence of violence at soccer matches likely exceeds any other sport (Young 2004).

Hooliganism has morphed into a subculture of soccer in many countries and has affected attitudes about the sport. Men with little education and working-class backgrounds seem to embrace such behavior and view it as their right to misbehave even if they harm the rights of others. Aggressive, masculine behavior seems strongly connected to people who lack education, have limited choice in occupation, and lack the skill to personally compete in professional soccer (Dunning 1999).

VIOLENCE IN SPORT

Violence pervades some sports because of their nature and the athletes they attract. The violence that takes place during an athletic contest may carry over into violent behavior off the field and then both athletes and society suffer the consequences. Young athletes may use the athletic arena to test their masculinity and to establish acceptance by peers.

Violence is highly visible in American sports because it is so prevalent in televised events. Violent plays are shown over and over in instant replays as the sports announcers exclaim over the hit, tackle, block, or body check. Athletes who deliver these violent acts are lionized by fans and teammates for their aggressive play. If a serious injury occurs, the tide shifts as people suspect the athlete's motives and admit that perhaps the game got out of hand.

On-Field Violence

American society seems to be confused about the place of violence in sports, particularly when the sport itself promotes aggressive play and physically abusing an opponent's body. Football is a collision sport. Wrestling, boxing, ice hockey, and lacrosse all require violence just to play the game. Even high-performance basketball involves heavy body contact and physical intimidation. Tackles, blocks, sacks, body checks, and jabs are clearly part of the culture of many sports. The place of violence becomes unclear when it involves acts prohibited by the rules of sport but often accepted by competing athletes. Examples of borderline violence include fistfights between players, hard body blocks in basketball, the brushback in baseball, or the intentional foul in basketball.

Many sports such as golf, tennis, volleyball, swimming, skiing, equestrian, dance, and track and field have little or no violence associated with them. These sports emphasize skill, are nonconfrontational, and lack body contact, traits that all factor into nonviolent activity. Add to these characteristics the tendency of these sports to be favored by participants with better education and financial resources, whose attitudes toward violence differ substantially from those of working-class athletes.

Masculinity is often rooted in bravery, willingness to risk bodily harm, toughness, and personal aggression. Boys grow up with role models who exhibit these traits. They are accepted by peers if they mimic these traits to prove their worthiness as men. Failure to do so can result in labels of sissy, wuss, or worse. Traditionally, sport was closely associated with warfare. Coaches who condition athletes to risk bodily harm for the good of the team often use the language and ethics of war. Think of the traditional headlines in the sports pages: "Vikings destroy Patriots . . . Eagles bury Giants . . . 76ers blow out Nets . . . Duke blitzes Wake Forest . . . Gators swamp Bulldogs . . . Oklahoma guns down the Longhorns . . ." and so on. Players give teammates the highest compliment when they say, "He's a guy you wanna go to war with."

In the hype leading up to the 2005 Super Bowl between the Philadelphia Eagles and the New England Patriots, television and newspapers featured stories on the "Hit Man," Rodney Harrison, who plays strong safety for the Patriots. Columnist Gary Shelton wrote for the *St. Petersburg Times* (2005), "This is the world of the Hit Man, the nastiest, dirtiest,

Rodney Harrison has amassed more fines than any other player has in NFL history, yet players and fans respect his playing style.

most frenzied player in the NFL. If you can count on nothing else in Sunday's Super Bowl, you can count on the Patriot's strong safety to go borderline mental. He will shove and scrap, bite, and bully. If you want to wager on who gets the first 15 yard penalty, he is the easy favorite."

Harrison isn't well liked around the league, but he draws attention. A poll by *Sports Illustrated* labeled him the dirtiest player in the league. He has been fined over $350,000 U.S. in his 11-year career, which is more than any other player has been fined. Yet among players, he draws respect and admiration. John Lynch, safety for the Denver Broncos, said, "He's one guy I would pay to see play" (Shelton 2005).

Rodney Harrison clearly overconforms to the image of a rough, aggressive player who takes violence in football to the limit. Rather than exclude

him from play, others in the game respect him for his physicality and fierce hits. He may leave broken bodies in his wake, but he's just playing the game the way it was meant to be played.

While some athletes push their violence to the limit, survive in the sport, and even earn respect from opponents and fans, others cross the line. In March of 2004, Canadian hockey player Steve Bertuzzi sucker punched another player from behind and was suspended for the rest of the season. In November of 2004, NBA players led by Ron Artest of the Indiana Pacers went into the stands to attack hecklers during a game. The attack began when, following a brawl between the Pacers and the opposing Detroit Pistons, a fan allegedly threw a cup on a stretched-out Artest. Artest was suspended, and though this was not the first time Artest was suspended for violent behavior, it drew the toughest penalty in NBA history: suspension without pay for the season. Artest lost about $5 million U.S. of salary.

Professional ice hockey struggled with its reputation for violence for years and could not seem to reconcile stricter rules and harsher penalties with the popularity of game fights. Many hockey supporters relish the breakout of violence and anticipate the potential fights. However, for the beginning of the 2005 season, the NHL adopted new rules, three relating to violence:

■ Instigation penalties: A player who instigates a fight in the final five minutes of a game will receive a game misconduct and an automatic one-game suspension. The player's coach will be fined $10,000 U.S. The suspension times and fines will double for each additional incident.

■ Officiating: Zero tolerance on interference, hooking, and hold obstruction.

■ Unsportsmanlike conduct: Players who dive, embellish a fall or a reaction, or fake injury in an attempt to draw penalties will be fined. Public complaints or derogatory comments toward the game will also result in fine (MSNBC.com 2006).

Off-Field Violence

It is not clear if on-field violent behavior leads to off-field violence. Common sense suggests that people who become accustomed to using physical intimidation and violence in sport naturally revert to those behaviors when facing conflict outside of sport. Athletes who hang out at bars, restaurants, or clubs are often targets for other tough guys, who bait them with insults and disrespect. The athlete, who feels his manhood is being challenged, may struggle not to respond with physical force. However, athletes who do respond physically may be simply reflecting cultural upbringing that was established outside of sport. Sport may not be the cause of violence, but rather a result of the athletes' upbringing or natural disposition, which led them to choose violent sport. As we saw in chapter 13, young males from lower socioeconomic classes tend to embrace sport to prove their masculinity. Any challenge to their manliness compels them to respond or lose face in front of their peers.

Alcohol consumption and binge drinking add to the problem of violence. In chapter 7 we discussed recent studies that show that athletes are more likely than nonathletes to binge. Athletes who are not in full command of their faculties are more likely to lose control and commit violent acts.

A sensitive topic for many athletes is the apparent rise in violence against women among male athletes. Most men would be quick to say that they respect women and certainly don't intend women harm. The National Coalition Against Violent Athletes was founded in 1997 by Kathy Redmond, who was raped on campus at the University of Nebraska by an athlete. She believes that athletes are not held to the general standards of behavior and are often protected by their coaches, athletic departments, or universities. Her coalition gathers data to help educate the public on the issues regarding athletes and violence. It also provides support and guidance for victims of violent abuse. Here are some statistics cited on the coalition's Web site, ncava.org:

- A three-year study showed that while male student-athletes make up 3% of the population on college campuses, they account for 19% of sexual assaults and 35% of domestic assaults on college campuses.
- Athletes commit one in three college sexual assaults.

Signing autographs and posing for pictures are safe forms of off-field behavior.

- The general population has a conviction rate of 60% for sexual assaults, while the rate for athletes is only 38%.

These statistics were gathered from 107 cases of sexual assault reported at 30 Division I schools between 1991 and 1993 (Crosset, Benedict, and McDonald 1995). Critics of this study say the sample size was relatively small and was not controlled for the use of alcohol, the use of tobacco, and the man's attitude toward women. Those three factors are the main predictors of a male's inclination to gender violence. More recent studies have corroborated the Crosset et al. study, and one researcher concluded that "a disproportionate number of campus gang rapes involve fraternities or athlete groups" (Simmons 2002). However, Todd Crosset (1999) reviewed the published research on violence against women by male athletes and concluded that while male athletes seem to be more frequently involved in sexual assaults than other male students, the differences between the two groups were not statistically significant.

Domestic violence is the number one crime perpetrated by athletes (Benedict and Yaeger 1998). In almost every case, the domestic violence involves male athletes who play violent sports physically abusing wives or girlfriends. In May of 2003, Super

Bowl champion Michael Pittman of the Tampa Bay Buccaneers used his Hummer to ram his wife's car while his wife, their 2-year-old son, and the sitter were in it. Pittman was already on probation for two domestic violence cases from 2001. Yet it is not clear that athletes are any more involved in serious crime than the general population is. In a follow-up study, Blumstein and Benedict (1999) showed that 23% of the males in cities with a population of 250,000 or more are arrested for a serious crime at some point in their life. That compares with the 21.4% of NFL football players who had been arrested for something more serious than a minor crime as reported in his earlier study (Benedict and Yaeger 1998). In fact, when Blumstein and Benedict compared NFL players with young men from similar racial backgrounds, they discovered that the arrest rates for NFL players was less than half that of the other group for crimes of domestic violence and nondomestic assaults. Is it difficult or nearly impossible to turn the violence off as soon as practice or the game is over? The majority of athletes who display violent on-field behavior don't continue their aggression

off the field. If they did, the court records and news media would surely let us know. We simply do not have enough research to address this question, nor do we have complete data on the incidence of domestic violence by athletes. Most families prefer not to publicize such incidents until they become frequent or incapacitating, and most women do not wish to press charges.

Some athletes do develop a sense of entitlement as their fame grows (Benedict and Yaeger 1998). In whatever city they're in, male athletes are surrounded by female groupies. The athletes often treat these women with disdain and yet are still tempted by their offers of sex. Wilt Chamberlain, a former great NBA player, boasted in his autobiography that he had slept with over 20,000 women . . . which, if true, shows a definite degree of deviance (ESPN 1999).

A notable case involved boxer Mike Tyson, who attacked and raped Desiree Washington, a church-going beauty queen with a squeaky-clean image. Although Tyson was convicted and sent to jail, Washington's career, psyche, and reputation were

Off-field violence isn't limited to rough on-field sports. The sophisticated world of figure skating was stunned by Tonya Harding's alleged role in the attack on fellow skater Nancy Kerrigan.

sullied forever. Typically, the male aggressor contends that his victim was asking for it and acting like a slut. Tyson of course claimed that he did not rape Washington, but once she filed charges he became so angry that he said, "I just hate her. Now I really do want to rape her" (Rivers 2003).

No case captured the public's attention as much as that of O.J. Simpson, who was accused but found innocent of killing his wife Nicole in 1994. As a football player, Simpson had won the Heisman Trophy in 1968 while in college at the University of Southern California and went on to stardom in the NFL for the Buffalo Bills and then the San Francisco 49ers. Simpson followed his football career as an on-air television sportscaster and was a familiar television personality. In spite of widespread suspicion of his guilt, Simpson was acquitted of all charges. However, in 1997 he was held liable in civil court for the deaths of Nicole and acquaintance Ron Goldman who was also in the house. O.J.'s case is often pointed to as the ultimate example of a professional athlete who avoided punishment because of his money and fame (Answers.com 2006).

Could reports of violent behavior by professional football and basketball players be rooted in the racist fears of the U.S. public? You'll recall from chapter 11 that table 11.3 showed the percentage of African Americans in 2004 in the NFL to be 69% and 76% in the NBA. With such dominance also comes some jealousy and suspicion from Whites about violent Black men since they see violent behavior on the football field or the basketball court. According to the National Opinion Research Center survey sponsored by the National Science Foundation at the University of Chicago, 56% of Caucasian Americans believe African Americans are more violent than they are (Lapchick 1999). Also, of the 1,600 daily newspapers published in the United States, fewer than half a dozen have African American sports editors in cities where there are pro franchises. The United States appears to have Caucasian American sports journalists writing for a Caucasian American audience that may already have prejudiced views of African American men.

While there is no question that violence occurs, when it involves football or basketball athletes, it receives exhaustive media coverage. Since African American men dominate those sports, if they are involved in violent behavior, it is practically guaranteed that the case will be widely publicized. Some African Americans such as Satch Sanders, who helped the Boston Celtics win eight world championships, are outraged by the violent portrayal of African American athletes. They point to the millions

of dollars that famous athletes donate to schools, charities, and youth foundations. Most professional athletes are solid family men who respect their wives, mothers, sisters, and women in general. Joyce Williams-Mitchell is the executive director of the Massachusetts Coalition of Battered Women's Service Groups and an African American woman who hates the violent image of athletes. She says, "It is a myth! Most batterers are men who control women through their profession, and they include police officers, clergymen, dentists, and judges. Athletes get the headlines, though, and an unfair public rap. Men from every profession, (regardless of race) have the potential to be batterers" (Lapchick 1999).

As already stated, we need more research before coming to any conclusions about violence and sport. Rather than rely on sensational examples from the press, we need solid data such as rates of occurrence to compare with the data for other groups of people. Drug and alcohol use should also be noted since they and not sport may be the cause of violence. No one is helped by sensationalized reporting or hidden facts. We need to address this issue as a society and take steps to prevent violence (Hughes 2004).

Consequences of On-Field Violent Behavior

Violent acts within sport shorten careers, permanently disable, and reduce the earning power of their victims. In professional football, spearing opponents by leading with the helmet and blows to opponents' heads have drawn the most attention in recent years. Quarterbacks are particularly susceptible to a blind-side rush, and the concussions suffered by prominent quarterbacks have crippled some teams and forced great athletes like Troy Aikman of the Dallas Cowboys into premature retirement.

Most professional athletes who suffer an injury try to keep playing or return to playing too soon. Then they often suffer further injury or their body compensates for the previous injury and thus predisposes them to further problems. It's a badge of honor to play with pain and injury and something that tough guys do. The sad result is that more and more athletes live the rest of their lives with bad backs, knees, or shoulders and a host of other complaints. Football players who carry the ball are running targets, and running backs have the shortest careers in the NFL, lasting an average of three or four years.

Violent on-field acts can rob big-time collegiate football teams of their best players. Professional football teams invest millions of dollars in their key players and have lots of money at stake. If the starting quarterback goes down, the team's fortunes are likely to plummet. League administrators are slowly realizing that protecting the players is crucial to keeping them on display and that curbing excessive violence helps the league. Likewise in the NBA, protecting players from violent fouls is crucial to the welfare of the league.

On-field violence presents a poor model to youth. Kids cannot withstand the same amount of physical abuse adults can. Kids have less mature bones and muscles and are more susceptible to injury, including career-threatening injury. Since younger athletes reach physical maturity at different rates, games may match athletes of vastly different size and weight. In youth and high school sport, clear rules against violence are needed to ensure the health of all players.

Reducing Violence

Earlier we discussed the stringent standards professional hockey has imposed since 2004, which clearly showed that the league believed changes in athlete behavior were necessary. Violence can be significantly reduced if those in charge of the sport agree that doing so is a worthy goal. Team owners have an investment in their athletes and can't afford to lose star players. Families don't want to see their kids injured or sentenced to a life of physical disability. League officials need to protect their superstars so they can continue to market them to potential spectators. Almost everyone in sport has a financial investment in the health and productivity of athletes and stands to gain by protecting them.

What can be done? Once violent acts are clearly defined in the minds of officials and coaches, penalties can be assessed right when the acts happen. Offenders can be immediately suspended from that game and future games. Players can also be fined, but forced inactivity carries more effect for most athletes. Coaches and teams who condone violent play can also be punished until they find the risks too great to allow such play any longer (NHL rules now punish coaches when players break the rules).

Educational programs like Mentors in Violence Prevention (MVP), founded in 1992 at Northeastern University, help reduce violence. MVP is the largest program nationally to use athletes to address violence against women (Lapchick 1999). Similar programs must be initiated in schools, churches, sport programs, and every other potential avenue. Professional sports must see it as being in their self-interest to minimize violence and must become leaders in the campaign against violence rather than waiting for others to take action.

Society must also tackle violence. Violent acts in the sports world may attract the headlines, but such acts also pervade business, profession, and education. When linked to social class and race, violence raises uncomfortable discussion that some people would rather avoid. But according to the U.S. Department of Justice, African American men have a one in three chance of spending time in prison during their lifetime (Chaddock 2003). Without addressing violence in light of race, ethnicity, sexual preference, or lack of education, American society may witness antisocial actions for years to come.

PERFORMANCE ENHANCEMENT THROUGH DRUGS

Perhaps no sport-related issue has received more attention in recent years than the use of drugs and performance-enhancing substances. This is not a new topic nor is there convincing evidence that drug

Ben Johnson of Canada was stripped of his gold medal in the 100 meter and banned from competition for life after testing positive for steroids at the 1988 Seoul Olympics.

use is more prevalent today than in the past. The differences are in the media reporting, the increasingly aggressive drug-testing programs, and the sophisticated methods abusers use to mask their actions.

One of the earliest mentions of performance-enhancing substances was made by Galenos, a Greek physician who practiced sports medicine and was born in 129 AD Reports from the early Olympic Games stated that athletes used herbs, animal proteins, and mushrooms to improve their performance. In the 19th century, French athletes reportedly drank a concoction of wine and cocoa leaves to reduce sensations of fatigue and hunger.

The Winter Olympics held in Oslo in 1952 was marred by heavy use of stimulants. The use of anabolic steroids was first reported in the 1960 Rome Olympics and again at the 1964 Summer Olympics in Tokyo. From that time until the 1980s, the illegal use of doping substances increased substantially because of lack of awareness and detection. In 1983, media attention focused on illegal drug use at the Pan American Games, where 19 athletes were found in violation. When Canadian Ben Johnson, winner of the 100 meters, tested positive for steroids and was disqualified at the 1988 Seoul Olympics, the problem of doping in sport received international attention (Lajis 1996).

Modern athletes may use three distinct types of drugs. First are the **prescription** or **over-the-counter drugs** that promote healing from sickness or injury or mask pain to allow the athlete to return to competition. Although elite athletes who mask their pain to continue competing may be at risk for long-term disability, they argue that it is their personal decision whether to risk the early return. Many athletes realize that a quick return is essential to keep their place on the team. Fans and the media applaud the athlete who guts it out after an injury, even though the athlete may be masking the pain through medication. Decisions to use restorative drugs should be made with honest medical advice. Young athletes should involve their parents in the decision rather than rely on the coach, trainer, and medical staff.

Stimulants, such as caffeine, cocaine, Benzedrine, Ritalin, and Methedrine, make up the second class of drugs in sport. Stimulants have been rampantly used in professional sport for decades. Players use them to get hyped up before competition and to heighten their arousal level. Speed or amphetamines are a fact of life in professional baseball, football, and basketball, and high-performance athletes feel pressured to take these substances just to stay competitive.

The third type of drugs in sport comprises **anabolic steroids** and related substances that increase muscles size, decrease fat, and produce secondary male sex characteristics. Anabolic steroids are faster and more effective than any physical training program for increasing size, strength, and speed. Weightlifters, track and field athletes, football players, and baseball players have all witnessed the miracle performances enhanced by steroids. There is evidence of chronic use of steroids by athletes in virtually every high-performance sport.

Other types of performance-enhancing substances used and abused by aspiring athletes include vitamins, health foods, human growth hormones, amino acids, and natural herbs. Athletes may also use blood doping, a technique in which oxygen-carrying red blood cells from blood previously withdrawn from an athlete are reinjected just before an event. Let's take a closer look at anabolic steroids and other performance enhancers.

Steroids

Steroids increase muscle size, speed, and power. They can also enhance masculinity, aggressiveness, well-being, and sexual prowess. For decades, sports fans have dismissed reports of drug use in sport. Americans prefer to accuse Eastern Communist countries led by East Germany as the main offenders in the Olympics. When evidence of illegal drug use became well publicized after the fall of the East German government, Americans merely nodded and assumed the bad guys had finally been caught.

But American Olympians had been quietly adding performance-enhancing substances to their own training regimens. In 2004, the world finally insisted on tougher drug testing before and during the Athens Olympic Games. Popular American athletes, particularly track and field athletes, were finally caught and labeled as drug cheats. Other athletes such as the premier sprinter Marion Jones and her partner, sprinter Tim Montgomery, were cast under a heavy cloud of suspicion. Montgomery was banned from the competition. Jones, along with dozens of others, was implicated in the investigation of BALCO Laboratories in California, and the final chapter of that network of illegal doping has yet to be written. Montgomery was banned following testimony from BALCO founder Victor Conte, who pleaded guilty to distributing steroids and was sentenced to four months in prison. Conte has also admitted supplying Jones and other Olympic and professional athletes with illegal drugs (ABC News 2004; Layden 2004).

Drug testing has evolved into random testing at any time, day or night, and when athletes least expect it. These policies are the only sure way to catch sophisticated violators who have learned how

In the Arena With . . . *Jose Canseco*

Professional baseball player Jose Canseco recently authored a controversial book, *Juiced: Wild Times, Rampant 'Roids, Smash Hits, and How Baseball Got Big* (2005). Canseco names other notable baseball players who he says were obviously using steroids and human growth hormones, although most of the other players have publicly denied any drug use. He believes most baseball players either have used steroids or are still doing so. According to Canseco, "The owners looked the other way even though they knew what was going on with steroids because the sudden increase in home run hitting brought baseball back to the front page after the disastrous player strike." But the owners "blackmailed me from baseball because I was the Chemist, the godfather of steroids in baseball."

In March of 2005, the U.S. Congress subpoenaed several prominent baseball players to appear for a full day of hearings probing the use of steroids in baseball. Members of the congressional committee lectured and generally decried the ruin of a game they grew up loving, but the recent rules MLB adopted for drug testing are still less stringent than the Olympic testing protocol.

Jose Canseco is convinced by his personal experience that properly using steroids and human growth hormones can benefit any athlete by increasing his strength, power, and ability to last longer as a major-league athlete. He goes on to say that anyone could benefit by using these drugs to slow the aging process. He also says that using these drugs improperly carries terrible risks, especially for young athletes.

---

to clean out their systems before competitions or anticipated tests. During the 2004 Athens Games, 22 athletes were caught in violation and sacrificed medals, reputations, and careers. That was twice the number of athletes who were disqualified in the previous Summer Games in Sydney. No U.S. athletes were involved, although American athletes came under heavy criticism since it was revealed that 24 American athletes had previously tested positive for banned substances between 1988 and 2000. Most of those cases involved stimulants, and each athlete was dealt with according to the drug-testing rules in effect at the time.

Concurrently, professional sports in the United States stepped up their effort to eliminate drug use. During contract discussions with MLB and other leagues, the player unions finally accepted significant penalties for drug use. Prominent athletes such as Barry Bonds were implicated for steroid use. While under grand jury testimony, Jason Giambi admitted to using steroids. Debates raged about home-run records that threatened to shatter those of Babe Ruth and Hank Aaron but were tainted by drug use. By the

summer of 2006, Bonds had in fact surpassed Babe Ruth's career home-run records and was second in baseball history only to Hank Aaron.

Bill Romanowski was a NFL star who won four Super Bowl rings and was named to the Pro Bowl twice. His book *Romo: My Life on the Edge—Living Dreams and Slaying Dragons* was released in 2005. According to *Publishers Weekly*, the book is about 30% football and 70% apothecary. Romanowski details his consistent drug use, which allowed him to play at a high level and return from injuries. He admits to using ephedrine, THG, DMSO cream, prescription-strength Motrin, and Naprosyn and claims he would do it all over again. Romanowski might have been an aberration, but his open account of years of drug use has made people pay attention to drug use in professional sports (Publishers Weekly 2005).

Bode Miller, who won the 2004 World Cup series in skiing, has made surprising comments to the media, saying that drugs such as erythropoietin (EPO) carry minimal risk and can help skiers if taken under supervision. While EPO is usually taken to boost endurance, Miller claims that it can help athletes by making the dangerous ski runs safer by improving instantaneous decision making (BBC Sport 2005).

Even the American hero Lance Armstrong, who fought cancer to reclaim his place as cyclist extraordinaire, has been accused of using drugs to capture the Tour de France, one of the most grueling physical tests in sport. Armstrong appeared on the national television program *Larry King Live* in August of 2005 to deny his use of any performance-enhancing substances and to bitterly denounce the inappropriate release of data from 1999, the year of his first victory, by the French sports newspaper *L'Equipe*. Testing done six years later on the B sample taken in 1999 showed evidence of EPO, a natural hormone produced in the kidneys. EPO increases the blood's ability to absorb and carry oxygen to cells, thereby increasing stamina in endurance races like the Tour de France, which requires cyclists to cover 2,500 miles (4,023 kilometers).

Without the A sample of urine, which was used up in 1999, the testing for EPO cannot be completed. There was no viable test for EPO in 1999, and so EPO testing was started seven years later with frozen sample of urine. Armstrong has never failed a drug test and has been tested more than any other cyclist both in and out of competition because of his prominent status and performance record. The controversy is unfortunate for both Armstrong and American sports fans, especially within a sport that has history of drug abuse. Millions of Armstrong fans are upset by the scurrilous charges brought against their hero who fought back from cancer to win a remarkable seven Tours de France (Cycling News 2005; Washington Post 2005).

Responding to Doping

Virtually every sport organization has begun to clarify and enforce the rules on drug use. The Olympics defines doping as "any method or substance that is harmful to athletes' health or capable of enhancing performance is doping." That broad definition is followed by numerous descriptions of doping methods and lists of illegal chemicals. Meanwhile, others press ahead to discover new masking agents that hide drugs and new combinations of substances that cannot be detected by current testing. As in most cases of illegal behavior, it seems the perpetrators are always just a step ahead of the enforcers.

Complicating the drug testing are debates about cold medicines that are banned but are still taken, perhaps simply by an athlete who contracts a cold just before a championship. Wouldn't the average citizen do the same if he caught a cold and needed to go to work? Gymnast Andreea Raducan was stripped of her gold medal in the all-around in the 2000 Summer Olympics because of a drug violation. The team doctor gave the 16-year-old Romanian two pills that contained nurofen, a common over-the-counter cold remedy.

Other controversies surround everyday vitamins consumed by average Americans. Are such vitamins illegal for athletes? Is Gatorade sold at grocery stores to help hydration and fight heat exhaustion an illegal aid? At American health food stores you can find and read the claims of thousands of agents that are not regulated by the U.S. Food and Drug

When an athlete such as Andreea Raducan is unknowingly given a banned substance by a trainer, should the athlete be punished?

Activity Time-Out: Justifying Athlete Drug Use

Some people like Jose Canseco believe it is foolish to try to ban substances. They suggest removing the rules and testing programs that don't seem to work anyway and allowing athletes to use substances with the advice of health professionals. The justification for allowing drug use in sport is that many nonathletes rely on drugs to deal with daily life. Preschoolers are put on Ritalin so they can focus. Parents take sleeping pills to sleep or tranquilizers and alcohol to relax. Other people use drugs to prevent pregnancy, cope with menopause, enhance sexual function, lower blood pressure, counter the aging process, fight migraines, and on and on. College students rely on caffeine or amphetamines to study for exams, and truck drivers take these drugs to stay awake on long hauls. Why should athletes be any different? What do you think? Would you continue down the same path of drug testing in sport, change the approach to drug testing in sport, or eliminate drug testing altogether?

Administration. The questions of illegal drugs are unending and sometimes so confusing that no solution seems possible.

There are signs of progress in drug testing and educational programs that combat the use of performance enhancers by athletes at all levels. Even high schools are considering drug testing for all students in cocurricular activities.

Under pressure from the U.S. Congress, MLB took major strides in 2005 to clean professional baseball of drug use. The league and players union agreed to a new drug policy that increases the penalty for failed drug test to 50 days of suspension for the first offense, 100 days for the second, and a lifetime ban (with appeal for reinstatement possible after two years) for the third offense (Associated Press 2006a).

The International Olympic Committee now forces all international governing bodies of sport to institute effective drug testing. Although the drug testing varies in different sports, it conforms to the basic IOC recommended format. Unannounced, random testing throughout the year, mandatory testing of competition winners, and minimum standards for frequency of testing have all led to more disqualifications now than in the past. Legal action such as that against the personnel at the BALCO Laboratories in California has helped offenses become publicized and thrown the weight of public support behind stronger enforcement.

Clearly the standard is set by the IOC, which has established doping as deviant behavior. No sporting organizations accept doping as proper and within the role of normal behavior (Luschen 2000). Continuing drug use in sport may lead to the following issues:

- A growing rejection of sport by fans, parents, and kids as a healthy, worthwhile activity.

- Withdrawal of financial support by corporations who follow public sentiment. If conventional wisdom lumps sport with other negative social activities, the benefits of being a corporate sponsor will fade quickly.

- Sport officials will accept that unless strong action is taken, athletics could be restricted to drug users, and athletes who refrain will only be also-rans.

- Drug use will affect the long-term health of former athletes long after use is discontinued. Athletes with shorter life spans and diminished quality of life will become commonplace.

- Young athletes will be enticed at an early age to follow the examples of their sport heroes.

- Female athletes who use drugs in early years may risk their ability to bear children later on.

- Genetic engineering may produce athletic capabilities only dreamed about and thus relegate performance enhancers.

Resolving these drug issues lies with sport leaders working cooperatively to ensure the heath and welfare of athletes. New attitudes and creative solutions to drugs must emerge for the sports world to avoid a rapid descent into competition dominated by chemicals. International sport bodies must work together on improving drug use in sport. Otherwise, if Americans solve some of the drug problems in their sport, they won't be able to compete with Chinese, German, or Russian athletes who may continue drug use.

The wrestling ritual of sweating off weight before the weigh-in and then gorging before the match can be considered an eating disorder.

The media can help by exposing doping in sports in a fair and unbiased manner. Blaming specific athletes is not useful if they are simply the victims of the situation. Coaches, sport administrators, officials, and sponsors must accept their share of blame and accept the need for change.

Parents can ban together to insist on consistent and fair policies for ensuring equal competition for their kids. Educational programs on doping should be available to families and required for sport participants.

Sport scientists can volunteer to provide guidance and recommend policies that support the philosophy of sport organizations. People who earn their living from sports or work with athletes to enhance performance can agree to a code of ethics that considers the welfare of athletes and sports in general.

Finally, sport participants can evaluate the value of an activity that may threaten their well-being. If athletes who love sports and value fair competition join together to restrict drug use in sport, they can catalyze powerful change in the sports world. The alternative is to withdraw from high-performance sport and move toward a society that values participation in sports regardless of the level of performance (Peretti-Watel et al. 2004).

EATING DISORDERS IN SPORT

An example of overconformity in sport is the incidence of athletes who develop eating disorders caused by or related to their sport. Athletes who are highly competitive often go to extreme lengths to maximize their chance for success. In some sports, maintaining lower body weights for either appearance or performance is clearly advantageous.

Athletes in sports that focus on physical appearance are at high risk for developing eating disorders. These sports include gymnastics, dance, figure skating, diving, and cheerleading. Other athletes at high risk are those in sports that reward body leanness such as cross country, wrestling, horse racing, and swimming. Power sports that rely on strength or body mass are less likely to encourage eating disorders, although there are cases of these disorders in every sport.

Most high achievers in sport are also highly disciplined and determined. They set lofty goals and spend many hours each day striving to reach them. They are rewarded for behavior that demands perfection, high motivation, attention to detail, and sometimes even obsession. If fellow athletes, coaches, and parents encourage these athletes to maintain thinness, their tendencies are only reinforced.

The three most common eating disorders found in athletes are anorexia nervosa, bulimia nervosa, and compulsive exercise. **Anorexia** is exhibited by people who starve themselves in order to maintain their perception of an ideal body weight. No matter how thin they are, they still regard themselves as fat. **Bulimia** is demonstrated by binge eating followed by purging. **Compulsive exercise** is characterized by overexercising rather than by undereating. These disorders may become so serious they lead to death. Other, more benign behaviors that may be precursors to these eating disorders include using diuretics, taking laxatives, dieting, fasting, following rigid patterns of eating certain foods, consuming inadequate protein, or being preoccupied with food.

Both men and women in any sport are susceptible to these disorders. Athletes are more at risk than nonathletes are. Depending on the sample of athletes and the study methodology, research shows that the percentage of female athletes who report eating disorders ranges up to 40%. In contrast, the percentage for male athletes is typically 10% or less (Nichols 1997; Sundgot-Borgen 1994).

Females clearly are more likely candidates for eating disorders. Research indicates that in the United States, 66% of high school girls and 17% of high school boys are on diets at any given time. These figures include both athletes and nonathletes. Of course, women who have careers in the entertainment or modeling industries also have a high incidence rate due to the pressure to limit their body weight (NFHS 2000; Quinn 2005).

Females who develop an eating disorder are likely candidates for **female athlete triad,** which includes disordered eating, amenorrhea, and osteoporosis or loss of bone density. Excessive exercise and restricted eating cause an energy deficit that stresses the body and changes its levels of hormones. The female athlete triad can affect the reproductive system, which shuts down the menstrual cycle, and lack of nutrients begins to destroy bone.

Before Title IX opened up athletic opportunities for women, eating disorders were relatively rare in sport. In the past, actresses, female entertainers, and models struggled with expectations to maintain low body weights and slim figures. Now athletes also feel those expectations, combined with pressure to perform in sports. In fact, some parents and coaches may partially cause eating disorders by sending messages to young female athletes about their body weight. Some research indicates that men may be especially insensitive to the feelings of their daughters, sisters, or wives and contribute to the problem (Women's Sports Foundation 2001a, 2001b).

National organizations, health professionals, coaching educators, and parent educators have all confronted the continuing problem of eating disorders. They've helped raise public awareness, and health professionals are now trained to recognize the signs of possible eating disorders. Coaches and parents know to look for warning signs and seek help at the first indication of a developing problem.

HAZING IN SPORT

According to the National Federation of State High School Associations, **hazing** is "any action or activity which inflicts physical or mental harm or anxiety, or which demeans, degrades or disgraces a person, regardless of location, intent or consent of participants" (NFHS 2006). Hazing is usually a rite of passage that must be endured to gain acceptance into a particular group like a fraternity or an athletic team. While hazing is not new, it has caught public attention as hazing practices moved from actions that were mostly annoying to actions that threatened physical or psychological harm. Activists fighting hazing liken their cause to that of sexual harassment.

A 1999 study of 244 college campuses completed by Alfred University and the NCAA found that approximately 80% of college athletes had been subjected to hazing (Alfred University 1999a). About half of these athletes were required to participate in drinking contests, while two-thirds were subjected to humiliating behavior. In the last 10 years, the media picked up on the story, widely reporting on hazing in colleges and high schools. In some cases legal action was initiated.

Today, both the NCAA and the National Federation of State High School Associations have express written policies against hazing and publish literature and sponsor educational seminars on combating hazing. In 2002, ESPN ran a weeklong television series on hazing in sport and followed it up with a companion piece on the Internet.

According to the study by Alfred University (1999b), the following athletes run the greatest risk for hazing:

Pop Culture: Deviant Behavior in the News

The spring of 2006 produced two big stories of deviant behavior in collegiate sports. The first was the arrest of three members of the Duke University lacrosse team for an alleged rape of an exotic dancer who was hired by team members to perform for them. Regardless of the outcome of the case, and whether the rape in fact occurred, the picture painted of privileged Duke students engaged in "Animal House" type behavior replete with alcohol, underage drinking, and exploitation of women persists. Just as people settled down from nightly news of the Duke case, Northwestern got into the act.

The Northwestern women's soccer team was suspended from all activities pending investigation of an alleged hazing of team members. A Web site displayed pictures allegedly of soccer players in various stages of undress, some with blindfolds on and others with hands taped behind their backs. It appeared that some were drinking alcohol. Hazing at Northwestern, as at most colleges, is clearly in violation of athletic department and university rules.

What links these two cases inextricably is that we used to think of "deviant behavior" as most likely to occur among males in team sports that were populated with players from so-called urban environments. Now, the incidents at Duke and Northwestern show clearly that athletes of all races, backgrounds, and academic ability appear to be involved in illegal activities (Associated Press 2006c; Brennan 2006).

- Male
- Non-Greek
- Swimmers or divers
- Soccer players
- On a residential campus
- Attend school in the U.S. East or South
- On a rural campus
- Lacrosse players
- In a state with no antihazing law

All athletes are at risk for hazing. Hazing can include excessively consuming alcohol, which is the most common behavior, enduring excessive physical punishment, acting as a personal servant to other players, going without sleep or food, engaging in or simulating sex acts, consuming disgusting food combinations, making prank phone calls, stealing or shoplifting, and being restricted from associating with certain people. More serious, life-threatening rituals include being violent toward others or being paddled, kidnapped, or abandoned.

For women, hazing tends to include more acceptable initiation rites such as extending practice sessions, taking oaths, doing volunteer work, dressing up for team functions, or participating in other activities that build the team. Men are much more liable to be threatened with extreme or harmful behavior.

According to ESPN.com, since 1980, most of the reported hazing incidents involve football players.

Incidents among football players were almost three times as many as those among baseball players, who were second in hazing incidents next to football players. Athletes in sports such as track, fencing, and golf were less likely to be hazed. Athletes in cross country, basketball, rowing, and tennis were less likely to be involved with alcohol use or other unacceptable or dangerous activities (Garber 2002).

Historically, many athletes and coaches believed that hazing was a benign ritual that built team unity, created camaraderie, and helped new athletes gain acceptance. But as the seriousness of hazing escalated, athletic teams and schools stepped in to ban hazing practices. According to www.stophazing. org, a Web site that monitors legal developments in hazing, all U.S. states except Arizona, Alaska, Hawaii, Montana, Michigan, South Dakota, Vermont, and Wyoming have banned hazing.

Some victims of hazing have died, such as Chuck Stenzel, the student at Alfred University whose death stimulated the national research on hazing. Some incidents end in lawsuits, such as one in which a California school district paid $675,000 U.S. to a Rancho Bernardo High School baseball player who was sodomized with a broom handle in the locker room after a game. Other victims have dropped sport or withdrawn from school to deal with the personal trauma they experienced (Farrey 2002a). The researchers who conducted the Alfred University study estimated that more than 1.5 million high school students are subjected to hazing each year. Of those, most were subjected to hazing in sport (24%); by peer groups or gangs (16%); in music, art, or theater (8%); or in church (7%). The number of student athletes in high school who are subjected to hazing totals 800,672 each year. Thankfully, due to media attention, comprehensive research by Alfred University, and educational programs for athletic personnel, parents, and athletes, the number of incidents seems to be decreasing. It is an issue worth monitoring for the future.

GAMBLING AND SPORT

Gambling on sport activities is nothing new. Accounts of gambling on sport are centuries old. In early colonial days, gambling focused on horse racing, cockfighting, boxing, and bearbaiting (Leonard 1980). As baseball gained popularity in the 19th century, local ball clubs began to pay some players under the table and fans began betting on games. When the national league formed near the end of the century, baseball became an openly professional game enjoyed by the masses and under the table payments were a thing of the past, but betting on games has survived (Stephan 1994).

The general public became keenly aware of illegal sports gambling when the infamous Black Sox scandal broke in the news. In the 1919 World Series, the Cincinnati Reds beat the Chicago White Sox in a disputed set of games. Investigations revealed that eight players on the White Sox were guilty of "dumping" the series in return for a financial payoff, thus dubbing the team the *Black Sox*.

College basketball suffered a similar scandal in the early 1950s when investigations revealed that eight colleges fixed some 86 games over three years. Thirty-two players were involved in the point-shaving scandal.

Pete Rose, one of baseball's all-time greats, has been banned from the sport and the Hall of Fame

Gambling on horse races, which has enjoyed popularity since Colonial days, continues to be a big industry in the United States. In 2005, total betting revenues on horse racing was $14.6 billion U.S., with 88% of that coming via track betting. An estimated $5.6 billion U.S. was wagered on the Kentucky Derby, arguably the most prestigious horse race in America (Ordine 2005).

because he bet on baseball during his career. He steadfastly denied the charges until it became clear he had no hope of reinstatement, at which time he admitted guilt.

Soccer scandal recently arose in Germany, the country that hosted the 2006 World Cup. Just a day before tickets were to be released for sale to the public for the 2006 event, a number of officials and players were implicated in a series of fixed games that had occurred in the previous year. The referees apparently made dubious calls, awarded suspect penalty shots, and conspired to change the outcome of the game (DW-World.DE 2005).

The problem with gambling on sports is that it calls into question the integrity of the performances by players, officials, coaches, and others. Players standing to gain sure money can be tempted to throw a game or shade the point spread. Once the public loses confidence in the integrity of the sport, its popularity is certain to decline. How many times have people watched a boxing match and been astounded at the decision or watched international judges at the Olympic Games show clear prejudices toward athletes from certain countries?

In the United States, 48 of 50 states allow some type of legalized gambling. Utah and Hawaii do not. Nevada is the only state where sport wagering is legal, although Oregon and Delaware have ventured into controlled sports gambling. Various media accounts estimate that the annual amount illegally wagered on sport in the United States is $80 to $350 billion U.S. In Nevada, the amount legally wagered on sport is just $2 billion U.S. per year (Weinberg 2003).

The NCAA and the major professional sport leagues have taken a strong stand against legalizing gambling in order to preserve the integrity of their games. Colleges are particularly sensitive to sports betting, and they mete out harsh penalties to students, athletes, coaches, or other administrators who violate NCAA rules. At the heart of their concern is that almost all gambling profits organized crime. Those profits are funneled into other illegal activities such as prostitution, supporting loan sharks, and selling drugs (NCAA 2004c).

In 1992 the U.S. Congress passed the Professional and Amateur Sports Protection Act to declare sports betting illegal in every state except Nevada, Oregon, and Delaware, which had preexisting laws. Though across the United States gambling has been recently legalized on riverboats and reservations, sports continue to be off-limits.

Not everyone believes sports gambling should be restricted. Mark Cuban, the controversial owner of the Dallas Mavericks of the NBA, has proposed a betting hedge fund. Hedge funds are loosely regulated investment funds favored by the wealthy since they typically require a significant minimum investment. Cuban compares sports betting to "betting" on the stock market. And people who buy stocks often do so knowing very little about the companies they are investing in. At least in sports, Cuban asserts, there is far better information about local sport teams than there is about local businesses; the local papers cover the sport teams every day (Cuban 2004). His proposal has drawn little support, and the NBA is clearly wary of introducing gambling into the sport (Cuban 2004; Hills 2004).

The strongest justification for legal sports gambling comes from those who suggest it can provide a bailout for local and state governments, who are searching for new revenue streams. When the governments promise to follow the example of Oregon and channel the profits into education or sport programs, there are public officials and many citizens who are tempted to embrace sports wagering if a significant revenue stream can be allocated to worthy causes such as education or youth sports. Proponents point out that currently illegal profits generated by sports gambling mostly go to illegal operations and organized crime, and this money could be used for worthier causes.

Those opposed to sports gambling believe that it will corrupt youth, offer an entrée to people from organized crime to become directly involved in sports, and take money from those who can't afford to lose it. They say that the benefits will go to bookies, a few gamblers, and offshore Internet betting sites. Those who will suffer include athletes who are pressured to throw games or shave a few points off the score, fans who lose faith in the legitimacy of games, gamblers who lose money, coaches who may become deceitful about their team's chances, and perhaps the American system of sports that will lose any semblance of integrity and eventually lose the fans that have made sports so successful.

A relatively new phenomenon in sports gambling is that of online betting, which so far is legal in the United States. A quick visit to the Internet reveals numerous opportunities to bet on virtually any sport. Betting begins at $5 U.S., and limits are set at $5,000 U.S. or in special circumstances up to $100,000 U.S. Fantasy football leagues have also become the rage in the United States. People select their own teams and then wager on their success each week. Fantasy team owners can select their players from any professional team and the composite performance of their players

No sport is immune from corruption. After a major judging scandal in pairs ice skating at the 2002 Winter Olympics, new judging procedures were put in place for the 2006 Winter Olympics.

(who play on many different teams) determines the success of their team. The future of online betting such as fantasy football is uncertain but clearly it will become an issue as it grows in popularity and receives more publicity.

Current laws, rules, and public opinion have rejected legalizing sports gambling, but as citizens have become more tolerant of gambling at casinos, on Native American reservations, and in state lotteries, the aversion to gambling seems to be subsiding.

While certain spectator sports such as horse racing, auto racing, and dog racing have long depended on gambling, most sports have steered clear of it. Stay tuned for continued strong debate.

CHAPTER SUMMARY

Deviance occurs in sports when athletes do not conform to accepted standards of behavior. Two distinct types of deviance were described: one in which athletes disobey the standards and a second in which athletes carry the standards too far.

The frequency of deviance occurring among athletes and coaches was compared to that occurring among the general population. In spite of abundant media publicity that makes it appear otherwise, there is evidence that athletes generally conform to expected standards of behavior and in fact probably exceed those standards.

Behavior is sometimes affected by the energy and intensity created during play. When those emotions overtake reason and control, people may act out of character. Coaches use emotional arousal to coax exceptional performances out of their athletes. Fans use the emotional release of sports to spice up everyday life. Hooliganism in soccer is an extreme example of this behavior.

Violence committed by athletes, whether committed on or off the field, is an issue of much debate. Some people believe violent acts within sport contribute to violent acts outside of sport. The facts, however, show that violence occurs among a relatively small percentage of athletes and is restricted to a handful of sports.

Drug use to enhance performance appears to be increasing in spite of strong actions to eliminate this practice. Doping has become more sophisticated, and testing with penalties seems unable to keep up with the creativity of athletes driven to excel by any means. In fact, there are some who believe it would be more honest and fair to athletes to simply allow the use of performance-enhancing substances and thus even the playing field. The current situation of enforcement trailing the ingenuity of athletes, coaches, and trainers who choose to cheat simply rewards the cheater in sports.

Eating disorders affect more female athletes than male athletes. People who participate in sports that emphasize physical appearance, such as gymnastics, ice skating, dance, and cheerleading, are at greatest risk for developing an eating disorder. Athletes in sports favoring leanness, such as wrestling, cross country, and swimming, are similarly at risk. The most common eating disorders are anorexia, bulimia, and compulsive exercise.

Hazing in sport has burst into prominence in the past 10 years due to widely publicized deaths, injuries, and humiliations suffered at the hands of athletic teammates. While hazing is not limited to athletes, researchers estimate that over 80% of college athletes are exposed to hazing, and in high school, nearly 25% of hazing victims are athletes. The alarming trend of growing numbers of serious incidents seems to have slowed due to wide publicity, educational programs, and state laws against hazing.

Gambling in sports is illegal in almost every U.S. state, and sport organizations at the professional and collegiate level have taken strong stands against it. Unfortunately, illegal betting on sports, encouraged by organized crime, has tarred the image of some sports in which fixed games and point-shaving have occurred. Arguments for and against legalizing sports gambling continue to this day.

18

Coaching Sport

Student Outcomes

After reading this chapter, you will know the following:

- Negative and positive influences of coaches
- Current standards, certification programs, and continuing education for coaches
- Differences in coaching at different levels of sport
- Personality, social orientation, and leadership style of coaches
- Challenges for the future of coaching

In looking at sport from every conceivable angle, we've examined the people who play sports and those who watch them. Now we'll examine a group that fills a critical role in sport: the coaches who provide the sport experience. No matter the level of competition, the coach significantly affects the experience of both athletes and spectators.

When you ask former athletes about their sport experience, they often mention significant coaches in their career. More than teammates, team owners, sport organizers, or parents, coaches are in the spotlight of athletic competition.

Coaches often help young people mature, set priorities, establish goals, learn sport skills, develop self-discipline, and so on. Because coaches typically work with younger athletes who are going through critical stages of personal development, they have a golden opportunity to influence young people. The fact that they are perceived as the keepers of the keys to the kingdom of athletic success doesn't hurt their potential to influence aspiring athletes.

INFLUENCE OF COACHES

Tom Crawford, who was formerly the director of coaching education for the USOC, cited this adapted quote from Hiam Ginott, a prominent psychologist and author who wrote two bestsellers, *Between Parent and Child* and *Between Parent and Teenager,* in the 1960s:

> "I have come to a frightening conclusion. I am the decisive element on the playing field. It is my personal approach that creates the climate. It is my daily mood that makes the weather. As a coach, I possess the tremendous power to make an athlete's life miserable or joyous. I can be the tool of torture or an instrument of inspiration. I can humiliate or humor, hurt or heal. In all situations, it is my response that decides if a crisis will be elevated or de-escalated, and an athlete humanized or dehumanized." (Mills 1997; Crawford substituted the word coach for teacher)

Those of us who have played sports would no doubt agree heartily. Coaches have been our heroes, role models, confessors, disciplinarians, mentors, teachers, leaders, and often our beloved friends. Their influence on us is incalculable, and we know how important they have been in our lives.

Like teachers, coaches have the opportunity to affect young people who are in the process of becoming an adult. The uncertainty young people face opens doors for coaches to suggest appropriate behavior and attitudes. The questioning of authority figures by teenagers presents coaches with opportunities to respond with patience and reason to influence rebellious minds. The battle with emotions uncovers feelings of inadequacy and the inability to manage feelings. Coaches can help athletes embrace these challenges, and they can suggest a course of action and reinforce good decisions.

Outstanding former athletes often do not make the best coaches. They may have learned skills easily and demanded much of themselves and thus are impatient with the performance of lesser athletes. Yet the public often seeks top former athletes to coach their children even when the former athlete has little training or experience in coaching. Educating the general public is the only way to combat this mistaken bias.

Coaching awards are almost always handed out to the coaches who win championships. However, the winning coach may win because he or she has the best talent (in his or her athletes), the best facilities, or the most money. It is easier to judge winning records than the more intangible results of coaching, but this approach reinforces an unhealthy emphasis on winning.

Positive Influences

Successful coaching cannot be described without comparing the coaching results with the expectations of the position. Obviously, success is defined differently for coaches of Little League teams than for managers of MLB teams.

In the public assessment of coaching success, wins and losses are typically the yardstick used. Yet we know that the best win–loss record does not always represent the best coaching job. Let's consider the criteria by which a coach might be more fairly judged, beginning with professional and high-performance sport. Currently, event outcomes are an accepted standard of measurement. Let's

A coach can be both a positive and negative influence on players. What qualities make a good coach?

look at other standards that should be considered for coaches in these situations.

Coaching success over several years with demonstrated consistency in performance regardless of the particular athletes participating is a more accurate indication of coaching ability. You may have heard coaches say they were more proud of their 20-year record than the number of conference championships they won. They realize that consistency over time is the real mark of excellence in coaching.

Innovative coaches who change their sport through their training methods, strategies, or other visible influences deserve to be recognized for their contribution. Regardless of their teams' win–loss record, the results of their innovation endure.

Coaches may be ultimately judged by the loyalty of their athletes even after those athletes' careers are over. Many former athletes keep in touch with good coaches who made a difference in their life. They rely on those coaches' counsel and support.

Leadership skills are critical for coaches at every level of competition. Successful leaders learn to adapt their skills to the group of athletes on a team and to individual athletes. This means not relying on

a single, fixed coaching or leadership skill, but tailoring that skill to the athletes. Coaches must develop leadership ability in training athletes' physical and technical skills, applying appropriate strategy, and setting a framework for the team to operate in a way that benefits the athletes as a group and as individuals.

Coaches who use democratic methods can allow greater athlete participation in setting group goals, arranging team practices, and plotting team tactics. This approach can foster significant growth, especially with younger players. However, it involves some risk by the coach, who has to allow the group to make certain decisions. Coaches of sports that require a great deal of independence by athletes can especially benefit from a more democratic approach. Team-sport athletes generally seem to prefer a more autocratic approach, in part because of the nature of the sport, the complexity of player interaction, and the dynamics of group interdependency (Riemer and Chelladurai 1995).

Coaches who work within an educational setting should be measured according to their contribution to the overall education of the young people in their

In the Arena With . . . *Bob Hurley*

The story of Bob Hurley is fascinating, instructive, and inspiring. Hurley has fashioned a career as a high school basketball coach at St. Anthony's Friars in Jersey City, New Jersey, by attracting kids off the streets to a small Catholic high school and forging them into a national power in high school sport.

Hurley's rules are firm, clear, and nondebatable. His methods are sometimes unorthodox, but they seem to work. Despite numerous offers to jump to the college coaching ranks, Hurley has stuck with his high school team. He not only saved the school's basketball program, he also helped raise money to save the school when it was threatened with bankruptcy.

Coaches earn their legacy through continuing superior achievements. Some coaches are blessed with gifted athletes for a few years and then are never heard from again. But the mark of a genius is to take kids year after year and turn them into consistent high performers. Hurley has done that for more than 20 years. At the same time, he's changed the lives of hundreds of kids who hang out on the mean streets of Jersey City.

Pick up a copy of the account of one season at St. Anthony's and see what you learn (Wojnarowski 2005).

charge. If the school district or university has clearly delineated the expected outcomes for student athletes, the task is much easier for the coach. Coaches can pay attention to more than athletic instruction. Their focus can be targeted toward enhancing the self-concept, self-awareness, and personal development of all athletes. The coach fills the role of adviser and supporter as athletes explore their potential through sport. Coaches help athletes make good decisions, figure out strategies, set performance goals, and learn from their mistakes.

Coaches who have a reputation for good sporting behavior contribute to the development of integrity in athletes. These coaches point out the requirements for moral behavior, and they allow athletes to make moral decisions and analyze the results of their choices.

The sidebar on Bob Hurley illustrates the commitment of a high school coach to players in a poor urban environment. While Hurley's record of wins and losses is impressive, the effect that his high school basketball team had on the lives of hundreds of young men is clearly more important.

Negative Influences

For all the positive influence coaches can have on athletes, there is another side of sport. Coaches who are inadequately prepared to be a coach or who coach for the wrong reasons may actually damage

young lives. Terry Orlick, a well-known sport psychologist, puts it this way:

"For every positive psychological or social outcome in sports, there are possible negative outcomes. For example, sports can offer a child group membership or group exclusion, acceptance or rejection, positive feedback or negative feedback, a sense of accomplishment or a sense of failure, evidence of self-worth or lack of evidence of self-worth. Likewise, sports can develop cooperation and a concern for others, but they can also develop intense rivalry and complete lack of concern for others." (1974)

For every positive coach who sets a good example, there are coaches who provide a negative example. Many coaches negatively influence young athletes, but the reasons they do so vary considerably. For instance, volunteer coaches who have little or no training may inadvertently make errors in judgment due to their lack of preparation for coaching. No matter how well intentioned, their lack of understanding of players and the coaching process may harm their athletes. In order to minimize the risk of poor coaching due to lack of preparation, parents, players, and communities must raise the expectations for coaches who accept the challenge of working with youth. Parents have the right to expect coaches to have a basic understanding of coaching, attend training sessions, and access appropriate distance learning coaching information on line. Other coaches who may be certified or have some level of experience can also create a negative environment. Perhaps the most common conflict occurs when the coaching philosophy clashes with the athletes' reasons for playing the sport. If the coach is focused on winning, some decisions will seem unfair to athletes who are more interested in the joy of playing than winning every contest.

Another common conflict is the routine use of physical punishment to discourage bad behavior, poor performance, or lack of effort. Athletes who must suffer endless running laps or push-ups soon learn to avoid physical activity whenever they can. Coaches who instill an aversion to physical activity in young athletes are setting those children up for a lifetime of inactivity.

In youth sport, there are often conflicts between parents and the coach. The parents may misunderstand the coach's intentions and may question the coach's methods and allocation of playing time. The solution is for coaches to share their philosophy before the season starts, hold regular parent meetings to discuss issues, and try to find common

ground with parents. Without the support of the parents, the coach's role is considerably more difficult and may even become impossible.

Coaches at higher levels of play may face many of the same issues as those who work with younger players. In addition, coaches whose employment depends on a winning record often make decisions that don't please every athlete on the team. Athletes who accept the competitive challenge to join a team where winning is clearly the focus must expect the coach to build a system that in the coach's judgment will produce the best results.

Because coaches are human beings with certain beliefs, prejudices, and personality quirks just like anyone else, athletes need to evaluate coaching behavior within the overall context of the situation. If the coaching philosophy and behavior are simply at odds with the athlete's reasons for playing, the athlete may prefer to change sports, schools, or private programs and find an organization where he feels more in tune with the program and the coaching personality.

At the extreme negative end of coaching behavior, you can find verbal, physical, and psychological abuse of athletes. **Abuse** is the willful infliction of

Expert's View: Addressing Coaching Abuse

It is helpful for coaches and athletes to be familiar with examples of abuse so they can recognize it, avoid it, and deal with it before it becomes a major problem. The Women's Sports Foundation has developed policy and position statements in the hope that leaders of sports governing bodies, youth sports programs, educational institutions, and athletic programs will adopt their own policies based on this information. Here are some common examples of abuse (Women's Sports Foundation 2004b):

- Verbal abuse may include public ridicule, profanity, or racial remarks. It may also include remarks about a player's appearance, body weight, or lack of courage.
- Physical abuse may include touching a player forcefully, unreasonable physical punishment, withholding food or water, holding endless practices until players get it right, or forcing an athlete to play with an injury or illness.
- Psychological abuse may include setting athletes up for failure by setting unrealistic goals such as an undefeated season; blaming seniors, captains, or star players for a team's poor performance; blaming a loss on one player's mistake late in the game; or benching athletes without explanation.
- In recent years, the media have publicized some unfortunate cases of hazing of athletes during preseason camps. In a few extreme cases, athletes died from physical abuse or alcohol abuse administered by teammates. Rules against hazing have now become common and punishments for both coaches and players are clear, including immediate dismissal. Coaches must not only make it clear that hazing is unacceptable, but they must also be vigilant for events that may take place in spite of their warnings. (See chapter 17 for more discussion on hazing.)

injury, pain, mental anguish, intimidation, or punishment, and it exists in the workplace, at home, in the government, and even in religious organizations. Adults who have power over younger people sometimes cannot resist the urge to use their power inappropriately.

Awareness of sexual abuse has risen, particularly with the increase of females in sport and the fact that more than half of their coaches are males. The Women's Sports Foundation has led the way in educating coaches, players, and parents on how to minimize the chances for sexual abuse through background checks, clear policy statements that delineate unacceptable behaviors, and a process for reporting and dealing with abuse if it occurs.

Verbal and physical abuse has always been an issue in sport, but athletes today are less tolerant of it and more likely to strike back or report it to authorities. Most educational institutions prohibit the use of degrading racial remarks, profanity, and public sanction or embarrassment, and offenders can lose their jobs.

The key to avoiding abuse and negative behaviors in coaching is for athletic organizations to delineate their expectations for coaches in writing and secure agreement from prospective coaches before hiring them. In addition, coaches should be trained in the policies and given specific examples of inappropriate behavior. A procedure for filing complaints against coaches should be spelled out and explained to coaches, parents, and athletes so that situations can be resolved and everyone's rights protected in the process. Finally, the consequences for a coach who exhibits abusive behavior should be spelled out and applied in situations where the charges are clearly proven.

STATUS OF COACHING

The number of young athletes who play sports has been estimated recently at about 40 million, which includes more than half of all kids age 5 to 10. To serve these young athletes, more than 3 million coaches work at all levels of ability. Roughly 500,000 of these coaches work in high school programs with varsity athletes. Yet out of all these coaches, it has been reported that less than 8% of high school coaches have had significant training in instruction, skill development, or other coaching skills, and even fewer coaches at the youth sport level have received significant training (Martens, Flannery, and Roetert 2002).

Coaches of college and professional athletes are more likely to have professional preparation for coaching than those who work with younger athletes. In most cases, they have graduated from college sport programs and served some time as an apprentice coach with other experienced coaches. However, at the professional level, many coaches have been outstanding sport performers who have little background in coaching. Their coaching methods are more likely the result of watching former coaches and imitating qualities that they admired.

It may be helpful to separate coaching into different levels when considering its history, current status, and future needs. Coaches of high-performance athletes tend to have the most preparation for coaching. Coaching is their chosen occupation and their career success depends on their knowledge and competency. They are highly motivated to seek every last bit of knowledge that may influence their chances for success. Because these coaches work with elite athletes, the number of positions available

The old standards of coaching—hat, whistle, and clipboard—are no longer sufficient in today's sports world. Today's coaches need good training and support systems.

is limited. The vast number of athletic coaches will never coach high-performance athletes.

Coaches of athletes who are most interested in participation than performance include almost all youth sport coaches and many at the high school level. These coaches enjoy being around young people and enjoy sport. At the youth level, they are typically volunteers; at the high school level they may be paid a modest stipend. Almost all of these coaches have other sources of income that represent their true profession. This group also includes some individuals who work for sport organizations, private clubs, and public parks.

Admittedly, there are some coaches who blend the goals of both participation and performance with adolescent or adult athletes. This group is likely to have some coaching preparation, and the demands of their competitive athletes force them to continue to upgrade their coaching skills. High school coaches in highly competitive sports such as football and basketball, particularly in sport-crazy communities, usually lean toward the performance model of coaching by virtue of the demand for winning teams.

Without drawing a black-and-white line between a description of the two major groups of coaches, those for performance and those for participation, it may be helpful to consider the significant differences between them. As we consider various topics, keep in mind not to lump the two groups together, especially when there are major differences between them.

Coaching As a Profession

Although we often refer to coaching as a profession, it is very difficult to make the case that it is indeed a profession. A profession is an occupation that

- dedicates itself to providing beneficial services to people;
- is based upon a generally accepted scientific body of knowledge;
- requires a rigorous course of study to transmit knowledge and skills;
- requires certification by demonstrating mastery of knowledge and ability to use the appropriate skills (membership is controlled by licensing after testing);
- has an accepted public code of ethics;
- monitors itself to sanction or remove those who do not live up to the expectations of the profession;
- provides and expects continuing education to members to ensure up-to-date information and skills; and

- establishes an organization to implement the standards, certification, and education of members (Martens, Flannery, and Roetert 2002; VanderZwaag and Sheehan 1978).

In general, coaching in the United States does not meet these standards. Many coaches are volunteers; they are untrained and coach only as a hobby. The problem in requiring volunteers to submit to more rigorous standards is that their numbers may simply decline, resulting in a huge coaching shortage for youth sport programs.

Full-time professional coaches who work at their craft would likely benefit in their career and in their compensation if coaching were to become a true profession. Raising the standards for coaching would likely improve the skill and knowledge of coaches and garner greater recognition by the public of the quality of the athletic experience. The casual, uncontrolled manner in which many coaches are hired simply does not merit public acceptance or regard for coaching as a profession when compared with law, medicine, engineering, or religion. However, there is no reason not to work toward making coaching a profession.

Coaching Standards

Standards for youth sport coaching are primarily set by the local community. Depending on the organizing group, coaches may be expected to have playing experience, coaching experience, or some level of coaching certification or training. On the other hand, organizations may simply require a willing volunteer. The level of expertise varies widely from sport to sport, community to community, and possibly year to year.

Because there is such a great need for youth sport coaches, most communities are only too happy to welcome volunteers and often have to persuade hesitant parents to coach. Without volunteer coaches, sport teams cannot operate and children lose a great opportunity. Parents who lack time, experience, or skill in coaching may agree to coach just to be sure that their kids can play on a team.

This situation creates two perplexing concerns. One is the lack of experience and training among coaches. The second is that even if the community sponsors coaching education or training for their volunteer coaches, the turnover rate is extremely high and training has to be repeated every year. Most volunteer coaches only continue while their own children are in the program. If they want to continue to spend time with their own kids in sport, they move to a higher level or become a fan and spectator.

High school coaching standards have suffered from a similar dilemma. In the 1970s, the demand for competent high school coaches skyrocketed due to the passage of Title IX, which ensured equal opportunities for girls in sport. Suddenly, high schools were faced with a critical coaching shortage. Added to the expansion of girls' teams were declining enrollments, a depressed economy, and fewer job openings for classroom teachers who might be coaching candidates. As the teaching staff aged, many retired from coaching yet kept their teaching jobs, further complicating matters. Principals were forced to change or reduce their standards for coaches just to find available bodies to staff their athletic programs.

It wasn't until 1995 that the first set of national coaching standards for high school coaches was crafted. Led by the National Association for Sport and Physical Education (NASPE), more than 140 sport organizations have agreed that these standards, referred to as National Standards for Athletic Coaches (NSAC), represent the core body of knowledge for coaching expertise. These standards were developed by reviewing and adapting scientific knowledge, practical coaching experience, and content of existing coaching education programs. The NSAC consists of 37 standards that are divided into eight domains of knowledge and competency (NASPE 2001).

- Injury prevention, care, and management
- Risk management
- Growth, development, and learning
- Training, conditioning, and nutrition
- Social-psychological aspects
- Skills, tactics, and strategies
- Teaching and administration
- Professional preparation and development

The hope is that by organizing these standards for coaching competency into one comprehensive and cohesive document, it can serve as a blueprint for coaching education programs and certification processes. A National Federation of State High School Associations (NFHS) coaching education task force along with the American Sport Education Program (ASEP) took the lead by recommending that state high school athletic associations mandate an ongoing professional development program for interscholastic coaches. By 2004, after working together since 1990, the NFHS and ASEP persuaded 35 states to offer coaching education courses. By offering the courses online, coaches could access them from virtually anywhere they could access the Internet (ASEP 2005).

Perhaps the most important contribution of these standards is that they identify the vast breadth of knowledge that is required of competent coaches. As these standards become more publicized and well known by sport administrators, school personnel, parents, and the general public, it is likely that more will be expected of athletic coaches. At the same time, we can hope that as more training is required, the compensation and general status of coaching will be elevated (Brylinsky 2002).

In the last 10 years, the USOC encouraged each of its national governing bodies to identify the coaching competencies needed for their sport. National models were developed that were similar to the NASPE standards but tailored specifically to volleyball, soccer, tennis, swimming, and other Olympic sports. Information was shared between national governing bodies and the result was a more developed model for coaching education and certification programs within the Olympic family.

What qualifications does this coach need? How would those qualifications change if he coached at the high school level? The college level?

Activity Time-Out: Domains of Coaching Knowledge

Interview a coach of your choice. Ask the coach to rate the eight domains of coaching knowledge from the most important (with a rating of 1) to the least important (with a rating of 8). Ask why certain domains rated very high and others rated low based on the coach's practical life experience in coaching. Be sure to consider the level of athletes the coach works with when evaluating the ranking of categories. The eight domains of coaching knowledge are the following (NASPE 2001):

- Injury prevention, care, and management
- Risk management
- Growth, development, and learning
- Training, conditioning, and nutrition
- Social-psychological aspects
- Skills, tactics, and strategies
- Teaching and administration
- Professional preparation and development

Coaching Educational Expectations

There is tremendous variation in the requirements for athletic coaches in school settings. According to ASEP, 36 states require coach education for nonteaching coaches. Only 15 states require coach education for all coaching candidates, and 15 states require no formal coaching education. For many school systems, coaches at least must have a bachelor's degree in teaching and a current teaching certificate, but with the lack of available coaches who are willing to work for very modest pay, large numbers of schools have opted to hire coaches who have some experience in the sport but lack any educational training in working with kids (Martens, Flannery, and Roetert 2002).

In most colleges and universities across the United States, the minimal standard for an athletic coach is a college degree. Because coaches will be working with college athletes and operating in a college setting, most athletic directors believe that a college background is a minimum standard. Beyond that, the requirements vary widely, including experience as an athlete in the sport, coaching experience at the high school or college level, or certification by a national governing body or other agency in that sport. Some coaches work their way into college coaching by serving as volunteer assistant coaches, interns, or graduate assistants to gain experience and a foothold in the profession.

Coaching in professional sport differs markedly from coaching within the educational system. In professional sport the required background can range from experience as a player at that level to years of successful coaching at a lower level of play. The educational requirements are typically not critical since the emphasis of a professional team is simply to win contests. However, the lack of preparation in coaching is a heavy weight for many professional coaches who are limited by their own personal experience in sport. For example, most coaches of professional tennis are excellent former players who rely on the coaching methods used by their coaches perhaps a decade earlier. Without any firsthand knowledge of current coaching science, they simply use coaching methods and information that are hopelessly out of date.

Coaching Certification

Now that standards for coaching have been developed, publicized, and disseminated, you might expect that there would be ways for prospective coaches to gain certification. In fact, there are at least three avenues to pursue, depending on the sport, the level of coaching, and the depth of coaching education that interests you.

A total of 179 institutions of higher education offer either an undergraduate major or minor in coaching education or a graduate degree in coaching. Most college programs are offered by state universities, although a few private colleges also offer programs. At a minimum, the typical undergraduate program requires six to eight courses, including principles of coaching, some sport science, sport-specific courses, and practical experience in coaching. Virtually every curriculum also requires a course in prevention, care, and treatment of injuries. Many students major in physical education, kinesiology, sport studies, or sport and exercise science and then minor in coaching education. For prospective coaches who hope to find employment at the high school or college level, these programs are the logical track.

A second possibility for coaching certification is to investigate the requirements in the sport you are interested in. Most national governing bodies have a certification program that evaluates coaching knowledge and competency. Various levels of competency may be identified for beginning coaches, and there are opportunities to advance with more study, experience, and demonstration of higher levels of coaching expertise. These coaching certifications may be slanted toward youth coaching, private coaching, or high-performance coaching. For example, professional tennis coaches are certified as having the skills to work at tennis clubs and public facilities.

A third possibility is to seek certification through a national agency that is neither offered by an educational institution nor affiliated with a particular sport. These programs are primarily targeted toward youth coaches, high school coaches, Special Olympic coaches, or coaches of athletes with disabilities.

ASEP is the sport education provider of the National Federation of State High School Associations (NFHS). Founded by Rainer Martens in 1976, ASEP is committed to improving amateur sport by encouraging coaches, officials, administrators, parents, and athletes to embrace a philosophy of "athletes first, winning second" and by providing education to put the philosophy to work. ASEP has continued to produce training materials on coaching education, offering courses and videos. In spite of the availability of these excellent materials, the barrier for many coaches and program administrators is simply finding the time to use them. ASEP has helped solve that problem by developing online courses that can be taken at the coach's leisure.

The National Youth Sports Coaches Association (NYSCA) also offers certification to coaches by partnering with many community organizations such as the YMCA, PAL, CYOs, JCC, Boys and Girls Clubs, and local park and recreation departments. NYSCA also offers an introductory instructional video for coaches, one-day clinics, and a Web-based course.

Certification for coaches is usually awarded by organizations after the prospective coach demonstrates competency through written tests of knowledge and understanding, a face-to-face course of instruction, or evaluation of their coaching or teaching. For beginning coaches, the focus is typically on an introduction to coaching philosophy, first aid, basic coaching principles, and ethics.

Program administrators should be aware of the different standards of these certification programs since they vary widely and typically measure only a small fraction of the competencies required for successful coaching.

Continuing Education for Coaches

Once coaches enter the profession, they have an obligation to expand their knowledge and keep up to date with new developments. Imagine how much coaching methods have changed over the last 25 years with advances in nutrition, physiology, sport psychology, sporting equipment, dealing with injuries, and performance-enhancing substances, to name just a few areas. While the strategy and tactics of most sports remain relatively constant, approaches to teaching them do not. Technique constantly changes as athletes invent new ways of performing, and for some sports, new skills are invented that were only dreamed of in the past.

Fortunately for interested coaches, many self-education resources are available. Here are a few of the options:

▪ Purchase books, videos, and DVDs for a personal coaching library.

Activity Time-Out: Coaching Certification

Interview a coach. Ask the following questions: Are you certified? How did you achieve that certification? Do you think it was a worthwhile experience? What changes would you make to that certification process now that you have had experience coaching? Be sure to identify the coach's sport, number of years coaching, and level of athletes coached.

- Review information online. Online courses are available, as are coaching discussion groups and networks of other coaches eager to exchange ideas. Information from international groups and other countries is also often available online.

- Attend coaching conferences sponsored by national governing bodies, state high school sport associations, and college sport associations held locally or at the state or national level. Experts in every imaginable area will tutor you and informal conversations with other coaches provide a wealth of knowledge.

- Subscribe to magazines, periodicals, or newsletters such as *Coach and Athletic Director Magazine, Scholastic Coach Magazine,* or one published by specific sport or coaching organization that delivers current coaching tips and information on a regular basis. Typically the information is screened by a panel of experts and written by experienced coaches or writers.

- Join a professional coaching organization in your sport, such as the United States Professional Tennis Association. Such organizations offer workshops, materials, and regular mailings to keep you on the cutting edge of your sport.

- Attend a coaching school offered by the NGB in your sport that offers a few weeks of intensive study and practical experience.

- Volunteer to assist an expert coach whom you admire.

- Take graduate courses in coaching education at a nearby college or university.

- Take a coaching course offered by ASEP or sign up for other national programs for coaching.

- Watch sport on television, observing the coaches' behavior.

- Consult specialists in fields about which you know little. For example, a sport psychologist may be willing to help you learn about the basics of mental toughness.

- Read books that chronicle the careers of popular coaches who have had success.

- Rent movies that feature coaches, such as *Friday Night Lights, Remember the Titans,* or *Glory Road.*

- Listen to interviews with coaches that you admire to see how they handle questions, criticisms, victory, and defeat.

Coaches have to work at their profession just as others work at theirs. You would be horrified if your personal physician who attended medical school 25 years ago did not keep up with advances in medicine. Coaching is no different and demands a lifetime of continuing education.

COACHING AT DIFFERENT LEVELS OF SPORT

It is unfair to lump all coaches together when considering what skills and competencies they ought to have. Different levels of athletes by age, skill, commitment, and sport require different coaching skills. In the following sections, we'll look closely at coaching at each level of participation and what makes a coach at that level successful.

Professional Sport

At the highest performance levels, coaches typically have a personal background of competing at that level. They also need to understand and accept the business aspect of sport, the commitment to winning that is required, and the criticism they will absorb if their team does not win. Since the athletes may be paid handsomely and may make several times more than the coach, motivation is sometimes a challenge. In addition, years of athletic training have inured some professional athletes to advice from coaches. And although these athletes are adults, they often are susceptible to lifestyle habits that interfere with their performance.

A perplexing conundrum exists in that although these athletes have reached the highest levels of sport, fundamental skills may be lacking. Coaches of professional athletes have to be skilled in teaching fundamental skills to athletes who are typically resistant to change.

Finally, the length of the season, the physical injuries, and the intensity of competition all take a toll on professional athletes. Coaches need to be well versed in the mental skills and strategies that can help athletes deal with constant challenges to maintaining a healthy psyche.

High-Performance Amateur Sport

Some children begin specializing before the age of 10 with the goal of reaching the highest levels of sport—the Olympics, international competition, or professional sport. Those who coach these athletes must be able to teach fundamental skills to young athletes who will stand up against top competition as they age and gain experience.

Coaches of young athletes also need a firm understanding of the growth and development of

The needs of professional athletes like former Olympian Nancy Kerrigan are very different from the needs of a beginner athlete. A good coach needs to know how to address those unique needs.

Finally, coaches of athletes with high aspirations must deal with parents and agents who also have opinions about the training and competitive schedule of the athletes. Their motives may be noble but less informed than that of the coach, so it falls to coaches to provide steady, responsible guidance, relying on specific experts to bolster their position when necessary.

Intercollegiate Sport

The requirements of college coaches vary depending on the college that employs them, the level of competition (Division I, II, or III), and the sport they coach. There is a wide range of expectations, facilities, levels of athletes, and compensation depending on those factors. Many smaller colleges hire part-time athletic coaches who are paid several thousand dollars for their work during the season. In contrast, large universities with highly competitive programs employ many full-time coaches who devote their time year-round to recruiting, off-season training, preseason training, and of course in-season practices and games.

The NCAA publishes and enforces a set of rules that college coaches must follow. Coaches must spend a significant amount of time verifying that their actions are within the rules to avoid embarrassing mistakes that could cost their employer dearly in penalties.

Building strength and endurance is also a key factor at this level because the athletes are capable of making huge gains in size, speed, and endurance. Year-round training is expected, especially for Division I athletes, although contact with a coach is limited by the NCAA during the off-season.

High School Sport

Coaches of high school athletes need to have a wide breadth of coaching knowledge and a keen understanding of young adults. Skills and strategy expertise are a must. Athletes who have developed bad habits need special care to learn new skills. Practical sports science knowledge such as injury prevention, physical training, and sports psychology

prepubescent athletes since their charges will be going through significant physical, emotional, and mental changes as they experience puberty.

Knowledge and understanding of the mental side of performance is essential for coaches since their athletes will be dealing with competitive pressure even at relatively young ages. Psychological skills that enhance performance must be taught and practiced along with physical skills. Burnout is common in intense competitive training, so coaches need to recognize warning signs and know how to deal with related problems.

Physical training and conditioning for elite levels of sport is quite intense and can be harmful if not properly designed and monitored. Injuries from overuse are common unless steps are taken to minimize their effect. Diet, nutrition, and strength training are all an essential part of high-performance training.

can be extremely helpful in teaching gifted athletes and dealing with psychosocial issues.

Generally, coaches of high school sport are former athletes who may also have played sports in college. They are hired to teach in the school system and offered a supplemental contract to coach after school. The remuneration for a season of coaching varies widely but may be as little as $1,000 U.S. for smaller sports like tennis and golf and up to $10,000 U.S. for sports like football in more affluent communities. Young teachers may coach several seasons and thus earn supplemental pay each season. However, teaching a full day and then adding coaching duties is challenging and exhausting. Many retire from coaching as their own families mature and they no longer enjoy the fast-paced schedule.

Coaching education for high school coaches is spotty, and aspiring coaches must seek out coaching clinics, workshops, and conferences on their own. Some sports offer easy access to education through books, videos, and seminars while other sports are poorly organized. Few states have rigorous standards for coaching, and many athletes have suffered under the tutelage of so-called warm-body coaches who accept the job under pressure but have minimal expertise or interest.

A typical high school coach usually likes kids, knows how to organize and administer the team, and can be a helpful adult role model during the critical adolescent years. It is more unusual for high school coaches to have a broad and deep knowledge of coaching and their sport. If they do, greener pastures at the collegiate level often beckon.

High school coaches who are dedicated to their sport often get involved in the sport at the community level and help develop youngsters as a feeder system for the high school team. They track potential athletes from an early age, offer advice, coach them in high school, and help them choose a college. For many dedicated coaches, this is a lifelong pursuit, and they gain so many friends and supporters over the years that a run for mayor is not out of the question. I've known more than one former coach who easily "retired" to the position of mayor or council member.

As athletes enter their preteen and teenage years, their coaches need to be strong both technically and strategically. They need to empathize with kids entering puberty, and they must be sensitive to the vast physical and emotional changes that accompany this period. Discipline and hard work will enable athletes to develop their individual talents. The coach must also help the athletes balance their dedication to sport with responsibilities to family, friends, and school.

Youth Sport

When kids are young and first exposed to sport, they need coaches who understand them, why they play, and what they expect out of sport. Coaches who are sensitive to their needs, concerned for each child's welfare, and able to produce success for each child to some degree are worth their weight in gold. Coaches of young beginners also need to be well schooled in teaching the basic strategy and skills of the sport so that children develop sound fundamentals.

Coaches of young athletes must help them understand the rules of the game, develop good sporting behavior, learn basic skills and strategies, and have fun. If they don't make sport attractive to children, even talented athletes will drop out since they haven't yet invested much time or effort. In addition, parents may need education in the philosophy of the program, unlike at other levels. When athletes are young and malleable, parental understanding of the sport and support of the program goals are critical, and attitudes about winning and losing are particularly crucial for parents to embrace and guide their youngsters.

A coaching personality that is fun, warm, and engaging is critical for young athletes. They want to enjoy time with their friends, test their skills, and celebrate games with a trip to the Dairy Queen regardless of whether they won or lost. Coaches should love to spend time with kids and enjoy their foibles without judging them or their parents.

Of course, even at different levels of coaching in youth sport, situations can vary. High-performance athletes who are very young such as gymnasts, tennis players, swimmers, and others who compete nationally and internationally present a coaching dynamic that is very challenging. Parents sacrifice huge amounts of money, and sometimes they uproot families to seek better competition. Their kids thus feel tremendous pressure to succeed. It takes special training and a special personality to work with young athletes and their families while dealing with the pressure for immediate success against the best competition in the world.

Coaching for Male or Female Athletes

Since the passage of Title IX and the opportunities for women as coaches has expanded, most research has focused on tracking the numbers of women in coaching rather than their coaching methods. Perhaps that is partly due to the fact that so many men have taken over women's teams. In any case, female athletes agree that they prefer a coach who is a quality person, a role model, assertive, cooperative,

What did Ashley McElhiney, the first female coach of a men's professional basketball team (the Nashville Rhythm), need to know about how males react to coaching styles?

not clear whether these differences are the result of cultural expectations or whether they are innate traits (Stewart 2005).

It is quite possible that girls who are exposed to male coaches and compete at highly competitive levels will be more likely to exhibit traits similar to those exhibited by boys simply because of their training and competitive experience. Nevertheless, it is important for coaches to recognize that differences exist and that coaching styles need to fit the needs of the athletes.

COACHING PERSONALITY

It may be unfair to lump all coaches together in a single group and attempt to describe their personalities, beliefs, and orientations. However, in every occupation certain similarities among practitioners give the impression of a stereotype that has some basis in fact.

determined, respected, willing to help, dedicated, responsible, energetic, and cool under pressure. They also prefer coaches who have a great personality. Not surprisingly, these traits do not differ significantly from those valued by male athletes (Holbrook and Barr 1997).

However, there are some indications that boys and girls react differently to coaching styles and that coaches should tailor their coaching methods to maximize the athletic experience for both genders. Craig Stewart has summarized the research on the need for different approaches in coaching female and male athletes (Stewart 2005). According to Stewart, girls are more intrinsically motivated by self-improvement and goals related to team success than boys. They are also more motivated by a cooperative, caring, and sharing team environment. Some female athletes can be turned off by coaches who overemphasize winning, and they seem to approach competition somewhat differently from male athletes (Garcia 1994). For example, girls seem to place more emphasis on playing fair and tend to blame themselves for a poor performance. Boys are more likely to break rules; strive to win at any cost; and blame other people or things for their defeats such as the weather, referees, or lucky breaks. It is

Coaches are not immune from stereotypes. Movies, television, and books often present coaches in a baseball cap with a whistle around the neck shouting profanities at their young charges. Of course, these representations are unfair, but they are based on years of observation by athletes, parents, and spectators.

Researchers have revealed that historically, male coaches have typically reflected certain personality traits. Sport psychologists Tom Tutko and Bruce Ogilvie and sport sociologist George Sage collected information in the 1970s that suggested that coaches tended to be moderately conservative; that is, they tended to value loyalty to tradition, respect authority, expect obedience, follow normal standards of conduct, and have strong religious orientation. Coaches in traditional team sports in highly competitive environments still tend to exhibit these characteristics because that style of authoritarian coaching fits with the so-called professional model of coaching (Lombardo 1999; Sage 1973).

Athletic coaches tend to be more conservative on most matters than the college students they coach, a situation that has often led to conflicts. However, when compared with other adults such as businesspersons or farmers, coaches were more to the middle of the road. Compared with other teachers at both the high school and college level, coaches tend to be among the most conservative of those groups.

The historical reasons for athletic coaches tending toward a conservative personality include the following (Lombardo 1999):

■ Coaches are typically former athletes who have seen their own coaches operate in a conservative atmosphere and they tend to perpetuate that style.

■ Coaches often have clear concepts of right and wrong based on strong religious and cultural backgrounds.

■ Coaches often come from working-class families where traditional values are emphasized as well as respect for authority and tradition.

■ Because most coaches are held accountable for their team's performance, they like to seize control of the team even if it means coaching in an authoritarian style.

■ In the past, many coaches had a strong military background that influenced their attitudes, beliefs, and habits. Since a volunteer army was instituted in the United States and fewer current coaches have had a military experience, this influence may have declined.

Since this research was conducted, sport has changed. In many instances the changes mirror changes in society. Women are now fully engaged in competitive sport, significant progress has been made in racial integration within sport, and scientific research on sport has added to the existing knowledge base for coaches.

Active coaches today have certainly been affected by their own athletic experiences, mentors, and life experience. If they model their coaching behavior on the past, they will likely encounter difficulties. Young athletes today have grown up in a world that is much different from that of their coaches. They have more personal freedom, are more likely to question authority, make decisions without parental knowledge or support, and often rely on peers for advice and counsel. The decline of stable two-parent families has contributed to some of these changes. Other general societal trends toward a more permissive environment have aided these changes, such as the fact that many families have both parents employed outside the home, thus giving kids a lot of independence.

Young athletes expect to enjoy their sport experience and often simply withdraw if they don't. They expect coaches to be attentive and interested in them as people rather than just sport performers. Authoritarian coaches may succeed in certain situations, but generally they have been forced to modify their coaching behaviors to adjust to today's athletes. Many coaches of women's teams also have learned to adapt to the needs of their athletes that are different from the needs of male athletes.

An in-depth look at the characteristics of coaches is likely to reveal some trends that may differ from those of the past. Coaches of certain sports that are more individual may have a different view than the traditional team coach. Consider the role of a tennis or golf coach who only deals with six or eight athletes compared with a football coach who presides over a squad with well over 100 athletes. Naturally, with such a large squad the opportunities for close interpersonal relationships are limited and the coach may be forced to adopt a role similar to that of the CEO of a small company.

Another factor is the shifting emphasis in professional sport from autocratic coaches to those who can manage a sizable business with the acumen of a savvy businessperson. The exorbitant contracts of star players and their influence on the success of the team have also shifted the balance of power from coach to outspoken players. A case in point is the breakup of the Los Angeles Lakers dynasty after the 2004 season and the firing of Phil Jackson, one of the most celebrated coaches in recent years. Because star player Kobe Bryant was unhappy with his role compared with that of Shaquille O'Neal, both Jackson and O'Neal were let go. Eventually, O'Neal was traded to the Miami Heat and Jackson was rehired by the Lakers for the 2005 season.

It is dangerous to generalize too much and stereotype groups of people. Athletic coaches are victims of those trends even though much of the conventional wisdom about coaching styles is outdated. In order to be successful in today's world, the majority of coaches have had to adapt their behavior to the coaching job they accept and align their coaching methods to the goals of the sponsoring organization and the expectations of the athletes entrusted to their care (Lin, Jui-Chia, and Esposito 2005; Lombardo 1999).

Coaches at other levels of competition, including nonrevenue sports at colleges, most high school sport, youth sport, and sport for athletes with disabilities, and older athletes are more likely to develop a humanistic or invitational style of coaching. They need to focus on the total development of the people

In the Arena With . . . *John Wooden*

John Wooden of UCLA was the most successful coach in the history of college basketball. His coaching records will likely stand the test of time. Imagine a young, eager coach setting out to equal or break Wooden's records of

- 10 national championships;
- an 88-game winning streak;
- four seasons with a record of 30–0; and
- a record of 885–203 in 40 years of coaching for a winning percentage of .813.

Wooden was a fine basketball player and is one of only two people inducted in the Basketball Hall of Fame as both a player and a coach (the other is Lenny Wilkens). He was a three-time All-American and was named College Player of the Year after leading Purdue to a national championship in 1932. What might seem remarkable today is Wooden's vital statistics of 5 feet 10 inches (1.8 meters) in height and 185 pounds (84 kilograms), yet he dominated college basketball.

Wooden was voted NCAA Coach of the Year six times, Sporting News Sports Man of the Year (1970), and *Sports Illustrated* Man of the Year (1973). His UCLA Bruins dominated college basketball through the 1960s and 1970s.

After stints as a high school coach and two years at Indiana State, Wooden was hired at UCLA in 1948. It took him 15 seasons to win the first of 10 national championships, a fact that should be instructive to young, impatient coaches and athletic directors with a "win or else" attitude.

Perhaps Wooden's most enduring legacy is the lessons he has taught us about coaching. His well-known "pyramid of success" outlined his building blocks for success and were the coaching bible for a generation of coaches. He believed in hard work, discipline, superb physical conditioning, drills run to perfection, and team play, and his teams proved how well those principles worked in real life.

Source: www.hoophall.com/halloffamers/Wooden.htm

they coach rather than on competition results. Coaches of sports that require independent thinking by athletes need to encourage and help players think for themselves. Those who subscribe to the invitational style need to ensure that every aspect of their program and coaching behavior is warm and welcoming to athletes. Sport participation for these athletes is an opportunity to test their limits and realize their potential as human beings.

Many successful coaches have written an autobiography or had someone write a biography of their life and coaching career. For aspiring coaches, these can be inspiring and instructive words. The trick, though, is to sort through the lessons learned by another coach who lived in a different era and pick out those that will stand the test of time. The days of authoritarian, no-nonsense coaching are gone no matter how suc-

cessful Vince Lombardi was years ago. Some coaches whose careers have stood the test of time and are worth investigating include the following:

- Football: Joe Gibbs, Don Shula, Bill Walsh, Marv Levy, Bill Parcells, Bill Belichick, Urban Meyer, Steve Spurrier, Pete Carroll, Bobby Bowden, Joe Paterno, and Eddie Robinson

- Basketball: John Wooden, Adolph Rupp, Rick Pitino, Phil Jackson, Lenny Wilkens, Mike Krzyzewski, Pat Summitt, Vivian Stringer, Geno Auriemma, John Chaney, John Thompson, Dean Smith, and Jim Valvano

- Other sports: Dick Gould, tennis; Doc Counsilman, swimming; Leroy Walker, track and field; Nick Bollettieri, tennis; Dan Gable, wrestling; Joe Torre, baseball; Earl Weaver, baseball; Billie Jean King, tennis; Tony DiCicco, soccer; Anton Torrance, soccer; and a host of others who may have coached at high schools or smaller colleges

An analysis of their lives and careers can be very instructive to aspiring coaches.

CHALLENGES FOR THE FUTURE OF COACHING

Coaching is difficult to describe and evaluate because it differs greatly from one situation to the next. The common identifiable theme is that coaches are part of sport to help athletes achieve their best performance and enjoy the experience. In other words, coaches are leaders of people engaged in sport participation.

The United States is different from other countries in that we have no generally accepted body of knowledge that coaches are expected to know. Most developed countries, particularly in Europe, have a coaching education plan in place that is approved by the government agency responsible for sport and typically administered by the governing body of each sport. Canada and Australia are examples of other countries that have programs. Their nationwide certification programs have five levels of coaching certification and to reach Level 3, a coach must complete approximately 100 hours of training in theoretical, technical, and practical areas.

In the United States, there is no process for coaches to gain certification from a neutral agency that verifies their knowledge and skill. It is up to the sport consumers to demand a minimum level of expertise from their coaches and to insist on change when coaches do not measure up to these expectations.

Perhaps the first and most important challenge, then, is to develop national coaching standards that differentiate among the levels of coaching knowledge necessary for various athletes according to skill, age, and level of performance. The NASPE coaching standards that were agreed upon by over 140 sport organizations should provide the framework for those standards.

Once these coaching standards are finalized and accepted, they should be adopted by every sport organization that is responsible for administering sport programs. Acceptance means not merely endorsing the standards as a wish list, but ensuring that all coaches who work in their programs meet the minimum standards.

Enforcement of such standards leads to a national certification process delivered locally that enables coaches to verify their understanding and ability to apply knowledge in practical situation. At some levels, the certification process could be available through an interactive online distance-learning system to ensure the widest possible accessibility.

Finally, once coaches have achieved certification, there must be a systematic method of continuing education to keep them current with new knowledge and allow more in-depth exploration of coaching skills and competency.

The second challenge is to launch a public-awareness campaign to support this coaching education and certification process. The public must be more informed about the need for improvement

Parent volunteers are vital to youth sport programs, but how do we make sure they can coach?

In the Arena With . . . *Pat Summitt*

Pat Summitt is likely the most famous and successful coach of women's basketball in history. She started her coaching career at the University of Tennessee at age 22 in 1975 and has outpaced all other coaches during the ensuing 31 years by fashioning a win–loss record of 882–172 for a winning percentage of 84%. Her NCAA tournament record is 89–19 for a winning percentage of 84%.

As a player, Summitt won a silver medal in basketball at the 1976 Olympics and was the coach of the gold-medal team in 1984. Her college teams at the University of Tennessee have won six national titles during her tenure.

With the advent of Title IX, women coaches began to gain equal footing with male counterparts. Summitt's exemplary coaching résumé has earned her respect and pay equal to any male coach. She has even been suggested as a prospect for several jobs coaching male players. She was the first female to receive the John Bunn Award, a prestigious award given by the Basketball Hall of Fame. She was inducted into the Women's Sports Foundation Hall of Fame in 1990.

In 1997, Summitt was honored by Hillary Clinton at a White House luncheon as one of the 25 most influential working mothers. She has cochaired the United Way of Knoxville, served as athletic director at the University of Tennessee, and is a member of the board of trustees of the Basketball Hall of Fame.

Sources: www.allamericanspeakers.com and www.coachsummitt.com

in coaching knowledge and application. They have the power as consumers to demand certain levels of competency by the coaches they rely on to serve them and their families.

A third challenge involves recruiting, training, and supporting the army of volunteer coaches who are the backbone of most youth sport programs. Because there is such high turnover of volunteer coaches, recruiting and training processes must be streamlined, easily accessible, and inexpensive. Efforts should also be made to reduce the resignations of volunteer coaches who quit as soon as their own kids graduate to another level. Perhaps a model of sharing coaching responsibilities with divided responsibilities and less time investment would encourage more experienced coaches to continue.

A related issue that needs to be addressed is making the coaching education and certification programs relevant enough to convince sport program administrators, parents, and prospective coaches that their time will be well spent. Unrealistic expectations will doom attempts to educate and certify volunteer

coaches who may simply turn down a coaching position instead; the effect would be a crisis of too few coaches available to staff youth sport programs.

A fourth challenge is to develop strategies for recruiting females into coaching at every level. Despite the explosion of girls' sport in the last 25 years, the number of women who coach female teams is less than one-third of all coaches. For many women, family responsibilities take priority, but in these days of shared parenting, men should accept more family responsibilities in order to help put prospective female coaches on the field. Many women could make significant contributions to coaching young people. We accept a similar role for women as teachers in schools, so why not entice them to our ball fields or gymnasiums? In addition, when recruiting and retaining female coaches it is necessary to make certain their compensation is equal to that of male coaches. We also need to encourage the media to promote successful female coaches as role models for aspiring coaches, such as Pat Summitt, who is profiled in the sidebar.

A fifth challenge is to ensure the safety of athletes from negative behavior or exploitation by athletic coaches. Background checks, credential reviews, and consistent monitoring with comprehensive performance reviews should be required by sport programs that employ coaches. Abuse of athletes by coaches must be defined, acknowledged, and eliminated so that every athlete at all levels has a healthy experience.

A sixth challenge is to develop a recognition system that is based on criteria other than just wins and losses. While the performance of their athletes is one measure of coaches' success, there are other measures that should be considered in the context of the goals of the program. If teaching fundamental skills is critical for young athletes, then coaches who are masters of skill acquisition should be widely recognized and rewarded. Volunteer coaches who invest so much discretionary time must also be rewarded through public recognition and perhaps granted incentives such as trips to the highest championships of their sport or further educational experiences at no cost to them.

A seventh challenge is to recruit and promote coaches from minority groups to provide role models for younger coaches and athletes. Based on Lapchick's *Racial and Gender Report Cards* (2004, 2005a, 2005b), with the exception of professional basketball very few sports have a representation of minority coaches that mirrors their presence in the population.

CHAPTER SUMMARY

The influence of coaches on younger generations is enormous. Testimonials from former athletes abound with praise for their coaches as mentors, advisers, and heroes. Coaching athletes through the stress of sport binds coaches and athletes together in a bond unlike other adult–child relationships.

Regrettably, there are also opportunities for coaches to have a negative impact on youths. Unrealistic demands from a coach may turn kids off of sport and activity, make them resentful of authoritarian discipline, damage their self-confidence, and confirm their worst suspicions about adults who are using them for their own self-interests.

We explored the current status of coaching in the United States and learned that standards for coaching have only recently been developed and accepted by over 160 different sport organizations. In spite of this landmark accomplishment, implementation of those standards is just beginning and few general certification programs are widely available or mandated by organizations that sponsor sport programs.

Youth sport is unique in that its hundreds of thousands of coaches typically have little if any background in coaching. Perhaps more distressing is that soon after they learn coaching skills on the job, they often resign from coaching as soon as their own children leave the team or sport.

We examined the skills and competencies that are useful for coaches at different levels of sport. We also acknowledged that the coach's philosophy should match the level of coaching required and the athletes' expectations.

While it is difficult to generalize about such a diverse population, athletic coaches typically exhibit fairly conservative personalities, particularly in team sports and at the professional level. Coaches who work with athletes who are more oriented toward participation rather than high performance are more likely to employ a democratic model for coaching than an autocratic model. Most aspiring coaches model their behavior after former coaches and their experience as athletes, and the majority accepts the values of hard work, discipline, respect for authority, and love of sport. Female coaches tend to be more committed to establishing a cooperative, caring team attitude than male coaches, who tend to focus heavily on winning or losing.

Finally, we wrapped up the chapter with a look at the challenges for coaching in the future. Unless some dramatic steps are taken in the next 25 years, it is possible that sport participation will decline as a result of dissatisfied athletes and families who expect more from coaches. While coaching does not yet merit acceptance as a profession, there is no reason why we cannot work toward that direction.

19

CHAPTER

Future Trends in Sport

Student Outcomes

After reading this chapter, you will know the following:

- Social trends that are likely to affect sport
- The conflict between performance sport and participation sport and the effects of money, sponsorship, facilities, programs, and sport popularity
- The influence of changing attitudes toward sport participation
- How spectatorship affects sport participation.
- Effects of technology on equipment, training, performance enhancers, and media support of sport
- How different social theorists would effect change in sport

One of my favorite professors in college, Lee "Pappy" Warren, professor of history at East Stroudsburg University, used to tell us, "There are four kinds of people in this world: Those that know, and know that they know; those that know, and don't know that they know; those that don't know, and know that they don't know; and those that don't know, and don't know that they don't know."

I've pondered those words over many years and have become convinced that Pappy was a wise man. He valued education, learning from the past, and self-study as the path toward enlightenment and a better society. After reading this book, noting current events in sport, working through the student activities, and discussing sport issues with others, you should be much closer to the first group identified in Pappy's saying: "Those that know, and know that they know." Your understanding of sport in society should be light years ahead of where it was when you began your studies. Yet, the picture is not complete without a peek at the trends that are likely to carve out the future of sport. This chapter considers those trends and invites you to predict where those trends will lead. Where you find the potential trends inconsistent with your personal beliefs, you may begin to form a plan of action to influence the future of sport in a way you believe will help society.

If you and I do nothing, it is possible that events and influences in our society will shape sport participation or lack of it in ways that we find unhealthy or even harmful. Those who profit financially from sport as entertainment, promote spectatorship, and ignore participation in sport by average citizens may take complete control over the sporting world. Given the potential for sport to enhance every citizen's quality of life, such a narrow focus would be a shame.

SOCIAL TRENDS

Social trends are difficult to predict since we have no way of knowing how outside influences in society are likely to affect our state of mind, our economy, or our values. Certain worldwide trends such as the rise in terrorism may drastically affect our lives in ways that are difficult to predict. Likewise, the shrinking of our world into a global economy of interdependence has the potential to either bring our world closer together in cooperation or split us wider apart in conflict.

Within our own society, certain social trends seem clear. First, our population is rapidly aging and the proportion of the populace that is older than 50 years will continue to skyrocket in the immediate future. Concerns for quality of life, health care, and productive use of leisure time after retirement will command the attention a large proportion of the population as they age. In addition to an aging population, we are also a declining population. Forecasts for the next 50 years show that Europe will continue to have a declining population. The United States will maintain its low birth rate, but that will be offset by a continued influx of immigrants, most of whom will be of Hispanic descent (Wottenberg 2003).

Second, the rights of all people regardless of age, race, gender, sexual preference, or disabilities will continue to be protected and discrimination laws are likely to be strengthened in the United States. The stage is set to not only protect the rights of every citizen, but also to enhance their quality of life by opening up avenues for new experiences and adventures.

Third, those who have benefited most from supporting performance sport will fight to protect their investment in sport. Rather than just protecting the status quo, they will bring ingenuity to strategies to expand the influence of performance sport. This group will continue to strengthen the bond between big-time collegiate sport, professional sport, and the Olympic Games.

The field of sport management is growing rapidly and will continue to expand as sport organizations search for ways to enhance their bottom line by enticing and serving consumers. Education on sport management is available in many universities and includes training in sport-related event management, finance, human resources, law, marketing, public relations, and program management. People training in sport management are playing an increasingly critical role in professional sport, amateur sport, nonprofit organizations such as the YMCA or YWCA, sporting goods manufacturers, sporting events, and sport facilities (Hoffman 2005).

Fourth, the natural human tendency to push against barriers will result in development of new materials and processes to produce better sport equipment, facilities, and training regimens so that elite athletes can challenge the frontier of athletic achievements. Records will continue to be broken as athletes benefit from scientific advances. Another key area of research will be the effort to rid sport of performance-enhancing substances that provide an unfair advantage to some athletes, create mistrust by fans and the media of great performances, and threaten the integrity of athletic competition at every level.

As the population continues to age, it will be important to find ways to keep our grandparents healthy and active.

Fifth, coaches will adapt to their athletes by increasing their coaching competency and adjusting their coaching philosophy toward meeting the needs of their athletes. At the same time, athletes will pressure coaches to endorse a certification process that indicates coaching knowledge, skill, and competency at various levels of coaching.

CONFLICT BETWEEN PERFORMANCE SPORT AND PARTICIPATION SPORT

There has always been keen competition between performance sport and participation sport. The competition centers on publicity, funding, accessibility, cost, facilities, coaching, and recruiting players into one track or the other. During the past century, performance sport has had the edge in just about every category. But things may change in this century as a result of our changing demographics, the shift to an older population, a potential national crisis in American health care, and in some cases public disinterest in performance sport.

However, it seems more likely that both categories of sport will grow steadily but perhaps for different reasons. Let's look at the potential for expansion of each one in turn.

Performance Sport

The institutions that support performance sport are strong, well funded, well established, and determined to perpetuate their roles. They are comprised of powerful businesspersons, athletic directors, college presidents, and commercial sponsors who have joined with the media to glorify the finest athletes in the world. The emphasis on superior athletes assaulting performance barriers is a captivating story. We love to see athletes running faster, jumping higher, hitting harder, or proving their power in sport, especially if their success can be attributed to hard work, dedication, or overcoming obstacles. Their success becomes our success and we rejoice in it.

Performance sport at the youth level will continue to thrive as youngsters and their families follow their dreams to achieve competitive success. Youth programs will grow as parents thrust their potential prodigies into sport training before they even enter school. The major barrier for many talented kids will continue to be the expense of such training and competition. Young people from modest financial backgrounds will thus continue to gravitate toward inexpensive sports, such as those in school-based programs. Sports such as skiing, tennis, golf, and many other Olympic sports will continue to beyond the financial reach of the working and middle classes.

High schools will continue to offer varsity programs and, particularly in affluent communities, will expect excellence from their athletic teams. The major team sports like football and basketball will continue to rely on high school programs to develop talent supplemented by off-season programs, camps, and leagues that keep kids playing one sport year-round.

Most colleges will struggle to fund their athletic programs but invest in them as a publicity and recruiting tool. College football and March Madness in basketball unite the college family like no other events. As a feeder system for professional sport, major colleges will continue to fight to retain the athletes in whom they invest time, money, and effort. The question of whether athletes should be paid to play beyond athletic scholarships will continue to be debated and likely some compromise will occur in the not-so-distant future. Athletes who are lured by the glamour and financial reward of leaving college early to turn professional will force the issue of financial compensation for what is essentially professional play.

Professional sport will continue to thrive. The investment in football, basketball, and baseball by corporate sponsors and television will continue to grow and advances in delivery of those sports through television will expand. As the popularity of those sports grows in other countries, gradual expansion of franchises to Europe is likely and the potential for true world championships will emerge. It is likely that women's professional basketball will increase in popularity as more people begin to appreciate the style of basketball they play, which emphasizes teamwork and passing.

A likely change in sport in North America will be the rising popularity of soccer. As immigrants continue to enter our country and the Hispanic population grows steadily, cultural interest in soccer will follow. The attraction of a sport that can accommodate both males and females as well as players of all sizes, shapes, and body types can appeal to millions of kids who lack the size or strength to compete in elite basketball or football. A new generation of Americans who played soccer as children will become adults who will likely encourage their own children to at least try the sport.

The owners of professional sport franchises and league officials will continue to convince cities to build more elaborate facilities to host their teams. City officials will scramble to attract professional franchises to their cities to enhance the economy and create fan interest. The parity of teams established by the NFL will continue to stir fan interest because

any team will have the chance to play in the Super Bowl if they make good management decisions.

Baseball will shift toward a similar philosophy, dooming the longtime dominance of big-market teams like the New York Yankees. Professional baseball will be forced to change if they have any hope of regaining their former title as America's pastime. Otherwise the decline in youth baseball participation, particularly in urban settings, forecasts a continued decline in popularity. Baseball officials and team owners must come up with a plan to ensure that every franchise has at least a possibility to be competitive through mandatory revenue sharing more like the NFL has. Olympic sports will continue down the path of professionalism. The finest athletes in the world will showcase their talents in bigger

Fiberglass poles were legalized in the 1950s, and later technology added carbon fiber to poles. The new materials immediately produced record-breaking vaults in world and Olympic competition. What technological advances will enhance sport performance in the next 10 years?

and better Games staged in countries that can offer the financial package to host them. Women's sport will grow in popularity through the Olympic movement, and led by soccer and basketball, professional leagues will grow in strength and popularity. Corporate sponsors will invest huge resources to support the Olympic Games and the emphasis will continue to shift from nationalism to corporate dominance.

The outlook for performance sport isn't all rosy. If drug testing and control of performance-enhancing substances do not improve, public disenchantment with professional sport could result as athletes continue to use illegal substances in the pursuit of exceptional performances.

Scientific advancements in equipment and sports medicine may enable athletes to perform at levels heretofore believed out of reach. If the public begins to see athlete performance as the result of technological achievements, it is possible that they will lose interest. The humanity of sport is a delicate balance of technology, financial interests, entertainment, and the athlete's struggle to achieve.

Youth programs will continue to struggle to provide development for superior athletes who come from modest financial circumstances. In the meantime, some parents will become frustrated with the demands made by excellence programs and coaches. Families who choose to expose their children to a wider range of activities will find themselves left out of excellence programs.

Kids who do not excel early in their sport career may become discouraged and withdraw from sport before they have a chance to blossom in it. The dropout rate for kids in performance sport will continue to be high.

Participation Sport

As Americans continue to struggle with health, people will begin to recognize how important exercise and sport are to controlling body weight, enhancing energy, resisting disease, improving physical appearance, and having a better quality of life.

Most youth sport programs attract large numbers of children between the ages of 6 and 8. More than half of them drop out of sport by age 14. By high school, only a fraction of those who continued in youth sport programs will make their high school varsity team. The system has a built-in rejection mechanism that forces the majority of young people to drop out of sport.

A possible solution is to expand the number of athletic teams sponsored by schools. Different teams could have different ability levels and training intensity. This system has been used successfully for generations by private schools that require every student to devote time each day to athletics and exercise.

A variation would be to sponsor complete intramural programs within schools to attract the masses of students who do not play varsity sport. The key is to find the money and facilities to support such an expansion. Lighted athletic fields that can be used for longer hours is one way universities have solved the problem of inadequate facilities, and high schools may soon follow that model. Rather than take pride in the win–loss record of a school's athletic teams, perhaps the model will shift to pride in the total number of students who play sport at any level.

Community programs that emphasize participation sport will also grow as young athletes search for opportunities to exercise, be with their friends, and have fun outside of school. The reduced emphasis on competition will be attractive to kids and families who have no aspirations as athletes but simply want to play sports and enjoy them. The demands for hours of practice, year-round devotion, expensive coaching, and specialization in just one sport will be discarded for the opportunity to play for recreation.

Extreme sports will continue to grow, as will sport activities that are focused on the player, informally organized, and novel in skills and strategy. Newer sports like street hockey, skateboarding, in-

Activity Time-Out: Mandatory Athletic Participation?

We do not cut students from academic classes for poor performance, but that is the model for sport. If sport is good for young people, why not require them to participate for at least an hour a day, three times a week? Why not provide sport programs that they can participate in no matter their skill level? Would you support either of these ideas? Justify your answer.

The 1998 Winter Olympics were the first Olympic Games to feature snowboarding as an event. What other sports will make their way to the Olympics?

line skating, and snowboarding will take their place among more traditional recreational sports such as biking, hiking, and other natural outdoor activities.

Coed teams may also encourage sport participation. Sports like softball, volleyball, soccer, tennis, and golf are just a few of the sports that adapt well to coed teams. The natural interest among teenagers to spend time with the opposite sex creates a natural drawing card to participation sport.

Young people aren't the only ones participating in sport. As health costs continue to climb, health insurers and employers will explore the benefits of encouraging physical activity among employees to minimize the health risks, loss of productive work days, and drain on health insurance programs. With older adults now numbering about 80 million of the total U.S. population of 290 million, their influence on every facet of society is going to be felt. Sport provides regular exercise, social interaction, and enhanced self-image, all important contributors to healthy living for older adults.

As with performance sport, participation sport faces roadblocks as well. The first roadblock is simply lack of interest in sport by those who played as children and dropped out. These adults need to be wooed back to sport with the offer of a different kind of experience. Leaders need to become more committed to increasing physical activity among young people, creating a change in consciousness among parents and kids through consistent marketing, and waging publicity campaigns on the value of sport programs based on participation rather than winning.

A second major roadblock is competition for money and facilities with traditional performance sport programs. Advocates of participation sport need to overcome this bias by enlisting the support of the masses since they certainly outnumber those involved in performance sport. School programs, extracurricular programs, community programs, and park and recreation programs are all ultimately supported by tax dollars from all citizens. Why shouldn't those dollars be spent to benefit more kids rather than be concentrated on a small majority of elite athletes?

Most sport leaders were competitive athletes and they tend to perpetuate similar programs. It will take a new breed of leaders who are dedicated to participation sport and are willing to change the status quo. They will also need patience, since it is not likely that change will happen quickly or without consistent pressure. They will also need to enlist the aid of some powerful allies such as physicians, health insurers, corporate leaders, and politicians.

Finally, activities other than sport will continue to compete for people's time. Entertainment via television or computers has become a powerful competitor. The lack of physical activity that results from submitting to the lure of spending hours in front of a screen may contribute to a national health crisis. Creative minds must work to educate people about the benefits of physical activity, and then it is up to sport organizers to make sport accessible, convenient, and fun for participants.

EFFECTS OF SOCIAL CHANGES

Significant social changes in the last 50 years have affected sport and will continue to do so. As discussed in chapter 11, the civil rights movement of the 1960s opened up sport to minorities. African Americans have become dominant in football and basketball, and Latinos account for one-third of the players in MLB. As more minorities move into the middle class, their children will begin to explore other sports such as tennis, swimming, golf, or volleyball—all sports that were once the exclusive provenance of affluent Whites. As these sports become more inclusive, positions of influence such as those held by coaches, organizers, and members of governing boards will include members of minority groups.

As discussed in chapter 12, the women's movement that ushered in Title IX in 1972 changed sport dramatically. The explosion in female participants has changed sport forever, but equity with male participants is still an elusive goal. Steady pressure to conform to the law will be required by women's rights advocates and female athletes must continue to be assertive.

Girls face some unique issues in sport. Puberty arrives an average of two years earlier in girls, affecting their physical capacity and sometimes their interest in sport. Teenage girls drop out of sport just when many boys, fueled by new levels of testosterone, are consumed by competitive sport. A clear transition from performance sport to participation sport needs to be available for girls at a younger age before they drop out for good.

Older women, too, will continue to have a significant effect on sport. Those who loved performance sport will prolong their careers with expanded professional, semiprofessional, and community leagues that offer strong competition. By far, though, most women who don sneakers and activewear are looking for healthy workouts to maintain physical appearance, control body weight, socialize, have fun, and increase their energy for the demands of daily living. New sports or variations on traditional sports must be ready for an influx of females to recreational participation sport. The recent surge of female participation in yoga, tai chi, strength training, and similar physical disciplines is an example of the new trends.

As mentioned previously, the aging of our society may be the most influential trend of all in sport. Age group competition for older adults will continue to grow as seniors seek the thrills of competitive sport and the challenge of testing themselves against others or the environment.

Other older adults are more interested in exercise simply to maximize good health, posture, and energy. Social interaction, fun, and release from stress are more important to these adults. Coaches and program leaders will need to continue to tinker with the formula for sport that meets the needs of these older athletes. More frequent but shorter workouts with less intensity seem to be the best schedule for older adults. Time to socialize time during or after activity is a strong attraction and should be made available in a comfortable setting.

Sexual preference will continue to be a topic of controversy in the coming years. Historically, sport has not been kind to gays and lesbians, particularly in performance sport. A relatively few successful homosexual athletes have publicly announced their sexual preference, but most have quietly concealed it to avoid controversy.

The Gay Games and local gay athletic organizations have exploded around the world. The Gay Games will be held in Montreal in 2006. More than 25,000 competitors are expected, making it the largest international sporting event in history.

What will it take to keep this athlete participating in sport throughout her life?

Activity Time-Out: Legalized Sports Betting

Do you favor legalized sports betting or not? Justify your answer with a historical perspective of betting on sport in terms of scandal, cheating, and mafia influence versus the potential benefits to social programs.

Gay and lesbians join local athletic clubs to enjoy physical activity, meet new people, receive emotional support, and have fun without the pressure of dealing with the historically homophobic sports world. As public acceptance of gays and lesbians grows, more athletes will have the courage to announce their sexual preference and insist on equal opportunities. The sports world will become more accepting of athletes, coaches, and sport administrators who embrace the gay or lesbian lifestyle.

Finally, mental and physical disabilities have historically eliminated people from sport participation. With the advent of laws that prevent discrimination against people with disabilities, sport participation has blossomed as well. The Special Olympics and the Paralympics have offered competitive and participation sport to people with disabilities at the national and international level. Local communities and schools have gradually sought to add sport programs for the people with disabilities and wherever possible have sought to include these athletes in existing programs. Some sports have been modified and others invented that are appropriate for those with handicaps. Education, financial support, and coaches' training are keys to sustaining the growth in opportunities for these athletes.

EFFECTS OF SPECTATORSHIP

Watching sport has always been a double-edged sword for sport. Some marketing studies have shown increases in participation that are attributed to increases in spectators and the popularity of star athletes. Certainly Michael Jordan's amazing career and resulting popularity raised the interest in basketball worldwide. Yet other sports such as soccer grew by leaps and bounds in the United States with virtually no heroes or stars until Mia Hamm and her teammates captivated fans with their remarkable international record.

It is clear that access to sport will increase in the future as more television coverage of sport is offered. Pay-per-view channels will carry selected sport programs, and channels exclusively devoted to sports such as golf and tennis are already available. The Internet will likely revolutionize spectatorship in the future as people will be able to follow their college teams, high school teams, and even youth sport teams like the Little League World Series from anywhere in the country.

The question is, will increased access create more sport fans, or will fans simply have more choices and spend more hours in front of the television or computer? If we believe that participation in sport will increase in the future, will spectatorship also increase?

Consider the average person who has time commitments to work, family, and the responsibilities of daily life. Carving time from that schedule for exercise and sport has proved to be the most perplexing barrier for most people. If they also increase the amount of time spent watching sport, something else will have to suffer; 10 hours of leisure time a week can only be split so many ways.

The power brokers in sport will mount a vigorous campaign to attract spectators in order to enhance their products. For them, participation is irrelevant; income from spectators, commercial sponsors, and media rights produce their revenue. One potential strategy for power brokers is to press for legalized sports gambling to get fans more actively involved in their favorite teams and players. Pressure on local and state governments to legalize gambling on sport will mount as the next natural step following the legalization of gambling at Native American reservations and offshore locations. Inducements such as allocating a percentage of gambling revenues toward education, youth sport programs, or other popular social programs will provide a dilemma for taxpayers who are suspicious of gambling interests. Internet gambling that so far is legal will attract some scrutiny as it grows and prospers.

EFFECTS
OF TECHNOLOGY

The relentless search for excellence in performance combined with the quest for sales of new products will continue to spur research and development of new sport equipment of every type. Field surfaces, court surfaces, and pool construction will continue to improve through technology. Likewise, implements such as tennis rackets, golf clubs, vaulting poles, baseball bats, footwear, and other similar equipment will continue to improve.

One positive effect of equipment advances will be the ease with which a beginning player can learn a new sport or an intermediate player can immediately improve. Consider that the larger heads of newer tennis rackets and golf clubs have added performance consistency to hundreds of thousands of weekend warriors' games. Ski design has done much the same thing through adjustments in length and design.

Similarly, for high-performance athletes, some technological advances will allow them to move faster, jump higher, hit harder, increase speed, and improve consistency. However, some of these advances may also come with increased risk to the body, which may not stand up to the increased forces of movement. Injury monitoring will become critical to prevent harm to elite athletes who embrace new technology. A good example of this risk is the rush to install synthetic turf on football fields 20 years ago. While athletes could run faster and jump higher, the rate of injuries exploded as joints simply could not withstand the force. Athletes and coaches forced a return to natural grass fields to protect their careers and their health.

Training methods based on scientific research will improve as we learn how to push the human body to the limit. Methods of strength and endurance training along with enhanced nutrition will equip athletes to perform better for longer periods of time. Along with improved performance will come better systems of training to prevent overuse injuries.

Drugs and other performance-enhancing substances will continue to be a hot topic. Athletes will always be tempted to shortcut training in favor of external substances that produce immediate results. The long-term negative effects of many substances will become clearer and drug-testing methods will continue to be refined. Unfortunately, based on history, we can expect that athletes and trainers will always be one step ahead of those who are responsible

What new training devices will help athletes become stronger and faster?

for testing and controlling performance-enhancing substances. It will be interesting to track the issue in the next 10 years and check to see if progress has been made in controlling the use of drugs.

Recovery from sport injuries will become quicker and there will be fewer permanent disabilities due to new procedures for joint and tissue repair and even replacement. Synthetic knees, hips, and ankles are becoming commonplace and other joints will follow. Participation in activity or even professional careers will be prolonged by surgical interventions we cannot yet imagine.

Coaches will eventually have access from the sidelines to the physical state of athletes. Assessment of head injuries, lack of conditioning, or risk of injury will be available; coaches will no longer have to rely on how athletes say they feel, but instead will have scientific assessment to rely on, even in the midst of competition.

A final, far-reaching issue is that of genetic engineering to produce exceptional athletes. The moral, ethical, and legal issues will be hotly debated in the coming years as science forges ahead in exploring options to alter genetic makeup. Imagine parents choosing the genetic makeup of their children or adjusting it during childhood. For most of us, these questions are too complicated to even comprehend and it is likely that the debate will rage for years.

EFFECTS OF THE ELECTRONIC MEDIA

In the last 25 years, the Internet has opened up possibilities that seemed impossible just a few decades ago. Here are a few ideas of what may happen in the next 25 years.

As mentioned previously, fans will have wider range of sports to watch on computers that will be hooked up to larger screens. The action will be on demand, meaning people do not have to plan their day around sport, but can watch when it fits their mood and schedule. It is virtually certain that fewer fans will watch the traditional big games that networks choose to feature, because they will now have access to all games. Anyone who supports a college team will be able to see that team in action on a given day. Fans of less popular sports will be able to watch their favorites rather than just what network television chooses to present. The trend has already begun in these directions and consumers will gradually demand even more choices.

The wildly popular fantasy teams and leagues that provide interactive entertainment will continue to grow. Live games that only allow you to watch passively can be replaced with exciting fantasy games with you positioned as the coach. Internet games that simulate professional sport shift the role of participants from spectator to coach who can pick the players on the team, choose the defense or offense, and call plays.

Athletes will be more accessible to their fans through online chat rooms and discussions. Where once they were hidden by game uniforms and helmets and protected from contact with fans, the athlete of the future will need to learn to be more open, accessible, and personable. Coaches will be "miked" at halftime so fans can overhear their tactical adjustments for the second half, athletes will be miked during competition, and fans will have an inside view of the sport experience like never before.

WILL SPORT CHANGE?

If you have any doubt whether sport will change in the future, look at the last 50 years. Since the 1950s, sport has expanded dramatically to become a huge corporate moneymaker. Professional football, basketball, baseball, ice hockey, tennis, and golf have made multimillionaires out of athletes and sustained the corporate organizations that regulate and control these sports. We once thought an athlete who earned $10,000 U.S. for a single season of play was amazingly rich. When Joe DiMaggio agreed in 1949 to the first $100,000 U.S. contract to play center field for the New York Yankees, we thought that was the zenith of sport compensation, yet today's superstars are signing contracts worth up to $10 million U.S. per year for up to seven years! Even taking inflation into account, athletes' salaries rose tenfold over the last quarter century, while the median real hourly earnings of the average American worker went *down* by about 5% (Lambert 2001).

As discussed, social changes have opened up opportunities for people of all races and ethnic groups, for women, and for athletes with disabilities. In spite of these significant changes, more are yet to come.

Who Will Lead the Way?

Those who follow functionalist theory would likely take the view that sport can be changed from the inside by improving the current sport culture through better marketing and promotion, presenting athletes as role models, making events more fan friendly, and trumpeting record-setting performances. This approach is the traditional conservative philosophy that maintains the status quo but improves it by producing more of what currently exists.

Reformists using functionalist theory are more likely to call for changes such as finally equalizing opportunities for females, minorities, and athletes with disabilities. They are likely to fight to control the use of performance-enhancing substances to ensure equal competition. Similarly, they may pressure collegiate athletics to pay athletes some modest wages in Division I programs while also limiting entry into the professional ranks until age 20 or so.

All of these actions suggest that sport can be improved by tinkering with the current model and adjusting to trends while maintaining the essential integrity of the model.

Those who subscribe to more radical changes in sport may use conflict theory to present their case. They may see a new model that opens sport as healthy recreation and cooperative physical activities to all citizens. They reject the current corporate structure, emphasis on winning, bottom-line mentality, and exploitation of athletes to benefit the power brokers who make millions from their performances.

Feminist theorists will push to improve the number of women in coaching, administration, media, and other key leadership positions and for equal pay for women in all aspects of sport.

Interactionist theorists see the changes in sport as coming from the bottom up. That is, athletes themselves will force change that better suits their needs. Two groups of athletes stand out as potential agents of change: youth and older adults. The professional model for sport does not fit the majority of athletes in either age group. Instead they will emphasize participation, healthy living, cooperation rather than competition, and accommodation of all skill levels. If changes within traditional sport are not forthcoming, it seems likely that both young and senior athletes will invent sport models of their own that better address their needs and interests. Extreme sports have already made a mark among young people, and perhaps similar changes will become popular with senior athletes.

Critical theorists might also affect youth and high school sport. If educators take the lead

on the value and place of sport, the programs might look very different. Intramural sports that include all students have the potential to grow in high schools as they have in colleges with increased student demand for use of facilities for physical recreation rather than reserving those facilities for a relatively few privileged athletes. Parents will have to insist on a new approach to youth sport that supports participation for every child regardless of economic level, ability, race, gender, or disability. Critical theorists will exert pressure to shift significant funding from performance sport to participation sport. The success of programs will be judged not by the win–loss record, but by the number of young people who participate and continue playing year after year.

Another significant change will be to establish standards of coaching at every level and avoid hiring coaches who are not appropriately certified. Public opinion could lead the way to this change to protect athletes who are directly affected by inadequate coaching. Parents are likely to insist on a level of coaching that reflects better education, a clear philosophy of coaching that parallels the goals of the specific program, and a more humanistic style of relating to athletes. Coaches who use outdated approaches and authoritarian methods of coaching will be more likely to struggle, especially in educational settings.

Who will lead changes in sport? Coaches? Athletes? Or you?

Critical theorists will also look at the current expenditure of public funds to support professional franchises, stadiums, and so-called sweetheart deals that entice wealthy franchise owners to move a team to a particular city. A reformist critical theorist would rather have that money spent on facilities or programs that directly benefit local citizens by offering opportunities to play sports rather than watch them. Compromises may be struck that allow some money to be spent on both participation and spectating if it can be shown that one approach also benefits the other.

The question of leadership still has not been answered. History will show that very few athletes become agents of change, especially during their playing days. Why risk all they have worked for unless they have suffered badly within the present system? A retiring NFL player who admits he cannot read in spite of a college degree might have cause, but of those who are frustrated, few have the courage or ability to express their frustration.

Coaches are not likely to rebel against a system that has been their life. Owners of professional teams, leaders in major sport organizations, and athletic directors have all invested their lives in the sport establishment.

Who Will Fight for Change?

Will it be you, someone who has studied sport, thought about it, and developed some strong opinions? Will it be parents who want a better experience for their progeny? Maybe it will be independent sport institutes like the Center for the Study of Sport at Northeastern University, politicians who believe they can advance their career by taking up the mantle of sport change, academic leaders at universities, sports writers, or sports commentators.

Or will changes occur as a reflection of a society that continues to adjust its values, economics, and political philosophies? Perhaps large coalitions of citizens will find themselves on the same side of arguments and band together to accomplish change. It seems clear from an analysis of demographics that U.S. society is heading quickly toward a large population dominated by older adults. That group has money, time, and a keen interest in sport as part of a healthy lifestyle. Exercise for its own sake will never be able to compete with the joy of sport or the social interaction it encourages. The fitness gym offers physical training benefits but lacks the universal appeal of games and sport. In the near future, a large proportion of our population will look to sport for help in blazing a new trail of longer, healthier lives.

What do you think?

CHAPTER SUMMARY

In this chapter we have examined the social trends that may affect the role of sport in our life. The major trends that were identified included aging of the population; protection for all people regardless of age, race, gender, sexual preference, or disability; continued expansion of performance sport by corporate sport leaders; enhancement of coaching competency; and technological improvement that may enhance sport performance.

Conflicts between consumers and leaders of performance sport versus those of participation sport were also considered. Those conflicts include struggles over fair shares of funding, use of facilities, public programs, and access for everyone.

We discussed the effect of opening sport participation to people of all ages, racial groups, ethnic groups, genders, sexual preferences, and disabilities. The demand for expanded programs and need for more financial support is a concern and likely to create a struggle among various advocacy groups.

Watching sport was considered both from a positive and negative point of view. While traditional performance sport will continue to try to grow its fan base and provide entertainment, we may find that a parallel growth in participation sport will conflict with their goals. Where spectatorship enhances participation and vice versa, the two groups will benefit from the synergy of working cooperatively.

Technological advances will affect the ability of athletes to generate exceptional performances and will ease the way for beginning athletes to take up a new sport. Performance-enhancing substances will continue to be a knotty problem for sport administrators, and time, money, and effort will be allocated to ensure equal competition for everyone. Improved methods of sports medicine will enable better treatment and recovery from injuries and will include replacement of body parts that break down from overuse.

Finally, we looked at how sport might change in the future, who will lead those changes, and what those changes might focus on. History provides some instructive lessons on how changes have occurred in the past, but peering into the future is more challenging. In the final analysis, changes in sport will be dictated by changes in our society, our needs, our values, and perhaps outside influences. Perhaps you will be a catalyst for change in your community!

Glossary

abuse—The willful infliction of injury, pain, mental anguish, intimidation, or punishment.

adult-organized sports—Sports that are organized by parents or other governing bodies. Activities are more structured and are played according to a fixed set of rules.

amateurs—Those who play for the intrinsic satisfaction of improving fitness, enjoying the competition, refining physical skills, working as part of a team, or simply embracing the challenge and excitement of testing skills against nature or other competitors; participation in sports is the key rather than the outcome.

Amateur Sports Act of the United States—Act of the U.S. Congress that established the United States Olympic Committee (USOC) and outlined its responsibilities.

American Association of People with Disabilities (AAPD)—The largest national, nonprofit, cross-disability organization dedicated to the 56 million Americans with disabilities.

Americans with Disabilities Act (ADA)—Landmark national legislation that protects the rights of Americans with disabilities.

anabolic steroids—Synthetic steroid hormones used to increase the size of muscles temporarily; illegal and sometimes abused by athletes.

anorexia—Eating disorder characterized by self-starvation.

appreciate—To increase in value.

athlete-organized sports—Sports that are organized by athletes without adult supervision. Activities are less structured and rules are made up as play progresses.

bed tax—A $1 U.S. fee on hotel rooms that goes into a special fund to help finance public sport stadiums.

biomechanics—The study of the structure and function of biological systems using principles of physics applied to human motion.

biophysical domain— Academic discipline of study of physical activity that includes physiology, biomechanics, nutrition, and sports medicine.

bulimia—Eating disorder characterized by overeating (binging) followed by purging, usually through laxative use or self-induced vomiting.

burnout—Exhaustion of physical or emotional strength as a result of prolonged stress that causes athletes to discontinue competitive sports.

capitalism—An economic system that is based on the accumulation and investment of capital by individuals who then use it to produce goods or services.

capital assets— Tangible property that cannot be easily converted into cash.

compulsive exercise—Eating disorder characterized by too much exercise rather than altered food intake.

conflict theory—Theory based on the work of Karl Marx that sees sport as being built on the foundation of money and economic power.

content research—Collecting information or pictures from articles, magazines, and TV programs and assigning the data to categories around a particular theme.

conventional stage—The second level of moral reasoning; most adults and society at large fall into this category, in which behavior is guided by what is acceptable to others.

corporate sport—Another name for the business of professional sport.

critical theories—Theories that study culture and determine the source of authority that one group has over another.

cultural capital—The skills and abilities people gain from education and life experiences. Cultural capital may include attitudes, expectations, and self-confidence.

depreciation—Decreased value over time of equipment, tools, or athletes (in sports).

deviant—Behavior that differs from the accepted norm.

direct spectators—People who attend live sporting events at a stadium, an arena, or another venue.

disability—A condition of mental or physical impairment that limits capacity in life.

economic capital—The financial resources a person has or controls.

economic model—Attempts to abstract from human behavior in a way that sheds insight into a particular aspect of that behavior.

electronic media—Media that include television, radio, and the Internet.

ethnicity—The cultural heritage of a group of people that arises from social customs.

ethnography—Data collected by researchers who immerse themselves in an environment and keep recorded conversations or notes.

exercise physiology—The study of human systems to enhance strength, speed, and endurance in performance.

extrinsic rewards—Rewards such as money, fame, and power.

female athlete triad—Includes disordered eating, amenorrhea, and osteoporosis.

feminist theory—Social theory that investigates the effect of gender within society.

figurational theories—The idea that we are all connected by networks of people who are interdependent on one another by nature, through education, and through socialization.

focus groups—Interviews with small groups of people.

functionalist theory—Looks at sport as a social institution that reinforces the current value system in a society.

games—An aspect of play that shows more evidence of structure and are competitive; the goals for participating are clear: they are mental, physical, or a combination of both; they are governed by informal or formal rules; they involve competition; winning is determined by luck, strategy, or skill; and they result in an end product such as prestige or status.

gender verification—Used for 30 years by the Olympics to test female athletes to ensure fair competition; discontinued in 1999 as demeaning, unnecessary, and unreliable.

hazing—Any action that inflicts physical or mental harm or anxiety or that degrades a person, regardless of location, intent, or consent of participants.

hegemony—Critical theory that focuses on dominance, which is the power that one individual or group has over others.

high-performance athletes—Athletes of any age who aspire to the highest levels of performance and typically become professional athletes.

historical research—Research that looks at trends in sport over time.

hooliganism—Rowdy, violent, or destructive behavior; often used to describe working-class men who disrupt soccer games with violence, excessive drinking, exchange of insults, destruction of property, and interruptions of the game.

indirect spectators—People who listen to or watch sports electronically by radio, television, or the Internet or who read about sports in newspapers or magazines.

interactionist theories—Theories that view society from the bottom up rather than the top down; they focus on the social interactions among people that are based on the reality people choose to accept.

interviews—Face-to-face personal questioning to elicit information, attitudes, or opinions.

intrinsic rewards—Rewards such as fun, health, self-satisfaction, and fitness.

lower class—Lowest level of the social class system; comprises unskilled laborers who essentially do work that is assigned and supervised by others.

masters—A classification in competitive sports for older athletes that usually starts at age 35 and above and is then divided into 5- or 10-year intervals.

middle class—Middle and largest level of the economic class system in the United States; includes skilled laborers, teachers, and people in the service industry.

minorities—A portion of the population that is different from others based on some criteria such as race.

motor learning and behavior—The study of relatively permanent changes in motor behavior that result from practice or experience.

naming rights—Corporations pay for the right to advertise their company through naming an athletic stadium or facility (e.g., American Airlines Arena in Miami).

nationalism—A spirit of loyalty and devotion to a nation; a strong characteristic of worldwide sports competition like the Olympic Games.

nutrition—The study to understand how food and drink affect performance.

obesity—Using a number called the body mass index (BMI), which calculates body weight compared to height, adults who are obese have a BMI higher than 30.

Olympic Games—An international sporting event held every four years that provides competition in most summer and winter sports.

overconformity—Behavior that goes beyond what is generally accepted. In sport, such behavior includes altering food intake or using supplements to meet an ideal body image.

over-the-counter drugs—Drugs bought at a store that are designed to promote healing from sickness or injury or to mask pain.

overweight—Using a number called the body mass index (BMI), which calculates body weight compared to height, adults who are overweight have a BMI between 25 and 29.9.

pedagogy—The study of the art and science of teaching.

personal seat licenses (PSLs)—Money spent by fans to purchase specific seats in a stadium.

philosophy of sport—The study of the definition, value, and meaning of sport.

play—Free activity that involves exploring our environment, self-expression, dreaming, and pretending. There are no firm rules and the outcome of the activity is unimportant.

politics—The art and science of government, of influencing governmental policy, or of holding control over a government.

postconventional stage—The highest level of moral reasoning; an autonomous, principled stage of thinking in which people adopt certain moral principles and hold to that behavior regardless of social punishment or reward.

preconventional stage—Basic level of moral understanding; being right means following authority with the understanding that there will be punishment if the rules aren't followed.

prescription drugs—Drugs prescribed by a doctor that are designed to promote healing from sickness or injury or to mask pain.

print media—Media that include newspapers, magazines, and books.

private funds—Monies raised from owner contributions, league contributions, bank loans, loans from local businesses, and personal seat licenses.

professional athletes—Paid performers who perform work by training to hone their physical skills to the highest level for competition with other elite athletes.

psychosocial domain—Academic discipline of the study of physical activity that includes psychology, motor learning and behavior, and pedagogy.

public funds—Monies raised from public sources, such as sales taxes, proximity and beneficiary taxes, general obligation and revenue bonds, and tax increment financing.

public tax funds—Tax funds collected by local or state governments that provide services to citizens.

qualitative data—Data collected through interviews or observations of individuals or groups or through analyzing societal characteristics and trends.

quantifiable studies—Studies producing data that can be counted and analyzed statistically.

race—Attributes that are passed along genetically.

racism—A belief that race is the primary determinant of human traits and that racial differences produce an inherent superiority of a particular race.

religion—The belief in a god or supernatural force that influences human life.

revenue-producing sports—Used in intercollegiate sports to describe those sport such as football and basketball that typically produce more revenue than expense for the university.

revenue sharing—Sports leagues share income from television contracts and other sources to protect smaller markets where income might be less.

social capital—Capital that depends on family, friends, and associates and includes resources based on group memberships, relationships, and both social and business networks.

social class—A category of people who share similar positions in society based on their economic level, education, occupation, and social interaction.

socialization—The process of interacting with other people and learning social customs, morals, and values.

social stratification—Class assignments based on levels of power, prestige, and wealth.

social theories—Theories used to compare trends in a particular area (like sport) with an overall social theory.

societal analysis—Using social theories to examine life from a social point of view.

sociocultural domain—Academic discipline of the study of physical activity that includes history, philosophy, and sociology.

sociology—The study of a society, its institutions, and its relationships.

sport—Institutionalized competitive activity that involves physical skill and specialized facilities or equipment and is conducted according to an accepted set of rules to determine a winner.

sport history—The study of the tradition and practices of physical activity and sport over time and within different countries, cultures, and civilizations.

sporting behavior—A gender-neutral term for sportsmanship.

sport psychology—The study of human behavior in sport, including enhancing performance and treating disorders that affect optimal performance.

sportsmanship—A behavior that is characterized by fair play and respect for others.

sport sociology—The study of sport and physical activity within the context of the social conditions and culture in which people live.

sport spectators—People who watch sports.

sport participation—Taking an active, participatory role in sports.

sport pyramid—A way of understanding sport as a pyramid containing the four elements of human activity: play, games, sport, and work.

sports announcers—Electronic media personalities who broadcast sports events.

sports medicine—Examines the prevention, care, and rehabilitation of injuries caused by participation in physical activity and sport.

sports writers—Journalists in the print media who specialize in sports.

stacking—The incidence of finding an unusual distribution of White and Black athletes in certain positions in sports that cannot be explained by a random distribution.

stimulants—Class of drugs that produces a temporary increase in functional activity or efficiency.

survey research—Research conducted through questionnaires.

Title IX—Landmark legislation passed in 1972 requiring any institution receiving federal funding to provide equal opportunities for males and females.

total salary cap—The total financial commitment a team is allowed to make to all players on the roster in combined salary and benefits.

underconformity—Behavior that does not conform to generally acceptable behavior. In sport, such behavior includes rule breaking, hazing, and drinking.

upper class—Highest level of the American economic class system; comprises the top 1% of households and controls approximately 35% of the nation's wealth.

upper-middle class—Second highest level of the social class system; comprises professionals such as physicians, attorneys, and managers who typically have significant amounts of discretionary income.

work—Purposeful activity that may include physical or mental effort to perform a task, accomplish something, overcome an obstacle or achieve a desired outcome. Sport can take on the characteristics of work as it moves toward the professional level.

youth sport—Sport participation by children ages 6 to 12.

References

Aaron, H. 1999. Time 100: Jackie Robinson. www.time. com/time/time100/heroes/profile/robinson01.html. Accessed August 13, 2005.

ABC News. 2004. BALCO Chief on sports doping scandal. December 3, 2004. http://abcnews.go.com/2020/ story?id=297995&page=1. Accessed May 22, 2005.

Ackman, D. 2005. ESPN's narrowing world of sports. www.forbes.com/business/2005/04/19/cx_da_ 0419topnews.html. Accessed November 21, 2005.

Acosta, V., and L. Carpenter. 2004. *Women in intercollegiate sport: A longitudinal study. 1977-2004.* Brooklyn: Brooklyn College.

Adherents. 2005. Internet initiative with statistics for religions of the world. www.adherents.com/rel_USA. html. Accessed November 15, 2005.

Alfred University. 1999a. High school hazing. How many students are hazed? www.alfred.edu/hs_hazing/howmanystudents.html. Accessed September 5, 2005.

Alfred University. 1999b. National survey of sports teams: Who is most at risk? Where are hot spots? www. alfred.edu/sports_hazing/mostatrisk.html. Accessed September 5, 2005.

Amateur Athletic Foundation of Los Angeles. 2005. *Gender in televised sports from 1989-2000.* Research report. www.aafla.org. Accessed November 10, 2005.

Amateur Athletic Foundation Olympic Primer. 2005. Issues of the Olympic Games. Olympic reports. www.aafla. org. Accessed September 9, 2005.

American Association of People With Disabilities. 2005. About AAPD. www.aapd-dc.org/docs/info.html. Accessed February 8, 2005.

Americans Disability Technical Assistance Centers. 2004. Historical context of the Americans with Disabilities Act. www.adata.org/whatsada-history.aspx.html. Accessed February 2, 2005.

American Sport Education Program. 2005. About ASEP. www.asep.com/about.cfm. Accessed March 1, 2005.

American Sports Data, Inc. 2000. *Organized youth team sports participation in the U. S. 2001.* Hartsdale, NY: SGMA.

American Sports Data, Inc. 2005. *American team sports: A status report.* Hartsdale, NY: SGMA.

Anastasio, D. 2000. *The pinky ball book.* New York: Workman.

Anspaugh, D.J., S. Hunter, and M. Dignan 1996. Risk factors for cardiovascular disease among exercising versus nonexercising women. *American Journal of Health Promotion* 5(10): 3.

Answers.com. 2005. Arthur Ashe, tennis player. www. Answers.com/Arthur-Ashe. Accessed September 10, 2005.

Answers.com. 2006. O.J. Simpson, football player, murder suspect, TV personality. www.answers.com/topic/ o-j-simpson. Accessed May 22, 2006.

Ariss, J. 2000. Good sportsmanship rules. Reprint from *Touching Base Magazine.* www.slopitch.org/sportsmanship.htm. Accessed May 10, 2004.

Ashe, A. Jr. 1977. An open letter to Black parents: Send your children to the libraries. *New York Times,* February 6, 1977, sec. 5, p. 2.

Ashe, A. Jr. 1988. *A hard road to glory.* New York: Warner Books.

Ashe, A. Jr. 1993. *Days of grace: A memoir.* New York: Knopf.

Assibey-Mensah, G. 1997. Role models and youth development evidence and lessons from the perceptions of African-American male youth. *Western Journal of Black Studies* 21 (4): 242.

Associated Press. 2006a. AP: Players could scrap new drug policy. mlb.com, May 9, 2006. http://mlb.mlb.com/NASApp/ mlb/news/article.jsp?ymd=20060509&content_ id=1445484&vkey=news_mlb&fext=.jsp&c_id=mlb. Accessed June 12, 2006.

Associated Press. 2006b. Mediation unsuccessful in Penn State bias lawsuit against coach. *USA Today,* May 15, 2006. www.usatoday.com/sports/college/womensbasketball/bigten/2006-05-15-psu-mediation_x.htm. Accessed June 1, 2006.

Associated Press. 2006c. Northwestern suspends women's soccer team. *Chicago-Sun Times,* May 15, 2006. www. suntimes.com/output/news/soccer15.html. Accessed May 20, 2006.

Associated Press. 2006d. Penn State coach accuses group of trying to exploit bias case. *USA Today,* May 18, 2006. www.usatoday.com/sports/college/womensbasketball/bigten/2006-05-18-portland_x.htm. Accessed June 1, 2006.

Association for Women in Sports Media (AWSM). 2000. Membership Directory. Farmington, CT: AWSM.

Audit Bureau of Circulations. 2005. Circulation falls at most newspapers. *USA Today,* November 8, 2005.

August, H. 2004. Many Elis break from norm, lean right. *Yale Daily News,* November 11, 2004. www.yaledailynews.com/article.asp?AID=27281. Accessed January 29, 2005.

Auman, G. 2004. Muslim basketball player quits USF team. *St. Petersburg Times.* www.sptimes.com/2004/09/16/Sports/Muslim_basketball_pla.shtml. Accessed January 24, 2005.

Badenhausen, K. 2004. *The best-paid athletes.* www.forbes.com/2004/06/23/04athletes1and.html. Accessed November 5, 2005.

Bahri, C. 2005. Spearheading the empowerment of Muslim women. www.happynews.com/news/1172005/spearheading-the-empowerment.htm. Accessed May 24, 2006.

Bairner, A. 2001. *Sport, nationalism, and globalization: European and North American perspectives.* Albany, NY: State University of New York Press.

Ball, D., and J. Loy. 1975. *Sport and social order: Contributions to the sociology of sport.* Reading, MA: Addison-Wesley.

Ballparks. 2006a. Bank of America Stadium. http://football.ballparks.com/. Accessed June 1, 2006.

Ballparks. 2006b. Busch Stadium. www.ballparks.com/baseball/national/stlbpk.htm. Accessed June 1, 2006.

Ballparks. 2006c. Gillette Stadium. http://football.ballparks.com/. Accessed June 1, 2006.

Barber, B., J. Eccles, and M. Stone. 2001. Whatever happened to the jock, the brain, and the princess? Young adult pathways linked to adolescent activity involvement and social identity. *Journal of Adolescent Research* 16 (5): 429-455.

Baseball Almanac. 2005. George Steinbrenner biography. www.baseball-almanac.com/articles/george_steinbrenner_biography.shtml. Accessed August 3, 2005.

BBC Sport. 2005. Miller "surprised" EPO is illegal. http://news.bbc.co.uk/sport2/hi/other_sports/winter_sports/4334612.stm. Accessed June 1, 2006.

Beane, B. 2003. *Going my way.* New York: Marlow.

Bell, J. 2004. NFL Tug-of-War over revenue. *USA Today.* July 6, 2004.

Beller, J., and S. Stoll. 1994. Sport participation and its effect on moral reasoning of high school student athletes and general students. *Research Quarterly for Exercise and Sport* Suppl. no. 65 (March).

Benedict, J., and D. Yaeger. 1998. *Pros and cons: The criminals who play in the NFL.* New York: Warner Books.

Best, C. 1987. Experience and career length in professional football: The effects of positional segregation. *Sociology of Sport Journal* 7 (4): 410-420.

Birrell, S. 2004. Feminist theories for sport. In *Handbook of sport studies,* ed. J. Coakley and E. Dunning, 61-75. London: Sage.

Bissinger, H. 2003. *Friday night lights.* New York: Da Capo Press.

Bloom, J. 2000. *To show what an Indian can do: Sport at Native American boarding schools.* Minneapolis, MN. University of Minnesota Press

Blumstein, A., and J. Benedict. 1999. Criminal violence of NFL players compared to the general population. *Chance* 12 (3): 12-15.

Booth, D., and J. Loy. 1999. Sport, status and style. *Sport History Review* 30 (1): 1-26.

Borzilleri, M.J. 2003. USOC targets positions, pay raises. *The Gazette* (Colorado Springs, CO), June 11, 2003.

Bowen, W., and S. Levin. 2003. *Reclaiming the game: College sports and educational values.* Princeton, NJ: Princeton University Press.

Bowles, W., and M. Jenson. 2001. Cultural capital. www.williambowles.info/mimo/refs/tece1ef.htm. Accessed January 1, 2006.

Brady, E., and R. Giler. 2004a. In a lot of cases, they have no other choice. *USA Today,* July 3, 2004.

Brady, E., and R. Giler. 2004b. To play sports, many U.S. students must pay. National Association of College Women Athletics Administrators. www.nacwaa.org/rc/rc_artilepr_paytoplay.php. Accessed January 1, 2005.

Brady, E., and M. Sylwester. 2004. Trends in girls sports. *USA Today,* June 17, 2004.

Brand, M. 2004. In athletics, level field must begin in classroom. *New York Times,* May 9, 2004.

Brennan, C. 2006. Northwestern, Duke matters sign of larger problem. *USA Today,* May 18, 2006, C2.

Brennan, D. 2001. Sanctity of sport. www.tothenextlevel.org. Accessed October 30, 2004.

Brigham Young University Athletics. 2006. www.byucougars.com/. Accessed June 7, 2006.

Brook, S. (2004). Euro final tops TV sports league. *Media Guardian,* December 23. http://forum.xbox365.com/ubb/ultimatebb.cgi?ubb=get_topic;f=4;t=016799 Accessed 10-14-2005.

Brown, G. 2000. Beating the odds. *NCAA News,* December 18, 2000.

Brown, G. 2005. Policy applies core principles to mascot issue. *NCAA News Online,* August 15, 2005. www2.ncaa.org/media_and_events/association_news/ncaa_news_online/2005/08_15. Accessed December 3, 2005.

Brown, M. 2001. The shoe's on the other foot. http://healthlibrary.epnet.com/GetContent.aspx?token=af362d97-4f80-4453-a175-02cc6220. Accessed June 8, 2006.

Brownfield, P. 2004. From "faster, higher, stronger" to "scantily clad." *FSUNews,* August 30, 2004. www.fsunews.com/vnews/display.v/ART/2004/08/30/41320d525e779?in_archive=1. Accessed February 10, 2006.

Bruce, T. 2000. Never let the bastards see you cry. *Sociology of Sports Journal* 17 (1): 69-74.

Brylinsky, J. 2002. National standards for athletic coaches. ERIC Clearinghouse on Teaching and Teacher Education Washington, DC. www.ericdigests.org/2004-1/coaches.htm. Accessed February 27, 2005.

Bucknell University. 2004. Celebration of Bison athletics: the Bison scholar athlete. News release. Bucknell University (Lewisburg, PA), April 29, 2004.

Bunker, L. 1988. Lifelong benefits of youth sport participation for girls and women. Speech presented at the Sport Psychology Conference, University of Virginia, Charlottesville.

Burnett, D. 2005. Sportsmanship checklist for kids. www.printablechecklists.com/checklist38b.shtml. Accessed June 1, 2006.

Cahill, B., and A. Pearl. 1993. *Intensive participation in children's sports.* Champaign, IL: Human Kinetics, 19-38.

Canseco, J. 2005. *Juiced: Wild times, rampant 'roids, smash hits, and how baseball got big.* New York: Regan Books/HarperCollins.

Carlson, D., and L. Scott. 2005. What is the status of high school athletes 8 years after their senior year? *Statistics in Brief: National Center for Education Statistics.* U.S. Department of Education. Washington, D., 1-19.

Carpenter, L., and V. Acosta. 2005. *Title IX.* Champaign, IL: Human Kinetics.

Carter, R. 2005. Ashe's impact reached far beyond the court. *SportsCenturyBiography.* http://sports.espn.go.com/espn/classic/bio/news/story?page = Ashe_Arthur. Accessed September 10, 2005.

Cary, P. 2004. Fixing kids' sports: Rescuing children's games from crazed coaches and parents. *U.S. News and World Report,* June 7, 2004.

Cauchon, D. 2005. Childhood pastimes are increasingly moving indoors. *USA Today,* August 12, 2005.

CBS News. 2004. Freddy Adu: Just Going Out to Play. www.cbsnews.com/stories/2004/03/25/60minutes/printable608681.shtml. Accessed October 10, 2004.

Center for Disease Control and Prevention. 2000. Youth risk behavior survey 1999. 9 (SSO5): 1-96.

Center for Disease Control and Prevention. 2006. Physical activity for everyone: Recommendations. www.cdc.gov/nccdphp/dnpa/physical/recommendations/. Accessed May 2, 2006.

Chaddock, G. 2003. U.S. notches world's highest incarceration rate. *Christian Science Monitor,* August 18, 2003.

Cherner, R. 2005. If you billed it around faith, they will certainly come. *USA Today,* July 22, 2005.

Children Now. 1999. Boys to men: Sports media messages about masculinity. http://publications.childrennow.org/publications/media/boystomen_1999_sports.cfm. Accessed June 1, 2006.

Christianity Today. 2002. Christian athletes in the 2000 Olympic Games in Sydney. www.christianitytoday.com. Accessed January 1, 2004.

CHSAA. *See* Colorado High School Activities Association.

Citizen Through Sports Alliance. 2005. Youth sports national report card. www.sportsmanship.org/News/1105%20Report%20Card-Fgrade.pdf. Accessed June 1, 2006.

Clarke, L. 2005. As interest wanes, tennis begins promotional push. *Washington Post,* July 18, 2005.

CNN Sports Illustrated. 2001. Jury rules for NFL. http://sportsillustrated.cnn.com/. Accessed May 22, 2001.

Coakley, J. 2004. *Sports in society.* 8th ed. New York: McGraw Hill.

Coakley, J., and P. Donnelly (eds.). 1999. *Inside sports.* London: Routledge.

Coakley, J., and E. Dunning (eds.). 2004. *Handbook of sports studies.* London: Sage Publications.

Cochrane, P., and B. Hoepper. 2005. *The finest sporting gesture in the history of sport.* Australia: The National Centre for History Education.

Coffman, S., 2004. *Welcome back to tennis 50+.* White Plains, NY: United States Tennis Association.

College Sports Information Directors of America (CoSIDA). 2001. Over 200 women sign up as members of Female Athletic Media Executives (FAME). *CoSIDA Digest,* April.

Colorado High School Activities Association. 2005. 2005-2006 Sporting behavior manual. www.chsaa.org/activities/sportsmanship/pdf/SportsmanshipManual.pdf. Accessed June 1, 2006.

Condor, R. 2004. Living well: When coaches and parents put too much emphasis on winning, kids drop out. *Post-Intelligencer* (Seattle, WA), September 30, 2004.

Crain, W. 1985. *Theories of development.* Englewood Cliffs, NJ: Prentice Hall, 118-136.

Crosset, T. 1999. What do we know and what can we do about male athletes violence against women: A critical assessment of the athletic affiliation and violence against women debate. *Quest,* August.

Crosset, T., J. Benedict, and M. McDonald. 1995. Male student-athletes reported for sexual assault: Survey of campus police departments and judicial affairs offices. *Journal of Sport and Social Issues* 19 (2): 126-140.

Cuban, M. 2004. My new hedge fund. *The Mark Cuban Weblog,* November 27, 2004. www.blogmaverick.com/entry/1234000570021684/. Accessed June 26, 2006.

Cycling News. 2005. More Armstrong allegations from *L'Equipe!* October 8, 2005. www.cyclingnews.com/features/?id = 2005/nelson_lequipe. Accessed May 23, 2006.

Davis, R. 2002. *Inclusion through sports.* Champaign, IL: Human Kinetics.

Decker, D., and K. Lasley. 1995. Participation in youth sports, gender and the moral point of view. *The Physical Educator* 53 (Winter 1995): 14-21.

Deford, F. 1976. Religion in sport. *Sports Illustrated,* April 19, 92-99.

Department of Justice. 2005. School violence rate stable, lowest level in a decade. www.ojp.usdoj.gov/bjs/pub/press/iscs05pr.htm. Accessed May 2, 2006.

Dobie, M. 2000. Race and sports in high school. In *Best newspaper writing 2000,* ed. C. Scanlon, 319-387. St. Petersburg, FL: Poynter Institute for Media Studies.

Dodds, T. 2000. Opening minds no harder than opening doors. *American Editor,* January-February.

Donnelly, P. 2004. Interpretive approaches to the sociology of sport. In *Handbook for sport studies,* ed. J. Coakley and E. Dunning, 77-91. London: Sage.

Drake Group. 2000. *The plan: Faculty group proposes college sports reform.* Meeting in Des Moine, IA, March 25, 2000. www.thedrakegroup.org. Accessed March 29, 2005.

Duncan, M., and M. Messner. 2005. Gender in televised sports: News and highlights shows, 1989-2004. Amateur Athletic Foundation of Los Angeles. http://www.aafla.org/9arr/ResearchReports/tv2004.pdf. Accessed June 1, 2006.

Dunn, M. 2005. Daily life in ancient Greece. http://members.aol.com/dunnclass/greeklife.html. Accessed January 10, 2006.

Dunning, E. 1999. *Sport matters: Sociological studies of sport, violence, and civilization.* London: Rutledge.

Dworkin, J., R. Larson, and D. Hansen. 2003. Adolescents' accounts of growth experiences in youth activities. *Journal of Youth and Adolescence* 32 (1): 17-36.

DW-World.DE. 2005. Referee scandal threatens Germany's World Cup. January 24, 2005. www.dw-world.de/dw/article/0,1564,1467560,00.html. Accessed January 31, 2005.

Edwards, H. 1973. *Sociology of sports.* Homewood, IL: Dorsey Press, 63-69, app. A.

Eitzen, S. 1992. Sports and ideological contradictions: Learning from the cultural framing of soviet values. *Journal of Sport and Social Issues* 16 (December): 144-149.

Eitzen, S. 2003. *Fair or foul: Beyond the myths and paradoxes of sport.* 2nd ed. Lanham, MD: Rowman & Littlefield.

Eitzen, S. 2004. Social control in sport. In *Handbook of sport studies,* ed. J. Coakley and E. Dunning, 370-381. London: Sage.

Eitzen, S., and G. Sage. 1978. *Sociology of American sport.* Dubuque, IA: William C. Brown.

Eitzen, S., and G. Sage. 2002. *Sociology of North American sport.* 7th ed. Boston: McGraw-Hill.

Elias, N., and E. Dunning. 1986. *Quest for excitement: Sport and leisure in the civilising process.* Oxford: Blackwell.

Entine, J. 2000. *Taboo: Why Black athletes dominate sports and why we're afraid to talk about it.* New York: Public Affairs.

Entine, J. 2004. Race and sport 1 and 2: The race to the swift—If the swift have the right ancestry. Peak Performance. www.pponline.co.uk/encyc/0657b.htm. Accessed December 16, 2004.

Ericson, J. 2000. Faculty group proposes college sports reform. News release. Drake University, March 16, 2000. www.drake.edu/events/collegesports/. Accessed March 29, 2004.

ESPN. 1999. *Wilt spoke of regrets, women and Meadowlark.* ESPN.com, October 13, 1999. http://espn.go.com/nba/news/1999/1012/110905.html. Accessed May 10, 2005.

Ewing, M., and V. Seefeldt. 1990. *American youth and sports participation.* Lansing: Youth Sports Institute at Michigan State University.

Fanbay.net. 2005. Women at the Olympics. www.fanbay.net/olympics/women.htm. Accessed September 25, 2005.

Farrey, T. 2002a. Laws get a workout. ESPN.com, June 3, 2002. http://espn.go.com/otl/hazing/friday.html. Accessed September 5, 2005.

Farrey, T. 2002b. Athletes abusing athletes. ESPN.com, June 3, 2002. http://espn.go.com/otl/hazing/monday.html. Accessed September 5, 2005.

Farrey, T. 2002c. They call it leadership. ESPN.com, June 3, 2002. http://espn.go.com/otl/hazing/tuesday.html. Accessed September 25, 2005.

Federation International Football Association. 2005. History of the FIFA World Cup. www.fifa.com/en/history/history/0,1283,5,00.html. Accessed November 12, 2005.

Feinstein, J. 2001. *The last amateurs: Playing for glory and honor in Division I.* Boston: Back Bay Publishers.

Feinstein, J. 2005. Interview sponsored by Time-Warner books. www.twbookmark.com/authors/98/692/interview11118.html. Accessed November 11, 2005.

Fejgin, N. 1994. Participation in high school competitive sports: A subversion of school mission or contribution to academic goals? *Sociology of Sport Journal* 11 (3): 211-230.

Fellowship of Christian Athletes. 2006. www.fca.org/aboutfca/. Accessed June 7, 2006.

Fine, G. 1987. *With the boys: Little League baseball and preadolescent culture.* Chicago: University of Chicago Press.

Fox Sports. 2006. Schools end use of slogan over drinking woes. Foxsports.com, May 16, 2006. http://msn.foxsports.com/cfb/story/5612364. Accessed May 22, 2006.

Frank, R. 2004. Challenging the myth: A review of the links among college athletic success, student quality and donations. Report to the Knight Commission on Intercollegiate Athletics. www.knightfdn.org/default/asp?story = athletics/reports/2004_frankreport/summary. Accessed November 16, 2004.

Frankel, D. 1998. Turner can't keep Murdoch from Dodgers. eonline.com, March 19, 1998. www.eonline.com/News/Items/0,1,2713,00.html. Accessed June 10, 2006.

Fullerton, R. 2003. Watching the pros vs. playing the game: How sports coverage affects community-level athletes. www.cces.ca/pdfs/CCES-PAPERSum-Smith-Fullerton-E.pdf. Accessed June 1, 2006.

Gale Group. 1999. Muhammad Ali. www.galegroup.com/free_resources/bhm/bio/ali_m.htm. Accessed August 24, 2005.

Game Face. 2002. *From the locker room to the boardroom: A survey on sports in the lives of women business executives.* February. Survey commissioned by Mass-Mutual Financial Group and Oppenheimer Funds. www.superednet.com/gameFace.html. Accessed May 15, 2005.

Garber, G. 2002. It's not all fun and games. ESPN.com, June 3, 2002. http://espn.go.com/otl/hazing/wednesday.html. Accessed September 5, 2005.

Garcia, C. 1994. Gender differences in young children's interactions when learning fundamental motor skills. *Research Quarterly for Exercise and Sport,* 66 (3), 247-255.

Gebicke, M., 1996. Director, Military Operations and Capabilities Issues. Letter to the Honorable John McCain, Chairman, Subcommittee on Readiness Committee on Armed Services, United States Senate. 6/14/1996 GAO/NSIAD-96-189R DOD Olympic Support.

Genel, M. 2000. Gender verification no more? *Medscape Women's Health Journal.* http://ai.eec.umich.edu/people/conway/TS/OlympicGenderTesting.html. Accessed December 16, 2005.

Gertz, S. 2004. Revisiting the pagan Olympic Games. *Christianity Today,* August 16, 2004. www.christianitytoday.com. Accessed October 10, 2005.

Gibbons, S. 2003. Sports news shortchanges female players, fans. Maynard Institute for Journalism, May 13, 2003. www.maynardije.org/columns/guests/030514_sportsnews. Accessed August 15, 2005.

Gibbins, S., V. Ebbeck, and M. Weiss. 1995. Fair play for kids: Effects on the moral development of children in physical education. *Research Quarterly for Exercise and Sport* 66: 247-255.

Goldberg, B. 2005. Baseball's hotbed. *HBO's Realsports,* September 28, 2005.

Gould, D. 1993. Intensive sport participation and the prepubescent athlete: Competitive stress and burnout. In *Intensive participation in children's sports,* ed. B.R. Cahill and A. Pearl, 19-38. Champaign, IL: Human Kinetics.

GovTrack. 2006. S. 1960: Integrity in Professional Sports Act. www.govtrack.us/congress/billtext.xpd?bill = s109-1960. Accessed June 8, 2006.

Greenberg, D. 2004. Urban girls and sports. Issues and action of women's sports foundation. www.womenssportsfoundation.org/cgibin/iowa/issues/disc/article.html?record = 774. Accessed August 15, 2005.

Griffin, P. 1998. *Strong women, deep closets: Lesbians and homophobia in sports.* Champaign, IL: Human Kinetics.

Gruneau, R. 1999. *Class sports and social development.* Champaign, IL: Human Kinetics.

Hackensmith, C. 1966. *History of physical education.* New York: Harper & Row.

Hamm, M. 2005a. Retiring U.S. soccer star Hamm to carry flag in closing ceremony. www.miafanclub.com/news/press.asp. Accessed August 11, 2005.

Hamm, M. 2005b. Mia Hamm. www.who2.com/mia-hamm.html. Accessed August 11, 2005.

Hargreaves, J., and I. McDonald. 2004. Cultural studies and the sociology of sport. In *Handbook of sport studies* ed. J. Coakley and E. Dunning, 48-60. London: Sage.

Harig, B. 2005. It pays to rip it and rip it. *St. Petersburg Times,* March 24, 2005.

Harris Interactive. 2001. Sports and women: Reaching this critical "casual fan." www.harrisinteractive.com/news/allnewsbydate.asp?NewsID = 391. Accessed August 15, 2005.

Harris Interactive. 2004. Trends and tudes. www.harrisinteractive.com/news/newsletters/k12news/HI_Trends&TudesNews2004_v3_iss09.pdf. Accessed June 1, 2006.

Harris Interactive. 2005. Professional football continues to be the nation's favorite sport. www.harrisinteractive.com/harris-poll/index.asp?PID = 622. Accessed May 8, 2006.

Harris, K. 2004. Pro athletes get in the political game. *Sun Sentinel* (Ft. Lauderdale, FL), October 29, 2004.

Harrison, C.K. 2004. *"The score," a hiring report card for NCAA Division IA and IAA football head coaching positions.* The Paul Robeson Center for Leadership, Academic, and Athletic Prowess.

Harris Poll. 2004. Survey of Americans with disabilities. National Organization on Disability, Washington, DC. www.nod.org. Accessed February 8, 2005.

Hawes, K. 1999. Women's sports enter NCAA arena. *NCAA News,* December 6, 1999. www.ncaa.org/wps/portal/!ut/p/kcxml/04_Sj9SPykssy0xPLMnMz0vM0Y_QjzKLN4j3CQXJgFjGpvqRqCKO6AKGph4QIUNTL31fj_zcVH1v_QD9gtzQ0IhyR0UAtMBstQ!!/delta/base64xml/L3dJdyEvUUd3QndNQSEvNElVRS82XzBfTFU!?CONTENT_URL = http://www.ncaa.org/news/1999/19991206/active/3625n32.html. Accessed June 1, 2006.

Hawes, K. 2001. Grant carried on the "idea" long after AIAW fell. *NCAA News,* May 21, 2001. www.ncaa. org/wps/portal/!ut/p/kcxml/04_Sj9SPykssy0xPLM-nMz0vM0Y_QjzKLN4j3CQXJgFjGpvqRqCKO6AKGp-h4QIUNTL31fj_zcVH1v_QD9gtzQ0IhyR0UAtMBstQ!!/ delta/base64xml/L3dJdyEvUUd3QndNQSEvNElVRS8 2XzBfTFU!?CONTENT_URL = http://www.ncaa.org/ news/2001/20010521/active/3811n05.html. Accessed June 1, 2006.

Health and Human Services. 1997. Shalala urges greater sports participation for girls; Releases first government report showing physical, mental and social benefits of sports and physical activity for girls. Health and Human Services press release, March 28, 1997. www. girlpower.gov/press/research/sports.htm. Accessed May 14, 2006.

Hechinger, F. 1980. About education. *New York Times,* February 19, 1980.

Hemery, D. 1986. *Sporting excellence, a study of sport's highest achievers.* London: Collin Sons.

Henley, K. 2005. A multiple-scandal test for big university. *Christian Science Monitor,* March 10, 2005. www.csmonitorservices.com/csmonitor/display. jhtml;jsessionid = JMZ3QKVHSCXU. Accessed May 25, 2006.

Henry, B., and P. Yeomans. 1984. *History of the Olympic Games.* Sherman Oaks, CA: Alfred Publishing.

Hills, C. 2004. Cuban hedges bet on NBA. *Focus on Family,* December 16, 2004. www.family.org/cforum/fosi/gam-bling/nac/a0034646.cfm. Accessed June 1, 2006.

Hoch, P. 1972a. *Rip off the big game.* New York: Doubleday.

Hoch, P. 1972b. The world of playtime, USA. *Daily World,* April 27, p. 12.

Hoffman, S.J. 1992. *Sport and religion.* Champaign, IL: Human Kinetics.

Hoffman, S., 2005. *Introduction to kinesiology.* 2nd ed. Champaign, IL: Human Kinetics.

Holbrook, J.E., and J. Barr. 1997. *Contemporary coaching: Trends and issues.* Carmel, IN: Cooper Publishing.

Holway, L. 2005. *A fight to the death: NCAA vs. AIAW.* Unpublished. Bryn Mawr, PA: Bryn Mawr College.

Houston Chronicle. 2004. Marvelous Messenger. www. chron.com/content/chronicle/sports/special/barri-ers/ashe.html. Accessed October 10, 2004.

Huff, D. 2005. Best by State: The top high school athletic programs in America. http://sportsillustrate. cnn.com/2005/magazine/05/11/top.high.map0516/. Accessed January 15, 2006.

Hughes, G. 2004. Managing black guys: Representation, corporate culture, and the NBA. *Sociology of Sport Journal* 21: 163-184.

Huizinga, J. 1950. *Homo Ludens: A study of the play element in culture.* Boston: Beacon Press.

Humphreys, J., and M. Plummer. 1996. The economic impact of hosting the 1996 Summer Olympics. www.

selig.uga.edu/forecat/Olympics/OLYMTEXT.HTM. Accessed November 11, 2005.

Huston, W. 2005. Sports is the opiate of the masses. *The American Daily,* January 18, 2005. www.american-daily.com/2951. Accessed January 18, 2005.

Hutchinson, E. 2004. Hornung was honest about Black athletes, many universities aren't. *AlterNet,* April 7, 2004. www.alternet.org/columnists/story/18358/. Accessed December 16, 2004.

Indiana Pacers. 2005. www.nba.com/pacers/. Accessed November 6, 2005.

Indianapolis Chamber of Commerce. 2006. Amateur Sports Capital of the World. www.indychamber.com/spor-tRec.asp. Accessed May 22, 2006.

International Council on Active Aging. 2006. www.icaa. cc/. Accessed May 15, 2006.

International Olympic Committee. 2006. Broadcast rights. www.Olympic.org/uk/organisation/facts/revenue/ roadcast_uk.asp. Accessed May 10, 2006.

IPSOS World Monitor. 2002. Trend Profiler II: Couch and field: Eight sports' global draw. First quarter, 2002. www.ipsos.ca/prod/wm/. Accessed October 21, 2004.

Issa, S. 2001. *Muslim girls' sports camp.* Los Angeles: Muslim Women's League.

Jenkins, B. 2004. Sportsline. *USA Today,* November 19.

Jenkins, C. 2000. Caught in gambling's web. *USA Today,* May 24.

Johnson, W. 1973a. And smile, smile, smile. *Sports Illustrated,* 38, 76-78, June 4.

Johnson, W. 1973b. Courting time in Peking. *Sports Illustrated,* 39, 12-15, July 2.

Johnson, W. 1973c. Sport in China. *Sports Illustrated,* 39 part 1, 82-100 September 24.

Josephson, M. 2004. Character counts: Sportsmanship survey. Josephson Institute of Ethics. Los Angeles, CA. www.charactercounts.org. Accessed December 8, 2004.

Journalism Jobs. 2002. 2002 RTNDA/Ball State University Salary survey. www.journalismjobs.com/salaries.cfm. Accessed April 4, 2005.

Kafka, P. 2004. *The Celebrity 100.* www.forbes.com/celeb-rity100/. Accessed September 19, 2004.

Katz, S. 2005. *Sub-mergent power: Struggles for equality under the AIAW/NCAA merger.* Unpublished. Bryn Mawr, PA: Bryn Mawr College.

Kidd, B. 1996. Taking the rhetoric seriously: Proposals for Olympic education. *Quest* 48(1): 82-92.

Kidd, B., and P. Donnelly. 2000. Human rights in sports. *International Review for the Sociology of Sport* 35 (2): 131-48.

Kidder, R. 2002. Sunday morning: Football or church? *Institute for Global Ethics Newsline,* June 3, 2002. www. globalethics.org/newsline/members/issue.tmpl?articl eid = 06030214064331. Accessed May 1, 2006.

King, C.R. and C. Fruehling. 2001. *Team spirits: The Native American mascots controversy.* Lincoln: University of Nebraska Press.

King, R. 2004. This is not an Indian. *Journal of Sport and Social Issues,* 28 (1): 3-10.

Klafs, C., and J. Lyon. 1978. *The female athlete.* 2nd ed. St. Louis: Mosby.

Knight Commission on Intercollegiate Athletics. 2001. A call to action: Reconnecting college sports and higher education. www.knightfdn.com. Accessed November 18, 2005.

Kopay, D. 1977. *The Dave Kopay story.* New York: Arbor House.

Kretchmar, R.S. 1994. *Practical philosophy of sport.* Champaign, IL: Human Kinetics.

Kruger, A., and J. Riordan, eds. 1995. *The story of worker sports.* Champaign, IL: Human Kinetics.

Lajis, R. 1996. The history of drug abuse in sports. www.prn2.usm.my/mainsite/bulletin/sun/1996/sun27.html. Accessed January 15, 2006.

Lambert, C. 2001. Has winning on the field become simply a corporate triumph? *Harvard Magazine,* September-October 2001. www.harvard-magazine.com/online/09014.html. Accessed May 23, 2006.

Lapchick, R. 1999. Race, athletes and crime. Special issue, *Sports Business Journal* [Online]. www.ucf.edu/sport/cgi-bin/site/sitew.cgi?page = /news/articles/article_13.htx. Accessed January 2, 2006.

Lapchick, R. 2001a. A grandfather's take on women's sports. *Women's Sports Foundation* [Online], November 8, 2001. www.womenssportsfoundation.org. Accessed December 10, 2004.

Lapchick, R. 2001b. Tennis opens up. www.bus.ucf.edu/sport/cgi-bin/site/sitew.egi%3Fpage%3D/news/articles/index.htx. Accessed December 10, 2004.

Lapchick, R. 2003. Just do it: Asian American athletes. *Asian-Nation: The landscape of Asian America.* www.asian-nation.org/sports.shtm. Accessed December 10, 2004.

Lapchick, R. 2004. *Race and gender report card.* Orlando: University of Central Florida.

Lapchick, R. 2005a. Race and gender report card for Major League Soccer for 2004. www.bus.ucf.edu/sport. Accessed January 3, 2006.

Lapchick, R. 2005b. Race and gender report card for Major League Baseball. www.bus.ucf.edu/sport. Accessed January 10, 2006.

Lapchick, R. and K. Mathews. 1999. *Race and gender report card.* Boston: Northeastern University Center for Study of Sport in Society.

Lapchick, R., and K. Mathews. 2002. *Race and gender report card.* Boston: Northeastern University Center for Study of Sport in Society.

Lausten, B.K. 2005. Mega events, both a bit of a myth and reality. http://medianet.djh.dk/sites/conferencepulse/folder.2005-11-03.1808955164/plonearticle.2005-11-10.1363578922. Accessed February 16, 2006.

Layden, T. 2004. Hanging from the BALCO-ny. *Sports Illustrated.* http://sportsillustrated.cnn.com/2004/writers/tim_layden/02/13/balco.indictments/index.html. Accessed May 22, 2005.

Lederman, D. 2005. The Faculty Role in Sports Reform. Insidehighered.com, November 9, 2005. www.inside-highered.com/news/2005/11/09/knight. Accessed June 6, 2006.

Le Fevre, D. 2002. *Best new games.* Champaign, IL: Human Kinetics.

Leisure Trends. 2004. Fun facts on leisure. www.leisure-trends.com/local/fun_facts.asp. Accessed June 1, 2006.

Leonard, L. 2000. The decline of the black athlete. ColorLines. www.arc.org/C_Lines/CLArchive/story3_1_03.html. Accessed December 4, 2005.

Leonard, W. 1980. *A sociological perspective of sport.* Minneapolis, MN: Burgess Publishing.

Levy, A. 2005. *Female chauvinist pigs: Women and the rise of raunch culture.* New York: Free Press.

Library of Congress. 2005. *Integrity in Professional Sports Act.* U.S. Senate, November 3, 2005. http://thomas.loc.gov/cgi-bin/query/z?r109:S03N05-0013:. Accessed May 25, 2006.

Lin, Z., C. Jui-Chia, and E. Esposito. 2005. Successful leadership in sport. *The Sport Journal.* www.thesport-journal.org/sport-supplement/vol13no1/05_success-ful_leadership.asp. Accessed September 5, 2005.

Lipsyte, R. 2003. Reform movements build in American college sports. *New York Times,* November 30.

Little League. (2005). About us. Mission and history. www.littleleague.org. Accessed May 10, 2005.

Lodriguss, J. 2005. Sports Photography. www.astropix.com/SPORTSPIX/NSC/NOTES.HTM. Accessed May 10, 2005.

Lombardo, B. 1999. Coaching in the 21st century: Issues, concerns and solutions. *Sociology of Sport* [Online]. htpp://physed.otago.ac.nz/sosol/v2i1/v2ila4.htm. Accessed September 5, 2005.

Lopiano, D. 1994. Equity in women's sports: A health and fairness perspective. *The Athletic Woman* 13 (2): 281-296.

Lopiano, D. 2001. Gender equity and the Black female in sport. www.womenssportsfoundation.org/cgi-bin/iowa/issues/disc/article.html?record = 869. Accessed December 18, 2004.

Loverro, T. 2002. Good riddance. *Washington Times,* December 12, 2002. www.nestofdeath.com/press/washTimes.html. Accessed May 2, 2006.

Loy, J., and D. Booth. 2004. Functionalism in sport and society. In *Handbook of sport studies,* ed. J. Coakley and E. Dunning, 8-25. London: Sage.

Luschen, G. 2000. Doping in sport as deviant behavior and its social control. In *Handbook for sport studies,* ed. J. Coakley and E. Dunning, 461-476. London: Sage.

Maguire, J. 1999. *Global sport: Identities, societies, civilizations.* Cambridge, UK: Polity Press/Cambridge Press.

Maguire, J., G. Jarvie, L. Mansfield, and J. Bradley. 2002. *Sport worlds: A sociological perspective.* Champaign, IL: Human Kinetics.

Malina, R., and S. Cumming. 2003. Current status and issues in youth sports. In *Youth sports: Perspectives for a new century,* ed. R. Malina and M. Clark, 7-25. Monterey, CA: Coaches Choice.

Marot, M. 2005. Spartans dig themselves too big a hole. *AP wire service,* April 5, 2005. www.cstv.com. Accessed May 12, 2005.

Martens, R., T. Flannery, and P. Roetert. 2002. The future of coaching education in America. www.nfhs.org/scriptcontent/va_Custom/vimdisplays/contentpagedisplay.cfm?content. Accessed January 9, 2006.

Martens, R., and V. Seefeldt, eds. 1979. *Guidelines for children's sports.* Repr., Washington, DC: American Alliance for Health, Physical Education, Recreation and Dance.

Martin, B. 1996. Ten reasons to oppose all Olympic Games. *Freedom* 57 (15): 7.

Martzke, R. 2000. DeVarona fights for fairness on principle: $50M, age, sex suit vs. ABC is "hardest thing I've done." *USA Today,* September 7.

Matus, R. 2004a. Islamic USF player: Dispute over uniform led to dismissal. *St. Petersburg Times*, September 11, 2004. www.sptimes.com. Accessed January 24, 2005.

Matus, R. 2004b. USF Controversy goes global. *St. Petersburg Times,* September 17, 2004.

McCain, John. 2004. McCain demands action by Major League Baseball on steroid testing. Press release: U.S. Senate Committee on Commerce, Science and Transportation, May 8, 2004. http://commerce.senate.gov/newsroom/printable.cfm?m?id = 220326. Accessed May 28, 2006.

McCallum, J. 2002. Citizen Barkley. *Sports Illustrated,* March 11, 34-38.

McCarthy, M. 2004. NBC Universal's gamble on Olympics pays off. *USA Today,* August 29, 2004.

McNamara, T. 2000. You're a dumb broad—and that's progress. *Columbia Journalism Review* 38 (5): 43.

Mediamark Research. 2003. Older Americans lead surge in physical fitness as walking surpasses team sports. Press release. http://www.mediamark.com/. Accessed October 12, 2005.

Menez, G. and A. Woo. 2005. Best high school athletic programs. *Sports Illustrated.com.* http://sportsillustrated.cnn.com/2005/magazine/05/11/top.high.school0516/. Accessed January 15, 2006.

Merriam-Webster's Collegiate Dictionary. 2001. 11th ed. Springfield, MA: Merriam-Webster.

Messner, M. 2002. *Taking the field: Women, men and sports.* Minneapolis: University of Minnesota Press.

Michener, J. 1987. *Sports in America.* Greenwich, CT: Fawcett.

Miller, R., and Associates. 2005. Sports business market research handbook. www.rkma.com. Accessed November 10, 2005.

Miller, T., ed. 2001. *Globalization and sport: Playing the world.* London: Sage.

Mills, R. 1997. Tapping innate resilience in today's classrooms. *Research/Practice.* Center for Applied Research and Educational Improvement. University of Minnesota. http://education.umnedu/CAREI/Reports/Rpractice/Spring97/tapping.html. Accessed May 23, 2006.

Miracle, A., and C. Rees. 1994. *Lessons of the locker room: The myth of school sports.* New York: Prometheus Books.

Moyes, G. 2000. Olympians I have known—John Landy. Reachout 2000 Olympic Media Archive. www.wesleymission.org.au/reachout2000/sermons/landy.asp. Accessed August 24, 2005.

MSNBC.com. 2006. A look at the NHL's new rules. www.msnbc.msn.com/id/8672777/. Accessed January 2, 2006.

Munich. 2005. Universal Pictures. http://movies.about.com/od/munich/. Accessed June 1, 2006.

Munoz, C. 2004. Dominican baseball. http://pegasus.cc.ucf.edu/~jtorres/domrep/baseball/. Accessed October 20, 2005.

Murphy, P., K. Sheard, and I. Waddington. 2004. Figurational sociology and its application to sport. In *Handbook for sport studies,* ed. J. Coakley and E. Dunning, 92-105. London: Sage.

Muse, W. 2000. Commentary: Who is responsible for learning in our society? *Auburn University News,* January 11, 2000. www.auburn.edu/administration/univrel/news/archive/1_00news/1_00brooks.html. Accessed May 18, 2006.

NASC. *See* Native American Sports Council.

National Association of Sport and Physical Education (NASPE). 2001. *National standards for athletic coaching.* Washington, DC: NASPE.

National Association of Youth Sports. 2005. www.youthsports@ncya.org. Accessed May 10, 2005.

National Basketball Association. 2005a. *NBA Basketball stars reunite for Basketball Without Borders Africa.* www.nba.com/bwb/starsreuniteafrica.html. Accessed January 1, 2006.

National Basketball Association. 2005b. *NBA Players from around the world: 2005-2006 season.* www.nba.com/players/international_player_directory.html. Accessed June 1, 2006.

National Collegiate Athletic Association. 2002. Fact Sheet. www.ncaa.org/about/fact_sheet.pdf. Accessed April 10, 2004.

National Collegiate Athletic Association. 2003. Estimated probability of competing in athletics beyond the high school interscholastic level. www.ncaa.org/wps/portal/!ut/p/kcxml/04_Sj9SPykssy0xPLMnMz0vM0Y_QjzKLN4j3NQDJgFjGpvqRqCKO6AI-YXARX4_83FR9b_0A_YLc0NCIckdFAEuT364!/delta/base64xml/L3dJdyEvUUd3QndNQSEvNElVRS82XzBfTFU!?CONTENT_URL=http://www.ncaa.org/research/prob_of_competing/. Accessed June 2, 2006.

National Collegiate Athletic Association. 2004a. NCAA Division I Manual, 2004-05. Constitution, Operating Bylaws, and Administrative Bylaws. Effective August 1, 2004. www.ncaa.org/library/membership/division_1_manual/2004-05/2004-05_d1_manual.pdf. Accessed February 3, 2005.

National Collegiate Athletic Association. 2004b. Participants in NCAA-sponsored sports. www.ncaa.org. Accessed October 10, 2005.

National Collegiate Athletic Association. 2004c. Sports wagering information packet. www.1.ncaa.org/membership/enforcement/gamblingPacket.html. Accessed February 3, 2005.

National Collegiate Athletic Association. 2005a. Division II national championships. *NCAA News,* January, 2005. www.ncaa.org. Accessed June 2, 2006.

National Collegiate Athletic Association. 2005b. What's the difference between Divisions I, II and III? www.ncaa.org/wps/portal/!ut/p/kcxml/04_Sj9SPykssy0xPLMnMz0vM0Y_QjzKLN4j3NQDJgFjGpvqRqCKO6AI-YegihqY-eECFDU099X4_83FR9b_0A_YLc0NDQiHJHAG7c3rg!/delta/base64xml/L3dJdyEvUUd3QndNQSEvNElVRS82XzBfTFU!?CONTENT_URL=http://www.ncaa.org/about/div_criteria.html. Accessed November 12, 2005.

National Council of Youth Sports (NCYS). 2006. A national multi-sport corporation. www.ncys.org. Accessed May 10, 2006.

National Education Association. 2005. Issues in education, school safety. www.nea.org/schoolsafety/index.html. Accessed May 2, 2006.

National Federation of High Schools. (1985). The case of high school activities. A survey of high school principals and students sponsored by Indiana University, Lilly Endowment and the National Association of Secondary School Principals. www.NFHS.org.

National Federation of State High School Associations. 2000. Sports medicine: National eating disorders screening program targets high school segment. www.nfhs.org/ScriptContent/VA_Custom/vimdisplays/contentpagedisplay.cfm?Content_ID=230&SearchWord=eating%20disorder. Accessed September 5, 2005.

National Federation of State High School Associations. 2003. Surveys resources: Participation sets record for fifth straight year. Press release, September 2, 2003.

www.nfhs.org/ScriptContent/VA_Custom/vimdisplays/contentpagedisplay.cfm?Content_ID=150&SearchWord=Surveys%20resources:%20Participation%20sets%20record%20for%20fifth%20straight%20year. Accessed November 14, 2005.

National Federation of State High School Associations. 2004a. The case for high school activities. www.nfhs.org/ScriptContent/VA_Custom/vimdisplays/contentpagedisplay.cfm?Content_ID=71&SearchWord=The%20case%20for%20high%20school%20activities. Accessed November 14, 2004.

National Federation of State High School Associations. 2004b. Sports participation for 2003-2004. www.nfhs.org/scriptcontent/va_custom/SurveyResources/2003-04_Participation_Survey.pdf. Accessed October 10, 2005.

National Federation of State High School Associations. 2006. Sexual harassment and hazing: Your actions make a difference! www.nfhs.org/staticcontent/pdfs/sexual_harassment_english.pdf. Accessed January 5, 2006.

National Organization for Women. 1966. Statement of purpose. www.now.org/history/purpos66.html. Accessed May 20, 2005.

National Osteoporosis Foundation (NOF). 1997. Osteroporosis prevalence figures: State by state report. Washington, DC: NOF, 1.

National Senior Games Association. 2005. www.nsga.com. Accessed March 21, 2005.

National Women's Law Center. 2002. *The battle for gender equity in athletics : Title IX at thirty.* June. Washington, DC.

Native American Sports Council. 2005. Native American professional athletes and Olympic athletes. www.nascsports.org. Accessed December 5, 2005.

NBA. *See* National Basketball Association.

NCAA. *See* National Collegiate Athletic Association.

Neuman, R. 2005. Adventures in Cybersound. www.acmi.net.au/AIC/ENC_BROADCASTING.html. Accessed November 10, 2005.

New England Patriots. 2006. www.patriots.com/stadium/index.cfm?ac=TicketSales. Accessed June 2, 2006.

NewsSmith. 1996. Post Olympics: What's next? www.smith.edu/newsmith/NSFall96/PostOlympics.html. Accessed May 10, 2006.

New York Times. 2004. University of Colorado reinstates football coach despite scandal. May 28, 2004. p.C12

NFHS. *See* National Federation of State High School Associations.

Nichols, K. 1997. What is the relationship between eating disorders and female athletes? www.vanderbilt.edu/AnS/psychology/health_psychology/sport.htm. Accessed September 5, 2005.

Nielsen Media Research. 2006. VNU's media and marketing guide for the Super Bowl. www.nielsenmedia.com/nc/portal/site/Public/menuitem.55dc65b4a7dff3f659361. Accessed May 9, 2006.

O'Brien, R. 2004. My sportsman choice: Hicham El Guerrouj. *SI.com,* September 24, 2005.

Ogilvie, B., and T. Tutko. 1971. Sport: If you want to build character, try something else. *Psychology Today,* October, 63.

O'Keefe, M. and T. Quinn. 2005. Yanks losing at money ball. *Daily News* (New York), December 4, 2005.

Olympic Charter. 2004. Fundamental principles of Olympism. #1. http://multimedia.olympic.org/pdf/en_report_122.pdf. Accessed October 14, 2004.

Ordine, W. 2005. Horse racing is betting on Internet wagering. Reprinted from *Baltimore Sun.* www.therx.com/blog_horse-racing-is-betting-on internet-wagering.php. Accessed May 23, 2006.

Orlick, T. 1974. The sports environment, a capacity to enhance, a capacity to destroy. Paper presented at the 6th Canadian Symposium of Sports Psychology. September. Halifax, Nova Scotia.

Otis, C. and R. Goldengay. 2000. *The athletic women's survival guide.* Champaign, IL: Human Kinetics.

Overberg, P., and H. El Nasser. 2005. Minority groups breaking patterns. *USA Today,* August 11.

Overman, S.J. 1997. *The influence of the Protestant ethic on sport and recreation.* Aldershot, UK: Avebury Press.

Palmer, A. 2006. Arnold Palmer. www.arnoldpalmer.com/en/. Accessed June 1, 2006.

Parker, S. 2004. Few make money. *USA Today,* September 1, 2004.

Payne, E., and L. Issacs. 2005. *Human motor development.* New York: McGraw-Hill.

Pearson Education, Inc. 2005. Internet access in the U.S. www.infoplease.com. Accessed February 10, 2006.

Peretti-Watel, P., V. Guafliardo, P. Vergeris, P. Mignon, J. Pruvost, and Y. Obadia. 2004. Attitudes toward doping and recreational drug use among French elite student-athletes. *Sociology of Sport Journal* 21 (1).

Persall, S. 2005. They call it Murderball. *St. Petersburg Times,* August 31, 2005.

Play the Game. 2005. Floating Olympic stadium could redress imbalance between rich and poor. www.playthegame.org/News/Up%20To%20Date/Floating_Olympic_stadium_could_redress_imbalance_between_rich_and_poor.aspx. Accessed February 16, 2006.

Pompeii, D. 2000. Marino never won the big one. *The Sporting News,* July 6.

Porter, E. 2004. Film examines court Jews who dominated basketball. *Forward,* November 26, 2004. www.thefirstbasket.com?Forward_article.html. Accessed July 29, 2005.

President's Council on Physical Fitness and Sports. 1999. Report on physical activity in the lives of girls. Physical and mental health dimensions from an interdisciplinary approach. Washington, DC: Author.

Pribut, S. and D. Richie. 2002. 2002: A sneaker odyssey. www.drpribut.com/sports/sneaker_odyssey.html. Accessed June 7, 2006.

Price, S.L. 1997. Is it in the genes? *Sports Illustrated,* December, 52 +.

PR Web. 2006. Advertising Super Bowl: Granchiser domination continues. www.prweb.com/released/2006/02/prweb343160.htm. Accessed May 31, 2006.

Publishers Weekly. 2005. http://reviews.publishersweekly.com/bd.aspx?isbn = 0060758635&pub = pw. Accessed June 8, 2006.

Quest. 2006. www.pastornet.net.au/quest/mission.htm. Accessed June 7, 2006.

Quinn, E. 2005. Eating disorders in athletes: About health and fitness. www.sportsmedicine.about.com/cs/eatingdisorders. Accessed September 5, 2005.

Reed, K. 2004. Backtalk: Elitism in youth sports yields physical fatness. *New York Times,* SportsDesk, February 1, 2004.

Rees, C., and A. Miracle. 2004. Education and sport. In *Handbook of sports studies,* ed. J. Coakley and E. Dunning, 277-290. London: Sage.

Relin, D. 2005. Who's killing kids' sports? *Parade,* August 7, 2005, 4.

Remember the Titans. 2000. htpp://en.wikipedia.org/wiki/Remember_the_Titans. Accessed May 10, 2006.

Rice, E., J. Hutchinson, and M. Lee. 1958. *A brief history of physical education.* New York: Ronald Press.

Riemer, H., and P. Chelladurai. 1995. Leadership and satisfaction in athletics. *Journal of Sport and Exercise Psychology* 17: 276-293.

Rigauer, B. 2004. Marxist theories. In *Handbook of sport studies,* ed. J. Coakley and E. Dunning, 28-47. London: Sage.

Rivers, C. 2003. Sports stars act like perks include abusing women. *Womens eNews.* www.womenenews.org/article/cfm/dyn/aid/1554/context/archive. Accessed February 4, 2005.

Robinson, R. 1999. *Rockne of Notre Dame: The making of a legend.* New York: Oxford University Press.

Ryan, J. 1995. *Little girls in pretty boxes: The making and breaking of elite gymnasts and figure skaters.* New York: Doubleday.

Sabo, D., K. Miller, M. Melnick, and L. Heywood. 2004. *Her life depends on it: Sport, physical activity and the health and well-being of American girls.* East Meadow, NY: Women's Sports Foundation.

Sage, G. 1972. Value orientations of American college and high school coaches. *Proceedings of the 75th Annual NCPEA for Men,* 174-186.

Sage, G. 1973. Occupational socialization and value orientations of athletic coaches. *Research Quarterly* 44 (October, 269-277.

Sage, G. 1998. *Power and ideology in American sport.* 2nd ed. Champaign, IL: Human Kinetics.

Sanchez, J. 2005. Latino Legends team announced. http://mlb.mlb.com/NASApp/mlb/news/article.jsp?

ymd = 20051026&content_id = 1260107&vkey = news_mlb &fext = .jsp&c_id = mlb. Accessed December 4, 2005.

Sandomir, R. 1997. Murdoch bids for Dodgers simply to bolster a lineup. *New York Times,* May 16, 1997. http://marshallinside.usc.edu/mweinstein/teaching/fbe552/552secure/notes/dodgers-murdoch. Accessed June 10, 2006.

Santa Fe Independent School District vs. Doe, U.S. Supreme Court. 2000. Ontario Consultants on Religious Tolerance. www.religioustolerance.org. Accessed July 3, 2005.

Scheiber, D. 2004. History of Olympic Games. *St. Petersburg Times* (St. Petersburg, FL), September 8, 2004.

Scheiber, D. 2005. Extreme evolution. *St. Petersburg Times* (St. Petersburg, FL), August 4, 2005, C1, C8.

Schrager, A. 2004. CU president testifying before Congress. www.9news.com/storyfull.aspx?storyid = 25369. Accessed October 15, 2005.

Schultz, J. 2004. Discipline and push-up: Female bodies, femininity, and sexuality in popular representations of sports bras. *Sociology of Sport Journal* 21 (2).

Schwartz, L. 2005a. Billie Jean won for all women. www.espn.go.com/sportscentury/features/00016060.html. Accessed June 2, 2006.

Schwartz, L. 2005b. Jackie changed the face of sports. www.espn.go.com/sportscentury/features/00016431.html. Accessed August 13, 2005.

Seefeldt, V., M. Ewing, and S. Walk. 1992. *Overview of youth sports programs in the United States.* Washington, DC: Carnegie Council on Adolescent Development.

Senn, A.E. 1999. *Power, politics, and the Olympic Games: A history of the power brokers, events, and controversies that shaped the Games.* Champaign, IL: Human Kinetics.

SGMA. *See* Sporting Goods Manufacturers Association.

Sharp, D. 1994. The women who took the jounce out of jogging. *Health Magazine,* September 25.

Sheehan, C. 2005. Kids obesity worse in rural areas. *CBS News,* March 14, 2005. www.cbsnews.com/stories/2005/03/14/health/main679946.shtml?CMP = ILC-SearchStories. Accessed November 8, 2005.

Shelton, G. 2005. This is the week of Hit Man. *St. Petersburg Times* (St. Petersburg, FL), February 3, 2005, 1C.

Shields, B., and G. Smith. 2005. Cheerleader-related injuries to children ages 5-18: United States 1990-2002. *Pediatrics* 117: 122-129.

Shields, D. 2002. Charles Barkley's head fake. *Slate,* November 22, 2002. www.slate.com/id/2074459/. Accessed March 15, 2004.

Shields, D. 2005. Bad behavior cited in youth sports study. *USA Today,* November 29, 13C.

Shields, D., and B. Bredemeier. 1995. *Character development and physical activity.* Champaign, IL: Human Kinetics.

Shults, B., and M.L. Sheffer. 2004. The changing role of local television sports. *The Sports Journal.* www.the-sportjournal.org/2004Journal/Vol7-No1/schultzscheffer.asp. Accessed May 26, 2006.

Simmons, K. 2002. Sex crimes on campus often silent. *Atlanta Journal Constitution* (Atlanta, GA), February 17.

Slater, R. 2003. *Great Jews in sport.* Middle Village, NY: Jonathan David.

Sleek, S. 2004. Psychologists help debunk the myth of Michael Jordan. www.umich.edu/ ~ paulball/webpage%20papers/Psychologists_Michael-Jordan.htm. Accessed December 16, 2004.

Smart, R., and M. Smart. 1982. *Children: Development and relations.* 4th ed. New York: MacMillan, 460-463.

Smith, A. 2002. The sports factor. *Radio Network in Great Britain,* October 20, 2002.

Smith, R. 1986. Toward a cognitive-affective model of athletic burnout. *Journal of Sport Behavior* 18(1): 3-20.

Speaker Series. 2005. *Bob Costas: Emmy-award winning sportscaster and Olympic host.* www.speakerseries.com/costas.htm. Accessed August 26, 2005.

Spears, B., and R. Swanson. 1978. *History of sport and physical activity in the United States.* Dubuque, IA: Brown.

Special Olympics. 2005. Athlete oath. www.specialolympics.org/Special + Olympics + Public + Website/English/About_Us/Athlete_Oath/default.htm. Accessed February 8, 2005.

Special Olympics. 2006. www.specialolympics.org. Accessed June 7, 2006.

Splitt, F. 2004. The faculty-driven movement to reform big-time college sports. Drake Group. www.thedrakegroup.org. Accessed January 20, 2005.

Sporting Goods Manufacturers Association. 2000. Organized youth team sports participation in the U.S. www.sgma.com. Accessed June 10, 2004.

Sporting Goods Manufacturers Association. 2001. Youth sports in America: The parental perspective. www.sgma.com. Accessed February 20, 2005.

Sporting Goods Manufacturers Association. 2003. Sports participation topline report. 2003 edition. www.sgma.com. Accessed March 10, 2004.

Sporting Goods Manufacturers Association. 2004. Sports participation topline report. 2004 edition. www.sgma.com. Accessed March 10, 2004.

Sporting Goods Manufacturers Association. 2005a. Extremesports: Ranking high in popularity. Press release, May 31, 2005. www.sgma.com/press/2005/1117636042-19826.html. Accessed August 4, 2004.

Sporting Goods Manufacturers Association. 2005b. Sports participation topline report. 2005 edition. www.sgma.com. Accessed February 25, 2005.

Sporting Goods Manufacturers Association. 2005c. Team sport in a state of flux: The ups and downs. www.sgma.com. Accessed February 20, 2005.

SportingNews.com. 2003a. Commission seeks fix for scandal-plagued U.S. Olympic Committee. June 19, 2003. www.sportingnews.com/soccer/articles/20030619/479205-p.html. Accessed June 10, 2004.

SportingNews.com. 2003b. What is power? www.sporting-news.com/features/powerful/whatis.html. Accessed January 17, 2005.

SportingNews.com. 2003c. 100 most powerful sports people of the year. www.sportingnews.com/features/powerful/completelist.html. Accessed January 17, 2005.

SportsBusiness Journal. 1999. Television viewers of 1999 Women's World Cup final. July 19-25. Taken from Women Sports Foundation, *Women's Sports and Fitness Facts and Statistics.*

Sports Doctor, Inc. (2000). Women's Issues. "The Female Athlete." http://www.sportsdoctor.com/articles/female9.html. Accessed June 8, 2006.

Staurowsky, E. 2000. *Women and men in the press box: The price of progress.* Ithaca, NY: Ithaca College.

Steeves, B. 2003. Top 15 frequently asked questions about stadiums. www.leg.state.mn.us/docs/2004/other/040634/Stadium/www.stadium.state.mn.us/faq.pdf. Accessed May 20, 2006.

Stephan, E. 1994. For love, for money, for real money. www.wwu.edu/~stephan./webstuff/es.19thBB.html. Accessed October 10, 2004.

Stevens, T. 2005. Ted Stevens Olympic and Amateur Sports Act. www.usolympicteam.com/12699_12720.htm. Accessed January 10, 2005.

Stevenson, C. 1997. Christian athletes and the culture of elite sport: Dilemmas and solutions. *Sociology of Sport Journal* 14: 241-262.

Stewart, C. 2005. Should boys and girls be coached the same way? www.coachesinfo.com/category/becoming_a_better_coach/13/. Accessed March 2, 2005.

StopHazing. 2005. Hazing and athletics 1998-2005. www.StopHazing.org/athletic_hazing/. Accessed September 5, 2005.

St. Petersburg Times. 2004. Graduation rates of bowl teams. December 8, 5C.

St. Petersburg Times. 2005a. Beijing already planning to wow the world in '08. August 30, 2005.

St. Petersburg Times. 2005b. Foreign players on opening day rosters for 2005. April 8, 2005.

St. Petersburg Times. 2005c. Always a diamond jubilee. February 9, 2005.

Suggs, W. 2002. Title IX at 30: In the arena of women's college sports, the 1972 law created a legacy of debate. *Chronicle of Higher Education* 48 (14): A38-42.

Sundgot-Borgen, J. 1994. Risk and trigger factors for the development of eating disorders in female elite athletes. *Medicine and Science in Sports and Exercise* 26: 414-418.

Sylvester, M. 2004. Percentage of Division I men's and women's programs that reported revenue. *USA Today*, September.

Television Bureau of Advertising. 2005. Top 25 network telecasts (sports). www.tvb.org. Accessed January 15, 2006.

Texas University Interscholastic League. 1998. Benefits of extracurricular activities. www.uil.utexas.edu/admin/benefits.html. Accessed November 14, 2004.

Thorpe, J. 2005. The official Jim Thorpe Web site. www.cmgww.com/sports/thorpe/index.php. Accessed September 1, 2005.

Topkin, M. 2004. Provacative poses divide U.S. women. *St. Petersburg Times*, (St. Petersburg, FL), August 25, 9C.

Tornoe, J. 2005. Olympic-style sporting tournament to showcase Hispanic athletes. http://juantornoe.blogs.com/hispanictrending/2005/11/olympicstyle_sp.html. Accessed December 4, 2005.

Tsiokos, C. 2005. Sports as the opiate of the masses. Population Statistics, September 4, 2005. www.populationstatistic.com/index.php?s = Sports + as + the + opiate + of + the + masses&submit = search. Accessed May 15, 2006.

Tuggle, C. 2003. Study shows ESPN still not paying much attention to women's sport. www.unc.edu/news/archives/aug03/tuggle080103.html. Accessed March 10, 2005.

Turco, D and T. Ostrosky. 1997. Touchdowns and fumbles: Urban investments in NFL franchises. *Cyber Journal of Sport Marketing.* www.ausport.gov.au/fulltext/1997/cjsm/v1n3/turco.htm. Accessed November 3, 2005.

United Cerebral Palsy. 2004. Americans With Disabilities Act fact sheet. www.ucp.org/ucp_generaldoc.cfm/1/8/11904/11904-11904/4522. Accessed February 8, 2005.

United States Census. 2005a. Report on percentage of working mothers in 1970s to 2004 in the United States. www.census/gov/employment. Accessed February 15, 2006.

United States Census. 2005b. Report on selected characteristics. Single mother head of households. Table FG5. www.census.gov/population/www/socdemo/msla.html. Accessed May 20, 2006.

United States Census. 2005c. USA statistics in brief—Race and Hispanic origin. www.census.gov/statab/www/racehisp.html. Accessed January 9, 2006.

United States Department of Health and Human Services. 2001. Overweight and obesity threaten U.S. health: Physical activity is critical. Press release, December 13, 2001. www.fitness.gov/sg_cta-obesity.htm. Accessed April 25, 2004.

United States Department of Labor. 2005. Athletes, coaches, umpires and related workers. www.bls.gov/oco/ocos251.htm. Accessed May 19, 2005.

United States Lacrosse Association. 2004. www.usalacrosse.org. Accessed February 10, 2004.

United States Olympic Committee. 2005. Corporate governance and documents. www.usoc.org. Accessed August 10, 2005.

United States Paralympics. 2005. What are the Paralympic Games? www.usparalympics.com/312.htm. Accessed February 8, 2005.

United States Tennis Association. 2003. Cost of junior competitive tennis. Unpublished. Key Biscayne, FL: High Performance Program.

United States Tennis Association. 2004. *USTA 2004 yearbook.* Lynn, MA: H.O. Zimman.

University of Colorado at Boulder. 2004. Preliminary action plan for the reorganization and oversight of intercollegiate athletics. www.colorado.edu/news/statements/athletics/reforms/reforms.html. Accessed April 21, 2005.

USA Today. 2005. Salary database for MLB. http://usatoday.printthis.clickability.com/pt/cpt?action = cpt& title = USATODAY.com + - + BA. Accessed September 19, 2004.

U.S. Census. *See* United States Census.

U.S. Department of Health and Human Services. *See* United States Department of Health and Human Services.

USTA. *See* United States Tennis Association.

VanderZwaag, H., and T. Sheehan. 1978. *Introduction to sport studies.* Dubuque, IA: Brown.

Vare, R. 1974. Buckeye: A study of coach Woody Hayes and the Ohio State football machine. *Harper Magazine Press*, 38.

Veronica, J. 1991. Power Players. *Rocky Mountain News,* July 28, 1991, 10M.

Wacquant, L. 2004. *Body and soul: Notebooks of an apprentice boxer.* New York: Oxford University Press.

Waldron, J. 2000. Stress, overtraining and burnout associated with participation in sport. Unpublished thesis. Lansing: Institute for the Study of Youth Sports at Michigan State University.

Wallechinsky, D. 1996. *Complete book of the Summer Olympics.* New York: Little, Brown.

Wall Street Journal. 2004a. National finances league. *St. Petersburg Times,* September 21, D-1.

Wall Street Journal. 2004b. Sole search: When the shoe doesn't fit. *St. Petersburg Times,* August 28. D-1.

Washington Post. 2005. UCI Criticizes Drug Allegations Against Armstrong. September 10, 2005. www.washingtonpost.com/wp-dyn/content/article/2005/09/AR2005090901949.html. Accessed December 3, 2005.

Watson, N., and D. Czech. 2005. The use of prayer in sport: Implications for sport psychology consulting. *Athletic Insight* 7 (4) (December). www.athleticinsight.com/Vol7Iss4/PrayerinSports.htm. Accessed May 24, 2006.

Weber, S. 1956. Krauss-Weber tests. *Pennsylvania Journal of Health, Physical Education and Recreation* (September): 14-15.

Webster's Sports Dictionary. 1976. Springfield, MA: G. & C. Merriam.

Weinberg, A. 2003. The case for legal sports gambling. www.forbes.com/2003/01/27/cx_aw_0127gambling.html. Accessed February 2, 2005.

Weinberg, R., and D. Gould. 1995. *Foundations of sport psychology.* Champaign, IL: Human Kinetics.

Weiner, B. 2004. First "masters" Sullivan finalist Raschker, 57, seeks lifetime fitness for aging Americans: In top five for America's top amateur athlete, breaking age stereotype. www.weinerpublic.com/page164.html. Accessed February 10, 2005.

Wendel, T. 2003. *The new face of baseball: The one-hundred-year rise and triumph of Latinos in America's favorite sport.* New York: Rayo/Harper Collins.

Wendel, T. 2005. When smiles leave the game. *USA Today,* August 23, 2005, A-13.

Wikipedia. 2005a. Bob Richards. http://en.wikipedia.org/wiki/Bob_Richards. Accessed August 11, 2005.

Wikipedia. 2005b. Cultural capital. http://en.wikipedia.org/wiki/Cultural_capital. Accessed January 1, 2006.

Wikipedia. 2005c. Grantland Rice. http://en.wikipedia.org/wiki/Grantland_Rice. Accessed June 15, 2005.

Wikipedia. 2005d. Muhammad Ali. http://en.wikipedia.org/wiki/Muhammad_Ali. Accessed August 24, 2005.

Wikipedia. 2006a. Centennial Olympic Park bombing. http://en.wikipedia.org/wiki/Centennial_Olympic_Park_bombing. Accessed May 22, 2006.

Wikipedia. 2006b. Munich massacre. http://en.wikipedia.org/wiki/Munich_Massacre. Accessed May 22, 2006.

Wikipedia. 2006c. Rupert Murdoch. http://en.wikipedia.org/wiki/Rupert_Murdock. Accessed May 20, 2006.

Wojnarowski, A. 2005. *The miracle of St. Anthony.* New York: Gotham Books.

WomenSport International. 2006. Interesting media coverage facts. www.sportsbiz.bz/womensportinternational/archives/2003/040103_wsf_media.htm. Accessed June 12, 2006.

Women's Sports Foundation. 1989. Minorities in sport: The effect of varsity sports participation on the social, educational and career mobility of minority students. New York.

Women's Sports Foundation. 1998. Research report: Sport and teen pregnancy. www.womenssportsfoundation.org/cgi-bin/iowa/issues/body/article.html?record = 883. Accessed June 2, 2006.

Women's Sports Foundation. 2001a. The female athlete triad. www.womenssportsfoundation.org/cgi-bin/iowa/issues/body/article.html?record = 721. Accessed June 2, 2006.

Women's Sports Foundation. 2001b. Research report: Health risks and the teen athlete. www.womenssportsfoundation.org/cgi-bin/iowa/issues/body/article.html?record = 771. Accessed June 2, 2006.

Women's Sports Foundation. 2004a. Women's Sports and Fitness Facts and Statistics. www.womenssportsfoundation.org. Accessed October 10, 2004.

Women's Sports Foundation. 2004b. Addressing the issue of verbal, physical and psychological abuse of athletes: The Foundation position. www.womenssportsfoundation.org/cgi-bin/iowa/iowa/issues/coach/article.html?record = 995. Accessed February 27, 2005.

Woods, R. 2004. *Coaching tennis successfully.* Champaign, IL: Human Kinetics.

Woodward, J. 2004. Professional football scouts: An investigation of racial stacking. *Sociology of Sport Journal.* 21: 356-375.

Woog, D. 1998. *Jocks: The true story of America's gay male athletes.* Los Angeles: Alyson Books.

World Police and Fire Games. 2006. www.2007wpfg.com/home/home.cfm. Accessed June 8, 2006.

World Sports for All Congress. 2002. Sport for all and elite sport: Rivals or partners? http://multimedia.olympic.org/pdf/en_report_555.pdf. Accessed September 15, 2004.

World Team Tennis. 2005. Billie Jean King. www.wtt.com/about/billie.asp. Accessed August 16, 2005.

Wottenberg, B.B. 2003. *It will be a smaller world after all.* Washington, DC: American Enterprise Institute.

Young, K. 2004. Sport and violence. In *Handbook of sport studies,* Chapter 25, J. Coakley and E. Dunning ed. London: Sage.

Index

Note: Page numbers followed by an italicized f or t refer to the figure or table on that page, respectively.

About the Author

Ronald B. Woods, PhD, is an award-winning performance coach with Human Performance Institute, a consultant to the United States Tennis Association, and an adjunct professor at the University of South Florida. He has 40 years of experience as a teacher, coach, and administrator of sports.

Previously, he spent 20 years with the United States Tennis Association. He was named the first director of player development of a program that assisted in the development of top junior players into touring professional players—including Pete Sampras, Venus and Serena Williams, and Jennifer Capriati. In 1996, the International Tennis Hall of Fame awarded him the Educational Merit Award.

He was honored by the United States Professional Tennis Association as National Coach of the Year in 1982 and named a Master Professional in 1984. He is a member of the American Alliance for Health, Physical Education, Recreation and Dance and was a member of the U.S. Olympic Coaching Committee for eight years. He received his PhD from Temple University.

*You'll find
other outstanding
sport sociology resources at*

www.HumanKinetics.com

In the U.S. call

1-800-747-4457

Australia	08 8372 0999
Canada	1-800-465-7301
Europe	+44 (0) 113 255 5665
New Zealand	0064 9 448 1207

HUMAN KINETICS
The Information Leader in Physical Activity
P.O. Box 5076 • Champaign, IL 61825-5076 USA